Clergy of the Church of England 1835

Part One: A to F

Map showing the Dioceses of England (and Wales) in 1835

CLERGY OF THE CHURCH OF ENGLAND

1835

A Biographical Directory

Part One: A to F

Compiled by Peter Bell

Published 2021 by Peter Bell

68 West Port, Edinburgh EH1 2LD

Scotland, UK

portsburghpress@gmail.com

0131-556-2198

ISBN (Part One):   978-1-871538-13-7

ISBN (Part Two):   978-1-871538-14-4

ISBN (Part Three): 978-1-871538-15-1

The right of Peter Bell to be identified as the compiler of this work has been asserted by him in accordance with the Copyrights, Designs & Patents Act 1988

Book production assistance by
Pixel Tweaks Publications
SELF PUBLISHING MADE SIMPLE
www.pixeltweakspublications.com

Cover: Photograph of Rev Bulkeley Bandinel, died 1861, Bodley's Librarian.
Public Domain image licensed under CC-PD-Mark

FOREWORD

Ten years ago I purchased a copy of the massive Report of the Ecclesiastical Revenues Commission, published in May 1835, with its detailed statistical information of every parish in England and Wales for the three years ending 1833. Among that information was a column listing the holder of every benefice in England and Wales, albeit abbreviated (e.g. T. Jones). Having made a list of these names, I decided that a biographical directory could be made from it, one in which both the professional and the personal lives of each cleric could be combined to their mutual benefit, along the lines of Venn's Alumni Cantabrigienses. If I had known what I was letting myself in for, I would probably never have begun!

The resulting Directory has been made possible only because of the existence of the Clergy of the Church of England Database, 1540-1835, a vast online database (abbreviated here as CCEd, or C followed by each cleric's unique identifying number). Compiled locally by record offices throughout England and Wales (but only England here), and not yet complete, the resulting information varies depending on what records survive. Details usually include university degrees, exact dates of ordination, and exact dates of the curacies, benefices and other appointments held by each man until c.1835; although the great problem of what Wikipedia calls disambiguation - the mixing of two or more men of exactly the same name - remains unresolved in too many cases.

For further information it is necessary to turn to existing sources, both printed and electronic, some printed and familiar (such as the registers for Oxford and Cambridge Universities, at a time when eighty percent of the clergy were graduates of those two places), but also to a number of less familiar titles as listed here under Existing Published Sources with Biographical Material, in which some biographical work has already been done by others, usually in a specific diocese.

Regarding the online resources, especially Ancestry.co.uk, all of these must be used with great caution. If used last of all they can often provide additional or expanded personal information, especially (it would seem) of wives and children. Few men warrant a Wikipedia entry, although each man has been checked online for any relevant information whatsoever. Contradictions occur frequently, and these have been noted only if currently unresolvable. New online information appears regularly (and some, especially online links, disappear), reminding us that biographical information is always in a state of change and incompleteness. This is why this is essentially a work in progress, and a first draft which I hope people will feel free to correct and add to where necessary (using the email link below).

A very specific source which must be noted is in the University of Durham's Special Collections Library in Palace Green, namely the Hudleston Index, consisting of thousands of hand-written index cards covering the Northern Province only. I now realise that so much of the information here about the Northern clergy (recorded ten years ago) comes from that source alone.

Special mention must also be made of the two volumes of York Clergy Ordinations for 1750-1799 and 1800-1849 respectively, which include ordination details of every man ordained in the (large) Archdiocese of York between 1750 and 1849. This is a model which should be adopted by every diocese, and would enable the missing dates, places of birth, and parentage to be filled in.

Writing this book on and off over a decade has, rather strangely, involved only a few people, but each of them important. Professor Arthur Burns, the director of the CCEd project responsible for this period of the long Eighteenth Century, allowed me at an early stage to access unpublished CCEd material, for which I am most grateful. With Emeritus Professor Ted Royle of York University I learnt enormous amounts about the workings of the Church of England in this period, for which I am again extremely grateful. My sister Judith has rescued me from computer problems and losses, and has proofed the whole work. Finally, my dear MaryCatherine Burgess has endured ten years of clerical trivia and monologue (which probably makes her a not inconsiderable authority on the men here).

Peter Bell

EDITORIAL METHOD & METHODOLOGY

The following model entry, accompanied by an interpretation, is rarely followed completely, as some vital information is invariably missing for most clergy. Many are anonymous, even after 200 years, and only persistent work (especially by a descendant) can produce fuller results.

> **HADEN** (Alexander Bunn) Bapt. Wednesbury, Staffs. 25/3/1783, | s. Rev. Alexander Bunn Haden, sen., and Mary Rotten. | St Edmund Hall, Oxford 1806, BA1810, dn10 (C&L), p11 (C&L), MA1813. | PC. Woore, Shropshire 1811-19 (res.), V. Brewood, Staffs. 1830 to death 16/8/1863, | leaving £1,000 | [C11358] | Married (1) Chetton, Shropshire 7/2/1826 Marianne Heptinstall (d.1850, 1st q.) (2) London 27/4/1859 Mary Ward (w). |

> **HADEN** (Alexander Bunn) Baptised Wednesbury, Staffordshire 25/3/1783, son of Reverend Alexander Bunn Haden, senior, and Mary Rotten. St. Edmund Hall, Oxford University 1806, Bachelor of Arts 1810, deacon 1810 (Coventry & Lichfield Diocese), priest 1811 (Coventry & Lichfield Diocese), Master of Arts 1813. Priest-in-Charge of Woore, Shropshire 1811-19 (resigned), Vicar of Brewood, Staffordshire 1830 to death 16/8/1863, leaving under £1,000 [Clergy of the Church of England Database 11358] Married (1) at Chetton, Shropshire 7/2/1826 Marianne Heptinstall (died 1850, 1st quarter) (2) in London 27/4/1859 Mary Ward (his widow). |

Names. In this example the father and son are identically named, an immediate cause of confusion. The father here was married twice, and this is his first wife. Mothers' names are often elusive, and often appear by their first name only, usually in the Census returns. The very many changes of surname are not normally noted here, although some doubled-barrelled names, and the many aristocratic titles, are usually cross-referenced. Future corrections should include a son's order in the male line (i.e. 2nd son). People with common surnames (not only Smith and Jones, but also Dixon, Carter, Wilkinson, &c.) when combined with identical forenames are a nightmare, and sometimes cannot be differentiated after 200 years.

Birth and Baptism. Not always differentiated in many original records, although attempted here. Baptism dates are recorded in the original ordination papers, and are given preference here if noted in CCEd. Saying that someone was, say, 60 at death in 1860, does not automatically make him born 1800, as birth and baptism dates could vary. Also the place of birth and/or baptism may not automatically be the parents' place of residence. Place names have been modernised wherever possible, though the original Report has some wild spellings and some joining of parishes which are not helpful in identifying them today.

Schools are not noted – something which should be rectified at a later date. Suffice it to say that the numbers at the 'Great Public Schools', especially Eton and Westminster, were high, especially among the clerical elite.

University. At this date, the vast majority of clergy were graduates of Oxford and (especially) Cambridge, as recorded in Foster and Venn respectively. Note that Foster gives the date of matriculation to the University; while Venn gives dates of admission to a particular college; matriculation at Cambridge was separate and is not noted here, but does account for children of 12 or 13 entering the university. Degrees did not have to be formally taken to make a man a university graduate, only matriculation. 'Ten Year Men' at Cambridge were extra-mural men, matriculating annually for 10 years, after which they could claim to be MA (Cantab.). Note that Foster described Doctors of Divinity as 'doctors', who are not Doctors of Medicine (who were MDs - as some were). Note also the number of men with legal degrees, or who were law students or actual lawyers of some sort before ordination. Non-graduates, known as literates (or 'literate persons'), were ordained at the discretion of the ordaining bishop.

Ordination. Deacons could only be ordained at the age of 23; priests at 24; and the vast proportion of men seem to have been ordained at this age, straight out of university. Bishops had to be 30 or more (and only George Murray, q.v., had a problem with this!).

Careers. Here I have followed a combination of CCEd and existing printed sources to ascertain the parishes in which a man was rector, vicar, or perpetual curate. (The Report also includes a number of 'miscellaneous' men who by rights should not really be there). Assistant or Stipendiary curacies are not noted (but are in CCEd), and information after 1835 (the cut-off date for CCEd) must be pieced together from all available sources, including early editions of The Clergy List (from 1840) and Crockford's (first useable edition 1860). The whereabouts of a man ordained and dying between 1835 to 1860 is the most difficult of all to track down.

Date of death. This is usually available, often from FreeBMD (Free Births, Marriages and Deaths) online; or alternatively that of burial, which is differentiated. Age at death is quoted when specifically given, and is not estimated from date of birth.

Wealth at death. This is available after January 1868 from the photographed printed records on Ancestry, and, as a printed legal document, is the most reliable of all documents. It gives all sums left at death as 'under' - which can be assumed here whenever a round figure is given. Many men did not leave a will at all; bishops can be found under their title, e.g. Samuel Winchester for Samuel Wilberforce, Bishop of Winchester.

Marriage. Marriages are included where known, and the absence of a wife here does not mean that a person was never married. Wives who had previously been married are designated Mrs., with their birth surname in brackets, whereas (w) – widow – indicates that a wife outlived her husband. Numbers of children vary with the original sources, which may or may not include those dying in infancy. Numbers of surviving children tend to be more reliable.

References. These are in square brackets. The CCEd is the unique reference number given to each individual in the Clergy of the Church of England Database 1540-1835, which is free to search. It can be assumed that Foster and Venn have been checked for every graduate clergyman - but the result, especially for a 'literate person', can be disappointing, or, in a few cases, almost non-existent.

Notes. Any miscellaneous information is included here, much of it trivial, but it may help to enliven what are often repetitive entries.

LIST OF ABBREVIATIONS

Abp.	Archbishop
b.	born
BA	Bachelor of Arts
BCL	Bachelor of Civil Law
BD	Bachelor of Divinity
Bapt.	baptised
Bp.	Bishop
C.	Curate
Cam.	Cambridge
CCEd/C	Clergy of the Church of England Database 1540-1835
Chap.	Chaplain
d.	died
dau.	daughter
DCL	Doctor of Civil Law
DD	Doctor of Divinity
D.L.	Deputy Lieutenant [of a county]
Dom. Chap.	Domestic Chaplain
Don. Chap.	Donative Chaplain [of a church outside the jurisdiction of the diocesan bishop]
dn.	deacon
d.s.p.	died without issue (*decessit sine prole*)
ERC	Ecclesiastical Revenues Commission [Report, 1835]
FreeBMD	Free Births Marriages and Deaths [online resource]
G/S	Grammar School
HEIC	[Honourable] East India Company
H/M	headmaster
Hon.	The Honourable/honorary
J.P.	Justice of the Peace
Lect.	lecturer
LLD	Doctor of Laws
LNCP	Library of Nineteenth Century Photographs [Online resource with many clergy]
MA	Master of Arts
Min.	Minister
M.P.	Member of Parliament
non-res.	non-resident [only when specified]
NPC	National Probate Calendar [from Jan. 1858]
ODNB	Oxford Dictionary of National Biography
Ox.	Oxford
p.	priest
PC.	Perpetual Curate
pop.	population
Preb.	Prebendary
Prof.	professor
q.	quarter [of the year; from FreeBMD]
R.	Rector
(res.)	resigned (only when specified)
R.N.	Royal Navy
s.	son (of)
Sec.	Secretary
S/M	schoolmaster
s.p.	without issue (*sine prole*)
Univ.	university
V.	Vicar
(w)	widow, indicating that she outlived her husband (whereas Mrs. indicates that she was previously married).

Entries will be found in Foster or Venn for all men at Oxford or Cambridge respectively unless otherwise specified.

OXFORD UNIVERSITY COLLEGES & HALLS

All Souls'
Balliol
Brasenose
Christ Church
Corpus Christi
Jesus
Lincoln
Magdalen College
Magdalen Hall
Merton
New College
New Inn Hall
Oriel
Pembroke
Queen's [The Queen's]
St Catherine's
St Edmund Hall
St John's
St Mary Hall
Trinity
University
Wadham
Worcester

CAMBRIDGE UNIVERSITY COLLEGES & HALLS

Christ's
Clare
Corpus Christi
Downing
Emmanuel
Gonville & Caius
Jesus
King's
Magdalene
Pembroke
Peterhouse
Queens'
Selwyn
Sidney Sussex
St Catharine's
St John's
Trinity College
Trinity Hall

BISHOPS OF THE CHURCH OF ENGLAND 1835

(appear in the text under their surname)

Bath and Wells (B&W)	George Henry Law
Bristol (Bristol)	Robert Gray [as Bristol and Gloucester after 1836]
Canterbury (Cant.)	William Howley
Carlisle (Car.)	Hon. Hugh Percy
Chester (Chester)	John Bird Sumner
Chichester (Chich.)	Edward Maltby
Coventry & Lichfield (C&L)	Hon. Henry Ryder [as Lichfield after 1836]
Durham (Dur.)	William Van Mildert
Ely (Ely)	Bowyer Edward Sparke
Exeter (Ex.)	Henry Phillpotts
Gloucester (Glos.)	James Henry Monk [as Gloucester and Bristol after 1836]
Hereford (Heref.)	George Isaac Huntingford (to 1832) [Hon. Edward Gray from 1832, not included here]
Lincoln (Lin.)	John Kaye
London (London)	Charles James Blomfield
Norwich (Nor.)	Henry Bathurst
Oxford (Ox.)	Richard Bagot
Peterborough (Peterb.)	Herbert Marsh
Rochester (Roch.)	George Murray
Salisbury (Salis.)	Thomas Burgess
Sodor and Man (S&M)	William Ward
Winchester (Win.)	Charles Richard Sumner
Worcester (Wor.)	Robert James Carr
York (York)	Hon. Edward Venables-Vernon (then Harcourt)

The four Welsh bishoprics (excluded from this survey) were:

Bangor (Bangor)	Christopher Bethell
Llandaff (Llandaff)	Edward Copleston
St Asaph (St Asaph)	William Carey
St David's (St David's)	John Banks Jenkinson

EXISTING PUBLISHED SOURCES WITH BIOGRAPHICAL MATERIAL

Al.Dub.	Alumni Dublinenses: a register of students, graduates … in the University of Dublin. Edited by G.D. Burtchaell and T.U. Sadleir. (1924).
ATV	Archbishop Thomson's Visitation Returns for the Diocese of York, 1865. Edited Edward Royle & Ruth M. Larsen. (York: Borthwick Institute for Archives, 2006).
Austin	The Church in Derbyshire in 1823-4: the parochial visitation of the Rev. Samuel Butler, Archdeacon of Derby, in the Diocese of Lichfield and Coventry. Edited M.R. Austin. (Derbyshire Archaeological Society, 1972).
Austin2	'A time of unhappy commotion': the Church of England and the people of central Nottinghamshire 1820-1870. (Chesterfield: Merton, 2010).
BBV	Bishop Bickersteth's Visitation Returns for the Archdeaconry of Craven, Diocese of Ripon, 1858. Edited Edward Royle. (York: Borthwick Institute for Archives, 2009).
Bennett1	Lincolnshire parish clergy c.1214-1968: a biographical register. Part I: The Deaneries of Aslacoe and Aveland. Compiled by Nicholas Bennett (Lincoln Record Society, 2013).
Bennett2	Lincolnshire parish clergy c.1214-1968: a biographical register. Part II: The Deaniers of Beltisloe and Bolingbroke. Compiled by Nicholas Bennett (Lincoln Record Society, 2016) And many more volumes to come!
Bertie	Scottish Episcopal Clergy 1689-2000. By David M. Bertie. (Edinburgh: T & T Clark, 2000). New edition in preparation.
Boase	Modern English Biography … of persons who have died between the years 1851-1900 … Compiled by Frederic Boase. (1908. Reprinted London: Cass, 1965). 6 volumes.
DEB	The Blackwell Dictionary of Evangelical Biography 1730-1860. Edited Donald M. Lewis. (Oxford, 1995). 2 volumes.
Fasti	Fasti Ecclesiae Anglicanae 1541-1857. By Joyce M. Horn [and others]. London, 1969-2014. 13 volumes. [Excludes the Welsh Dioceses]
Foster	Alumni Oxonienses: the Members of the University of Oxford, 1715-1886. Compiled by Joseph Foster. (1888-92. Reprinted Bristol: Thoemmes, 2000). 4 volumes.
Gelling	A history of the Manx Church (1698-1911). By John Gelling (Douglas, IoM: The Manx Heritage Foundation, 1998).
Hodson	Visitations of the Archdeaconry of Stafford 1829-1841. Edited David Robinson (HMSO for Historic Manuscripts Commission, 1980).
Kaye	Lincolnshire parish correspondence of John Kaye, Bishop of Lincoln, 1827-53. Edited R.W. Ambler. (Lincoln Record Society, 2006).
LFBI	Landed Families of Britain and Ireland. [The very beginnings of an extraordinary project by Ben Kingsley to link country houses and their owners – obviously including many clergy here. Only on letter 'B' at time of writing – unfortunately.] landedfamilies.blogspot.com/
McClatchey	Oxfordshire clergy, 1777-1869 … By Diana McClatchey (Oxford, 1960).

Platt	The Diocese of Carlisle, 1814-1855: Chancellor Walter Fletcher's Diocesan Book, with additional material from Bishop Percy's notebooks … Edited by Jane Platt (Surtees Society, 2015).
Romilly	Romilly's Cambridge diary 1832-42. Edited J.P.T. Bury. (Cambridge, 1967).
Romilly2	Romilly's Cambridge diary 1842-1847. Edited M.E. Bury & J.D. Pickles. (Cambridgeshire Records Society, 1994).
Romilly3	Romilly's Cambridge diary 1848-1864. Edited M.E. Bury & J.D. Pickles. (Cambridgeshire Records Society, 2000).
Smart	Biographical Register of the University of St. Andrews 1747-1897. By Robert N. Smart. (St. Andrews University Library, 2004).
Snell	The Snell Exhibitions. From the University of Glasgow to Balliol College, Oxford. By W. Innes Addison. (Glasgow: James Maclehose, 1901).
Venn	Alumni Cantabrigienses … Part 2 from 1752 to 1900. Compiled by J.A. Venn (1922-54. Reprinted Bristol: Thoemmes, 2001). 6 volumes.
Wilberforce	The Diocese Books of Samuel Wilberforce, Bishop of Oxford 1845-1869. Edited Ronald and Margaret Pugh. (Oxfordshire and Berkshire Record Societies, 2008).
Wilberforce2	The letter-books of Samuel Wilberforce, 1843-68. Transcribed and edited by R.K. Pugh. (Buckingham Record Society & Oxfordshire Record Society, 1970).
Wilberforce3	Bishop Wilberforce's Visitation Returns for the Archdeaconry of Oxford in the year 1854 … Edited E.P. Baker. (Oxfordshire Record Society, 1954).
YCO	York Clergy Ordinations 1750-1799. Compiled by Debbie Usher (York: Borthwick Institute, 2002) [and] York Clergy Ordinations 1800-1849. Compiled by Sara Slinn (York: Borthwick Institute, 2001). [The latter has a most important Introduction.]

Clergy of the Church of England 1835

Part One: A to F

Parishes underlined (thus) are the ones held in plurality by one clergyman in the early 1830's

ABBISS (John) Born Wandsworth, London 13/7/1789, s. John Abbiss and Mary Parkin. Trinity, Oxford 1810, BA1814, dn15 (Salis.), MA1817, p19 (London). R. St Bartholomew the Great, City of London 1819 to death (unm.) 8/7/1883, leaving £28,013-2s-9d. [C65626. Boase] Port. online.

ABBOT, ABBOTT (John) Bapt. Exeter 15/9/1799, s. John White Abbot and Elizabeth Bowlins. Pembroke, Oxford 1817, BA1821, dn22 (Ex.), MA1823, p23 (Ex.). V. Exeter St David 1826-31, R. Meavy, Devon 1831-72. Died Plymouth 1/3/1882 aged 82, leaving £7,418-6s-9d. [C139148] Married (1) Catherine Ross (d.1857) (2) Bathford, Som. 11/5/1859 Rosetta Gray Soady (d.1862), 1s. (3) St Germans, Cornwall 1864 (2nd q.) Jane Watson Skardon (w), with further issue.

ABBOTT (Philip) Born Morland, Westmorland 2/5/1785, s. Christopher Abbott and Betty Harding. Literate: dn10 (York for Chester), p11 (Chester). Usher Clitheroe G/S, Lancs. 1812, H/M 1841-52; PC. Colne, Whalley, Lancs. 1817-21, PC. Downham, Whalley 1818-52 (with H/M Downham Free G/S), PC. Newchurch in Rossendale, Whalley 1825-33. Died (a widower) 4/9/1852 aged 66 [C83004. Boase. YCO] Married Lowther, Westmorland 29/12/1808 Elizabeth Holmes, w. clerical son. J.P. Lancs. 1823.

ABBOTT, ABBOT (William) Bapt. St Lawrence in Thanet, Kent 5/9/1770, s. Rev. William Abbot and Jane Friend Taddy. King's, Cambridge 1789, Fellow 1792-1815, BA1793, dn95 (London), MA1796, p96 (N. LF30or.). Assistant Master Eton College 1797-1806; R. of Horstead, Surrey 1815 and R. Coltishall, Norfolk, 1815 to death 4/2/1846 aged 76 [C5215] Married (1) Newington, Surrey 19/7/1815 Margaret Ann Morris (d.1832) (2) Horstead 20/8/1832 Mary Ann Donna (d.1843).

ABDY (Charles Boyd) Born Essex, s. Rev. Thomas Abdy and Mary Hayes. Jesus, Cambridge 1806, BA1811, dn11 (London), p12 (London), MA1814. R. Theydon Garnon, Essex 1812 [blank in ERC] (with RD) to death. Dom. Chap. to 2nd Baron Braybrooke 1817. Died (unm.) 20/8/1843 [C1161]

ABDY (John Channing) Born Southwark, London 9/4/1792, s. Rev. William Jarvis Abdy and Elizabeth Perkins. Worcester, Oxford 1810, BA1813, dn15 (C&L for Win.), MA1816, p16 (Salis. for Win.). R. Horsleydown St John, Southwark, Surrey 1823-45. Probate granted 21/2/1845 [C8292] Married London 1821 Maria Smith (a minor poet), w. clerical s. Albert Channing Abdy.

A'BECKETT, *later* **A'BECKETT TURNER (Thomas)** Born West Lavington, Wilts. 7/6/1751, s. Thomas A'Beckett and Philippa Turner. BNC, Oxford 1768, BA1772, dn74 (London), MA1778, p82 (C&L for Cant.). PC. Wootton Underwood, Bucks. 1782 to death (unm.) 4/6/1838 aged 87 [C8291. Foster, *Gentleman's Magazine* and ERC under Turner] 'Very rich'.

ACASTER (John) Bapt. Brotherton, Yorks. 10/10/1779, s. Thomas Acaster and Mary Foulds. Literate: dn02 (York), p03 (York). V. York St Helen Stonegate 1815 to death. Dom. Chap. to 2nd Earl of Mexborough 1818. Died (a widower) 3 or 6/7/1854 aged 74 [C84040. Boase. YCO] Married York 27/5/1813 Anne Whitelock, with issue. Port. and memorial plaque online.

ACKLAND (Thomas Gilbank) Born London 8/6/1792, s. Rev. Thomas and Elizabeth Ackland. St John's, Cambridge 1807, BA1811, dn13 (London), MA1814, p14 (London), DD 1829. V. St Mildred Bread St. w. St Margaret Moses, City of London 1818 to death. Chap. to HRH Duke of York 1816. Died 20/2/1844 aged 53 [C1167. ODNB] Married Covent Garden, London 16/5/1811 Harriet Clinton Baddeley.

ACKROYD (John) Bapt. Bowling, Yorks. 3/11/1766, s. James Ackroyd and Mary Waddington. Literate: dn97 (York), p98 (York). R. Egmere w. Holkham, Norfolk 1825. Probate granted 13/12/1847 [C110596. YCO]

ACKROYD, AKROYD (Jonathan) Bapt. Illingworth, Yorks. 10/5/1795, s. Jonathan Ackroyd (a member of the largest worsted manufacturing family in Britain) and Betty Charnock. Literate: dn26 (York), p27 (York). Chap. (and builder) of the Donative of Christ Church, Skircoat, Halifax, Yorks. 1827-?40, V. Grinton, Yorks. 1848-?50. Died Hounslow, Middx. 16/3/1858 aged 64, leaving under £200 [C114772. YCO] Married (1) Halifax 19/1/1816 Susan Crawshaw (d.1831), 8 ch. (1 clerical) (2)

Huddersfield 1840 (4th q.) Susan Beaumont, 2 further ch. A delinquent clergyman, being imprisoned in Jan. 1843 at Bury Assizes for obtaining money under false pretences, 'the profession [thereby] being relieved of one of its greatest blots'.

ACTON (William) Born Southampton. St John's, Cambridge 1804, LLB1812, dn20 (Chester *or* Glos.), p22 (Lin.). R. Ayot St Lawrence, Herts. 1823-30 (res.), R. Weston Colville, Cambs. 1832 to death 30/11/1864 aged 76, leaving £5,000 [C5216] Married West Wratting, Cambs. 9/12/1823 Henrietta Watson (dau. of a knight), with issue.

ADAMS (Benjamin) Bapt. Newcastle under Lyme, Staffs. 10/1/1759, s. Benjamin Adams (a linen draper, *J.P.* and Mayor) and Elizabeth Slade. Emmanuel, Cambridge 1776, BA1782, dn82 (Peterb. for C&L), p92 (C&L). V. Barlaston, Staffs. 1792 to death 25/1/1834 (CCEd says 14/3/1834) aged 76 [C8282] Married Jane Thompson. A Freeman of Newcastle-under-Lyme 1790.

ADAMS (Dacres) Born Westminster, London 26/7/1806, s. William Dacres Adams and Elizabeth Meynell-Mayow. Christ Church, Oxford 1824, BA1827, dn29 (Ex.), p30 (Ex.), MA1832. V. Pinhoe, Devon 1832, V. Bampton, Oxon. (2nd Portion) 1837 (with RD of Witney) to death 8/12/1871 aged 65, leaving £7,000 [C139150. LFBI 30] Married 15/8/1832 Anna Marie Fulford, with clerical son William Fulford Adams.

ADAMS (George) Born Chastleton, Oxon. 6/10/1805, s. Rev. James and Maria Adams. St John's, Oxford 1824, BA1828, dn28 (Ox.), MA 1832, BD1837. R. Chastleton 1832, R. Farndon, Northants. 1838 to death 17/1/1855 [C21361]

ADAMS (Henry) From Buckler's Hard, Hants., s. Henry Foster Adams. Wadham, Oxford 1785 (aged 21), BA1789, p93 (C&L for Win.), MA 1794. PC. Lemington, Glos. [C137279] 1797-1805 (res.), R. Hatch Beauchamp, Som. 1798 to death. Dom. Chap. to 2nd Baron Montagu of Beaulieu for 49 years. Died 27/4/1839 aged 74 [C8293]

ADAMS (Henry) Born Holborn, London 18/11/1770, s. Patience [*sic*] Thomas Adams and Martha Marsh. St John's, Oxford 1788, BA1792, dn93 (Lin.), p94 (Ox.), MA1796, BD1801. R. Arley, Warwicks. 1803-15, R. Bardwell, Suffolk 1815 to death 3/2/1852, *s.p.* [C5265]

ADAMS (Richard) Bapt. Hannington, Wilts. 1/12/1762, s. Rev. Simon and Catherine Adams. Christ Church, Oxford 1782, BA1787, dn87 (Lin.), p88 (Lin.). R. Edingthorpe, Norfolk 1789 and V. Deopham, Norfolk 1799. Died? [C42564]

ADAMS (Stephen Lewis) Born Blackawton, Devon 19/9/1759, s. Rev. Thomas Adams and Elizabeth Creed. Pembroke, Oxford 1777, BA1781, dn82 (Ex.), p84 (Ex.), MA1784. PC. Slapton, Devon 1787, R. Moreleigh, Devon 1795 and V. Blackawton 1803 to death. Dom. Chap. to 1st Baron Ribblesdale 1803. Died 12/1/1834 aged 77 [C137753] Married (1) Blackawton 12/8/1794 Mary Hayne (2) Blackawton 5/4/1821 Dorothy Hawkins.

ADAMS (Thomas Coker) Bapt. Ansty Hall, Stanton, Warwicks. 14/12/1782, s. Simon Adams and Sarah Coker. Merton, Oxford 1801, BA1804, dn07 (C&L), p08 (Win. for C&L), MA1809. PC. Shilton, Warwicks. 1809 w. R. Saxelby, Leics. 1809, V. Ansty 1809, V. Foleshill, Warwicks. 1822 to death. Dom. Chap. to 5th Earl of Aylesford 1820. Died 26/10/1851 [C5220. Boase] Married Bath 16/9/1806 Mary Withington, w. issue. Founded the Asylum for Juvenile Offenders at Stretton upon Dunsmore, Warwicks. An archer.

ADAMS (William) Born Shrewsbury, Shropshire 1766, s. John Adams and Grace Cay. Pembroke, Oxford 1779), BA1783, MA1785, dn89 (Chester for Ox.), p95 (Ox.), BD and DD1808. S/M Shrewsbury G/S 1798; V. Halstead, Essex 1804, R. Abington Pigotts, Cambs. 1808 to death 29/3/1850 [C9318] Married Holborn, London 14/1/1796 Frances Cay.

ADAMSON (Sandford John Cyril) Born Padiham, Whalley, Lancs. 2/10/1798, s. Rev. John and Maria Adamson. St Bees 1819, dn21 (Chester), p22 (Chester). PC. Padiham 1823-65. Died Altham, Lancs. 10/6/1873 (a widower) aged 74, leaving £2,000 [C83008] Married Whalley 2/3/1829 Nancy Brooks, *s.p.* In 1871 Census he lived alone with a female servant.

ADDINGTON (William Leonard, 2nd Viscount Sidmouth) Born Palace of Westminster

13/11/1794, s. Henry. 1st Viscount Sidmouth and Ursula Mary Hammond. Christ Church, Oxford 1812, dn20 (Salis.), p20 (London). R. Poole Keynes (o/w Poole St Michael), Glos. 1821-33 (res.). Died Albury, Surrey 25/3/1864, leaving £12,000 [C83214. Boase. LFBI 44] Married 20/4/1820 Mary Young (a clergy dau.) with issue. Succ. to title 1844.

ADDISON (Edward) Bapt. Saxthorpe, Norfolk 25/6/1775, s. Leonard Addison and Ann Tilson. Corpus Christi, Cambridge 1792, BA 1797, dn97 (Nor.), Fellow 1798-1824, p99 (Nor.), MA1800, BD 1807. PC. Cambridge St Benedict 1816-21, R. Landbeach, Cambs. 1821 to death 27/5/1843 [C6494]

ADDISON (John) Born Calcutta c.1782, s. Eldred Addison and an unknown Indian woman. Trinity, Cambridge 1799, LLB1805, dn09 (Ex. for London), p10 (London). R. Ickenham, Middx. 1815 (and RD) to death 18/2/1859, leaving £4,000 [C113072] Married Billericay, Essex 7/2/1816 Maria Adams, with issue.

ADDISON (William) see under **FOUNTAINE**

ADNUTT (Robert Thomas) Born Nailstone, Leics. 3/1/1802, s. Rev. Thomas Adnutt and Mary Catherine Green. Emmanuel, Cambridge 1819, BA1825, dn25 (Lin.), p26 (Lin.), MA 1828. R. (and patron) of Croft, Leics. 1826 and R. Cadeby, Leics. 1826 to death 25/5/1872, leaving £3,000 [C5281] J.P. Leics.

AFFLECK (Robert, Sir, 4th Bart.) Born Dalham Hall, Newmarket, Suffolk 27/1/1765, s. Rev. James Affleck (Finedon House, Northants.) and Mary Proctor. Christ Church, Oxford 1783, BA1787, MA1790, dn92 (Nor.), p93 (Nor.). V. Westow, Yorks. 1796-1833 (and S/M Hemsworth G/S 1796), R. Treswell, Notts. (Two Medieties) 1796-1837, Prebend of Tockerington in York Minster 1802-51, V. Doncaster, Yorks. 1807-17, V. Silkstone, Yorks. 1817-35 (res.). Dom. Chap. to Archbishbp of York 1807; Dom. Chap. to 3rd Earl Harcourt 1817. Died Dalham Hall 7/5/1851 [C84058. Boase. LFBI 50] Married Marylebone, London 16/5/1800 Maria, dau. Sir Elijah Impey (Chief Justice of Bengal, Newick Park, Sussex), with 9 ch. (1 clerical - James Danby Affleck). Succ. to the title 1833.

AHIER (Jean Thomas) Bapt. Jersey, Channel Islands 21/8/1781, s. Philippe Ahier and Marie Le Gallais. Literate: dn04 (Win.), p05 (Win.). R. Jersey Holy Trinity 1811-50. Died 25/3/1850 'of inanition' (malnutrition)[C69120]

AINGER (William) Born Whittlesea, Cambs. c.1785, s. William Ainger and Mary Boyce. St John's, Cambridge 1803, BA1807, dn08 (Salis. for Ely), p09 (Nor. for Ely), Fellow 1809, MA 1810, BD1817, DD1822. PC. St Bees, Cumberland and founder and first Principal of St Bees Theological College 1816-40, V. Castle Carrock, Cumberland 1816-[31], V. Sunninghill, Berks. 1817-30, Canon of Chester Cathedral 1827 and R. Northenden, Cheshire 1829 to death (St Bees) 20/10/1840 aged 55 [C2864. T. Park, *St Bees College* (2nd edn. St Bees, 2007) shows a portrait bust] Married Harpenden, Herts. 10/7/1817 Elizabeth Humphries, w. clerical s. George Henry Ainger.

AINSLIE (George) Born Mayfair, London 28/7/1803, s. Sir Robert Sharpe Ainslie, 2nd Bart., *M.P.*, and Elizabeth Wanger. Emmanuel, Cambridge 1821, BA1825, dn28 (Cant. for London), MA1829, p29 (London), incorporated at Oxford 1849. R. South Willingham, Lincs. 1830-37, V. Barkway w. Reed, Herts. 1837-8, PC. St Philip, Clerkenwell, London 1851-4 (res., 'perhaps on having a breakdown' - LFBI). Died unmarried 14/5/1875 aged 71, leaving £18,000. Sec. of the Incorporated Church Building Society 1857-75; and London Diocesan Secretary of the Additional Curates' Society [C5327. LFBI 63 and photo.].

AINSWORTH (Thomas) Born Manchester Oct. 1795, s. John Ainsworth (a militia officer) and Mary Bancroft. Trinity, Cambridge 1814, BA1819, dn19 (Chester), p20 (Chester), MA 1822. PC. Hartford, Cheshire 1825 (living at Hartford Hall) to death 15/5/1847 aged 51 [C83016] Married (1) 1820 Elizabeth Bentley (killed 1832 falling from a gig) (2) 1837 Ann Rawstrawn, with issue.

AIREY (Henry Holme) Born Kendal, Westmorland 2/2/1797, s. Rev. Thomas and Alice Airey. Literate: dn21 (Chester), p21 (Chester). S/M Sedbergh School 1823-30; PC. Selside, Kendal 1831 to death 20/7/1867 aged 70, leaving £1,500 [C83017] Married Liverpool 17/9/1829 Sarah Rigg (w). Brother Thomas, below.

AIREY (John) Literate: dn08 (Car.), p09 (Car.). PC. Hugill (o/w Ings), Westmorland 1813 (and H/M Hugill G/S 1829-34) to death 20/6/1845 aged 66 [C4438] Married Kendal, Westmorland 16/11/1809 Sarah Smith, with clerical son.

AIREY (Thomas) Born Selside, Westmorland 9/5/1789, s. Rev. Thomas Airey and Alice Airey. Merton, Oxford 1810, migrated to Trinity, Cambridge 1811, BA1814, dn23 (Chester), p24 (Chester), MA1817. PC. Grayrigg, Kendal, Westmorland 1828-34 (disputed; res.). Died Holme Park, Lambrigg, Westmorland 10/7/1864, leaving £600 [C83021. Venn confuses father and son - who is PC. Peel, Lancs. at C100757] Married Kendal 9/2/1831 Isabella Holme (w), with clerical son of father's name. Brother Henry Holme, above. *J.P.*

AIREY (William) Bapt. Morland, Westmorland 23/10/1800, s. John Airey and Elizabeth Fothergill. Queen's, Oxford 1818, BA1822, dn24 (York), p25 (York), MA1826. V. Hexham, Northumberland 1826-45, V. Bramley, Hants. 1845 to death 16/3/1869 aged 68, leaving £4,000 [C114808.YCO] Married Hexham 5/2/1846 Anna Bushby, *s.p.*

AISLABIE (William James) Bapt. London 12/7/1768, s. Rawson Aislabie (merchant) and Frances Reason. Pembroke, Cambridge 1785, BA1789 [adm. Middle Temple 1788], MA1792 [called to the Bar 1793] dn00 (York). R. Holywell cum Needingworth, Hunts. 1804 to death (Cheltenham, Glos.) Probate granted 16/6/1843 [C5331. YCO] Married Kirkmichael, IoM 11/11/1797 Jane Heywood.

AITKENS (Robert Ellis) Born Westminster, London 26/11/1774, s. Robert Aitkens and Augusta Ellis. Trinity, Oxford 1793, BA1796, MA1800, p02 (C&L). PC. Atlow, Derbys. 1803, PC. Okeover, Staffs. 1802, PC. Hanley, Staffs. 1830-49 (where his house was fired by Chartists: *www.staffspasttrack.org.uk › Homepage › Disorder and Unrest*). Died 11/3/1849 [C8307] Married Mary Mere, w. clerical s. Charles Houghton Aitkens.

AKROYD see under **ACKROYD**

ALBAN (Thomas) Peterhouse, Cambridge 1786 (aged 24), a 'Twenty Year Man'. PC. Edgton and Sibdon Carwood, Shropshire 1795-1804 (res.), R. Culmington, Shropshire 1800-04 (res.), R. Snead, Montgomery 1801-35, V. Eaton under Haywood, Shropshire 1810-31 (res.), R. Llandrillo yn Rhos, Denbigh 1816 to death 13/4/1835 [C102229] Clerical son of same name.

ALCOCK (Charles) Born Slindon, Sussex, s. Rev. Charles Alcock, sen. New, Oxford 1814 (aged 19), BA1818, dn18 (Ox.), p20 (Ox.), MA 1822, Fellow. V. Empshott, Hants. 1823, R. and V. Great (w, Little) Witchingham, Norfolk 1835. V. Adderbury, Oxon. 1836 to burial 20/11/1857 aged 62 [C21369] Wife Mary, w. 1 son (died).

ALDER (St John) Born Dublin, s. John Alder (a mariner). TCD1802 (aged 16), BA1807, dn18, MA1818, p19. R. (and patron) of Bedhampton, Hants. 1823 to death 23/12/1864 aged 79, leaving £12,000 [C69189. Al.Dub.] Married Bloomsbury, London 6/6/1818 Harriot Eliza Reid.

ALDERSON (George) Bapt. Bowes, Yorks. 25/4/1747, s. Rev. William Alderson and Isabella Perkin. Literate: dn69 (Chester), p71 (York). R. Birkin, Yorks. (and Preacher throughout the Diocese of York) 1788 to death 8/5/1835 (CCEd says 31/7/1835) aged 88 [C83072. YCO] Married Cockfield, Durham 24/7/1778 Eleanor Humphries, w. clerical son William, below?

ALDERSON (George) Bapt. Eckington, Derbys. 13/6/1799, s. Rev. Jonathan Alderson (below) and Anna Maria Hodgson. Pembroke, Cambridge 1817, BA1822, dn22 (York), p23 (York), MA1856. PC. Wingerworth, Derbys. 1826-9, (succ. his father as) V. (and patron) of Hornby, Catterick, Yorks. 1829 to death. Dom. Chap. to Duke of Leeds at Hornby Castle 1841. Died 31/8/1879 aged 80, leaving £120,000 [C8288. YCO] Married York 30/11/1837 Henrietta Kearsley, with clerical son.

ALDERSON (Jonathan) Born Aston, Yorks. 6/8/1769, s. Rev. Christopher (R. Eckington, Derbys.) and Elizabeth Alderson. Pembroke, Cambridge 1788, BA1792, dn92 (C&L), p93 (C&L), MA1795. R. Langton on Swale, Yorks. 1793-1812, V. Hornby, Yorks. 1804-29, R. Harthill cum Winsley, Yorks. 1812 to death. Dom. Chap. to Lord Conyers, later Duke of Leeds. Died 10/9/1848 [C8285] Married 7/6/1798 Anna Maria Hodgson (a clergy dau.), with clerical son George (above). His brother William, below. *J.P.* North Riding.

ALDERSON (Joseph) Bapt. King's Lynn, Norfolk 18/9/1761, s. Joseph and Mary Alderson. BNC, Oxford 1779, BA1782, MA1785, dn87 (C&L), p87 (C&L). R. Hevingham, Norfolk 1787 and R. Oxwick, Norfolk 1810 death 12/2/1833 (CCEd thus) [C8297]

ALDERSON (Robert Jervis Coke) Born Bungay, Suffolk 4/8/1792, s. Robert and Henrietta Maria Alderson. Exeter, Oxford 1820, BA1825, dn25 (Ox.), p26 (Ox.), MA1827. R. Ipswich St Matthew, Suffolk 1831, R. Bodham, Norfolk 1832, R. Baconsthorpe, Norfolk 1832-68 [all blank in ERC], R. Wetherden, Suffolk 1844 to death (Capel St Mary, Suffolk) 19/8/1868, leaving £800 [C110756] Married Barningham Town, Norfolk 18/12/1832 Sophia Sara Mott, w. issue.

ALDERSON (Samuel Hurry) Bapt. Great Yarmouth, Norfolk 14/6/1789 (nonconformist baptism), s. Robert Alderson (barrister) and Elizabeth Hurry. Caius, Cambridge 1805, BA 1810, Fellow 1811-22, MA1813, dn21 (Nor.), p22 (Nor.). R. Risby w. Fornham St Genevieve, Suffolk 1830-63, R. Bredfield, Suffolk 1832-5 [vacant in ERC], V. Lowdham and Pettistree, Notts. 1834, R. Rise, Suffolk 1835-9, RD. Chap. to the Lord Chancellor 1830. Died Risby 27/1/1863, leaving £14,000. [C110757] Married Rougham, Suffolk 4/12/1821 Jane Frances Bennet, with issue.

ALDERSON (William) Born Aston cum Aughton, Yorks. 31/7/1773, s. Rev. Christopher (R. Eckington, Derbys.) and Elizabeth Alderson. Pembroke, Cambridge 1790, BA1795, dn96 (C&L), p97 (C&L), MA 1804. PC. Tissington, Derbys. 1811-52, (succ. his father as) R. Aston cum Aughton 1811 to death. Dom. Chap. to Lord Conyers, later Duke of Leeds Died 30/9/1852 aged 79 [C8286] Married Eastwood, Rotherham, Yorks. 23/2/1813 Harriet Walker, s.p. His brother Jonathan, above. J.P. West Riding.

ALDERSON (William) Born Birkin, Yorks. 28/3/1774, s. Rev. George (above?) and Elizabeth Alderson. Sidney, Cambridge 1792, then St Catharine's 1796, BA1796, dn96 (York), p98 (York). V. Hornby, Yorks. 1800-4, PC. Seaton Ross, Yorks. 1826 and R. (and patron) of Everingham, Yorks. 1827 to death 10/1/1839 aged 64 [C136043, YCO] Married York 23/10/1802 Elizabeth Robinson, with clerical son, below (and a possible second marriage 1837?)

ALDERSON (William Thompson) Born Holme on Spalding Moor, Yorks. 26/7/1806, s. Rev. William Alderson (above) and Elizabeth Robinson. Sidney, Cambridge 1825, then St. Catharine's 1826, BA1829, dn29 (York), p30 (York). (first) Curate Alverthorpe, Wakefield, Yorks. 1831-41. Chap. Wakefield House of Correction 1841-76. Died Goole, Yorks. 27/11/1892 aged 86, leaving £7,637-7s-1d. [C122865. YCO] Married Wakefield 12/9/1850 Eliza Sibbald Dykes, with clerical son of same name.

ALDRICH (Charles) Bapt. Stowmarket, Suffolk 4/8/1782, s. John Aldrich and Amy Cook. [NiVoF] PC. Wingfield, Suffolk 1813-14 (res.), PC. St Ives, Ewny Lelant, Cornwall 1825. Died (a widower) Plymouth 9/1/1864, leaving £600 [C110759] Married (1) 17/4/1807 Agnes Maria Blake (d.1808) (2) Brixham, Devon 2/12/1815 Susanna Bartlett France; w. clerical s. William. Brother William, below.

ALDRICH (John Cobbold) Born Stowmarket, Suffolk 18/3/1807, s. John Aldrich and Mary Cobbold. Lincoln, Oxford 1825, BA1828, dn30 (Nor.), MA1831, p31 (Nor.). PC. Ipswich St Lawrence, Suffolk 1831 to death 17/8/1874 aged 67, leaving £800 [C110760] Married Capel St Mary, Suffolk 11/2/1832 Sarah Maria Barthorpe (w), with issue. Fine photo. online.

ALDRICH (Stephen John) Born Chichester 17/8/1779. Literate: dn99 (London), p99 (London). R. Chickney, Essex 1799 to death 1843 (1st q.) [C2858] Married Great Chesterford, Essex 9/9/1794 Sarah Bustead, w. issue.

ALDRICH (William) Born Stowmarket, Suffolk 25/5/1763, s. Rev. William Aldrich, sen. and Mary Hall. Jesus, Cambridge 1781, dn85 (Nor.), BA 1786, p88 (Nor.). V. Stowmarket 1788-1837, R. Boyton St Andrew, Suffolk 1807, R. Hintlesham, Suffolk 1818-19? [but is this perhaps the man below?] Chap. to Prince Regent 1812. Died 22/7/1837 aged 74 [C110767] Married Wanstead, Essex 4/7/1799 Catherine Baynes, with issue. Doubtless related to the other Stowmarket men here.

ALDRICH (William) Bapt. Stowmarket, Suffolk 10/3/1781, s. John Aldrich and Amy Cook. Magdalen, Oxford 1799, BA1802, dn03

(Nor.), MA1805, p05 (Nor.), BD1815. R. Ipswich St Mary at Elms, Suffolk 1805 and R. Boyton, Wilts. 1823-[41]. Died Ipswich 3/11/1859, leaving £4,000 [C110766] Married Ipswich 31/8/1784 Maria Meyer (w), with clerical son, below. Brother Charles, above.

ALDRICH (William Wogan) Born Stowmarket, Suffolk 30/9/1800, s. William Aldrich (above) and Maria Meyer. Trinity Hall, Cambridge 1821, dn24 (Nor.), p25 (Nor.), LLB 1828. PC. Butley w. Capel St Mary, Suffolk 1825, R. Boyton, Suffolk 1841 to death 9/11/1864 aged 67, leaving under £200 [C110768] Married Orford, Suffolk 22/11/1830 Lucy Dorothy Mingay Rope (w).

ALFORD (Charles) Born Ashill, Somerset 24/1/1787, s. Rev. Thomas Alford and Sarah Coles. Balliol, Oxford 1805, BA1809, dn10 (B&W), p11 (B&W). R. West Quantoxhead (o/w St Audries), Som. 1814 to death (Exeter) 10/11/1869 aged 83, leaving £300 [C31119] Married St Audries 1815 Elizabeth Symes (w), with issue Charles Richard Alford, Bishop of Victoria, Hong Kong. Surrogate 1820. Port. online.

ALFORD (Henry) Born Curry Rival, Som. 3/12/1782, s. Rev. Samuel Alford (Dean of St Buryan, Cornwall) and Mary Bush. Wadham, Oxford 1800, BA1804, MA1811, barrister 1811, Fellow, dn13 (Salis.), p14 (Salis.). R. Ampton, Suffolk 1826-42 R. Wingfield, Wilts. 1833-5, R. Aston Sandford, Bucks. 1836-50. Died Tunbridge, Kent 23/9/1852 [C41254. Boase] Married (1) Tamworth, Staffs. 20/12/1809 Sarah Eliza Paget (dau. of a banker, she d. 1860 at the birth of their son Henry, the future Dean of Canterbury) (2) 11/8/1831 Susannah Barber, Denmark Hill, London. Brother, below.

ALFORD (Samuel) Born Curry Rival, Som. 6/3/1776, s. Rev. Samuel Alford, sen. (Dean of St Buryan, Cornwall) and Mary Bush. Queen's, Oxford 1794, BA1797, dn98 (B&W), MA1800. PC. Muchelney, Som. 1822-[45]. Died 22/3/1854 [C23616] Married Charmouth, Dorset 1802 Rebecca Shute, with issue. Brother, above. Port. online.

ALGAR (Joseph) From Canterbury, Kent, s. Joseph Algar. Wadham, Oxford 1806 (aged 18), BA1809, dn10 (B&W), p11 (B&W), MA1815. R. Orchardleigh, Som. 1818 and Min. Frome Christ Church, Som. 1819 to death. Probate granted 7/5/1839 [C31121]

ALINGTON (John) Born Graveley, Herts. 4/5/1795, s. Rev. William Alington and Sarah Williamson. Balliol, Oxford 1813, BA1817, dn19 (Lin.), p21 (Lin.), MA1822. R. (and patron) of Little Barford, Beds. 1822 (living at Little Barford Manor, and Letchworth Hall, Herts.) Died there 11/12/1864 aged 81, leaving £20,000 [C5338. LFBI 87] Married (1) Little Stanmore, Middx. 3/10/1822 Eliza Frances Plumer (d.1838), w. issue (2) Letchworth 27/3/1841 Elizabeth Tufnell.

ALINGTON (John) Born Swinhope, Lincs. 11/6/1801, s. Rev. Marmaduke Alington (below) and Ann Emeris. Magdalen, Oxford 1818, BA 1822, Fellow, dn24 (Ox.), p25 (Ox.), MA1825, LLD. R. Croxby, Lincs. 1832 and R. Candles-by, Lincs. 1834 to death 1/6/1883, leaving £5,617-5s-7d. [C5339. LF87] Married Spilsby, Lincs. 12/6/1835 Charlotte Sophia Bellingham, with clerical sons.

ALINGTON (Marmaduke) Born Swinhope, Lincs. 2/9/1760, s. Rev. Henry Alington and Frances Baron. Emmanuel, Cambridge 1778 [adm. Gray's Inn 1778] BA1782, dn83 (Lin.), p84 (Lin.). R. Stenigot, Lincs. 1785-1837, R. Walsoken, Lincs. 1787 and R. Thorganby, Lincs. 1787 to death (Swinhope House) 3/8/1840 aged 79 [C42582. LFBI 88] Married Louth, Lincs. 15/8/1794 Ann Emeris (a clergy dau.), with clerical son John (above). Brother, below. *J.P.* Lincs. 'for over 50 years'.

ALINGTON (William) Bapt. Aston, Herts. 10/12/1761, s. Rev. Henry Alington and Frances Baron. Peterhouse, Cambridge 1779, BA1783, dn84 (Lin.), p85 (Lin.), MA1809. R. Swinhope, Lincs. 1785-1837, R. (and patron) of Twywell, Northants. 1799, R. Little Barford, Beds. 1809-[22]. Chap. to 14th Baron St John of Bletso 1809. Died 13/12/1849 aged 88 [C5340. LF87] Married 2/7/1788 Sarah Williamson (dau. of a banker, Baldock, Herts.), with issue. Brother, above.

ALISON (Archibald) Born Edinburgh 13/11/1757, s. Andrew Alison (Lord Provost of Edinburgh) and Margaret Harte. Glasgow Univ. 1770, then Snell Exhibitioner Balliol, Oxford 1775, dn79 (Ox.), p82 (Durham), BCL 1784, LLD1791. Inc. Sudbury, Northants. --, PC. Kenley, Shropshire 1791 1800, Prebend of

Yetminster Secunda (or Inferior) in Salisbury Cathedral 1791-1839, R. West Lavington, Wilts. 1792-5, V. Ercall Magna (Great/High Ercall), Shropshire 1795-1800, R. Rodington, Shropshire 1799-1800; Min. Cowgate Chapel, Edinburgh 1800-31. Died 17/5/1839 [C9320. ODNB as 'writer on aesthetics'. Bertie. Snell] Married Thrapston, Northants. 19/6/1784 Dorothea Gregory (dau. of a physician), with distinguished issue (inc. Sir Archibald Alison, Bart., *q.v.* ODNB). *F.R.S.(Edin.)*. (1784).

ALLANSON (Thomas) Bapt. Allerston, Yorks. 21/5/1781, s. Francis and Grace Allanson. Literate: dn07 (Car. for York), p08 (York). PC. Dishforth, Yorks. 1818-53, PC. Monk Fryston, Yorks. 1821-39, V. Wistow, Yorks. 1827-39, R. Kirby on the Moor, Yorks. 1839 to death (Kirby Hall, Boroughbridge, Yorks.) 4/10/1859 aged 78, leaving £800 [C84082. YCO. Venn distinguishes him from a contemporary namesake, but has no details] Married Beverley, Yorks. 1810 Margaret Reddie, with issue.

ALLEN (Charles Jefferys) Born Stocklinch Manor, Bridgwater, Som. 9/12/1796, s. Jefferys Allen, *M.P.* and Susan Burlton. St Catharine's, Cambridge 1819, dn20 (Glos. for B&W), p21 (Salis.). R. Stocklinch Ottersey 1821 to death (unm.) 4/2/1875 aged 77, leaving £20,000 [C31123. LFBI 101]

ALLEN (Edward) From Bloomsbury, London, s. William Allen. BNC, Oxford 1804 (aged 17), BA1808, dn09 (Win. for Roch.), MA 1810. R. (and patron) of Hartley, Kent 1826 to death 4/1/1870. Will not traced [C1547]

ALLEN (George) Bapt. Dent, Yorks. 18/9/1791, s. of William Allen (a labourer) and Mary Oversby. Literate: dn16 (York), p17 (York). V. Kirkburn, Yorks. 1826-65, PC. Great and Little Driffield, Yorks. 1833-76. Died there 28/11/1881 aged 90, leaving £1,788-4s-6d. [C128573. YCO. ATV] Married (1) Alice (2) Heslerton, Yorks. 26/5/1818 Jane Vicker-man, w. clerical son.

ALLEN (James Thomas) Born Leominster, Heref., s. Rev. Thomas Allen. Balliol, Oxford 1791 (aged 18), BA1795, dn95 (Heref.), p97 (Peterb.), MA1798. R. Kelmarsh, Northants. 1797, R. Shobdon, Heref. 1799 to death. Probate granted 4/6/1844 aged 72 [C102235]

ALLEN (John) Bapt. Burton on Trent 23/6/1771, s. Jonah and Alice Allen. Christ Church, Oxford 1790, BA1794, dn94 (C&L), p95 (C&L), MA1797. S/M Crewkerne, Som. and V. Bledington, Glos. 1799 to death 22/5/1841 [C8313]

ALLEN (John) [NiVoF] PC. (Upper) Arley, Staffs. 1824 to death (from a carriage accident, Ilfracombe, Devon) 23/8/1850 [C8319]

ALLEN (John Taylor) Bapt. Salford, Lancs. 24/2/1784, s. James Allen (a hatter and hose manufacturer) and Elizabeth Taylor. BNC, Oxford 1801, BA1805, MA1807, dn11 (Chester), p12 (Chester). [Chetham's Librarian, Manchester 1812-21] PC. High Leigh, Cheshire 1821-6, PC. Clitheroe, Whalley, Lancs. (with S/M Clitheroe Free G/S) 1826-35, R. Alresford, Essex 1838-41, V. Stradbroke, Suffolk 1841 [income £1,140] to death 12/8/1861, leaving £5,000 [C83079. Boase] Married Hempstead, Glos. 2/1/1821 Mary Eleanora Drake (of Rochdale, a clergy dau.), with clerical son.

ALLEN (Joseph, *later* Bishop of Bristol, *then* of Ely) Bapt. Manchester 6/12/1770, s. William Allen (a bankrupt banker of Davyhulme Hall, Eccles, Lancs.) and Nelly Livesey. Trinity, Cambridge 1788 [adm. Lincoln's Inn 1788] BA1792, Fellow 1793, MA1795, dn99 (Nor.), p00 (Nor.), DD1829. Canon of Westminster Abbey 1806-36, V. Battersea St Mary, South London 1808-35, V. St Bride, City of London 1829-35, Bishop of Bristol 1834-6, Bishop of Ely 1836 to death 20/3/1845 [C51859. Not noted in ODNB?] Married Frodsham, Cheshire 19/5/1807 Margaret Ashley, with issue. Port. online.

ALLEN (Richard) Literate: dn84 (York), p85 (York). V. Wharram Percy, Yorks. [pop. 44] 1787 and PC. Great w. Little Driffield, Yorks. 1798 to death 23/1/1833 aged 74 [C84088. YCO] Probably married York 28/2/1781 Mary West. His unpublished diaries survive for 1828, 1830, 1832.

ALLEN (Robert) Born Lymington, Hants., s. Robert Allen (a Barbados plantation owner). New, Oxford 1812, LLB1819. R. Barcombe, Lewes, Sussex 1826 (and Prebend of Exceit in Chichester Cathedral 1841, value £5-3s-8d.) to death (while living in Wandsworth, London). Died Lymington 19/7/1877 aged 84, leaving £10,000 [Not yet in CCEd. LBSO] Wife Mary.

ALLEN (Samuel James) Born St Katharine's by the Tower, London 16/6/1798, s. Samuel Allen (a sailmaker) and Mary Brown. Pembroke, Cambridge 1816, BA1820, dn21 (Chester), p22 (Chester), MA1824. PC. Salesbury, Blackburn, Lancs. 1822 (and sometime H/M of Burnley Free G/S), V. Easingwold, Yorks. 1839 to death. Dom. Chap. to Lord de Tabley. Died 29/4/1856 aged 58 [C83080. Boase. DEB. Long obituary in the *Gentleman's Magazine*] Married Blackburn 16/5/1829 Mary Carr. 'A learned antiquary and a clever draftsman', he completed T.D. Whitaker's *History of Richmondshire* (1823).

ALLEN (Stephen, sen.) Born King's Lynn, Norfolk 25/9/1755, s. Rev. Stephen and Elizabeth Allen. Christ's, Cambridge 1771, no degree, dn78 (Nor.), p80 (Nor.). V. Dunton cum Doughton, Norfolk 1789-1800, PC. King's Lynn St Margaret w. St Nicholas 1791, V. Houghton, Norfolk 1799-1817, R. Haslingfield, Cambs. 1800-47, R. Wolterton w. Wickmere, Norfolk 1801. Died 15/3/1847 aged 92 [C1026] Married Gretna Green, Scotland 28/10/1772 (aged 17 years 1 month) Susanna Sharpin, East Dereham, Norfolk, with clerical son (below). 'Credited with having lost a fortune in his youth through extravagance' (Venn).

ALLEN (Stephen, jun.) Born King's Lynn, Norfolk 6/9/1775, s. Rev. Stephen Allen, sen. (above) and Susanna Sharpin. Trinity, Cambridge 1792, BA1797, dn98 (Nor.), p00 (Nor.), MA1800. (succ. his father as) V. Dunton cum Doughton, Norfolk 1800-55, R. Wolterton, Norfolk 1841-50. Died Erpingham, Norfolk 27/4/1855 aged 80 [C109949] Married with issue.

ALLEN (Thomas Dawson) Born Westminster, London, s. Andrew Allen. University, Oxford 1804 (aged 18), BA1809, MA1810, dn11 (Ox.), p12 (Ox.). R. North Cerney, Glos. 1826 to death 11/10/1875 aged 89. Will not traced [C21372] Married Cheltenham, Glos. 26/8/1840 Mrs Jane Henry, a clergy widow.

ALLEN (Thomas Lingen) Bapt. Hereford 23/5/1803, s. Rev. William (Holland House, Hereford) and Elizabeth Allen. Worcester, Oxford 1824, BA1828, dn29 (Heref.), p31 (Bristol for Heref.), MA1835. PC. Sutton St Michael, Heref. 1831-64-. Died (Brislington, Bristol) 17/4/1886, leaving £1,618-1s-10d. [C8073] Married Hereford 1/5/1845 Elizabeth Gwillim, with issue.

ALLEN (William) Born London Dec. 1773, s. Mundeford Allen. Trinity, Cambridge 1793, BA1797, dn97 (Nor.), p98 (Nor.), MA1800. V. Narborough w. Narford, Norfolk 1799 and V. Appleton, Norfolk [income £8] 1834 to death (a bachelor) 30/5/1864 age 91, leaving £2,000 [C110833]

ALLEN (William) Bapt. Hatton Garden, London 3/2/1775, s. Joseph and Elizabeth Allen. St John's, Oxford 1793, BA1797, dn98 (Ox.), p99 (Chester for Ox.), MA1801. PC. Peel (o/w Little Hulton), Lancs. 1814 (and H/M Bolton G/S at some date, living at Peel Hall) to death 4/3/1834 (CCEd thus) [C83081 and 22212] J.P. A member of the British Association for the Advancement of Science.

ALLFREE (Edward Mott) Bapt. Hurstmonceux, Surrey 30/9/1773, s. Edward Allfree and Ann Mott. St Alban Hall, Oxford 1790, then Wadham 1794, BA1794, MA1799. R. Warden, Sheppey, Kent 1808-20 (res.) (and S/M Maidstone, Kent G/S 1808-20 - res.), R. Canterbury St Andrew w. St Mary Bredman, Kent 1818, Minor Canon of Rochester Cathedral (and S/M Rochester Cathedral School) 1819, R. Strood, Kent 1821-32, V. Shorne, Kent 1832. Dom. Chap. to 2nd Earl Romney 1818-32. Died 1837 (4th q.). [C45] Married Hurstmonceux 21/6/1802 Ann Westenholt, with issue.

ALLGOOD (James) Born Chipchase Castle, Northumberland 29/1/1796, s. James Allgood and Martha Reed. University, Oxford 1813, then St Mary Hall, BA1819, dn19 (Nor. for Bristol), p21 (Bristol), MA1821. V. Felton, Northumberland 1827 and R. Ingram, Northumberland 1829 to death. Dom. Chap. to 1st Viscount O'Neill 1829-41. Died (unm.) 27/4/1850 aged 54 [C8074]

ALLIES (Thomas) Born Midsomer Norton, Som. 9/1/1785, s. James Allies and Hannah Dudden. St Edmund Hall, Oxford 1805, BA1808, dn10 (Salis.), MA1812. R. Wormington, Glos. 1826. Died Malvern, Worcs. 25/7/1838 [C32507] Married (1) Bristol 13/4/1812 Frances Elizabeth Fripps (d.1813), 1s. (2) Clifton, Bristol 16/3/1815 Caroline Hilhouse, w. further issue. Ports. online.

ALLKIN (Herbert) Bapt. Uttoxeter, Staffs. 9/3/1800, s. John and Dorothy Allkin. St Bees adm. 1825. (first) PC. Hyde, Stockport, Cheshire 1833 to death 1849 (1st q.) aged 49 [C83083]

Married Manchester 20/8/1834 Sarah Berkenshaw Peacock, 1s. Port. online.

ALLOTT (George) Bapt. South Kirkby, Yorks. 30/10/1776, s. Rev. John Allott (Hague Hall) and Ann Hammersley. St. Catharine's, Cambridge 1795, BA1799, dn99 (York), p00 (York), MA1814. PC. Bolton upon Dearne, Yorks. 1800-48, (succ. his father as) V. South Kirkby 1813 to death 13/6/1848 aged 71 [C84106. YCO. LFBI 112] Married South Kirkby 10/10/1805 Mary Emmerson, with clerical son John Allott.

ALLPORT (Josiah) Born Walsall, Staffs. 1784, s. Joseph Allport. [NiVoF] Literate: dn11 (Llandaff), p12 (Llandaff). H/M Bell's Foundation G/S, Newland in Forest of Dean 1811-17; PC. Bream, Glos. 1813-19 (res.), PC. Atherstone, Mancetter, Warwicks. 1825-30 (res.), PC. Ashted St James, Birmingham 1829-59, V. Sutton upon Trent, Notts. 1859 to death. Edited the *Protestant Journal* 1831-4. Died 16/2/1867, leaving £200 [C3617. Boase. DEB] Married Bristol 16/1/1812 Judith Wreford (w), and had issue.

ALLSOPP (Thomas) Bapt. Loughborough, Leics. 1/6/1770, s. Thomas Allsopp (attorney) and Anne Davis. Emmanuel, Cambridge 1787, BA1792, dn93 (C&L), p94 (Nor.), Fellow 1794, MA1795, BD1802. V. Fressingfield w. R. Withersdale, Suffolk 1809 to death 31/10/1845 aged 75. [C8289] Married Mendham, Suffolk 30/11/1813 Ann Brettingham, with issue.

ALLWOOD (Philip) From London, s. of Thomas Allwood. Magdalene, Cambridge 1787 (aged 18), BA1791, p93 (C&L), MA1794, BD1801, Fellow. PC. Wandsworth St Ann, London 1824 to death 14/3/1838 aged 69 [C8290]

ALMOND (Robert White) Born London 25/12/1785, s. Robert (of Nottingham, absentee plantation owner, Jamaica) and Mary Almond. Trinity, Cambridge 1803, then Queens' 1803, BA1808, dn09 (Salis. for York), p10 (York), MA1813. R. Nottingham St Peter 1814 to death 24/9/1853 aged 69 [C83221. YCO. LBSO] Married Nottingham 3/5/1808 Sarah Maria Russel, w. clerical s. William Russel Almond. Astronomer.

ALSTON (Vere John) Born Kempston, Beds.. 26/6/1788, s. Thomas Alston (Odell Caster, Odell, Beds.) and Elizabeth Raynsford. St John's, Cambridge 1806, BA1810, dn11 (Ex.), p12 (Ex.). V. Cowesby, Yorks. 1816-[32], V. Odell [blank in ERC] 1829 to death. Dom. Chap. to 2nd Marquess of Bute 1813. Died (and buried) Calais 24/5/1863, leaving £2000 (in 1847 his wife having taken a carriage to London with the family silver to avoid the creditors) [C5382. LDB! 117] Married (1) Combe Florey, Som. 14/8/1813 Elizabeth Mary Barnard (a clergy dau., d.1845), w. clerical son, also Vere John (2) Hinwick, Beds. 2/10/1845 Mrs Maria (Longuet) Orelebar: www.thekingscandlesticks.com › webs › pedigrees

AMBLER (Richard) Bapt. Shrewsbury, Shropshire 4/7/1781, s. Richard Ambler and Mary Gosnell. University, Oxford 1800, migrated to Christ's, Cambridge 1818, BA1824, p24 (Heref.). PC. Churchstoke, Montgomery (Hereford Diocese) 1831-45, V. North Lydbury, Shropshire 1834-7. Died Montgomery 1845 (3rd q.) [C102241] Married Lucy Harriet Clack, w. issue.

AMBROSE (John) From London, s. John Ambrose and ?Jane Bradbury. University, Oxford 1784 (aged 16), BA1791, MA1791 (as Ambrosse), dn91 (Salis.), p92 (London for Salis.). R. Blisworth, Northants. 1797-1839 [but parish sequestrated and Ambrose absent in France, and then in prison for debt]. Died 15/6/1839 [C83224] Married to 'a considerably younger wife', with issue. 'He disgraced a profession he should have adorned', as the following extraordinary article shows: www.blisworth.org.uk/images/Articles/Ambrosse-2.htm

AMPHLETT (John) Bapt. Hadsor Hall, Worcs. 25/1/1756, s. of William and Christian Amphlett. Worcester, Oxford 1774, BA1778, dn78 (Ox.), p80 (Wor.), MA1781, BD1790, DD 1791. R. Hadsor 1780-1808, V. Dodderhill w. Elmbridge, Worcs. 1789 and R. Hampton Lovett, Worcs. 1814 to death 26/6/1834 (CCEd says 14/8/1834) [C22214] Clerical son Joseph. Brother Martin, below.

AMPHLETT (Joseph) Bapt. Ombersley, Worcs. 7/9/1788, s. Thomas Amphlett and Elizabeth Nott. Trinity, Oxford 1806, BA1810, MA1813, dn23, p25. PC. Wythall, Worcs. 1824 and R. Hampton Lovett, Worcs. 1834 to death (King's Norton, Worcs.) 13/9/1859, leaving

£1,500 [C8317] Married King's Norton 21/1/1820 Martha Gem, with issue.

AMPHLETT (Martin) Born Hadsor, Worcs. 1/8/1767, s. William and Christian Amphlett. Worcester, Oxford 1790, BA1794, dn94 (Wor.), p96 (Wor.). R. Ryhall w. Essendine, Rutland 1807 to death (Stamford, Lincs.) 21/11/1834 aged 66 [C109117] Brother John, above.

AMPHLETT (Richard Holmden) Born Hadsor, Worcs. 18/8/1782, s. Richard Amphlett and Lydia Holmden. University, Oxford 1800, BA1805, dn05 (Heref.), p06 (Heref.), MA1807. R. Hadsor 1808, R. Birlingham w. Nafford, Worcs. 1812-14 (res.). Probate granted 2/4/1842 [C102242. LFBI 124] Married (1) Bloomsbury, London 15/1/1807 Sarah Paul (d.1823), w. clerical s. (2) Malvern, Worcs. 10/2/1827 Jane Dudley, w. further issue.

ANDERSON (Charles John, Sir, 8th Bart.) Born Kilnwick Percy Hall, Yorks. 5/10/1767, s. Rev. Sir William Anderson of Broughton, 6th Bart. and Anne Maddison. University, Oxford 1787, BA1791, dn91 (Lin.), p93 (Lin.), MA 1797. R. Lea, Lincs. 1795-1846, R. Donington on Bain, Lincs. 1797-1829-, Prebend of Thorngate in Lincoln Cathedral 1812-46, V. Scawby, Lincs. 1829 w. R. Bradley, Lincs. 1829 to death. Dom. Chap. to Lord Banff 1797. Died (a widower) 24/3/1846 aged 78 [C5389. LFBI 127] Married Scawby 13/12/1802 Frances Mary Nelthorpe (dau of a baronet) with issue. 'An amiable, sporting parson'. Inherited title in 1799.

ANDERSON (Edward) Bapt. Birdhopecraig Presbyterian Chapel, Northumberland 25/5/1784, s. Edward Anderon and Catherine Dacre. Queens', Cambridge 1803, BA1807, dn07 (Car.), p08 (Car.), Fellow 1808, MA1810, BD 1819. PC. Cumwhitton, Cumberland 1808-21, Minor Canon Carlisle Cathedral 1809-21 (res.), R. Hickling, Notts. 1821 to death 5/1/1843 aged 58 [C2866. Platt] Married Arthuret, Cumberland 11/6/1822 Ann (dau. of the famous Archdeacon Paley of Carlisle), w. clerical son.

ANDERSON (James Stuart Murray) Born Bombay. Balliol, Oxford 1817 (aged 17), BA 1821, MA1823, dn23 (Chester for Bristol), p24 (Bristol). PC. Brighton St George, Sussex 1831-51, R. Tormarton w. Acton Turville, Wilts. 1851-69 [income in CR65 £1,020] w. Hon. Canon Bristol Cathedral 1856 to death. Chap. in Ordinary 1836; British Chap. at Bonn 1859-65. Died Bonn 22/9/1869 aged 69, leaving £1,500 [C8077. Boase] Married 24/7/1823 Barbara Charlotte Wroughton, with clerical son in EpCoS.

ANDERSON (Mason) Bapt. Tittleshall, Norfolk 11/5/1790, s. William Anderson and Martha Mason. Ordained 31/5/1813 at Hoxton Academy for Congregationalists. Literate: dn28 (Salis.), p29 (Salis.). R. Sherrington, Wilts. 1831 to death 1/5/1873 aged 82, leaving £9,000 [C83225] Married Chalfont St Giles, Bucks. 4/8/1818 Charlotte Grimsdale (w), with clerical son.

ANDERSON (Richard) Bapt. West Witton, Leyburn, Yorks. 16/1/1792, s. John and Elizabeth Anderson. Lincoln, Oxford 1810, BA1815, dn15 (Chester), p16 (Chester). PC. West Witton 1822-64, V. Burneston, Yorks. 1834-54 (res.), PC. Leeming, Yorks. 1868-79. Died (a widower) Aisken House, Bedale, Yorks. 24/10/1884 aged 92, leaving £1,338-16s-0d. [C168171. Boase. Not in Foster] Wife Emma, and clerical son. A sporting parson.

ANDERSON (Robert) MA but NiVoF, dn21 (London), p22 (London). (first) Min. Brighton Holy Trinity [Proprietary Chapel] 1826-47. Died? [C2860]

ANDERSON (Thomas) Born Woodford, Essex 1795, s. John Anderson (who had slave plantations) and Susanna Fraser. Exeter, Oxford 1812, BA1816, MA1819, dn20 (Lin.), p21 (Lin.). R. (and patron) of Felsham, Suffolk [blank in ERC] 1822 to death 4/12/1872, leaving £60,000 [C42899] Married Northaw, Herts. 22/12/1819 Lydia Gould, with clerical son. J.P. www.natgould.org/thomas_anderson_1795-1872

ANDREW (James) Bapt. Hampsthwaite, Yorks. 27/10/1780, s. of William (a yeoman farmer) and Elizabeth Andrew. Literate: dn06 (York), p07 (Car. for York). PC. Whitby, Yorks. 1818-43, PC. Aislaby, Whitby, Yorks. 1825-6 (res.). Died Whitby 3/12/1843 aged 63 [C84130. YCO] Married Whitby 1819 Janet Chapman (of a banking family), with issue (including clerical son John Chapman Andrew in the New Zealand Parliament, q.v. Wiki).

ANDREWES (Gerard Thomas) Born Bloomsbury, London 27/12/1794, s. Rev.

Gerard Andrewes and Elizabeth Maria Ball. Trinity, Cambridge 1813, BA1817, dn18 (Cant.), p19 (Ely for Cant.), MA1820. R. All Hallows, Bread St. w. St John the Evangelist, City of London 1819 to death. Chap. to House of Commons 1839-49. Died 22/6/1851 [C6502] Married Westminster, London 10/6/1819 Elizabeth Catherine Heberden, w. issue.

ANDREWES, later UTHWATT (William) Born Great Linford Manor, Bucks. 26/8/1793, s. Henry Uthwatt Andrewes (banker) and Judith Yates. St John's, Cambridge 1812, BA 1816, dn16 (Lin.), MA1819, p19 (Lin.). R. Lillingstone Dayrell, Bucks. 1832-48, V. Stowe, Bucks. 1833-76, R. Maids Moreton, Bucks. 1848 to death. Dom. Chap. to Duke of Buckingham. Died 20/9/1879, leaving £80,000 (as Uthwatt) [C5398. LF139] Married 1832 Mary Long (Thorphinsty Hall, Westmorland (w) (a clergy dau.), 1 dau. J.P.

ANDREWS (George) From Reading, Berks., s. Rev. William Andrews. Trinity, Oxford 1810 (aged 18), then Corpus Christi, BA1815, MA 1827, dn27 (Ex.), MA1827, p28 (London). V. Hough on the Hill, Lincs. 1812-22, V. Sutton Courtenay w. Appleford, Oxon. 1832, R. Castor, Northants. 1851 to death 4/3/1864 aged 72, leaving £4,000 [C83226] Widow Catherine Mary.

ANDREWS (Robert Gordon) Bapt. Oxted, Surrey 16/10/1785, s. Rev. Nicholas Andrews and Sarah Castleman. St John's, Cambridge 1803, then Corpus Christi, BA1808, MA1812, dn12 (Ox.), p22 (Lin.). H/M Grantham G/S. V. Hough on the Hill, Lincs. 1822 to death (Grantham) 11/11/1842 [C5425] Married Leighton Buzzard, Beds. 1/1/1817 Jane Elizabeth Wilson, 2 clerical sons.

ANDREWS (Thomas) Born Clerkenwell, London 1776, s. William Andrews. Magdalen Hall, Oxford 1800 (aged 24), BA1806, MA1807, dn08 (Glos.), p08 (Glos.). PC. Cogges, Oxon. 1810, PC. Bredhurst, Kent 1828 to death 1855 [C137598 and C22066] Married Rachel Bright, w. clerical s. Thomas Desborough Andrews.

ANGUISH (George) Born London 7/2/1764, s. Thomas Anguish (barrister) and Sarah Henley. Caius, Cambridge 1781, BA1786, dn86 (Nor.), p88 (Nor.), MA1789. V. Moulton St Mary w. Tunstall, Norfolk 1788-1813, V. Potter Heigham, Norfolk 1789-1803, Canon of 5th Prebend in Norwich Cathedral 1790-1820 (res.), R. Gisleham, Suffolk 1797-1833, R. Ashby, Suffolk 1803-10, R. Lound, Suffolk 1810-16. Died unmarried 5/7/1843 (but LFBI suggests a £20,000 bequest must have been to his mistress and natural ch.). Lived at Somerleyton Hall (which he had inherited) [C1027. LFBI 144]

ANLEZARK (Robert) Born Pleasington Hall, Duxbury, Lancs., s. James Richard Anlezark and Margaret Ainsworth. A Congregational Minister at Stockport, Cheshire 1793-1801. St Edmund Hall, Oxford 1804 (aged over 40), migrated to Christ's, Cambridge 1806, dn08 (Bristol), BA 1809, p09 (Peterb.), MA1812. PC. Stafford St Chad 1825 and PC. Castle Church, Staffs. 1820 to death 24/11/1845 aged 83 [C114840] Married (1) Stockport 20/12/1798 Elizabeth Ryle (d.1802), w. issue (2) Bermondsey, London 8/6/1802 Mary Warren (d.1820) (3) Cannock, Staffs. 21/8/1826 Beatrice Bolton, w. further issue. 'A man of great stature and bulk.' Port. online.

ANNESLEY (Arthur) Born Chewton Mendip, Somerset 30/10/1769, s. Rev. Arthur Henry Annesley and Alice Dighton. Trinity, Oxford 1786, BA1790, dn92 (B&W), p93 (B&W), MA 1793. R. Clifford Chambers, Glos. 1793 and PC. Chilcompton, Som. 1802. Died 9/2/1845 aged 75 [C24462] Married Reading, Berks. 14/1/1800 Elizabeth Vere Tyndale, w. clerical s. Francis Vere Annelsley.

ANSON (Frederick) Born Shugborough Hall, Great Haywood, Staffs. [LFBI 149] 23/3/1779, s. George Anson (born Adams), *M.P.*, and Hon. Mary Venables Vernon. Christ Church, Oxford 1797, then All Souls, Fellow 1799-1803, BA 1801, dn02 (Car.), p03 (Car.), MA1804, BD and DD1839. V. Sudbury, Derbys. 1803-36, V. Marston upon Dove, Beds. 1804, V. Longford, Derbys. 1809, Prebend of Halloughton in Southwell Minster 1826-37, then of Oxton Secunda 1827, Dean of Chester 1839 (and R. Doddleston, Cheshire 1843) to death. Dom. Chap. to 3rd Baron Vernon 1817. Died 8/5/1867, leaving £45,000 [C4442, Boase. Kaye] Married Little Missenden, Bucks. 2/5/1807 Mary Anne Levett (a clergy dau.), with clerical son, also Frederick. Brother, below.

ANSON (Henry) Born Shugborough Hall, Great Heywood, Staffs. [LFBI 147] 19/12/1773, s. George Anson (born Adams), *M.P.*, and Hon. Mary Venables Vernon. Christ Church Oxford 1791, BA1795, dn97 (Car.), MA1798. R.

Gresham, Norfolk 1798-1801, R. Oxnead w Buxton, Norfolk 1801-54, R. Swanton Abbot, Norfolk 1807-26, R. Skeyton, Norfolk 1807-54, PC. Bylaugh cum Whitwell, Norfolk 1826-7, R. Lyng cum Whitwell, Norfolk 1827 to death (unm.) 17/10/1854. Dom. Chap. to 2nd Earl of Lichfeld 1819 [C4443] Brother, above.

ANTROBUS (William [Thomas]) Bapt. in an Independent Chapel, Cockermouth, Cumberland 30/1/1760, s. William Antrobus (innkeeper) and Ann Fearon. St John's, Cambridge 1778, BA1782, MA1785, Fellow 1786-95, dn89 (Ely), p90 (Ely), BD1792. R. St Andrew Undershaft w. St Mary Axe, City of London 1794 [net income £1,576] and R. Acton, Middx. 1797 to death. Examining Chap. to Bishop of London. Lived latterly Springfield Park, Acton. Died Brentford, Middx. 10/1/1853 aged 93 [C99080. Boase] Married St James, Piccadilly, London 15/5/1803 Hannah Elizabeth Bowles (a clergy dau.), with issue. Involved in lawsuit with the *H.E.I.C.* which lasted 20 years.

APPERLEY (Thomas) From Wrexham, Denbigh, s. Thomas Apperley. BNC, Oxford 1792 (aged 18), BA1796, dn96 (Chester), p98 (Chester). R. Stoke Lacy, Heref. 1811-33 [sequestrated in ERC], V. Ocle Pychard, Heref. 1815 [blank in ERC] Died? [C102616]

APTHORP (Frederick) Born Croydon, Surrey 8/9/1778, s. Rev. East Apthorp (Prebend of St Paul's Cathedral) and Elizabeth Hutchinson. Jesus, Cambridge 1795, BA1799, dn01 (London for Ely), p02 (Ely), MA1802. V. Bicker, Lincs. 1802, Prebend of Farndon cum Balderton in Lincoln Cathedral 1802-53, R. Gumley, Leics. 1807-53, V. Farndon cum Balderton >< Lincs. 1809-51. Dom. Chap. to 1st Earl of Dunraven and Mount-Earl 1807-8. Died Gumley 12/8/1853 aged 74 (living at Hanslope Park, Bucks.). [C5440] Married St George's Hanover Square, London 22/11/1803 Susan Hubbard, with clerical son, below.

APTHORP (George Frederick) Born Gumley, Leics. 29/1/1804, s. Rev. Frederick Apthorp (above) and Susan Hubbard. Emmanuel, Cambridge 1821, BA1826, dn27 (Lin.), p27 (Lin.). V. Bierton cum Broughton, Bucks. 1832-4, Minor Canon of Lincoln Cathedral 1834 (then Senior Vicar 1833, then Prebend 1865-77), PC. Greetwell, Lincs. 1833-8, R. Thorpe on the Hill, Lincs. 1833-77, V. Ashby Puerorum, Lincs. 1837-60. Died (Pott Shrigley, Cheshire) 15/6/1877, leaving £18,000 [C5441] Married Lincoln Jan. 1839 Mary Barbara Beaty, with clerical sons George Francis, and Charles Pretyman Apthorp.

ARCHER (Thomas) From Oxford, s. John Archer. Pembroke, Oxford 1797 (aged 16), then Merton, BA1803, dn03 (Salis.), p04 (Win.), then Peterhouse, Cambridge 1807. V. Whitchurch, Bucks. 1812 to death 22/5/1843 aged 63 [C5447]

ARDEN (Francis Edward) Born Longcroft Hall, Yoxall, Staffs. 3/6/1777, s. Rev. John Arden and Margaret Elizabeth Hamar. St John's, Cambridge 1795 [as Edward], BA1799, dn99 (Nor.), p01 (Nor.). R. Gresham, Norfolk 1801-55, V. Paston, Norfolk 1806-29, R. Burgh by Aylsham, Norfolk 1829-31 (res.), R. Borough Green, Cambs. --, PC. West Beckham, Norfolk 1853 to death (Gresham) 27/12/1855 [C110900. LF170] Married Blickling, Norfolk 17/10/1803 Rachel Pinckard, with clerical sons Francis Edward, jun., and Henry Cotton Arden. Succ. to the Longcroft Hall estate in 1824. Brother below.

ARDEN (Thomas) Born Longcroft Hall, Yoxall, Staffs. March 1796, s. Rev. John Arden and Margaret Elizabeth Hamar. Trinity, Cambridge 1815, BA1819, dn20 (Glos.), p20 (Glos.). R. Bessingham, Norfolk 1832-42, V. Walton on Trent, Derbys. 1858 to death. Chap. to the Magdalen Asylum, Birmingham 1850-3. Died 8/10/1860, leaving £1,000 [C8323] Married /Longdon, Staffs. 98/4/1834 Isabella Mary Cooper, w. issue. Brother above.

ARKWRIGHT (Joseph) Born 9/8/1791, s. Richard Arkwright (s. of the inventor, Willersley Castle, Derbys. [LFBI 175]) and Mary Simpson. Trinity, Cambridge 1810, BA1814, dn15 (C&L), p16 (C&L), MA1817. V. Latton, Essex 1820-50, R. Thurlaston, Leics. 1824-45. Died (Mark Hall, Latton, Essex) 29/2/1864, leaving £400,000 - the largest amount left by any clergyman here [C5449. Boase. LFB1 173] Married Walthamstow, Essex 29/10/1818 Anne Wigram (dau. of a baronet), with clerical son John Julius Arkwright. Master of the Essex Foxhounds; and 'one of the largest farmers in Essex'.

ARMISTEAD, ARMITSTEAD (William) Bapt. Whitehaven, Cumberland 23/3/1799, s. Rev. Richard and Agnes Armistead. St John's, Cambridge 1819, BA1823, dn23 (York), p24

(York). PC. Lorton, Cumberland 1826-64, PC. Garstang, Lancs. 1835 [specifically noted in C4446 against Venn; Foster has a second man]. Died Edinburgh 15/2/1870 (unm., of bronchitis), leaving £8,000 [C4446. YCO]

ARMISTEAD see also **ARMITSTEAD**

ARMITAGE (Braithwaite) Born 29/3/1804, s. Whaley Armitage and Eleanora Haistwell. Trinity, Cambridge 1823, BA1827, dn27 (Heref.), p28 (Heref.). V. Peterchurch, Heref. 1832-75. Died Lewisham, Kent (a widower) 6/11/1878, leaving £1,500 [C42999] Married Bloomsbury, London 28/9/1831 Ann Susanna Longden, 2s., 1 dau.

ARMITAGE, ARMYTAGE (John Wentworth) Born Northampton 23/4/1793, s. John Armitage and Anne Thursby. Emmanuel, Cambridge 1812, BA1816, dn16 (York), p17 (York), MA1819. PC. Hickleton w. Bulwell, Notts. 1817 to death (unm.) Doncaster, Yorks. 12/4/1865, leaving £18,000 [C130472. YCO. ATV] Known as 'Divine Jack'! 'Out of health.'

ARMITSTEAD (James) Bapt. Giggleswick, Yorks. 7/9/1806, s. John Armitsead and Ann Carr. Wadham, Oxford 1825, BA1829, dn29 (Lin.), p30 (Lin.), MA1831. PC. Barlings, Lincs. 1830 to death (Fiskerton, Lincs.) 24/5/1843 aged 37 [C43000]

ARMITSTEAD, ARMISTEAD (John) Born Cranage Hall, Goostrey, Cheshire 24/2/1801, s. Rev. John Armistead and Mary Simpson. Trinity, Oxford 1819, BA1823, dn24 (Chester), p25 (Chester), MA1826. PC. (and patron) of Church Hulme (now Holmes Chapel), Sandbach, Cheshire 1825-8, V. (and patron) of Sandbach 1828 [total income in CR65 £1,307] to death 19/4/1864 aged 65, leaving £6,000 [C168178. LFBI 179] Married Chester 27/5/1828 Hester Susannah Massie (of Coddington, Cheshire, a clergy dau.), 8 ch (2 clerical: John Richard, and William George). J.P. Cheshire. 'A tireless mountain of a man'; a keen education-alist, cricketer and gardener', 'he is said to have postponed the celebration of Ascension Day by one week because it would have prevented him attending an English cricket match.'

ARMITSTEAD see also **ARMISTEAD**

ARMSTRONG (Charles Edward) Born Bombay 6/1/1807, s. Charles Edward Armstrong ('of Maidenhead') and Dorothy Wood. Worcester, Oxford 1827, BA1831, dn31 (York), p32 (York), MA1833. PC. Frickley w. Clayton >< Pontefract, Yorks. 1832-62, Master of Holgate's Hospital [almshouses], Hemsworth, Yorks. 1832 to death 2/4/1872 aged 65, leaving £5,000 [C130474. YCO] Married Bath 18/4/1838 Mary Anne Clayton (Enfield Old Hall), with issue. Succeeded to his grandmother's estates in Otley, Yorks. 1852.

ARMSTRONG (John) Born Dockray, Wigton, Cumberland 31/10/1794, s. of a labourer. Literate: dn19 (Durham), p20 (Durham). PC. Westoe, Durham, 1827-30 (res.), PC. Wallsend, Northumberland 1830 to death 7/12/1871 aged 77, leaving £1,500 [C130280] Married Darlington, Yorks. 5/2/1823 Mary Wilson (w), with issue.

ARMSTRONG (Matthew) Bapt. Hagbourne, Berks. 5/3/1758, s. William Armstrong and Christian Philips. Wadham, Oxford 1775, BA 1779, dn80 (Ox.), p87 (Salis.). R. Marsh Baldon, Oxon. 1788-1800 (res.), R. Toot Baldon, Oxon. 1790, R. Shaw cum Donnington, Berks. 1826 to death 12/5/1837 [C22235] Married Courtenay, Berks. 13/10/1785 Ann Philips. Confusion with man below.

ARMSTRONG (Matthew) Christ's, Cambridge 1808, then Queens' 1809, BA1813, p13 (Chester 1808, then Queens' 1809, BA 1813, p13 (Chester for C&L), MA1817. PC. Buckland (near Dover), Kent 1821 to death 1837 [C8401] Confusion with the man above.

ARMSTRONG (William) Bapt. Raskelf, Yorks. 17/8/1772, s. James Armstrong (a farmer). Jesus, Cambridge 1791, BA1795, dn95 (York), p98 (Ely). R. Stanford le Hope, Essex 1801-41. Died (Gravesend, Kent) 13/10/1844 [C84156. YCO]

ARMSTRONG (William Archibald) Bapt. Marylebone, London 24/12/1770, s. Edmund Armstrong and Frances Armstrong, Trinity, Cambridge 1788, BA1793, dn93 (Ex. for Salis.), p00 (London). R. South Hykeham, Lincs. 1819 to death (Cheshunt, Hants.) 23/4/1837 aged 66 [C5455] Married St George's Hanover Square, London 2/5/1796 Charlotte Eleanor Mary Hassell, w. issue. J.P. Herts. and Middx. F.S.A.

ARMYTAGE see under **ARMITAGE**

ARNOLD (Charles) Bapt. Stamford, Lincs. 27/5/1802, s. Thomas George Graham (medical doctor) and Elizabeth Arnold. Caius, Cambridge 1820, BA1824, dn25 (Peterb.), Fellow 1825-8, p26 (Nor. for Peterb.), MA1827. R. Wakerley, Northants. 1826-8, R. Tinwell, Rutland 1827-84, Hon. Canon Peterborough Cathedral 1854 (and RD 1866-81). Died 2/10/1884, leaving £15,573-1s-3d. [C8402] Married London 25/6/1828 Ellen Burrows, with issue. Brother Thomas Kerchever, below.

ARNOLD (Richard Aldous) Born Lowestoft, Suffolk 12/12/1792, s. Aldous Charles Arnold and Margaret Doughty. Trinity, Oxford 1811, BA1816, dn17 (Nor.), p19 (Nor.), BCL. R. Ellough, Suffolk 1830-77, PC. Great Redisham, Suffolk 1830-64-. Died (Ellough) 29/4/1877, leaving £30,000 [C110904] Married Chesterfield, Derbys. 1/12/1816 Charlotte Elizabeth Thomas, w. clerical sons Charles Thomas, and Frederick Montague Arnold.

ARNOLD (Thomas Kerchever) Bapt. Stamford, Lincs. 6/3/1800, s. Thomas George Graham (medical doctor) and Elizabeth Arnold. Trinity, Cambridge 1816, BA1821, Fellow 1823, dn24 (Ely), MA1824, p27. R. Lyndon, Rutland 1830 to death 9/3/1853 [C6506. ODNB. Boase] Educationalist, especially as a writer of school text books. Brother Charles, above. 'Remarkable for an almost feminine gentleness of manner, and for the unaffected simplicity of his life,' etc.

ARROWSMITH (Joseph) Bapt. Bolton upon Swale, Yorks. 8/4/1787, s. Joseph and Dorothy Arrowsmith. St John's, Cambridge 1804, BA 1810, dn10 (York), p13 (Durham). V. Fishlake, Yorks. 1822 to death 5/3/1846 [C84162. YCO] Married Haughton-le-Skerne, Durham 27/11/1810 Mary Robson, with issue.

ARSCOTT (John) Bapt. Plympton St Maurice, Devon 1/4/1777, s. John Arscott. Exeter, Oxford 1796, dn99 (Ex.), BA1800, p01 (Ex.), MA1816. PC. Plympton St Maurice 1801-[45], R. Rame, Cornwall 1804, V. Mevagissey, Cornwall 1824. Died Plympton 1845 (3rd q.) aged 68 [C139172 as Anscott]

ARTHUR (George Frederick) Born Plymouth 1805, s. John Arthur. Trinity, Oxford 1823, BA 1827, dn28 (B&W), p29 (Ex.), MA 1832. V. Tamerton Foliot, Devon 1830 to death 7/12/1870 aged 65, leaving £12,000 [C41263] Married Bishop's Hull, Som. 18/4/1841 Elizabeth Julia Walter (w).

ARTHUR (James) Bapt. Piltom, Devon 5/2/1797, s. William and Grace Arthur. Pembroke, Cambridge 1817, dn21 (Ex.), BA 1821, p23 (Ex.). R. (and patron) Atherington, Devon 1829 to death 8/11/1878 aged 81, leaving £1,500 [C139176] Married by 1827 Mary Judd Brent Burnard, w. clerical s. Thomas Frederick Arthur.

ARTHUR (John) Bapt. Lostwithiel, Cornwall 27/3/1759 (CCEd says born St Ives, Cornwall 27/10/1759), s. John Arthur (of Truro). Exeter, Oxford 1778, BA1782, dn82 (Ex.), p84 (Ex.). V. (St.) Colan, Cornwall 1790-1836 [not noted in CCEd], V. St Neots, Cornwall 1806 [CCEd says Hunts.] to death 12/12/1836 aged 77 [C5492] Married St Ives 1792 Dorothy Stephens, with issue.

ARUNDELL, *born* **JAGO (Francis Vyvyan Jago)** Born Launceston, Cornwall 24/9/1780, s. Thomas Jago and Catherine Bolt. Exeter, Oxford 1797, BA1801, dn03 (Ely), p04 (Ex.), MA1809. R. Landulph, Cornwall 1805 to death. Chap. to the British factory at Smyrna in 1822 for 14 years, where he collected antiquities, and about which he wrote extensively). Died 5/12/1846 aged 66 [C145302 under Jago. ODNB under Arundell - changed name 1815] Married Marylebone, Lodon 17/10/1818 Anna Maria Morier (dau. of the Consul General at Constantinople). Fine portrait online.

ARUNDELL (William Harris) Born Cheriton Fitzpaine, Devon 27/10/1797, s. Rev. John Arundell. Caius, Cambridge 1817, BA 1821, dn22 (Ex.), p23 (Ex.), MA1824. Preacher throughout the Diocese of Exeter 1813, R. (and patron) of Cheriton Fitzpaine 1824 [income in CR65 £1,052] to death 5/5/1873 aged 75, leaving £12,000 [C139178] Married (1) Woolfardisworthy, Devon 1840 (4th q.) Louisa Hole (a clergy dau., d.1845), w. clerical s. William Henry (2) Clifton, Bristol 23/11/1847 Sarah Peach Kettle (w), more ch.

ASHBRIDGE (Joseph) Literate: p78 (C&L). PC. Temple Normanton (o/w Derby St Peter, Normanton Chapel) 1793-1836, V. Ault Hucknall, Derbys. 1798-1836 (non-res.) and V. Heath, Derbys. 1822-36 [C9329. Austin] to burial 10/3/1836 aged 82 [C8396. Austin]

ASHBURNER (John) [NiVoF] V. Linton, Kent 1800 and V. Otham, Kent 1831 to death. Probate granted 18/5/1849 [C150210 is confused with Denny Ashburnham, below]

ASHBURNER (Robert) Bapt. Dalton in Furness, Lancs. 10/2/1760, s. John Ashburner and Margaret Atkinson. Literate: dn85 (Chester), p91 (Chester). PC. (Kirkby) Ireleth, Dalton 1791-1840 (and S/M there), PC. Rampside, Dalton 1807-8 (res.). Died Ireleth 6/6/1840 aged 81 [C168185] Married Dalton 1/6/1797 Hannah Bellman, with issue (one of whom, Margaret, kept a child's diary 1814-19, transcribed in *Trans. Cumberland and Westmorland Antiquarian and Archaeological Soc.*, N.S. (Volume 43) 1943).

ASHBURNER (William) [NiVoF] PC. Ufton, Warwicks. 1807. Died 1838 [Not yet in CCEd] 'Late a lodger of Ulverston, Lancs.'; and an 'occasional dealer in boots' [*sic*. books?]

ASHBURNHAM (Denny) Born Westminster, London 29/5/1773, s. Sir William Ashburnham, 5th Bart. and Alicia Woodgate. Clare, Cambridge 1799, BA1804, p20 (Ely for Chich.), MA1828. V. Ditchling, Sussex 1820 and R. Catsfield, Sussex 1823 to death (Regent's Park, London) 2/3/1843 aged 69 [C2861 is confused with John Ashburner, above] Married (1) 20/2/1802 Mrs Ann/Nancy (Dickson) Bancroft (d.1818), w. issue (2) Holborn, London 7/5/1819 Mary Hill (a minor) (3) Marylebone, London 10/7/1828 Harriet Luckie (a minor), w. issue. Brother, below.

ASHBURNHAM (John, Sir, 7th Bart.) Born Westminster, London 26/12/1770, s. Sir William Ashburnham, 5th Bart. and Alicia Woodgate. Clare, Cambridge 1810, BD1815. R. Guestling, Sussex 1798-1854, V. Cocking, Sussex 1796-8, Gates Prebend and Chancellor of Chichester Cathedral 1796 and V. (and patron) of Pevensey, Sussex 1816 to death 1/9/1854 [C2862. Boase. LFBI 201] Married (1) Hollington, Sussex 4/7/1804 Fanny Foster (d.1838), with issue (2) Anne Harman, *s.p*. Brother, above. Succ. to the baronetcy 1843. Confused with John *Ashburner*, above.

ASHE (Robert) Bapt. Langley Housem, Langley Burrell, Wilts. 11/1/1781, s. Robert Ashe and Thermuthis Martyn. Trinity, Oxford 1799, BA1803, dn03 (Salis.), MA1811. R. Langley Burrell 1807-55 [C83234] and R. Harnhill, Glos. 1825-33 (res.). Died Langley House 12/2/1855 aged 74 [C137434. LFB! 204] Married (1) Purton, Wilts. 30/8/1803 Mary Jane Jenner Watts (d.1811), w. clerical sons Robert Martyn, and Edward Ashe (2) Bath, Som. 1/11/1814 Mrs Elizabeth (Selby-Lowndes) Harman (Winslow, Bucks., d.1829) (3) Box, Wilts. 2/12/1830 Elizabeth Rous Pybus.

ASHFIELD (Charles Robert) Bapt. Slapton, Bucks. 17/2/1790, s. Rev. Charles Ashfield and Mary Wodley. BNC, Oxford 1808, BA1812, dn13 (Lin.), p14 (Lin.), MA by 1827. R. St Benet Fink, City of London 1818-34, V. Keynsham, Som. 1819-25 (res.), R. Dodington, Som. 1821-31, R. Great Blakenham, Suffolk 1827-71, R. Loddon, Norfolk1830, R. Whitton cum Thurleston, Suffolk 1830-4, R. Burgate, Norfolk 1834 to death 11/8/1871. Will not traced [C5497] Married Dinton, Bucks. 25/6/1817 Ann Goodall, and issue. *J.P.* Suffolk.

ASHFORD (John) Bapt. Birmingham 7/5/1787, s. Richard and Ann Ashford. St John's, Cambridge 1825, a Ten Year Man, dn24 (York), p25 (York). V. Kirkby Wharfe, Yorks. 1832 to death 2/11/1856 aged 68 [C130477. YCO] Wife Ann, with issue.

ASHLEY (John) Bapt. Frodsham, Cheshire 20/3/1779, s. Robert Wainwright (attorney) and Ann Ashley. Trinity, Cambridge 1796, then Jesus 1798, BA1801, Fellow 1802-10, dn03 (Peterb.), MA1804, p04 (Peterb.). V. Guilden Morden, Cambs. 1809, V. Eckington, Worcs. 1812-30, R. (and patron of) Great Wenham (Wenham Magna), Suffolk 1830, Canon of Ely Cathedral 1841-58, R. Teversham, Cambs. 1843 to death. Chap. to Bishop of Ely 1836. Died 24/4/1859 aged 81, leaving £12,000 [C99556] Married Whitegate, Cheshire 21/6/1819 Hannah Dutton, with issue. Brother below.

ASHLEY (Thomas) Born Frodsham, Cheshire, s. Robert Wainwright (attorney) and Ann Ashley. BNC, Oxford 1/91 (aged 19), BA 1794, MA1797, dn98 (Ox.), p98 (Ox.), BD1810. R. West Shefford, Berks. 1818 to death (a bachelor) 15/4/1851 aged 79 [C22241]. Brother above.

ASHTON (Ellis) Born Woolton Hall, Liverpool 15/4/1789 (bapt. in a Presbyterian Chapel), s. NicholasAshton (the owner of the Dungeon Salt Works, and High Sheriff of Lancashire) and Catharine Hodson. BNC,

Oxford 1807, BA 1811, Fellow 1813-24, MA 1813, dn13 (Ox.), p13 (York for Chester), BD1821. V. Huyton, Prescot, Lancs. 1813-69 (and RD of Prescot 1845-69) and R. Begbroke, Oxon. 1823 to death. Chap. to Archbishop of Canterbury 1848-62. Died Huyton 11/7/1869 aged 80, leaving £16,000 [C22079. Boase has an interesting note. YCO] Married Hope, Derbys. 12/8/1817 Mary Woodroœ, w. issue (2) Toxteth Park, Liverpool 1/5/1834 Frances Colquitt.

ASHWORTH (Thomas Alfred) Born Pendleton, Salford 1/1/1805, s. Richard John Daventry Ashworth (barrister) and Ann Macaulay. Trinity, Cambridge 1823, BA1828, dn28 (Chester), p30 (Chester), MA1831. V. Farnworth, Lancs. 1831-6. Joined the Irvingite or Catholic Apostolic Church and moved to London. Insane and living at Moorcroft House, Hillington, Middx., dying there 5/2/1884 aged 79, leaving £4,750-0-5d. [C168190] Married Lytham, Lancs. 28/5/1828 Harriet Halstead, with issue (including a son also insane, and in the same private asylum).

ASKEW (Henry) Bapt. Bloomsbury, London 8/7/1767, s. Anthony Askew (physician) and Elizabeth Holford. Emmanuel, Cambridge 1786, BA1790, dn90 (B&W), p94 (Nor. for B&W), MA1799. R. Greystoke, Penrith, Cumberland 1798 [blank in ERC] to death 25/12/1852 aged 87. Built Glenridding House, Ulswater, Lancs. [C4457. Platt. LFBI 213] Married Ulverston 29/7/1799 Anne Sunderland, 3 ch. Venn recounts him meeting the ghost of Corby Castle!

ASPINALL (James) Born Liverpool 22/6/1795, s. John Bridge Aspinall (Cleongar Hall, Cheshire) and Nancy Clarke. St Mary Hall, Oxford 1816, BA1820, dn20 (Chester), then Queen's, p21 (Chester), MA1823. Chap. Liverpool St Michael 1826-31, (joint) Minister Liverpool St. Luke 1831 'for 5 years', R. Althorpe, Lincs. 1839 to death. Dom. Chap to Lord Clonbrock for over thirty years. Died 15/2/1861 aged 65, leaving £3,000 [C168191. ODNB. Boase] Married Birkenhead, Cheshire 3/10/1816 Harriet Lake (d.1860), with issue. *J.P.* for Lindsey.

ASTLEY (Francis Bickley, *also known as* Thomas Bickley') Born Eastcote Barston, Warwicks. 8/12/1782, s. Francis Dugdale (Everly, Wilts.) and Mary Astley. Oriel, Oxford 1802, BA1806, dn07 (Salis.), p09 (Salis.), MA1809. R. Manningford Abbas, Wilts. 1810-56, R. Bishopstrow, Wilts. 1820-31, R. Everleigh, Wilts. 1830 to death. Dom. Chap. to 2nd Earl of Ailesbury 1820-30; to 1st Marquess 1830. Died 29/10/1856 [C41267] Married Placé, Mayenne 19/7/1813 Mary Anne Ludford, with issue.

ASTLEY (Henry Nicholas) Born Melton Constable Hall, Norfolk [LFBI 219] 5/1/1767, s. Sir Edward Astley, 4th Bart. and Anne Milles. Adm. Lincoln's Inn 1785. Christ's, Cambridge 1785, BA1789, dn91 (Nor.), p91 (Nor.), MA 1792. R. East Barsham w. Little Snoring (o/w Nareing), Norfolk 1791-1854, R. Bintree, Norfolk 1799-1804, R. Foulsham, Norfolk 1803-33 (res.). Died Walsingham, Norfolk 14/8/1854 aged 87 [C110914. LFBI 219] Married Exeter 22/2/1798 Sarah Pitman (an Exeter clergy dau.), w. clerical s. Henry L'Estrange Milles Astley.

ASTON (Walter Hutchinson, 9th Baron Aston of Forfar - a Scottish feudal or prescriptive barony). Born London 15/9/1769, s. Walter Aston, 8th Lord Aston of Forfar and Ann Hutchinson. Christ Church, Oxford 1789, BA 1793, dn95 (Ox.), MA1796, p96 (York). V. Tardebigge, Worcs. 1821, V. Tanworth, Warwicks. Died 21/1/1845 [C22244. YCO] Married 15/6/1802 Elizabeth Haines (a clergy dau.), *s.p.* Succ. to title 1805: title extinct on his death. *J.P.* Worcs.

ATCHESON (Anthony Singleton) Born Holborn, London 8/11/1800, s. Nathaniel Atcheson and Elizabeth Singleton Eden. St John's, Cambridge 1815, dn23 (Heref. for London), SCL1824, p24 (London), BA1826. R. Teigh, Rutland 1830 to death 18/6/1876, leaving £5,000 [C109223] Married Melcombe Regis, Dorset 23/8/1831 Ellen Bradley, with issue.

ATHERLEY (Arthur) Born Southampton, Hants. 8/2/1794, s. Arthur Atherley and Lady Louisa Kerr (dau. of the 5th Marquess of Lothian). Trinity, Cambridge 1812, BA1812, MA1816, dn18 (Chester for Chich.), p18. V. Heavitree, Exeter (and Preacher throughout the Diocese of Exeter) 1820 and Middleton Prebend of Chichester Cathedral 1833 to death (London) 14/2/1857 [C61097. LF226] Married Littlehampton, Sussex 8/11/1821 Amelia Elizabeth Dawkins, with issue.

ATHILL, ATTHILL (Lombe) Bapt. Great Yarmouth, Norfolk 5/2/1788, s. Edward Athill (merchant) and Mary Turner. Caius, Cambridge 1805, BA1810, dn11 (London [for Nor.?]), p12 (Nor.). PC. (and patron of) Rumburgh w. South Elmham St Michael, Suffolk 1823-50. Died Halesworth, Suffolk 20/3/1864 aged 76, leaving £5,000 [C111031] Married Halesworth 15/8/1831 Harriet Pizzey.

ATHOW (John) Bapt. Hoe, Norfolk 21/1/1776, s. Robert and Alice Athow. Jesus, Cambridge 1801, BA1803, dn07 (Nor.), p08 (Nor.). R. Norwich St Edmund the King 1808-17 (res.), R. Hulcott, Bucks. 1817 to death 9/4/1842 aged 66 [C5508] Married Norwich 1/6/1815 Maria Anne Fromow, w. issue.

ATKINS (Henry) From Wykeham, Hants., s. Samuel Atkins. New, Oxford 1793 (aged 17), dn97 (Win.), BA1798, p99 (Win.), MA1800. V. Arreton, IoW 1815-42, PC. Chichester St Bartholomew, Sussex 1832, Windham Prebend 1828 then Wightring Prebend in Chichester Cathedral 1834 to death. Dom. Chap. to 2nd Earl of Onslow 1814. Died Kingsteignton, Devon 8/10/1842 aged 67 [C61100]

ATKINSON (Christopher) Born Leeds 5/4/1773, s. Rev. Miles Atkinson (V. Kippax, Yorks.) and Mary Kenion. Magdalene, Cambridge 1791, BA1796, dn96 (London), p97 (York), MA1799. PC. Elland cum Stainland and Fixby, Leeds 1802 and PC. Leeds St Paul 1811 to death 15/5/1843 aged 70 [C84174. YCO] Married Leeds 6/2/1802 Elizabeth Wilson (w), w. clerical son, also Christopher. Brother Thomas, below.

ATKINSON (Henry) Born Bacton, Norfolk 1/11/1770, s. Henry Atkinson (attorney). Caius, Cambridge 1788, BA1793, Fellow 1793-6, dn93 (Nor.), p96 (Nor.). R. (Great w. Little) Wacton, Norfolk 1800 (non-res.) and R. Crostwight, Norfolk 1804 to death 1/1/1846 [C111052] Married North Walsham, Norfolk 24/6/1799 Maria Hepworth (a clergy dau.).

ATKINSON (Henry Arthur) Bapt. Knight's Enham, Hants. 11/3/1788, s. Rev. Arthur and Penelope Atkinson. Queen's, Oxford 1805, BA 1809, dn11 (Ox.), Fellow 1811-22, MA1812, p12 (Ox.). V. Chetwode w. Barton Hartshorn >< Bucks. 1812, PC. Portsea St George, Hants. 1827, PC. Escomb, Co. Durham 1848 to death 12/6/1867, leaving under £100 [C5342]

ATKINSON (Hugh) Literate: dn82 (Car.), p85 (Car.). PC. Asby, Westmorland 1788 (and S/M there 1782) to death 29/3/1834 aged 81 (CCEd says 10/6/1834) [C4458. Platt] Married Kirkby Thore, Westmorland 6/1/1793 Mary Sewell, s.p. 'A truly pious and peaceable pastor', etc.

ATKINSON (Jeremiah) Bapt. Ennerdale, Cumberland 18/1/1786, s. Jonathan Atkinson and Hannah Bowman. Literate: dn09 (York), p10 (Chester). PC. Loweswater, Cumberland 1828 to death 23/2/1858 aged 72. No will traced [C4459. YCO. Platt] Wife Frances, with issue.

ATKINSON (John) [BA but NiVoF] Literate: dn83 (Car.), p83 (Car.). PC. Barton St Mary w. Barton St Cuthbert >< Yorks. 1803 (and S/M Hartforth Free School 1804) to death 4/6/1835 aged 75 (CCEd says 14/9/1835) [C168197] Married Warcop, Westmorland 13/10/1796 Anne Breeks, with clerical son John Breeks Atkinson (below).

ATKINSON (John) From Kendal, Westmorland, s. of Thomas Atkinson [pleb]. Queen's, Oxford 1786 (aged 16), BA1791, dn94 (C&L), p95 (Chester), MA1795. PC. South Cowton, Gilling, Yorks. 1795-1834. Died? [C8408].

ATKINSON (John) [NiVoF] R. Gate Burton, Lincs. 1808-28, V. Owersby w. Kirkby and Osgodby >< Lincs. 1828 to death (Pontefract, Yorks.) 5/4/1837 aged 73. Dom. Chap. to Lord Mexborough [C5511]

ATKINSON (John Breeks) Born Barton, Yorks. 3/9/1798, s. Rev. John Atkinson (three above) and Anne Breeks. Sidney, Cambridge 1816, BA1821, dn21 (Chester), p22 (Bristol for Win.), MA1824. PC. Richmond Holy Trinity, Yorks. 1822-35, PC. Carisbrooke, West Cowes, IoW 1827-73, R. Kingston, IoW 1831 to death (Cowes) 23/5/1880 aged 82, leaving £4,000 [C8085] Married 1836 Kincardine Castle, Aberdeenshire Jane Isabella Johnston, with issue. Surrogate.

ATKINSON (John Wilson) Born Bradford, Yorks. 23/11/1800, s. Rev. William Atkinson. Jesus, Cambridge 1819, BA1824, dn24 (York), p25 (York). PC. Walton, Ainsty of York 1827-36 [C130481] and V. Burham, Kent 1828 to death 11/1836 [C7076. YCO]

ATKINSON (Richard) Bapt. Hatfield, Yorks. 23/10/1793, s. Benjamin Atkinson. St Catharine's, Cambridge 1814, BA1818, dn18 (Nor.), p19 (Nor.), MA1823. R. Claxby w. Normanby le Wold, Lincs. 1820 and PC. Usselby. Lincs. 1820 to death (Harrogate, Yorks.) 18/9/1860, leaving £5,000, living at Wyburn Hall, Yorks. [C5512]

ATKINSON (Thomas) Born Kirkby Ireleth, Lancs. 10/12/1751, s. Thomas Atkinson and Eleanor Crossfield. Literate: dn74 (Chester), p76 (York). S/M Sancton Free G/S School 1777; PC. Filey, Yorks. 1786-1833, PC. Sancton, Yorks. 1794, V. North Newbald, Yorks. 1794 and V. Saundby, Yorks. 1835 to death 6/3/1835 (CCEd says 21/8/1835) aged 83 [C84196. YCO] Married (1) Lorton, Cumberland 18/9/1775 Jane Fisher (a clergy dau., d.1788), w. issue (2) North Newbald 3/5/1790 Anne King ('then aged 17'), with further issue.

ATKINSON (Thomas) Born and bapt. Leeds 10/6/1780, s. Rev. Miles Atkinson and Mary Kenion. Magdalene, Cambridge 1797, BA1802, dn02 (London for York), p04 (York), MA1814. PC. Thornton, Yorks. 1805-15 (exchanged with Rev. Patrick Bronte for) PC. Hartshead cum Clifton, Dewsbury, Yorks. 1815-66. Died 28/2/1870 aged 90, leaving £2,000 [C84198. YCO. BBV] Married Kirkheaton, Yorks. 23/12/1817 Frances Walker (w), Lascelles Hall, Huddersfield, *s.p.* Brother Christopher, above. He and his wife were godparents to Charlotte Bronte.

ATKINSON (Thomas) From Brampton, Cum-berland, s. Thomas Atkinson. Queen's, Oxford 1810 (aged 20), BA1814, dn14 (Ex.), p15 (Ex.). 'S/M in the Diocese of Exeter' 1817; R. Exeter St Edmund the Martyr 1822 to death 9/6/1841 aged 51 [C139184]

ATKINSON (William) Born Horton, Yorks. St Catharine's, Cambridge 1782, BA1787, dn88 (Ely), MA1790, p91 (Ely), then Jesus, Fellow 1792. R. Warham All Saints w. Waterden, Norfolk 1792 [C111045], V. Canewdon, Essex 1809 to death 24/3/1847 aged 80 [C99557]

ATKINSON (William) Bapt. Orton, Cumberland 21/1/1793, s. of a yeoman farmer. Literate: dn17 (Chester), p18 (Chester). S/M Tebay G/S; PC. Blawith, Lancs. 1818 to death 6/7/1841 aged 49 [C168208] Married Orton 27/11/1814 Elizabeth Wilson, with issue.

ATLAY (Charles) Born Stamford, Lincs. 29/11/1794, s. Rev. Richard Atlay (schoolmaster, below) and Sarah Robinson. St John's, Cambridge 1811, BA1816, dn17 (Lin.), MA 1819, p19 (Lin.). R. Stamford St George w. St Paul 1823-40, R. Barrowden, Rutland 1840 to death 29/11/1870, leaving £12,000 [C5516] Married Westminster, London 31/7/1840 Mary Priscilla Barnes. Brother, below. His nephew was Bishop of Hereford.

ATLAY (Henry) Born Stamford, Lincs. 7/8/1785, s. Rev. Richard Atlay (schoolmaster, below) and Sarah Robinson. St John's, Cambridge 1802, BA1806, dn08 (Lin.), Fellow 1808, MA1809, p09 (Lin.). R. Stamford St George w. St Paul 1814-23, R. Wakeley, Northants. 1814-26, R. Tinwell, Rutland 1826-27 (res.), R. Great Ponton, Lincs. 1826-34 (res.), R. Great Casterton w. Pickworth, Rutland 1827 (and RD 1840) to death. Dom. Chap. to 2nd Marquess of Exeter 1827. Died 21/2/1861, leaving £4,000. [C5517] Married Cambridge 4/1/1815 Elizabeth Rayner Hovell, of Brighton (dau. of a barrister), with clerical son. Brother, above.

ATLAY (Richard) Born Sheriff Hutton, Yorks. 17/5/1751, s. John Atlay (farmer) and Mary Herrison. St John's, Cambridge 1769, BA1773, dn73 (Lin.), p75 (C&L), MA1776. H/M Stamford G/S, Lincs. 1781-1832; R. Stamford St John w. St Clement 1785 and V. Stamford Baron St Martin 1787 to death. Dom. Chap. to 2nd Earl of Clarendon 1787. Died 'suddenly, at the Mermaid Inn, Wansford, Northants.' 19/12/1832 (CCEd say 22/1/1833) [C5518] Married Northampton 7/1/1783 Sarah Robinson, with clerical sons Charles Atlay, and Henry Atley, above.

ATTWOOD, ATWOOD (Thomas George Patrick) Born Westminster, London 10/4/1803, s. Rev. Thomas Alexander Attwood and Grace Burtenshaw, Pembroke. Oxford 1821, BA 1825, dn26 (Salis.), p27 (Salis.). V. Froxfield, Wilts. 1828 to death 21/12/1869, leaving £1,000 [C83460] Married Collingbourne Ducis, Wilts. 21/6/1831 Elizabeth Wilson, with issue. Port. online.

ATWOOD (Francis [Thomas]) Born Hammersmith, London, s. of Thomas Atwood and Kitty Loveday. Trinity, Cambridge 1817, dn22 (Chester for London), BA1823, p23 (Chester for London), MA1826. PC. Hammersmith St Paul, Middx. 1826-56, V. Great Ludford (Ludford

Magna), Lincs. 1828-9, R. Sixhills, Lincs. 1828-9, R. Butterleigh, Devon 1830-1, V. (Great) Grimsby, Lincs. 1831 to death 6/8/1856 aged 57 [C5520. Kaye] Married Hammersmith 21/6/1827 Lucy Howard, w. clerical son Francis John Atwood.

AUBER (Robert Henry) Bapt. Camberwell, London (in the French Huguenot Church) 11/3/1774, s. Isaac Auber and Marie Gahlié. Pembroke, Cambridge 1782, BA1796, dn96 (Salis. for Win.), then Trinity Hall 1796, p00 (London). R. Wanlip, Leics. 1831-7. In Camberwell 1846 and 1854. Died North Petherton, Som. 14/7/1859, leaving £3,000 [C5527]

AUBERTIN, AUBERTON (Peter) Born Chipstead, Surrey 4/2/1775, s. Henry Aubertin (a merchant, from Lausanne, Switzerland). St John's, Cambridge 1794, BA1798 (as John Auberton), dn98 (Win.), p99 (Win.). R. Chipstead 1809 to death 9/11/1861, leaving £20,000 [C69222] Married Banstead, Surrey 6/7/1809 Henrietta Lambert, with clerical son Peter.

AUBIN (Philip) From Jersey, Channel Islands, s. Thomas Aubin. Pembroke, Oxford 1819 (aged 21), then Jesus 1822, BA1822, dn22 (Ox.), MA1823, p23 (Ox.), BD1830. R. Jersey St Ouen / Owen 1824-6 (res.), R. Jersey St Clement 1826 to death 2/9/1842 [C22085]

AUCKLAND (Robert John Eden, 3rd Baron) see under **EDEN**

AUFRERE (George John) Born Hoveton Hall, Hoveton, Norfolk 22/9/1769, s. Anthony Aufrere, J.P., and Anna Norris. Corpus Christi, Cambridge 1788, BA1792, dn92 (Nor.), p93 (Nor.). V. Ridlington w. East Ruston, Norfolk 1794-1836, V. Bacton, Norfolk 1810-23 (res.). Died Ridlington 30/1/1853 aged 83 [C110850. LFBI 252] Brother, below.

AUFRERE (Philip Duval) Born Hoveton Hall, Hoveton, Norfolk 7/4/1776, s. Anthony Aufrere, J.P., and Anna Norris. Pembroke, Cambridge 1795, dn98 (Ely for Nor.), BA1800, p00 (Nor.). R. Eccles by the Sea, Norfolk 1806-8 (res.), V. Hempstead, Norfolk 1806-8 (res.), V. Bacton, Norfolk 1806-10 (res.), R. Scarning (Mediety), Norfolk 1808 and R. Bawdeswell, Norfolk 1810 to death (Mundesley, Norfolk) 4/6/1848 aged 73 [C99558. LFBI 252] Married (1) Smallburgh, Norfolk 25/11/1802 Mary Beevor (a clergy dau., d.1818) (2) Wells-next-the-Sea, Norfolk 29/6/1819 Ann Margaret Smith (a clergy dau.), w. issue. Brother, above.

AUSTEN (Charles) From Ensbury, Dorset, s. Rev. Charles Austen, sen. University, Oxford 1814 (aged 20), BA1818, dn18 (London for Bristol), p19 (Chester for Bristol). R. Tollard Royal, Wilts. 1823 to death 31/5/1860, leaving £2,500 [C51986]

AUSTEN (Henry Thomas) Born Steventon, Hants. 8/6/1771, s. Rev. George Austen and Cassandra Leigh (and thus the brother of Jane Austen). St John's, Oxford 1788, BA1792, MA 1796 [co-founder of a bank 1804 and bankrupt 1816] dn16 (Salis. for Win.), p17 (Salis. for Win.). R. Steventon, 1820-3, S/M Farnham G/S 1823-7, PC. Bentley, Hants. 1824. Dom. Chap. to 1st Earl of Moray 1817. Died Tunbridge Wells, Kent 12/3/1850. [C69225] Married (1) Marylebone, London 31/12/1797 his widowed cousin Eliza de Feuillide (née Hancock, she d.1813, her husband having been guillotined) (2) Chelsea, London 1820 Eleanor Jackson: www.jasna.org/persuasions/printed/opno1/grey.htm

AUSTEN (John) From Poole, Dorset, s. Henry Austen. BNC, Oxford 1783 (aged 17), then Oriel 1787, dn88 (Bristol), p90 (Bristol), BA1798, MA1803. R. Tarrant Keynston, Dorset 1806 to death 7/9/1856 aged 91 [C50987]

AUSTEN (John) Born Wilmington, Kent 6/6/1777, s. Francis Motley Austen (a cousin of Jane Austen) and Elizabeth Wilson. Oriel, Oxford 1794, BA1799 (Senior Wrangler), dn00 (Chich. for Cant.), p01 (Cant.). R. Crayford, Kent 1806-13 (and Preacher throughout the Diocese of Canterbury 1806), R. Chevening, Kent 1813-51, R. Pulborough, Sussex 1822 [net income £1,376]. Dom. Chap. to 4th Duke of Dorset 1806; to 4th Earl Stanhope 1817. Probate granted 6/10/1851 [C153053. Boase] Married Seal, Kent 7/9/1813 Harriet Lane, with issue. Brother William, below.

AUSTEN (John Thomas) Born Kent 11/6/1794, s. John Austen and Harriet Hussey. St John's, Cambridge 1811, Fellow 1817, BA 1817 (Senior Wrangler), dn19 (London for Roch.), MA1820, p20 (Chester for Roch.), BD1828, incorporated at Oxford 1834. V. Aldworth, Berks. 1832-48, R. West Wickham, Kent 1848 (and Hon. Canon of Canterbury

1873) to death 10/6/1876 aged 82, leaving £7,000 [C1551. Boase] Married IoW 28/10/1834 Charlotte Sophia Tilson (w), with issue.

AUSTEN (William) Bapt. Lamberhurst, Kent 24/12/1787, s. Francis Motley Austen and Elizabeth Wilson (and thus another cousin of Jane Austen). BNC, Oxford 1806, BA1810, MA 1814. S/M Upton Lovell Endowed School 1814; R. Horsted Keynes, Sussex 1815-40. Died Southampton 5/4/1854 [C61111] Married Southampton 17/12/1793 Elizabeth Matilda Butler Harrison, with issue. Brother John, above.

AUSTIN (Anthony) From Wotton under Edge, Glos., s. Anthony Austin. Oriel, Oxford 1804 (aged 19), BA1808, MA1811, dn12 (Glos.), p13 (Glos.). R. Hardenhuish, Wilts. 1823, R. Alderley, Glos. 1831-[46]. Died? [C83463]

AWDRY (Jeremiah) Bapt. Lacock, Wilts. 21/6/1774, s. John Awdry and Sarah Susannah Darbyshire Roston. Oriel, Oxford 1791, BA 1795, dn97 (Salis.), MA1798, p98 (Ex. for Salis.). V. Felsted, Essex 1798, S/M Upton Lovell, Wilts. 1814. Lived at Seagry House, Chippenham, Wilts. Died Bath 4/2/1859 aged 84, leaving £20,000 [C83465] Married (1) Swindon, Wilts. 31/5/1799 Maria Emilia May (d.1814), w. clerical s. Charles Roston Edridge Awdry (2) Salisbury 6/10/1823 Rosina Osborne Weller (d.1830), w. further issue (3) Walcot, Bath 10/9/1835 Mary Sibella Wilkinson, w. yet more issue. *J.P.*

AYCKBOWN, AYCKBOWM (Frederick) Born Dublin June 1793, s. John Dedrich Ayckbown (of German extraction) and Mary Barnes. TCD1810, BA1816. R. Chester Holy Trinity 1825 to death 23/8/1862 (Tibbermore, Perthshire), leaving £12,000. Chap. Chester Gaol 1820; Dom. Chap. to Marquess of Westminster [C168212 as Ayckbourn. Al.Dub.] Married (1) Onchan, IoM 13/1/1833 Marianne Hutchinson (d.1842 'at the baths of Biberich, Duchy of Nassau'), with issue (including Emily Harriet Elizabeth Ayckbown, *aka* Mother Emily, founder of an Anglican order of nuns, *q.v.* ODNB) (2) Inveresk, Midlothian 8/1/1846 Charlotte Spens (w), with further issue. Excellent family photo. (with dog) online.

AYLING (William) Born Tillington, Sussex 18/7/1792, s. John Ayling. University, Oxford 1811, BA1815, MA1817. R. Barlavington, Sussex 1832. Died 1853 (3rd q.) [C61114] Married Lambeth, Surrey 12/5/1840 Eleanor Willett Hanbury.

AYRES (Thomas) Born Marston Magna, Dorset. St John's, Cambridge 1825, dn29 (Lin.), SCL, p29 (Lin.). R. Stockwood, Dorset 1832-56, R. Melbury Bubb, Dorset 1856 to death 22/5/1860, leaving £450 [C43029] Married Puckington, Som. 1840 Rebecca Mary Dowling (w), with issue.

BABER (Henry Hervey) Born Slingsby, Yorks. 22/8/1775, s. Thomas Baber (a London barrister) and Elizabeth Berriman. All Souls, Oxford 1795, BA1799, dn98 (Lin.), p00 (Lin.), MA1805. [At Bodleian Library from 1796. Keeper of Printed Books, British Museum 1812-37] Vice-Principal St Mary's Hall, Oxford 1805. R. Stretham cum Little Thetford, Cambs. 1827 to death 28/3/1869 aged 94, leaving £12,000 [C5542. ODNB as a philologist. Boase] Married City of London 27/1/1809 Ann Smith (a banker's dau.), with clerical son. *F.R.S.*

BABINGTON (Charles Maitland) Born Dumfries 3/5/1775, s. Rev. William Babington (an Irish-born Scottish Episcopalian) and Jane Maitland. Glasgow Univ. 1791 and Balliol, Oxford (Snell Exhibitioner) 1793, BA1797, dn99 (Win. for Salis.), p99 (Salis.), MA1800. R. Peterstow, Heref. 1809-41, Prebend of Little Withington in Hereford Cathedral 1814-18 (res.), Inc. Dumfries Qualified Chapel 1818-40. Chap. to Marquess of Queensbury. Died Dumfries 5/8/1841 [C83466. Bertie. Snell] Married (1) Sunninghill, Berks. 13/8/1799 Lilias Staig (a banker's dau., she d.1823), w. issue incl. 3 pairs of male twins and a general (2) Dumfries 30/6/1825 Catherine Newall (dau. of a lawyer). Photo. online.

BABINGTON (John Albert) Born Rothley, Leics. 6/9/1791, s. Thomas Babington, *M.P.*, and Jean Macaulay. St John's, Cambridge 1810, BA1814, dn14 (Peterb.), p15 (Peterb.), MA1817. R. Cossington, Leics. 1820-59, V. Rothley 1823-35, V. Thrussington, Leics. 1843-5, Hon. Canon of Peterborough 1847-85, Min. Brighton St Mary, Sussex 1865, R. Walton le Wolds, Leics. 1867-73. Dom. Chap. to 3rd Baron Calthorpe 1823. Died Brighton 16/10/1885 aged 94, leaving £4,572-15s-9d. [C5543] Married (1) Paston, Northants. 21/4/1818 Maria Frances Pratt (a clergy dau., d.1851), w. issue (2) Clifton, Bristol 9/8/1855 Eleanor Elliott.

BABINGTON (Matthew Drake) Born Rothley, Leics. 11/7/1788, s. Rev. Matthew Babington and Elizabeth Drake. Trinity, Cambridge 1807, BA1812, dn12 (Lin.), p13 (Lin.), MA1816. PC. Swinnington St George, Whitwick, Leics. 1828-51, PC. Oaks Chapel, Charnwood, Leics. 1838-51 (and RD). Chap. Messina, Italy, dying there 26/7/1851 [C5545] Married Shepsted, Leics. 7/6/1820 Hannah Fleetwood Churchill, with issue.

BACKHOUSE (John Barnes) Bapt. Caldbeck, Cumberland 16/4/1766, s. John Backhouse and Dorothy Cautley. Trinity, Cambridge 1785, dn88 (London for Cant.), BA1789, p89 (Cant.), MA 1792. R. Cheriton w. V. Newington, Kent 1790-3, R. Edburton, Sussex 1792-6, R. Deal, Kent 1795 and R. Little Chart, Kent 1811 to death. Dom. Chap. 4th Duke of Dorset 1811. Died Deal 14/9/1838 [C114949] Married St Pancras, London 31/1/1793 Sarah Drake Brockman (a clergy dau.), with issue. *J.P.* Kent and Cinque Ports.

BACON (Isaac) Born Bridekirk, Cumberland 27/2/1763, s. John Bacon [*pleb*]. Queen's, Oxford 1781, BA1785, dn88 (Salis. for Peterb.), Fellow, MA1789, p98 (Salis. for Cant.). R. Blechingdon, Oxon. 1807. Died 1837 aged 74 [C22088]

BACON (Robert) Born Holt, Suffolk c.1767. Emmanuel, Cambridge 1799, dn02 (Nor.), p03 (Nor.), LLB1806. PC. Fring, Norfolk 1809 and R. Wolverton 1836 to death 21/5/1861, leaving £1,000 [C1029. Boase corrected?] Wife Susan, and issue.

BADELEY (Joseph) Bapt. Walpole, Norfolk (Independent chapel) 28/7/1772, s. Samuel Badeley and Esther Shrimpton. Literate: dn16 (Nor.), p16 (Nor.). R. Halesworth cum Chediston, Suffolk 1831-5. Died 12/9/1837 aged 65 [C111616] Married Westminster, London 27/3/1797 Eliza Smith, w. issue. Brother below

BADELEY (Samuel) Bapt. Walpole, Norfolk 28/7/1772 (Independent Chapel), s. Samuel Badeley and Esther Shrimpton. Trinity Hall, Cambridge 1787, LLB1795, dn99 (Nor.), p00 (Nor.). V. Ubbetson, Suffolk 1800 to death (Yoxford, Suffolk) 8/8/1854 aged 84 [C111065] Had issue. Brother above.

BADNALL (William) Born Highfield Lodge, Leek, Staffs. 13/10/1803, s. Richard Badnall (silk merchant, banker and *J.P.*) and Harriet Hopkins. BNC, Oxford 1821, BA1825, dn26 (C&L), p ( ), MA1828. (first) PC. Wavertree Holy Trinity, Childwall, Liverpool 1827 to death. Chap. to HRH Duke of Cambridge 1827. King's Preacher in Lancashire 1830. Died 28/7/1859 aged 55, leaving £1,000 [C8422] Married Childwall 16/7/1833 Elizabeth Rose Parr, with clerical son. Port. online.

BAGGS (Isham) Born Dublin, s. of John Baggs. Merton, Oxford 1773 (aged 17), BA 1777, dn78 (Ox.), p88 (B&W). In Ireland 1808-10; Chaplain R.N. 1810; Chap. to the House of Assembly, Jamaica. R. Wark, Northumberland 1819 to death 6/2/1848 aged 92, leaving £5,000 [C22259] Married (1)South Brent, Devon 27/5/1795 Sarah Hunt (d.1802) (2) Ardeley, Herts. 18/7/1804 Editha Pearman; with issue.

BAGNALL (Samuel) Bapt. Eccles, Lancs. 9/9/1801, s. of Thomas Bagnall and Mary Freeman. BNC, Oxford 1820, migrated to Downing, Cambridge 1822, dn24 (Chester), BA1825, p25 (Chester), MA1829. PC. Aston by Sutton, Runcorn, Cheshire 1826-44, PC. Weston Point, Runcorn 1844 to death (Frodsham, Cheshire) 13/11/1876 aged 76, leaving £600 [C168214] Married (1) Carlisle 23/8/1842 Elizabeth Anne Donald (d.1868), w. issue (2) Southport, Lancs. 30/5/1876 Eleanor Burgess.

BAGNELL (William Webber) Born Ireland 1791. Trinity, Cambridge 1809, BA1812, dn15 (B&W), p16 (Ex.). PC. Clyst Honiton >< Devon 1821 to death 7/12/1874 aged 83, leaving under £200 (Will proved by a labourer's wife) [C41801] Married (1) Clyst Honiton 10/2/1825 Martha Brock (d.1827) (2) Plymtree, Devon 29/11/1836 Mary Ann Webber.

BAGOT (Ralph) Bapt. Blithfield, Staffs. 22/3/1797, s. Rev. Walter Bagot (Pype Hayes Hall, Erdington, Birmingham) and Ann Swinnerton. Christ's Church, Oxford 1815, migrated to Peterhouse, Cambridge 1817, LLB 1822, dn22 (Win.), p23 (Win.). V. Wolstanton, Staffs. 1824-35-, unbeneficed after 1852. Died Pype Hayes Hall 20/7/1866 aged 69, leaving £9,000 [C8695. LFBI 312] Married Wolstanton 3/9/1845 Mary Adams Sneyd, w. issue. www.holmesacourt.org/hac/4/11967.htm

BAGOT (Richard, Bishop of Oxford, *then* of Bath and Wells) Born Daventry, Northants. 22/11/1782, s. William, 6th Bart. and 1st Baron Bagot and Hon. Elizabeth Louisa St John's (dau. 2nd Viscount Bolingbroke and St John's). Christ Church, Oxford 1799, BA1803, then Fellow All Souls 1803-6, MA1806, dn06 (London), p06 (Ex.), DD (Lambeth) 1829. R. Leigh, Staffs. 1806-30, R. Blithfield, Sussex 1807-20, Prebend of Pipa Parva in Lichfield 1812-28 (res.), Canon of 2nd Prebend in Worcester Cathedral 1817-22 (res.), Canon of Windsor 1820-7, Dean of Canterbury 1827-45, Bishop of Oxford 1829-45 (w. V. Cuddesdon, Oxon. appended); translated ('on the edge of a nervous breakdown') to Bath and Wells 1845 to death (although his See was administered for a time by Bishop Monk of Gloucester and Bristol, *q.v.*, following Bagot's complete breakdown). Dom. Chap. to Frances, Countess of Jersey 1806. Died 15/5/1854 [C8423. ODNB. Boase. LFBI 312] Married St George's Hanover Square, London 22/12/1806 Lady Margaret Villiers (dau. 4th Earl of Jersey), 8s. (3 clerical), 4 dau. 'He was of a modest, retiring and nervous disposition'.

BAGOT DE LA BERE (John) see under **EDWARDS (John)**

BAGSHAW(E) (Edward Benjamin) Born Brigg, Lincs. 15/10/1800, s. Sir William Chambers Darling (later Bagshawe), *M.D.*, and Helen Ridgard. Magdalene, Cambridge 1818, BA1823, dn23 (Glos.), p25 (B&W), MA1827. H/M Norton G/S 1823; R. Eyam, Derbys. 1826-62. Lived at Bath after 1862, dying there 3/1/1884, leaving £3,519-14s-4d. [C8697. LFBI 314] Married Walford, Heref. 8/6/1826 Jane Partridge (Bishopswood, Heref.), with issue.

BAGSHAW, BAGSHAWE (William) Born Ford Hall, Chapel-en-le-Frith, Derbys. 6/1/1763, s. Samuel Bagshaw and Catherine Caldwell. BNC, Oxford 1783, BA1787, dn89 (C&L), p90 (C&L), MA1790. PC. Chapel en le Frith 1790-92, PC. Wormhill, Derbys. 1791, V. Buckminster w. Sewstern, Leics. 1801, V. Garthorpe, Leics. 1813-20 (res.). Dom. Chap. to Margery, Baroness Saltoun 1813. Died Sheffield 11/11/1847 [C8436. LFBI 314. W.H. Greaves-Bagshawe, *The Bagshawes of Ford: a biographical pedigree* (1886)] Married Staveley, Derbys. 12/11/1798 Anne Foxlowe Murray, with issue. Port. online.

BAGSHAWE (Edward Benjamin) Born Brigg, Lincs. 15/10/1800, s. Sir William Chambers Darling (later Bagshawe), *M.D.* (of Norton, Derbys.) and Helen Ridgard. Magdalene, Cambridge 1818, BA1823, dn23 (Glos.), p25 (B&W), MA1827. H/M Norton G/S 1823; R. Eyam, Derbys. 1826-62. Lived at Bath after 1862, dying there 3/1/1884, leaving £3,519-14s-4d. [C8697] Married Walford, Heref. 8/6/1826 Jane Partridge (Bishopswood, Heref.), with issue.

BAILEY (Henry [Ives]) Born Briston, Norfolk 23/4/1778, s. William and Ann Bailey.

Literate: dn14 (York), p15 (York). PC. Drighlington, Yorks. 1816 (and S/M there 1814), V. North Leverton w. Apesthorpe, Notts. 1844-68. Died there 7/12/1870 aged 92, leaving £9,000 [C130798. YCO] Married Bradford, Yorks. 6/8/1824 Sarah Rand, with clerical son.

BAILEY (John) From Lancashire. St John's, Cambridge 1780, BA1785, dn85 (Chester), p87 (Chester). V. Great Stukeley, Hunts. 1790 to death 26/11/1837 [C168216]

BAILEY (Rishton Robinson) Bapt. Norwich 8/5/1780, s. William and Margaret Bailey. [In 21st Fusilliers]. Literate: dn13 (Nor.), p13 (Nor.), migrated to Jesus, Cambridge 1820 (aged 38 - a Ten Year Man). PC. Culpho, Suffolk 1815 (w. Chap. Woodbridge House of Correction 1815), Chap. St Peter ad Vincula, Tower of London (and Chap. to the Forces there) 1827 to death (Maidstones Grange, Womingford, Essex) 28/3/1840 aged 59 [C111067] Married 5/9/1804 Harriot Rolfe, w. clerical s. of same name (who d.1833). Port. online.

BAILEY see also **BAYLEY, BAYLY,** and below

BAILLIE (John, Hon.) Born Mellerstain House, Berwickshire 3/1/1810, s. George Baillie, *M.P.* (brother to 10th Earl of Haddington) and Mary Pringle. Trinity, Cambridge 1829, dn33 (York), BA1834, p34 (Lin. for York), MA 1853. V. Wetwang w. Fimber, Yorks. 1834-41, V. Lissington, Lincs. 1837-52, Prebendary of Wistow in York Minster 1852, V. Nunburnholme, Yorks. 1852-4, Canon Residentiary of York Minster 1854-88, R. Elsdon, Northumberland 1854-76 with RD of Rothbury [total income £1,460], R. Wivenhoe, Essex 1867, PC Cupar Fife 1879-88, Prebendary of St Ninian's Cathedral, Perth 1887 to death (York) 7/8/1888 aged 78, leaving £7,071-3s-11d. [C43041. YCO. Bertie] Married 4/4/1837 Cecilia Mary, dau. Rev. Charles Hawkins (Canon of York), 9 ch. (1 clerical). *J.P.* for Perthshire. 'Raised to the rank of an Earl's younger son' 1859.

BAILYE (Hugh) Bapt. Lichfield, Staffs. 13/4/1761, s. William Bailye and Frances Hand. Christ Church, Oxford 1778, BA1782, dn83 (C&L), p85 (C&L), MA1809. V. Hendon, Middx. 1790 (res.), Prebend of Gaia Minor in Lichfield Cathedral 1802-16 (2nd Canon Residentiary 1816 and Chancellor 1818), V. Alrewas, Staffs. 1818-30 (res.), V. Hanbury, Staffs. 1832 to death 9/6/1833 aged 72 [C8438] Married Lichfield 30/5/1785 Ann Grundy (w).

BAINBRIDGE (Thomas) Probably bapt. Dent, Sedbergh, Yorks. 19/3/1758, s. John Bainbridge. Literate: dn86 (Lin.), p87 (Lin.). R. Addlethorpe, Lincs. 1809. Died Ledborough, Yorks. 10/4/1844 aged 85 [C430452]

BAINES (Cuthbert Johnson) Born Penzance, Cornwall, s. Cuthbert Baines and Lydia Veale. Pembroke, Oxford 1793 (aged 18), BA1797, dn98 (Chester), MA1800. V. St Ives w. Old Hurst and Woodhurst, Hunts. 1802 [blank in ERC] to death 13/10/1840 aged 63 [C5574] Had issue. Brother below.

BAINES (James Johnson) Born Falmouth, Cornwall 30/11/1778, s. Cuthbert Baines and Lydia Veale. Pembroke, Oxford 1796, migrated to Christ'#s, Cambridge 1797, BA1801, MA1804, dn04 (Ely), p05 (Bristol for Ely). V. Burwell St Mary, Cambs. 1808 to death 14/2/1854 [C5574] Married Barnwell, Cambs. 15/5/1809 Harriet Bullen (a clergy dau.), with issue. Brother above.

BAKER (Charles) Bapt. Deal, Kent 4/12/1775, s. John Baker and Elizabeth Brumsall. Jesus, Cambridge 1796, BA1800, then Clare, Fellow 1800-10, dn00 (Glos.), p02 (Ely), MA1803. R. Charlton by Dover, Kent 1803-11, PC. Ash, Kent 1803-10, V. Tilmanstone, Kent 1803 to death 22/8/1842 aged 66 [C99559] Married London 11/10/1809 Anna Catherine Turing.

BAKER (Charles William) Born Salisbury 22/12/1771, s. Rev. John Baker and Sarah Cooper. St Edmund Hall, Oxford 1794, no degree? dn95 (Salis.), p96 (Salis.). R. Tellisford, Som. 1804. Died Freshford, Som. 6/10/1861, leaving £80,000 [C32521] Married Freshford 19/3/1801 Alice Susannah Wittington, with clerical son. Brother below.

BAKER (Francis) Born Salisbury, Wilts. 4/4/1773, s. Rev. John Baker and Sarah Cooper. Merton, Oxford 1791, BA1794, dn95 (Salis.), p97 (Salis.). V. Coombe Bissett, Wilts. 1803, V. South Newton, Wilts. 1812-27, V. Wylye, Wilts. 1826 to death 1840 [C83488] Brother above.

BAKER (George) Bapt. Wolborough, Devon 17/4/1776, s. of a merchant. Sidney, Cambridge 1794, BA1798, dn98 (Ex.), p00 (Ex.). V. (and patron) of South Brent, Devon 1810 to death 1/8/1845 aged 69 [C139475] Had issue.

BAKER (Henry) Born 20/1/1757, s. Sir William Baker (Governor of Hudson's Bay Company, then *M.P.*, of Brayfordbury House, Herts.) and Mary Tonson. Clare, Cambridge 1775, BA1780, dn80 (Lin.), p81 (Lin.), MA 1783. R. Stevenage, Herts. (and Preacher throughout the Diocese of Lincoln) 1781 to death (*hanged himself*) 19/4/1833 (CCEd says 25/6/1833) [C5577]

BAKER (Henry de Foe) Bapt. Esher, Surrey 30/9/1790, s. Rev. William Baker (R. Lyndon, Rutland) and Mary Mockett. St Catharine's, Cambridge 1807, BA1811, dn12 (Peterb.), p12 (Peterb.), MA1814. V. Greetham, Rutland 1821 (and Warden of Brown's Hospital [almshouses], Stamford, Lincs. 1844-5) to death 3/7/1845 aged 56 [C109230] Married Tiverton, Devon 15/9/1828 Harriet Boulten, w. clerical son of same name.

BAKER (James) Bapt. Whitburn, Durham 28/8/1788, s. Benjamin Baker. New, Oxford 1807, BA1811 [admitted Lincoln's Inn 1811] dn13 (Ox.), p13 (Durham), MA1815, Fellow 1817-18. Chancellor of Diocese of Durham 1818-54, V. Durham St Mary le Bow w. St Mary the Less 1822-8, R. Nuneham Courtenay, Oxon. 1825-54, R. Wheatfield, Oxon. 1831-5. Died 6/9/1854 aged 66 [C22094. Boase]

BAKER (John) Born Kent 27/2/1787, s. John Baker and Mary Gilder. St John's, Cambridge 1803, LLB1810, dn11 (Cant.), p12 (Cant.). V. Thorp Arch, Yorks. 1820 and V. Westbourne, Sussex 1828 to death 2/1/1844 (CCEd says 7/3/1843) [C130800] Married Harewood, Yorks. 13/10/1814 his cousin Frances Tattersall (a clergy dau.).

BAKER (Lawrence Palk) Bapt. Layston, Herts. 10/11/1784, s. John Baker (surgeon) and Mary Gilder. St John's, Cam-bridge 1803, BA 1807, MA1810, dn11 (Ely), p16 (Bristol), BD 1817. V. Impington, Cambs. 1823-5, R. Medbourne cum Holt, Leics. [pop. 33] 1825 to death 29/1/1870, leaving £5,000 [C5579]

BAKER (Ralph Bourne) Born Hilderstone Hall, Staffs. 11/10/1803, s. William Baker, *J.P.*, and Mary Bourne. Trinity, Cambridge 1822, BA 1826, dn26 (C&L), p27 (C&L), MA1829. R. (and first) V. Hilderstone, Staffs. 1833-60 (res. ill-health) w. RD of Stone 1840-60, then RD of Stoke, V. Brompton Chapel, Kensington, London 1860-3. Examining Chap. to Bishop of Meath 1852-72. Died Hasfield Court, Glos. 25/5/1875, leaving £140,000 [C8429. LFBI 340 and photo.] Married Taney, Co. Dublin 28/3/1845 Frances Crofton Singer (w) (dau. of the Bishop of Meath), w. issue. In 1865 his brother left him a pottery factory, together with all his money and the estates of Hasfield Court, Glos. and Fenton House, Hampstead, London. *J.P.* Staffs. 1850 and Glos. 1869.

BAKER (Richard) Bapt. Cawston, Norfolk 28/9/1773 (CCEd thus), s. Rev. Richard Baker, sen. Pembroke, Cambridge 1790, BA1795, dn96 (Nor.), p99 (Nor.), MA1800. R. Botley, Hants. 1803 to death 5/12/1853 aged 18 [C69387] Had issue.

BAKER (Richard Henry) Bapt. North Chapel, Sussex 28/11/1783, s. James Baker and Ann Coleman. Wadham, Oxford 1801, dn06 (Win.), p07 (Ex. for Win.), BCL1808. PC. Linchmere, Sussex 1808, V. West Hanney (o/w Hannay cum Lyford), Berks. 1817 to death (Linchmere) 7/3/1849 aged 64 [C83493] Married 13/9/1832 Elizabeth Bowler (w).

BAKER (Robert George) Born London 29/10/1788, s. Sir William Baker (Bayfordbury, Herts.) and Sophia Conyers. Trinity, Cambridge 1806, BA1810, dn11 (Lin.), p13 (Lin.), MA1813. R. Springfield, Essex 1823-7, R. Monken Hadley, Middx. 1819, R. Little Berkhampstead, Herts. 1825-34, R. Stevenage, Herts. 1833-4, V. Fulham All Saints, Middx. 1834-72, Prebend of St Paul's Cathedral, London 1846 [value £2] and RD of Fulham 1851-71. Died 21/2/1878 aged 89, leaving £40,000 [C5580. Boase] Married (1) 16/6/1818 Emma Franks (d.1864) (2) Fulham 6/7/1865 Mary Catherine Henrietta Sulivan.

BAKER (Thomas) Bapt. Great Yarmouth. Norfolk 22/12/1768, s. John Baker. University, Oxford 1788, BA1792, dn92 (Nor.), p94 (Nor.), MA1795. R. Little Cressingham, Norfolk 1801, R. Rollesby, Norfolk 1801 to death 1841? [C111156]

BAKER (Thomas) Born Dublin 22/2/1784, s. Capt. Benjamin Baker (Stamford, Lincs.) and Amelia Barnard. Oriel, Oxford 1803, BA1807, dn07 (Ox.), p08 (Durham), MA1810. R. Great Stainton (o/w Stainton le Street), Durham 1808, R. Stockton upon Tees 1809-10, R. Whitburn,

Durham 1810 [income £2,188] to death. Dom. Chap. to Bishop of Durham. Died 14/2/1866 aged 82, leaving £4,000 [C134499] Married Marylebone, London 5/5/1808 Julia Priscilla King (a Shropshire clergy dau.), probably *s.p.*

BAKER (Thomas) Born Croydon, Surrey 28/11/1798, s. Thomas Baker (formerly Thomas Baker Elsley, a shipbroker). Christ's, Cambridge 1817, dn21 (Bristol), BA1822, p23 (Chester), MA1825. R. Rodmell, Sussex 1825-36, R. Bexhill, Sussex 1827, R. Hartlebury, Worcs. 1835 [income £2,188] (w. Hon. Canon of Worcester 1835 and RD of Kidderminster) to death 7/6/1877, leaving £5,000 [C61157 has several men here] Married Chichester 7/6/1825 Elizabeth Lloyd Carr (dau. of a Bishop of Chichester), 7s., 1 dau.

BAKER (William) Born (St) Gluvias, Cornwall 28/4/1763, s. Richard Baker. Exeter, Oxford 1781, SCL, dn91 (Ex.), p92 (C&L for Ex.). R. Gerrans (o/w St Gerrins) 1807 to death 16/3/1844 aged 81 [C139478]

BAKER (William Dew) Bapt. Newland, Glos. 27/5/1799, s. James Baker and Elizabeth Freeman. Literate: dn22 (Llandaff), p23 (Landaff). V. Cherry Willingham ><, Lincs. 1832 to death 1848 (1st q.) [C3623] Married Bristol 19/7/1825 Harriet Harris.

BAKER (William Innes) Bapt. Bristol 20/9/1779, s. Rev. William Baker and Mary Innes. New, Oxford 1799, dn04 (Ox.), p05 (Ox.), BCL1807, LLB, DCL. R. Lasborough, Glos. 1805, R. Heyford Warren, Oxon. [blank in ERC] 1820. Died Bicester, Oxon. 4/1/1859. No will traced [C22098] Married Holborn, London 7/7/1823 Elizabeth Payne, with issue.

BAKER (William Lake) Born London 19/12/1787, s. John Baker and Elizabeth Young. Magdalene, Cambridge 1805, BA1809, dn11 (London), MA1812, p13 (London). R. (and patron of) Hargrave, Northants. 1818 to death 27/1/1865 aged 77, leaving £3,000 [C43048] Married Chingford, Essex 15/1/1819 Harriet Elizabeth Lewis, with issue.

BALDOCK (Richard) Bapt. Easting, Kent 9/2/1806, s. Thomas Baldock and Mary Harris. St John's, Cambridge 1825, BA1829, dn30 (London for Cant.), p32 (Cant.), MA1832. R. Kingsnorth, Kent 1832 (w. RD of Lympne 1858) to death (a widower) 14/1/1886 aged 79, leaving £7,238-9s-4d. [C114961] Clerical son.

BALDWIN (Gardner/Gardner) Born Ireland 22/5/1792 (bapt. Wigan, Lancs.), s. William Baldwin (an attorney) and Frances Kearney. BNC, Oxford 1810, BA1814, dn15 (Chester), p18 (Chester), MA1825. V. Leyland, Lancs. 1824 to death 24/10/1852 [C109231] Married (1) Tattenhall, Cheshire 21/11/1821 Elizabeth Orton, w. clerical sons Thomas Rigbye Baldwin, and Octavius de Leyland Baldwin. J.P. Lancs. 1826.

BALE (Sackville Stephens) Bapt. Westminster, London 7/11/1753, s. Rev. Sackville Spencer Bale and Lousia Godde (Goode?). Christ Church, Oxford 1771, dn76 (Ox.), p77 (Ox.), BCL1778, LLB. R. Chiddingstone, Kent 1783, (succ. his father as) R. Withyham, Sussex 1815 to death. Dom. Chap. to 1st Viscount Sackville 1782. Died 28/9/1836 [C22275] Married Sevenoaks, Kent 29/12/1788 Alicia Otway, with issue.

BALFOUR (James) St Bees admitted 1820, dn21 (Chester), p22 (Chester). PC. Lower Peover, Cheshire 1823-[38]. Died Manchester 1843 (2nd q.)? [C168226] Married Liverpool 8/7/1823 Sophia Harrison, w. issue.

BALLARD (John) Bapt. Winchester, Hants. 14/2/1782, s. Rev. John Ballard, sen. and Mary Goodridge Waller. St John's, Oxford 1800, dn05 (Ox.), p06 (Ox.), then New, BCL1809. R. Cropready, Oxon. 1811-51, R. Wood Eaton, Oxon. 1823. Died London 11/5/1851 [C22101] Married Marylebone, London 11/5/1811 Sophia Weyland, with clerical son, also John. 'Though he also held Wood Eaton, [he] was resident and zealous. His manner, however, appears to have been overbearing, particularly towards nonconformists. Besides activities as an agriculturalist and as a Conservative, a Savings Bank Trustee, and a Poor Law Guardian, he ran a clothing club, asserted his right to tithes, and re-seated his church.'

BALLEINE (George) Bapt. Jersey, Channel Islands 6/9/1786, s. George and Elizabeth Balleine. Literate: dn09 (Win.), p10 (Win.). R. Jersey St Ouen 1815, R. Jersey St Peter 1815-29. R. Jersey St Mary w. Gorey 1829. Died Jersey 15/7/1856 [C69393] Married Jersey 14/12/1820 Marie Anne Le Petevin, and had issue. Fine oil port. online.

BAMFORD (Robert Walker) Bapt. Ulverston, Lancs. 29/7/1798 (aged 2), s. Robert Bamford. S/M Bluecoat Hospital [School], Liverpool. Literate: dn19 (Durham), p20 (Durham *or* Salis.), then Trinity, Cambridge 1821 (a Ten Year Man), then Emmanuel 1829, BD Lambeth 1830. V. Bishopton, Durham 1825 and Minor Canon Durham to death 30/4/1838 aged 42 [C83641] Married Giggleswick, Yorks. 10/10/1822 Alice Holgate (w), with clerical son.

BAMPFIELD (John) Bapt. Branscombe, Devon 5/12/1770, s. Rev. Isaac Bampfield. Pembroke, Oxford 1790, BA1797, dn01 (Ex.), p02 (B&W). R. Bradford, Devon 1803. Probably died 1842 (2nd q.) [C32600]

BAMPFYLDE (Charles Francis) Born London, s. Sir Charles Warwick Bampfylde, 5th Bart. and Catherine Moore (dau. of a naval baronet). Balliol, Oxford 1806 (aged 19), dn10 (B&W), p11 (B&W), BCL1820, DCL. R. Hemington w. Hardington, Som. 1814 and R. Dunkerton, Som. 1820. Chap. to Prince Regent 1814. Probate granted 28/3/1855 [C32602] Married Marylebone, London 9/11/1820 Ann Row, with issue. Known As 'The Devil of Dunkerton', and 'the worst man in the West of England.'

BAMPFYLDE (Richard [Warwick]) Bapt. Exeter 5/2/1759, s. Sir Richard Warwick Bampfylde, 4th Bart. and Jane Codrington. BNC, Oxford 1776, BA1781, dn82 (Ex.), p83 (Ex.), MA1783. R. Poltimore w. Huxham, Devon 1783 and R. Black Torrington, Devon 1783 (both family livings) to death. Dom. Chap. to Mary, Lady Bellenden 1782. Died 15/9/1834 aged 76 [C139481]

BAND (Charles Edward) Bapt. Whimple, Devon 1/2/1803, s. Edward Wright Band and Sarah Elizabeth Drew. St John's, Cambridge 1820, BA1823, dn26 (B&W), p27 (B&W), MA 1828. PC. Sheldon, Devon 1827-66, R. Combe Raleigh, Devon 1827 to death 22/10/1878 aged 75, leaving £18,000. Lived at Wookey House, Somerset [C41803] Married (1) Sidbury, Devon 4/6/1827 Henrietta Maria Bourke Fellows (a clergy dau., d.1841), w. clerical s. (2) Honiton, Devon 1862 Susannah Maria Cobham [Venn differs here], with further issue.

BANDINEL (Bulkeley) Born Oxford 21/2/1781, s. Rev. James Bandinel (V. Netherbury, Dorset) and Margaret Dumaresq (both families from the Channel Islands). New, Oxford 1800, dn04 (Glos.), BA1805, p05 (Ox.), Fellow 1805, MA1807, BD and DD1823. Chaplain *R.N.* on HMS *Victory* 1808 [Deputy, then Bodley's Librarian 1813-60]. R. Haughton le Skerne, Durham 1822-55 (non-res., net income £1,279) and Preacher throughout the Diocese of Durham 1822. Died Oxford 6/2/1861. Will not traced [C22102. ODNB and photo. of this large man Boase] Married Sutton Courtenay, Hants. 24 or 25/5/1813 Mary Phillips, *s.p.* An important librarian; and an autocrat.'

BANFATHER (Henry) Bapt. Norwich 4/6/1794, s. John Banfather. Literate: dn17 (Nor.), Pembroke, Cambridge 1818, p18 (Nor.), then Jesus 1826, BD1828 (a Ten Year Man). PC. (and patron) of Sprowston, Norfolk 1818-78 [pop. 25], R. (and patron) of Beeston St Andrew, Norfolk [no church, pop. 37] 1849 to death 30/9/1885 aged 91, leaving £18,247-0s-6d. [C1030] Married Norwich 22/1/1834 Mary Corbould, with issue.

BANISTER (John) Born Sittingbourne, Kent 2/9/1786 (CCEd thus), s. Thomas Banister. Worcester, Oxford 1806, BA1809, dn09 (Nor.), p10 (Nor.), MA1812. PC. West Worldham, Hants. 1828-64-, R. Kelvedon Hatch, Essex 1832 to death (Alton, Southampton) 11/7/1870, leaving £3,000 [C8450] Had clerical issue.

BANISTER see also under **BANNISTER**

BANKES (Edward) Born Kingston Lacy Hall, Wimborne, Dorset 13/8/1795, s. Henry Bankes, *M.P.*, and Frances Woodley. Trinity Hall, Cambridge 1812, LLB1818, dn18 (Chester for Bristol), p18 (London). R. Winterbourne Tomson, Dorset 1818, R. Corfe Castle, Dorset 1818-54 (handed over to his son), V. Stoke Bliss, Heref. 1820-3, 5th Prebend Norwich Cathedral 1820, Canon Residentiary Gloucester Cathedral 1821-67 [value £700], V. East Farleigh, Kent 1828-32, Canon (and 1st Prebend) Bristol Cathedral 1832 [value £800] to death. Chaplain in Ordinary 1820 to death. Died Gloucester 24/5/1867 aged 71, leaving £60,000 [C1031. Boase. LFBI 357] Married (1) St James's Westminster, London 6/4/1820 Lady Frances Jane Scott (dau. of 1st Earl of Eldon, Lord Chancellor, she d.1838), w. clerical s. Eldon Surtees Bankes (2) Stow, Glos. 3/9/1839 Hon. Maria Rice (dau. of a Dean of Gloucester), 5 ch. Inherited Soughton Hall, Northop, Flintshire;

J.P. and *D.L.* Flint. The epitome of the pluralist clergyman!

BANKS (Jabez) Born Thorpe Bassett, Yorks. 10/5/1795, s. William (a labourer) and Dinah Rose (?). Literate: dn18 (York), p19 (York). Chap. of the Donative of Bempton, Yorks. 1820 and R. Ergham, Yorks. 1837 to death (Bridlington, Yorks.) 30/11/1859, leaving £1,000 [C130802. YCO] Married (1) Acaster Malbis, Yorks. 22/3/1818 Jane Thompson (d.1841), w. issue (2) York 26/3/1842 Mary Dunn.

BANKS (John) From Keswick, Cumberland, s. John Banks. Literate: dn78 (Lin.), p79 (Lin.), then Christ's, Cambridge 1789 (a Ten Year Man), BD1800. S/M Boston School, Lincs. 1790-1825; PC. Dalby, Lincs. 1808 and R. Bratoft, Lincs. 1808 and V. Cammeringham, Lincs. 1813 to death (Spilsby, Lincs.) 26/3/1842 aged 78 [C5605] *F.S.A.*

BANKS (Joseph Staines) Born Cambridge 19/5/1766, s. Samuel Banks. Trinity Hall, Cambridge 1782, LLB1788, dn92 (Lin. for Ely), p93 (Ely). V. Hemingford Grey, Hunts. 1794 to death. Dom. Chap. to 5th Duke of Manchester 1814. Died 19/8/1848 aged 82 [C5604] Clerical son, below.

BANKS (Samuel Horatio) Born Hemingford Grey, Hunts. 30/12/1798, s. Rev. Joseph Staines Banks (above). Trinity Hall, Cambridge 1815, LLB1821, dn23 (Peterb. for Ely), p28 (Ely), LLD1841. V. Dullingham, Cambs. 1828 and V. Cowlinge, Suffolk 1829 to death (unm.) 18/8/1882, leaving £846-4s-2d. [C6512]

BANKS (Thomas) Bapt. Ormskirk, Lancs. 18/8/1769. Literate: p97 (Llandaff for Chester). PC. (Great) Singleton, Kirkham, Lancs. 1797 (where he also kept a boarding school at Singleton Lodge) to death 1843 aged 73 [C3625]

BANNISTER, BANISTER (James Dawson) Bapt. Cowgill, Dent, Yorks. 30/3/1798, s. Dawson and Ann Bannister. St Bees admitted 1819, dn21 ([Chester]), p22 (Chester). PC. Pilling, Fleetwood, Lancs. 1825-76 (res.). Died Goosnargh, Lancs. 9/1/1883 aged 84, leaving £1,157-4s-10d. [C168231] Married Dean, Lancs. 15/2/1835 Nancy Coop, with clerical son.

BARBER (John) Born Manchester 1800, s. John (a company clerk) and Betty Barber. St John's, Cambridge 1819, BA1823, dn24 (Chester), p25 (Chester for Cant.), MA1826. (first) PC. Wilsden cum Allerton, Bradford, Yorks. 1828-39, PC. (North) Bierley, Yorks. 1839 (where he trained literate clergy) to death. Chap. to Bishop of Gibraltar 1842. Died (unm.) 21/4/1868 aged 67 [C130804. BBV] S. Slinn, 'Archbishop Harcourt's recruitment of literate clergymen: Part 2.' *Yorkshire Archaeological Journal*, 81 (2009), especially p.295]

BARBER (John Hurt) Born Lambeth, Surrey 10/4/1793, s. John Barber and Susannah Swanscombe. Wadham, Oxford 1817, BA1820, dn20 (Nor.), p20 (Nor.), MA1823. R. Aston Sandford, Bucks. 1821, R. Little Stukeley, Hunts. 1827-60. Died 28/1/1872 aged 78, leaving £25,000 [C5609] Married 12/9/1820 St George's, Hanover Square, London Lady Millicent Acheson (w) (dau. of 1st Earl of Gosford, Armagh).

BARBER (Thomas) Bapt. Gouldrop, Beds. 1773, s. Isaac Barber. St John's, Cambridge 1798, BA1802, Fellow 1803-23, dn04 (Peterb.), MA1805, p06 (York). R. Houghton Conquest, Beds. 1821 to death 30/10/1836 [C5611. YCO] Married Kempston, Beds. 17/6/1824 Frances Moore (a clergy dau.). Described in Venn as 'an energetic rector with a strong will and of singular bodily vigour; enforced order in the Church by the power of his lungs, and in the streets by the weight of his arm'.

BARBER (William) Probably bapt. Kirby Muxloe, Leics. 25/8/1778, s. Richard Barber and Ann Willatt. St John's, Cambridge 1796, BA1800, dn01 (C&L), p02 (C&L), MA1803. PC. Hanley, Staffs. 1802, PC. Quarndon, Derbys. 1802 and V. Duffield, Derbys. 1819 to death 19/5/1858 aged 80, leaving £1,500 [C8454] 2 clerical sons.

BARDGETT (Joseph) Born Oxford, s. Joseph Bardgett [*pleb*]. All Souls, Oxford 1795 (aged 19), then Merton BA1800, MA1804, Chaplain to 1825. R. Melmerby, Cumberland 1821-30 and V. Broughton with Elslack, Yorks. 1824 to death (Whitehaven, Cumberland) 12/4/1830 aged 55 (CCEd says 27/5/1830) [C4476. Platt] Had issue.

BARFOOT (Henry) Bapt. Witham, Lincs. 11/9/1787, s. Henry Barfoot and Mary Sharpe. Trinity, Cambridge 1807, then Clare, BA1812, dn12 (Lin.), p12 (Lin.), MA1815. V. Leake,

Lincs. 1831 to death 2/11/1864 aged 77, leaving £3,000 [C5613] Married Marylebone, London 11/9/1833 Mary Kempin.

BARHAM (Richard Harris) Born Canterbury 6/12/1788, s. Richard Barham and Elizabeth Fox. BNC, Oxford 1807, BA1811, p13 (Chester for Cant.), p14 (Chester for Cant.). R. Snargate, Romney Marsh, Kent 1817-24 (where his church was used as a depot by smugglers), Minor Canon of St Paul's, London 1822 (Senior 'Cardinal' 1833),V. St Mary Magdalen Old Fish Street w. St Gregory by St Paul, City of London 1824-42, Priest-in-Ordinary 1824 to death 17/6/1845 C114967. ODNB. R.D.H. Barham, *The life and letters of the Rev. Richard Harris Barham* (1870. 2v.)] Married Ashford, Kent 13/9/1813 Caroline Smart, w. clerical son. Author of *'The Ingoldsby Legends'*. Good colour ports. at: www.myjacobfamily.com/favershamjacobs/richardharrisbarham.htm

BARING (Frederick, Hon.) Born 31/1/1806, s. 1st Baron Ashburton (financier and *M.P.*) and his American wife Anna Louisa Bingham. Christ's, Cambridge, BCL, dn29 (Win.), p30 (Win.). R.&V. Itchen Stoke w. Abbotstone, Hants. 1830. Died London 4/6/1868, leaving £80,000 [C69399] Married Westminster, London 24/4/1831 Frederica Mary Catherine Ashton, with issue.

BARING-GOULD (Charles) see under **GOULD**

BARKER (Alleyne Higgs) Bapt. Swannington, Norfolk 3/2/1807, s. Rev. William Alleyne Barker (V. Abbotsbury, Dorset) and Ann Ramell. Christ's, Cambridge 1825, BA1829, dn29 (Lin. for Bristol), p31 (Bristol), MA 1832. R. Wouldham, Kent 1831-53, V. Rickmansworth, Herts. 1853 to death 6/6/1884 aged 79, leaving £1,680-5s-0d. [C7149] Married (1) London 29/12/1837 Mary Elizabeth Gale (a clergy dau., d.1845), w. issue (2) Paddington, London 6/5/1845 Marianna Burmester, with further issue.

BARKER (Anthony Auriol) Born and bapt. Baslow, Derbys. 8/4/1799, s. Rev. John Barker and Jane Whyte. Peterhouse, Cambridge 1817, BA1821, dn22 (Chester for C&L), p24 (C&L), MA1833. (succ. his father as) PC. Baslow 1824 and PC. Beeley, Derbys. 1824 to death. Dom. Chap. to Dowager Countess Galway. Died 21/12/1853 aged 54 [C8689] Married (1) Sheffield, Yorks. 4/4/1825 Sophia Stanley (d.1840), w. issue (2) Whitehaven, Cumberland 15/7/1846 Agnes Parker (a naval dau.); w. further issue. Brother Frederick, below.

BARKER (Benjamin) Bapt. Redgrave, Suffolk 12/6/1778, s. Benjamin and Ann Barker. Queens', Cambridge 1796, BA1800, dn03 (B&W), p03 (Nor.). R. Caston, Norfolk 1803, R. (and patron) of Rockland All Saints w. Rockland St Andrew, Norfolk 1803 and R. (and patron) of Shipdham, Norfolk 1820 to death 20/1/1850 aged 71 [C32612] Married Norwich 18/4/1811 Catherine Pillans, w. issue. Brother James Rickard Barker, below.

BARKER (Charles) Bapt. Hollym and Withernsea, Yorks. 8/3/1791, s. Rev. Robert Barker. St Catherine's, Cambridge 1810, BA 1814, dn14 (York), p15 (York), MA1817. (succ. his father as) V. Hollym and Withernsea 1816 (living at Hollym House) to death before 12/1/1857 [C130807. YCO] Married Doncaster, Yorks. 8/11/1838 Mary Anne Atkinson, with issue.

BARKER (Frederick, *later* Bishop of Sydney) Born Baslow, Derbys. 17/3/1808, s. Rev. John Barker and Jane Whyte. Jesus, Cambridge 1826, BA1831, dn32 (Chester), p35 (Chester), MA1839, DD1854. PC. Overchurch (o/w Upton), Cheshire 1832-4, PC. St Mary, Edge Hill, Liverpool 1835-54, V. Baslow 1854, Bishop of Sydney, NSW and Metropolitan of Australia 1854 to death (San Remo, Italy) 6/4/1882, leaving £3,364-5s-4d [C168233. ODNB and photo. Boase. *Australian Dictionary of Biography. Online Edition*] Married (1) Baslow 15/10/1840 Jane Sophia Harden (d.1876), of Brathay Hall (2) 22/1/1878 Mary Jane Woods (w); *s.p.* 'Barker was an imposing evangelical (6 feet 5½ inches tall), and was known as the "High Priest."' Brother Anthony Auriol Barker, above.

BARKER (James Rickard) Bapt. Redgrave, Suffolk 6/4/1775, s. Benjamin and Ann Baker. Corpus Christi, Cambridge 1792, then Trinity 1793, dn06 (Nor. as James), BA1807, MA1810. R. Newmarket All Saints, Suffolk 1806-38 (and Newmarket St Mary Nov.-Dec. 1834, 1835), V. Great Abington, Cambs. 1828-45, R. Wood Ditton, Cambs. 1834 (only), V. Leatherhead, Surrey 1834. Died 1/7/1850 aged 75 [C1341. Venn very confused] Married Burwell, Cambs.

21/11/1796 Elizabeth Turner. Brother Benjamin Barker, above.

BARKER (John, *later* Sir John Barker-Mill, 1st Bt.) Born Wareham, Dorset 4/12/1803, s. John Barker and Mary Mill. BNC, Oxford 1822, migrated to Downing, Cambridge 1825, dn27 (B&W for Win.), BA1828, p28 (Llandaff for Win.), MA 1831. V. Longstock, Hants. 1828-36, V. King's Somborne, Hants. 1831-6. Dom. Chap. to Bishop of Norwich. Died (Mottisfont Abbey, Hants.) 20/2/1860 aged 56, leaving £90,000 [C41605] Married Keynsham, Som. 14/8/1828 Jane Swinburn, *s.p.* As distant heir to the 10th Baronet, he changed his name (1835), and the baronetcy was recreated for him 1836. Trained racehorses, played cricket; 'and was by all accounts a jolly chap, known for his cherry-coloured cravats and his loud check trousers'.

BARKER (Ralph) Bapt. Knaresborough, Yorks. 17/3/1798 (nonconformist chapel), s. William and Jane Barker. Peterhouse, Cambridge 1817 (as Barber), dn21 (Nor.), BA1822, p22 (Nor.). PC. Longton, Lancs. 1827-31. V. Cottingham w. Skidby, Yorks. 1832-[41], V. Pagham, Sussex 1850 (with RD of Chichester 1858) to death. Co-editor of the *Protestant Guardian* (1827-29) and of the *Quarterly Educational Magazine* (1847-9). Died 9/3/1871 aged 73, leaving £1,000 [C111197. Boase] Married Norwich 10/6/1823 Jane Elisabeth Beevor, w. issue.

BARKER (Samuel) Bapt. Hull 27/5/1781, s. Rev. John Barker. Trinity Hall, Cambridge 1798 (for one year, 'but it proved too expensive'), dn03 (London for York), p07 (Lin.). Sinecure R. Carleton St Peter, Norfolk 1832 to death (a widower, Lakenheath, Suffolk) 14/9/1859 aged 78, leaving under £200 [C5620. YCO] Had issue. Possibly brother William, below.

BARKER (Thomas) Born York 25/11/1779, s. Rev. Thomas Barker, sen. and Lucy Wycliffe. Trinity, Cambridge 1797, then Magdalene 1798, then Queens' 1799, dn02 (York), BA1802, p04 (York), MA1806. PC. Kilburn, Easington, Yorks. 1804 and V. Thirkleby, Yorks. 1804-64. Died London 21/4/1868 aged 88, leaving £16,000 [C84506. ATV. YCO] Married by 1814 Jane Flower, with issue. Mentioned negatively in ODNB under his daughter Lucette Elizabeth Barker, a painter and illustrator 'whose [commercial] career he tried to suppress'.

BARKER (William) Born Hull, s. Rev. John Barker. Magdalene, Cambridge [*not* Oxford] 1789, BA1794, dn96, p97 (London), MA1800. R. Silverton, Devon 1806 and V. Broad Clyst, Devon 1819 to death. Dom. Chap. to 4th Earl of Aberdeen 1819. Died 3/12/1838 aged 66 [C69404] Had clerical son. Possibly brother Samuel, above.

BARLEE, *born* BUCKLE (Edward Buckle-) Bapt. Worlingworth, Suffolk 6/9/1788, s. Rev. William Buckle and Ann Smith. St John's, Oxford 1807, BA1811 (as Buckle), p12 (Nor.), MA1830 (as Edward Buckle-Barlee). R. Worlingworth w. Southholt 1815. Died Vaud, Switzerland 6/9/1854 [C111206] Married City of London 2/2/1818 (the Jewish) Justina Levy, 10 ch. (inc. Sir Frederick Palgrave Barlee, Colonial Secretary in Western Australia). Brother below.

BARLEE, *born* BUCKLE (William) Born Wrentham, Suffolk 1791, s. Rev. William Buckle and Ann Smith. Trinity, Oxford 1810, BA1813 (as Barlee - having assumed this name), dn16 (London) p17 (London). R. West Chiltington, Sussex 1830. Died 1850 (4th q.) [C151405] Married Dickleburgh, Norfolk 26/9/1822 Margaret George Lee (w), 14 ch. Brother above.

BARLING (Thomas) Born London 11/3/1769, s. Philip (*or* Thomas?) Barling and Rachel Clitherow. Pembroke, Cambridge 1787, BA 1791, dn92 (Nor.), p93 (Nor.). R. Howe w. Little Poringland, Norfolk 1793 to death 25/7/1836 aged 67 [C111209] Married (1) Chiswick, London 25/7/1803 Anna Clarke Lavender (d.1830), w. issue (2) Shoreditch, London 3/3/1834 Priscilla Southcombe.

BARLOW (Francis George, *later* George Francis) Born London, s. Francis Barlow and Alethea Masterman. Oriel, Oxford 1785 (aged 16), BA1789. MA 1791 (as George Francis), dn91 (London), p92 (London). R. Tooting Graveney, Wilts. 1798-1801, R. Edwardstone, Suffolk 1800-6, R. Sotterley, Suffolk 1805, R. Burgh (St Botolph), Suffolk 1814 to death (Woodbridge, Suffolk) 24/3/1850. [C69405] Married Lower Tooting, Surrey 21/5/1798 Harriet Mount, 10 ch.

BARLOW (John) Born South Mimms, Herts. (his mother's home) 20/11/1798, s. Rev. Thomas William Barlow and Anne Brockett. Trinity, Cambridge 1816, BA1820, dn22 (Ely for

Cant.), p23 (Ely for Cant.), MA1823. R. Little Bowden (Bowden Parva), Northants. 1830-43 [Sec. to the Royal Institution 1843-60]. Chaplain in Ordinary, Kensington Palace 1854 to death 8/7/1869 aged 70, leaving £40,000 [C6520. Boase] Married 1/10/1824 Cecilia Anne Law ('daughter of a wealthy nabob'), *s.p.* An important and well-connected scientist. *F.R.S.* 1834. Fine photo and excellent article at: www.rigb.org/our-history/people/b/rev-john-barlow

BARLOW (Robert Joseph) Born Dublin, s. John Barlow (from Lancs.) and Anne Wilson. TCD1820 (aged 16), BA1826, MA1830. V. Rudby in Cleveland w. Middleton and East Rounton (o/w Hutton Rudby), Yorks. 1831 to death 23/6/1878 aged 75, leaving under £100 [C130812. ATV. Al.Dub. A. Barrigan, *Remarkable but still true: the story of the Revd. R. J. Barlow in the time of the cholera* (Guisborough: The author, 2007)] Married Marianne Webb, with issue.

BARLOW (William) Born 4/12/1789, s. Admiral Sir Robert Barlow and Elizabeth Garrett. [Col. in the Madras Infantry] Trinity, Cambridge 1806, BA1811, dn20 (Chester for Roch.), p20 (London for Roch.), MA1820. V. Canterbury St Mary Bredin 1824-28, R. Weston-super-Mare, Som. 1829-40, R. Coddington, Cheshire 1834-40 and Canon of Chester 1834-48, R. Northenden, Cheshire 1840 to death (Bath) 8/12/1848 [C1562] Married (1) Marylebone, London 24/11/1824 Louisa Adeane (d.1837), w. ch. (2) Rochester 27/7/1846 Anne, dau. Rev. Hon. Frederick Hotham.

BARMBY (James) Born Idle, Yorks. 24/1/1773, s. of Henry Barmby [*pleb*]. University, Oxford 1791, BA1795, dn95 (B&W), p97 (B&W), MA1800, Fellow by 1803. S/M then H/M Bradford G/S, Yorks. 1803-18; R. Melsonby, Richmond, Yorks. 1816 to death 16/9/1852 aged 79 [C32625] Married Bradford 1/9/1819 Beatrix Pollard, with clerical s. of same name.

BARNARD (Charles Drake) Bapt. Withersfield, Suffolk 25/5/1768, s. Rev. Thomas Barnard and Melosina Rosenhagen. Trinity, Cambridge 1785, BA1789, dn90 (Lin.), p92 (London for Lin.). R. Bigby, Lincs. 1792-1832, V. Barnetby le Wold, Lincs. 1792-1833, R. Ashby by Partney, Lincs. 1809-17, V. Roxby w. Risby, Lincs. 1816. Dom. Chap. to 5th Earl of Oxford and Earl Mortimer 1816. Died 2/1/1833 (CCEd says 8/1/1833). [C5623] Married 10/3/1805 Mrs Anne Maria (Parkhurst) Foulis. *s.p.* Brother Robert, below.

BARNARD (Edward) Born 30/9/1763, s. Rev. Edward Barnard (Provost of Eton College) and Susannah Haggart. St John's, Cambridge 1781, MA1803, dn03 (B&W), p03 (B&W). PC. Harefield, Middx. 1803-7, R. Everdon, Northants. 1807-9, V. Bexley, Kent 1808-25, Prebend of Preston Wynne in Hereford Cathedral 1809-40, Prebend of Yatton in Wells Cathedral 1812-17, V. Alverstoke, Hants. [net income £1,287] 1825 to death 23/10/1840 [C32637] Married St James's, Westminster, London 22/7/1784 Mary Ann Beadon (a clergy dau.), with clerical son, below.

BARNARD (Henry Watson) Born Chislehurst, Kent 10/1/1793, s. Rev. Edward Barnard (above) and Mary Ann Beadon. St John's, Cambridge 1811, BA1815, dn15 (Heref.), p16 (St Asaph), MA1818. V. Pilton, Som. 1816, Prebendary of Yatton in Wells Cathedral 1817-55, V. Compton Bishop, Som. 1826-30, V. Yatton, Som. 1830-46 (and Preacher throughout the Diocese of Bath and Wells 1830), V. St Cuthbert, Wells 1833 to death. Dom. Chap. to 2nd Earl of Chatham 1816. Died (Granada, Spain, of cholera) 9/7/1855 aged 63 [C32629] Married Pilton 7/9/1819 Eleanor Clerk, with clerical son.

BARNARD (Mordaunt) Bapt. Litcham, Norfolk 13/12/1795, s. Rev. Thomas Barnard (V. Great Amwell, Herts.) and Everilda Dorothea Martin. Christ's, Cambridge 1813, BA1817, dn18 (London), p20 (Peterb. for York), MA1833. PC. Barnoldswick (o/w Gill), Yorks. 1820-40 [C130814], V. (and patron) of Great Amwell 1826-64, PC. Colney, Herts. 1826, V. Ridge, Herts. 1832, R. (and patron) of Little Bardfield, Essex 1845-64, R. Preston Bagot, Warwicks. 1867-75, RD of Bocking. Died St Leonards on Sea, Sussex 29/10/1885 aged 89, leaving £34,699-15s-11d. [C109247. YCO] Married (1) Marylebone, London 15/4/1821 Margaret Louisa Maria Bolton (dau. of an army officer, she d.1857), with issue (2) Linton, Cambs. 11/9/1866 Adelaide Sophia Barnard (w) (a clergy dau., of Bigby, Lincs.); with clerical son. J.P. Essex. Surrogate.

BARNARD (Robert) Born Withersfield, Suffolk 12/8/1760, s. Thomas Henry and

Melosina Rosenhagen. Trinity, Cambridge 1776, BA1782, dn87 (Ely), p87 (Ely), MA1788. R. Lighthorne, Warwicks 1787-1834, 9th Prebend of Winchester 1793-1834, R. & V. Witney, Oxon. 1797 to death 25/2/1834 (CCEd says 13/3/1834) aged 73 [C3267] Married Lighthorne 31/10/1793 Louisa Peyto-Verney, dau. 14th Baron Willoughby de Broke (their son - also Robert - inheriting the title and changing his name). Brother Charles Drake Barnard, above.

BARNEBY (Thomas) Bapt. Brockhampton, Heref. 14/8/1773, s. Richard and Betty Barneby. Oriel, Oxford 1791, BA1795, then BNC, MA1797, dn97 (Ox.), p98 (Ox.), BD1810. R. Edwin Loach w. Tedstone Wafer, Heref. 1811 and R. Stepney St Dunstan, London 1815 to death 11/5/1842 aged 69 [C22370]

BARNES (Francis) [NiVoF] R. Glaston, Rutland 1788. This is probably - but not conclusively - the controversial Master of Peterhouse, Cambridge (13/1/1744 to 30/4/1838), elected 1788 (to death) [C43101]

BARNES (Frederick [William]) Born St Merryn, Cornwall 9/6/1771, s. Ven. Ralph Barnes ('Old Ugly') and Ann Blackall. Christ Church, Oxford 1790, BA1794, MA1797, dn98 (Ox.), p99 (Chester), BD1805, DD1811. PC. Oxford St Michael 1799, PC. Cowley, Oxford 1803, V. Colebrooke, Devon 1805, V. Colyton, Devon 1807-53-, Canon of Christ Church, Oxford (7th Prebend) 1810-59, R. Cheriton Bishop, Devon 1823. Died 19/8/1859. No will traced [C22110] Brothers below.

BARNES (George) Bapt. Marylebone, London 25/12/1769, s. Thomas and Catherine Barnes ('of Hull'). St John's, Cambridge 1792, BA1796, then Queens', dn98 (Ely), Fellow 1799 (and Tutor), p01 (Ely), BD1808. [Failed candidate for the College Presidency]. R. Grimston, Norfolk 1816 to death 9/12/1846 [C99562] Married Cambridge 3/11/1817 Eliza Tucker Atkinson (a clergy dau.?)

BARNES (George) Born Harberton, Devon 11/12/1782, s. Ven. Ralph Barnes ('Old Ugly') and Ann Blackall. Exeter, Oxford 1799, BA 1803, Fellow 1805, MA1806, p08 (Ex.), BD 1814, DD1818. R. St Mary Major, Exeter 1809, (first) Archdeacon of Bombay 1814, R. Sowton, Devon 1826 (w. Archdeacon of Barnstaple 1830) to death 29/6/1847 aged 64 [C139490] Married Bombay 1817 Harriet Penelope Rivett-Carnac, with issue. Brothers above and below.

BARNES (Henry) Bapt. Monmouth 15/9/1783, s. Henry and Louisa Barnes. Oriel, Oxford 1801, then Exeter, BA1806. V. Monmouth and Rockfield 1822. Minister of the Episcopal Chapel at St Servan, France to death 23/7/1837 aged 53 [C3629. LBSO - claimed slave compensation] J.P. Heref. and Monmouth. D.L. Herefordshire.

BARNES (James) [NiVoF]. V. Warton, Lancaster, Lancs. 1823 to death 11/12/1837 aged 41 [C168245] Note another cleric of this name PC. Langho, Lancs. 1803 and PC. Samlesbury, Lancs. 1803 to death 1/5/1829 [C138649]

BARNES (John) Born Wigton, Cumberland 29/12/1798. St. Bees admitted 1822, dn25 (Car.), p25 (Car.). PC. Wreay, Carlisle, 1832-5, PC. Kirkandrews-on-Esk 1832, PC. Bassenthwaite, Cumberland 1835 to death 1852 (but other possibilities) [C2872. Platt] Wife Anne (b. Jamaica), with issue.

BARNES (Joseph) Bapt. Isell, Cumberland 3/3/1779, s. Thomas Barnes. S/M Dalston Free G/S, Cumberland 1796. Literate: dn02 (Durham), p03 (Durham). S/M Durham G/S 1803; V. Berwick upon Tweed, Northumberland 1805 (and Minor Canon Durham Cathedral 1810) to death 5/12/1853 aged 74 [C4480] Married Alston, Cumberland 1801 Isabella Young, with issue.

BARNES (Theophilus) Bapt. Exeter, Devon 9/9/1774, s. Ven. Ralph Barnes (Archdeacon of Totnes, 'Old Ugly') and Ann Blackall. Exeter, Oxford 1791, Fellow 1794, BA and MA1798, dn98 (Ox.), p99 (Ex.). R. Exeter St Petrock, Devon 1798. R. Castleford, Yorks. 1803-50, R. Stonegrave, Yorks. 1815-50 (non-res. for 40 years), Prebend of Fridaythorpe in York Minster 1826 to death. Dom. Chap. to 1st Baron Glenbervie 1815; sometime chaplain and private secretary to 1st Earl of Liverpool. Died Castleford (a widower) 9/2/1855 aged 79 [C22373] Married York 29/4/1815 (or Saxton in Elmet, Yorks. 2/5/1815?) Charlotte Davison Bland (Kippax Park, Yorks.), with issue. J.P. until 1837. Brothers above.

BARNES (William) [NiVoF] R. Burgh [in the Marsh] cum Winthorpe, Norfolk 1812 to death 27/8/1838 aged 68 [C43104]

BARNES (William) Literate: dn17 (Chester), p19 (Chester), MA1830 (Lambeth). R. Richmond St Mary, Yorks. 1823-38, R. Brixton Deverill, Wilts. 1838 to death 14/4/1858 aged 63, leaving £4,000 [C150317] Married 1821 Elizabeth, dau. Richard Bootle-Wilbraham, M.P.

BARNETT (Matthew) Literate: dn88 (Lin.), p89 (Lin.). V. Cranwell, Lincs. 1799-1833, V. North Willingham, Lincs. 1821-33, R. Little Ludford (Ludford Parva), Lincs. 1823 to death 24/9/1833 [CCEd 43105. Kaye]

BARNWELL (Charles Barnwell) Bapt. Mileham Hall, Mileham, Norfolk 12/7/1801, s. John Barnwell (formerly Harring, a merchant) and Catherine Barnwell. Caius, Cambridge 1819, BA1823 dn24 (Nor.), p25 (Nor.). R. (and patron) of Mileham 1825 to death (Norwich) 27/11/1882 aged 81, leaving £1,327-13s-3d. [C111270] Married elbrigg, Norfolk 28/10/1829 Sophia Wyndham (Cromer Hall, Norfolk). Took the (second) name Barnwell 1822. J.P. Norfolk.

BARNWELL (John) Born Demerara, British Guiana, s. Edward Barnwell (slave connections). Pembroke, Oxford 1818 (aged 18), BA1821, dn24 (Bristol), p24 (Bristol). V. Stogursey, Som. 1826-32, R. Sutton Valence, Kent 1832, R. Holford, Som. 1832 [total income £1,145] to death 16/9/1866, leaving £12,000 [C1342. LBSO] Married Dinton, Bucks. 4/5/1826 Emilia Goodall, with clerical son.

BARON (John) Born Wigan, Lancs. 16/7/1795, s. John Baron (solicitor) and Ellen Jackson. BNC, Oxford 1816, BA1820, dn20 (Ches.), p21 (Chesh), MA1822. V. Walsall St Matthew, Staffs. 1822-37 (res.). Lived in Clifton, Bristol. Died Weston super Mare, Somerset 7/2/1867 aged 71, leaving £5,000 [C160186] Married Stockport, Cheshire 24/4/1823 Anna Maria Prescot (a clergy dau.), with issue. The following shows the mess that amateur genealogists can get themselves into: www.genealogy-specialists.com › English Counties › Staffords-hire

BARON (John Samuel) Born St Dominica, West Indies 25/4/1788, s. John Baron. Queen's, Oxford 1810, BA1813, dn13 (Lin.), p14 (Lin.), MA1816. PC. Brill w. Boarstall, Bucks. 1814.

Dom. Chap. to 2nd Baron Kensington 1815. Died 24/4/1866, leaving £1,500 [C43112] Married Norwood Green, Middx. 9/7/1812 Sarah Harris Parker, with clerical son.

BARRETT (Jonathan Tyers) Bapt. Lambeth, Surrey 6/5/1784, s. Bryant Barrett (a wax chandler) and Elizabeth Tyers. Peterhouse, Cambridge 1801, BA1806, Fellow 1806, dn07 (Win.), p08 (Win.), MA1809, DD1821. V. Norton Mandeville, Essex 1815-16, R. Beauchamp Roding ><, Essex 1822, V. Lambeth St John's the Evangelist, Surrey 1824-32, Mapesbury Prebend of Apesbury in St Paul's Cathedral 1825, R. Attleborough, Norfolk 1839 to death (Brandon House, Suffolk) 6/3/1851 aged 66 [C69398] Married Lambeth 13/9/1809 Mary Slade, w. issue. The Vauxhall Pleasure Gardens in London were at one time in his joint ownership. He was Secretary of the Society for the Conversion and Religious Instruction of Negro Slaves (from 1822).

BARRINGTON (Lowther John, Hon.) Born Sedgefield, Co. Durham 17/7/1805, s. Rev. George Barrington, 5th Viscount Barrington and Elizabeth Adair. Oriel, Oxford 1822, BA 1825, MA1829, dn30 (Lin.), p30 (Lin.). R. Chesham Bois, Bucks. 1830-9, R. West Tytherley, Hants. 1839-50, R. Watton-at-Stone, Herts. 1850-86 (and RD of Welwyn), Hon. Canon of St Albans Cathedral 1868 to death. Chap. to Bishop of Jerusalem 1868 to death. Died London 10/3/1897 aged 91, leaving £7,198-18s-8d. [C43116. Boase. LFBI] Married St James, Westminster, London 26/10/1837 Lady Catherine Georgiana Pelham (dau. of 2nd Earl of Chichester), w. clerical s. Ythil Arthur.

BARROW (Anthony) Born Kendal, Westmorland 19/6/1755, s. Robert Barrow and Elizabeth Dodeson. S/M Blawith G/S, Ulverston, Lancs. 1780. Literate: dn80 (C&L for Chester), p80 (Chester). PC. Rusland, Lancs. 1780-1802, PC. Kentmere, Westmorland 1802-16 (res.), PC. Lindale, Cartmel, Lancs. (and S/M) 1815 to death 5/1/1834 aged 78 ('after a lingering illness') [C8692] Married Blawith 31/6/1787 Martha Redhead, w. clerical s. (three below).

BARROW (Francis) Bapt. Strood, Kent 14/10/1791, s. Francis Barrow and Elizabeth Kirby. Wadham, Oxford 1809, BA1813, MA 1816, p16 (London). V. Sandwich St Mary, Kent 1823-4 (res.), PC. Margate Holy Trinity, Kent 1829-[46]. Dom. Chap. to Marquess of Huntley.

Died Cranbrook, Kent 7/2/1858, leaving £14,000 [C87] J.P. for Kent and the Cinque Ports.

BARROW (James) Born Southwell, Notts. 21/18/1793, s. Richard Barrow. St John's, Cambridge 1811, BA1815, dn17 (Salis.), p17 (Salis.), MA1818, Fellow. R. North (and South) Lopham, Norfolk 1823-61, R. North Wingfield, Derbys. (a family living) 1861-78 [income £1,400]. Living at Southwell 1880; died there 12/4/1881 aged 87, leaving £90,000 [C84665] Married Marylebone, London 8/1/1824 Louisa Malet, with issue. 'An easy-going man'.

BARROW (James) Bapt. Colton, Lancs. 17/10/1801, s. Rev. Anthony Barrow (above) and Martha Redhead. St Bees admitted 1824, dn25 (Chester), p26 (Chester). PC. Rusland, Colton 1826 to death (Kendal, Westmorland) 19/5/1846 aged 45 [C168259] Married Colton 25/5/1830 Mrs Charlotte (Burns) Dawson, with issue.

BARROW (Richard) Bapt. Dent, Sedbergh, Yorks. 22/10/1747, s. John Barrow (landowner, but as *pleb*!) and Isabel Hodgson. Literate: dn70 (York), p72 (York), then St John's, Cambridge 1773 (a Ten Year Man, BD1783). V. Bleasby, Notts. 1774-8, S/M Southwell G/S, Notts. 1774-85, a Vicar-Choral of Southwell Minster 1774-1838, V. South Muskham, Notts. 1778-1838, R. South Wheatley, Notts. 1778-1838, V. Upton, Notts. 1780-4, R. Halloughton, Notts. 1782, V. Rolleston, Notts. 1784-5, R. Beelsby, Lincs. 1785-86, R. Barnoldby le Beck, Lincs. 1785-1838, V. Rampton, Notts. 1798 (and Prebend of Eaton in Southwell Collegiate Church 1815) to death. 'One of the greatest pluralists of the Georgian age'. Died Southwell 23/2/1838 aged 90 [C43120. YCO. Kaye. Austin2. LFBI 412 and port.] Married Southwell 1/1/1778 Mary Hodgkinson, with clerical son. Brother below.

BARROW (William) Bapt. Dent, Sedbergh, Yorks. 15 *or* 16/12/1754, s. John Barrow [landowner, but as *pleb*!] and Isabel Hodgson. Queen's, Oxford 1774, BA 1778, dn79 (Ox.), p80 (Lin.), MA1783, DCL 1785. Prebend of Eaton in Southwell Minster 1815, R. North Wingfield, Derbys. 1822, R. Waltham, Lincs. 1825-30 (res.), R. Beelsby, Leics. 1830, Archdeacon of Nottingham 1830-2 (res.). Bampton Lecturer 1799. Died 19/4/1836 aged 82 [C9064. LFBI 412. Austin2] Married 5/1/1791 Elizabeth Anne Probyn, *s.p.* Brother above.

BARRY (Gaius) Born Upton Scudamore, Wilts. 8/2/1771, s. Richard Barry (the Third) and Elizabeth Holloway. Literate: dn95 (Peterb. for Salis.), p96 (Salis.). Minor Canon of Bristol Cathedral 1812, R. Little Sodbury, Glos. 1819. Died Bedminster, Som. 5/10/1850 aged 80 [C41812] Married Walcot, Bath 12/10/1801 Harriett Squire, with clerical son.

BARRY (Henry) Bapt. Hereford 1781, s. Rev. Henry William Barry and Catherine Roberts. All Souls, Oxford 1799, BA1803, then Queen's, MA1806. R. Draycot Cerne, Wilts. 1812-50, R. Upton Scudamore, Wilts. 1812-50. Dom. Chap. to Elizabeth, Dowager Duchess of Devonshire 1812. Buried Draycot Cerne, Wilts. 20/8/1850 [C84667] Married Westminster, London 8/12/1817 Elizabeth King, w. issue.

BARTER (Charles, sen.) Bapt. Sandford, Devon 14/2/1750, s. Rev. William Barter. Balliol, Oxford 1770, dn73 (Ex.), BA1774, p75 (Ex.). V. (and patron) of Cornworthy, Devon 1775 and V. Buckland Monachorum, Devon 1783 to death 26/4/1846 aged 96 [C139494] Married Tiverton, Devon 2/2/1785 Catherine Sweet, with clerical sons, below.

BARTER (Charles, jun.) Born Cornworthy, Devon 1786, s. Rev. Charles Barter, sen. (above) and Catherine Sweet. Balliol, Oxford 1803, BA1807, Fellow 1811, MA1812, dn12 (Ox.), p13 (Ox.), Fellow. R. Sarsden w. Churchill, Oxon. 1817-69, RD of Chipping Norton, R. Cornwell, Oxon. 1829 to death 24/6/1868 aged 82, leaving £1,500 [C22112] Married Sarsden, Oxon. 21/11/1817 Elizabeth Catherine Langston (w), and issue. Brother, below.

BARTER (William Brudenell) Born Cornworthy, Devon 1788, s. Rev. Charles Barter, sen. (above) and Catherine Sweet. Christ Church, Oxford 1805, BA1809, then Oriel, Fellow 1811, MA1813, dn15 (Heref. for Win.), p15 (B&W for Win.). R. Highclere, Hants. 1816 and R. Burghclere W. Newton, Hants. (and Preacher throughout the Diocese) 1825 to death. Dom. Chap. and family tutor to 2nd Earl of Carnarvon 1816. Died Southampton 16/11/1858 aged 71, leaving £9,000 [C22113. Boase] Married (1) High Littleton, Som. 16/7/1800 Martha Hodges Mogg (d.1805) (2)

Stogumber, Som. 1/5/1825 Sarah Sweet Escott, w. issue. Brother above.

BARTHOLOMEW (John) Born Exeter 25/8/1790, s. Rev. Robert Bartholomew and Ann Churchill. Corpus Christi, Oxford 1809, BA1813, dn17 (Ex.), p17 (Ex.), MA1820. PC. Withycombe Raleigh, Devon 1817, PC. Sowton, Devon 1819, V. Lympstone, Devon 1820 and R. Morchard Bishop, Devon 1831-65, Prebend 1831 and Canon Residentiary of Exeter 1840-65, Archdeacon of Barnstaple 1847 [total income £1,681] to death (a widower) 24/9/1865, leaving £16,000 [C136720. Boase] Married Marylebone, London 30/7/1822 Ann Eliza Farquharson, with 2 clerical sons.

BARTLETT (John) Born Bucks., s. John Bartlett (banker). Queens', Cambridge 1811, BA1816, dn17 (Chester), MA1820, p21 (Chester for C&L). PC. Buildwas, Shropshire 1822 and V. Spratton, Northants. 1823 to death (Madeley, Shropshire) 17/11/1861 aged 67, leaving £40,000 [C8840] Married Wellington, Shropshire 26/9/1822 Susannah Ball Reynolds, with issue.

BARTLETT (Thomas) Born Rotherfield Greys, Henley-on-Thames, Oxon. 24/2/1789, s. Thomas Bartlett (bapt. in an Independent Chapel) and Lucy Hunt. St Edmund Hall, Oxford 1809, dn12 (Salis.), BA1813, p14 (Glos.), MA 1816. R. Kingston, Kent 1816-52, Canterbury All Saints w. St Mildred w. St Mary de Castro, Kent 1828, R. Chevening, Kent 1851-4, V. Luton, Beds. 1854-7, R. Burton Latimer, Northants. (but living at Tunbridge Wells, Kent) 1857 to death. Dom. Chap. to 2nd Marquess of Cholmondeley 1828-50. Six Preacher at Canterbury 1832-72. Died 28/5/1872, leaving £800 [C42. ODNB. Boase] Married (1) by 1815 Catherine Sarah Cowper (d.1863), w. clerical s. George Philip (2) Uckfield, Sussex 1864 Lucinda Grace Hoare (w).

BARTLETT (Thomas Oldfield) Born Wareham, Dorset 1/4/1788, s. Thomas Bartlett and Ann Vincent. 'Sometime an attorney at law'. Literate: dn16 (Bristol), p16 (B&W). R. Swanage 1817-41, R. Sutton Montis, Som. 1820. Died 27/2/1841. Married 1817 Elizabeth Leach, at least 6 ch. (1 handicapped - note the early use of this term) [C8129] Brother two below?

BARTLETT (William) Born Bristol, s. Simeon Summers Bartlett and Mary Taylor. St John's, Oxford 1787 (aged 19), BA1792, dn93 (Bristol), p94 (Bristol), MA1814. V. East Stoke w. Syerston, Notts. 1804-35 and V. Newark on Trent, Notts. 1814 to death 11/5/1835 (CCEd says 2/6/1835) aged 65. Dom. Chap. to 1st Viscount Carleton 1814 [C84562] Married East Harptree, Som. 30/10/1800 Sarah Wright, with issue.

BARTLETT (William Oldfield) Born Wareham, Dorset 18/3/1797, s. Thomas Bartlett and Ann Vincent. Merton, Oxford 1814, BA 1818, dn20 (Glos. for Bristol), p21 (Chester for Bristol), MA1822. V. Worth Maltravers, Dorset 1822 and R. Great Canford (Canford Magna), Dorset 1826 to death 21/5/1842 [C52016] Married Wareham 18/2/1823 Gloria Brice, with issue. Brother two above.

BARTON (Charles) Bapt. Gloucester 15/9/1766, s. William Barton [*pleb - sic*] and Mary Chapman. Corpus Christi, Oxford 1782, BA1786, dn89 (Glos.), MA1789, BD1798. p90 (Ox.), DD1805, Fellow. R. Halstead, Kent 1806-7, V. Rainham, Kent 1807, R. Pluckley, Kent 1807-16, R. Bocking, Essex 1816 (and Dean of Bocking - a Peculiar - 1816) and R. Monks Eleigh, Suffolk 1816 to death(unm.) 6/3/1834 (CCEd says 11/3/1834), leaving £120,000 [C22390]

BARTON (Charles) Bapt. Ardwick, Manchester 15/6/1796, s. James Bartlett and Dorothy Ann Howell. [MA but NiVoF]. R. Saxby, Lincs. 1824-32, V. Elsham, Lincs. 1832. Died Bideford, Devon? Probate granted 8/12/1852 [C43128] Married Stockport, Cheshire 30/6/1825 Frances Jane Hoyle, w. clerical son Charles John Wood Barton.

BARTON (Henry Jonas) Born Aldingham, Lancs. 21/2/1797, s. Rev. James Barton and Eleanor Parr. BNC, Oxford 1814, BA1818, MA 1820, dn22 (Wor.), p23 (Wor.). V. Latton w. Eisey, Wilts. 1830, R. Wicken, Cambs. 1838-72 (and RD of Preston), Hon. Canon of Peterborough Cathedral 1854 to death 27/8/1872 aged 75, leaving £4,000 [C84669. LBSO] Married Reading, Berks. 1/5/1827 Emma Elizabeth Warner, w. issue.

BARTON (John) Born Liverpool 27/4/1798, s. Rev. Henry Barton and Mary Davies. St Mary Hall, Oxford 1822, dn25 (Chester), BA1826, MA1828. (succ. his father as) R. Eastchurch, Kent [income £1,724] 1827 to death (Walmer,

Kent) 11/3/1858, leaving £7,000 [C136723] Married Ulverston, Lancs. 2/8/1825 Eleanor Yarker, w. clerical s. John Yarker Barton.

BARTON (Matthew) Bapt. Swineshead, Lincs. 15/4/1774, s. James Barton. St John's, Cambridge 1792, BA1797, dn97 (Lin.), p01 (Peterb.), MA1819. R. Clipsham, Rutland 1816 to death 6/8/1845 [C43113] Married Frances Williams (a clergy dau.), with issue.

BARTON (Miles) Bapt. Hoole, Ormskirk, Lancs. 22/9/1786, s. Rev. Roger Barton and Mary Davies. Literate: dn10 (Chester), p11 (Chester). (succ. his father as) R. (and patron) of Hoole 1812 to death (New Brighton, Cheshire) 31/10/1848 [C168264] Married Winwick, Lancs. 25/4/1814 Mary Robertson Chippendale, many children.

BARTON (Robinson Shuttleworth) Born Preston, Lancs. 16/1/1786, s. Rev. James Barton and Ann Shuttleworth. TCD1814, dn15 (York for Chester), p15 (Chester), then St John's, Cambridge 1840 (a Ten Year Man: BD1842). PC. Goosnargh, Lancs. 1815-22, V. Alconbury cum Alconbury Weston, Hunts. 1822-38, R. Heysham, Lancs. 1838 to death (Malvern, Worcs.) 4/6/1858 aged 72, leaving £5,000 [C43134. YCO. Al.Dub.] Married Flixton, Lancs. 16/8/1830 Jane Baron, and had issue.

BARTON (Thomas) Bapt. West Peckham, Kent 5/2/1787, s. Thomas and Mary Barton. Literate: dn11 (York), p12 (York). PC. Kingston on Soar, Notts. 1827, R. Sutton Bonington, Notts. 1845 to death 14/3/1848 [C130822. YCO] Was married with issue.

BARWICK (John) Born c.1768, s. John and Margaret Barwick. Corpus Christi, Cambridge 1785, BA1789, dn90 (Nor. for Cant.), p92 (C&L), MA1805. V. Charing, Kent 1799-1834, R. Boughton Malherbe, Kent 1804, PC. Egerton, Charing 1816 to death 18/5/1834 (CCEd thus) aged 67 [C8841] Married Charing 28/4/1791 Frances Anne Marshall, w. issue.

BASELEY (Thomas) Born Monks Kirby, Warwicks. 12/5/1768, s. Rev. Henry Baseley, (R. Knibworth, Leics.) and Susannah Trubshaw. St John's, Cambridge 1785, migrated to BNC, Oxford 1787, then Merton, BA1790, dn90 (Lin.), p92 (Lin.), migrated back to Cambridge, MA1796. V. Harrold, Beds. 1792-9, R. Little Woolston, Bucks. 1796-1834. Chap. to Bishop of Lincoln 1796. Died Chelsea, London 7/10/1844 [C43228] Married St James, Piccadilly, London 20/3/1790 Sarah Adams, with issue. Involved in legal proceedings 1807, and seemingly attempted to solicit his appointment as Dean of Salisbury, 'offering ample financial remuneration'.

BASKETT (John) Born Wimborne Minster, Dorset 30/12/1773, s. Rev. John Baskett, sen. (R. Compton Abbas, Dorset) and Hannah Palmer. Jesus, Cambridge 1793, BA1797, dn97 (Bristol), p98 (Bristol). V. Tarrant Monkton w. Tarrant Launceston, Dorset 1822-?37, R. Compton Abbas, Dorset 1827-52, R. Spetisbury, Dorset 1852 to death (Wimborne Minster) 17/2/1855 aged 81 [C52007] Married Poole. Dorset 29/4/1825 1835 Elizabeth Bristowe, w. issue.

BASKETT (Kingsman) Born Pocklington, Yorks. 16/10/1758, s. Rev. Kingsman Baskett, sen. (schoolmaster) and Jane Purbeck. Trinity, Cambridge 1776, BA1781, dn82 (York), Fellow 1782, MA1784, p85 (Peterb.). V. Arrington, Cambs. 1787, R. Great Loughton, Bucks. 1797-1833 (and Chap. to the Hull Charterhouse [almshouses] 1800-33), V. Aysgarth, Yorks. 1797 to death 20/1/1833 aged 77 (CCEd says 10/7/1833) [C42186. YCO] Married Dorothy Bourne. 'A sound scholar and a Whig of the old school'.

BASLEY (Daniel) From Oxford, s. Daniel Basley [*pleb*] and Mary Colcutt. Merton, Oxford 1800 (aged 20), BA1804, dn04 (Lin.), p05 (Lin.). R. Cranford St John's, Northants. 1815-[47]. Died Cowley, Oxon. 5/10/1868, leaving £5,000 [C43230] Married (1) Oxford 26/2/1805 Sarah Hewitt (d.1838), w. issue (2) Welwyn, Herts. 11/7/1839 Ann Maria Hill (w), and further issue.

BASNETT, BASSNETT (Richard) Bapt. Manchester 10/11/1799, s. of Thomas Bassnett (a smallware trader) and Mary Adamson. Trinity, Oxford 1819, BA1822, dn23 (Chester for York), p23 (York), MA1825. PC. Manchester St Thomas, Gorton 1831 to death 20/10/1864 aged 65, leaving £14,000 [C130824. YCO] Married Manchester 2/2/1829 Marianne Brotherton, with issue.

BASNETT, BASNET (Thomas Still) Born Nottingham 29/10/1792 (bapt. in a Presbyterian

Chapel), s. of Thomas (a surgeon) and Elizabeth Basnett. St John's, Oxford 1811, BA1815, dn16 (Ely for York), p17 (York), MA1820. PC. Halam, Notts. 1821, PC. West Ravendale Chapel, East Ravendale, Lincs. 1822-65, R. Bonsall (o/w Bonteshill), Derbys. 1827-33, Vicar Choral of Southwell Collegiate Church with V. Rolleston, Notts. 1840-1, R. Waltham, Grimsby, Lincs. 1841 (and RD of Great Grimsby No.2 District) to death 13/2/1865, leaving £1,500 [C130823/1308974. Kaye] Married St George's Hanover Square, London 3/3/1830 Jane Elizabeth Beard (w), with issue. Surrogate.

BASSETT (Henry) Born Glentworth, Lincs. 12/4/1778, s. Richard Bassett. Balliol, Oxford 1797, BA1801, dn01 (Lin.), p02 (Lin.). R. (and patron) of North Thoresby, Lincs. 1802, V. Glentworth 1802, V. Saxby w. Firsby, Lincs. 1805 to death 1/5/1852 [C43227] Married Lincoln 1/10/1811 Caroline Fardell.

BASTARD (John) Bapt. Blandford, Dorset 23/1/1781, s. John Bastard and Isabella Benjafield. Wadham, Oxford 1799, BA1803, dn04 (Bristol), p05 (Bristol). R. Fifehead Neville, Dorset 1817-62, R. Stratfield Saye, Berks. 1818, R. Stratfield Turgis, Berks 1829. Died London 3/1/1862, leaving £80,000 (having inherited a fortune from Lord Rivers) [C8130] Married St George's Hanover Square, London 16/5/1807 Anna Charlotte Clarke, w. issue

BASTARD (Philemon Pownell) Born Ashburton, Devon, s. Edmund Pollexfen Bastard, *M.P.*, and Jane Pownall. Balliol, Oxford 1812 (aged 19), BA1816, dn16 (London), p17 (London). R. Hanworth, Middx. 1819. Probate 12/8/1846 [as Bestard] [C114986] Married Wimbledon, Surrey 24/9/1816 Mary Ann Park.

BATCHELER (Thomas John) Born Horstead, Norfolk 5/3/1795 (CCEd thus), s. Thomas Horatio Batcheler and Jane Beevor. Caius, Cambridge 1814, dn18 (Nor.), p19 (Nor.), a Ten Year Man 1819 (BD1834). PC. Arminghall, Norfolk 1833-60. Died London 23/7/1874. Will not traced [C1032] Married Norwich 27/10/1831 Catherine Barnwell Herring, with issue.

BATEMAN (Gregory) Born Covent Garden, London 31/10/1772, s. Gregory Bateman and Mary Welch. Trinity, Cambridge 1791, BA 1795, dn95 (Lin. for Peterb.), p97 (Ex. for Peterb.). R. Great Hormead, Herts. 1797-1800, R. Pilton, Rutland 1800 and R. Easton by Stamford, Northants. 1805 (and S/M Gouldhurst G/S 1833) to death 21/4/1848 [C43241] Married Peterborough 9/9/1823 Alice Richmond, w. issue.

BATEMAN (Rowland) From Bedford, Co. Kerry, s. Colthurst Bateman. TCD 1791 (aged 18), BA1804, p11 (Ex.). R. Silton, Dorset 1815. Died? [C52020. Al.Dub.] Married Clifton, Bristol 29/3/1826 Catherine Frances Elizabeth Mitford (d.1831).

BATES (Charles Cecil) Bapt. Holborn, London 3/3/1771, s. Joah and Sarah Bates. Christ's, Cambridge 1807, BA1812, MA1815, dn15 (Heref. for Ely), p16 (Ely). V. Castleton, Derbys. 1818 to death (London) 4/1/1853 [C6527]

BATES (George Ferne) Bapt. City of London 1/10/1775, s. Rev. Henry Bates (R. Freckenham, Suffolk). Queens', Cambridge 1801, BA 1805, dn05 (London), p06 (London), MA1808. V. South Mimms, Middx. 1812-41, R. West Malling, Kent 1814 to death. Chap. to HRH Duke of Kent 1814. Died 18/11/1841 aged 66 [C43. DEB] Married Wateringbury, Kent 27/5/1834 Justina Fraser.

BATES (William) Bapt. Bridgnorth, Shropshire 7/3/1775, s. John Bates. Pembroke, Oxford 1792, BA1796, dn98 C&L), MA1800, p08 (Win.). PC. Jackfield (o/w Tachfield), Shropshire 1808, R. Willey, Shropshire 1823, R. Beckbury, Shropshire 1824. Died? [C9100]

BATESON (Christopher) Bapt. Horton in Ribblesdale, Yorks. 14/12/1791, s. Henry Bateson (farmer) and Elizabeth Proctor. Pembroke, Cambridge 1809, BA1814, dn14 (Chester), p15 (Chester). PC. Westhoughton, Lancs. 1816 to death 25/3/1842 aged 50 [C168269] Married Giggleswick, Yorks. 30/12/1812 Alice Holgate, with issue.

BATH AND WELLS (George Henry Law, Bishop of) see under **LAW**

BATHER (Edward) Bapt. Meole Brace, Shrewsbury, Shropshire 2/4/1780, s. Rev. John Bather and Martha Hannah Hallifax (a clergy dau.). Oriel, Oxford 1798, BA1803, dn03 (Heref.), p04 (Heref.), MA1808. V. Meole Brace 1804-47, Archdeacon of Salop (w. Prebend of

Ufton Cantoris in Lichfield Cathedral) 1828 to death 3/10/1847 [C9101. ODNB. DEB] Married (1) Standish, Glos. 16/4/1805 Emma Hallifax (d.1825) (2) Shrewsbury 27/3/1828 Mary Butler (dau. of the H/M of Shrewsbury School, later Bishop of Lichfield, *q.v.*); *s.p.*

BATHURST (Charles, Hon.) Born 21/1/1802, s. Henry, 3rd Earl Bathurst and Lady Georgiana Lennox. Christ Church, Oxford 1821, dn25 (Ox.), p26 (Cashel for Ox. - in Oxford), then All Souls 1830, BCL1830, DCL 1835. R. Siddington, Glos. 1830, R. Southam, Warwicks. 1830. Died 28/2/1842 aged 40 [C9102] Married 31/7/1830 Lady Emily Caroline Bertie (dau. 5th Earl of Adingdon, *s.p.*

BATHURST (Henry, sen., Bishop of Norwich) Bapt. London 16/10/1744, one of the *36* ch. of s. Benjamin Bathurst, *M.P.* (Lydney Park, Glos., a slave trader, and brother of 3rd Earl Bathurst) and (his second wife) Katherine Brodrick. New College, Oxford 1761, BCL1768, p69 (Ox.), then Christ Church DCL1776. R. Dunkerton, Norfolk 1789-74, R. Sapperton, Norfolk 1773-5, 1785-1833, R. Great Witchingham, Norfolk, and Norwich St John's Maddermarket 1775-86, Canon of 7th Prebend in Christ Church, Oxford 1775-95, 2nd Prebend of Durham Cathedral 1795-1805, Bishop of Norwich (where 'the neglect of his See was shocking') 1795 to death (London) 5/4/1837 (leaving 2,650 bottles of wine) [ODNB. C22412. *Memoirs of the late Dr Henry Bathurst, Lord Bishop of Norwich*, ed. T. Thistlethwaite (1853)] Married Kilfenora, Co. Clarke 15/8/1780 Grace Coote (dau. of the Dean of Kilfenora), 8s. (incl. below), 3 dau. A good whist player and huntsman; and 'the only liberal' on the Episcopal Bench (because he favoured Catholic Emancipation). His statue in Norwich Cathedral is of him serenely seated, with hands clasped.

BATHURST (Henry, jun.) Born Northampton 4/5/1781, s. Rt. Rev. Henry Bathurst (Bishop of Norwich, above) and Grace Coote (dau. of Dean of Kilfenora). New, Oxford 1797, BCL1804, dn04 (Glos.), p05 (Ox.). Chancellor of Norwich 1805-9, R. Ashby w. Oby and Thurne, Norfolk 1829, R. North Creake, Norfolk (and Preacher throughout the Diocese of Norwicdh) 1809, Archdeacon of Norwich 1814-44, R. Hollesley, Suffolk 1829. Died Chelten-ham, Glos. 10/9/1844 [income then £1,907] [C22411]

BATHURST (William Hiley) Born Mangotsfield, Glos. 25/8/1796, s. Hon. Charles Bathurst and Charlotte Addington. Christ Church, Oxford 1814, BA1818, dn19 (Ox.), p20 (London), MA1822. R. Barwick in Elmet, Yorks. 1820-[52], but living at Lydney Park, Glos. (on the site of a Roman villa which he excavated). Died Chepstow, Monmouth 25/11/1877 aged 81, leaving £50,000 [C22410. Boase] Married Roundhay, Yorks. 2/9/1828 Mary Anne Rhodes, with clerical son. Port. online.

BATLEY (William Lashmar) Bapt. Clerkenwell, London 20/11/1785 (in a Lady Huntingdon's Connection Chapel), s. Henry Batley and Awdry Lashmar. Peterhouse, Cambridge 1803, BA1808, dn08 (Win.), p08 (Win.), Fellow, MA 1811. R. Woodford, Northants. 1817 to death 30/10/1856 aged 73, leaving £3,000 (left unadministered until 1875) [C43250] Married Ferring, Sussex 14/11/1815 Eliza Henty with issue.

BATTEN (Joseph Hallet) Born Penzance, Cornwall 25/8/1778, s. Rev. Joseph Batten (Congregational minister) and Anne Luke. Trinity, Cambridge 1794, BA1799, Fellow 1801, MA1802, dn07 (Lin.), p09 (Lin.), DD1815. [Professor of Classical Literature at the East India Company's College at Haileybury 1805, then Principal 1815-37]. R. Beesby in the Marsh, Lincs. 1810-37, R. Gretford w. Wilsthorpe, Lincs. 1810 (and Welton Brinkhall Prebend in Lincoln Cathedral 1814-32) to death. Dom. Chap. to 10th Earl of Westmoreland 1810. Died Brighton 11/10/1837. [C43315] Married (Bengeo, Herts.) 4/7/1807 Catherine Maxwell (of Ardwell, Wigtownshire), and had issue. F.R.S. 1816. Port. online.

BATTISCOMBE (Richard) Born New Windsor, Berks. 10/4/1798, s. Robert Battiscombe and Susannah Griffenhoofe. Merton, Oxford 1815, BA1819, dn21 (Glos.), p22 (Glos.), MA1823. R. Southmere, Norfolk 1833 [no church and blank in ERC] to death (Hacton House, Upminster, Essex) 29/11/1873 aged 75, leaving £35,000 [C41817] Married Lawhitton, Cornwall 10/11/1823 Ann Marshall, with issue.

BATY (William) Bapt. Kirklinton, Cumberland 4/1/1768, s. Rev. William Baty, sen. and Jane Graham. Worcester, Oxford 1788, BA 1791, MA1794. R. Whitfield, Northants. 1814 to death 19/6/1834 (CCEd thus) [C43318]

BAUGH (Job Walker) Bapt. Stokesey, Shropshire 9/10/1788, s. Job Walker Baugh (alderman of Ludlow, Shropshire) and Elizabeth Sayce. St John's, Cambridge 1787, BA1791, dn92 (C&L for Salis.), p93 (Salis.), MA1794. R. Frilsham, Berks. 1793-5, V. Diddlebury w. Westhorpe, Shropshire 1795, R. Moccas, Heref. 1797-1812, Prebend of Nonnington in Hereford Cathedral 1802 and R. Ripple, Worcs. (and Preacher throughout the Diocese of Hereford) 1812 to death. Dom. Chap. to Bishop of Bristol 1812, and Chancellor of the Diocese of Bristol [total income over £2,100]. Died 1/9/1838 aged 69 [C9103] Married Clapham, Surrey 17/5/1808 Charlotte Hibbert.

BAUGH (Richard) Bapt. Neen Sollars, Shropshire 6/1/1765, s. Edward Baugh. Pembroke, Oxford 1782, BA1786, dn90 (Ox.), p91 (Ox.). R. Wheathill and Burweston, Shropshire 1799-1800 (res.), R. Ludlow, Shropshire 1803 to death 20/5/1837 (*suicide*) [C102703]

BAWDEN (Richard) Born South Molton, Devon 3/8/1770, s. John Bawden. Exeter, Oxford 1788, BA1792, dn94 (Ex.), p95 (Ex.), MA1795. R. Warkleigh, Devon 1795 and R. Satterleigh, Devon 1795 to death 1841 (2nd q.) [C139510]

BAXTER (Robert William) From London, s. Rev. George Baxter. Jesus, Oxford 1781 (aged 16), BA1785, MA1787, dn90 (Ox.), p91 (Ox.), BD1796. R. Northampton St Peter 1802 to death (St Pancras, London) 1850 (1st q.) [C22419] Married Newbold Pacey, Warwicks. 22/11/1810 Elizabeth Clavering.

BAYLAY (Charles Frederick Rogers) Born Chudleigh, Devon 5/11/1806, s. Rev. William Frederick Baylay (below) and Ann Nicholson. Trinity, Cambridge 1823, BA1828, dn29 (Ely for Roch.), p30 (C&L for Ely), MA1831. V. Woodnesborough, Kent 1833-47, R. Kirkby upon Bain, Leics. 1846 (and RD) to death (Horncastle, Lincs.) 3/4/1890 aged 84, leaving £19,010-13s-3d. [C1343] Married Ramsgate, Kent 14 or 20/6/1833 Ann Luke (dau. of a baronet), and had issue. Port. online.

BAYLAY (William Frederick) Born Stoke Damerel, Devon 21/4/1778, s. Richard Baylay (shipowner) and Mary Foster. Emmanuel, Cambridge 1797, BA1802, MA1805, dn06 (Win.), p07 (Win.), incorporated Oxford 1834. V. Dartmouth, Devon 1809-11, V. Margate St John the Baptist, Kent 1810, 2nd Prebend of Canterbury Cathedral 1826-45 and 6th Prebend of Rochester Cathedral 1827 (only), V. Wilmington, Kent 1828-32, RD 1840. Chap. of House of Commons in 1821. Died (Bishops Teignton, Devon) 5/1/1845 aged 66 [C1344] Married Greenwich 5/8/1802 Ann Nicholson, with clerical son, above. *F.R.S.* Port. online.

BAYLES (Philip) Born Essex, s. Thomas Bayles and Mary Dennis. Corpus Christi, Cambridge 1792, BA1796, dn97 (London), p99 (London), MA1800. R. Colchester St Mary at the Walls, Essex 1804 to death 2/3/1855 aged 81 [C114993]

BAYLEY (Arden) Born Quinton, Northants. 28/6/1795, s. Rev. Edward Bayley and Mary Easton. Exeter, Oxford 1813, BA1819, dn19 (C&L), p21 (Chester for C&L). R. Edgcote, Northants. 1827 (and RD of Brackley) to death (Banbury, Oxon., a widower) 23/2/1876, leaving under £200 [C9107] Married Wardington, Oxon. 13/9/1824 Harriet Bartholomew, with issue.

BAYLEY (Henry Vincent) Born Hope Hall, Manchester 6/12/1777, s. Thomas Butterworth Bayley (*q.v.* ODNB) and Mary Leggatt. Trinity, Cambridge 1795, BA1800, Fellow 1802, dn03 (Chester), p03 (Chester), MA1803, DD1824. R. Stilton, Hunts. 1804-5, V. Hibaldstow, Lincs. 1806-14, Prebend of Crackpole St Mary and Sub-Dean of Lincoln Cathedral (which he repaired and improved) 1805-28, Prebend of Liddington in Lincoln Cathedral 1823, V. Messingham and Bottesford, Lincs. 1811-27, V. Great Carlton, Lincs 1812, Archdeacon of Stow 1823-44, R. West Meon, Hants. 1826-44, Prebend of Westminster Abbey 1828. Chap. to Bishop of Chester. Died (blind) West Meon 12/8/1844 [C43328. ODNB. Kaye] Married Eccles, Lancs. 17/6/1807 Hannah Touchet (Broomhouse, Manchester), *s.p.* A distinguished classical scholar.

BAYLEY (Kenneth Champaign) Bapt. Bloomsbury, London 9/4/1798, s. Sir John Bayley (later 1st Bt.) and Elizabeth Markett. Oriel, Oxford 1817, migrated to Caius, Cambridge 1820, dn22 (Nor.), p24 (London). R. Acrise, Kent 1826-45, R. Weybridge, Surrey 1828-45, R. Copford, Essex 1845 to death 2/6/1861 aged 62, leaving £6,000 [C69413] Married Hythe, Kent 23/6/1831 Charlotte

Drake Brockman (Beachborough, Kent), with issue.

BAYLEY see also **BAILEY, BAYLY** and below

BAYLIE (John) Born Cripplegate, London 23/11/1792, s. William (a tobacconist) and Eleanor Baylie. Literate: dn20 (Chester for York), p21 (York). R. Bloxwich, Staffs. 1826 to death 6/9/1865, leaving under £200 [C9110. YCO] Widow Emily.

BAYLIFFE (William) Born Sheffield 18/6/1760, s. Rev. George Bayliffe (an Independent Minister for 44 years). Trinity, Cambridge 1779, BA1783, dn83 (C&L), p84 (York). R. Blore Ray, Suffolk 1786 to death (Ashbourne, Derbys) 24/2/1836 aged 76 [C9112. YCO]

BAYLIS (Joseph) Bapt. Kingswood, Wilts. 9/6/1762, s. Rev. Joseph Baylis and Hannah Furnley. Queen's, Oxford 1780, dn83 (Salis.), p85 (Ox.), BA1786, migrated to Queens', Cambridge 1794, MA1794. R. Gloucester St Mary de Crypt w. All Saints and St Owen 1788-1834, R. Gloucester St Mary de Lode 1788, V. Mickleton w. Ebrington, Glos. 1821 to death. Dom. Chap. to 6th Duke of Beaufort 1821. Died 19/1/1834 [C22420] Married Gloucester 15/12/1785 Susannah Packes, with issue.

BAYLY (Francis Turner) Born Devizes, Wilts. 26/2/1774, s. Rev. Francis Bayly and Mary Turner. Balliol, Oxford 1792, BA1796, dn97 (Salis.), p98 (Salis.). R. Gloucester St Aldate 1804 and Gloucester St John's the Baptist 1804 (and Chap. of the Workhouse) to death 28/9/1854 [C83486] Married Devizes 13/11/1805 Marianne Lediard, with clerical son Thomas.

BAYLY, BAILY (John) Born Frome, Somerset 11/8/1767, s. Benjamin Bayly. St John's, Cambridge 1787, BA1790, dn90 (Ex.), p91 (Ex.), MA1793. V. (and patron) of Chilthorne Dormer, Som. 1803-46 and V. St Merryn, Cornwall 1790 to death (Bath) 20/5/1857 aged 89 [C32693]

BAYLY (William) Born Warminster, Wilts. 17/7/1778, s.William Bayly and Susanna Seagram. New, Oxford 1796, Fellow 1798, BA 1800, p02 (Glos.), MA 1806, BD & DD1816. H/M Midhurst G/S for 22 years; V. Hartpury, Glos. 1803 to burial 2/2/1838 [C69433/41820] Married Swindon, Wilts. 13/7/1802 Louisa Maria Goodenough, w. issue. Port. online.

BAYNES (Adam) Bapt. Rickinghall Inferior, Suffolk 5/12/1784, s. Rev. William Baynes and Penelope Dove. Sidney, Cambridge 1802, BA 1807, dn08 (Nor.), p08 (Nor.). R. Adstock, Bucks. 1809 to death 27/6/1860 aged 76, leaving £10,000 [C43333] Married St Margaret's, Westminster, London 5/10/1811 Harriet Sophia Ross, with issue.

BAYNING (Henry Townsend, 3rd Baron) see under **TOWNSEND**, *later* **WILLIAM-POWLETT (Henry)**

BAYNTUN (Henry) Bapt. Milton Lilbourne, Wilts. 30/4/1769, s. Rev. Henry and Ann Bayntun. Pembroke, Oxford 1819, dn92 (London for Salis.), p92 (Nor. for Salis.), BA 1793, MA1795. R. Bromham, Wilts. 1792 to death (Bromham House, Kew, Surrey) 3/2/1857 aged 89 [C111321]

BAYTON (William Stevens) From Hambleton, Hants., s. John Bayton. St Edmund Hall, Oxford 1794 (aged 22), migrated to St John's, Cam-bridge 1810. R. Ford, Sussex 1815 and R. Madehurst, Sussex 1815 to death (Chichester) 17/1/1848 [C61380] Married Chichester 21/1/1808 Martha Guy (w), and had issue.

BAZELY (Charles Henry Baker) Bapt. Dover, Kent 7/12/1802, s. Admiral John Bazely and Harriett Baker. Clare, Cambridge 1819, BA 1824, dn26 (Lin. for Cant.), MA1827, p27 (London for Cant.). R. Southchurch, Essex 1828-33. Died 17/11/1836 [C43337] Married London 27/2/1830 his cousin Agnes Bazely (of Manton Manor and Kearsley Court, Kent).

BEADON (Frederick) Born London 6/12/1777, s. Rev. Edward Beadon. Trinity, Oxford 1796, BA1800, dn02 (B&W), p03 (B&W), MA1804, LLD. V. Weston super Mare, Som. 1806-11, Prebend of Warminster in Wells Cathedral 1807-10 (then of Compton Bishop 1809), R. North Stoneham, Hants. 1811-79, PC. Titley, Heref. 1811-76, Canon Residentiary Wells Cathedral 1812 (Chancellor 1823-79), R. Sulham, Berks. 1814-23. Died 10/6/1879 aged 101 and six months. No will traced [C32707. ODNB. Boase. G.W. Norman, *Memoir of the life of the Rev. Frederick Beadon* (Bromley, 1879)]

Married Hants. 12/10/1803 Marianne Wilder, w. clerical s., below.

BEADON (Frederick Fleming) Born North Stoneham, Hants., s. Rev. Frederick Beadon (above) and Marianne Wilder. Oriel, Oxford 1823, BA1829, dn29 (Win.), p33 (Win.), MA 1833. V. Compton Bishop, Som. 1830, V. Pilton, Som. 1833. Died Swathling Grange, South Stoneham, Southampton 26/12/1880 aged 75, leaving £14,000 [C41821] Married (1) Wells 5/4/1838 Augusta Tudway (d.1849), with issue (2) Wold, Northants. 8/5/1851 Mary Anna Elizabeth Carroll, with further issue.

BEADON (George Griffith) Born Dunster, Somerset, s. George Beadon and Charlotte Griffiths. Literate: dn21 (Chester), p22 (Chester). V. Othery, Som. 1822, R. Axbridge, Som. 1823-75. Died (unmarried) Crowcombe, Som. 31/1/1886 aged 88, leaving £868-8s-4d. [C32709]

BEADON (John Watson) Born City of London, s. Rev. Edward Beadon (R. North Stoneham, Hants.) and Mary Watson. St John's, Cambridge 1784 (aged 17), then Jesus 1787, BA1788, Fellow 1794-8, dn94 (Glos. for Win.), MA1791, p95 (Bristol for Win). V. Fordham, Cambs. 1798-9, Precentor of Brecon Collegiate Church (w. Prebend of Llanveneth) 1797-1835, V. Odiham, Hants. 1798-1824, Prebend of Litton in Wells Cathedral 1805-35 (and Precentor 1812), R. Farley Chamberlayne, Hants. 1813-35, V. Arreton, IoW 1813-15, V. Pilton, Som. 1813-16, R. Christian Malford, Wilts. 1815 (w. Residentiary Canon in Wells Cathedral 1827-8) 1815 to death. Dom. Chap. to Bishop of Gloucester (later) Bath and Wells 1811. Died 30/3/1835 (CCEd says 11/4/1835 thus) aged 70 [C32711] Married Umberleigh, Devon 1010/1798 Juliana Bassett Davie.

BEADON (Richard John) Born Taunton, Som. 4/4/1804, s. Robert Beadon and Helen Petten. Queen's, Oxford 1822, BA1826, dn27 (B&W), p28 (B&W), MA1829. V. Holcombe Burnell, Devon 1832, PC. Cothelstone, Som. 1832-5, R. Shirwell, Devon 1835 to death 13/12/1882 aged 78, leaving £14,600-4s-3d. [C41823] Married Barnstaple, Devon 15/4/1848 Charlotte Elizabeth Chichester, with issue.

BEAGUE (Richard Bowden) From Dulverton, Devon. Emmanuel, Cambridge 1806, BA1810, Fellow 1812, MA1813. V. ('Treasurer') of Brompton Regis (o/w King's Brompton), Som. 1820 to death (Dulverton) 3/5/1847 [C32715]

BEARD (James) From Gorton House, Gorton, Manchester, s. Thomas Beard, J.P. Queens', Cambridge 1810 BA1815, dn17 (Lin.), p18 (Lin.), MA1818. R. Cranfield, Beds. 1820-44 (and Preacher throughout the Diocese of Lincoln). Died London 5/12/1860 aged 68, leaving £9,000 [C43343] Married (1) Eccles, Lancs. 23/10/12820 Elizabeth Hobson (d.1823), w. issue (2) Manchester 8/5/1832 Susamma Wilson.

BEATH (Henry) Born Thickenham, Surrey c.1804, s. Patrick Ballingall Beath (below) and Mary Courtenay. St John's, Cambridge 1822, BA1827, dn27 (Win.), p28. V. Billingshurst, Sussex 1832-60. Died there 20/10/1877, leaving £1,500 [C61383] Married Capel, Surrey 16/10/1827 Mary Crews, with issue.

BEATH (Patrick Ballingall) Born Falkland, Fife 17/3/1767, s. Henry Beath and Elizabeth Ballingall. Literate: p04 (Chichester), [MA but NiVoF]. V. Ilketshall St Margaret, Suffolk 1812, Donative Chap. of Capel, Dorking, Surrey 1814. Buried 24/5/1847 [C61405] Married Southwark, Surrey 9/3/1799 Mary Courtenay, w. clerical son, above.

BEATY (Robert) Born Cumberland. Literate: dn06 (Car.), p07 (Car.). PC. Tatham Fells, Lancs. 1821 to death (Brampton, Cumberland) 16/4/1839 aged 70 [C4495]

BEAUCHAMP (Brian) Bapt. Twickenham, Middx. 19/8/1776. King's, Cambridge 1794, Fellow 1797-1801, dn98 (Lin.), BA1799, p01 (London for B&W). R. Hawkridge w. Withypool, Som. 1801 to death (Thorverton, Devon) 15/6/1834 (11/11/1834 in CCEd) [C32726] Married Tiverton, Devon 4/6/1801 Catherine Portberry Wood.

BEAUCHAMP, *born* BEAUCHAMP-PROCTOR (Henry William Johnson) Born Chaseley, Worcs. 28/7/1793, s. William Henry Beauchamp-Proctor and Frances Mary Davie. Worcester, Oxford 1811, BA1815, dn16 (Heref.), MA1818. V. Latton w. Eisey, Wilts. 1819-26, V. White Ladies Aston, Worcs. 1829-[39]. Died 25/1/1863 aged 69, leaving £1,500 [C84674. Foster corrected] Married 16/10/1821

Catharine Vernon (a clergy dau.), with clerical son. Brother below.

BEAUCHAMP, *born* **BEAUCHAMP-PROCTOR (James)** Born Forthampton, Glos. 1/7/1804, s. William Henry Beauchamp-Proctor (Chaseley, Worcs.) and Frances Mary Davie (and ward of Rev. Willoughby Bertie Beauchamp, Buckland, Surrey). Clare, Cambridge 1823, BA1828, MA1828, dn29 (Ox.), p30 (Ox.). R. Crowell, Oxon. 1830-74, V. Shirburn, Oxon. 1832-74. Died Hurst, Berks 25/11/1891, leaving £2,872-8s-2d. [C22427] Married 2/10/1833 his cousin Margaret Sophia ('pleasing and well-spoken of', the sister of Sir George Beaumont, 8th Bart.), with issue. Brother above.

BEAUCHAMP-PROCTOR (Thomas William Henry) Born Langley Park, Norfolk 11/6/1790, s. Sir Thomas Beauchamp Proctor, 2nd Bt. and Mary Palmer. Christ's Cambridge 1808 (as Proctor), BA1812, dn13 (Nor.), p14 (Bristol), MA1820. R. Buckenham w. Hassingham, Norfolk 1814-63, R. Chedgrave, Norfolk 1817-38, PC. Langley, Norfolk 1817-38 [ERC as Tutt], R. Carleton St Peter w. Ashby 1838 to death 9/5/1863 aged 73, leaving £7,000 [C111325] Wife Caroline Esther. Doubtless related to the two men above.

BEAUCLERK (Frederick [de Vere], Lord) Born London 8/5/1773, s. 5th Duke of St Albans and Lady Catherine Ponsonby. Trinity, Cambridge 1790 [as a nobleman], MA1792, dn95 (Nor.), p97 (Nor.), DD1824. V. Kimpton, Herts. 1797-1827 (res.), V. Redbourn, Herts. 1826, V. St Alban St Michael, Herts. 1827 to death 22/4/1850 [C43465] Married 3/7/1813 Hon. Charlotte, dau. of 12th Viscount Dillon, 4 ch. A famous if notorious cricketer (and President of the MCC 1826); a gambler; and 'completely devoid of Christian charity'; like Talleyrand 'a cleric without, it would seem, the faintest interest in being a clergyman or any kind of Christian'; described as 'an unmitigated scoundrel'; a 'foul-mouthed, dishonest man who was one of the most hated figures in society ... he bought and sold [cricket] matches as though they were lots at an auction'. Another described him as 'cruel, unforgiving, cantankerous and bitter':
https://en.wikipedia.org/wiki/Lord_Frederick_Beauclerk

BEAUFORD (Henry Walter) Born Tavistock, Devon 8/12/1780, s. Henry Beauford. Exeter, Oxford 1799, BA1802 dn03 (London) p04 (Ex.). R. Eaton Socon, Beds. 1808-[61]. Died 12/3/1865, leaving £14,000 [C43468] Married 28/4/1790 Isabella Elizabeth Linton, with issue.

BEAVER (James) Bapt. Lewknor, Oxon. 21/12/1760, s. Rev. James Beaver and Jane Skeeler (a clergy dau.). Corpus Christi, Oxford 1773 (aged 12 - *sic*), BA1777, MA1781, p84 (Win. for C&L), BD1790. Army and naval chaplain (present at Battle of Copenhagen where he acted with conspicuous bravery); R. Childrey, Berks. 1800 to death (Dieppe, France) 25/2/1840 - 'latterly his time had been altogether passed on the Continent' – in debt? [C9114] Married St Mary Ash, Surrey 4/1/1803 Henrietta Mary Halsey, w. issue.

BECHER (John Thomas) Bapt. Cork 23/12/1769, s. Michael Becher (of Cork) and Catherine French. Christ Church, Oxford 1788 [Lincoln's Inn 1788] BA1792, dn92 (York), p94 (Car. for York), MA1795. PC. Thurgarton w. Hoveringham, Notts. 1799-1848, V. Rampton, Notts. 1801-4, V. Midsomer Norton, Som. 1802-27, Prebend of South Muskham, Notts. 1818-30 then Vicar General of Southwell Collegiate Church 1830, R. Barnborough, Yorks. 1830 to death (Southwell) 3/1/1848 aged 78 [C4496, ODNB. YCO. J. O'Neill, *The life and times of John Thomas Becher of Southwell, 1769-1848* (Burton Joyce: The author, 2002)] Married Southwell 6/1/1802 Mary Drake (a clergy dau.), with issue. J.P. and Chairman of North Notts. Quarter Session 1806-36. Writer on social reform.

BECHER (Sherard) Bapt. Southwell, Notts. 4/9/1773, s. Rev. William Becher and Elizabeth Lucas. St John's, Cambridge 1791, BA1795, dn96 (Glos. for York), p97 (York), MA1798, BD1808, Senior Fellow 1808-52. (succ. his father as) V. Whittington, Derbys. 1798-1811, Vicar Choral of Southwell Collegiate Church 1802, V. East Markham w. R. West Drayton, Notts. 1811 to death (unm.) 28/2/1852 aged 78 [C9116. YCO]

BECKETT (George) Born 10/2/1793, s. Sir John Beckett, 1st Bart. (of Leeds and Somerby Park, Lincs.) and Mary Wilson (dau. of a Bishop of Bristol). Trinity, Cambridge 1809, BA1815, dn16 (Chester for York), p17 (Chester for York), MA1819. PC. Chapelthorpe, Yorks. 1818-27, Prebend of Corringham in Lincoln Cathedral 1822-43, V. Gainsborough, Lincs.

1822 and R. Epworth, Lincs. 1823 to death. Dom. Chap. to 1st Viscount Sidmouth 1823. Died 13/4/1843 aged 50 [C43493. YCO]

BECKLEY (Thomas) From Lymington, Hants., s. Thomas Beckley (surgeon) and Mary Baskett. New, Oxford 1808 (aged 18), BA1812, dn13 (Glos.), MA1815. R. Long Stratton St Michael, Norfolk 1823. Dom. Chap. to 5th Earl de la Warr 1813. Died (Lymington) 28/12/1871 aged 81, leaving £16,000 [C69442] Wife Mary, and clerical son.

BECKWITH (Edward James) Bapt. Norwich 23/6/1770, s. Edward Beckwith [*pleb*] and Mary Corbwell. Magdalen, Oxford 1787, BA 1790, then New, MA1793, dn93 (Ox.), p95 (Ox.). Minor Canon of St Paul's Cathedral 1797-1833 [Foster adds: and of Westminster Abbey?], R. St Alban Wood Street w. St Olave Silver Street, City of London 1800 and V. Tillingham, Essex 1817 to death. Dom. Chap. to 5th Earl of Abingdon 1815. Priest in Ordinary in the Chapel Royal 1833. Died 7/1/1833 aged 62 (CCEd says 8/3/1833) [C22434] Married Great Haseley, Warwicks. 16/2/1794 Jane Chard, w. clerical s. Edward George Ambrose Beckwith.

BECKWITH (Henry) Born Houghton le Spring, Durham (his mother's home) 29/11/1806, s. William Beckwith. Jesus, Cambridge 1826, BA1830, dn30 (Nor.), p31 (Nor.). PC. Eaton Constantine, Shropshire 1832 to death 22/10/1888 aged 81, leaving £4,111-2s-9d. [C9118] Married Shrewsbury 7/9/1836 Ann Rose Eyton (a clergy dau. and relict).

BECKWITH (Henry Arthur) Born Norwich 24/3/1797, s. of organist and composer John 'Christmas' Beckwith and Mary Elizabeth Cox. Magdalen, Oxford 1814, BA1818, dn20 (Ox.), MA1820, Chaplain New College, p21 (Ox.). V. Collingham, Yorks. 1827 and Vicar Choral of York Minster 1829 and V. York St Martin Coney Street 1829 to death. Dom. Chap. to Lord Harewood. Died Collingham 19/10/1838 aged 41 (typhus) [C22435] Married Holborn, London 27/1/1823 Mary Pownall, with issue.

BECKWITH (Thomas Francis) Born East Retford, Notts. 1792. Literate: dn13 (Lin.), p14 (Lin.), then St Catharine's, Cambridge 1814, a Ten Year Man (BD1832). V. East Retford 1821 to death 16/3/1853 aged 63 [C43494] Married Doncaster, Yorks. 1/8/1822 Anne Sutton Carter (a clergy dau.), with clerical issue.

BEDFORD (Richard Gordon) Bapt. Crediton, Devon 9/9/1767, s. Ricard Bedford [*pleb*]. Queen's, Oxford 1786 (as Richard), dn91 (Heref.), p93 (Ex.), then re-entered Oxford 1833 (as Richard Gordon), BA1833, MA 1835. V. Marden, Wilts 1813, V. Bathampton and Bathford, Som. 1816, V. Bristol St George Brandon Hill 1832-44. Probate granted 27/1/1844 [C8134]

BEDFORD (Thomas) From Worcester, s. William Bedford. Oriel, Oxford 1780 (aged 19), BA1784, dn84 (Wor.), p85 (Wor.), MA1787. R. Worcester St Helen 1786 and R. Worcester St Alban 1801 to death 1/1/1836 aged 76 ('found a corpse' by his servant) [C120449]

BEDFORD (William Riland) Bapt. Birmingham 2/3/1795, s. William Bedford. University, Oxford 1812, BA1815, dn17 (C&L), p19 (Glos.), MA1819. R. Sutton Coldfield, Warwicks. 1822 [blank in ERC]. Died 6/7/1843 [C19580/9120]

BEEBEE (James) Born Leominster, Hereford c.1753, s. Rev. Thomas Beebee and Hannah Meredith. Wadham, Oxford 1773, dn77 (Heref.), BA1777, p79 (Heref.). PC. Wisteston in Arden, Heref. 1788 and R. Presteigne, Radnorshire 1816 to death. Chap. to Presteigne Gaol 1816. Died 23/1/1841 aged 86 [C102896]

BEED (John Bishop) Bapt. Bishop's Hull, Som. 8/9/1771, s. John Bishop Beed. All Souls, Oxford 1790 ('civilian'), dn03 (Roch. for Cant.), p03 (Chich.). V. Felpham, Sussex 1805-32 and R. Middleton, Sussex 1832 to death 1847 (2nd q.) [C16407] Wife Esther, w. issue.

BEEKE (Henry) Born Kingsteignton, Devon 6/1/1751, s. Rev. Christopher Beeke and Mary Yard. Corpus Christi, Oxford 1769, BA1773, Fellow Oriel 1775, MA1776, dn76 (Ex.), BD 1785, DD1800. Regius Professor of Modern History 1801-13. V. St Mary the Virgin, Oxford 1782-90, V. Lamberhurst, Sussex 1784, V. Ufton Nervet, Berks. 1789-1819, Dean of Bristol 1813-37, V. Weare, Som. 1819. Died (unm.) Torquay 9/3/1837 [C1452. ODNB as 'a writer on taxation and finance'. LBSO] Important botanist and economist, being the first person to lecture on the latter subject at Oxford.

BEESLY (James) From Kimbolton, Hunts., s. James Beesley. St Edmund Hall, Oxford 1804 (aged 21), BA1808, p09 (Salis.), MA1810. V.

Feckenham, Worcs. 1826 (and S/M Feckenham School) to death 3/2/1855 [C120451] Married by 1829 Mary Fitzgerald (Queen's Co.), with issue (incl. the positivist writer Edmund Spencer Beesly).

BEETHAM (John Tidy) Born Bunny w. Bradmore, Notts. 17/8/1790, s. Rev. William Beetham (below) and Isabella Tidy. Christ's, Cambridge 1807, BA1812, dn13 (York), p14 (York). V. Bunny w. Bradmore 1823 to death 9/3/1864, leaving £12,000 [C130832. YCO]

BEETHAM (Matthew) Born Kirkby Lonsdale, Westmorland 2/6/1769, s. Richard and Agnes Beetham. Literate: dn97 (York), p98 (York). PC. Sheen, Staffs. 1816 to death 1848 (3rd q.)? [C9123. YCO]

BEETHAM (William) Born Kirkby Lonsdale, Westmorland 21/9/1758, s. of William Beetham (a husbandman) and Margaret Holme. Sidney, Cambridge 1781, dn81 (Chester), p85 (Roch. for York). V. Bunny w. Bradmore, Notts. 1785-1801, PC. Thrumpton, Notts. 1787-98, V. Ruddington, Notts. 1798-1801, R. Costock, Notts. 1801 and R. Keyworth, Notts. 1801 to death 10/8/1833 aged 75 [C84623] Married 1785 Isabel Tidy, with clerical s. John Tidy Beetham (above).

BEEVOR, later LOMBE (Edward Rigby) Born Norwich 16/11/1799, s. James Beevor (a brewer) and Mary Rigby. Trinity, Cambridge 1816 (did not reside), then Corpus Christi 1819, BA1823, dn23 (Nor.), p24 (Nor.). R. Winfarthing, Norfolk 1824 [blank in ERC], R. (and patron) of Hevingham, Norfolk 1837 to death 5/8/1878 (as Beevor) aged 78, leaving £14,000 [C11378 under Beevor. A. Carter, *The Beevor story* (Norwich, 1993)] Widow Marie Felicie Honorine. Name changed 1847.

BEEVOR (Miles) Born Hethel, Norfolk 22/18/1756, s. Thomas Beevor. University, Oxford 1774, BA1778, dn78 (Nor.), MA1781, p82 (Nor.), BD & DD1815. R. Toftrees w. South Creke, Norfolk 1784-5, V. Ketteringham, Suffolk 1786-1835, R. Bircham Newton w. Bircham Tofts, Norfolk 1789 and R. Hethel 1792 to death 29/12/1834 (CCEd says 2/1/1835) [C111381] *J.P., D.L.*

BELCHER (Paul) Bapt. Heather, Leics. 4/10/1771, s. Rev. Paul, sen. ad Ann Belcher. St John's, Cambridge 1789, BA1793, dn93 (Lin.), p95 (Lin.), MA 1796. H/M Ashmole G/S, Derbys. 1796-1836; V. Mayfield, Leics. 1816 and R. Heather 1823 to death. Dom. Chap. to 1st Baron Ravensworth 1823. Died 1836 [C9125] Married Stanton, Derbys. 26/6/1799 Lydia Elizabeth Greaves (a clergy dau.).

BELFIELD (Finney) Born Paignton, Devon 16/9/1758, s. Rev. Samuel Belfield and Eleanor Churchward. Oriel, Oxford 1775, BA1778, MA 1781, dn81 (Ex.), p83 (Ex.). V. Stoke Gabriel, Devon 1787, R. Exbourne, Devon 1793. Probate granted 18/3/1846 [C138532] Married Bristol 1782 Eleanor Belfield Daniel, w. clerical s. John Belfield.

BELGRAVE (Thomas) From Louth, Lincs., s. Thomas Belgrave. St John's, Cambridge 1806, BA1810, dn11 (Lin.), p12 (Lin.), MA 1817, Fellow. R. (and patron) of North Kilworth (o/w Kilworth Abbas), Leics. 1812 (and RD) to death 28/3/1854 (of apoplexy, 'when on horseback') aged 67 [C43513] Married South Kilworth 26/10/1812 Maria Holmes, with issue.

BELL (Edward John) Born Newcastle upon Tyne 6/12/1791, s. Richard and Mary Bell. Christ Church, Oxford 1809, BA1814, dn15 (B&W), p19 (Salis. for Win.). V. Wickham Market, Suffolk 1827 to death 28/4/1842 [C41825]

BELL (George) From Southwark, Surrey, s. of a Surveyor of Excise. Trinity, Cambridge 1778 (aged 18), BA1783, p84 (Lin.), p85 (Peterb.), MA1787. V. Bloxham, Oxon. 1789-1852, V. Kimpton, Herts 1793-7. Died 19/4/1852 aged 92 [C22440] 'A well-known champion of the rights of the poor'.

BELL (James) Literate: dn89 (Chester), p90 (Chester). R. Lympne, Kent 1802-40. Probably died 1839 (4th q.)? [C123402]

BELL (John) Bapt. St Olave, City of London 18/1/1758, s. John and Susannah Bell. St John's, Oxford 1776, BA1780, dn80 (Ox.), p82 (Ox.), MA1784, BD1789, DD1797. V. Kirtlington, Oxon. 1801-3, R. Bainton, Yorks. 1802 to death 13/7/1833 (CCEd thus) [C22514]

BELL (John) Born Wakefield, Yorks. 25/1/1776, s. Robert Bell. Queen's, Oxford 1794, BA1798, MA1801. S/M Salisbury Cathedral School; R. Knightwick w. Doddenham, Worcs. 1813-[52]. Died? [C120455] Had issue.

BELL (John) Born Newburn, Northumberland 29/6/1805, s. Matthew Bell. University, Oxford 1822, BA1827, dn28 (Durham), p29 (Durham), MA1832. V. Rothwell, Yorks. 1829 [income £990] (with RD of Wakefield) to death. Chap. to Earl of Mexborough. Died Durham 14/10/1869, leaving £14,000 [C136738. BBV] Married Newcastle upon Tyne 20/12/1828 Isabella Elizabeth (dau. of Sir Charles Loraine, 5th Bart., Kirkharle Hall, Durham), with clerical son.

BELL (Philip) Born Wallington, Norfolk 3/3/1751, s. Henry Bell. Caius, Cambridge 1770, BA1774, dn74 (Nor.), Fellow 1774-7, p76 (London for Nor.), MA1777. R. Runcton Holme w. South Runcton and Wallington 1778-1834, V. Stow Bardolph w. Wimbotsham, Norfolk 1779 to death 3/5/1834 (CCEd says 5/6/1834) [C111386] Married Thornham, Norfolk 8/12/1784 Elizabeth Collison, with issue.

BELLAIRS (Henry) Born Stamford, Lincs. 29/8/1790, s. Abel Walford Bellairs and Susanna Lowley. [A midshipman (wounded twice at Trafalgar); afterwards in the 15th Hussars] St Mary Hall, Oxford 1816, dn17 (Salis.), p18 (Salis.), BA1820, MA1823. R. Bedworth, Warwicks. 1830-64-, V. Hunsingore, Yorks. 1832-72 [joint income £1,033], RD of Monk's Kirby 1852, Hon. Canon of Worcester 1853 to death. Dom. Chap. to Earl of Strafford. Died Paignton, Devon 17/4/1872 aged 82, leaving £12,000 [C9133. Boase] Married Twickenham, Surrey 30/5/1811 Dorothy Parker Mackenzie, w. clerical sons Henry Walford, and Charles Bellairs. *J.P.*

BELLAMAN (John) Literate: dn88 (Chester), p90 (Lin.). PC. South Kyme and North Kyme, Lincs. 1806-38, V. Ewerby, Lincs. 1806 and V. Kirkby [on the] Green, Lincs. 1808 to death (Little Hale, Lincs.) 21/8/1838 aged 80 (*or* 27/10/1837) [C43758] *F.S.A.*

BELLAMY (James William) Born Rotherham, Yorks. 15/11/1788, s. John Bellamy and Ann Pindar. Queens', Cambridge 1807, BA1812, dn13 (London), p14 (London), MA1815, incorporated at Oxford 1829, BD1821. R. St Mary Abchurch w. St Lawrence Pouteny, City of London 1816-44 (and RD), Twiford Prebend of Harleston in St Paul's Cathdral 1817-74, H/M Merchant Taylors' School, London 1819-45, R. Sellindge, Kent 1822 to death 2/3/1874, leaving £50,00 [C115237. Boase] Married London 8/7/1815 Mary Coates Cherry (dau. of the previous H/M of Merchant Taylors' School). Their son was President of St John's College, Oxford. *F.R.S.* 1834.

BELLAS (Lancelot) Bapt. Long Marton, Westmorland 15/3/1792, s. Richard Bellas. Queen's, Oxford 1811, BA1815, dn18 (Salis. for Cant.), p18 (Cant.), Fellow, MA1819. R. Bramshott, Hants. 1832 to death 18/6/1869 aged 76, leaving £3,000 [C69480] Married Bolton, Westmorland 12/10/1815 Ann Nicholson, with issue. Brother below.

BELLAS (Thomas) Born Long Marton, Westmorland 26/1/1790, s. Richard Bellas. Queen's, Oxford 1809, BA1813, dn15 (Car.), p16 (Car.), MA1816. V. Appleby St Michael (o/w Bondgate), Westmorland 1823-80, V. Warcop, Westmorland 1843-51 (res.). Died (Appleby) 15/3/1880 aged 90, leaving £3,000 [C4504. Platt] Married Appleby St Lawrence 13/5/1822 Elizabeth Wilkinson, with issue. *J.P.* and *D.L.* Brother above.

BELLI (Charles Almeric) Born Bath 8/12/1792, s. John Belli (Private Secretary to the Governor-General of India) and Elizabeth Stuart Cockerell. Christ Church, Oxford 1810, BA1814, MA1816, dn16 (London), p16 (Salis. for London), V. Prittlewell, Essex 1816-22, (absentee) Precentor of St Paul's Cathedral 1819-86, V. Witham, Essex 1820-1, R. Aldham, Essex 1821-3, R. Paglesham, Essex 1822-60, V. South Weald, Essex 1823-77. Died 6/1/1886, leaving £233,356-9s-5d. [C84696. Boase] Married London (by the Bishop of London) 14/11/1827 Frances Willan.

BELLMAN (Edmund) Bapt. Wetheringsett, Suffolk 28/4/1792, s. Rev. Rayner Bellman and Elizabeth Childe. Caius, Cambridge 1790, BA 1795, dn95 (Nor.), p97 (Nor.), MA1798, Fellow 1798-1802. R. Pettaugh, Suffolk 1801-43, R. Helmingham, Suffolk 1812 and V. Framsden, Essex 1812 to death. Dom. Chap. to Lord Dysart. Died 25/12/1843 [C111387] Married Thorpe Episcopis, Norfolk 26/11/1811 Fanny Harvey (Thorpe Lodge, Norfolk), w. 3 clerical sons.

BELOE (Henry Parr) Bapt. St Margaret's, Westminster, London 28/6/1792 (born

20/10/1790), s. Rev. William Beloe and Mary Ann Rix. Benet Hall, Corpus Christi, Cambridge 1808, BA1812, dn14 (Nor.), p16 (Ex.). R. Bermondsey St Mary, London 1824, R. Guildford Holy Trinity and St Mary, Surrey 1824 to death 21/5/1838 [C69481] Married Guildford, Surrey 19/1/1834 Elizabeth Elkins, with issue. Frequent contributor to the Reviews.

BENEZET (Edward Porten) Bapt. Marylebone, London 25/11/1767, s. Claude Benezet and Ann Allen. Corpus Christi, Cambridge 1785, BA 1789, dn90 (Cant.), Fellow 1790-2, p91 (Cant.), then St John's, MA1792. V. Newton by Castle Acre, Norfolk 1798-1834, V. Bungay Holy Trinity, Suffolk 1803-34. Died Reading, Berks. 3/9/1831 [C99569]

BENN (John) Bapt. Hensingham, Cumberland 28/9/1765, s. Anthony Benn and Margaret Lowther Spedding. University, Oxford 1782, BA1786. R. Farringdon, Hants. 1797 to death 9/5/857 aged 99 [C69482] Married Farringdon 27/12/1790, Elizabeth Thornton Heysham, their dau. being a friend of Jane Austen.

BENNET (James Thomas) Born Barton, Suffolk 16/11/1796, s. Philip Bennet and Jane Judith Keddington. Balliol, Oxford 1813, BA 1817, dn19 (Nor.), p21 (Nor.), MA1831. R. (and patron) of Cheveley, Cambs. 1831 to death 12/7/1868 aged 71, leaving £4,000 [C111396] Married Doncaster, Yorks. 6/4/1826 Henrietta Eliza Jackson, with clerical son.

BENNETT (Henry) [NiVoF] V. Martock, Som. 1798 to death 29/6/1835 'at an advanced age' (CCEd says 7/12/1835) [C32803]

BENNETT (Henry) Born Sparkford Hall, Cadbury, Somerset 30/10/1795, s. James Bennett and Mary Clutterbuck. Trinity, Cambridge 1814, LLB1822, dn22 (Glos), p23 (Chester). R. South Cadbury (a family living) 1831-66, R. (and patron) of Sparkford, Som. 1836 to death. Chap. at Naples 1830-33 and various other European cities. Died Weymouth, Dorset 1/9/1874 aged 79, leaving £7,000 [C41826] Married St Petersburg 20/7/1821 Emily Moberly (dau. of the British Consul-General), 14 ch. (incl. Rev. James Arthur Bennett):

BENNETT (Henry Leigh-) Born London 17/5/1795, s. Rev. John Leigh (below) and Harriet Eliza Bennett. Christ Church, Oxford 1812, BA1817, dn18 (Peterb.), MA1819, p19 (Peterb.). R. Croughton, Northants. 1819, V. Thorpe, Surrey 1849-74. Died Thorpe Place, Chertsey, Surrey 31/8/1880, leaving £12,000 [C109464] Married Windsor, Berks. 11/9/1845 Caroline Crutchley, with issue.

BENNETT (Hugh) Born Whitfield, Leics. 18/3/1772, s. Rev. John Bennett (V. Bromsgrove). Worcester, Oxford 1790, BA1794, dn95 (Ox.), p96 (Ox.), MA1797. V. Elmley Castle, Worcs. 1800-60, PC. Newborough, Staffs. 1809, PC. Marchington, Staffs. 1809. Died Great Budworth, Cheshire 11/4/1860, leaving £1,500 [C9345] Married Marchington 1/3/1813 Mary Mousley, with clerical son.

BENNETT (John Leigh-) Bapt. Bradwell, Glos. 28/4/1768, s. Rev. Woolley Bennett and Rachel Capps. BNC, Oxford 1787, BA1790, dn91 (Ox.), p92 (Ox.), MA1796 (as Bennet). V. Lechlade, Glos. 1795-1832 (res.), V. Thorpe, Surrey 1806-35, R. Letton, Heref. 1809. Died Thorpe Place, Chertsey, Surrey 27/4/1835 (CCEd says 1/10/1835) [C22520] Married Harriet Eliza Bennett. Clerical s. Henry Leigh (above). Brother Woolley Leigh (below).

BENNETT (Samuel) Born Boreham, Essex 23/4/1775, s. Samuel Bennett and Mary Butterfield. Peterhouse, Cambridge 1793, then Queens' 1795, BA1797, dn97 (London), MA 1800, p00 (London), DD1823. V. Great Wakering, Essex 1804-22, R. Walton on the Hill, Surrey 1822 (with Chap. to the British Embassy at Constantinople 1835) to death. Chap. to HRH Duke of Kent. Died Pera, Turkey 26/3/1847 aged 71 [C69485] Married Writtle, Essex 1/10/1801 Mary Anne Craneis, with issue.

BENNETT (Thomas Leigh) Bapt. Soho, Westminster, Lonbdon 14/7/1775, s. Thomas Leigh Bennett and Grace Home. Christ's, Cambridge 1793, BA1797, dn00 (Lin.), p01 (Lin.), MA1802. R. Allexton and Skeffington, Leics. 1802, R. Letton, Heref. 1809, V. Nettlebed w. Pishill, Oxon. 1814-44, V. Long Sutton (or Sutton St Mary), Lincs. (with Preacher throughout the Diocese) 1816 to death (Highmoor Hall, Nettlebed) 12/12/1844 aged 69 [C23376]

BENNETT (William) From Danbury, Essex, s. John Bennett. St John's, Oxford 1782 (aged 18), BA1786, dn86 (Ox.), MA1793, p95 (Ely),

BD1795. R. (West) Cheam, Surrey 1813-[56]. Died? [C22522]

BENNETT (William) Bapt. Ely, Cambs. 13/10/1765, s. William Bennett. Trinity, Cambridge 1783, BA1787, dn88 (Ely), p89 (Ely), MA 1811. Minor Canon of Canterbury 1801, V. Stone in Oxney, Kent 1801-20, V. Littlebourne, Kent 1820-4, R. Canterbury St George the Martyr w. St Mary Magdalen 1824-6, V. Milton w. Sittingbourne (o/w Milton Regis), Kent 1826-34, R. Milton, Kent 1834-44. Died 6/6/1852 aged 87 [C99570] Married Canterbury 4/10/1808 Elizabeth Chafy (a clergy dau.), of Swalecliffe, Kent.

BENNETT (William Coles) Born Salisbury 29/9/1794, s. William Bennett. Queen's, Oxford 1811, BA1816, dn17 (Salis.), MA1819, p20 (Glos.). V. Corsham, Wilts. 1832 to death 29/12/1857, leaving £600 [C28137] Married Bath 3/6/1828 Frances Otto Edwards (w), and issue.

BENNETT (Woolley Leigh-) From Finmere, Oxon., s. Rev. Woolley Leigh Bennett, sen. and Rachel Capps. Merton, Oxford 1794 (aged 19), BA1797, dn98 (Ox.), p98 (Ox.), MA1808. R. Foscott, Bucks. 1802-19, R. Water Stratford >< Bucks. 1818 to death 1839 (1st q.) [C22524] Married Cork 1810 Margaret King, with issue. Brother John Leigh, above.

BENSON (Christopher) Born Cockermouth, Cumberland 16/1/1788, s. Thomas Benson (solicitor). Trinity, Cambridge 1804, BA1809, dn11 (Durham), p13 (Durham), MA1815, then Magdalene, Fellow 1820. V. Ledsham w. Fairburn, Yorks. 1822-7, R. St Giles-in-the-Fields, London 1824-6, Canon of 9th Prebend in Worcester Cathedral 1826-68, Master of the Temple [Church] 1826-45, PC. Cropthorpe, Worcs. 1826-40 [blank in ERC], V. Lindridge, Worcs. 1842-9. Died Ross on Wye, Heref.) 25/3/1868, leaving £30,000 [C115254. ODNB. Boase] Married St George's Hanover Square, London 27/7/1826 Bertha Maria Mitford (w). Note a contemporary Oxford namesake.

BENSON (Edmund) Born Salisbury, Wilts. 19/7/1754, s. George Fowles Benson and Margaret Abbott. Queen's, Oxford 1778, dn80 (Heref.), p81 (Heref.), BA1782, MA1786. V. Eldon, Yorks. 1790, R. Salisbury St Edmund 1794-1802, Vicar Choral Salisbury Cathedral 1797-1835, V. Wilsford, Wilts. 1802-35, PC. Homington, Wilton 1812 to death 9 or 19/1/1835 (CCEd thus) [C16429] Married Devizes, Wilts. 17/3/1785 Ann Hunt, with issue.

BENSON (Francis) Bapt. 19/10/1787, natural s. of Ann Sergent (who married 1797) Benjamin Benson (a schoolmaster from Leyland, Lancs.). Hertford, Oxford 1809, then Queen's 1814, BA1814, dn14 (York), p15 (Chester for York), MA1820. PC. Worsbrough, Yorks. 1815-21, PC. Beltingham, Northumberland 1830 and PC. Greenhead, Haltwhistle, Northumberland 1831 to death 21/4/1845 aged 57 [C130839. YCO]

BENSON (Henry Bristowe) Born York 9/8/1793, s. Rev. Robert Benson (V. Heckington, Lincs.) and Lucinda Fretwell. Christ's, Cambridge 1810, BA1815, dn16 (Lin.), p17 (Lin.), MA1819. (succeeded his father as) V. Heckington 1822-32. Died 18/10/1855 [C43776] Married Utterby, Lincs. 15/10/1835 Mary Catherine Harrold (of Utterby House). *J.P.* Lincs.; Chairman of Louth Board of Guardians.

BENSON (Isaac) Bapt. Windermere, Westmorland 17/5/1795, s. Joseph Benson and Agnes Stewartson. St Bees admitted 1818, dn20 (York), p21 (York). PC. West Acklam, Stockton on Tees, Yorks. 1823-64 (and S/M) and PC. Middlesbrough 1823 to death (Stockton on Tees) 22/12/1864, leaving £1,500 [C84771 has others mixed in and a wrong death date. ATV] Married (1) Kendal, Westmorland 30/6/1826 Dorothy Agnes Garnett (d.1869), with issue (2) Durham Nov. 1862 Sarah Siddle. Surrogate. Photo. of memorial plaque online.

BENSON (John) Born Halifax 26/7/1783, s. Rev. Joseph Benson (*q.v.* ODNB) and Sarah Thompson. St John's, Cambridge 1801, BA 1805, dn06 (Win.), p07 (Win.), MA1808. PC. Withington, Shropshire 1819, R. Norton-sub-Hamdon, Som. 1823 to death 27/8/1860, leaving £5,000 [C9352] Married (1) Willoughby Waterleys, Leics. 14/2/1809 Mary Levett (a clergy dau., d.1812) (2) Pulverbach, Shropshire 12/9/1816 Frances Gilpin (a clergy dau.), with issue.

BENSON (Joseph) Born Heversham, Westmorland **1/8/1777, s.** John Benson [*pleb*] and Agnes Mansergh. St Edmund Hall, Oxford 1801, BA1807, dn07 (Win.), p08 (Win.), MA 1807, then Queen's BD & DD1819. PC.

Hounslow, Heston, Middx. 1830-51, R. St Breock, Cornwall 1851 to death 1/3/1861, leaving £1,000 [C69488] Left a son.

BENSON (Martin, sen.) Bapt. Canterbury Cathedral 1/1/1761, s. Rev. John Benson (Prebend of Canterbury) and Susannah Oliver. Jesus, Cambridge 1778, BA1782, dn83 (Cant.), MA1785, p85 (Cant.). V. King Charles the Martyr, Tunbridge Wells, Kent 1786-1829, R. Ogarskirk, Kent 1788-91, R. St Dunstan-in-the-East, City of London 1789-91, R. Merstham, Surrey 1791 to death. Registrar of the Diocese of Gloucester. Died 1/4/1833 aged 72 [C1575] Married (1) His cousin Mary Benson (a clergy dau.) (2) Marylebone, London 11/3/1815 Mrs Harriet (Yorke) Aldersley (Stoke Park, Guildford, Surrey). Son of same name, below.

BENSON (Martin, jun.) Born Tunbridge Wells, Kent 1789, s. Rev. Martin Benson, sen. (above) and Mary Benson. Jesus, Cambridge 1808, BA1812, dn12 (B&W for Roch.), p13 (Chester), MA1816. PC. Heath and Reach, Beds. 1826 to death 11/8/1834 aged 45 (CCEd says 15/3/1835) [C1576] Married Dunstable, Beds. Rebecca Osborne.

BENSON (Thomas) Born Cockermouth, Cumberland Oct. 1802, s. Rev. John Benson. St John's, Cambridge 1819, BA1824 [admitted Inner Temple 1824] dn30 (Peterb.), p31 (Peterb.), MA1834. R. North Fambridge, Essex 1832 to death 9/6/1887, leaving £686-4s-9d. [C109466] Botanist.

BENSON (William) From Cockermouth, Cumberland, s. Jonathan Benson [*pleb*]. Queen's, Oxford 1779 (aged 18), BA1783, dn18 (Salis. for Ox.), p85 (Chester for Peterb.), MA1786, BD 1797, DD1820. V. Ashby St Ledgers, Northants 1785-1840, R. Hampton Poyle, Oxon. 1801 and R. South Weston, Oxon. 1801 to death 1839 (4th q.)? [C22527]

BENT (Hugh) Bapt. Sandford, Crediton, Devon 27/12/1786, s. Rev. George Bent and Hannah Honycombe. Exeter, Oxford 1805, BA1809, dn09 (Ex.), p11 (Ex.), MA1813. R. High Bray, Devon 1814 and R. Jacobstowe, Devon 1814 with PC. Sandford 1814 to death. Dom. Chap. to Elizabeth, Baroness Graves 1814. Died 8/6/1836 [C139994] Married (1) Sandford 24/3/1814 Sarah Lane (d.1822), w. issue (2) Bideford, Devon by 1829 Emily Hutton, w. further issue.

BENTINCK, *or* CAVENDISH-BENTINCK (William Harry Edward Cavendish, Hon.) Born London 2/2/1784, s. Lord Edward Charles Cavendish-Bentinck (and thus grandson to 2nd Duke of Portland) and Elizabeth Cumberland. Christ Church, Oxford 1802, BA1805, Student [Fellow], dn07 (Ox.), p08 (York), MA1808. R. Sigglesthorne, Hull, Yorks. 1808-68, Canon of Westminster 1809 and Archdeacon of Westinster 1854-64 [total income £1,450], RD of Westminster 1842 to death. Dom. Chap. to Archbishop of York 1810. Died Sigglesthorne 29/9/1868 aged 84, leaving £80,000 [C22530 under Bentinck. Boase. YCO] Married St George's Hanover Square, London 19/7/1814 Frances Constable (a clergy dau.), *s.p.*

BENYON (Edward Richard) Bapt. Lausanne, Switzerland 14/12/1802, a naturalised British subject (and nephew of the richest commoner in England Richard Benyon de Beauvois, worth an estimated £7 million, living at Colford Park, Suffolk). St John's, Cambridge 1819, BA1824, dn26 (Nor.), p26 (Bristol for Nor.), MA 1827. R. Downham, Essex 1827-39, R. North Ockenden, Essex 1827-39, R. Culford, Ingham and Timworth, Suffolk 1839 (living at Culford Hall, Bury St Edmunds) (and R. Eldon 1841-5) to death. Dom. Chap. to 3rd Earl of Chichester 1827. Died London 7/7/1883 (widower w. 13 servants) aged 81, leaving £50,167-12s-4d. [C8143. LNCP] Married Eyton, Heref. Jane Evans (or Benson?).

BERE (Richard) Born Morebath, Devon 6/9/1761. Sidney, Cambridge 1783, dn84 (B&W), BA1786, p86 (Ex.), BD1793, Fellow. V. Carhampton, Som. 1802-32, V. Morebath 1813-31, R. Skilgate, Som. 1817 to death 29/8/1831 (CCEd says 5/5/1832) [C32820] Doubtless a clerical relation below.

BERE, BEARE (William Baker) From Rill House, Morebath, Devon, s. Montague Baker Bere (barrister) and Anne Clarke (a clergy dau.). Emmanuel, Cambridge 1819, dn23 (Glos.), BA1824, p25 (B&W), MA1827, LLD. PC. Upton, Som. 1826 and V. Morebath, Devon 1832 to death 5/10/1844, aged 44 [C41830] Married Ugborough, Devon 15/8/1834 Mary Emily Sprye (a clergy dau.), with issue. Doubtless a clerical relation above.

BERENS (Edward) Born Hextable, Kent 1/8/1777, s. Joseph Berens and Elizabeth

Hulse. Christ Church, Oxford 1795, BA1798, then Oriel, Fellow, MA1801, dn01 (Ox.), p02 (Ox.). V. Shrivenham, Berks. 1804-59, R. Englefield, Berks. 1817 (and RD 1829), Prebend of Slape in Salisbury Cathedral 1829-55, Archdeacon of Berkshire 1832-55 (res.). Dom. Chap. to Bishop of Bristol, Exeter and then of Lincoln 1803-17. Died Shrivenham 7/4/1859, leaving £45,000 [C22539. Boase] Married 30/12/1805 Catherine Courtenay.

BERENS (Edward Riou) From City of London, s. Joseph Berens and Charlotte Benyon. Christ Church, Oxford 1825 (aged 18), then St Mary Hall, BA1831, dn31 (London for Cant.), MA1832, p32 (Cant.). R. Broxted, Essex 1833, R. Wickford, Essex 1833, R. Downham, Essex 1839 [joint income £1,083] to death 31/7/1866 aged 58, leaving £35,000 [C106691] Married Woodmansterne, Surrey 21/8/1849 Sarah Frances Walpole, with issue.

BERESFORD (Gilbert) Bapt. Ashborne, Derbys. 10/10/1774, s. Richard Beresford and Alice Garle. St John's, Cambridge 1791, BA 1795, dn99 (C&L), p99 (C&L), MA1799. R. Fordwich, Kent 1799-1802, R. Saxelby, Leics. 1800-9, R. Bedworth, Warwicks. 1802-9, R. Trowbridge, Wilts. 1809-13, R. Aylestone, Leics. 1813-19 (and again 1838-43), St Andrew, Holborn, London 1819-38, R. Hoby w. Rotherby, Leics. 1838 to death (Hoby) 2/6/1843 aged 69 [C2349] Married Hoby 15/10/1805 Anne Browne (a clergy dau.), with issue. 'For the correction of a somewhat misleading account of his character, given in Cobbett's *Rural Rides*, see the article by J. Beresford in *The Times Lit. Supplement*, Jan. 29 1931'.

BERESFORD (James) From Upham, Hants., s. Richard Beresford. Merton, Oxford 1783 (aged 18), BA1786, dn88 (Chester for Ox.), p89 (Roch.), MA1798. R. Hawridge, Bucks. 1789-92 (res.), R. Kibworth Beauchamp, Lincs. (and Preacher throughout the Diocese of Lin.) 1812-40, V. Snettisham, Norfolk 1812-15 (res.). Died 29/9/1840 [C1577]

BERIDGE (Basil) Bapt. Algarkirk, Lincs. 19/1/1797, s. Rev. Basil Bury Beridge and Dorothy Tanfield. Magdalen, Oxford 1815, dn22 (Lin.), p22 (Lin.). R. (and patron) of Algarkirk cum Fosdyke 1822 [a family living since 1636, income £1,363], Prebend of Leighton Ecclesia in Lincoln Cathedral (and Preacher throughout the Diocese, and RD) 1872 to death (Combe Bury, Surrey) 20/7/1881, leaving £65,627-6s-3d. [C43800. Boase] Married (1) Tathwell, Lincs. 30/12/1823 Bettina Mary Elizabeth Chaplin (d.1823) (2) St George's Hanover Square, London 21/8/1828 Judith Pulteney; *s.p.* J.P.

BERKELEY (John Rowland) Born Writtle, Essex 22/12/1781, s. Rev. Rowland Berkeley and Elizabeth Wathen. New, Oxford 1800 (aged 19), BA1805, dn06 (Ox.), p07 (Glos.), MA1808, Fellow. R. Much Cowarne, Heref. 1813 to death (unm.). Probate granted 2/4/1850 [C22541]

BERKELEY, *born* TOMKYNS (Richard [Bohun]) From Claines, Worcs., s. Rev. Richard Tomkyns. New, Oxford 1787 (aged 19), BA1791, Fellow, dn94 (Ox.), p95 (Ox.), MA 1797. R. Great Horwood, Bucks. 1816 to death 1840 [C37922 as Tomykns] Name changed 1832.

BERKIN (Henry) Born Bristol, s. William and Mary Berkin. St Edmund Hall, Oxford 1804 (aged 25), BA1808, dn08 (Glos.), p09 (Glos.), MA1812. PC. Kilgwrrwg, Monmouth 1810 (non-res.), PC. Llandogo, Monmouth 1810-18, PC. Penterry, Monmouth 1810 (non-res.), (first) PC. Dean Forest Holy Trinity, Glos. 1817, V. High Offley, Staffs. 1833-4 (res.). Died 19/10/1847 [C3653] Married Clifton, Bristol 1803: https://books.google.co.uk/books?isbn=0953443728

BERNARD (William) St John's, Oxford 1807, dn10, p11, Fellow. R. Clatworthy, Som. 1810 to death 1857 (3rd q.) [Probably C41831 but NiF] Married Combe Flory, Som. 9/5/1816 Charlotte Matilda Perring, with issue.

BERNEL (Nicholas) Literate: dn08 (Win.), p08 (Win.). R. Guernsey St Saviour, Channel Islands 1818. Died? [C70727]

BERNERS (Henry Denny) Born Marylebone, London 18/8/1769, s. Charles Berners and Catherine Laroche. St Mary Hall, Oxford 1787, dn93 (Nor.), p94 (Nor.), BCL1794. R. Harkstead, Suffolk 1794-1833 (res.), R. Woolverstone w. Erwarton, Suffolk 1801-34, Archdeacon of Suffolk 1819-46. Living at Woolverstone Hall, Suffolk. Will proved 25/2/1852 [C1035. LBSO] Married Millbrook, Hants. 8/7/1799 Sarah

Jarrett (born Jamaica), with clerical son, below. Claimed slave compensation:

BERNERS (Henry William Wilson, 10th Baron) see under **WILSON**

BERNERS (Ralph) Bapt. Sutton, Suffolk 3/4/1802, s. Ven. Henry Denny Berners, Archdeacon of Suffolk (above) and Sarah Jarrett. Trinity, Oxford 1820, then Magdalen, BA1823, dn26 (Ox.), MA1826, p27 (Nor.). Donative R. Kings Walden, Herts. 1831 [Not in ERC]. Died Nice 31/1/1858, leaving £14,000 [C22546] Married 27/6/1832 Eliza Cuyler (dau. of a military baronet).

BERRY (Joseph Walter) Bapt. Thriplow, Cambs. 6/3/1802, s. Rev. Butler Berry (V. Foxton, Cambs.) and Mary Raynard. Peterhouse, Cambridge 1820, BA1824, dn25 (London), p26 (London), MA1827. V. Foxton, Cambs. (sequestrator 1832) 1835 to death 30/3/1875 aged 77, leaving £800 [C65236] Married Peterborough 1861 (4th q.) Sarah Noble (w).

BERRY (William) From St Marylebone, London, s. Dennis Berry. Trinity, Oxford 1801 (aged16), migrated to Magdalene, Cambridge 1806, BA1810, dn10 (Salis. for Win.), p11 (Win.). V. Brooksby, Leics. 1831-5 [C8140], R. Bircham Newton w. Bircham Tofts, Norfolk 1835 to death (Kelmarsh, Northants.) 23/11/1869 aged 84, leaving £3,000 [C70728] Widow Sarah.

BERTIE (Frederick, Hon.) Born London 12/2/1793, s. 4th Earl of Abingdon and Charlotte Warren. Jesus, Cambridge 1814, BA1816, dn16 (Ox.), p17 (Ox.). R. Wytham, Berks. 1817-68, R. Albury, Oxon. 1817-68, PC. South Hinksey w. Wootton, Berks. 1820 (all family livings). Chap. to HRH Duke of Clarence 1817. Died Thame, Oxon. 4/2/1868 aged 74, leaving £7,000 [C22540] Married Shiplake, Oxon. 17/10/1825 Lady Georgina Anne Emily (w), dau. of Lord Mark Kerr, with issue.

BESLY, BESLEY (John) Bapt. Tiverton, Devon 4/3/1802, s. of William and Jenny Besly. Balliol, Oxford 1817, BA1821, Fellow 1823, dn23 (Ox.) [Tutor at Rugby School 1823-8] p24 (Ox.) [Sub-Librarian at Bodleian Library 1828-31] MA1826, DCL 1835. V. Long Benton, Northumberland 1830-68 and R. Aston sub Edge, Glos. 1831 to death (Long Benton) 17/4/1868 aged 66, leaving £25,000. Proctor in Convocation for York 1836-45, 1855-64 [C22634. Boase] Married (1) Rugby, Warwicks, 10/12/1829 Elizabeth Margaret Kennedy (d.1834) (2) ?Devon June 1835 Mrs Frances Bint.

BEST (Francis) Born and bapt. York 2/4/1775, s. Rev. Francis Best, sen. (R. South Dalton, Yorks.) and Mary Dobinson. Peterhouse, Cambridge 1793, then Clare, BA1797, dn97 (York), p99 (York), MA1803. (succ. his father as) R. South Dalton 1802 to death (unmarried) 16/4/1844 aged 69 [C84811. YCO. Venn has a long and delightful quote about 'Parson Best'].

BEST (Samuel, Hon.) Born London 2/12/1803, s. William Best, 1st Baron Wynford (of Wynford House, Dorset) and Mary Anne Knapp. King's, Cambridge 1822, dn25 (Lin.), Fellow 1825-6, BA1826, p26 (Win.), MA1840. R. Blandford St Mary, Dorset 1830 and R. Abbotts Ann, Hants 1831 (and Preacher throughout the Diocese of Winchester and RD of Andover) to death. Dom. Chap. to his father 1831. Died 20/1/1873, leaving £25,000 [C70731. Boase. A. Geddes, *Samuel Best & the Hampshire labourer* (Andover, c.1981)] Married (1) St James's, Westminster, London 11/4/1826 Charlotte Willis (d.1833, dau. Sir James Burrough), w. issue (2) 24/2/1835 Emma Duke (a military dau), w. further issue. Port. online.

BEST (Thomas) Born Cradley, Worcs. 23/6/1787, s. Rev. Thomas Best, sen. Worcester, Oxford 1806, BA1810, dn10 (Ox.), p12 (Ox.), MA1816. PC. Sheffield St James 1817 to death (unm.) 10/3/1865, leaving £1,000 [C9357. ATV] Surrogate.

BEST (Thomas) Born Haselbury, Som., s. Thomas Best. Jesus, Cambridge 1818 (aged 23), dn21 (London for Bristol), p22 (Glos.), LLB 1825. R. Kirby on Bain, Lincs. 1827-45, R. East Barkwith, Lincs. 1828-43. Died (Andover) 18/11/1880 aged 85, leaving £30,000 [C41833. Kaye]

BETHELL (George) Bapt. Wallingford, Berks. 1/8/1779, s. Rev. Richard Bethell and Anne Clitherow. King's, Cambridge 1798, BA1802, Fellow 1801-1807 [Assistant Master Eton College 1802-17, Fellow of Eton 1818-57, Vice Provost 1851-7] dn03 (Salis.), p05 (Nor.) MA1805. R. Burnham, Bucks. 1822-33, R.

Worplesdon, Surrey 1833 to death. Dom. Chap. to 1st Marquess Wellesley (later 1st Duke of Wellington) 1813. Died Eton 16/3/1857 aged 78. [C43833. Boase] Married Fulmer, Bucks. 23/12/1807 Anne Lightfoot, w. issue.

BETHUNE (George Maximilian) Bapt. Worth, Sussex 5/1/1792, s. Rev. George Bethune and Catherine Bethune [*sic*]. University, Oxford 1791, BA1794, MA1801, BCL and DCL809. R. Wanstrow, Som. 1797-1824, R. Brumsted, Norfolk 1803, (succ. his father as) R. Worth 1803, V. Frant, Sussex 1815, R. Nuthurst 1819-22. Dom. Chap. to 2nd Earl of Abergavenny 1807. Died East Grinstead, Sussex 9/12/1840[C32914] Married 10/6/1797 Anne Marie Ewart, with issue.

BETTON, *born* BRIGHT (John Bright) From Shrewsbury, s. Richard Bright. Christ Church, Oxford 1792 (aged 19), BA1796, dn97 (C&L), MA1799, p00 (C&L). PC. Lydbury w. Norbury, Shropshire 1800 to death 22/12/1833 (CCEd says 21/5/1834) [C9359] Changed name on inheriting the Tollerton estate 1807.

BETTS (Thomas D'Eye) Born Wortham Hall, Wortham, Suffolk 1789, s. Rev. George Betts. Caius, Cambridge 1807, BA1812, dn12 (Nor.), p13 (Nor.). R. Colney, Norfolk 1821-3, R. Martlesham, Suffolk 1832 to death 13/3/1859, leaving £1,500 [C111388. K. Doughty, *The Betts of Wortham in Suffolk, 1480-1905* (1912)]. Married 30/1/1826 Harriet Doughty, Theberton Hall, Suffolk (a clergy dau.), with issue.

BEVAN (Evan) Literate: dn94 (Heref.), p99 (Heref.). PC. Great Washbourne, Glos. 1825, PC. Oxenton, Glos. 1826. Died? [C102834]

BEVAN (Frederick Stephen) Born Fosbury, Wilts. 11/10/1779, s. Silvanus Bevan ('The Banker', of Riddlesworth Hall, Norfolk) and Louisa Kendall. Emmanuel, Cambridge 1799 [admitted Lincoln's Inn 1799] BA1803, MA 1807, dn07 (Nor.), p09 (Nor.). R. Carleton Rode, Norfolk 1821 to death 26/9/1859 aged 79, leaving £60,000 [C111417] Married St George's Hanover Square, London 17/3/1806 Anne Elizabeth (dau. Sir Robert John Buxton, 1st Bart.?), *s.p.*

BEVAN (James) [NiVoF] PC. Tipton (o/w Tibbington), Staffs. 1812. Probate granted 4/5/1847 ('now resident at Builth, Brecon')

[C9362] Married Broseley, Worcs. 19/7/1820 Jane Corbet.

BEWICK (Calverley John) Bapt. Clapham, Surrey 23/1/1765, s. Benjamin Bewick (merchant) and Anne Glesell Christ Church, Oxford 1782, BA1786, dn89 (Roch.), p89 (Lin.), MA 1812. R. Hallaton cum Blaston, Leics. 1789 (and Preacher throughout the Diocese) and V. Lodington, Leics. 1812 to death (Hallaton Hall) 5/5/1843 [C1578] Married (1) Holborn, London 16/8/1788 Mary Elizabeth Buckworth-Herne, *divorce petition* 1807 (2) Holborn, London 12/12/1815 Caroline Newman, with issue.

BEWSHER (Thomas) Bapt. Appleby in Westmorland St Michael 3/12/1775, s. William and Jane Bewsher. Literate: dn05 (York), p06 (York). PC. Barmby Marsh, Yorks. 1805; S/M Penrith Free G/S 1816-24; R. Knarsdale, Northumberland 1824 to death 28/2/1853 aged 77 [C4509. Platt, YCO] Married 1807 Mary Jolly, with issue. Brother, below.

BEWSHER (William) Bapt. Appleby in Westmorland St Michael 11/2/1769, s. William and Jane Bewsher. Queen's, Oxford 1795, p99 (Ex. for Chester), BA1801, MA1802, BD and DD1825. PC. Crossc(w)ake (o/w Stainton), Westmorland 1799 to death (Brighton) 2/9/1834 aged 65 [C8142] Brother, above.

BICKER (John) Born Swefling, Suffolk 20/6/1785 (bapt. Stainburn, Yorks. 20/8/1820), s. John and Ann Bicker. Literate: dn20 (York), p28 (Nor.). PC. Wingfield, Suffolk 1832 to death (apoplexy) 18/3/1836 aged 52 [C111419. YCO]

BICKERSTETH (Edward) Bapt. Kirby Lonsdale, Westmorland 3/1/1787, s. Henry Bickersteth (surgeon) and Elizabeth Batty. A solicitor in Norwich 1812-15. Literate: dn15 (Nor.), p15 (Glos.). Travelled in West Africa for the Church Missionary Society after 1816 (then one of their Secretaries). Min. of Sir George Wheler's Proprietory Chapel, Spitalfields, London 1829-30, R. Watton at Stone, Herts. 1830 to death 28/2/1850 aged 63, leaving £14,000 [C5536. T.R. Birks, *Memoir of the Rev. Edward Bickersteth, late Rector of Watton, Herts.* (1851. 2 vols.)] Married Norwich 1812 Sarah Bignold, with clerical sons the Bishops of Exeter, and of South Tokyo. Brother, below.

BICKERSTETH (John) Born Kirby Lonsdale, Westmorland. 19/6/1781, s. Henry

Bickersteth (surgeon) and Elizabeth Batty. Trinity, Cambridge 1807, BA1811, dn11 (Bristol), p11 (Bristol), MA1813. V. Acton, Suffolk 1811-37, R. Sapcote, Leics. 1837 to death 2/9/1855 aged 74 [C8144] Married 16/6/1812 Henrietta Lang, Leyland, Lancs. Brother, above.

BIDDULPH (Henry) Bapt. Warmington, Staffs. June 1796, s. Sir Theophilus Biddulph, 5th Bart. (of Arlescott, Warwicks) and Hannah Prestridge. St John's, Oxford 1813, then Magdalen, BA1817, MA1819, dn19 (Ox.), p20 (Ox.), Fellow 1820-33, BD1829. R. Birbury (or Birdingbury, a family living), Warwicks 1826 and R. Standlake, Oxon. (non.-res.) 1832 (and RD of Southam) to death 19/9/1867 aged 81, leaving £6,000 [C9398] Married 1834 Emma Susan Nuttall, with issue.

BIDDULPH (John) From Birbury, Warwicks., s. Sir Theophilus Biddulph, 4th Bart. and his cousin and wife Jane Biddulph. University, Oxford 1785, BCL1792, dn29 (C&L), p30 (C&L). R. (and patron) of Frankton, Warwicks. 1830-7, V. Lillington, Warwicks. 1831-3 (res.). Died Frankton 19/8/1837 [C9400 is confused but the *Gentleman's Magazine* sorts things out]. Married Sophia, dau. Rev. Sir Charles Wheler, 7th Bart., with clerical son.

BIDDULPH, *later* BIDDULPH-FORESTER (Thomas Shrapnel) Born Amroth Castle, Pembroke 12/12/1789, s. Rev. Thomas Tregenna Biddulph (below, St Mary Redcliffe, Bristol) and Rachel Shrapnel. Worcester, Oxford 1812, dn16 (Glos.), BA1816, p16 (B&W), MA1819. R. Brockley, Som. 1823-34, Prebend of Llangloedd in Brecon Collegiate Church 1834 to death (Dartford) 24/12/1866 aged 77, leaving under £100 [will under B-F.]. Lived at (the immense) Amroth Castle [C33040] Married (1) 1811 Caroline Field (d. in childbed 1813), 1 spinster dau. (2) Great Malvern, Worcs. 2/3/1819 Charlotte Stillingfleet, with further issue. Brother Zachariah Henry, below.

BIDDULPH (Thomas Tregenna) Bapt. Claines, Worcs. 27/7/1763, s. Rev. Thomas Biddulph and Martha Tregenna (a clergy dau.). Queen's, Oxford 1780, BA1784, dn85 (Ex.), MA1787, p88 (Salis.). V. Bengeworth, Worcs. 1793-1803 (non-res.), PC. St James, Bristol 1800 (and Don. Chap. Durston, Som. 1813) to death 19/6/1838 [C26734. ODNB. DEB - a long entry] Married Bradford on Avon, Wilts. 9/2/1789 Rachel Shrapnel, with clerical son, above. Evangelical leader in the South-West.

BIDDULPH (Zachariah Henry) Born Stockwell, Som. 24/1/1792, **s.** Rev. Thomas Tregenna Biddulph and Rachel Shrapnel. St Edmund Hall, Oxford 1809, then Magdalen, BA1813, Fellow, dn15 (Ox.), MA1815, p18 (Ox.), BD 1823. V. Old Shoreham and New Shoreham, Sussex 1828 and also V. ('Treasurer') Backwell, Som. 1828 to death 21/11/1842 [C22670. DEB] Married Bristol 1/6/1833 Harriet Davis. Brother Thomas Shrapnel Biddulph, above.

BIDMEAD (Uriah) Bapt. Bisley, Glos. 12/2/1765. St Catharine's, Cambridge 1815 [did not matriculate]. Literate: dn18 (Nor.), p20 (Nor.). PC. Little Berwick, Shropshire 1832-45, R. Great Hanwood, Shropshire 1835 to burial 9/1/1849 aged 89 [C32131]

BIDWELL (Edward Tomson) Born Thetford, Norfolk 1/9/1794, s. Shelford Bidwell and Mary Tomson. Jesus, Cambridge 1810, then Clare 1812, Fellow, dn16 (Lin.), p17 (Lin.), BA1818, MA1818. V. Orcheston St Mary, Wilts. 1827 to death 1852 (1st q.) [C43841] Brother below.

BIDWELL (George) Born Thetford, Norfolk 23/3/1787, s. of Shelford Bidwell and Mary Tomson. Clare, Cambridge 1804, BA1809, dn10 (Ely for Nor.), Fellow 1810-12, p11 (Ex.), MA 1814. R. Stanton All Saints w. Stanton St John the Baptist, Suffolk [income in CR65 £1,019] 1811 to death 20/10/1865 aged 78, leaving £20,000 [C99571] Married Stanton Dec. 1811 his first cousin Elizabeth Nunn, with clerical issue. J.P. Brother above. Archaeologist and antiquarian.

BIEDERMANN (George Augustus) Bapt. Woodbastwick, Suffolk 22/4/1782, s. Henry Augustus Biedermann and Mary Aldridge. Christ's, Cambridge 1805, BA1806, MA1809. R. Michaelstow y Fedw, Monmouth 1818, R. Flemington, Glamorgan 1818, R. Llanvihangel, Glamorgan 1818, R. Dauntsey, Wilts. 1829 to death (Plymouth) 30/3/1859 aged 77, leaving £1,500 [C3695] Married (1) Gloucester 13/10/1813 Helen Price (d.1830), with issue (2) Maria (d.1835), 1 dau. (3) 30/5/1837 Selina Stewart, with further issue.

BIGGS (George) Bapt. Pedmore, Worcs. 16/11/1779, s. Thomas Biggs and Theodisia Hesketh. Queen's. Oxford 1799, BA1803, dn03 (Wor.), p04 (Wor.), MA1807. V. Halesowen, Warwicks. 1805 and R. Upton Warren, Worcs. 1807 to death. Dom. Chap. to 1st Baron Lyttelton 1807. Died 29/2/1836 [C99571] Married Stratford-on-Avon, Warwicks, 10/11/1821 Mary Margaret Bree, w. clerical s. George Hesketh Biggs. Brother below.

BIGGS (Thomas Hesketh) Bapt. Pedmore, Worcs. 2/3/1792, s. Thomas Biggs and Theodosia Hesketh. University, Oxford 1810, BA1814, p16 (Heref.). V. Dormington w. Bartrestree, Heref. 1822, R. Whitbourne, Heref. 1826 (w. V. Donnington, Heref. 1826) to death 3/1/1833 (CCEd thus) [C102924] Brother above.

BIGING (John Keal) From Penn, Somerset, s. William Biging. St John's, Oxford 1812 (aged 18), BA1817, dn17 (Salis.), p18 (Salis.), MA1828. R. Stourton, Wilts. 1828-32, R. Penselwood, Som. 1832 to death (Bath) 1841 (2nd q.). Probate granted 4/9/1841 [C41837]

BIGLAND (John) Born Lowick, Lancs. 19/2/1798, s. of a yeoman farmer. St Bees admitted 1820, dn21 (Chester), p22 (Chester). PC. Finsthwaite, Cartmel, Lancs. 1822 to death (unm.) 4/2/1871 aged 72, leaving £200 [C168307]

BILLINGTON (John) Bapt. Ashford, Kent 30/8/1797, s. John Billington and Sarah Tritton. University, Oxford 1814, BA1818, dn21 (Cant.), MA1821, p22 (Cant.). V. Boughton Aluph, Kent 1821 and R. Kenardington, Kent 1821 to death. Dom. Chap. to 12th Earl of Caithness 1821. Died Ashford 22/5/1873, leaving £45,000 [C111824] Married Felbrigg, Norfolk 21/7/1829 Maria Wyndham (w), and had issue.

BINFIELD (Henry) Born Hampstead, London, s. Rev. Henry Binfield, sen. Pembroke, Cambridge 1779 (aged 17), BA1784, dn74 (C&L), p86 (C&L). PC. Farewell, Staffs. 1804 and PC. Armitage, Staffs. 1804 to death. Dom. Chap. to 1st Marquess of Anglesey 1820. Died (Longdon, Staffs. 6/12/1848 aged 76 (CCEd says 14/12/1838) [C9407]

BINGHAM (John Batt) Born Great Gaddesden, Herts. 28/8/1787, s. Ven. John Bingham (Archdeacon of London) and Agnata Dörrien. BNC, Oxford 1805, BA1809, dn10 (Lin.), p11 (Lin.), MA1819. R. St Martin's Ludgate, City of London 1819-68 (w. Preacher throughout the Diocese of London) and V. Great Gaddesden 1820 to death. Dom. Chap. to 5th Earl de la Warr 1820. Died 10/4/1872 aged 84, leaving £60,000 [C43850] Married Manchester 28/6/1834 Frances Johnson, with issue.

BINGHAM (Richard) Born Runwell, Essex 1/4/1765, s. Rev. Isaac Moody Bingham and Catherine Tonge. New, Oxford 1783, BA1787, dn87 (Ox.), BCL1801. PC. Gosport Holy Trinity, Hants. 1792-1838, V. Great Hale (o/w Hale Magna), Hants. 1796-1858, and Prebend of Chichester 1807 to death 18/7/1858 aged 94, leaving under £200 [ODNB. C22680. Boase] Married 10/11/1788 (against parental opposition) Lydia Mary Anne Douglas (a naval dau.), with clerical son, also Richard. J.P. for Hants. A very litigious man, engaged in building speculation in Gosport, he was imprisoned for 6 months for illegally obtaining a license for a non-existent public house.

BINGHAM (Thomas) Born Derbys., s. Rev. James Bingham. St John's, Cambridge 1783, BA1788, dn88 (C&L), p89 (C&L), MA1827. R. Norbury, Derbys. 1788-1834 (res.) [blank in ERC] (with Snelston, Derbys. 1827-34), V. (and patron of) Ab Kettleby, Leics. 1827 [blank in ERC] to death. Dom. Chap. to Barbara, Baroness Grey de Ruthin 1827. Died Bath 26/12/1849 aged 65. [C9410] D.L. Derbys.

BINNEY (Hibbert) Born Halifax, Nova Scotia, Canada 2241792, s. Hon. Hibbert Newton Binney and Lucy Creichton. King's College, Nova Scotia, BA1811, MA1814, dn16 (London), LLD1827, DCL1834. In England from 1823. V. Hackthorne, Lincs. 1827 and R. Cold Hanworth, Lincs. 1827, Min. Trinity Chapel Knightsbridge, London 1834, V. Newbury, Berks. 1838 to death 6/7/1857 [C53853. Wilberforce2. *Dict. Canadian Biog.*.] Married 25/9/1818 Henrietta Amelia Stout (a Canadian), one of their sons (also Hibbert) becoming 4th Bishop of Nova Scotia.

BIRCH (Charles) Bapt. Bristol 28/9/1784, s. Richard abd Frances Birch. Magdalene, Cambridge 1813, no degree, dn15 (Nor.), p16 (Nor.). R. Happis-burgh, Norfolk 1830 to death 27/10/1852 [C111441]

BIRCH (Charles Edward) From Battle, Surrey, s. Ven. Thomas Birch, Archdeacon of Lewes (below) and Maria Rosara Gordon. St John's, Oxford 1825 (aged 18), BA1829, dn30 (Chich.), p31 (Chich.), MA1833. R. Wiston (o/w Wissington), Suffolk 1832 to death 21/12/1887, leaving £817-1s-1d. [C61684] Married Old Machar, Aberdeenshire 2/7/1833 Marianne Burnett (w), with issue.

BIRCH (Edward) From Middlesex. St John's, Cambridge 1818, BA1823, dn23 (London), p23 (London), MA1826. R. West Hackney, London 1827-46 (res.), R. Windlesham w. Bagshot, Surrey 1846-64. Died Upper Norwood, Surrey 13/8/1870 aged 70, leaving £800 [C115271] Married Stoke Newington, Hackney 13/3/1829 Marianne Luddington, with clerical son.

BIRCH (Henry William Rous) Born Calcutta 1794, s. John Brereton Birch and Louisa Judy Rous. BNC, Oxford 1812, BA1815, dn17 (Chester for London), MA1818, p18 (London). V. Reydon, Suffolk 1820, PC. (then V. 1829) Southwold, Suffolk 1820-54, V. Yoxford 1821 and R. Bedfield, Suffolk 1821 to death 10/1/1854 [C111443] Married Woodford, Essex 25/8/1818 Lydia Mildred [surname], w. clerical son (and Sir Arthur Nonus Birch).

BIRCH (Samuel) Bapt. City of London 31/5/1781, s. Samuel Birch (Lord Mayor of London, 'confectioner and occasional dramatist', *q.v.* ODNB) and Mary Birch. St John's, Cambridge 1798, dn03 (Lin.), Fellow 1804-9, p05 (Lin.), BA1812, MA1815, DD1828. R. St Mary Woolchurch Haw w. St Mary Woolnoth, City of London 1808-48, Twyford Prebend in St Paul's Cathedral 1819-48, V. Little Marlow, Beds. 1833 to death. Chap. to the Lord Mayor of London 1808-9 and to his father 1814-15. Died 24/6/1848 [C43859] Married 15/4/1811 Margaret Browning (Woburn Place, London), with issue (including Samuel Birch, egyptologist and orientalist). Professor of Geometry at Gresham College, City of London 1808-48.

BIRCH (Thomas) Born Alford, Lincs. 1766, s. Rev. Thomas Birch, sen. (V. Thoresby, Lincs.) and Marianne Burnett. St John's, Cambridge 1785, dn89 (Lin.), p90 (Ox.), BA1792, LLD 1797, DD. V. (and Dean of) Battle (Abbey), Sussex 1801, PC. Northmoor, Oxon. 1801-33, Archdeacon of Lewes 1823 and V. Westfield, Sussex 1828 to death 25/2/1840 [C22712] Married 30/1/1804 Maria Rosara Gordon (w) (a Scot), 4s. (incl. Charles Edward (above), 5 dau.

BIRCH (Thomas Wickham) Bapt. Oving, Sussex 2/8/1792, s. Rev. Charles Birch and Anne Seymer. St Edmund Hall, Oxford 1810, then Christ Church BA1814, dn15 (B&W), p15 (B&W), MA1818. R. Stoke Wake, Dorset 1817 and R. Chesselbourne, Dorset 1820 to death. Dom. Chap. to Henry, Lord Willoughby de Broke 1820. Died (as Wickham Birch) 7/3/1872 aged 79, leaving £10,000 [C41842]

BIRCH (William) [NiVoF] V. Burford, Oxon 1826. Died? [C22714 and probably 9445, who is the only other Rev. William Birch noted at this time, and is an identifiable figure, d.1840]

BIRD (Charles John) Born Hereford 11/7/1777, s. William Bird, *J.P.*, and Hannah Boulton. Magdalene, Cambridge 1794, BA1799, dn99 (Heref.), p01 (Bristol for Heref.), MA 1802, R. Dyndor, Heref. 1801-54, R. Mordiford, Heref. 1804 (and RD of Ross) to death. Dom. Chap. to Grace, Countess of Clanbrassil 1804. Died 6/12/1854 aged 77, living at Drybridge House, Heref. [C52092] Married (1) Bath 19/5/1803 Harriet Jones (of Upton Castle, Pembrokeshire), w. issue (2) 4/2/1823 Rachel Glover (a clergy dau.), 1 dau.

BIRD (Christopher) Born Morland, Westmorland 3/12/1778, s. Christopher and Margaret Brocklebank. St John's, Cambridge 1800, dn02 (Nor. for York), p02 (London for York), migrated to St Alban Hall, Oxford 1803, BA1806, then St John's, Cambridge again 1809, MA1810. Tutor to the Beaumont family. PC. Allendale, Northumberland 1806-22, R. High Hoyland, Yorks. (1st Mediety 1807, 2nd then both 1811), V. (and patron) of Chollerton, Northumberland 1821-67 and V. Warden, Northumberland 1827 (and RD of Chollerton, total income £996) to death 10/5/1867 aged 88, leaving £25,000 [C130848/42887. YCO. BBV] Married Lambeth, Surrey 25/10/1808 Anne Harrison, with issue, including clerical son, also Christopher.

BIRD (Godfrey) Bapt. Great Waltham, Essex 19/9/1796, s. Rev. Godfrey Bird and Susanna Greave. University, Oxford 1814, BA1818, dn19 (London), p20 (Lin.), MA1821. R. Great Wigborough, Suffolk (and RD of Mersea) 1832 to death 25/10/1879, leaving £6,000 [C42880 mixes father and son] Married 14/8/1832 Sarah Jane Edwards, with 15 ch.

BIRD (John) Born Wigan, Lancs. 20/6/1784, s. John Bird. Hertford, Oxford 1807, BA1811, then BNC, p11 (Chester), MA1824. S/M 1811; PC. Upholland (as Holland in ERC), Wigan, Lancs. 1821 to death 24/3/1844 aged 59 [C168312] Married (1) Wigan 26/6/1811 Margaret Scott (2) Manchester 26/6/1827 Catherine Prescott Braithwaite. A popular and conscientious man, who also kept a boarding school.

BIRD (John) Born Plumbland, Cumberland 11/6/1791, s. Rev. John Bird, sen. Trinity, Cambridge 1808, then Peterhouse 1812, BA 1814, dn19 (Lin.), p20 (Lin.), MA1834. V. Ainstable, Cumberland 1832 to death (Keswick, Cumberland) 23/3/1853 aged 62 [C4510. Platt] [C140006] Married 1/10/1816 Mrs Elizabeth Brisco Morland, with issue.

BIRD (John Thorisby) Born Worsted, Norfolk 25/4/1768, s. William Bird (grocer) and Elizabeth High. Caius, Cambridge 1785, BA 1790, dn90 (Nor.), p92 (Nor.). R. Bradfield St Clare, Suffolk 1795-1815, R. Rockland St Peter, Norfolk 1799-1839, PC. Beccles, Suffolk 1812-17, R. Riddlesworth w. Gasthorpe, Norfolk 1815-39, R. Knettishall, Suffolk 1826 to death 3/2/1839 [C111450] Married East Harling, Norfolk 18/6/1801 Elizabeth Rodwell, w. issue.

BIRD (William) Bapt. Leigh, Staffs. 12/7/1763, s. John Bird. St Edmund Hall, Oxford 1791, BA1795, dn95 (C&L), p95 (C&L), MA1798. S/M Church Eaton, Staffs. 1801-47; PC. Stretton, Staffs. 1806 to death 12/3/1847 [C9448]

BIRDS (William Taylor) Born Ellesmere, Shropshire 13/7/1797, s. David Birds and Catherine Moss Taylor. Queens', Cambridge 1817, BA1821, dn21 (Chester), p21 (Chester), MA1841. PC. Penley, Flintshire 1823-34 (res.), R. Preston upon the Wild/Weald Moor, Shrewsbury 1826 to death 27/5/1860 aged 61, leaving £450 [C9450] Married Paddington, London 20/12/1830 Lydia Dagley, w. clerical son James Adey Birds.

BIRDWOOD (Christopher) Born Plymouth. Devon 16/11/1775, s. Richard Birdwood and Ann Travers. Exeter, Oxford 1794, BA1798, dn98 (Ex), p99 (Ex), MA1800. V. Cadbury, Devon 1802 and R. Bratton Clovelly, Devon 1816. Died Plymouth 1845 (4th q.) [C140006] Married 1817 Sophia Grigg, with issue.

BIRDWOOD (William Ilbert) Bapt. Dartington, Devon 2/4/1775, s. Roger Birdwood and Bridget Anne Ilbert. Balliol, Oxford 1793, BA1797, dn97 (Ex.), p99 (Ex.), MA1815. R. Throwleigh, Devon 1807 to death 13/3/1841. Involved in an adulterous affair with a married woman 1798/9, for which he was fined £500 and costs [C115272, which says Throwley, Kent] Married Slapton, Devon 10/2/1807 Dorothea McCarmick Allen, with military issue.

BIRKETT (James, sen.) Literate: dn74 (Carlisle for Durham), p75 (Durham). PC. Ovingham, Northumberland 1791 to death 1834 [C4515] Married Mary Ions, w. clerical son, below. Engraved port. online: https://www.flickr.com/photos/newcastlelibraries/4081555200

BIRKETT (James, jun.) Bapt. Ovingham, Northumberland 28/4/1798 (CCEd thus), s. Rev. James Birkett, sen. (above) and Mary Ions. Christ Church, Oxford 1816, BA1820, dn21 (Ox.), p22 (Durham), MA1823. Chap. Mickley, Ovingham 1827, (succ. his father as) PC. Ovingham 1834 to death 13/8/1838 aged 40 [C22635]

BIRKETT (John) From Cumberland. St John's, Cambridge 1818, BA1822, MA1825, dn26 (Ely), Fellow 1827, p27 (Ely). R. Laceby, Lincs. 1832; S/M Cheltenham College 1853-70. Died 19/6/1878, leaving £6,000 [C6538]

BIRKETT (Joseph) Bapt. Keswick, Cumberland 27/3/1755, s. John Birkett and Ann Askew. St John's, Cambridge 1773, BA1777, dn78 (Nor. for Salis.), p81 (Ely for Salis.). Army Chaplain; V. Stranton, Durham 1796 to death 7/9/1833 aged 78 [C107784] Married Whitehaven, Cumberland 12/4/1795 Anne Robinson, with clerical issue. Venn notes he gave away the produce of his extensive garden to the poor.

BIRKETT (Robert) Bapt. 2/4/1777. Literate: dn02 (C&L for Durham), p04 (Chester). PC. Unsworth, Prestwich, Lancs. 1804 to death (a widower) 22/7/1863 with issue, leaving £5,000 [C170814] Confusion with the man below.

BIRKETT or **ATKINSON (Robert)** Bapt. Troutbeck, Westmorland 21/10/1777, natural s. of Agnes Birkett and William Atkinson (a soldier). Literate: dn01 (York), p02 (York). S/M Auckland Free G/S 1805-14; V. (Church) Kelloe, Durham 1814 to death 19/7/1851 aged 73 [C84855. YCO] Married 1801 Eleanor Parker (a clergy dau.), with issue. Confusion with the man above.

BIRKETT (Thomas) Born Leigh, Lancs. 14/2/1792, s. Rev. Daniel and Elizabeth Birkett. Literate: dn15 (Chester), p16 (Chester). PC. Astley, Leigh 1822-53, PC. Penwortham, Preston, Lancs. 1824-31, V. South Tawton, Devon 1831 to death 2/10/1856 [C168316]

BIRT (John) From Gloucester, s. William Birt. Christ Church, Oxford 1806 (aged 18), BA 1809, dn11 (Ox.), MA1812, p12 (Ox.), Chaplain 1811-13, BD1819, DD1822. Vicar-Choral Hereford Cathedral 1812-16, PC. Brockhampton 1813-14, R. Putley, Heref. 1814-25, H/M King's School Canterbury 1819 and R. Canterbury St Alphege w. St Mary Northgate 1824-32, V. Faversham Kent 1832 (and S/M there) to death 11/5/1835 aged 58 [C7822] Married 1834 a Miss de Fer, of Canterbury.

BISCOE (Robert) From Lympsfield, Surrey, s. Vincent Hilton Biscoe and Anna Catharina Noel. Christ Church, Oxford 1819 (aged 17), BA1823, MA1825, dn27 (Ox.), p28 (Ox.). PC. Littleton, Worcs. 1831, R. Whitbourne, Heref. 1833, Prebend of Pratum Minus in Hereford Cathedral 1834. Died Bromsgrove 14/11/1870 aged 69, leaving £9,000 [C22771] Left issue.

BISCOE (William) Born Bletchingly, Surrey 17/4/1805, s. Joseph Seymour Biscoe and Stephana Law. Queens', Cambridge 1826, dn30 (Heref.), p30 (Heref.), BA1831, MA1834. R. Donnington, Heref. 1831-45, V. Combe Bisset, Wilts. 1843-57, V. Edlington, Lincs. 1857-68, R. Exhall-cum-Wixord, Warwicks. 1868 to death 6/11/1877, leaving £450 [C120975] Married 29/10/1835 Caroline Trewecke Wooldridge (a naval dau.), with clerical sons.

BISHOP (Henry) Born Cambridge, s. Robert Bishop (an Oxford draper). Wadham, Oxford 1796, migrated to St John's, Cambridge 1799 (aged 21), BA1800, dn01 (London), p02 (London), MA1803. V. Ardleigh, Essex 1806-51, RD, V. Cretingham, Suffolk 1821-3, V. Great Clacton w. Little Holland, Essex 1823-45. Dom. Chap. to Baron Gordon 1821. Probate granted 27/1/1851 [C111454] Married Copford, Essex 28/4/1807 Christian Kelly (from Douglas, IoM), with clerical son, also Henry.

BISHOP (John) Bapt. Gloucester 14/9/1794, s. William and Betty Bishop. Pembroke, Oxford [but NiF], migrated to Trinity Hall, Cambridge 1811, dn12 (Glos.), p12 (Glos.) V. Brookthorpe, Glos. 1820-8, V. Gloucester St Mary de Lode and Holy Trinity 1828 (and Minor Canon of Gloucester, and Precentor) to death 3/7/1838 aged 51 [C138620]

BISHOP (William) Bapt. Holborn, London 1/3/1776, s. Samuel Willson Bishop. Wadham, Oxford 1793, BA1797, then Oriel, MA1801, dn10 (Ox.), p02 (Ox.). V. Oxford St Mary the Virgin 1810-19, R. Ufton Nervet, Berks. 1819-47. Probate granted 2/3/1847 [C22775] Founded an educational charity which survives.

BISHOP (William) Bapt. Birmingham 9/1/1778, s. Rev. John and Elizabeth Bishop. Literate: dn19 (York), p20 (York). PC. Thornton, Bradford, Yorks. 1820 to death 1839 (2nd q.?) [C130851. YCO. S. Slinn, 'Archbishop Harcourt's recruitment of literate clergymen: Part 2'. *Yorkshire Archaeological J.*, 81 (2009), p.281, n.19].

BISS, BISSE (Henry) Bapt. Hereford 10/2/1792, s. James Bisse. Worcester, Oxford 1810, BA1814, dn15 (Ox.), p15 (Ox.), MA1817, Fellow. Min. Southampton St Mary 1829, PC. Southampton Holy Trinity, Hants. 1835 (res.), R. Winford, Som. 1850 to death (Wilton upon Wye, Heref.) 1858 (1st q.). No will traced [C22776]

BISSELL (John) Bapt. Tattenhall, Cheshire 14/12/1766, s. Rev. William and Mary Bissell. BNC, Oxford 1787, BA1790, dn92 (Heref.), p92 (Heref.), MA1816, BD1816. S/M Kington G/S, Heref. 1792-1827; V. Leintwardine w. Adforton, Heref. 1799 (non-res.) and V. Brampton Bryan, Heref. 1800 to death 6/11/1838 aged 71 [C102979] Left a widow Margaret. J.P. and Chairman of Herefordshire Quarter Sessions.

BISSETT (John Collinson) Bapt. Croydon, Surrey 13/10/1785, s. Alexander and Sarah Bissett. St Edmund Hall, Oxford 1803, BA 1808, dn09 (Win.), p11 (Win.), MA1819. S/M Croydon Free G/S 1812; V. Addington, Surrey 1821. Buried 28/4/1852 as Bisset) [C70748]

BISSILL (William) From Knipton, Leics. Chorister at Southwell Minster, Notts. St John's, Cambridge 1781, BA1786, MA1791, dn87 (Lin.), p88 (Lin.). V. Whissendine, Rutland 1803 and R. Folksworth, Hunts. 1820 to death 1832 aged 73 [C43932]

BISSLAND (Thomas) Born Greenock, s. Thomas Bissland. Glasgow Univ. 1815-18, then Snell Exhibitioner Balliol, Oxford 1818 (aged 19), BA1821, dn21 (Ox.), p22 (Ox.), MA1824. PC. Edmonton St Paul, London 1828, R. Hartley Maudit, Hants. 1833 to death 25/4/1834 (CCEd thus) [C22131. Snell] Married (1) Edmonton, Middx. 1/7/1824 Amelia Eliza Johnson Barton (d.1829) (2) Holybourne, Hants. 1829 Christiana Grace Turnour Gibson (a clergy dau.), with issue.

BLACK (Richard) Bapt. Hull 12/4/1773, s. William Black. Jesus, Cambridge 1791, BA 1795, dn96 (Lin.), p00 (Glos. for Nor.), MA 1805. R. Merton, Norfolk 1800-3, V. Great Canfield, Essex 1801-10, V. Uffington, Berks. 1810-14, V. Catmore, Berks. 1810-37, V. Hutton, Essex 1814-37, R. Copdock w. Washbrook, Suffolk 1814 to death. Dom. Chap. to 3rd Baron Walsingham 1813. Died 30/1/1837. [C43936] Left issue.

BLACK (William) From Liverpool, s. Patrick Black. BNC, Oxford 1787 (aged 21), BA1791, dn94 (Ox.), MA1794, p94 (Ox.). R. Lillington, Dorset 1797 [C22822], R. Blaisdon, Glos. 1798. Died? [C140748]

BLACK (William Hennell) Born Dumfries, Scotland 16/1/1790. Literate: dn15 (Lin.), p19 (Lin.). PC. Wormegay, Norfolk 1819 [blank in ERC] (and Min. Tavistock Chapel, London 1820-1) to death (Plymouth) 9/2/1834 (CCEd says 13/5/1834) [C111458] Married Whissonset, Norfolk 11/8/17 Mary Biscall, w. issue.

BLACKALL (Samuel) Bapt. Exeter 6/2/1770, s. Theophilus Blackall and Elizabeth Ley. Emmanuel, Cambridge 1787, BA1791, dn94 (Ely), MA1794, p94 (Ely), Fellow 1794, BD 1801. R. North Cadbury, Som. 1812 (and Prebend of Combe 1 in Wells Cathedral 1826) to death 11/3/1842 aged 71 [C33046] Married Clifton, Bristol 15/1/1813 Susannah Lewis, with clerical son Samuel. This is the man romantically (if briefly) attached to Jane Austen:

BLACKBURN (Edward) Literate: dn94 (Chester), p95 (Chester). PC. Ingleton Fell (otherwise Chapel le Dale), Bentham, Yorks. 1814 to death 3/7/1835 (CCEd thus) [C168319]

BLACKBURN (John) Bapt. Louth, Lincs. 17 *or* 23/8/1787, s. John Blackburn and Ellin Winder. St John's, Cambridge 1811, BA1815, [in 1815 the Bishop of Chester refused to ordain him because of his views contrary to Article 16: Sin after Baptism], dn15 (Ely), p16 (Nor.), MA 1818, incorporated at Oxford 1832. PC. Attercliffe cum Darnall, Yorks. 1817-52, Prebend of Riccall in York Minster 1851, R. Yarmouth, IoW 1853 to death (widower) 12/4/1870 aged 82, leaving £3,000 [C6546] Married (1) St Peter Le Poer, City of London 17/4/1816 Elizabeth Walton Curteis (d.1834), w. clerical son (2) St Pancras, London 2/9/1835 Sophia Rivington (d.1839), with further issue. Surrogate IoW and Hants. 1853. Online photo. Invented the Parabolic Sounding Board to help church acoustics: en.wikipedia.org/wiki/Sounding_board

BLACKBURNE (Thomas) Born Prestwich, Lancs. 29/12/1790, s. John Blackburne (but 'of St Margaret's, Westminster, London'). BNC, Oxford 1809, BA1814, dn15 (Chester), p16 (Chester), MA1815. R. Crofton, Yorks. 1817, V. Eccles (w. Pendleton), Salford, Lancs. 1818-37 [and it was to his vicarage that the fatally injured William Huskisson was taken, and died, when run over at the opening of the Liverpool and Manchester Railway on 15/9/1830], R. Bygrave, Herts. 1832, R. Prestwich, Manchester 1836 to death. Chap. to the Prince Regent 1818. Died West Derby 5/8/1847 [C43957] Married Newton, Lancs. 2/9/1819 Emma Hesketh, with clerical son.

BLACKDEN (Benjamin George) Born Uttoxeter, Staffs. 6/11/1791, s. Benjamin Blackden (of High Wycombe, Bucks.) and Elizabeth Cayley. St John's, Cambridge 1809, then Queens' 1809, BA1814, dn15 (London), MA1818, p18 (Ox.). R. Thorpe, Derbys. 1824 to death 10/4/1832 [C9468] Married Charteris, Cambs. 31/1/1826 Mary Denny, with issue.

BLACKETT, *later* BLACKETT-ORD (John Alexander) Born Wylam, Northumberland 27/10/1803, s. Christopher Blackett and Alice Ingham. Christ Church, Oxford 1823, BA1827, dn29 (Nor.), p29 (Nor.). V. Heddon on the Wall, Northumberland 1830-48, R. Wolsingham,

Durham 1848-51. Died Whitfield Hall, Haltwhistle, Northumberland 10/5/1865, leaving £14,000 [C111512] Married Cheltenham, Glos. 4/4/1842 Anne Jane Hamilton, with clerical son.

BLACKLEY (Thomas) Bapt. Canterbury, Kent 25/1/1782, s. John and Elizabeth Blackley. Literate: dn14 (Ex. for York), p16 (York). V. Rotherham, Yorks. 1826 to death 26/1/1842 aged 60 [C130854. YCO] Had issue.

BLACKMORE (John) Born Parracombe, Devon 21/6/1764, s. John Blackmore. Exeter, Oxford 1782, BA1786, dn87 (Ex.), p88 (Ex.). R. Oare, Som. 1809, R. Combe Martin, Devon 1833 to death 1842 aged 78 [C33050] Grandfather of R. D. Blackmore, author of *Lorna Doone*.

BLACKMORE (Richard White) Bapt. Shaftesbury, Dorset 1/1/1794, s. Rev. Richard Blackmore and Jane ?White. Merton, Oxford 1809, BA1813, dn14 (Salis.), p15 (Salis.). Chap. to the Russia Company 1819-47 [income £1,200]; R. Donhead St Mary, Wilts. [income £1,200 in CR65] 1847 to death. Died 28/6/1882 aged 90, leaving £8,252-9s-3d. [C91224. Boase] Married a Russian lady. Sympathtic writer on the Russian Church and its liturgy.

BLACKSTONE (Frederick Charles) Born Wymering, Hants. 11/8/1795, s. Rev. Charles Blackstone and Margaret Bigg-Wither. New, Oxford 1812, dn18 (Heref.), BCL1819, p19 (Ox.), Fellow. V. Worting, Hants. 1819-32 (res.), V. Heckfield, Hants. 1825 to death 29/4/1862, leaving £4,000 [C22883] Married Clifton, Bristol 20/3/1826 Elizabeth Rankin, with issue.

BLACOW (Richard) Bapt. Broughton, Preston, Lancs. 8/9/1765, s. Henry Blacow and Janet Cardwell. Trinity, Cambridge 1783, BA 1788, dn93 (Chester), p98 (Chester), MA1814 [admitted Lincolns Inn]. PC. Childwall, Lancs. 1793, PC. St Mary the Virgin, West Derby, Lancs. [CCEd calls this Westerby] 1798-1845 and PC. Liverpool St Mark 1815 to death 23/12/1845 [C168323] Married Patience Rochfort (dau. of and Irish *M.P.*, she d. 1817). Twice in prison in 1811 for contempt of Court; fined and imprisoned at Lancaster Assizes in 1821 for libelling Queen Caroline (details of the trial online).

BLADES (Thomas) Born Garsdale, Dent, Yorks. 9/9/1759, s. John Blades and Agnes Garthwaite. Literate: p86 (York). PC. Langford, Notts. 1802-37 and PC. Garsdale 1803 to death 14/7/1837 aged 77 [C84864. YCO] Married Garsdale 15/7/1845 Mary Dawson, with issue.

BLAGDEN (Thomas Nixson) Bapt. Chichester 6/6/1784, s. John Blagden and Frances Nixson. Queen's, Oxford 1802, then Magdalen, BA1805, dn07 (Win.), MA1808, p08 (Ox.), BD1815, Fellow. V. Washington, Sussex 1828, PC. Mid Lavant, Sussex 1834, R. Ashurst, Sussex 1836 to death (Thakeham, Sussex) 19/3/1865 aged 82 ('after a long and painful illness'), leaving £9,000 [C22886] Married Portsmouth 18/12/1832 Ann Arnaud (w), with issue.

BLAIR (Robert) Born 24/8/1759, s. Gilbert Blair (Edinburgh barber and wigmaker) and Lilias Henry. Edinburgh University 1775-6, 1778-9, dn89 (Car.), then Pembroke, Cambridge 1792, p92 (Salis.), DD St Andrews 1802. R. Barton St Andrew, Norfolk 1792 to death. Secretary to the British Legation at Florence and Naples 1837-38. Died London 22/12/1838 [C4520. Smart]

BLAKE (Henry William) Bapt. Norwich 13/1/1799, s. Thomas Blake (barrister) and Theodora Martha Columbine. Corpus Christi, Cambridge 1817, BA1821, Fellow 1822, dn23 (Nor.), p23 (Lin.), MA1824. R. Thurning, Norfolk 1824 to death 28/11/1857 aged 58 [C43970] Married (1) Horsford, Norfolk 23/11/1821 Louisa Day (d.1843), w. issue (2) Mitford Norfolk 1846 (3rd q.) Mary Heitland, with further issue.

BLAKE, *later* **JEX-BLAKE (William Jex)** Born Swanton Abbotts, Norfolk 23/11/1786, s. William Blake. Caius, Cambridge 1803, BA1808, dn09 (Nor.), p10 (Nor.). R. Banningham, Norfolk 1814 and R. Great Hautbois, Norfolk 1827 to death 23/10/1857 [C111514] Married 11/6/1811 Maria Lobbock (The Hall, Swanton Abbotts), with issue.

BLAKE (William Robert) Bapt. Midhurst, Sussex 28/2/1800, **s.** Henry James Blake. Merton, Oxford 1818, BA1822, dn23 (Nor.), p24 (Nor.). V. Great Barton, Suffolk 1826 [blank in ERC] to death (a bachelor) 6/12/1867, leaving £8,000 [C111516]

BLAKELOCK (Ralph) Born Red Hall, Leeds 1803, s. Ralph Blakelock (a former army officer) and Elizabeth Sturdy. St Catharine's, Cambridge 1820, BA1825, MA1828, Fellow 1828-34 [admitted Middle Temple 1830] dn31 (Lin.), p32 (Lin.). R. Gimmingham, Norfolk 1833-92 [vacant in ERC], Hon. Canon of Norwich Cathedral 1864-71, Archdeacon of Norfolk 1869-74. Died 1/3/1892, leaving £8,635-9s-8d. [C43971. Boase] His son became an Oratorian priest. Established allotments for labourers, and thus 'the father of the allotment movement'.

BLAKISTON (George Frank) Born London 3/11/1758, s. Rev. John Blakiston and Francis Gartrop. St John's, Cambridge 1776, BA1780, dn81 (St David's), p83, MA1784, BD1789, DD 1806, Fellow. PC. Northmore, Oxon. 1790-7, R. Belbroughton, Worcs. 1798, V. Baschurch, Shropshire 1806 to death 21/3/1837 [C9478] Married Oxford 18/5/1801 Ann Hornsby, with issue.

BLANCHARD (John) Born Nottingham 27/3/1790, s. Rev. John Blanchard and Ann Hoskins. Jesus, Cambridge 1808, BA1813, dn13 (York) p14 (York), MA1816. PC. North Dalton, Yorks. 1815-27, V. Lund, Yorks. 1826 and R. Middleton on the Wolds, Yorks. 1827 (and RD 1843) to death (Lund) 18/11/1862 aged 72, leaving £5,000 [C130859. YCO] Married Smalley, Derbys. 27/5/1824 Anne Radford (w), with clerical s. Henry Dacre Blanchard.

BLAND (Miles) Born Sedbergh, Yorks. 11/10/1786, s. Thomas and Esther Bland. St John's, Cambridge 1804, BA1808, Fellow 1808, dn09 (Nor.), tutor 1809-23, p10 (Salis. for Ely), MA1811, BD1818, DD1826. R. Lilley, Herts. 1823 (and Prebend of Combe V11 in Wells 1826) to death (Ramsgate, Kent) 27/12/1867 aged 81, leaving £16,000 [C41848. ODNB. Boase] Married (1) Ramsgate, Kent 22/7/1823 Ann Templeman (2) Emma Russell, of Binfield, Berks; clerical s. also Miles. *J.P.* Beds., and Herts. *F.R.A.S.*, *F.R.S.* (1827), *F.S.A.* 'A strong Tory'.

BLAND (Stephen) Born Keighley, Yorks. 14/5/1786, s. Joseph Bland and Susanna Butterfield. H/M Burnsall Free G/S 1805-49. Literate: dn10 (York), p10 (York). V. Kirkby Malham, Yorks. 1811 to death. Dom. Chap. to 8th Earl Ferrers 1827. Died Skpiton, Yorks. 26/1/1862 aged 78. Will not traced [C124440. YCO date of birth is wrong] Married 25/2/1813 Lydia Cockshott, w. clerical son. Dates of birth and death here are contested.

BLAND (Thomas) Bapt. Dufton, Westmorland 8/3/1761, s. John and Elizabeth Bland. Literate: dn88 (Durham), p89 (Durham). V. Alwinton w. Holystone, Northumberland 1798-[1833]. Died before 1838 [C134136] Married Lancaster 6/3/1791 Jane Bleasdale, with issue.

BLAND (Thomas) [NiVoF] V. East Rudham w. West Rudham, Lincs. 1805, V. Toftrees, Norfolk 1805. Probate 15/12/1851 [C111520]

BLAND (William Handley) Bapt. Newark on Trent, Notts. 28/4/1807, s. Thomas Bland (physician, Grantham, Lincs.) and Emma Sheppard. Caius, Cambridge 1824, BA1830, dn30 (Lin.), p31 (Lin.), MA1833. V. Braceby, Lincs. 1832 [parish not in ERC?] w. V. Sapperton, Lincs. 1832-89, V. Middle Rasen Drax, Lincs. 1832-79. Died Braceby 29/12/1889. Will not traced [C44060] Married Grantham, Lincs. 10/3/1834 Louisa Ann anners, with issue.

BLANDFORD (Joseph [Jessop]) Bapt. Covent Garden, London 4/10/1781, s. of Joseph (a lawyer) and Elizabeth Blandford. St John's, Cambridge 1800, then Trinity Hall 1801, dn04 (York), p05 (London for York), LLB1808. PC. Maplebeck, Notts. 1820-49, R. Kirton, Notts. 1821-49, V. Carlton le Moorland 1827 w. V. Stapleford, Lincs. 1827-49, PC. Wellow, Notts. 1827-32. Died Kirton 14/9/1849 aged 67 [C44061. YCO] Wife Mary, with issue (inc. a dau. Julia, who married John Blackwood, the Edinburgh publisher).

BLATCH (James) Bapt. Colchester, Essex 17/10/1774, s. James and Elizabeth Blatch. Balliol, Oxford 1792, then Magdalen, BA1796, MA1798, p09 (Ox.), BD1810. V. Basingstoke (w. Basing and Up Nately), Hants. 1814 to death 23/6/1864, leaving £45,000 [C22891]

BLATHWAYT (Charles) Born Langridge, Bath 6/1/1800, s. Rev. George William Blathwayt and Isabella Pye. Exeter, Oxford 1817, migrated to Queens', Cambridge 1818, BA1823, dn23 (Chester), p24 (Salis.), MA1828. R. Langridge 1825-65, PC. Redlynch, Som. 1865-72. Died Kensington, London 15/1/1874, leaving £300 [C41849] Married Westminster, London Anne Linley Rose (w), and had issue.

BLAYNEY (Rowland) Born Whitchurch, Shropshire, s. Rev. Richard Blayney. Hertford, Oxford 1783 (aged 27), dn84 (Bristol), p85 (Bristol), then St Alban Hall, BA1787. Chap. of the Donative of Birch in Rusholme, Manchester 1795 to (burial) Manchester 6/6/1838 aged 84 [C52096] Married Eccles, Lancs. 25/11/1794 Ann Tunnadine.

BLEECK (William) Born Warminster, Wilts. 10/12/1801, **s.** John Bleeck and Sarah Slade. Magdalen Hall, Oxford 1821, dn24 (Salis.), BA 1825, p26 (B&W). R. Huish, Wilts. 1830 [income £25] to death 27/12/1874 aged 72, leaving £5,000 [C41851] Married (1) Wilcot, Wilts. 26/6/1828 Charlotte Goodman (d.1830), w. issue (inc. the orientalist Arthur Henry Bleeck) (2) Huish, Wilts. 31/5/Martha Young (w), with further issue.

BLENCOWE (Edward Everard) Bapt. King's Lynn, Norfolk 5/6/1805, s. John Prescott Blencowe and Pleasance Everard. St Alban Hall, Oxford 1825, BA1829, dn29 (Nor.), p30 (Nor.). R. West Walton (1st Mediety, o/w Walton Elienses), Norfolk (and RD) 1831-69, R. Stow Bardolph, (o/w Stow under Wimbotsham) Norfolk 1869 to death (unm.) 31/10/1895 aged 89, leaving £3,081-17s.-0d. [C111553] Lived with his sister.

BLENCOWE, BLENCOE (Thomas) Bapt. Marston, Northants. 15/11/1782, s. Samuel Jackson Blencowe ND Anna Bree. Oriel, Oxford 1800, BA1804, dn06 (Peterb.), MA1807, p07 (Peterb.). V. Marston St Thomas w. Warkworth 1809 to death (unm.) 1840 (1st q.) [C109966]

BLENKARNE (James) Born Ashby-de-la-Zouche, Leics. c.1757, s. James Blenkarne. Emmanuel, Cambridge 1774, BA1778, dn79 (Lin.), MA1781, p83 (Lin.). H/M St Olave's G/S Southwark 1790-1833; V. St Helen Bishopgate, City of London 1799-1836, Chap. Guy's Hospital 1815. President of Sion College 1818. Dom. Chap. to 4th Duke of Grafton 1811. Died 7/2/1836 aged 78 [C44070] Married (1) Cambridge 16/3/1778 Mary Stone (d.1798), w. clerical s. Charles James (2) Shoreditch, London 29/5/1797 Mary Bruton (d.1805), w. further issue (3) Southwark, Surrey 19/6/1806 Elizabeth Savage L'Heureux, 1s.

BLENNERHASSETT (John) Born Ballyseedy, Co. Kerry 3/3/1803, s. Arthur Blennerhassett and Dorcas Twiss. TCD1821, BA1824, MA, dn27 (B&W for Bristol), p28 (Bristol). R. Ryme Intrinseca, Dorset 1830 (and V. Hermitage 1834-85) to death 5/9/1890 aged 87, leaving £2,818-18s-3d. [C8211. Al. Dub.] Married Heddington, Wilts. 21/10/1834 Elizabeth Houssemayne du Boulay (w), whose twin sister married his brother William (below). Left issue: www.blennerhassettfamilytree.com/INSCRIPTIONS-at-Ryme-Intrinseca-

BLENNERHASSETT (William) Born Ballyseedy, Co. Kerry 10/7/1800, s. Arthur Blennerhassett and Dorcas Twiss. TCD1816, BA1821, dn25 (Ex.), p26 (Ex.), MA1827. V. Iwerne Minster, Dorset 1832 (with Chap. of the Donative of Wooland, Dorset noted in ERC only) to death 27/4/1860, leaving £1,500 [C8212 with one 't'. Al.Dub.] Married Donhead St Mary, Wilts. 21/4/1835 Emma Sophia Houssemayne du Boulay (w), whose twin sister married his brother John (above). Left issue.

BLICK (Charles) Born Sutton Coldfield, Warwicks. 28/1/1785, s. Francis Blick and Ann Buswell. St John's, Cambridge 1801, BA1805, Fellow 1807-49, MA1808, dn11 (Ex. for Ely), Proctor 1814, BD1816, Senior Bursar 1816-46. R. Wentworth (o/w Wingford), Cambs. 1821-47, R. Brandesburton, Yorks. 1847 to death 10/6/1852 [C6550] Doubtless related to the man below.

BLICK (Francis) From Coventry, Warwicks., s. Francis Blick. St John's, Cambridge 1770 (aged 16), BA1774, dn76 (Wor.), MA1777, p78 (Wor.). PC. Wissett (le Roos), Suffolk 1795, PC. Tamworth w. Glasvote and Hopwas, Staffs. 1796, R. Walton on Trent, Derbys. 1800, Prebend of Pipa Parva in Lichfield Cathedral 1828. Died 3/4/1842 [C9481. S. Wood, *Tamworth, the parish, town and Napoleon: the writings of the Reverend Francis Blick from 1796 to 1811* ([2010])] Doubtless related to the man above:

BLIGH (John) Born Bodmin, Cornwall 12/9/1788, s. Richard Blight and Hester Stone. St John's, Cambridge 1807, BA1811, dn11 (Ex.), p13 (Lin.), MA1826. S/M Kimbolton G/S 1827; PC. Barham w. Long Stow (o/w Stow Longa), Hunts. 1826-76, V. Easton, Kimbolton, Hunts. 1826-76, V. of Spaldwick, Hunts. [sequestrator] 1826-38. Died Long Stow 10/8/1876 aged 87, leaving £3,000 [C44073] Married (1) Kimbolton

16/7/1812 Mary Codling (2) Kimbolton 29/1/1841 Eliza Bird, w. issue. Brother below.

BLIGH (Reginald) Born Bodmin, Cornwall 1/1/1779, s. Richard Blight and Hester Stone. St John's, Cambridge 1797, BA1801, dn01 (Win.), Fellow 1802-33, p03 (Win.), MA1804, BA1813. R. West Buckland, Devon 1807-31, R. Cockfield, Suffolk 1831 to death 4/2/1841 [C70759] Brother, above. Another clergyman of same name in Yorkshire.

BLISS (George) Born Oxford 10/3/1782, s. Robert Bliss (bookseller, and grandson of Nathaniel Bliss, Astronomer-Royal) and Martha Ogilvy. Christ Church, Oxford 1799, BA1803, dn05 (Glos.), MA1805, Chap. 1805-9. p06 (Ox.). Prebend of Highleigh in Chichester Cathedral 1808-24 (res.). PC. Funtington, Sussex 1818 to death (with S/M Chichester Cathedral School). Probate granted 21/8/1856 [C61924/7901] Married Chichester 17/6/1823 Elizabeth Barton Hack (a Quaker). ttps://sites.google.com/site/funtingtonarchive/general-history/george-bliss

BLISS (Philip) Born Chipping Sodbury, Glos. 21/12/1787, s. Rev. Philip Bliss, sen. St John's, Cambridge 1806, BCL1815, dn17 (Ox.), p18 (Ox.), DCL1820. [Assistant librarian 1810 then Sub-Librarian, Bodleian Library 1822-8]. Registrar of the University 1824-53. Principal of St Mary Hall, Oxford 1848-57. R. Avening, Glos. 1830 ('but had little interest in parish work'), Died (presumably unm.?) 18/11/1857. Dom. Chap. at Studeley Priory 1830-55 [C22899. ODNB fails to mention his ordinations. Boase]. According to one writer, his 'prominence and diligence in university business and his polished manners made him the embodiment of the traditions of *ancien régime* Oxford.'

BLOFELD (Thomas Calthorpe) Born Hoveton, Norfolk 16/8/1778, s. Thomas Blofeld (barrister). St John's, Cambridge 1795, then Pembroke, BA1801, dn01 (Nor.), p02 (Nor.), MA1805. V. Bishop Norton >< w. Atterby, Lincs. 1802 (non-res.), V. & R. Flemington, Norfolk 1803-19, V. Hoveton St Peter and St John's 1819-55, RD Waxham 1842-51, R. Drayton w. Hellesdon, Norfolk 1851-5. Died (Hoveton House) 25/3/1855 [C44075] Married Walton, Norfolk 7/5/1802 Mary Caroline (dau. of Francis Grove, the antiquary), with clerical issue.

BLOMBERG (Frederick William) [Reputedly the illegitimate son of George 111 (whom he strongly resembled), and was certainly brought up in the Royal household (*q.v.* P.B. Dewar & R. Powell, *Royal bastards* (2011)]. Bapt. Rochester 22/9/1761 as s. Friedrich Karl August von Blomberg and Catherine Layng. St John's, Cambridge 1777, BA1782, dn84 (Ely), p85 (St Davids in Oxford), MA1785, DD1822. R. Shepton Mallet, Som. 1787-1834, 6th Prebend of Bristol Cathedral 1790-1828, V. Bradford on Avon, Wilts. 1793-1834, V. Banwell, Som. 1799-1809, V. Bristol St Augustine 1803-10, Prebend of Westminster 1808-22, Prebend of Weldland and Canon Residentiary of St Paul's, London 1822 and V. St Giles Cripplegate, City of London 1822 to death. Chap. in Ordinary from 1793. Died 23/3/1847 aged 85 [C33072] Married Walcot, Bath 23/5/1787 Mary Floyer. A great musician. Some dates here are contested.

BLOMFIELD (Charles James, Bishop of Chester, *then* Bishop of London) Born Bury St Edmunds, Suffolk 29/5/1786, s. of Charles Blomfield (schoolmaster) and Hester Pawsey. Trinity, Cambridge 1804, BA1808, Fellow 1809, dn10 (Bristol), p10 (Bristol), MA1811, BD1818, DD1820. R. Dunton Bucks. 1811 [72 parishioners 'and old woman, who could not read, to serve as clerk'], V. & R. Great and Little Chesterford, Essex 1817, R. Tuddenham, Suffolk 1817, R. St Botolph Bishopsgate, City of London 1829 (which he retained as Bishop of Chester), Archdeacon of Colchester 1822-4, Bishop of Chester 1824-8, Bishop of London 1828-56 (res. on a pension of £6,000pa after 'premonitory symptons of paralysis caused by slipping on the polished floor of one of the rooms at Osborne'). Instrumental in setting up and organising the *Ecclesiastical Revenues Commission* (on which this present book is based), and the most important prelate in the CoE during this period. Died Fulham Palace (22 servants) 5/8/1857 [C8145. Boase. A. Blomfield *A memoir of Charles James Blomfield, DD, Bishop of London* ... (1863. 2v.). M. Johnson, *Bustling intermeddler? the life and work of Charles James Blomfield* (Leominster, 2001)] Married (1) Hemblington, Norfolk 6/11/1810 Anna Maria Heath (d.1818), only 1 ch. lived (2) St George's Hanover Square, London 29/5/1819 Mrs Dorothy (Cox) Kent ('a young attractive widow'), 11 ch. Consecrated 196 churches, and edited five plays of Aeschylus. Brother below.

BLOMFIELD (George Becher) Born Bury St Edmunds, Suffolk 28/11/1801, s. of Charles Blomfield (schoolmaster) and Hester Pawsey (and thus brother of Charles James, Bishop of London, above). Trinity, Cambridge 1819, then Christ's 1821, BA1824, dn24 (Chester) p25 (Bangor for Chester), MA1827. R. Tattenhall, Cheshire 1826-34, Canon Residentiary of Chester 1827-85, R. Coddington, Cheshire 1827-34, R. Stevenage, Herts. 1834-74 [total income £1,573], RD of Hitchin. Died Mollington Hall, Cheshire 25/12/1885 aged 84, leaving £7,065-18s-2d. [C44077] Married (1) Chester 9/1/1827 Frances Maria Massey (d.1837), 7 ch. (2) Chester 18/1/1847 Mary Anson (dau. of the Dean of Chester, she d.1852) (3) St George's, Hanover Square, London 1854 (2nd q.) Elizabeth Ellen Feilden, Mollington Hall. Cheshire; had clerical issue. *J.P.* for Herts. Book collector.

BLOOMFIELD (Samuel Thomas) Born Wisbech, Cambs. 19/1/1783, s. Samuel Bloomfield. Sidney, Cambridge 1804, BA1808, dn08 (Lin.), p08 (Lin.), MA1811, DD1829, incorporated at Oxford 1845. V. Bisbrooke, Rutland 1814 (and Hon. Canon of Peterborough 1854) to death (Wandsworth, London) 28/9/1869 aged 85, leaving £25,000 [C14078 under Bloomfield. Boase] Civil List pension of £200 from 1846.

BLOW (William) Born Cottingham, Yorks. 29/10/1789, s. William and Anna Blow. Sidney, Cambridge 1813, BA1817, dn18 (York), p19 (York). R. Goodmanham w. Eastrop, Yorks. 1819-70 (a family living) to death (Cleethorps, Lincs.) 29/6/1870, leaving £40,000 [C130865. YCO] Wife Elizabeth, w. clerical son, also William. *J.P.* and *D.L.*

BLOXAM (Richard Rouse) Born Alcester, Warwicks. 19/4/1765, s. Richard Bloxam and Susannah Rouse. Christ Church, Oxford 1782, BA1787, dn87 (St David's), MA 1790, p93 (C&L) BD& DD1810. V. Brinklow, Warwicks. 1793, S/M Rugby School 1804 and V. Bulkington, Warwicks. 1803 to death. Dom. Chap. to 3rd Earl of Harrington 1802. Died 28/3/1840 [C9484] Married Soho, London 10/4/1796 Anne Lawrence (sister of the painter), with clerical sons the botanist Rev. Andrew Bloxam (*q.v.* ODNB), and John Rouse Bloxam.

BLOXHAM, BLOXAM (Matthew) Born Merrydown, Warwicks. 19/4/1775, s. Anton Bloxham.Worcester, Oxford 1793, BA1797, dn98 (Wor.), p02 (Wor.). (first) PC. Ide Hill, Sundridge, Kent 1807 to death18/2/1846 [C120477] Married Battersea, London 5/11/1807 Maria Astle, *s.p.*

BLUCK (John) Born 1789. Literate: dn18 (Nor. for York), p20 (Chester for York). R. Grays Thurrock, Essex 1823-4 (res.), R. Westley Waterless, Cambs. 1824, R. Bowers Gifford, Essex 1827, R. Walsoken, Norfolk by 1845. Died (St Bartholomew's Hospital, London) 26/3/1857, leaving £2,000 [C6552. YCO] Married Mansfield, Notts. 1828 Eliza Ellis, with issue.

BLUETT (Buckland) Born Bampton, Devon 27/2/1754, s. Gilbert Bluett. Exeter, Oxford 1773, BA1776, dn76 (Ex.), p78 (Ex.), MA1795. R. Churchstanton, Devon 1784 (and RD of Dunkeswell 1836) to death. Dom. Chap. to 1st Baron Suffield 1787. Died 13/6/1837 aged 83. [C140016] Married Pitminster, Som. 26/7/1809 Frances Mallach. Brother below.

BLUETT (Thomas Lovell) Bapt. Falmouth, Cornwall 15/5/1767, s. Richard Bluett and Sarah Lovell. Sidney, Cambridge 1787, BA1791, dn92 (London), p94 (Ex.). V. Mullion, Cornwall 1831 to death 2/4/1834 aged 66 [C22904] Married Madron, Cornwall 14/2/1795 Sarah Vigurs, with clerical son of same name. Brother above.

BLUNDELL (James) S/M Leigh Free School 1804. Literate: dn06 (Chester), p07 ([Chester]). R. Crowland (o/w Croyland Abbey), Lincs. 1808-34, PC. Whaplode Drove Chapel, Lincs. 1812 to death 20/8/1834 (CCEd thus) [C44083]

BLUNDELL (William) Born Liverpool 24/9/1764, s. Bryan Blundell (merchant). Sidney, Cambridge 1789, BA1794, dn94 (Ox.), p94 (Ox.). Minister Liverpool St Anne Richmond 1802 to death 11/11/1842 aged 78 [C22906. ODNB] Probably married Liverpool 3/9/1803 Sarah Dickson, with issue [but there is an alternative wife!]

BLUNT (Henry) Born Dulwich, Surrey 12/8/1794, s. Henry (Chelsea, London) and Mary Blunt. Pembroke, Cambridge 1812, BA 1817, Fellow 1817, dn18 (London), p18 (London), MA1820. V. Clare, Suffolk 1819-33 (res.), PC. Upper Chelsea [now Holy Trinity, Sloane Street], London 1832-6, R. Streatham,

Surrey 1835 to death. Chap. to 5th Duke of Richmond 1820. Died 20/7/1843 [C70775] Married Chelsea, London 21/12/1820 Julia Anne Nailer, with issue.

BLUNT (John) From Birmingham, s. Joseph Brazier Blunt. St John's, Cambridge 1784 (aged 18), BA1788, Fellow 1789-94, dn88 (C&L), MA 1791, p91 (C&L). S/M Newcastle under Lyme G/S 1791-1812; PC. Blurton, Staffs. 1801-43, V. Lilleshall, Shropshire 1816 to death 14/6/1843 aged 77 [C9488] His son John James Blunt was Lady Margaret Professor of Divinity, Cambridge University (*q.v.* ODNB - 'no details are known of his mother').

BLYTH (Charles Dethick) Bapt. Solihull, Warwicks. 26/8/1796, s. Rev. Thomas Blythe. St John's, Cambridge 1815, BA1819, dn19 (Ox.), p21 (Ox.), MA1824, BD1829. R. Sutton, Beds. 1830 to death 13/3/1884 aged 87, leaving £6,386-16s.-7d. [C22908] Married Pensax, Worcs. 18/11/1830 Barbara Clutton.

BLYTH (Edward Gwyn) Born Burnham Westgate, Norfolk 27/2/1800, s. Henry Blyth and Sarah Etheridge. Christ's, Cambridge 1818, BA1822, dn23 (Nor.), p24 (Nor.), MA1825. R. Burnham Deepdale, Norfolk 1824 (and RD of Burnham 1844) to death 1/1/1855 aged 54 [C11563] Married Westminster, London 25/6/1829 Mary Susanna Kerslake, w. clerical son Edward Kingslake Blyth.

BLYTH (Thomas) From Doddeshill, Worcs., s. Rev. John Blyth. St John's, Cambridge 1779 (aged 17), BA1782, dn83 (C&L), MA1785, p85 (C&L). PC. Knowle, Warwicks. 1783, PC. Over Whitacre, Warwicks. 1785, PC. Packwood, Warwicks. 1786, R. Elmdon, Warwicks. 1789-1802 (res.), R. Whitchurch, Warwicks. 1801. Died? [C9488] Wife Elizabeth and issue.

BOAK (John) From Lowther, Westmorland, s. John Boak [*pleb*]. Queen's, Oxford 1784 (aged 24), dn84 (B&W), p85 (B&W). R. Swalecliffe, Kent 1826 to death *post* 1840 [C33127] Had issue.

BOARD (Richard) Born City of London 16/10/1765, s. Richard Board. Hertford, Oxford 1784, dn88 (Ox.), p89 (Ox.), BCL1791. R. Brockley, Som. 1795-1823 (res.), V. Westerham (and V. Edenbridge 1800, then separated), Kent 1792 to death 5/12/1859 aged 96, leaving £10,000 [C36] Had issue.

BOCKETT (Joseph) Born Hampstead, London 8/10/1794, s. John Halsey Bockett and Rebecca Bradney. Trinity, Oxford 1811, BA 1815, dn17 (Salis.), p18 (Salis.), MA1818. V. Shinfold and Shallowfield, Berks. 1818-[23], R. Stoodleigh, Devon 1816 to death. Dom. Chap. to Bishop of Rochester. Died Exeter 16/7/1880 aged 85, leaving £25,000 [C91228] Married Bishops Hull, Som. 13/5/1828 Rachel Barker. His parish charity survives.

BODDINGTON (John Compton) Bapt. West Haddon, Northants. 30/9/1787, s. Robert Boddington and Martha Compton. Literate: dn21 (York), p22 (York). PC. Great Horton, Bradford 1822 to death (Cheltenham) 16/3/1851 aged 62 [C130868. YCO] Married Great Berkhampstead, Herts. 15/10/1812 Sarah Summers, with issue.

BOGIE (Brackenbury Dickson) Born Halifax, Yorks. 7/5/1803, s. Rev. James Bogie (Wesleyan Minister) and Margaret Dickson. TCD, BA1828, dn28 (Lin.), p28 (Lin.). R. Lusby, Lincs. 1828 to death 25/6/1890. Will not traced [C44089. Al.Dub. Married Spilsby, Lincs. 1/101837 Ann Hubbard, and had issue.

BOHUN, *born* BROWNE (John Francis Browne-) Bapt. Beccles, Suffolk 21/6/1766, s. Le Grice Browne Bohun and Elisabeth Price. Magdalen, Oxford 1774, BA1788, dn88 (Nor.), p90 (Nor.), MA1791. R. Depden, Suffolk 1796-1836, R. Rumburgh, Suffolk 1805-16 (res.). Died London 18/2/1836 aged 70 [C111583] Married Great Yarmouth 1791 Ann Mannoch, w. issue.

BOLDEN, BOLDON (John Satterthwaite) Bapt. Heversham, Westmorland 3/9/1805, s. John Bolden (formerly Lennard) and Mary Satterthwaite. Trinity, Cambridge 1823, BA 1828, dn31 (Chester), p32 (Chester), MA1832. PC. Shireshead, Cockerham, Lancs. 1832-8 [in Australia 1840-7] R. (and patron) of Preston Bissett, Bucks. 1863-73 (res.). Died Bradford Abbas, Dorset 12/3/1892 aged 86, leaving £5,490-6s-1d. [C168338] Married Stockport, Cheshire 27/5/1835 Eliza Andrew (of Compsall, Cheshire), with clerical issue. Also a shorthorn cattle breeder - hence the Australian family venture: adb.anu.edu.au/biography/bolden-john-satterthwaite-1801

BOLDERO (George) Bapt. Ixworth, Suffolk. 8/7/1781, s. George Boldero and Hester

Griffin. Caius, Cambridge 1799, BA1804, dn04 (Nor.), p06 (Nor.), MA1819. PC. Ixworth 1804 to death (Brussels) 17/1/1836 aged 55 [C103260] Married Bocking, Essex 22/4/1830, Amelia Campion, with issue. J.P. Suffolk.

BOLLAND (John Gipps) Born Clapham, London 25/10/1788, s. John Bolland and Elizabeth Gipps. Trinity, Cambridge 1806, BA1811, dn11 (Win.), MA1815, p15 (Salis. for Win.). R. Fetcham, Surrey 1818 to death 21/7/1833 (CCEd says 14/1/1834) [C70807] Married Barnwood, Glos. 18/6/1816 Maria Walters.

BOLLAND (William) Bapt. Leeds 5/10/1785, s. Thomas Bolland and Rebecca Powell. Trinity, Cambridge 1802, BA1806, Fellow 1808, MA 1809, dn11 (Bristol), p11 (Bristol). V. Swineshead, Lincs. 1811 and V. Frampton, Lincs. 1811 (and Min. Waltham Cross Chapel 1833) to death 13/3/1840 aged 54 (he was thrown out of his carriage and landed on his head, *q.v. Gentleman's Magazine*) [C7147] Married (1) Shrewsbury, Shropshire 9/2/1819 Sarah Pritchard (d.1827), w. clerical s. William (2) Llanaber, Merioneth 28/8/1828 Jennet Meredith, w. further issue.

BOLTON (Horatio) Bapt. Hollesley, Suffolk 2/6/1793, s. Rev. William Bolton (R. Bramcaster, Norfolk, below) and Mary Woodthorpe. Caius, Cambridge 1814, BA1818, dn19 (Nor.) p21 (Nor.), MA1823. V. Docking, Norfolk 1829 and V. Ashby w. Oby and Thurne, Norfolk 1829 to death (Thorpe, Norwich) 15/6/1873, leaving £14,000 [total income, £1,318] [C111586. Boase] Married Burnham Westgate, Norfolk 13/11/1832 Elizabeth Mary Blyth, *s.p.* 'An excellent chess problem composer'.

BOLTON (William) Bapt. Coddenham, Suffolk 17/4/1753, s. Samuel Bolton. Trinity, Cambridge 1771, BA1775, dn77 (Peterb. for Nor.), p79 (Nor.), MA1780. V. Holkham, Norfolk 1780-4, R. Hollesley, Suffolk 1783-1829, R. Brancaster, Norfolk 1804 to death 8/3/1840 aged 85 [C109971] Married Little Oakley, Essex 12/12/1776 Mary Woodthorpe, with clerical son Horatio, above.

BONAKER (William Baldwin) From Prussia House, Evesham, Worcs., s. William Bonaker. Wadham, Oxford 1803 (aged 17), BA1807, dn09, MA1810, p10 (Glos.). V. Church Honeybourne w. Cow Honeybourne, Worcs. 1817 to death 1/7/1869 aged 84, leaving £7,000. A notorious non-resident, he was sequestrated in 1847 for negligence, and then reinstated after legal cases in church courts [C120485 has wrong surname] Married Marylebone, London 5/2/1838 Louisa Smith.

BOND (Essex Henry) From Kent, s. Capt. Essex Henry Bond and Mary Young. Queens', Cambridge 1822, BA1826, dn26 (Ely for Win.), p27 (Win.). PC. Merton, Surrey 1827 to death 11/2/1848 aged 52 [C6557] Married Merton 3/11/1835 Mary Rider Boys, with issue.

BOND (Henry) Born Bristol 3/5/1804, s. Canon William Bond and Jane Biggs. Christ's, Cambridge 1824, dn28 (B&W), BCL1829, p29 (B&W), LLB1830. V. ('Treasurer') South Petherton, Som. 1829 (and Prebend in Wells Cathedral 1864) to death 27/9/1875, leaving £18,000 [C41857] Married Cheltenham 4/4/1850 Editha Augusta Mary, dau. Hon. Henry Pomeroy, w. issue.

BOND (John) Bapt. Crediton, Devon 14/11/1780, s. Rev. John Bond, sen. Oriel, Oxford 1789, BA1793, dn93 (Ex.), p94 (Ex.), MA1795. R. Saltfleetby, Lincs. 1802-50 [C171384], PC. Nether Exe, Devon 1813 and R. Romansleigh, Devon 1829 to death 1855 (2nd q.) [C140366. ERC links them]

BOND (John) Born Bathweston, Som. 7/4/1801, s. Rev. William Bond (R. Tyneham, Dorset (below) and Jane Biggs. Wadham, Oxford 1820, BA1824, dn24 (Bristol), p26 (Bristol), MA1828. V. Weston, Bath 1826-81, Prebend of Cudworth in Wells Cathedral 1844-82 (res.), RD of Keynsham 1852 (then of Bath 1864-73), R. Keynsham, Som. 1854-64. Died (Tyneham) 26/1/1898 aged 96, leaving £128,984-2s-6d. [C8187] Clerical son of same name.

BOND (William) Born Steeple, Dorset 10/9/1757, s. John Bond, *M.P.*, and Mary Dummer. Wadham, Oxford 1775, BA1779, dn80 (Ox.), p82 (Ox.), MA1783. R. Steeple w. Tyneham 1795 to death, R. Corfe Castle, Dorset 1800-18 (and Preacher throughout the Diocese), Canon Residentiary of 5th Prebend, Bristol Cathedral 1818. Dom. Chap. to 1st Baron Carrington 1800-28. Died 5/3/1852 [C22917] Married Stockton, Wilts. 23/4/1794 Jane Biggs, with clerical son (above).

BONNER (George) Born Booths Hall, Knutsford, Cheshire 17/3/1785, s. John and Frances Bonner. Emmanuel, Cambridge 1803, dn07 (Car. for York), p08 (Lin.), re-admitted 1816, LLB1821. PC. Cheltenham St James, Glos. 1830 to death 25/6/1840 aged 56 [C44100. YCO]

BONNETT (Charles Shrubsole) Born St James's, Piccadilly, London 26/6/1787, s. Stephen Bonnett (merchant). Sidney, Cambridge 1809, BA1814, dn14 (Nor.), p14 (Nor.), MA1817. R. Avington, Hants. 1820 to death. Dom. Chap. to Duke of Buckingham and Chandos. Died 24/3/1860 aged 73, leaving £1,500 [C70809] Married Westminster, London 28/9/1819 Louisa Joanna Tappenden, with issue.

BONNEY (Henry Kaye) Born Tansor, Northants. 22/5/1780, s. Rev. Henry Kaye (*or* Key) Bonney, sen. (R. King's Cliffe, Northants.) and Bridget Morgan. Emmanuel, Cambridge 1797, BA1802, dn02 (Peterb.), p04 (Peterb.), MA 1805, DD1824. PC. Thurlby 1804-23, Prebend of Nassington in Lincoln Cathedral 1807, V. Nassington w. Yarby, Lincs. 1810-29, (succ. his father as) R. King's Cliffe 1810-62, R. Woodnewton 1813, Archdeacon of Bedford and Canon Residentiary 1821-45 ('indefatigable'), Dean of Stamford 1827, Archdeacon of Lincoln 1845 to death. Dom. Chap. to 10th Earl of Westmoreland 1810, and to Bishop of Bristol / Exeter / Lincoln 1820. Died (King's Cliffe) 24/12/1862, leaving £14,000 [C44101. ODNB. Boase] Married 15/5/1827 Charlotte Perry (of Moor Hall, Essex), *s.p.* Brother, below.

BONNEY (Thomas Kaye) Born Tansor, Northants. 20/6/1782, s. Rev. Henry Kaye (*or* Key) and Bridget Morgan Bonney. Clare, Cambridge 1799, BA1803. dn05 (Peterb.), Fellow 1805-16, MA1806, p07 (Peterb.), MA 1806, p07 (Peterb.), etc. R. Normanton, Rutland 1814-63, R. Coningsby, Lincs. (and Preacher throughout the Diocese of Lincoln) 1815-63, R. Normanton, Rutland 1814-63 (with Prebend of Welton Beckhall in Lincoln Cathedral 1823-63), Archdeacon of Leicester 1831 to death (Normanton, unm.) 7/4/1863 aged 80, leaving £14,000 [C44102. Boase] Brother, above.

BOODLE (Richard) Born Chipping Ongar, Essex 29/8/1778, s. of John Boodle (surgeon) and Susanna Meetkerke. Jesus, Cambridge 1796, BA1800, dn01 (London), p03 (London), MA1803. V. Barkway w. Reed, Herts. 1809-15, V. Totternhoe, Beds. 1813-14, R. Radstock, Som. 1814 and V. Compton Dando, Som. 1818 to death 26/2/1853 [C33131]. Married St George's Hanover Square, London 22/3/1815 Mary Boodle.

BOOKER (Luke) Born Nottingham 20/10/1762, s. of a scholmaster. Literate: dn85 (C&L - no title), p89 (Wor.), LLD by 1805. S/M Dudley Free G/S 1789; R. Tedstone Delamere, Heref. 1805, V. Dudley, Worcs. 1812 to death. Chap. in Ordinary from 1814. Prolific author and poet. Died 1/10/1835 (CCEd thus) [C120480. ODNB] Married (1) West Bromwich, Staffs. 5/1/1796 Anne Blakemore (d.1806), w. issue (2) Worcester 25/6/1811 Phillis Anne Moxam (d.1817), further issue (3) Kinver, Staffs. 3/11/1818 Elizabeth Grant (d.1827), more issue (4) Cheltenham 3/9/ 1829 Elizabeth Barclay, w. clerical s. John Kay Booker. *J.P.*

BOON (Robert) From Northants. St John's, Cambridge 1779, BA1784, MA1787, Fellow 1788-1810, dn91 (Lin.), p92 (Lin.), BD1794, Bursar 1798-1809. R. Sockerston, Leics. 1793 and R. Ufford w. Bainton, Northants. 1808 (and Chap. of Horningsea, Cambs. 1799-1802) to death 3/1844 aged 85 [C44108] Married Stamford, Lincs. 15/8/1815 Mary Edwards.

BOONE (James Shergold) Born Sunbury on Thames, Middx. 30/6/1799, s. Thomas Boone and Rose Ann Shergold. Christ Church, Oxford 1816 [admitted Lincoln's Inn 1819] BA1820, MA1823, dn26 (London), p28 (London). S/M Charterhouse. Min. St John's, Paddington, London 1832 to death 26/3/1859, leaving £10,000 [C116505. ODNB. Boase] Married (1) Totteridge, Herts. 24/4/1824 Ellen Cotterill (d.1840) (2) Paddington, London 11/1/1842 Julia Maria Cox; *s.p.* Brother below. Editor of the *British Critic*; and miscellaneous writer.

BOONE (Thomas Charles) Bapt. Sudbury on Thames, Middx. 1/1/1797, s. Thomas Boone and Rose Ann Shergold. Peterhouse, Cambridge 1818, dn22 (London), p22 (London), BA1823. V. Kensworth, Herts. 1830 to death 23/4/1851 [C44109] Married Paddington, London 11/9/1832 Amy Brown, with issue. Brother above.

BOOTH (Ebenezer) Bapt. Kirkburton, Yorks. 20/4/1772, s. John Booth [*pleb*]. Queen's, Oxford 1790, BA1794, dn94 (York), p96

(Chester). PC. (and patron) of <u>Salford St Stephen</u>, Lancs. 1805-36, Fellow of Manchester Collegiate Church 1832 to death 1844 (3rd q.) aged 72 [C84910. YCO] Married High Hoyland, Yorks. 22/2/1814 Sarah Wood, with issue.

BOOTH (George) Born Masborough House, Rotherham, Yorks. 12/11/1791, s. William Booth and Sarah Key. Trinity, Cambridge 1809, migrated to Lincoln, Oxford 1811, BA1813, dn15 (York), then Magdalen, Fellow 1816-34, MA1816, p16 (Peterb. for York), BD1823, etc. V. <u>Findon</u>, Sussex 1833 to death 21/6/1859 aged 67, leaving £1,500 [ODNB. C61935. YCO] Married Marianne Usborne, w. issue. 'An accomplished Latin scholar and linguist'.

BOOTH (George) Born Richmond, Surrey, s. John Booth. St John's, Cambridge 1826, dn30 (C&L for Ely), BA1831. PC. <u>Atherstone, Mancetter</u>, Warwicks. 1832. Died? [C9500]

BOOTH (Thomas Willingham) Bapt. Ingoldmells, Lincs. 2/3/1806, s. John Booth and Hannah Franklin. BNC, Oxford 1824, BA1828, dn29 (Lin.), p30 (Lin.). V. <u>Friskney</u>, Lincs. 1830 (a family living) (and RD) to death 6/11/1869 aged 63, leaving £3,000 [C44115] Married Sibsey, Lincs. 3/1/1824 Mary Anne Pacey, with clerical son. Online photo. and of wife. *J.P.*

BOOTHBY (Charles) Born Dublin 20/2/1786, s. Major Sir William Boothby, 7th Bart. (Ashbourne Hall, Derbys.) and Rafaela del Gardo. [Capt. of Engineers; lost a leg at Battle of Talavera 1809 (so had a 'cork leg'); prisoner of war in France]. St Mary Hall, Oxford 1815, migrated to Trinity Hall, Cambridge 1815, dn16 (Salis.), p16 (Salis.), BA1819 (Oxon). V. <u>Bleasby</u>, Notts. 1819, V. <u>Sutterton</u>, Lincs. 1819-46, Prebend of Muskham North in Southwell Collegiate Church 1829, R. Poynton, Cheshire 1829-31. Dom. Chap. to 1st Baron Ravensworth 1831. Died Sutterton 19/8/1846 aged 60 [C44886. C. Boothby, *A prisoner of France: the memoirs, diary and correspondence of Charles Boothby, Captain Royal Engineers, during his last campaign* (1898); *Under England's flag from 1804 to 1809: the memoirs [etc.]* Compiled by the last survivors of his family (1900)] Married Algarkirk, Lincs. 24/10/1820 Marianne Catherine Beridge (a clergy dau.), 7 ch. (inc. clerical and military). *J.P.* Holland, Lincs. and Chairman of Quarter Sessions.

BOOTY (William) Born Walsingham, Norfolk 27/10/1750, s. William Booty and Sarah Pettingale. Caius, Cambridge 1769, BA1773, dn73 (London), p75 (London), MA1776. V. <u>Chaddleworth</u>, Berks. 1805 to death. Chap. to HRH Duke of Gloucester. Died (Brimfield, Herts.) 4/12/1840 aged 90. [C91234]

BORASTON (Gregory) Born Wolverley, Worcs. 17/3/1768, s. Rev. William Boraston and Mary Haddock. Queen's, Oxford 1786, BA 1791, dn91 (Wor.), p92 (Wor.), MA1793. R. <u>Broughton Hackett</u>, Worcs. 1794. Buried Claines, Worcs. 18/9/1851 [C120483] Married (1) Walcot, Bath 7/7/1794 Mary Catherine Leslie, w. issue (2) Cheltenham 28/12/1809 Ann Hind.

BORRADAILE (William) Bapt. City of London 10/8/1792, s. William Borradaile and Ann Delapierre. BNC, Oxford 1809, BA1814, dn15 (Cant.), MA1816, p16 (Cant.). V. <u>Wandsworth</u>, London 1823. Buried 23/3/1838 [C70842] Married Donnington, Heref. 17/7/1827 Agnes Sarah Blizard Shaw (a clergy dau.), w. issue.

BORROWS (William) Bapt. Derby 18/11/1781, s. William and Catherine Borrows. St Edmund Hall, Oxford 1808, BA1812, p13 (Ox.), MA1815. PC. <u>Clapham St Paul</u>, Surrey 1815. Died 1852 (2nd q) [C22936]

BORTON (Charles) Bapt. Bury St Edmunds, Suffolk 5/10/1801, s. James Borton (attorney) and Ann Jenks. Caius, Cambridge 1818, BA 1823, dn24 (Nor.), p25 (Nor.), MA1828. V. <u>Wickhambrook</u>, Suffolk 1829-53, V. Hartest w. Boxted, Suffolk 1853-78. Died 11/11/1884 aged 83, leaving £51,160-9s-11d. [C111601] Married Barley, Herts. 6/2/1834 Harriet Blachley, with military issue.

BORTON (John Drew) Bapt. Diss, Norfolk 14/6/1769, s. John Borton (a furrier) and Mary Kerry. Caius, Cambridge 1785, BA1790, Fellow 1790-1805; S/M Pearse School, Cambridge 1791-3; MA1793, dn03 (Lin.), p03 (Lin.). R. <u>Blofield</u>, Norfolk 1804-47, RD, V. <u>Felmingham</u>, Norfolk 1830-4 (res.). Died 9/5/1847 [C44894] Married Beccles, Suffolk 1804 Louisa Carthew (a clergy dau., Woodbridge Abbey, Suffolk), with clerical son of his name.

BOSANQUET (Edwin) Born Marylebone, London 10/12/1799, s. William Bosanquet and

Charlotte Elizabeth Ives. Corpus Christi, Oxford 1819, BA1823, dn24 (London), p25 (London), MA1826, incorporated at Cambridge. R. Ellisfield, Hants. 1830-[48], R. Forscote, Bath 1848-70. Died 30/8/1872 aged 72, leaving £1,500 [C70845] Married 2/8/1831 Eliza Terry (Dumner House, Hants.), with issue.

BOSCAWEN (John Evelyn, Hon.) Born Westminster, London 11/4/1790, s. 3rd Viscount Falmouth and Elizabeth Anne Crewe. Christ Church, Oxford 1808, BA1811, dn13 (Ox.), p14 (Ox.), then All Souls MA1818. R. Wootton, Surrey 1818, Canon of 12th Prebend in Canterbury Cathedral 1822, R. Dunsfold, Surrey 1827, V. Ticehurst, Sussex 1833. Died Wootton 12/5/1851 [C22938] Married 4/5/1814 Catherine Elizabeth Annesley, with issue (incl. 6th Viscount Falmouth).

BOSWELL (Martin) Born London 11/3/1791, s. Bruce Boswell, R.N., and Mary Lindsay. Trinity, Cambridge 1809, then Clare 1811, Fellow 1817, BA1817, dn18 (Ely), p19 (Ely). PC. St George's Chapel, Forest of Bere, Hants. 1831-52, unbeneficed to death (Iver, Bucks.) 14/5/1871, leaving £25,000 [C6561] Married Chatteris, Cambs. 12/6/1823 Dorothea Chatfield, with issue.

BOSWORTH (Joseph) Bapt. Etwall, Derbys. 6/1788, s. Thomas Bosworth. Literate: dn14 (York), p15 (York). Aberdeen University, MA, LLD 1838, migrated to Trinity, Cambridge 1823 (a Ten Year Man: BD1834), DD1839, incorporated at Christ Church, Oxford 1857, PhD (Leyden) 1831. Rawlinson Professor of Anglo-Saxon, Oxford University 1859-76. Compiled the first Anglo-Saxon dictionary, and endowed the Elrington and Bosworth Chairs at Cambridge. V. Little Horwood (or Horwood Parva), Bucks. 1818-33 (res.), V. Waith, Lincs. 1841-58, R. Water Stratford, Bucks. 1858 to death. Chap. at Amsterdam 1829-32 and Rotterdam 1832-40. Died (Oxford 27/5/1876, leaving £14,000 [C44897. ODNB. Boase. YCO] Married (2) Leckhampton, Glos., 8/12/1853 Mrs Anne Margaret (Elliot) Elrington (d.11863) (3) 5/12/1867 Mrs Emily Stonhouse, d.s.p. F.R.S. 1829, F.S.A., etc.

BOUCHER (Henry) Born Salisbury, Wilts. 12/8/1797, s. William Boucher. Wadham, Oxford 1815, BA1819, dn15 (B&W), p17 (B&W), MA1821. V. Hilton, Dorset 1821-38. Died Thornhill House, Sturminster, Dorset 25/10/1880 aged 83, leaving £34,403-8s-2d. [C52108] Married Cheriton, Kent 27/10/1833 Frances Drake Brockman.

BOUCHER (Richard) Bapt. City of London 14/2/1754, s. John Boucher and Elizabeth Torriano (dau. of a baronet). Trinity, Cambridge 1770, BA1775, dn76 (London), MA1778, p78 (Lin.). R. Brightwalthon (o/w Bright Waltham), Berks. 1778, R. East Ilsey, Berks. 1795-1803 (res.). Dom. Chap. to 12th Baron Teynham. Died 9/2/1841 [C44899]

BOUDIER (John, sen.) From Jersey, Channel Islands, s. John Boudier. Pembroke, Oxford 1778 (aged 28), dn80 (Ox.), BA1782. V. Jersey St Ouen/St Owen 1785-95 (deprived), V. Glendon, Northants. 1818 to death (Wellingborough, Northants.) 28/5/1833 [C22951] Married Mary Keysting, with clerical son below.

BOUDIER (John, jun.) Born Wellingborough, Northants. 29/10/1786, s. Rev. John Boudier, sen. (above) and Mary Keysting. Sidney, Cambridge 1805, BA1809, dn09 (Peterb.), p10 (Lin. for Peterb.), MA1814. V. Warwick St Mary 1815-72 (and RD of Warwick), R. Farmington (o/w Thormerton), Glos. 1825-58, Hon. Canon of Worcester Cathedral 1852 to death. Dom. Chap. to 3rd Earl Brooke and Warwick 1816. Died 7/11/1874 aged 88, leaving £7,000 [C44900. Boase] Married 10/6/1816 Marianne Rooke, with issue. Surrogate.

BOULBY (John) Born Aislaby, Whitby, Yorks. 18/4/1802, s. John Boulby and Rebecca Noble. Literate: dn25 (York), p26 (York). PC. Aislaby 1826 (a family living) 1828 to death Jan. 1843 [C130873. YCO] Married Scarborough, Yorks. 16/3/1830 Mary Stonehouse, with clerical son.

BOULTBEE (Charles) Born Baxterley, Warwicks. 31/3/1783, s. Joseph Boultbee and Catherine Dabbs. Literate: dn16 (Salis.), p17 (Salis.), then Trinity, Cambridge 1818, a Ten Year Man. V. Kirdford, Sussex 1819-22, R. Blackborough, Devon 1830-3, R. Bondleigh, Devon 1830-2, R. Baxterley, Warwicks. 1832 to death (Atherstone, Warwicks.) 6/8/1833 (CCEd says 20/2/1834) aged 50 [C9509] Married St George's Hanover Square, London 11/7/1812 Laura, dau. Hon. William Frederick Wyndham, with issue.

BOULTBEE (Richard Moore) Bapt. Rotherby, Leics. 25/5/1794, s. Joseph Boultbee

(Springfield House, Knowle, Warwicks.) and Elizabeth Margaret Alice Moore. Merton, Oxford 1811, BA 1815, dn17 (Ox.), MA1818, p19 (Glos.), BD 1825. V. Elham, Kent 1828-30 (res.), R. Barnwell, Northants. 1829-60. Died Bath 8/4/1874 aged 79, leaving £7,000 [C22952] Married (1) Oxford 19/2/1816 Mary Pegge (d.1844), 7 ch. (2) Walcot, Bath 4/6/1848 his cousin Rosalind Boultbee. Online photo.

BOULTBEE (Thomas) Born Shirburn, Oxon. 25/5/1793, s. Joseph Boultbee (Baxterley, Warwics.) and Sarah Elizabeth Lane. Christ Church, Oxford 1783, BA1787, dn24 (Chester), p25 (Chester). R. (and patron) of Bidford on Avon, Warwicks. 1830-77 and R. (and patron) of Salford Priors, Warwicks. 1830-64-. Died Kings Pyon, Heref. 23/3/1883 aged 89, leaving £452-7s-9d. [C9510] Married Liverpool 7/12/1815 Eliza Pownall, w. clerical son Thomas Pownall Boultbee.

BOULTON (Anthony) Born Hampstead, London 5/6/1788, s. Henry Boulton (barrister, of Cottingham, Northants. - who had married five times) and Susannah Forster. Sidney, Cambridge 1807, BA1811, dn11 (Peterb.), p12 (Peterb.), MA1829, DD1841, then St John's 1844. R. Glendon, Northants. 1814, R. Preston Capes, Northants. 1832-6, R. Sampford Peverell, Devon 1847 (w. Chap. to Tiverton Gaol and House of Correction) to death 23/5/1854 aged 65 [C41862] Married Alphington, Devon 29/6/1819 Harriet Lane (her father-in-law Henry Boulton having married *her* sister!). Photo. online.

BOULTON (George) Born Uppingham, Rutland 12/8/1761, s. Henry Boulton and Mary Preston. Pembroke, Cambridge 1779, BA1783, dn84 (Lin.), p85 (Lin.), MA1787. R. Garthorpe, Leics. 1785-7, R. Oxenden, Northants. 1786-1843, V. Weston Favell, Northants. 1787, R. Preston Capes, Northants. 1828-32, R. Charwelton, Northants. 1832. Chap. to 5th Duke of Dorset 1828-32. Died (Oxenden) 16/8/1843 aged 82 [C44906] Married 8/12/1791 Mary Walker, with issue.

BOURCHIER (Charles Spencer) Born Sandridge, Herts. 22/2/1791, s. Charles Bourchier and Elizabeth Preedy (clerg dau.). St John's, Cambridge 1808, BA1812, dn14 (London), p15 (London), MA1838. V. Sandridge 1823 and R. Great Hallingbury, Essex 1838 to death [total income £1,020]. Dom. Chap. to Earl of Plymouth. Died 22/7/1872 aged 81, leaving £7,000 [C106696] Married St James's. Westminster, London 13/4/1814 Eliza Harman, with issue.

BOURCHIER (Edward) Born Bramfield, Herts. 13/7/1776, s. Rev. Edward Bourchier, sen. and Mary Wollaston. St John's, Cambridge 1793, BA1798, dn99 (Win.), p00 (Win.), MA 1802, incorporated at Oxford 1830. R. Bramfield 1800 to death 28/4/1840 [C44909] Married Holborn, London 7/2/1804 Harriet Jenner (dau. of a barrister), and had issue.

BOURDILLON (Thomas) Bapt. Covent Garden, London 26/7/1772, s. Thomas Jacob Bourdillon and Ann Eastgate. Queens', Cambridge 1789, BA1794, Fellow 1795, dn96 (Ely), MA1797, p97 (Ely). V. Fen Stanton cum Hilton, Hunts. 1802-53 (res.), H/M Macclesfield G/S 1828-9. Died 11/3/1854 aged 89 [C44910] Married Clapham, London 19/4/1802 Anne Ellen Dewar, with issue. Photo. online.

BOUSTEAD see under **BOWSTEAD**

BOUTELL (Charles) Born Tittleshaw, Norfolk 19/9/1771, s. Charles Boutell. Sidney, Cambridge 1795 (no degree?), dn95 (Nor.), p97 (Nor.). R. Repps w. Bastwick, Norfolk 1804-48, R. Litcham w. East Lexham 1848 to death (South Kensington, London) 26/7/1855 aged 83 [C111604] Married Aspal, Suffolk Mary Chevallier 2/4/1838, w. issue (including a clerical son of same name, an authority on monumental brasses).

BOUTFLOWER (Henry Crewe) Born Salford, Lancs. 25/10/1796, s. of John Johnson Boutflower (surgeon) and Harriet Crewe. St John's, Cambridge 1814, BA1819, dn21 (Chester for C&L), p22 (Chester for C&L), MA1822. PC. Little Bolton All Saints, Lancs. 1828-34 (res.), PC. Bury St John's, Lancs. 1832-57 (and H/M Bury School 1823-57 - 'scholarly but ineffective'), R. Elmdon, Warwicks. 1857 to death. Dom. Chap. to Viscount Strathallan. Died West Felton, Shropshire 4/6/1863 aged 66, leaving £800 [C9496. ODNB. Boase] Married Ashbourne, Derbys. 21/6/1825 his cousin Harriet Boutflower, 2s, 4 dau. 'A conscientious clergyman and a good preacher', etc. Asthmatic.

BOUVERIE (Edward) Born Ash, Hunts. 15/8/1782, s. Bartholomew Bouverie, *M.P.*, and

Mary Wyndham Arundell. Christ Church, Oxford 1800, BA1804, MA1806, dn06 (Salis. for Win.), p07 (Win.). V. Coleshill, Berks. 1808 and Prebend of Preston in Salisbury Cathedral 1826 to death. Chap. in Ordinary 1820 to death. Dom. Chap. to 2nd Earl of Radnor 1806-19. Died 22/7/1874, leaving £35,000 [C70868. Boase] Married 20/11/1811 Lady Frances Charlotte Bouverie, w. issue. Brother William Arundell, below.

BOUVERIE (Frederick Pleydell-, Hon.) Born 16/11/1785, s. 2nd Earl of Radnor and Hon Anne Duncombe. Oriel, Oxford 1803, BA1805, p09 (Ox.), then All Souls, MA1810. R. Pewsey, Wilts. 1816, Prebend of Netherbury in Ecclesia in Salisbury 1816, R. Hambledon, Surrey 1823 (only), R. Stanton St Quentin, Wilts. 1823-6 (res.), R. Whippingham, IoW 1826 to death. Dom. Chap. to 3rd Earl of Radnor 1816. Died 6/6/1857 [C22957] Married Thames Ditton, Surrey 1/2/1814 Elizabeth Sullivan (dau. of a baronet), with issue.

BOUVERIE (John) Born London 13/1/1779, s. Edward Bouverie (Delapre Abbey, Northampton) and Harriott Fawkener. St John's, Cambridge 1797, BA1802, dn02 (Win.), p03 (Win.), MA1805. R. Tydd St Mary, Lincs. 1806-55, R. Woolbeding, Sussex (living at Woolbeding House) 1808 (and Prebend of Centum Solidorum in Lincoln 1822) to death (unm.) 9/6/1855 [C44915]

BOUVERIE (William Arundell) Born Marylebone, London 6/2/1797, s. Hon. Bartholomew Bouverie, M.P., and Mary Wyndham Arundell. Christ Church, Oxford 1813, BA1817, then Merton, Fellow, MA1820, dn21 (Ox.), p22 (Ox.), BD1829. R. Hambledon, Surrey 1823, R. West Tytherley, Hants. 1829-39, R. Denton, Norfolk 1839-77, Hon. Canon of Norwich 1847 (and RD of Brooke), Archdeacon of Norfolk 1850-69 [total income £1,013]. Died 22/8/1877, leaving £100,000 [C22958. Boase] Married Blithfield, Staffs. 8/2/1831 Frances Sneyd. Brother Edward, above.

BOUWENS (Theodore) Born Marylebone, London 11/5/1798, s. Jacob Charles Philip Bouwens (a Dutchman) and Margery Rycroft. Merton, Oxford 1817, BA1820, dn22 (Lin.), MA1823, p23 (Lin.). R. Stoke Hammond, Bucks. 1823, Prebend of Brampton in Lincoln Cathedral 1823-69, R. Bedford St Mary, Beds. 1825. Chap. to Bishop of London 1825. Died London 18/2/1869, leaving £35,000 [C44916] Married Camden, London 3/8/1841 Julia Lambert, with issue.

BOWDEN (Henry Joseph) From Fulham, London, s. 'J. Bowden'. Queens', Cambridge 1823, BA1827, dn31 (B&W), p31 (B&W). PC. Chilton Polden, Som. 1831-5, PC. Edington, Som. 1831-5, PC. High Bray, Devon 1835. Became a Catholic priest 1852. Died 18/11/1869. No will traced [C418863] Was also in the Army at some date

BOWDLER (Thomas) Born Hayes, Kent 13/3/1782, s. John Bowdler (and nephew of Thomas Bowdler the elder, *the original bowdleriser or expurgator*) and Harrietta Hanbury. St John's, Cambridge 1798, BA1803, dn03 (London), p04 (London), MA1806. R. Hopton Wafers, Shropshire 1806-20, R. Ridley and Ash, Kent 1811-22, R. Addington, Kent 1821-34, PC. Sydenham St Bartholomew, Kent 1832-43 [new parish not in CCEd], Prebend of St Paul's Cathedral 1849 to death 12/11/1856. Chap. of St Katharine's Hospital [almshouses], Regent's Park, London. Secretary of the Incorporated Church Building Society 1846-56 (which his father had been instrumental in founding). Edited a bowdlerised version of Gibbon's *Decline and Fall of the Roman Empire* [C52. ODNB. Boase. LNCP] Married 22/7/1806 Phoebe Cotton, 9 ch.

BOWEN (Jeremiah) Bapt. Cambridge 20/10/1801, s. Benjamin Bowen and Ann Nightingale. All Souls, Oxford 1821, BA1825, (o/w West Lynn), Norfolk 1830, R. Walton Lewes, Norfolk 1863 to death (Cambridge) 23/9/1875, leaving £1,500 [C9513. Boase] Married (1) Wonersh, Surrey 17/6/1828 Sarah Norton Cole (d.1854), w. issue (2) Southampton 12/6/1856 Sarah Jane Shepherd Mugridge.

BOWEN (John) From Swansea, s. Thomas Bowen. Oriel, Oxford 1767 (aged 20), dn69 (St David's), p71 (Glos.), BA by 1817. Priest-Vicar Wells Cathedral 1776-92, PC. Godney, Som. 1778-1835, V. Bishop's Lydeard, Som. 1780-96 (res.), V. Mudford, Som. 1796-1828, R. Bawdrip, Som. 1828 to death. Minister of Margaret Chapel, Bath, 'where he resided for many years'. Dom. Chap. to 8th Lord Cranstoun 1785. Died 17/9/1835 (CCEd thus) [C141006] J.P.

BOWEN (Thomas) [MA but NiVoF] PC. Temple Guiting w. Cutsdean, Glos. 1810 to death, V. Guiting Power w. Farmcote, Glos. 1835. Died 26/11/1848 aged 79 [C146885]

BOWEN (William Mogg) Born Taunton, Som. 1768, s. Benjamin Bowen. All Souls, Oxford 1774, BA1788, dn90 (Salis.), p92 (Salis.), MA1799, BD & DD1803. H/M St Albans G/S 1803; V. Shipton Bellinger, Hants. 1812. Died St Albans (widower) 12/8/1857 aged 93 [C91237] Married Elizabeth Anne Bovingdon, w. clerical son w. father's name. Oil port. by Danniel Maclise online. *J.P.* Mayor of St Albans 1825.

BOWER (Edward) Born Clifton, Bristol 23/12/1801, s. Rev. Henry Bower (below) and Lucy Smith. Jesus, Cambridge 1820, BA1824, dn25 (B&W), p26 (B&W), MA1828. R. Closworth, Som. 1828 to death 27/12/1874, leaving £14,000 [C41866] Widow Elizabeth Anne.

BOWER (Henry) Born Orchard, Somerset 28/7/1773, s. Thomas Bower and Anne Catherine Napier. Queen's, Oxford 1791, BA 1795, dn96 (Bristol), MA1798, p01 (Salis.). R. Orchard Portman, Som. 1806 [blank in ERC], R. Staple Fitzpaine w. Bickenhall, Som. 1811 [blank in ERC], V. Taunton St Mary Magdalen, Som. 1819 [blank in ERC] to death. Dom. Chap, to 4th Earl of Rosebery 1819. Died ('much loved') 21/1/1840 [C52110] Married Clifton, Bristol 8/7/1800 Lucy Smith, with clerical son (above).

BOWER (John) Bapt. Lostwithiel, Cornwall 27/6/1786, s. James Bower and Elizabeth Eliot. Exeter, Oxford 1804, BA1808, dn09 (Ex.), p12 (Ex.), MA1815. V. (and patron) of Lostwithiel 1816 to death 21/12/1872 aged 86, leaving £16,000 [C140377]

BOWER (John William) Born Welham, Yorks. 22/5/1799, s. of Robert Bower (landowner) and Elizabeth Amy Clubbe. Trinity, Cambridge 1817, BA1822, dn22 (Lin.), p23 (Lin.). R. Barmston, Yorks. 1829 to death 3/4/1859 aged 59, leaving £9,000 [C44935] Married Scorborough, Yorks. 3/9/1828 Eugenia Hall, with issue. *J.P.* East Riding.

BOWER (Joseph) Bapt. Chesterfield, Derbys. 2/3/1774, s. Joseph Bower and Ann Plant. Queen's, Oxford 1792, dn94 (C&L), BA1796, p00 (York). PC. Waverton, Cheshire 1804 to death 21/11/1844 [Note: Revenues from this parish annexed to the Bishop of Chester]

[C9515. YCO] Married Tibshelf, Derbys. 23/11/1808 Elizabeth Chambers, with issue.

BOWERBANK (Thomas, *or* William) Bapt. Mansfield, Notts. 13/3/1803, s. Rev. William Bowerbank (schoolmaster) and Rebecca Carpendale? St John's, Cambridge 1823, dn27 (York), BA1828. R. (and patron) of Salmonby, Lincs. 1827 to death 1840 (4th q. - as William)[C4528 as William. YCO] Confusion: probably two men in CCEd and/or Venn].

BOWERBANK (Thomas Frere) Born St Clement Dane, Westminster, London 11/4/1781, s Rev. Edward and Mary Bowerbank . Queen's, Oxford 1799, BA1802, MA1805. V. ('Lecturer') Chiswick, London 1811 to death 25/12/1856 [C116518] Married (1) Mellow. Wilts. 4/5/1810 Judith Anne Guy (d.1841) (2) Hammersmith, Middx. 4/6/1846 Catherine Jane Bland; *s.p.*

BOWERS (George Hull) Born Staffs. 1794, s. Francis Bowers and Mary Victoria Hull. Literate: dn17 (Lin.), p18 (Lin.), then Clare, Cambridge 1819 (a Ten Year Man, BD 1829), DD1849. PC. Elstow, Beds. 1819-32, R. St Paul, Covent Garden, Westminster, London 1831-48, Dean of Manchester 1847 [income £2,000] to death. Chaplain Bedford House of Correction 1823. Died Leamington Spa, Warwicks. 27/12/1872 aged 78, leaving £7,000 [C44939. ODNB. Boase] Married (1) Biddenham, Beds. 21/9/1826 Harriet Agnes Addington (d.1838), with clerical s. (2) St George's Hanover Square, London 4/7/1854 Isabella Norreys. Co-founder of Marlborough College.

BOWES, *later* FOORD-BOWES (Timothy Fysh) Bapt. Beverley, Yorks. 17/5/1777, s. Canon Barnard Foord and Anne Bowes. Trinity, Cambridge 1794, BA1799, dn99 (London for York), p01 (York), MA1802, DD1835. R. (and patron) of Cowlam, Yorks. 1802-61, R. Oake, Som. 1803 and R. Barton le Clay, Beds. 1820 to death. Chap. in Ordinary 1820 (and Deputy Clerk of the Closet). Died Folkestone, Kent 27/9/1861 aged 84, leaving £6,000 [C40106 as Bowes. YCO] Married York 13/4/ 1803 Juliet Topham.

BOWLBY (Thomas) Born Auckland, Co. Durham 27/9/1762, s. of the Registrar to the Dean and Chapter of Durham. St John's, Cambridge 1780, BA1784, dn85 (Lin. for Durham), p86 (York for Durham), MA1787.

PC. Penshaw, Durham 1798 to death. Dom. Chap. to Catherine, Countess Dowager of Morton 1785. Died 28/1/1835 aged 73 [C44982. YCO] Married Croxdale, Co. Durham 3/3/1786 Eleanora Elizabeth Salvin (Sunderland Bridge House), with issue (some clerical). A fine drawing in D. Cross, *Joseph Bouet's Durham: drawings from the age of reform* (Durham, 2005).

BOWLE (Charles) Bapt. Idmiston, Wilts. 22/8/1769, s. Edward Bowle and Anne Pyle. Queen's, Oxford 1787, BA1791, dn92 (Bristol), p93 (Bristol), MA1794. V. Milborne Port, Som. 1825-35, V. Morden, Dorset 1834-41. Buried Wimborne, Dorset 2/2/1841 [C41868] Married Wimborne 21/12/1792 Sarah Gutch, with issue.

BOWLES (Charles Bradshaw) Bapt. Hull 3/10/1806, s. Humphrey Bowles and Harriet Atkinson. Exeter, Oxford 1825, BA1828, dn30, MA1831, p31 (Nor.). PC. Pirbright, Surrey 1832, V. Woking, Surrey 1837-66, RD of North East Stoke 1850, R. Wisely w. Pyford, Surrey 1866-7. Lived at Tunbridge Wells, Surrey. Dom. Chap. to Catherine, Countess Dowager of Morton 1785. Died Brighton 26/8/1885 aged 78, leaving £7,138-6s-8d. [C70977] Married (1) Willlingale Doe, Essex 9/7/1835 Sophia Deedes (d.1844), with issue (2) Worksop, Notts. 9/6/1846 Mary Charlotte Eyre (dau. of a baronet), with further issue. Lived at Bradshaw Hall, Derbys.

BOWLES, *born* RUSHOUT (George Rushout, Hon.) Born Burford, Oxon. 30/7/1772, s. John Rushout, 1st Baron Northwick and Rebecca Bowles. Christ Church, Oxford 1789, BA1792, then All Souls 1797, Fellow. R. Burford (1st and 3rd Portions) 1799-1834 (res.). Died 17/10/1842 aged 70 [C37715. Foster as Rushout-Bowles] Married 1803 Lady Caroline Stewart (d.1818), dau. of 7th Earl of Galloway, w. issue. Name changed 1817.

BOWLES (William Lisle) Born Kings Sutton, Warwicks. 24/9/1762, s. Rev. William Thomas Bowles and Bridget Grey (a clergy dau.). Trinity, Oxford 1781, BA1786, dn88 (Salis.), MA1792, p92 (Salis.). R. Chicklade, Wilts. 1795-7, V. Dumbleton, Glos. 1797, R. Bremhill w. Foxham and Highway, Wilts. 1804-50, Prebend of Major Pars Altaris in Salisbury 1805 (Canon Residentiary 1826) to death. Dom. Chap. to Bishop of Carlisle and Salisbury; Chap. in Ordinary to Prince Regent. Died 7/4/1850 aged 88 [C91239. ODNB] Married Magdalen Wake (a clergy dau.). A major minor poet:

BOWMAN (Isaac) Bapt. Penrith, Westmorland 14/7/1799, s. of William Bowman (an innkeeper) and Ann Robinson. Literate: dn22 (Chester), p23 (Chester). PC. Formby, Lancs. 1833-47, PC. Holme Cultram, Cumberland 1850, PC. Walton, Carlisle 1854-64-, RD of Brompton. Died (Clifton) 7/11/1876 aged 77, leaving £10,000 [C168352] Lived unmarried in Southport with his unmarried sister.

BOWMAN (John) Bapt. Brantingham, Yorks. s. Rev. Thomas Bowman. Trinity, Cambridge BA1786, dn87 (York), p88 (Bristol for York), MA1789, St John's Fellow 1789. DD. R. Great Poringland 1792-1813 (res.), R. Bixley w. Framlingham Earl >< Norfolk 1813 and PC. ('Chaplain') Norwich St Peter Mancroft 1826 to death 5/7/1848 aged 86 (as John Watson Bowman)[C111608] Identified with the Countess of Huntington's Connection.

BOWMAN (John) Bapt. Whitehaven, Cumberland 14/7/1799, s. of Richard Bowman (a mariner) and Mary Richardson. Literate: dn21 (York), p22 (York). (first) PC. Lathom, Ormskirk, Lancs. 1832-40, PC. Buttershaw, Bradford, Yorks. 1842 to death 14/11/1858, leaving under £100 [C130877. YCO. BBV] Married Birkin, Yorks. 3/1/1832 Hannah Sophia Wood Davison, with issue. Brother below.

BOWMAN (William) Bapt. 2/11/1800, s. Richard Bowman (a mariner) and Mary Richardson. Whitehaven, Cumberland. Literate: dn23 (York), p24 (York). PC. Queenborough, Kent 1826. Died? [C130878. YCO] Had issue. Brother above.

BOWNESS (George) Bapt. Orton, Cumberland 26/5/1778, s. Leonard and Sarah Bowness. Literate: dn01 (Chester), p02 (Chester). R. Rokeby, Yorks. 1823 to death 26/6/1858 aged 80, leaving £7,000 [C168359] Married Orton 1814 Isabella Parker (a clergy dau.), with issue. Another (lay)man in Orton of this name w. confusion.

BOWREMAN (Thomas) Born IoW 8/3/1774, s. Thomas Bowreman and Mary How. [NiVoF] R. (and patron) of Brooke, IoW 1798. Died Ningwood House, IoW 6/1/1844 aged 71 [C70976] Married 1798 Elizabeth Hicks, and issue.

BOWSKILL (William Westfield) Bapt. Warton, Lancs. 20/12/1750, s. Edmund Bowskill. Trinity, Cambridge 1770, BA1775, dn75 (London), p79 (London). V. Mountnessing, Essex 1802-39. Buried 7/5/1839 [C116521] Wife Sarah, and issue.

BOWSTEAD, BOUSTEAD (John) Born Great Salkeld, Cumberland 24/12/1754, s. Thomas Bowstead (a yeoman farmer) and Grace Rebanks. The 'learned and highly respected' S/M Bampton Free G/S, Cumberland 1776 'for 56 years'. Literate: dn77 (Car.), then Jesus, Cambridge, 1779, p81 (Car.), then Peterhouse 1786 (a Ten Year Man, BD 1791). PC. Mardale, Westmorland 1800-30, R. Great Musgrave, Westmorland 1832 (with Prebend of Bobenhull in Lichfield Cathedral 1841 a few days before he died, by his nephew the Bishop of Lichfield) to death 1/11/1841 aged 87 [C4526 has a long MI transcribed. Platt] Married Bampton 7/6/1778 Peggy Mounsey, with clerical son Thomas Stanley (below). Brother Rowland below.

BOWSTEAD (Rowland) Born Great Salkeld, Cumberland 13/9/1766, s. Thomas Bowstead (a yeoman farmer) and Grace Rebanks. Literate: dn95 (Chester), p96 (Chester). Writing Master Lancaster Royal G/S to 1802; PC. Littledale, Lancs. 1798-1843, V. Ulceby, Lincs. 1818 [C170821] Died 27/11/1843 aged 77 [C44995] Married Hawkshead, Lancs. 2/6/1789 Agnes Sawrey. Brother John, above.

BOWSTEAD, BOUSTEAD (Thomas) Born Sedbergh, Yorks. 30/1/1804, s. Thomas and Margaret Boustead. St. John's, Cambridge 1822, BA1827, dn27 (York), p28 (York), MA 1834. PC. Sledmere, Yorks. 1833 and V. Kirby Grindalythe, Yorks. [both entries blank in ERC] 1833 to death (unmarried) 2/8/1867 aged 63, leaving £4,000 [C130875. YCO]

BOWSTEAD (Thomas Stanley) Born Bampton, Westmorland 1787, s. Rev. John Bowstead (above) and Peggy Mounsey. St John's, Cambridge 1807, BA1813, dn14 (Chester), p15 (Chester), MA1816, BD1834, DD1838, incorporated at Oxford 1848. 'Highly successful' H/M Wigan G/S 1813-17; (joint) PC. Liverpool St Philip 1820, V. Tarvin, Cheshire 1842 (and Prebend of Melton Ross w. Scamlesby in Lichfield 1842) to death (Bampton) 28/2/1852 aged 64 [C168361] Married Melbourne, Derbys. 2/10/1821 Caroline Fisher, with issue.

BOWYER (Henry) Born Marylebone, London 9/3/1786, s. Admiral Sir George Bowyer, 1st/5th Bart. and Henrietta Brett. Christ Church, Oxford 1805, BA1809 [M.P. for Abingdon 1809-11], dn12 (Salis.), p12 (Salis.). R. Sunningwell, Berks. 1812 to death. Dom. Chap. to Earl of Rosebery 1819. Died unm. 18/10/1853 [C6572]

BOWYER-SMITH (Edward, Sir, 10th Bart.) see under **SMITH**

BOYCATT, *otherwise* **BOYCOTT (William)** Born Burgh St Peter, Norfolk, s. Rev. William Boycatt, sen. and Anne Smythe. Queen's, Oxford 1814 (aged 16), migrated to Corpus Christi, Cambridge 1815, migrated back to Magdalen, Oxford 1816 (aged 18), BA1820, dn21 (Ox.), p22 (Ox.), MA1822. R. (and patron) of Wheatacre Burgh (o/w Burgh St Peter) 1829 to death (Ormesby St Margaret, Norfolk) 30/10/1871 aged 73, leaving £8,000 [C22978] Married Honingham, Norfolk 25/9/1829 Elizabeth Georgiana Beever, w. clerical s. Arthur William (and also Charles Cunningham Boycott, land agent for Lord Erne in Ireland, from whom the term 'to boycott' derives).

BOYER (John William Robert) Bapt. Loughborough, Leics. 2/1/1775, s. Thomas Boyer and Lucy Charge. Trinity, Cambridge 1792, BA1797, p98 (Lin.). PC. Woodhouse, Leics. 1798-1834, PC. Quorn, Leics. 1798, R. Swepstone w. Sanreston, Leics. 1832 to death 8/10/1843 aged 68 [C9525] Married Morcott, Rutland 1/6/1803 Charlotte Pochin, many ch.

BOYLES (Charles Gower) Born Plymouth, Devon, s. Admiral Charles Boyles and Mary Dorothea Hawker. Exeter, Oxford 1812 (aged 17), BA1816, dn18 (Glos. for Win.), p19 (Salis. for Win.), MA1822. R. Buriton, Hants. (w. Petersfield Chapel, and Preacher throughout the Diocese of Salisbury) 1829 to death 30/5/1845 aged 50 [C70979]

BOYS (Daniel) Born Westminster, London 1/9/1777, s. Thomas Boys ('a gold-wire drawer'). St John's, Cambridge 1795, BA1799, dn03 (B&W), p03 (B&W), MA1810. V. Bendeden, Kent 1805 and V. Brookland, Kent 1810 to death. Dom. Chap. to Earl Tyrconnel 1809. Died Benenden 11/9/1857 aged 80

[C33478] Married Benenden 9/11/1807 Sarah Rider Richardson, with issue.

BOYSE (John) Bapt. Shirvell, Devon 27/4/1770, s. Henry and Ann Boyse. St Mary Hall, Oxford 1789, dn93 (Ex.), p94 (Ex.). R. Culborne (o/w Kitnor), Som. 1821 [blank in ERC], V. Old Cleeve, Som. 1848, Prebend of St Endellion Collegiate Church, Cornwall. Died 1850 (3rd q.) [C33519]

BRACKENBURY (Charles) Born Scremby Hall, Spilbsy, Lincs. 11/12/1783, s. Charles Brackenbury and Anne Caroline Hairby. Jesus, Cambridge 1802, BA1806, dn07 (Lin.), p08 (Lin.). R. Aswarby, Lincs. 1828 and R. (and patron) Wilsford, Lincs. 1831 to death 7/12/1848 [C45008. Kaye] Married Aswarby 1812 his cousin Janetta Brackenbury, w. child. Brother below.

BRACKEBNBURY (Henry) Born Scremby Hall, Spilbsy, Lincs. 11/12/1790, s. Charles Brackenbury and Anne Caroline Hairby. Jesus, Cambridge 1809, BA1813, dn12 (Lin.), p15 (Lin.), MA1816. R. (and patron) Scremby 1816-62, V. Dunholme w. St John's, Newport, Lincs. 1837-49. Died Scremby Hall 14/5/1862, leaving £9,000 [C45009] Married (1) 28/5/1821 Anne Atkinson (Austhorpe Hall, Leeds, d.1858) (2) St George's Hanover Square, London 1859 (4th q.) Julia Charlotte Hare Cropper (Laceby House, Lincs.), with issue. Brother above.

BRACKENBURY (Robert Carr Nichelson) Born Spital, Lincs. 2/9/1803, s. Sir John Macpherson Brackenbury ('Consul for the Province of Andalusia at Cadiz') and Sophia Nichelson. Lincoln, Oxford 1822, BA1826, dn28 (London for Cant.), p29 (Cant.), MA1829. R. Canterbury St Margaret 1828, R. Kirmington and Brocklesby, Lincs. --- . Chap. to Earl of Yarborough 1837; to Duke of Cleveland. Died (Mentone, 'in the Empire of France') 2/2/1863, leaving £3,000 [C116529] Married Swallow, Lincs. 2/3/1848 Anna Maria Holliwell (a clergy dau., who later remarried), s.p.

BRADBURNE (Thomas) Bapt. Lichfield 3/7/1783, s. Samuel Bradburne and Ann Fern. Christ's, Cambridge 1801, BA1805, dn06 (C&L), p07 (C&L), MA1808, Fellow 1810-29. Priest-Vicar and Prebend of High Offley in Lichfield Cathedral 1808-15, R. Toft and Caldecote, Cambs. 1827-40 (sequestrated for non-res., 'this order was rescinded but again reinforced 1842').

Died Wall, Staffs. (a bachelor) 19/12/1859 aged 76, leaving £8,000 [C6568].

BRADDON (John) Born Stowford, Devon 17/2/1755, s. John Braddon and Mary Martin. Exeter, Oxford 1773, BA1777, dn78 (Ex.), p79 (Ex.). PC. Germansweek, Cornwall 1787, PC. Broadwoodwidger, Devon 1787 (and Chap. of the Donative of Werrington 1788) to death 1842 (2nd q.) [C140383] Married at Paul, Cornwall 8/9/1788 [but some say St Paul, Covent Garden, London] Mary Ann Smith, s.p.

BRADFORD (Edward) Probably bapt. Norwich 20/9/1753, s. Miles and Sarah Bradford. Corpus Christi, Cambridge 1770, BA1775, Fellow 1776-98, dn76 (Peterb.), p77 (Ely), MA 1778, BD1786. Private tutor Harrow School 1776-80; V. Babraham, Cambs. 1793, R. Stalbridge, Dorset 1795 to death (London) 2/6/1837, aged 83 [C52116] Married Doulting, Som. 24/4/1802 Sarah Jeffery Paget.

BRADFORD (John) Bapt. Pinhoe, Devon 13/8/1758. Clare, Cambridge 1776, BA1780, dn81 (Ex.), p82 (Ex.). R. Exeter Holy Trinity 1813 to death 21/12/1836 aged 79 [C140385]

BRADFORD (William) Bapt. Doncaster, Yorks. 30/5/1780, s. Thomas Bradford and Elizabeth Otter. St John's, Oxford 1802, BA 1806, MA1809, R. Storrington, Sussex 1811 (and RD) to death. Chap. in Ordinary 1819. Died 1857 (2nd q.) aged 77 [C62030. Boase] Married Clifton, Bristol 17/7/1812 Martha Wilmot, w. issue.

BRADFORD (William Mussage) Bapt. Henley, Oxon. 20/6/1773, s. Henry Bradford [*pleb*] and Sarah Bland. Christ Church, Oxford 1791, BA1795, MA1798, p04 (Lin.). R. Hedsor, Bucks. 1814 to death (Beaconsfield, Bucks.) 19/8/1840 aged 66 [C56055] Married Bodfary, Flintshire 21/9/1803 Mary Wharton, with clerical son, below. *J.P.* Bucks.

BRADFORD (William Mussage Kirkwall) Born Beaconsfield, Bucks. 7/5/1806, s. Rev. William Mussage (above) and Mary Wharton. Magdalen Hall, Oxford 1825, BA1830, dn30 (Lin.), MA1832, p32 (Lin.). R. Hambleden, Bucks. 1832, R. West Meon, Hants. 1844 (and RD) to death. Dom. Chap. to Lord Cranworth. Died Hove, Sussex 10/4/1872 aged 66, leaving £7,000 [C45056] Married Hambleden, Bucks.

1/7/1834 Mary Ridley (w); their military son was created a baronet.

BRADLEY (Charles) Bapt. Halstead, Essex 22/2/ 1789, s. Thomas Bradley and Ann Charlesworth. St Edmund Hall, Oxford 1810, no degree noted, dn12 (London for Salis.), p18 (Lin.). Took pupils 1810-25. V. Glasbury, Brecon 1823-71, PC. Clapham St James, London 1829-55. 'Very eminent as a preacher'. Died (Cheltenham, Glos.) 16/8/1871, leaving £4,000 [C45060. ODNB. Boase. DEB. A.G. Bradley, *Our centenarian grandfather* (1922)] Married (1) 29/12/1809 Catherine Shepherd (d.1831), w. clerical s. Charles (2) 1840 Emma Linton, ch. incl. George Bradley, Dean of Westminster; and Herbert Bradley, moral philosopher.

BRADLEY (Joseph) Born Walpole, Suffolk 28/7/1782. Literate: dn16 (Nor.), p16 (Nor.). R. Halesworth w. Chediston, Suffolk 1831 to death 14/2/1835 [C111616]

BRADLEY (William) Bapt. Lindal, Cartmel, Lancs. 11/5/1760, s. William Bradley. Trinity, Cambridge 1779, BA1783, dn83 (Nor.), p86 (Nor.). V. Rendham, Suffolk 1796-1800, R. Aldeburgh w. Hazelwood, Suffolk (and Preacher throughout the Diocese of Norwich) 1799-1833, V. Friston cum Snape, Suffolk 1818 to death (Woodbridge, Suffolk) 29/10/1833 aged 73 (CCEd says 19/11/1833) [C111618]

BRADLEY (William) From Liverpool, s. John Bradley. BNC, Oxford 1810 (aged 17), BA1814, MA1817, dn17 (Lin.), p19 (Lin.). H/M Atherstone G/S, Warwicks. 1818; PC. Baddesley Ensor, Warwicks. 1819-67, PC. Nether Whitacre, Warwicks. 1826-67 (and Chap. of the Donative of Merevale, Warwicks. 1826, RD of Polesworth. Dom. Chap. to Earl Howe. Died Bath 7/11/1867, leaving £12,000 [C9531] Had issue.

BRADNEY (John Hopkins) Born Blackfriars, London 31/1/1795, s. Joseph Bradney and Elizabeth Hopkins. Trinity, Cambridge 1812, BA1816, dn18 (Salis.), MA1819, p20 (B&W). V. Charlton Adam (o/w East Charlton), Som. 1823-[40]. Lived at Leigh House, Bradford on Avon, Wilts. Died (Bath) 16/3/1861 aged 66, leaving £50,000 [C33529] Married (1) Sidmouth, Devon 10/6/1819 Elizabeth Kekewich (d.1820), 1 dau. (2) York 17/5/1827 Mary Preston (d.1831), 3 ch. (3) 24/5/1832 Mary Boland, with further issue. *J.P.* Wilts and Somerset:

BRADRIDGE (Henry) From Ashprington, Devon, s. Henry Bradridge. Wadham, Oxford 1807 (aged 20), BA1811, MA1814. R. Greatworth, Northants. 1816. Died June 1848 aged 62 [C109980] 'An Inquest was held on the body of the Rev. Henry Bradridge, aged 62 years, residing at Sampson, in Torbryan, who drowned himself at Broadhempston, on Friday last. He had been out of his mind for the last five years, and had been attended by a man who seldom or ever lost sight of him, but on the day named he left his residence unobserved and was found the following day in a quarry-pit with six feet of water; when taken up a rope was round his neck with a large stone attached to it. An Inquest was held on Monday … and the Jury returned a verdict that the deceased drowned himself whilst labouring under insanity'.

BRADSHAW (William) Born Halton, Lancs. 1798, s. William Bradshaw. Lincoln, Oxford 1818, dn22 (Chester), p23 (Chester), no degree. PC. Over Kellet, Bolton le Sands, Lancs. 1825 to death 26/11/1861 aged 65, leaving £3,000 [C168367] Married Over Kellet 16/5/1842 Elizabeth Ewan (w), with issue.

BRADSTOCK (Rowland Thomas) Bapt. Birlingham, Worcs. 21/6/1793, s. Rev. Rowland Bradstock and Elizabeth Collet. University, Oxford 1814, BA1817, MA1820, p29 (Ex.). R. Thelbridge, Devon 1829 to death on or about 3/1/1860, leaving £1,500 [C120500] Married Norton Canes, Staffs. 22/9/1829 Harriet Hawkes (w), w. issue.

BRAGGE (Champness Pleydell) Bapt. Thorncombe, Devon 4/10/1795, s. John Bragge and Hannah Ann Aspden. St Mary Hall, Oxford 1813, migrated to Jesus, Cambridge 1815, dn15 (B&W), p17 (B&W), LLB1820. R. West Chelborough, Dorset 1822-43, R. Walditch, Dorset 1823-39, R. Chilton Cantloe, Som. 1839 to death (all family livings). Died Sadborow House, Thorncombe 26/7/1843 aged 50 [C41876] Brother below.

BRAGGE (John) Bapt. Thorncombe, Devon 10/10/1791, s. John Bragge and Hannah Ann Aspden. Merton, Oxford 1809, migrated to Trinity Hall, Cam-bridge 1811, dn13 (Salis. for Bristol), p14 (B&W), LLB1816. R. (and patron) of (West) Chelborough, Dorset 1821-2, V.

Burstock, Dorset (a family living) 1822-72, V. Thorncombe 1833 (a family living) to death 16/1/1875 aged 85, leaving £3,000 [C41877] Brother above.

BRAHAM, *later* MEADOWS (William Spencer Harris) Born Soho, London 3/5/1802, s. John Braham and Anna Selina Storace. Lincoln, Oxford 1822, BA1826, dn26 (Ely), MA1829. V. Willesborough, Kent 1829, R. Canterbury St George the Martyr and St Mary Magdalen 1840, Minor Canon of Canterbury Cathedral, R. Peldon, Essex [post-1851], V. Chigwell, Essex 1855 (and RD) to death. Dom. Chap. to Earl Waldegrave. Died 2/9/1883, leaving £643-3s-0d. [C6573] Married Edenham, Lincs. 13/10/1839 Martha Burchell Martin (of Godmanchester, Hunts.), with issue.

BRAMSTON (John) Born Roxwell, Essex 12/5/1802, s. Thomas Gardiner Bramston, *M.P.*, and Maria Anne Blaauw. Oriel, Oxford 1820, BA1824, then Exeter, Fellow 1825-30, MA 1826, dn26 (London), BD1827, p27 (London). V. Great Baddow, Essex 1830-40, V. Witham, Essex 1840-64- (lived there), Hon. Canon of Rochester, RD of Witham, Dean of Winchester 1872-83. Chap. to Bishop of St Albans 1872-89. Died 13/11/1889 aged 86, leaving £23,824-16s-8d. [C116535. Boase] Married (1) Marston Bigot, Som. 6/1/1832 Clarissa Sandford Trant (d.1844), their dau. Mary Eliza was a minor novelist; and clerical s. John Trant Bramston (2) Witham 1846 (3rd q.) Anna Hanbury. Port. online.

BRANSON (Henry John) Born Doncaster, Yorks. 26/2/1803, s. John Branson (physician) and Maria Jackson. Caius, Cambridge 1822, dn26 (Lin. for York), BA1827, p27 (York), MA 1830. PC. Doncaster Christ Church 1829-45, R. Armthorpe, Doncaster 1834 to death 1/6/1884 aged 81, leaving £1,238-2s-6d [C9536. YCO] Married Dirleton, East Lothian 10/11/1836 Lucy Mansel, with issue.

BRASIER (John Henry) Born Camberwell, London 16/4/1778, s. John Brasier. Sidney, Cambridge 1796, BA1800, dn01 (Nor. for C&L), p02 (Nor.). PC. Sandhurst, Berks. 1832 to death 30/1/1850 [C9538]

BRASIER (John [Isaac]) From Drayton, Shropshire, s. John Brasier and Sarah Margaret Jervis. Trinity, Cambridge 1800, LLB1806, dn06 (C&L), p08 (C&L). R. Whitmore, Staffs, 1809 and R. North Cleobury, Shropshire (a family living) 1819 [blank in ERC] to death (Ross, Heref.) 11/10/1848 [C9537]

BRASS, *later* BRASSE (John) Bapt. Richmond, Yorks. 26/3/1787, s. George Brass (stonemason and church sexton) and Jane Tutin. Trinity, Cambridge 1807, BA1811, Fellow 1813, dn13 (Bristol), MA1814, p15 (Bristol), BD1824, DD1829. V. Aysgarth, Yorks. 1817-24, V. Stotfold, Beds. 1824 to death (Cheshunt) 26/7/1833 (CCEd thus) [C8149. ODNB as educationalist] Married Richmond 1817 Isabella Milner, with issue. Lame from birth.

BRASSEY (Willoughby) Born Leyton, Essex 23/10/1787, s. Nathaniel Brassey and Mary Lee. Emmanuel, Cambridge 1807, no degree, dn17 (Nor.), p18 (Nor.). R. Belstone, Devon 1828-36. Died Melcombe Regis, Dorset 5/11/1845 aged 58 [C111635] Married Barking, Essex 1816 Anne --. Freemason

BRAY (Edward Atkyns) Bapt. Tavistock, Devon 26/12/1778, s. Edward Bray (solicitor) and Mrs Mary (Brandreth) Turner. Called to the Bar (Middle Temple) 1806. Literate: dn11 (Nor.), p11 (Nor.), then Trinity, Cambridge 1811 (a Ten Year Man: BD1822). V. Tavistock 1812 and PC. Brent Tor, Devon 1812 to death 17/7/1857 [C111636. ODNB as miscellaneous writer and poet. Boase] Married York 26/10/1822 Mrs Anna Eliza (Kempe) Stothard, (novelist, *q.v.* ODNB), *s.p.*

BRAYSHAW (Timothy) Bapt, Idle, Yorks. 20/2/1803, s. James Brayshaw (manufacturer) and Jane Bailey. St John's, Cambridge 1824, BA1828, dn28 (York), p29 (York), MA1831. R. Addingham, Yorks. 1831, PC. Eastwood, Keighley, Yorks. (with S/M Keighley G/S) in 1845 to death 21/9/1853 [C130885.YCO] Married Otley, Yorks. 10/4/1841 Dorothea Brown, with clerical son.

BREAY (John George) Born Plymouth, Devon 9/4/1796, s. John Breay [a Baptist] and Mary Didham. Bapt. Dowles, Shropshire 14/6/1815 in a dissenting chapel. Literate: dn19 (Chester for York), p20 (York). Queens', Cambridge 1825, BA1824. PC. Haddenham, Cambs. 1826, V. Birmingham Christ Church 1832 (and Prebend of Tachbrook in Lichfield Cathedral 1835) to death (Edgbaston, Birmingham from 'overwork') 5/12/1839 aged 43 [C6570. YCO. *Memoir of the Rev. John George Breay ... With a* *selection from his correspondence* (2n edn. 1841)] Married 10/7/1827 Phillis Hariott Peyton, w. issue.

BREE (William Thomas) Born Coleshill, Warwicks. 6/6/1786, s. Rev. William Bree (R. Allesley, Warwicks.) and Elizabeth Mallory. Oriel, Oxford 1804, BA1808, dn10 (C&L), p11 (C&L), MA1816. R. Allesley 1823 to death 25/2/1863, leaving £16,000 [C9544] Married Knowle, Warwicks. 26/2/1822 Helena Maria Boultbee, with clerical son in same place - both keen entomologists.

BREEDON (Henry) Born Bear Court, Pangbourne, Berks. 22/10/1791, s. Rev. John Symonds Breedon and Jane May. Balliol, Oxford 1810, BA1814, dn15 (Glos.), MA1817, p17 (Glos.). R. Pangbourne, Berks. 1817 to death 6/4/1845 aged 53 [C141023] Married Thanet, Kent 28/11/1818 Elizabeth Julia Usborne, w. issue.

BREEKS (John) Bapt. Warcop, Westmorland 12/7/1769, s. John [*pleb*] and Margaret Breeks. Queen's, Oxford 1787, BA1792, dn94 (Ox. for Win.), p95 (C&L for Win.), MA1796. R. Swindon, Glos. 1805-7 (res.), V. Carisbrook (w. Newport Chapel and Northwood. IoW) 1822 to death 1845 (1st q.) [net income £1,123] [C23074]

BRERETON (Charles David) Born Brinton, Norfolk 4/7/1790, s. John Brereton and Anna Margaretta Lloyd. Queens', Cambridge 1808, BA1813, dn13 (Nor.), p14 (Nor.), MA1816. R. Norwich St Edmund 1816, R. Hulcott, Bucks. 1817-19, R. Little Massingham, Norfolk 1820-68, RD of Lynn 1842, R. (and patron) Bixley and Framingham Earl 1848-63. Died Massingham 15/10/1868 [C45297] Married Stowlangtoft, Suffolk 29/6/1819 Frances Wilson (Stowlangtoft Hall, the dau. of a silk merchant), 11 ch. (inc. clerical son of same name). 'Well known as a writer on agricultural questions and the administration of the Poor Law'.

BRERETON (Henry) Born Alton Barnes, Wilts. 1782, s. Rev. John Brereton and Mary Mimms. Queen's, Oxford 1802, BA1806, dn07 (Bristol), p08 (Salis.). R. Haslebury, Dorset 1822. Died Uxbridge, Middx. 2/4/1867, leaving under £200 [C8192] Married (1) St George's Hanover Square, London 19/12/1804 Theresa Elizabeth Cowdery (d.1858), with issue (2) Hackney, London 1/2/1859 Anne Willis, with further issue. Brother below.

BRERETON (Thomas) Born Alton Barnes, Wilts., s. Rev. John Brereton and Mary Mimms. New, Oxford 1805 (aged 19), dn09 (Ox.), BCL 1815, p16 (Ox.). S/M Bedford G/S 1817-32; V. Steeple Morden, Cambs. 1830 to death 7/3/1865 aged 79, leaving £7,000 [C6574] Married Bedford 16/12/1831 Louisa Milbourne Dyson (w), with issue. Brother above.

BRERETON (Thomas [William]) Born Acton, Cheshire 1776, s. Rev. Joseph Brereton. Merton, Oxford 1793, BA1798, dn00 (London), p08 (Nor.). R. Framsden, Suffolk 1812 to death 6/1/1858. Will not traced [C111638. F. as Thomas] Married 15/1/1802 Mary Wayleth, with clerical son.

BRETT (John) Born Essex. Emmanuel, Cambridge 1810, BA1814, dn16 (Salis. for London), MA1817, p17 (London). R. (and patron) of Mount Bures, Essex 1818 to death 16/11/1853 aged 61 [C91402] Had issue.

BRETT (Joseph) Bapt. Norwich 19/6/1774, s. John Brett (wool stapler). Caius, Cambridge 1790, BA1796, dn97 (Nor.), MA1799, p00 (Nor.). PC. Cringleford, Norfolk 1805 and R. Wolferton, Norfolk 1831 to death 13/4/1835 (CCEd thus) [C111641] Married Norwich 27/8/1798 Honor Mary Barton.

BRETT (Joseph George) Born Stockwell, Surrey 1790, s. Joseph George Brett and Isabella Maria Christiana Forbes. Jesus, Cambridge 1812, dn19 (London for Cant.), LLB1820, p20 (Peterb. for Cant.). (first) PC. Hanover Chapel, Regent Street, London 1832 to death (Chelsea, London) 20/5/1852 [C111829] Married Boughton Malherbe, Kent 4/11/1813 Dorothy Best (dau. of an M.P., Chilston Park, Kent), with issue (inc. 1st Viscount Esher).

BREWSTER (John, sen.) Born Newcastle upon Tyne 18/1/1754, s. Rev. Richard Brewster (V. Heighington, Durham) and Isabella Baxter. Lincoln, Oxford 1772, BA1775, dn76 (C&L for Peterb.), MA1778, p78 (Durham). V. Heighington 1791, V. Greatham on Tees, Durham 1791-1818 (res.), V. Stockton on Tees 1799-1805, R. Redmarshall, Durham 1805-9, R. Boldon, Durham 1809-14, R. Egglescliffe, Durham 1814 to death. Dom. Chap. to 8th Viscount Falkland 1785. Died 28/11/1842 aged 89 [C9550. ODNB] Married Stockton 16/6/1791 Frances Robinson (w), with son, below.

BREWSTER (John, jun.) Born Greatham, Durham 26/7/1792, s. Rev. John Brewster, sen. (above) and Frances Robinson. University, Oxford 1810, BA1813, dn15 (Durham), p16 (Durham), MA1816. (succ. his father as) V. Greatham 1818-60 and V. Laughton w. Wildsworth, Gainsborough, Lincs. 1820 to death (Greatham) 17/3/1860, leaving £7,000 [C45550] Married St George's Hanover Square, London 24/5/1821 Elizabeth Lockley.

BRICE (Edward) Born Poole, Dorset, s. Rev. George Tito Brice and Frances Hyde. Wadham, Oxford 1803 (aged 18), BA1806, dn07 (Win. for Bristol), p09 (Salis. for Bristol). Chaplain *R.N.*; R. Thorneyburn, Northumberland 1829-33, PC. Humshaugh, Northumberland 1832-68. Died 1/7/1873 aged 89. Will not traced [C8194. In ERC as Price].

BRICE (Henry Crane) Bapt. Winterbourne, Bristol 22/9/1797, s. of Edward Brice (banker, sugar refiner, and Mayor of Bristol) and Mary Crane. Christ's, Cambridge 1820, dn24 (B&W), BA1825, p25 (Bristol), MA1830. R. Bristol St Peter 1829 to death 4/5/1867 aged 69, leaving £3,000 [C8151] Married Britford, Wilts. 18/10/1827 Martha Maria Augusta Roberts (w).

BRICKENDEN (Francis Hungerford) Bapt. Dynedor, Hereford, s. Rev. Francis and Ann Brickenden. Worcester, Oxford 1793, BA1796, dn97 (Heref.), p98 (Ox.), MA1799, BD1810. PC. Aconbury, Heref. 1820, PC. Dewsall w. Callow, Heref. 1820, R. Winford, Som. 1830. Died Hereford 1838 (1st q.) [C23082] Married Hereford 14/7/1829 Ann Coyle.

BRICKNELL (William Gerard) Born West Meon, Hants. 30/4/1763, s. John Bricknell. Literate: licensed from 1790, then Trinity, Cambridge 1792 (a Ten Year Man). V. Hartley Witney, Hants. 1831 to death 13/6/1844 aged 80 [C70998. Others say Gerald]

BRICKNELL (William Simcox) Bapt. Oxford 19/3/1806, s. Thomas Fox Bricknell and Sarah Simcox. Worcester, Oxford 1822, BA 1827, MA1829, dn29 (Glos.), p30 (Glos.). (first) PC. Grove, Berks. 1836-88, V. Eynsham, Oxon. (a family living) 1845 to death 1888 (2nd q.) aged 82. Will not traced [C141378] Married Salford, Oxon. 16/7/1833 Elizabeth Nash Skillicorne, with issue. A leading anti-Tractarian.

BRIDGE (Bewick) Born Linton, Cambs. 30/3/1767, s. William and Ann Bridge. Peterhouse, Cambridge 1786, BA1790 (Senior Wrangler), dn90 (Ely), Fellow 1792-1833, p92 (Ely), MA1793, BD1811. [Prof. of Mathematics at East India Company's College, Haileybury 1806-16]. V. Cherry Hinton >< Cambs. 1816 to death 15/5/1833 (26/10/1833 in CCEd) aged 66 [C6567. ODNB. *Gentleman's Magazine* is fulsome] *F.R.S.* (1812).

BRIDGEMAN (Henry Edmund, Hon.) Born Dover, Kent 18/10/1795, s. Sir Orlando Bridgeman (later 1st Earl of Bradford), *M.P.*, and Lucy Elizabeth Byng (dau. of 4th Viscount Torrington). Trinity, Cambridge 1814, MA 1817, p20 (Chester). R. Backwell, Som. 1820-3 (res.), R. Marston Bigot, Som. 1820-1 (res.), R. Castle Bromwich, Warwicks. 1821-34 [not noted in CCEd], R. Kingston Deverill, Wilts. 1820-3 (res.), R. Teddington, Middx. 1820-36, R. Blymhill, Staffs. 1823-36. Died (Barnes, Surrey) 15/11/1872, leaving £900 [C9556] Married 25/8/1820 Louisa ElizabethGeorgina Simpson (w), 7 ch.

BRIDGES (Brook George, Sir, 6th Bart.) Born 12/10/1802, s. Sir Brook William Bridges, 4th Bart. (Goodnestone Park, Kent) and Eleanor Foot. Oriel, Oxford 1821, BA1825, dn26 (Peterb.), p27 (Peterb.). R. Orlingbury, Northants. 1827-37, R. Blankney, Lincs. 1854-78. Died 1/4/1890 aged 87, leaving £57,338-14s-4d. [C109984. Boase] Married Marylebone, London 15/11/1832 Louisa Chaplin; 'without legitimate issue'. Assumed title 1875. Related to man below somehow.

BRIDGES (Brook Henry) Born 1/6/1769, s. Sir Brook William Bridges, 3rd Bart. and Fanny Fowler. Christ Church, Oxford 1788, BA1792, dn93 (Ex. for Cant.), p93 (B&W for Cant.), MA 1794. R. Danbury, Essex 1793 and R. Woodham Ferrers, Essex 1795 to death, Prebend of Hendridge in Wells 1800 to death 20/9/1855 aged 86 [C33567] Married 1/7/1795 Jane Hales (dau. of a baronet), with clerical son. Related to man above somehow.

BRIDGES (Charles) Born Northampton 26/3/1794, s. John Bridges (of Maldon, Essex). Queens', Cambridge 1812, dn17 (Nor.), BA 1818, p18 (London), MA1831. R. Old Newton, Suffolk 1823-49, RD 1844-9, R. Melcombe Regis, Dorset 1849-56, R. Hinton Martell, Dorset 1856 to death 2/4/1869 aged 75, leaving

£12,000 [C45554. ODNB. Boase] Married Ipswich 25/4/1851 Harriet Torlesse. Prominent evangelical.

BRIDGES (Nathaniel) From Orlingbury, Northants., s. Rev. Brooke Bridges. University, Oxford 1767 (aged 17), then Magdalen, BA 1770, MA1773, dn78 (Ox.), p78 (Ox.), BD1780, DD1784. R. Wadenhoe, Northants. 1783, V. Willoughby, Warwicks. 1792-1835 [C9557], PC. Hatton, Warwicks. [C120501] 1792 to death. Probate granted 19/9/1834 (CCEd says died 12/3/21835) [C9557. DEB].

BRIDGES (Nathaniel) Bapt. Maldon, Essex 25/3/1789. Queens', Cambridge 1812, BA, dn12 (Nor.), MA by 1813, p13 (Nor.). V. Henstridge, Som. 1813 to death 22/3/1871, leaving £9,000 [C33573] Married 1815 Alicia Jane Enraght.

BRIGGES (Jonathan) From Painswick, Glos., s. Jonathan Brigges. St Mary Hall, Oxford 1771 (aged 23), BCL1794, LLB. R. Stapleford, Herts. 1784, V. Thornborough, Bucks. 1790 and V. Bradwell, Bucks. 1802 to death 24/12/1833 (CCEd thus) [C45556] Married Great Harwood, Bucks. 11/9/1798 Elizabeth Bradbery.

BRIGGS (John) Bapt. Calverton, Bucks. 4/11/1771, s. Rev. John Briggs and Judith Porteous. Admitted Middle Temple 1788. King's, Cambridge 1790, Fellow 1793-1806, dn94 (Lin.), BA1795, p96 (York), MA1798, Fellow of Eton College 1822. R. Methley, Yorks. 1801-5, R. Burstead Parva, Essex 1806-20, V. St Albans St Peter (and Preacher throughout the Diocese of Lincoln) 1820, R. Quainton, Bucks. 1820-2 (res.), R. Southmere, Norfolk 1824-30, R. Creeting St Mary w. St Olave, Suffolk 1829. Dom. Chap. to 3rd Baron Holland 1820. Died Eton College 5/5/1840 [C6569. YCO. LBSO - probably but not certainly] Married St George's Hanover Square, London 15/7/1806 Isabella Ekins (dau. of a Dean of Carlisle), w. issue.

BRIGGS (William Tomkyns) Born London 25/7/1779, s. William Briggs and Amelia Tomkyns. Pembroke, Cambridge 1798, dn02 (Ely), BA1802, p04 (Lin.), MA1805. S/M Merchant Taylors' School 1805-7; V. Thursby, Cumberland 1813-30, Lecturer Carlisle Cathedral and Carlisle St Cuthbert 1813-31, Minor Canon of Carlisle 1823, V. Addingham, Cumberland 1830-4, PC. Hampton Wick, Middx. 1831-4, PC. Putney, Surrey 1834-35

(res.). Sometime Chaplain to Lord Gambier. Died Brighton 12/7/1862 aged 84. Will not traced [C2879. Platt] Wife Anne (married 1818).

BRIGHT (John) Bapt. Houghton le Spring, Co. Durham 14/1/1763, s. John Bright and Elizabeth Stonhewer (a clergy dau.). Pembroke, Cambridge 1780, BA1785, dn85 (Peterb.), MA 1789, p92 (Peterb.). R. Alderton, Northants. 1792-1833, R. Grafton Regis cum Alderton, Northants. 1792 (with Prebend of Coombe and Harnham in Salisbury Cathedral 1826) to death 22/7/1833 (CCEd says 10/9/1833) [C85948] Had issue. Brother, below.

BRIGHT (Thomas Stonhewer) Born Durham 3/2/1766, s. John Bright and Elizabeth Stonhewer (a clergy dau.). St John's, Cambridge 1784, BA1788, dn89 (Ely for Dur.), p90 (Dur.), MA1791. R. Forton, Staffs. 1804 (and Prebend of Carfarchell in St David's Cathedral 1805-20, then of Mathry 1820) to death 29/1/1838 aged 72 [C9559] Brother, above.

BRINDLE (Joseph) Bapt. Warrington, Lancs. 22/4/1798, s. John Brindle and Mary Ann Stoehr. Literate: dn22 (Chester), p22 (Chester). PC. Thelwall, Runcorn, Cheshire 1829 to death 22/10/1868 aged 70, leaving £450 [C168381] Married Standish, Lancs. 28/7/1823 Ann Croston ('under age'), with issue.

BRISCALL (Samuel) Bapt. Stockport, Cheshire 8/4/1778, s. James Briscall and Alice Compton. Brasenose College, Oxford 1797, BA1801, MA1804, dn05 (Ox.), p06 (Ox.), BD1814. Army chaplain in the Peninsula War and as Wellington's personal chaplain 1814 attended the Waterloo Ball. R. South Kelsey, Lincs. 1822. Died 7/10/1848 [C23109]

BRISCO (Joseph) Literate: dn76 (Car.), p77 (Car.). PC. Soulby, Kirkby Stephen, Westmorland 1803-34 and V. Crosby Ravensworth, Westmorland 1810-34, appointed PC Kirkby Stephen but died 21/3/1834 (CCEd thus) [C4543. Platt] Married 1777 Elizabeth Bewsher (aged 19), with issue.

BRISCOE (William Lea) Bapt. Kingswinford, Shropshire 20/4/1760, s. Rev. Benjamin Briscoe and Elizabeth Lea. Worcester, Oxford 1779, BA1783, dn83 (Glos.), MA1792, BCL and DCL 1793. V. Ashton Keynes w. Leigh, Wilts. 1786 to death 16/12/1834 (CCEd thus) [C91409]

BRISTOL (Bishop of) see under **GRAY (Robert)**

BRITTON (James, sen.) Bapt. Dudley, Staffs. 14/8/1759, s. John Britton and Mary Pasmore. Christ Church, Oxford 1777, BA1781, dn83 (Car. for Durham), p83 (Durham), MA1784, BD and DD1819. S/M Durham Cathedral School 1782-1812; V. Bossall, Yorks. 1808 and V. East Acklam, Yorks. 1819-36, V. Great Bardfield, Essex 1829. Died (Clifton, Yorks.) 1/5/1836 aged 77 [C130324. F. as Briton] Married Brancepeth, Durham 2/1/1790 Isabella Mills (dau. of a banker and wine merchant), with clerical son, below.

BRITTON (James, jun.) Born Durham 25/10/1790, s. Rev James Britton, sen. (above) and Isabella Mills. Christ Church, Oxford 1809, dn12 (Chester for York), BA1813, MA 1815, p14 (York). V. Great Bardfield, Essex 1829-40. Died (Great Ouseburn, Yorks) 18/51871 aged 80. Bankrupt 1844. No will traced [C130889. YCO] Married City of London 22/8/1818 Julia Down (dau. of a London banker), and had issue.

BROADLEY (Robert) Born Southwark, Surrey 14/3/1777, s. Peter Broadley and Sarah Wybrands. St John's, Oxford 1794, BA1798. R. Cattistock, Dorset 1805-51, V. Stinsford, Dorset 1820-1 (res.), R. Melbury Stampford, Dorset 1823-9 (res.), R. Bridport, Dorset 1829 to death. Dom. Chap to 3rd Earl of Ilchester 1820. Died 25/4/1851 [C52122] Married before 1807 Anna Maria Hayes, w. issue.

BROCK (Thomas) Probably born Guernsey, Channel Islands, s. Henry Brock and Susan de Saumarez. Pembroke, Oxford 1794 (aged 17), BA1799, MA1801. R. Guernsey St Pierre du Bois 1803 to death 29/12/1850 aged 73 [C71009] Married 23/8/1802 Mary Judith Carey, with clerical son of father's name. Commissary (or official) of Guernsey 1832. Photo. online.

BROCKLEBANK (John) Born Whitbeck, Cumberland s. Rev. John Brocklebank, sen. Literate: dn97 (Chester), p99 (Lin.), then Pembroke, Cambridge 1804 (aged 29), a Ten Year Man, BD 1814 (re-admitted 1817?). PC. Compton Abdale, Glos. 1806-24 (res.), R. Teversham, Cambs. 1817-43, V. Melbourn, Cambs. 1817-24 (res.), R. Willingham, Cambs. 1824 to death (Teversham) 26/5/1843 [C45576] Married Ulverston 1791 Agnes Brade, with son below.

BROCKLEBANK (Robert Brade) Bapt. Whitbeck, Cumberland 23/4/1794, s. Rev. John Brocklebank (above) and Agnes Brade. Trinity, Cambridge 1813, dn17 (Chester), BA1817, p18 (Chester), MA1820. PC. Malpas St Chad, Cheshire 1822 to death (unmarried) 29/6/1859, leaving £5,000 [C168389]

BROCKLEBANK (William) Born Whitbeck, Cumberland 25/12/1771, s. William Brocklebank and Sarah Walker. Literate: dn93 (Car.), p95 (Car.). V. Norton Disney, Lincs. 1799 to death 1851 (4th q.) [C4574] Married (1) Mary Troughton, w. issue (2) by 1825 Elizabeth Piggett, w. further issue.

BROCKMAN (Julius Drake) Born Newington, Kent 24/10/1768, s. Rev. Ralph Drake and Caroline Brockman. Oriel, Oxford 1787 (aged 18), BA1790, dn92 (Cant.), p92 (Cant.). R. Cheriton w. Newington 1793 to death 1849 (3rd q.) [C154766] Married Elmstead, Kent 10/1/1793 Harriet Locke (an Irish clergy dau.), w. son below.

BROCKMAN (Thomas) Born Cheriton, Kent 21/11/1806, s. Rev. Julius Drake Brockman (above) and Harriet Locke. Trinity, Cambridge 1824, BA1828, dn30 (Lin.), p31 (London for Cant.). V. Brenzett, Kent 1831, V. Sandwich, Kent 1831 to death. Chap. to Marquess Camden. Died Wadi Beni Jabor, Muscat 26/7/1846 [C45579] Travelled in Arabia under the auspices of the Royal Geographical Society, keeping diaries and sketch books.

BRODIE (Robert) Born Newcastle upon Tyne 23/9/1790, s. Hugh and Alice Brodie. St Edmund Hall, Oxford 1813, dn17 (B&W), BA 1817, p17 (B&W), MA1821. PC. Mangotsfield, Dorset 1822-59 (and PC. Downend, Dorset 1831 - not in CCEd). Living in Chichester from 1862. Died Clifton, Bristol 23/12/1873, leaving £1,500 [C41883] Wife Anna Marie Lisle, w. issue.

BRODRICK (William John, 7th Viscount Middleton) Born 8/7/1798, s. Rt. Rev. John Brodrick (Archbishop of Cashel) and Mary Woodward. Balliol, Oxford 1816, BA1820, dn22 (Bangor for Cant.), p22 (Win.), MA1823. R. Castle Rising, Norfolk 1825, R. Bath 1839-54, Dean of Exeter 1863-7. Chap. in Ordinary to the Queen 1847. Died 29/8/1870 aged 72, leaving £80,000 [C71014. Boase under Midleton] Married (1) 16/3/1824 Lady

Elizabeth Anne Brudenell (dau. of 6th Earl of Cardigan, she d.1824) (2) 31/3/1829 Harriet Brodrick (w) (dau. of 4th Viscount Middleton); with clerical son. Succ. to title 1863.

BROMBY (John Healey) Born Hull 18/10/1770, s. John Bromby (merchant) and Isabella Mallinson. Sidney, Cambridge 1788, BA1792, Fellow, dn93 (York), MA1795, p97 (London for York). V. (Kingston upon) Hull Holy Trinity 1798-1868 (nearly 70 years; with Master of the Charterhouse [almshouses], Hull 1849) and V. Cheswardine, Shrewsbury 1821 to death (Hull) 25/3/1868 aged 97 (then the oldest clergyman in England), leaving £14,000 [C9595. Boase. YCO] Married Covent Garden, London 4/8/1806 Jane Amis, with clerical son Charles Henry Bromby, first Bishop of Tasmania. Surrogate 1799.

BROMFIELD (Thomas Ross) Born and bapt. Dunchurch, Warwicks. 5/10/1807, s. Rev. Henry Bromfield and Mary Downing. Trinity, Oxford 1785, BA1789, dn90 (C&L), p92 (C&L), MA 1792. V. Napton on the Hill, Warwicks. 1793, V. Grandborough, Warwicks. 1804, Prebend of Basset Parva in Lichfield Cathedral 1823-32, then of Gaia Minor 1832 to death (Boulogne) 2/7/1842 aged 74 [C9598] Married Chislehurst, Kent 7/6/1793 Sarah Belcher, with clerical son Henry Bromfield.

BROMHEAD (Charles French) Born Lincoln 18/5/1795, s. Sir Gonville Bromhead, 1st Bart. and Jane ffrench. Trinity, Cambridge 1812, BA 1816, Fellow 1818, MA1819, dn21 (Ely), p22 (Ely), bursar 1825-8. V. Cardington, Beds. 1829 to death (unm., Worthing, Sussex) 2/8/1855 aged 60 [C6577]

BROMHEAD (Edward) Born Lincoln 30/10/1746, s. Benjamin Bromhead and Margaret Bordman. Corpus Christi, Oxford 1765, no degree, dn68 (Ox. for Salis.), p70 (Peterb.). V. Repham, Lincs. 1771 to death 16/1/1835 aged 88 (CCEd says 25/3/1835), leaving £129,000 [C23113] Married 11/6/1776 Catherine Ayre, 1s, 2 dau.

BROMLEY, *born* DAVENPORT (Walter Davenport) Born London 5/3/1787, s. Davies Davenport, *M.P.*, and Charlotte Sneyd. Christ Church, Oxford 1804 (aged 16), BA1808, dn10 (Ely for Chester), MA1811. V. Ellaston, Staffs. 1811-30 (res.), R. Baginton, Warwicks. 1824 to death 1/1/21862 (living at Wooton Hall, Derbys.) [C10487. Foster under Davenport] Married (1) St George's Hanover Square, London 28/7/1818 Caroline Barbara Gooch (a clergy dau., she d.1827), with issue (including William Bromley Davenport, *M.P.*) (2) St James's Westminster, London 2/2/1829 Lady Louisa Mary Dawson (dau. of 1st Earl of Portarlington). Took additional surname 1822.

BROMWICH (Thomas) Bapt. Pattingham, Staffs. 10/3/1754, s. Rev. John I'Anson Bromwich and Mary Raban. Literate: dn76 (Peterb.), p78 (Chester for Peterb.). V. Wymington, Beds. (non-res.) 1782-1834 (res.). Died (unmarried) Lichfield 20/12/1838 (having 'unhappily' 'lost the use of one side') [C45583] The *Gentleman's Magazine* entry is genealogically exhaustive!

BRONTE, *born* BRUNTY (Patrick) Born Drumballyroney, Co. Down 17/3/1777, eldest of 10 ch. of Hugh Brunty (farm labourer/farmer) and Eleanor / Alice McClory. Ran a school 1793. St John's, Cambridge 1802, BA1806, dn06 (London), p07 (Salis. for London). PC. Hartshead, Yorks. 1811-15, PC. Thornton le Dale, Yorks. 1815-20, V. Haworth, Yorks. 1820 to death 7/6/1861 aged 84 (all his 6 ch. having predeceased him), leaving £1,500 [C91415. ODNB and port. Boase. BBV. J. Lock and W.T. Dixon, *A man of sorrow: the life, letters and times of the Rev. Patrick Bronte* (1965); *The letters of the Rev. Patrick Bronte* / edited D. Green (2005)] Married Guiseley, Yorks. 29/12/1812 Maria Branwell, of Penzance, Cornwall; the parents of the Bronte sisters.

BRONWIN (Brice) Bapt. Pullam, Norfolk 3/9/1786, s. Rev. Brice Bronwin, sen. and Elizabeth Cooper. Literate: dn16 (York), p17 (York). PC. Denby, Penistone, Yorks. 1820-[52]. Died (unm.) Paddington, London 20/11/1869 aged 83, leaving £6,000 [C130891. YCO]

BROOK, *born* SHAW (John Kenwood Shaw) Born Westminster, London, s. John Shaw. Trinity, Oxford 1774 (aged 15), BA1778, then All Souls, Fellow 1782-96, MA1782. R. Eltham, Kent 1783 and R. Hurstpierpoint, Sussex 1815 to death 16/12/1840 [C62282. F. as John Kenward Shaw] Took additional name 1786.

BROOKE (Charles) Bapt. Ufford Place, Woodbridge, Suffolk 21/6/1765. s. Francis Brooke. Pembroke, Cambridge 1783 (aged 18), BA1788, dn88 (Nor.), p90 (Nor.), MA1791. V.

Hoxne w. Denham, Suffolk 1790-4 (res.), R. Bloxhall, Suffolk 1798 and R. Ufford 1803 to death 30/3/1836 [C111656] Married Earl Soham, Suffolk 13/12/1809 Charlotte Capper (a clergy dau.). Claimed the dormant barony of Cobham.

BROOKE (John) Born Haughton Hall, Shifnal, Shropshire 1/3/1803, s. George Brooke. BNC, Oxford 1821, BA1825, dn26 (St Asaph), p27 (C&L), MA1827. V. Shifnal 1831-47. Died 27/1/1881, leaving £18,880-12s-5d. [C9605] Clerical son. Horticulturalist.

BROOKE (Joshua) Bapt. Gamston, Notts. 13/1/1761, s. Rev. Samuel and Mary Brooke. Literate: dn85 (Bristol), p87 (London for York), then Trinity Hall, Cambridge 1788 (a Ten Year Man, BD1798). Master of St Leonard's Hospital [almshouses], Newark on Trent, Notts. 1788-1851; R. Hammeringham w. Scrayfield, Lincs. 1790-1801, V. Colston Bassett, Notts. 1800-34 (and Usher, Newark Free G/S 1803), R. Gamston, Notts. 1812 to death 12/3/1851 aged 90 [C52124.YCO] Married Newark, Notts. 1795 Sarah Bailes, with clerical son. A Liveryman of the Company of Stationers of London 1782.

BROOKE (Thomas) Born Liverpool 8/9/1790, s. James Brooke and Anne Parkinson. Christ's, Cambridge 1811, dn14 (Chester for Lin. *or vice versa?*), BA1815, p15 (Bangor for Chester). PC. Lane End, Stoke, Staffs. 1817-26, PC. Longton, Lancs. 1817-26, PC. Wistaston, Cheshire 1825 to death 25/2/1873 aged 83, leaving under £100 [C9609] Married Nantwich, Cheshire 10/2/1818 Maria Lowe, at least 11 ch. *J.P.* Cheshire. Photo. online.

BROOKE (Zachary) Bapt. Cambridge 24/12/1766, s. Rev. Zachary Brooke, sen. (Lady Margaret Professor of Divinity, *q.v.* ODNB) and Susannah Hanchett. St John's, Cambridge 1783, BA1788, Fellow 1789-1801, MA1791, dn91 (Lin.), p93 (Ely), BD1799. V. Ickleton (o/w Icklington), Cambs. 1793-1802, V. Great Hormead, Herts. 1800 to death. Dom. Chap. in Ordinary 1795. Died 12/4/1842 aged 76 [C45592] Married Cambridge 16/12/1800 Elizabeth Gunning (a clergy dau.), w. issue.

BROOKES, BROOKS (Jonathan) Born Liverpool 1/9/1775, s. Joseph Brookes (brewer). Trinity, Cambridge 1793, BA1798, dn98 (Chester), p99 (Chester), MA1802, incorporated at Trinity, Oxford 1839. R. Liverpool Parish Church (1st Mediety 16/10/1829, then 2nd Mediety 14/11/1829) and Archdeacon of Liverpool 1848 to death 28/9/1855 [C168394. Boase] Married Walton-on-the-Hill, Liverpool 11/3/1805 Anna Maria Heathcote (a clergy dau.), with clerical issue. An active *J.P.* from 1814 and Chairman of Quarter Sessions for many years. A statue of him is in St George's Hall, Liverpool.

BROOKLAND (William James) Born c.1776, s. Rev. William James and Eleanor Brookland. Merton, Oxford 1794, BA1798, dn99 (Salis.), p99 (Salis.). V. Beaminster Chapel, Netherbury, Dorset 1804 to death 8/3/1842, leaving £1,058-6s-0s (probate granted 30/6/1887) [C91473] Married (1) South Wraxall, Wilts. 11/5/1802 Mary Margaret Le Cras (d.1815) (2) Lymington, Hants. 20/11/1819 Eleanor/Ellen Mason (w), w. child.

BROOKS (George William) Born Marylebone, London 28/3/1803, s. John Brooks and Harriet Sophia Egerton. Christ Church, Oxford 1821, BA1825, dn27 (Lin.), p27 (Lin.), MA1857. R. Great Hampden w. Great Kimble, Lincs. 1827. 'Late of Flitwick, Beds.' Died Scarborough, Yorks. 6/7/1871 aged 68, leaving £450. Chap. to Duke of Leeds. [C45596] Married St George's Hanover Square, London 28/8/1832 Jane Mary Shepherd, with issue.

BROOKS (Joshua William) Born Westminster, London 31/10/1789, s. Rev. John Boover Brooks and Martha Watson. Literate: dn19 (York), p20 (York). V. Clarborough, Notts. 1827-43, R. Grove, Notts. 1838-43, V. St Mary, Nottingham 1843-64 (and RD of Nottingham No.3 1854-64), R. Great Ponton, Lincs. 1864 (and Prebendary of Aylesbury in Lincoln Cathedral 1858) to death. Dom. Chap. to Viscount Galway; and to 2nd Baron Fitzgerald and Vesey. Died 15/2/1882 aged 92, leaving £11,145-17s-7d. [C130892. Boase. YCO. Austin2] Married (1) York 26/10/1824 Sarah Fearby, with issue (2) Sandal Magna, Yorks. 1/1/1829 Frances Summerscales, with further issue. Millennialist. Photo. online.

BROOKS (William) From Coventry, s. Samuel Brooks. St John's, Cambridge 1769 (aged 17), BA1775, dn75 (Ox.), p76 (Ox.), MA1779, BD 1784. R. Coventry St John's, Warwicks. 1779 and R. East Farndon, Northants. 1797 to death 14/11/1833 (CCEd thus) [C9614]

BROOKSBANK (Edward Hawke) Born Healaugh Manor, Tadcaster, Yorks. 19/12/1789, s. Benjamin Brooksbank and Philippa Clitheroe. Queens', Cambridge 1809, BA1813, dn13 (York), p14 (York), MA1816. R. (and patron) of Healaugh 1814-63, V. Tickhill, Yorks. 1819-56 (res. on inheriting the Healaugh estate) Died Healaugh 5/8/1883 aged 93, leaving £31,493-16s-7d. [C130893. YCO corrected] Married (1) Wakefield, Yorks. 3/5/1825 Hannah Heywood (d.1846), Stanley Park, Yorks., with issue (2) Tickhill, Yorks. 5/12/1848 Mary Parker, s.p. J.P.

BROOKSBY (Thomas) Bapt. Newark on Trent, Notts. 2/12/1768, s. Samuel Brooksby. Jesus, Cambridge 1787, BA1791, dn92 (York), MA1794. p94 (Nor.). V. Haughey, Suffolk 1798, R. South Hanningfield w. West Hanningfield, Essex 1801 to death 4/11/1842 [C87322. YCO] J.P. Chelmsford, Essex 'for 33 years'.

BROTHERHOOD (William) From Markfield, Leics., s. John and Ann Brotherhood. Magdalene, Cambs. 1787, BA1791, dn93 (Lin.), MA1794. V. Rothwell cum Orton, Northants. 1828 to death 1835 aged 70 [C45599] Married Markfield 6/9/1785 Ann Adnutt (d.1804), with issue.

BROUGHTON (Brian) From Hammersmith, London, s. Charles Broughton. New, Oxford 1785 (age 18), BA1789, dn89 (Ox.), p90 (Ox.), MA1792. PC. Long Ditton, Surrey 1811 to death 8/1/1838 aged 70 [C23128]

BROUGHTON (Clement Francis) Born Betley, Staffs., s. Alexander Day Broughton and Susanna Sneyd. Emmanuel, Cambridge 1823, BA1828, dn28 (C&L), p29 (C&L), MA1832. V. Uttoxeter, Staffs. 1829-54, V. (and patron) of Norbury, Derbys. 1854 to death (Snelston, Derbys.) 16/8/1879 aged 74, leaving £7,000 [C9507] Married (1) Eccleshall, Staffs. 27/6/1843 Annie Louise Sanders (d.1851), with issue (2) St Pancras, London 16/2/1854 Mary Jane Pennell, w. clerical s. Walter Basil.

BROUGHTON (Henry Delves, Sir, 8th Bart.) Born Broughton Hall, Broughton, Staffs. 10/1/1777, s. Rev. Sir Thomas Delves Broughton, 6th Bart. and Mary Wicker. Oriel, Oxford 1794, migrated to Jesus, Cambridge 1799, BA1801, dn02 (C&L), p03 (C&L), MA 1805. PC. (and patron of) Broughton 1803-51, R. Cheadle, Cheshire 1807-29, PC. Haslington, Cheshire 1829-31-. Died Doddington Hall, Cheshire 3/11/1851 aged 74 [C9571. Boase] Married Cheltenham, Glos. 15/6/1807 Mary Pigott (of Bevere, Worcs. and Ireland), 18 ch. (1 clerical). Online portrait. Succeeded 1847.

BROUGHTON (Thomas Delves) Born Lawton, Cheshire 18/2/1801, s. Thomas Delves Broughton and Elizabeth Lester Rowlls Legh. BNC, Oxford 1819, migrated to Trinity, Cambridge 1820, then Downing 1821, BA1821. R. Bletchley, Bucks. 1832 (and RD) to death (Buxton, Derbys.) 10/8/1859, leaving £8,000 [C45605] Married 2/4/1834 Frances Corkran (dau. of a member of the Council of Bombay), 'with legal issue'.

BROWN (Abner William) Born Jamaica 30/9/1800, s. James Brown (of Gattonside House, Roxburgh) and Ann Mellor. Admitted Lincoln's Inn 1817. Literate: dn30 (Peterb.), p31 (Peterb.), then Queens', Cambridge 1836, BA 1831, MA 1846. V. Pytchley, Northants. 1832-51, RD of Weldon, V. Gretton, Northants. (and Hon. Canon of Peterborough) 1851 to death. Surrogate for Peterborough Diocese 1854. Died 15/9/1872 aged 72, leaving £1,859-3s-5d. [C109986. LBSO] Married Old St Pancras, London 30/6/1824 Maria Sarah Dangerfield, with clerical son. Brother James Mellor, below.

BROWN (Charles) Born Tooting, Surrey 21/11/1780. Trinity, Cambridge 1797, BA1802, dn04 (Win.), p04 (Win.), MA1805. R. Whitestone, Devon 1813 to death 31/10/1856 aged 75 [C71019] Married Tooting 14/5/1807 Mary Clarke, with issue.

BROWN (Edward) Bapt. Stamford, Lincs. 13/10/1787, s. Edward Brown. Christ Church, Oxford 1805, BA1809, dn10 (Ox.), Student [Fellow], MA1812, p12 (York). R. Sheering, Essex 1824-43 (res.). Purchased Lyndon Hall, Rutland. Died unm. 17/9/1862, leaving £400,000 [C23607. YCO. LFBI 386]

BROWN (Edward) Born London, s. Edward Brown. Magdalen Hall, Oxford 1815 (aged 19), BA1819, dn19 (Lin.), p20 (Lin.), MA1822. V. Binbrook St Gabriel, Lincs. 1821-[45]. Died? [C45612]

BROWN (James) [NiVoF] V. Osmotherley, Yorks. 1828 to death 10/6/1838 aged 74 [C130238. Venn distinguishes him from a contemporary Cambridge namesake. YCO possible as dn01 and p03?] Left a widow.

BROWN (James) Bapt. Mendham, Suffolk 8/7/1773, s. Crispin Brown and Christiana Cossey. St John's, Cambridge 1792, BA1796, dn97 (Nor.), MA1799, Fellow 1799-1813, p03 (Nor.), BD1806. PC. Norwich St Andrew 1807 and V. Minting, Lincs. 1811 (and Hon. Canon of Norwich 1849) to death. Chap. Norfolk County Gaol 1825. Died 2/10/1856 aged 83 [C45623. Kaye] Married Norwich 23/9/1812 Catherine Anne Landy, with issue.

BROWN (James Humphrey) Bapt. Shotley, Notts. 9/8/1788, s. Rev. Simpson Brown. Literate: dn17 (Durham), p19 (Durham) [CCEd adds MA, so a Ten Year Man]. V. Dalton le Dale, Durham 1832 to death 31/12/1867 aged 79, leaving £4,000 [C130327, CR65 says Joseph] Married Redmarshall, Co. Durham 2/5/1826 Mary Anne Heysham (w) (a clergy dau.), with issue.

BROWN (James Mellor) Bapt. Kingston, Jamaica 14/7/1796, s. James Brown (of Gattonside, Roxburgh) and Ann Mellor. Queens', Cambridge 1825, dn29 (Nor.), p29 (Nor.), BA 1830. PC. Low Ford (o/w South Hylton), Durham 1831-33 [but see also William Chaplin, *supra* 1833-]. R. Isham, Northants 1839 to death 10/2/1867 aged 71, leaving £3,000 [C111668. LBSO] Married (1) Kirby Hill, Yorks. 4/8/1824 Mary Smith, Givendale Grange, Yorks. (2) York 11/5/1831 Elizabeth Helen Newton, Guisborough, Yorks.; 2 clerical son Henry. Brother Abner William Brown, above. As a 'scriptural geologist' he warrants an online entry.

BROWN (Jervase/Gervaise) Bapt. Ashby Folville, Leics. 9/11/1770, s. Richard Brown and Ann Brigg. Magdalene, Cambridge 1792, BA1796, dn96 (Lin.), p97 (Lin.), MA1799. V. Ilkeston, Derbys. 1802-40-, PC. Awsworth, Nuttall, Notts. 1812, R. Fenny Bentley, Derbys. 1821-42 and V. Ashby Folville 1823 to death (Ashbourne, Derbys.) 15/5/1842 aged 71 [C9684] Married Westminster, London 13/10/1827 Sarah Evans.

BROWN (John) From Hartshill, Warwicks., s. William Brown. Trinity, Cambridge 1795, BA 1799, Fellow 1801-48-, MA1802, Tutor 1807-24, Vice-Master 1839-42. R. Bottisham, Cambs. 1828 to death (Sowe, Coventry) 17/8/1850 [C6581]

BROWN, *born* **CAVE (John Cave-)** Born Stretton-en-le-Field, Leics. 20/9/1767, s. John Cave. Pembroke, Cambridge 1785, BA1790, dn90 (C&L), p92 (C&L), MA1793. R. Stretton en le field 1792 to death 23/3/1843 [9578] Married Great Glen, Leics. 1/5/1788 Margaret Haymes. His father inherited the Stretton estates and took the additional surname 1752.

BROWN (John Henry) Bapt. Southwark St Olave, Surrey 9/7/1788. Emmanuel, Cambridge 1806, BA1810, dn12 (Nor.), p12 (Nor.), MA 1814. R. Middleton in Teesdale, Durham 1829 [entry blank in ERC] to death 21/9/1874 aged 86, leaving £6,000 [C111665 has another man in here also. Venn says 'probably' PC. Liverpool St Augustine 1847] Married (1) St James's, Westminster, London 17/7/1817 Henrietta Barber (d. before 1829), with issue (2) Henllam, Denbigh 3/9/1833 Marianne Peel (of Stapenhill, Derbys.), with further issue. Note also an unrelated John Henry Browne, below.

BROWN (Joseph) Born London 26/12/1785. St Andrews University, MA1802, dn07 (S&M), p07 (S&M). Chap. Castletown (with S/M Castletown G/S), IoM 1807-18; V. Kirk Michael, IoM 1818 to death 27/1/1860 aged 74. Will not traced [C7230. Smart is unhelpful. Gelling] Married 1809 Janet Stobs, with issue.

BROWN (Lancelot Robert) Born Hemingford Abbots, Cambs. 1786, s. Rev. Thomas Brown, (R. Conington, Cambs., and s. of 'Capability' Brown the landscape gardener) and Susannah Dickins. St John's, Cambridge 1803, BA1808, dn09 (Nor.), p10 (Nor.), MA1819. R. Kelsale w. Carlton, Suffolk 1810-68, R. Thorington, Suffolk 1821-50, R. Saxmundham, Suffolk [income £1,268] 1826 to death (Torquay, Devon) 11/2/1868 aged 88 [total income £1,268], leaving £9,000 [C111670] Married Beccles, Suffolk 17/3/1809 Anna Maria Sparrow Bence, with issue.

BROWN (Robert) Bapt. IoM 10/2/1792, s. Robert Brown (a Manx sea captain) and Jane Drumgold. Literate: dn16 (S&M). Chaplain Braddan St Matthew, Douglas, IoM 1816-32 (and S/M Douglas G/S 1817-36), V. Braddan 1836 to death ('found dead by the roadside') 28/11/1846 aged 54 [C7231. Gelling] Married 21/4/1819 Dorothy Thompson, 'a Scottish lady living in Douglas', many ch. 'A pronounced evangelical'.

BROWN (Thomas) Bapt. Easingwold, Yorks. 17/7/1759, s. Robert Brown. Literate: dn82 (York), p83 (York). PC. Blacktoft, Pocklington, Yorks. 1785-1839, PC. Seaton Ross, Yorks. 1794. Died 1/3/1839 aged 80 [C87259. YCO]

BROWN (Thomas) Born Kirby Ravensworth, Yorks. 12/5/1748. [NiVoF?] V. Tideswell, Derbys. 1796-[1837]. Died? [C21485] Married Kirby Ravensworth 15/3/1784 Esther Lax, w. clerical son George Best Brown.

BROWN (Thomas) From Gameringham, Lincs., s. Hezekiah Brown. Oriel, Oxford 1797 (aged 18), BA1801, dn01 (Lin.), p03 (Lin.), MA 1804. V. Hackthorne, Lincs. 1813-21 (res.), R. Leadenham, Lincs. 1821 to death (Grantham, Lincs.) 1836 aged 56 [C45957]

BROWN (Thomas) Born London, s. George Brown (surgeon). Pembroke, Cambridge 1819, dn23 (Nor.), BA1824, p24 (Nor.). R. Hemingston, Suffolk 1824 to death 18/11/1884, leaving £661-17s-1d. [C111672] Had issue. J.P.

BROWN (Thomas Woodcock) From Leics. St John's, Cambridge 1817, BA1821, dn22 (Lin.), p23 (Lin.). V. Hornighold, Lincs. 1823 to death (Blaston, Leics.) 24/10/1850 aged 52 [C45959]

BROWN (Walter) Bapt. Newport, Shropshire 12/9/1774, s. Walter Brown [*pleb*]. Christ Church, Oxford 1790, BA1794, MA1797, dn98 (Ox.), p00 (Ox.). R. Bladon w. Woodstock, Oxon. 1801 (only), Canon of Canterbury Cathedral 1805-34, R. Stonesfield, Oxon 1810 and R. All Hallows Lombard Street, City of London 1810 to death 13/1/1834 (CCEd says 3/12/1833) [C23146] Ruskin's tutor at Christ Church.

BROWN (William) From Iffley, Oxon., s. William Brown. Magdalen Hall, Oxford 1779 (aged 18), BA1783, MA1786, dn95 (Lin.), p96 (Lin.), BCL1799. R. Horton, Bucks. 1796. Died? [C45962]

BROWNE (Alexander) Born Rochester, Kent 18/2/1780, s. Rev. Nicholas Browne. Lincoln's Inn 1796. Christ's, Cambridge 1797, then St John's 1800, BA1803, dn03 (Roch. for Cant.), p04 (Roch. for Cant.), MA1807. V. Rodmersham, Kent 1815-46, R. Flempton w. Hengrave, Suffolk 1845 to death. Prison Chap. Chatham dockyards 1806-32? Died 27/7/1851 aged 71 [C1674] Married Lynstead, Kent 18/7/1807 Susanna Fairman.

BROWNE (Arthur) Bapt. Norwich Cathedral 21/1/1798. St John's, Cambridge 1813, BA 1819, Fellow 1821, dn21 (Nor.), MA1822, p22 (Nor.). V. Marham, Norfolk 1827 to death (Brighton) 4/4/1868 aged 70, leaving £3,000 [C111679] Married St Pancras, London 8/7/1840 Henrietta Eliza Daubent.

BROWNE (Charles) Bapt. Thelnetham, Suffolk 5/6/1763, s. Rev. Charles Browne (R. Blo'Norton, Norfolk). Pembroke, Cambridge 1780, BA1785, dn95 (Nor.), p87 (Nor.), MA 1789. PC. Leiston cum Sizewell, Suffolk 1796-1834, (succ. his father as) R. Blo' Norton 1817 to death 4/5/1834 aged 70 (CCEd says 8/8/1834) [C111692] Had issue.

BROWNE, BROWN (Corbet) Bapt. Upton Magna, Shropshire 22/9/1776, s. Rev. Corbet Browne, sen. and Jane Gregory. St John's, Cambridge 1794, BA1798, dn99 (C&L), p01 (C&L). PC. Withington 1801, (succ. his father as) R. Great Upton (or Upton Magna) 1808 to death 17/4/1854 aged 77 [C9575] Married Wem, Shrop-shire 29/7/1799 Sarah Dickin (of Loppington House).

BROWNE (George Adam) Born Gibraltar 26/6/1774, s. Peter Browne. Trinity, Cambridge 1791, BA1795, Fellow 1797, MA1798, dn98 (Peterb.), Bursar 1802-23, p03 (Peterb.), Proctor 1808, Vice-Master 1842. V. Chesterton, Cambs. 1817-36, R. Rettendon, Essex 1838 to death. Chap. to HRH Duke of Sussex. Died 4/7/1843 [C6584] An 'ardent freemason'.

BROWNE (Henry) From Leicester. Lincoln, Oxford 1779 (aged 19), dn82 (Lin.), BA1783, p83 (Lin.), migrated to King's, Cambridge 1820. R. Hoby, Leics. 1784-1838 (succ. his uncle as) R. Aylestone (o/w Elston), Leics. (and Preacher throughout the Diocese of Lincoln) 1820 to death. Dom. Chap. to 5th Earl of Aylesford 1820. Died 16/3/1838 aged 78 [C45969]

BROWNE (Henry) Bapt. Higham, Norfolk 24/6/1804, s. Rev. John Henry Browne. Corpus Christi, Cambridge 1822, BA1826, dn27 (Nor.), MA1830, p31 (Chich.). V. Rudgwick, Sussex 1831-3, R. Earnley 1833-54 (and RD 1838-45), Principal of Chichester Theological College 1842-7 (and Prebend of Waltham in Chichester 1842-70), PC. Chichester St Bartholomew 1850-

4, R. Pevensey, Hants. 1854 [income £1,153] to death. Chap. to Bishop of Chichester 1847-70. Died Titchwell, Norfolk 19/6/1875, leaving £4,000 [C62289. ODNB. Boase]

BROWNE (Henry Albert) Bapt. Holborn, London 11/12/1800, s. William Loder Browne and Katharine Hunter. Queen's, Oxford 1818, BA1822, dn27 (Lin.), p28 (Lin.). R. Newton by Toft, Lincs. [pop. 82] and R. Toft next Newton [pop. 85] 1835 to death 2/10/1883, leaving £1,663-19s-6½. [C45970. Kaye] Married (1) Wraby, Lincs. 1/6/1830 Frances Margaret Micholson (d.1838), w. issue (2) Marylebone, London 22/2/1845 Eliza Anne Blake (d.1866) (3) Westminster, London 5/5/1870 Sarah Alice Casson.

BROWNE (John) Bapt. Ripon, Yorks. 4/6/1769, s. Rev. Richard Browne. St John's, Cambridge 1789, BA1793 ('name off' 1796), dn93 (York), p94 (York). S/M Bakewell G/S, Derbys.; PC. Taddington, Bakewell, Derbys. 1804 and PC. Ashford, Derbys. 1828 to death 1836 aged 60 (CCEd says 20/2/1837) [C21484 but confusion here. YCO]

BROWNE (John Geoffrey) Born 1797, s. Col. Dominick Geoffrey Browne, *M.P.* (of Castle Macgarrett, Co, Mayo) and Margaret Browne. TCD, BA1818, dn22, p22. R. Kiddington (o/w Cuddington), Oxon. 1823 to death 26/19/1877 aged 80, leaving £300 [Not traced in CCEd. Al.Dub.] Married (1) 1823 Anne Elizabeth Lindsay (d.1855), with issue (2) 1867 Emma Hill (w) (a clergy dau.), with further issue. 'Good natured; hot headed; ultra low church' (Wilberforce).

BROWNE (John Henry) Bapt. Norwich 5/9/1767, s. Simon Browne (a schoolmaster) and Anne Loder. Pembroke, Cambridge 1793, dn93 (Nor.), p94 (Nor.). LLB1800. S/M Hingham G/S, Norfolk; V. Runhall, Norfolk 1815 and V. Crownthorpe, Norfolk 1817 to death 1/5/1843 aged 65 [C111688] Married Norwich 17/1/1795 Charlotte Ann Penleaze, w. issue.

BROWNE (John Henry) Bapt. Maidstone, Kent 28/6/1780, s. Samuel Daniel (chemist) and Jane Browne. Pembroke, Cambridge 1798, then St John's 1800, BA1803, dn03 (York), p04 (York), MA1806, Fellow 1808-14. PC. Thrumpton, Notts. 1804-11, R. Weston, Notts. 1811, R. Cotgrave, Notts. 1811-58 and Archdeacon of Ely 1816-58 (and Canon and 6th Prebend of Ely 1817-18). Died Cotgrave 2/11/1858 aged 79, leaving £10,000 [C5032. YCO] Married Willington, Derbys. 9/9/1813 Elizabeth Ward Spilsbury, with clerical son of father's name. Note also an unrelated John Henry Brown, above.

BROWNE, BROWN (John Rowlls) Born London 26/3/1776 , s. of an 'irregular liason' between Rev. John Brown and a Miss Rowlls. St John's, Cambridge 1794, BA1798, dn00 (Win.), p00 (Win. as John Rolls Browne), MA 1802 (as Rowlls, 'his mother's name'). V. Prestbury, Cheshire 1800 to death 29/5/1843 aged 67 [his headstone reads Brown] [C71022 as Brown] Married (as John Rowles Browne) 1810 Frances Anne de Hulton. *J.P.* for Cheshire.

BROWNE (Matthew) [NiVoF] R. Elton on the Hill, Notts. 1803-12 (res.), V. Hinckley, Leics. 1812. Died? [C45976] Married 1814 Mrs Lucy Towers, with issue.

BROWNE (Thomas) From Abbots Bromley, Staffs., s. Rev. Thomas Browne, sen. St Edmund Hall, Oxford 1791 (aged 18), BA1795, MA1798. PC. Coppenhall, Penkridge, Staffs. 1830 to death 3/10/1849 aged 76 [C11127]

BROWNE (Thomas) Bapt. Troutbeck, Westmorland 16/12/1792, s. George Browne and Elizabeth Benson. St Bees admitted 1817, dn17 (York), p20 (York). PC. Carlton in Cleveland, Northallerton, Yorks. 1823-54, PC. Faceby, Stokesley, Yorks. 1823 to death 1866 (1st q.) aged 73. Will not traced [C130900. YCO] Married Normanby, Yorks. 31/8/1822 Mary Jackson, with issue.

BROWNE (Thomas Powell) Bapt. Bradley, Staffs. 27/8/1800, s. Rev. Thomas and Elizabeth Browne. St Edmund Hall, Oxford 1818, BA1823, dn23 (Chester for C&L), p24 (C&L). R. Gratwich, Staffs. 1826 and R. Kingstone, Staffs. 1828. Died 1853 (4th q.) [C9688] Married Bradley 20/10/1828 Sarah Dibble.

BROWNE (William) Bapt. Benhall, Suffolk 31/3/1757, s. Richard Browne. St John's, Cambridge 1777, dn80 (Nor.), BA1784, p84 (Nor.). S/M Framlingham, Suffolk 1784; R. Dallinghoe, Suffolk 1787-1827 (res.), R. Great Glemham and Little Glemham, Suffolk 1826-33,

R. Thetford, Norfolk 1811, R. Marlesford, Suffolk 1823 to death 16/9/1833 [C111696]

BROWNE (William Frederick) Born Westminster, London, s. Rev. Richard Browne. Christ Church, Oxford 1774 (aged 16), BA1778, dn78 (Ox.), MA1781, BD and DD1800. R. Launton, Oxon 1779, Prebend of Wanstrow in Wells Cathedral 1785. Died? [C23154]

BROWNE see also under **BROWN**

BROWNING (Frederick) Bapt. Burnham, Bucks. 6/5/1791, s. Rev. John Browning. King's, Cambridge 1810, Fellow 1813-23, BA 1815, MA1818, dn17 (Ex. for Salis.), p20 (Salis.). Prebend of Uffculme in Salisbury Cathedral 1823 and R. Titchwell, Norfolk 1824 to death (Witham Hall, Bourne, Lincs.) 3/12/1858 aged 66, leaving £450 [C45980] Widow Wilhelmina.

BROWNLOW (William) Born City of London 5/3/1798, s. William Brownlow and Patience Brown. Pembroke, Oxford 1819, BA1822, dn24 (Lin.), p25 (Lin.), MA1826, incorporated at Cambridge MA1852. R. Wilmslow, Cheshire 1829-72 [income £1,150] Died Bath 4/10/1876 aged 75, leaving £9,000 [C45981] Married Bloomsbury, London 9/6/1829 Frances Chambers, with clerical son.

BROWNRIGG (Thomas) Literate: dn91 (Chester), p92 (Chester). PC. Boston Spa, Tadcaster, Yorks. 1818 to death 1849 (2nd q.) [C109996] Married (2?) 1844 (3rd q.) Ann Winterburn (he being aged 76 and she 30).

BRUCE (Courteney Boyle) Bapt. Broome, Norfolk 7/11/1800, s. Rev. Adair Adam Bruce and Martha Porter. Peterhouse, Cambridge 1819, BA1824, dn24 (Nor.), p25 (Nor.). R. South Elmham St James, Norfolk 1828, R. Homersfield, Norfolk 1832. Dom. Chap. to HRH the Duke of York. Died 1854 (4th q.) [C111645] Married Bungay, Suffolk 27/8/1828 Margaret Augusta Kelso (a military dau.), with issue.

BRUCE (James) Peterhouse, Cambridge 1818 (aged 24), no degree, dn22 (Chester). R. Creeksea w. Althorne, Essex 1831 to death (Ipswich) 21/10/1859 aged 80, leaving £1,500 [C116591]

BRUNT (John) Born Biggleswade, Beds. 19/11/1793, s. William Brunt and Sarah Heapy. Peterhouse, Cambridge 1817 (a Ten Year Man), St Bees admitted 1819, dn20 (Glos. [for Chester?]), p21 (Chester). PC. Cleator, Cumberland 1822 to death (The Trumpet House, Whitehaven) 16/9/1844 [C147208] Married Leek 1816 Mary Davenport, with issue.

BRUNTY (Patrick) see under **BRONTE**

BRUNWIN (Martin John) From Bradwell, Essex, s. of Layzell Brunwin and Ann Carter. Corpus Christi, Cambridge 1796, BA1800, dn00 (London), p02 (London). R. Bradwell by Coggeshall, Essex 1813 to death (Park House, Bradwell) 20/11/1839 aged 62 [C116590] Married Buxhall, Suffolk 3/6/1812 Mary Ann Tweed, with clerical son Peter Maxey Brunwin.

BRYAN (Charles) Born Badminton, Glos. 13/10/1784, s. Thomas Bryan. Oriel, Oxford 1802 (aged 17), BA1806, dn07 (Glos.), p08 (Glos.), MA1809. R. South Normanton, Derbys. 1811-19 (res.), R. Woolaston w. Alvington, Glos. 1813 to death, V. Preston, Lydbury, Glos. 1820-53-. Died Bath 17/5/1859, leaving £1,500 [C141745] Married Helston, Cornwall 28/4/1814 Eleanor Kempthorne, w. issue.

BRYAN (George) Bapt. Stoke Dry, Rutland 14/9/1800, s. Thomas and Mary Bryan. St John's, Cambridge 1818, BA1823, dn24 (Lin.), MA1826, p26 (Lin.). PC. Mumby St Leonard's Chapel, Lincs. 1826-79 and V. Huttoft, Lincs. 1833-82. Died (Alford, Lincs.) 16/2/1889 aged 89, leaving £987-0s-10d. [C45986] Married Hogsthorpe, Lincs. 29/3/1830 Lucy Frashney, *s.p.*.

BRYAN (Guy) Bapt. Stepney, London 5/3/1782, s. Guy Bryan and Henrietta Driffield. Peterhouse, Cambridge 1799, BA1803, Fellow 1803, dn07 (Lin. for Ely), MA 1807, p10 (London). R. South Normanton, Derbys. 1811-19, R. Woodham Walter, Essex 1819 to death. Dom. Chap. to 3rd Marquess of Lansdowne 1811 Died (a widower) 22/4/1870 aged 88, leaving £1,500 [C9552] Married Tottenham, London 5/3/1818 Selina Eardley Wilmot (Bruce Castle, Tottenham), with clerical son. F.S.A.

BRYAN (Richard) Born West Down, Devon 9/10/1779, s. Joshua Bryan and Faith Short. Oriel, Oxford 1798, BA1802, dn03 (Ex.), p03 (Ex.), MA1807. V. West Down 1808-45, V. Cheldon, Devon 1831, R. Eggesford, Devon 1819. Chap. to HRH Duke of Kent 1819. Died

West Down 16/5/1845 [C136724] Married South Molton, Devon 7/7/1807 Sarah Hawell, Sarah, and had issue.

BRYANS (Francis) Born Co. Down, s. of Richard Bryans (a Cheshire landowner with land also in Co. Tyrone) and Ann Pillar. TCD 1815 (aged 15), BA1821, migrated to St Edmund Hall, Oxford 1823 (aged 22), dn23 (Chester), MA 1823, p24 (Chester), incorporated at Cambridge 1868. PC. Farndon, Cheshire 1830-38, V. Backford 1838 to death 3/5/1877 aged 76, leaving £4,000 [C168406] Married (1) Walton-on-the-Hill, Liverpool 27/12/1827 Sarah Clough (d.1830), w. ch. (2) Gresford, Denbigh 10/10/1833 Harriette Barker (d.1861), with issue (3) Bonhill, Dunbarton 23/10/1867 Mrs Janetta Frazer (Robertson) Buchanan [photo. of her online]; with clerical son.

BRYDGES (Anthony Egerton-) Born Lee Priory, Kent 16/1/1802, s. Sir Samuel Egerton Brydges, 1st Bart. and Mary Robinson (a clergy dau.). Trinity, Cambridge 1821, BA1827, dn27 (London for Cant.), p27 (London for Cant.), MA1831. R. Denton, Kent 1827-35, PC. Swingfield, Kent 1827-35. Sequestrated for debt and imprisoned in the Fleet Prison (discharged 1840, 'having become a lunatic'). Died 16/5/1849 aged 47 [C116595]

BRYER (Thomas) Literate: p13 (Chester). PC. Marton, Lancs. 1814-43 (and H/M of Baines Endowed School). Probably died Blackpool 4/4/1857 aged 69 [C168407 confuses with Marton, Cheshire] Married Birmingham 4/4/1815 Emma Carless, many ch.

BRYMER (William Thomas Parr) Born Halifax, Nova Scotia 14/11/1795, s. Alexander Brymer (colonial official and rum importer) and Harriot Parr. Trinity, Cambridge 1814, BA1820, dn19 (Chester), p21 (Chester for B&W), MA 1823. R. Charlton Mackrell, Som. 1821, 4th Prebend of Wells 1834 (Residentiary Canon 1840), Archdeacon of Bath 1839, all to death 19/8/1852 [C33612] Married Bathwick, Som. 26/6/1821 Jane Anne Wilkinson. 'Superintended the affairs of the entire Diocese during the incapacity of Bishop Law' (q.v.).

BUCHANAN (Gilbert) Of American parentage. Queens' Cambridge 1783, dn83 (Roch.), p83 (Roch.), LLB 1789, LLD1806. R. Woodmansterne, Surrey 1783 and V. Northfleet, Kent 1796 to death. Dom. Chap. to Hester, Countess of Chatham 1786; Chap. to the London Light Horse Volunteers. Died 31/12/1833 (CCEd says 4/2/1834) [C1679] *J.P.* Surrey and Chairman of the Croydon Bench.

BUCK (Charles) Born Sheerness, Kent 1/1/1796 (bapt. in an Independent chapel), s. Charles and Elizabeth Buck. St Edmund Hall, Oxford 1816, BA1820, p20 (Glos.), MA1826. R. Bristol St Stephen 1830 to death (Durdham Down, Glos.) 28/10/1858, leaving £6,000 [C41919] Married Bristol 8/8/1821 Anne Davis (w).

BUCK (John) Born Hingham, Norfolk 17/7/1757, s. Rev. John Buck. Caius, Cambridge 1774, BA1779, dn79 (Nor.), p81 (Nor.). R. Great Fransham, Norfolk 1791-1834, R. West Newton, Norfolk 1797 and V. Appleton, Norfolk (as sequestrator) 1797 to death 3/7/1834 (CCEd says 12/7/1834) [C222707] Married Hingham, Norfolk 16/10/1787 Elizabeth Jodrell (a clergy dau.).

BUCKINGHAM (James) Born West Buckland, Devon 8/11/1769, s. James Buckingham and Elizabeth Crang. St Mary Hall, Oxford 1788, BA1792, dn92 (C&L for Ex.), p94 (Ex.), BCL and MA1828. V. Burrington, Devon 1814-32 (a family living), R. Doddiscombsleigh, Devon 1828 to death 1856 (2nd q.) [C9703] Married Rose Ash, Devon 1/8/1796 Mary Tanner, and had issue.

BUCKINGHAMSHIRE (Augustus Edward Hobart-Hampden, 6th Earl of) see under HOBART

BUCKLAND (John) From Newton, Devon, s. Rev. William Buckland. Corpus Christi, Oxford 1762 (aged 15), BA1765, MA1769, dn69 (Ox.), p71 (Ox.), Fellow, BD & DD 1778. PC. Warborough, Oxon. 1797 and R. Southwark St George, Surrey 1809 to death (Warborough) 20/4/1837 aged 91 [C23606]

BUCKLAND (John) Born Axminster, Devon 14/7/1785, s. Rev. Charles Buckland and Elizabeth Oke. Trinity, Oxford 1802, BA1806, dn08 (Salis.), MA1809, p13 (Salis.). R. Trusham, Devon 1821 to death (Chertsey, Kent) 24/11/1859 aged 74, leaving £5,000. [C91481] Married Kensington, London 23/7/1816 Frances Arnold, with clerical son. Brother of William, Dean of Westminster, 'the evolutionary geologist', below.

BUCKLAND (William) Born Axminster, Devon 12/3/1784, s. Rev. Charles Buckland and Elizabeth Oke. Corpus Christi, Oxford 1801, BA1805, MA1808, Fellow 1808-25, Waynflete Professor of Mineralogy, Oxford University 1813-56. BD1816, Professor of Geology, Oxford University 1818-56, Christ Church DD1825. R. Stoke Charity, Hants. 1825 [C71027], Canon of 1st Prebend Christ Church Cathedral, Oxford 1825-45 (res.), Dean of Westminster 1845 to death 15/8/1856 [C23261. ODNB. Boase. T. Buckland, *Memoir of the Very Rev. William Buckland, D.D., F.R.S., Dean of Westminster* (1858). Anna B. Gordon, *The life and correspondence of William Buckland, D.D., F.R.S., sometime Dean of Westminster, twice President of the Geological Society, and first President of the British Association* (1894). N. Rupke, *the great chain of history: William Buckland and the English school of geology, 1814-1850* (Oxford, 1983)] Married Abingdon, Oxon. 30/11/1825 Mary Morland (a geologist in her own right), and had issue (including Frank Buckland, 'the practical naturalist', whose many eccentricities included the eating of all and any living creature; as noted in: www.oum.ox.ac.uk/learning/htmls/**buckland**.htm. Brother John (above).

BUCKLE (Robert Bentley) Born Sowerby, Yorks. 6/1/1802, s. Edward Buckle and Frances Bentley. Sidney, Cambridge 1820, BA1824, dn26 (Lin.), MA1827, p28 (Ely). R. Buckland Ripers, Dorset 1831-40, R. Moreton, Dorset 1831-7, Archdeacon of Dorset (and Preacher throughout the Diocese of Bristol) 1836-62, R. Upwey, Dorset 1837-88, Prebendary of Stratton in Salisbury Cathedral 1841 to death (Upwey) 16/9/1893 aged 91, leaving £10,839-19s-1d. [C6590] Married Abbotsbury, Dorset 5/6/1828 Caroline Louisa Barker, with issue.

BUCKLE (Thomas Starling) Born Norwich 2/4/1774, s. John Buckle (ironmonger) and Editha Maria Starling. Caius, Cambridge 1791, BA1796, dn97 (Nor.), p98 (Nor.), MA1800. R. Bramerton, Norfolk 1798-1827, R. Beighton, Norfolk 1827 to death (Hethersett, Norfolk) 16/10/1844 aged 71 [C111717]

BUCKLE (William Lewis) Born Banstead, Surrey, s. Oxon., s. Rev. William Buckle and Grace Stewart. Lincoln, Oxford 1808 (aged 16), BA1811, dn13 (Ox.), p14 (Ox.), MA1815. R. Adwell, Oxon 1817-65, R. Easington, Oxon. 1819-32, R. Shirburn and Pyrton 1823-32, V. (and patron of) Banstead 1832 to death 9/5/1865 aged 74, leaving £7,000 [C23262] Married Holborn, London 18/2/1822 Mary Freeman Manley, with issue.

BUCKLEY (Henry William) Born Marylebone, London 23/3/1800, s. Col. Edward Pery Buckley and Lady Georgiana West (dau. of 2nd Earl de la Warr). BNC, Oxford 1816, BA1820, then Merton, Fellow 1821-32 (Warden 1826), MA1822, dn23 (Ox.), p24 (Ox.). V. Lower Eatington (o/w Ectington), Warwicks. 1831-3, R. Hartshorne, Derbys. 1833 to death 23/11/1892, leaving £1,918-3s-7d. [C9704] Married Sept. 1831 Charlotte Margaret Johnstone, with clerical son.

BUCKLEY (John) Literate: dn88 (Chester), p90 (Chester). PC. Friarmere, Rochdale, Yorks. 1790 to death 14/1/1837 aged 76 (CCEd thus) [C168413]

BUCKOLL (James) Bapt. Brighton, Sussex 23/1/1775, s. Stephen Buckoll and Johanna Howel. Wadham, Oxford 1791, dn97 (Glos.), p99 (Glos.), BCL1800. R. Siddington St Mary, Glos. 1806, V. Great Limber (Limber Magna), Lincs. 1830 to death 12/5/1844 aged 67 (having been thrown from his 'pony phaeton' on 10th April) [C81267] Married Horsham, Sussex 15/7/1801 Sarah Dubbins, w. clerical son.

BUCKSTON(E) (German) Born Bradbourne, Derbys. 9/1797, s. Rev. George Buckston (Bradbourne Hall) and Frances Walhouse. St. John's, Cambridge 1815, BA1820, dn21 (Chester for C&L), p23 (Glos. for C&L). V. Brassington, Derbys. 1824, (succ. his father as) V. (and patron of) Bradbourne w. Ballidon 1827 and V. Sutton on the Hill, Derbys. 1836 to death 17/4/1861, leaving £30,000 (and living in a mansion close to the church) [C9585] Married Doncaster, Yorks. 10/5/1820 Ellen Margaret Ward (a clergy dau.).

BUCKWELL (William) Bapt. Great Badminton, Glos. 27/1/1799, s. John Buckwell and Ann Isaac. Literate: dn26 (York), p27 (York). PC. Longnor, Staffs. 1830-51-, PC. Earl Sterndale, Derbys. 1833-51-, PC. Hartington, Derbys. 1834. Died (Youlgreave, Derbys.) 8/7/1860, leaving £1,500 [C9708, YCO] Married Alstonefield, Derbys. 7/4/1834 Dorothea Blackwall Cantrell (w), and issue.

BUCKWORTH (John) Bapt. Colsterworth, Lincs 17/1/1779, s. of Thomas (a baker - *pleb*) and Alice Buckworth. St Edmund Hall, Oxford 1801, dn04 (Chester for York), BA1805, p05 (York), MA1810. V. Dewsbury, Yorks. 1806 to death 4/5/1835 (CCEd thus) aged 56 [C87108. YCO. I. Clarkson, *Memoir of the Revd John Buckworth, late Vicar of Dewsbury* (1856); S. Slinn, 'Archbishop Harcourt's recruitment of literate clergymen: Part 2', *Yorkshire Archaeological Journal*, 81 (2009)] Married Dewsbury 28/1/1806 Rachel Halliley. A major evangelical and one of the founders of the Elland Clerical Education Society: 'A fine preacher and hymn writer'.

BUDD (Henry) Born Newbury, Berks. 25/9/1774, s. Richard Budd (a London physician) and Mary Stabler. Admitted Lincoln's Inn 1793. St John's, Cambridge 1793, dn97 (Lin.), BA1798, p98 (Salis. for Lin.), incorporated at Oxford 1797. Min. and Chap. of Bridewell Prison Precinct 1801-31 (res.), R. White Roding, Essex 1808 to death 27/6/1853 [C45996. ODNB. Boase. DEB. H. Robinson and T. Harding, *A memoir of the Rev. Henry Budd, MA., comprising an autobiography, letters, papers and remains* (1855)] Married (1) Bridewell Chapel 22/2/1803 Eliza Henrietta Lewin (d.1806) (2) Kensington, London 25/5/1815 Jane Hale Twin (d.1821), with issue (3) Clapham, London 20/10/1829 Jane Waldron (d.1838), with further issue. Evangelical; one of the founders of the Prayer Book and Homily Society 1812. Brother, below.

BUDD (Richard) Born London, s. Rev. Richard Budd, sen. and Mary Stabler. Christ Church, Oxford 17918), then Corpus Christi, BA1795, p99 (Ox.), Fellow, MA1799, BD1807. R. Ruan Lanihorne, Cornwall 1809 to death ('suddenly') 15/9/1850 aged 70 [C23266] Married Veryan, Cornwall 6/5/1813 Harriet Ann Tryst, w. issue.Brother, above.

BUDDICOM (Robert Pedder) Born Liverpool 11/9/1781, s. Robert Josiah Buddicom (surgeon) and Frances Pedder. Pembroke, Cambridge 1801, then Queens' 1803, BA1806, Fellow 1807, dn07 (Peterb.), p08 (Peterb.), MA1809. (first) Chap. St George, Everton, Liverpool 1814-40, V. St Bees and Principal of the Theological College 1840 to death ('suddenly') Great Alne, Warwicks. 2/7/1846 aged 66, 'while visiting a relative' [C110001. T. Park, *St Bees College* (2nd edn. St Bees, 2007) port.] Married West Bromwich, Staffs. 17/5/1814 Ellin Barber, with clerical issue. F.S.A. 'His learning was deep and sound and his classical knowledge extensive'.

BUDWORTH (Philip) From High Laver, Essex, s. Rev. Richard Budworth and Mary Velley. Trinity Hall, Cambridge 1801, then Jesus 1804, dn07 (B&W), p09 (Salis. for London). R. (and patron) of High Laver 1809 to death (a widower, Greensted Hall, Essex) 5/12/1861, leaving £300 [C33618] Married Shelley, Essex 3/8/1812 Elizabeth Darby (a clergy dau.), with issue.

BULL (George Stringer) Born Stanway, Essex 12/7/1799, s. Rev. John Bull (R. Pentlow, Essex) and Margaret Towndrow. [In the Royal Navy 1810-16; and missionary and S/M in Sierra Leone 1818] Literate: dn23 (Chester for York), p24 (York). PC. Bierley (or Byerley), Bradford, Yorks. 1826-39, V. Doddesden, Birmingham 1840-7, R. St Thomas, Birming-ham 1847-64, V. Almeley, Hereford 1864 to death. 'The demagogic Parson Bull, my archbishop', who worked with Richard Oastler to alleviate the lot of factory children. Died 20/8/1865, leaving £2,000 [C130904. ODNB. Boase. YCO. J.C. Gill, *The ten hour parson* (1959), *idem, Parson Bull of Byerley* (1963 and port.)] Married 5/12/1825 Mary Frances Coulson, with issue. Brother William Howie Bull, below.

BULL (Henry) Born Inworth, Essex, s. Rev. John Bull and Catherine Boys. Peterhouse, Cambridge 1791, BA1795, dn96 (London), MA 1798, p98 (London), Fellow 1798. R. Salcott, Essex 1810-12, V. Littlebury, Essex 1813 and V. Salcott Virley 1824 to death. Dom. Chap. to Harriet, Dowager Countess of St Germans 1824. Died 13/3/1840 [C116626] Married Wallington, Herts. 7/10/1817 Elizabeth Oswin Sisson, w. issue. Brothers John, and Nicholas, below.

BULL (Israel) Bapt. Aylesbury, Bucks. 16/10/1767, s. Farmor and Mary Bull. Oriel, Oxford 1789, BA1793, MA1797, dn97 (Lin.), p98 (Lin.). R. Fleet Marston, Bucks. 1832 to death (Dorney, Berks.) 27/12/1851 aged 85 [C45999] Married Aylesbury 28/7/1808 Rebecca Kennedy.

BULL (John) Born Great Yeldham, Essex 2/12/1766, s. Rev. John Bull (R. Pentlow, Essex) and Catherine Boys. Christ's, Cambridge 1785, BA1789, dn89 (London), p90 (London), MA 1892. (succ. his father as) R. Pentlow 1802-

34, R. Tattingstone, Suffolk 1816 to death 24/9/1834 aged 67 (CCEd says 9/10/1834) [C111786] Clerical sons William Howie Bull and George Stringer Bull, here. Brothers Henry (above), and Nicholas (below).

BULL (John) Born Oxford, s. John Bull (surgeon). Christ Church, Oxford 1808 (aged 18), BA1812, MA1814, dn17 (Ox), p18 (Ox.), BD1821, DD1825. PC. Binsey, Oxon. 1820-1, Prebend 1823, then Canon Residentiary Exeter Cathedral 1824, Archdeacon of Cornwall 1826, then of Barnstaple 1826-30, Prebend of Fenton in York Minster 1826-58, Canon of 3rd Prebend, Christ Church Cathedral, Oxford 1830, R. Staverton, Northants. 1830 to death (Oxford) 21/2/1858 aged 68, leaving £80,000 [C23270. Boase]

BULL (Nicholas) Born Pentlow, Essex 10/5/1775, s. Rev. John Bull and Catherine Boys. Trinity, Cambridge 1793, then Christ's 1793, scholar [Fellow], dn97 (London), p99 (London), MA by 1804. V. Ickleton, Cambs. 1803 and V. Saffron Walden, Essex 1804 to death 31/7/1844 aged 68 [C71033] Married Reading, Berks. 13/5/1807 Susanna Tanner, w. clerical s. Alfred Nicholas Bull. Brothers Henry and John, above.

BULL (Samuel Neville) Born London, s. John Thompson Bull and Susanna Woodgate. Literate: dn12 (Peterb.), p12 (Peterb.), MA (a Ten Year Man). V. Dovercourt w. Harwich, Essex 1826 and V. Ramsey, Essex 1827 to death 1855 (4th q.) [C110006.] Married Soho, London 27/12/1799 Frances Comber. Surrogate.

BULL (Thomas) From Carlton, Bucks., s. William Bull [*pleb*]. St Edmund Hall, Oxford 1781 (aged 20), BA1785, dn85 (Lin.), p86 (Lin.). V. Renhold (o/w Raynold), Beds. 1787-97, V. Elveden, Suffolk 1796 to death (Diss, Norfolk) 19/2/1841 [C46004]

BULL (William Howie) Born Stanway, Essex 1796, s. Rev. John Bull (R. Pentlow, Essex, above) and Margaret Towndrow. St John's, Cambridge 1814, BA1819, dn19 (London), p20 (London), MA1825. PC. Sowerby, Yorks, 1827-49, V. Old Newton, Suffolk 1849-60, V. Billinghurst, Sussex 1860-74. Died East Preston, Sussex. 11/1/1888 aged 91, leaving £1,827-13s-8d. [C116630] Married Leighton Buzzard, Beds. 12/10/1825 Sarah Bridges, with issue. Brother George Stringer Bull, above.

BULLEN (Edward) From Barnwell, Cambs., s. Rev. John Bullen. Trinity Hall, Cambridge 1815, SCL1818, dn19 (Lin.), p20 (Lin.). R. Gunby St Peter, Lincs. 1824-30, R. Eastwell, Leics. 1831 to death 21/9/1884, leaving £569-5s-8d. [C46007] Married Stickney, Lincs. 20/3/1826 Jane Batchelor (w), with issue. A sporting parson.

BULLEN (Henry St John's) Born Bury St Edmunds, Suffolk 24/6/1773, s. Henry Bullen and Ann Hockley. Trinity, Cambridge 1790, BA1795, dn96 (Nor.), p97 (Nor.), MA1798. R. Quarrington, Leics. 1801-5; S/M Bury St Edmunds G/S, H/M Leicester Free G/S 1802; R. Tuddenham, Suffolk 1805-17, R. Dunton, Beds. 1817 and R. Wreslingworth, Beds. 1821 to death. Dom. Chap. to 1st Marquess of Bristol 1821. Died 24/8/1836 [C46009] Married Windsor 1800 Sarah Clode.

BULLEN (John) Bapt. Southwark, London 8/3/1793, s. John Bullen and Mary Louisa Hall. St John's, Cambridge 1810, BA1814, dn16 (Salis. for Ely), MA1817, p19 (Ely). R. Bartlow, Cambs. 1828 to death 3/5/1863, leaving £2,000 [C6592]

BULLER (John) Born Morval, Cornwall 22/12/1777, s. Edward and Mary Buller. Corpus Christi/(Bennet Hall), Cambridge 1796, dn00 (Ex.), LLB1802, p02 (London for Ex.). R. St Stephen by Saltash, Cornwall 1803-15, V. Perranzabuloe, Cornwall 1818 and V. St Just in Penwith, Cornwall 1825 to death (Plymouth) 26/10/1846 [C116633] Married Mary Susan Coles (a clergy dau.).

BULLER (Richard) Born Teingrace, Devon 21/12/1804, s. James Buller and Mary Templar. Oriel, Oxford 1822, BA1826, dn28 (Ex.), p29 (B&W), MA1829. R. Lanreath, Cornwall 1829-83 (a family living) to death (Pounds, Devon) 19/6/1883 aged 78, leaving £1,644-13s-9d. [C41923] Married Marylebone, London 12/7/1830 Elizabeth Hornby, with military issue.

BULLER (William Beadon) Born Nether Stowey, Somerset c.1796, s. Robert Beadon Buller and Ann Poole. St John's, Cambridge 1814, BA1818, dn19 (B&W), p20 (B&W), MA1821. V. ('Treasurer') Over Stowey 1820 and V. Middlezoy, Som. 1822 to burial 1/1/1856 [C33622] Married Bath 6/4/1831 Mary Anne Jane Sheppard.

BULLIVANT (Henry) From Marston Trussel, Northants., s. Rev. John Bullivant. St John's, Cambridge 1803, then Jesus 1804, LLB1809, dn08 (Lin. for Peterb.), p09 (Lin. for Peterb.). (succ. his father as) R. Marston Trussel 1809 and V. Lubbenham, Leics. 1812 to death 6/7/1842 aged 57 [C46012] Married Croyland (or Crowland) Abbey, Lincs. 27/5/1814 Frances Everard (Leasingham, Lincs.), with issue.

BULLOCK (Charles Penry) Born Bristol, s. Charles Penry Bullock and Catherine Morgan. Queen's, Oxford 1799 (aged 22), BA1803, dn03 (B&W), MA1806, p07 (Bristol). PC. Bristol St Paul 1822-[49]. Buried 11/9/1849 [C8200] Married Bedminster, Som. 10/2/1804 Ann Willoughby, with issue.

BULLOCK (Edward) From Drayton, Cambs., s. Rev. Richard Bullock (R. St Paul's, Covent Garden, London). Christ Church, Oxford 1792 (aged 17), BA1796, then Oriel MA1798, dn99 (Ox.), p00 (Ox.). R. Belleau, Lincs. 1819, R. Fontmell Magna, Dorset 1812-19, PC. Spilsby, Lincs. 1812-13, R. Hambledon, Surrey 1833 to death 11/1/1850, *s.p.* [C23273. Bennett2]

BULLOCK (James) Bapt. Hereford 29/11/1794, s. Rev. James, sen. and Jane Bullock. BNC, Oxford 1814, BA1817, dn17 (Ox.), p18 (Ox.), MA1820. PC. Grendon (Bishop), Heref. 1823-30 (res.). Died? [C23275]

BULLOCK, born WATSON (John) Born Virginia, USA 1775, s. Jonathan Josiah Christopher Watson (of Middlesex). Clare, Cambridge 1794, BA1798, dn98 (Ex. for Nor: as Watson), p99 (Nor. as Watson), MA1801, Fellow 1802-6. R. Radwinter, Essex 1806 and R. Faulkbourn, Essex 1818 (and RD) to death 12/8/1844 aged 70 [C116022] Married Dedham, Essex 1806 Mary Roberts Watkinson, with issue. Name changed 1810.

BULLOCK (Thomas) From Shepperton, Middx., s. Henry Bullock. St Edmund Hall, Oxford 1820 (aged 20), dn23 (Salis.), p24 (Salis.), then St Alban Hall, BA1830. R. Castle Eaton, Wilts. 1828-46, R. Chisledon, Wilts. 1830 to death. Dom. Chap. to 16th Earl of Suffolk. Died 29/10/1846 aged 48 [C91483] Married Marlborough, Wilts. 3/7/1828 Ellen Maurice, w. issue.

BULMER (Edward) Born Hereford, c.1793. St John's, Cambridge 1815, BA1819, dn19 (Glos. for Heref.), p20 (Heref.), MA1822. Vicar Choral and Minor Canon, Hereford Cathedral 1820 [income £19], R. Putley, Heref. 1825, R. Moreton on Lugg, Heref. [pop. 77] 1839 to death (Holmer, Heref.) 22/1/1875 aged 82, leaving £25,000 [C103896] Married Hereford 31/5/1831 Isabella Susanna Whitfield, with issue.

BULMER (Peter) Bapt. York 3/4/1757, s. George Bulmer (silk weaver) and Sarah Heron. Jesus, Cambridge 1777, dn79 (York), BA1781, p81 (Lin. for York), then St Catharine's, MA 1813. V. Thorpe St Peter, Lincs. 1781-1834, V. Wainfleet All Saints, Lincs. 1791, V. Orby, Lincs. 1813 to death. Dom. Chap. to 1st Baron Muncaster 1812. Died Liverpool (where he was curate at the Parish church 'for the latter 18 years') 5/4/1834 aged 78 (CCEd says 14/7/1834) [C46015. YCO. Bennett2] Married Ripon, Yorks., 11/2/1783 Hannah Kidd with issue:
www.bulmerfamilies.com/getperson.php?personID=I73&tree=T1025

BULMER (William) Born York 23/9/1778, s. Francis (a butter factor) and Helen Horseman. Magdalene, Cambridge 1796, BA1801, dn01 (Ely), p02 (York), MA1804, Fellow. Probationer 1801 then a Vicar Choral of York Minster 1802-51, V. York Holy Trinity in Goodramgate with St John's Del Pike and St Maurice without Monkbar 1802, V. York St Martin, Coney Street 1803-29, PC. York St Sampson 1821-52, V. York St Mary, Bishophill Junior 1829-52, V. Ferry Fryston, Yorks. 1852 to death (Brotherton, Yorks., a widower) 9/7/1869 aged 90, leaving £5,000 [C87123. YCO] Married (1) Leeds 21/11/1811 Elizabeth Frances Clarke (2) Isleham, Cambs. 4/1/1833 Eleanor Anne Eamonson.

BULTEEL (Courteney James Cooper) Born Yealmpton, Devon 27/1/1805, s. John Bulteel and Elizabeth Perring. Balliol, Oxford 1823, BA1828, dn28 (B&W), p31 (B&W), MA1831. R. Holberton, Devon 1830-80, V. Ermington (w. Kingston), Devon 1833 to death. Dom. Chap. to 4th Baron Ducie 1834. Died Holberton 24/3/1880 aged 75, leaving £1,000 [C41933] Married Plympton St Mary, Devon 9/5/1840 Caroline Macdonald (w), w. issue.

BULWER (Augustine Earle Lloyd) Born Heydon, Norfolk 2/11/1796, s. Rev. Augustine Bulwer and Bridget Lloyd. Pembroke, Cambridge 1813, BA1820, dn20 (Nor.), p23 (Nor.). R. Cawston, Norfolk 1821 to death 28/7/1855 aged 58 [C111794] Married Cawston, Norfolk 14/5/1833 Mary Blanche Bulwer [*thus*] (a clergy dau.), with issue. Obviously related to the man below.

BULWER (Edward Earle) Bapt. Heydon, Norfolk 17/5/1771, s. William Wiggett Bulmer and Mary Earle. Pembroke, Cambridge 1789, BA1791, dn95 (Nor.), p95 (Nor.), MA1799. V. Guestwick, Norfolk 1797 and R. Salle, Norfolk 1818 to death 14/3/1847 aged 75 [C111795] Clerical son. Obviously related to the man above.

BUNCE (John Bowes) Bapt. Sandwich, Kent 27/12/1774, s. Rev. Wheler Bunce and Elizabeth Nairne. St John's, Cambridge 1791, BA1796, dn97 (Ex. for Cant.), MA1799. p99 (Win. for Cant.). Chaplain *R.N.* 1799; V. Canterbury St Dunstan 1801 and V. Sheldwich, Kent 1818 to death. Master of Eastbridge (o/w St Thomas) Hospital [almshouses], Kent 1823-50. Died Canterbury 22/6/1850 aged 75 [C123447] Married Deal, Kent 30/4/1818 Ann Pratt (of Hurworth, Co. Durham), w. clerical son, also John Bowes Bunce.

BUNTING (Edward Swanton) Bapt. Yelden, Beds. 17/7/1791, s. Rev. Edward Bunting and Sarah Creak. Clare, Cambridge 1809, BA1813, Fellow 1813, MA1816, dn17 (Lin.), p19 (Lin.), BD1830. R. Datchworth, Herts. 1829 and R. Yelden 1830 to death 27/3/1849 aged 57 [C5537] Married Loughborough , Leics. 19/1/1842 Elizabeth Middleton (dau. of a banker), *s.p.*

BURDETT (Dean Judd) Born Gilmorton, Leics. 4/9/1785, s. Rev. Robert Burdett and Martha Judd. Jesus, Cambridge 1804, BA1808, dn08 (Lin.), p09 (Lin.). R. Gilmorton 1809 to death there 26/12/1850 aged 65 [C46024] Married Misterton, Leics. 8/11/1808 Sophia Wotton, with issue.

BURDON (George) Bapt. Winchester, Hants. 3/2/1769, s. John Burdon. Queen's, Oxford 1788, then Trinity 1788, BA1791, dn91 (C&L for Win.), p93 (Lin. for Win.), MA1803. Chaplain *R.N.* 1798; R. Falstone, Northumberland 1815 to death (Ramsgate, Kent) 22/7/1834 [C9716] Married Farnham, Surrey 26 or 28/12/1815 Maria Susan Locke (a clergy dau.), with issue. Sydney Smith wrote: 'The poor man, who had seen some service at sea, became restless, expensive, drunken, embarrassed and eventually insane in his retirement'.

BURFORD (William John, *sometimes* James) Born Chigwell, Essex 8/4/1775, s. Rev. Peter Thomas Burford and Anne Broughton. H/M Chigwell School 1813-50; Christ's, Cambridge 1791, BA1798, dn98 (London), p99 (London), MA1802, DD1825. V. Tottington, Norfolk 1800-50, R. Magdalen Laver, Essex 1832 to death (Brompton, London) 8/6/1852, leaving (as John) under £100 (unadministered) [C111801] Married by 1804 Harriet Court (a clergy dau.), w. clerical s. William James Burford.

BURGES (George) Bapt. Wisbech, Cambs. 16/2/1765, s. George Burges and Ann Hume. Magdalene, Cambridge 1782, then St John's 1783, BA1787, dn87 (Ely), p91 (Ely). V. Halvergate, Norfolk 1812-53, V. Tunstall, Norfolk 1812, R. Moulton St Mary, Norfolk 1813 to death 24/1/1853 aged 89 [C99604. Boase] Married Mitcham, Surrey 14/4/1825 Eliza Myers.

BURGESS, Thomas, Bishop of St David's, *then* of Salisbury) Born Odiham, Herts. 18/11/1756, s. William Burgess ('a respectable grocer') and Elizabeth Harding. Corpus Christi, Oxford 1775, BA1778, MA1782 (and tutor), Fellow 1783, dn84 (Ox.), p84 ([Ox.]), BD1791, DD1803. Prebend of Durham 1794, R. Winston, Co. Durham 1795, Bishop of St David's 1803 (where he revitalised the Church in the Diocese, and where he built St David's College, Lampter to raise the abysmal standards of the Welsh clergy); translated (rather reluctantly) to Salisbury (aged 68) 1827 to death 19/2/1837 [C23281. ODNB. J.S. Harford, *The life of Thomas Burgess, DD* (1840). D.T.W. Price, *Bishop Burgess and Lampter College* (Cardiff, 1987)]. Married Durham 1/10/1799 Margery Bright (sister of the Marchioness of Winchester), *s.p.*

BURGESS (William) Bapt. Maidwell, Northants. 15/1/1780 (CCEd thus), s. William Burgess and Diana Church. Literate: dn17 (Nor.), p18 (Nor.). V. Kirby le Soken w. Walton le Soken and Thorpe le Soken, Essex (and Preacher throughout the Diocese of London) 1823 to death (Thorpe) 29/4/1862, leaving £25,000 [C111802]

BURGH (Allatson) Bapt. Holborn, London 28/12/ 1769, s. Rev. Allatson Burgh, sen. and

Elizabeth Copibger. University, Oxford 1787, BA1791, MA1794. R. Oake, Somerset 1797-1803, V. St Lawrence Jewry w. St Mary Magdalen Milk Street, City of London 1815 (and Preacher throughout the Diocese of London) to death (Hampstead, London) 1856 (3th q.) [C28919] Married Shoreditch, London 10/2/1794 Sarah Davenport. 'An odd fellow ... and as diverting as Punch'.

BURGIS (William Persehouse) Born Offenham, Worcs., s. Rev. Robert Burgis and Elizabeth Persehouse. Worcester, Oxford 1783 (aged 17), BA1788 (as William), dn89 (Wor.), p90 (Wor.). R. Winfrith Newburgh, Dorset 1800, R. Upwey, Dorset 1802 to death 1837 (3rd q.) [C52138] Married Market Drayton, Shropshire 19/10/1815 Elizabeth Grinsell, with issue.

BURMESTER (Alfred) Bapt. City of London 8/3/1787, s. (Hieronimus) Henry Burmester (Gwynne House, Woodbridge, Essex) and Mary Maynard. Trinity, Cambridge 1806, BA1810, dn10 (Bristol for Ely), p11 (Ely), MA1823. R. (and patron) of Mickleham, Surrey 1813 to death 26/8/1867 aged 80, leaving £12,000 [C52139] Married St Feock, Cornwall 23/9/1828 Elizabeth Jane Daniell, w. issue. Brother below.

BURMESTER (George) Bapt. London 11/11/1794 (in a Prebyterian Chapel?), s. Henry Burmester and Mary Maynard. Balliol, Oxford 1814, BA1820, MA1821 [barrister Middle Temple 1821-9 (res.)], dn28, p29. R. (and patron) of Little Oakley, Essex 1830 to death 9/1/1892 aged 97, leaving £4,836-16s-4d. [C62319] J.P. Essex. Surrogate. Brother above.

BURN (Edward) Born Killileagh, Co. Down 29/11/1762, s. Charles Burn. St Edmund Hall, Oxford 1784, dn85 (C&L), p86 (C&L), BA1790, MA1791. PC. Ashted St James Chapel 1810-29 (res.), PC. Birmingham St Mary 1810-37, R. Smethcott, Shropshire 1830 to death 20/5/1837 [C9719] Was married with issue: https://en.wikipedia.org/wiki/Edward_Burn

BURN (Richard) Bapt. Hesket in the Forest, Cumberland 15/1/1781, s. Rev. Richard Burn, sen. Literate: dn10 (Car.), p12 (Car.). (succ. his father as) R. Kirkandrews on Eden w. Beaumont, Cumberland 1815 to death 1846 (2nd q.) [C4568. Platt] Married before 1804 Mary Burton (or Hodgson?), with issue.

BURNABY (Andrew) Bapt. Asfordby, Leics. 4/8/1785, s. Rev. Thomas Beaumont Burnaby and Catharine Clarke. Jesus, Cambridge 1803, BA1808, dn09 (C&L), p10 (Win.), MA1817. R. (and patron) of Asfordby 1825 to death 29/10/1856 aged 71 [C9588]. Doubtless related to the man below.

BURNABY (Frederic George) Born Rotherby, Leics. 18/9/1803, s. John Richard Burnaby (army officer) and Mary Ann Fowke. Caius, Cambridge 1822, BA1827, dn27 (Lin.), p27 (Lin.), MA1830. V. Lowesby, Leics. 1828-45, V. Plungar, Leics. 1831-59 and V. Barkstone, Leics. 1831-59 (RD1847). Died Asfordby House, Melton Mowbray, Leics. 31/1/1880, leaving £20,000 [C46055] Married Marylebone, London 13/1/1830 his cousin Anna Maria Atkins (dau. of an *M.P.*). Doubtless related to the man above.

BURNABY (Robert) Born Leics. 21/11/1796, s. Rev. Thomas Burnaby and Lucy Dyott. St John's, Cambridge 1813, BA1818, dn19 (Lin.), p20 (Lin.). PC. Leicester St George 1827 to death there 15/7/1863 aged 66, leaving £5,000. Chap. Leicester Gaol 1803-6 [C46058] Married York 18/11/1841 Sarah Anne Blow (a clergy dau.), w. clerical s. Robert William Burnaby.

BURNE (Charles) Bapt. Lifton, Devon, s. Rev. Walter Burne and Mary Stacy. Oriel, Oxford 1795 (aged 18), BA1799, dn99 (Ex.), p08 (Ex.). Chaplain *R.N.* (present at Trafalgar). R. (and patron of) Tedburn St Mary, Devon 1808 to death 24/9/1852 aged 75 [C140418] Married Tedburn St Mary, Devon, 2/2/1820 Elizabeth Tothill (a clergy dau.), w. clerical son of the same name in the same parish. 'Maritime Memorial' in Church noted online.

BURNE (William Way) Born Westminster, London 28/12/1775, s. Thomas Burne and Elizabeth Bearsley. St Edmund Hall, Oxford 1793, BA1797, dn99 (C&L). MA1800, p00 (C&L). R. Grittleton, Wilts. 1802 to death 26/9/1858, leaving £250,000 [C9721] Married Tormarton, Glos. 27/11/1806 Caroline Newdigate Poyntz (a clergy dau.).

BURNET (John) Born Dublin 1800, s. of John Burnet and Elizabeth Comas. TCD1816, BA1822, LLB1827, LLD1847. PC. Sutton St George, Prestbury, Cheshire 1834, V. Bradford, Yorks. 1847 (with Chap. to Bradford Poor Law Union, and RD of Bradford 1857) to death

(Hawkshead, Lancs.) 7/3/1870 aged 69, leaving £3,000 [C168424. Al.Dub. BBV] Married Dublin 1825 Elizabeth Jane King, w. clerical son. Surrogate.

BURNET (Richard) Born Strand, London 2/10/1772, s. Charles Burnet. St John's, Cambridge 1792, BA1797, dn97 (Lin.), p98 (Lin.). H/M Bungay G/S, Suffolk 1805; V. Bethersden, Kent 1823 to death 1857 (1st q.) [C81658] Married Sudbury, Suffolk 14/6/1804 Catherine Naylor, with issue.

BURNETT (Joseph Bernard) Born Flanders ('a subject of the Crown'). [MA but NiVoF] Literate: p14 (Salis. for Win.). PC. Pinner, Middx. 1817-30 (res.), R. Houghton, Hants. 1831-65. Died Droxford, Hants. 1/6/1881 aged 91, leaving £8,581-1s-5d. [C71046. Venn notes a Joseph Edward with whom he may be confused?] Married Guildford, Surrey 3/6/1817 Charlotte Haydon, with issue.

BURNEY (Richard Allen) Bapt. Covent Garden, London 22/11/1773, s. Charles Rousseau Burney and Hester Burney (dau. Dr Charles Burney, musicologist, *q.v.* ODNB). Magdalen Hall, Oxford 1796, BA1799, MA 1807. R. Rimpton, Som. 1802-36, V. Buckland Dinham, Som. 1817-29. Dom. Chap. to 2nd Viscount Dungannon 1817. Died 29/3/1836 [C28929] Married 1811 Elizabeth Leyton Williams, with issue.

BURNS (James) Bapt. Colton, Lancs. 8/7/1764, s. Edward Burns (and Agnes Benson?). Literate: dn90 (Chester), p91 (Chester). PC. Egton cum Newland, Ulverston, Lancs. 1792-1833. Buried there 25/5/1833 aged 69 (CCEd says 7/6/1833) [C168326] Married with issue.

BURNSIDE (John) Bapt. Nottingham 7/10/1792, s. John Burnside (merchant) and Ann Stanford. Trinity, Cambridge 1810, BA 1814, dn15 (York), p16 (York), MA1817. R. Plumtree, Notts. 1816 [income £1,113] to death 24/12/1864 aged 72, leaving £180,000 [the richest clergyman in the Northern Province] [C130909. YCO] Married by 1820 Henrietta Anne Julia Thompson, with issue.

BURRARD (George, Sir, 3rd Bart.) Born Lymington, Hants. 6/4/1769, s. of Lieut.-Col. William Burrard ('a blinded and crippled army officer') and Mary Pearce. Trinity, Oxford 1786, then Merton, BA1790, dn92 (Ox.), p93 (Ox.), MA1793. R. Fobbing, Essex 1801-22, R. Yarmouth, IoW 1801-41 with V. Shalfleet, IoW 1801-35, V. Middleton Tyas, Yorks. 1804 and R. Burton (le) Coggles, Lincs. 1822 to death. 'Chaplain-in-Ordinary 1801 to 4 sovereigns'. Died (Walhampton, Hants.) 17/5/1856 aged 87 [C23611. Boase. Bennett2] Married (1) 18/9/1804 Elizabeth Ann Coppell (from Jamaica, she d.1815), with issue (2) Yarmouth 1/5/1816 Emma (dau. Rear-Admiral Joseph Bingham), w. further issue. Succeeded to title 1840.

BURRIDGE (William) From Ruishton, Somerset, s. John Burridge and Elizabeth Knight. Exeter, Oxford 1796 (aged 18), BA 1802, dn02 (B&W), p06 (B&W). V. Bradford, Som. 1829 to death 22/1/1858, leaving under £800 [C33630] Married Blandford Forum, Dorset 30/10/1806 Mary Waters, with issue.

BURRILL, BURRELL (Joseph) Bapt. Masham, Yorks. 7/12/1763, s. Joseph Burrill and Elizabeth Calvert. Literate: dn88 (York), p89 (York). R. Broughton Sulney, Notts. 1808 to death 1/3/1853 [C87137. YCO] Married Masham, Yorks. Lucinda Wrather, with issue. 'H/M of the G/S, proprietor of a boarding school, and a farmer'.

BURRINGTON (Gilbert) Bapt. Chudleigh, Devon 13/4/1753, s. Rev. Gilbert Burrington, sen. and Maria Savery. Balliol, Oxford 1771, BA1774, dn75 (Ex.), p77 (Ox.), MA1777. V. Chudleigh 1785-1840, Prebend of Exeter Cathedral 1798 and R. Woodleigh, Devon 1832 to death. Dom. Chap. to 1st Earl Morley 1832. Died 26/9/1840 [C23612]

BURROUGHES (Jeremiah) Born Burlingham, Norfolk 13/10/1795, s. James Burkin Burroughes (Hoveton Hall, Norfolk) and Christabel Negus. Emmanuel, Cambridge 1813, BA1817, dn19 (Nor.), p19 (Nor.), MA1820. R. Burlingham St Andrew w. St Edmund 1819 (a family living, pop. 85) and R. Burlingham St Peter 1830-72 (a family living, pop. 30), RD of Blofield 1847-69. Died Lingwood, Norfolk 19/5/1872, leaving £14,000 [C111816] Married Beeston St Lawrence, Norfolk 31/7/1828 Pleasance, dau. Sir Thomas Hulton Preston, 1st Bart. (Beeston Hall, with issue. *J.P.* Norfolk.

BURROUGHES (Walter) Bapt. Norwich 10/9/1798 (CCEd thus), s. Rev. Ellis Burroughes and Sarah Nasmyth Marsh. Clare, Cambridge 1816, BA1820, dn21 (Nor.), p22 (Nor.), MA1823, Fellow. R. (but see above) Burlingham St Peter, Norfolk 1820. Lived unbeneficed at Morningthorpe, Norfolk. Died (Hastings) 5/12/1850 aged 52 [C111818]

BURROUGHS, *born* SALUSBURY (Lynch) Born Cotton Hall, Denbigh. 10/10/1763, s. Robert Salusbury and Gwendolen Davis. St John's, Cambridge 1779, BA1783, MA1786, dn86 (Glos.), p87 (Lin.). V. Offley, Herts. 1787-1835, R. Graveley w. Chivesfield, Herts. 1803-19 (res.). Dom. Chap. to 1st Earl of Beverley 1803. Died (Welbury, Herts.) 10/8/1837 [C46101 under Salusbury] Married (1) Bloomsbury, London 29/7/1790 Jane Offley (d.1815), with issue (2) London 1820 Anne Dickie. Name changed 1804.

BURROUGHS, BURROWS (William Francis) Born Portsea, Hants.2/6/1795, s. Francis Burroughs (born Marsh) and Mary Brown. Magdalen Hall, Oxford 1820, dn21 (Win.), p22 (Win.). V. Christchurch, Hants. 1830-64-, PC. Corhampton, Hants. 1833. Died Whitchurch, Hants. 22/2/1871 aged 75, leaving £800 (as Burrows) [C71148. Forster as Burrows] Married (1) Droxford, Hants. 23/8/1821 Elizabeth Jackson (d.1835), w. issue (2) Wilton, Wilts. 22/10/1838 Frances Stockwell (w), w. further issue. Surrogate 1831. Photo. online.

BURROW (Thomas) Bapt. Exeter 13/3/1766, s. James Burrow. Oriel, Oxford 1784, BA1788, dn88 (Ex.), p90 (Ex.), MA1802. 'Perpetual V'. Bampton (2nd Portion), Oxon. 1799 to death 1837 aged 71 [C140422]

BURROWS (Joseph) Bapt. Marston, Cheshire 17/5/1783, s. Thomas Burrows and Jane Potts. BNC, Oxford 1803, BA1807, MA1809, dn10 (Ox.), p11 (Ox.), Fellow, BD1817. R. Collingtree, Northants. 1818-20 (res.), R. Steeple Aston, Oxon. 1832 to death 22/9/1862, leaving £25,000 [C24283] Married 1832 Sarah Emma Shorter (w), apparently an exemplary clerical wife. 'A man "of the old school", unwilling to meet the increased demands on his office. He preached the same sermons repeatedly. The parishioners complained in 1854 about the paucity of services and in 1855 about the lack of parish visiting …' (*British History Online*).

BURROWS (Samuel) From Staffs. St Catharine's, Cambridge 1782, BA1786, dn86 (C&L), p87 (C&L), MA1789. R. (and patron). Highley, Shropshire 1790-1844, R. Sheinton, Shropshire to death 26/2/1844 [C9619] Clerical son of same name.

BURSLAM, BURSLEM (Charles Shaw) Bapt. Chester 14/11/1774, s. James Burslam and Sarah Shaw. Literate: dn03 (Chester). PC. Little Budworth, Cheshire 1816 to death 1/3/1853 [C168432] Married Liverpool 6/2/1827 Mary Tabitha Jones, with issue.

BURT (Robert Gascoyne) Born Twickenham, Middx., s. Rev. Robert Burt and Sarah Gascoyne (with slave connections: details online). Exeter, Oxford 1810 (aged 18), BA1814, dn15 (Roch.), p16 (Chester for Roch.), MA1818. R. (and patron) of St Mary Hoo, Kent 1816 (a family living) and R. (and patron) of High Halstow, Kent 1825 [total income in CR65 £1,377] to death. Dom. Chap. to Charlotte Mary Gertrude, Baroness Rayleigh 1823. Died 18/2/1875 aged 83, leaving £35,000 [C1694] Married Westminster, London 19/3/1829 Joanna Curd Smart.

BURTON (Charles) Born Rhodes Hall, Middleton, Lancs. 18/1/1793, s. Daniel Burton (a 'substantial' Wesleyan calico printer) and Esther Matthews. Glasgow University. Methodist itinerant preacher. St John's, Cambridge 1815, dn16 (Chester), p17 (Ex. for Chester), LLB 1822, incorporated at Magdalen Hall, Oxford, BCL and DCL 1829. R. (and patron) of Chorlton cum Medlock All Saints, Manchester 1820-66 (where he built the church at the cost of £18,000, which burnt down 1850), Minister Tavistock [Proprietory] Chapel, St Martins in the Fields, London 1832. Died (Durham) 6/9/1866 aged 73 (typhus), leaving under £100 [C140423. ODNB. Boase, M. Wells. *The Reverend Charles Burton: a biography of Manchester's forgotten man of the cloth* (Harton: The author, Yorks., 2014 and port.) Married Burslem, Staffs. 5/8/1813 Sarah Walker ('a wealthy woman from the Potteries'), with clerical issue. F.L.S. 'for discovering in Anglesey a plant new to science'. 'Firmly evangelical.'

BURTON (Charles James) Born Daventry, Northants. 30/3/1792, s. Edward Burton and Elizabeth Mather. Lincoln, Oxford 1809, then Queen's, BA1813, dn15 (C&L for Roch.), p16 (Salis. for Cant.), Fellow 1816-18, MA1818. PC. Ash, Kent 1817-21, V. Nonington w. Wymynwold, Kent 1817-21, Lydd, Kent 1821-87 [income £1,650], RD and Preacher throughout the Diocese of Canterbury, Chancellor of Carlisle Diocese 1855-87 [and notorious for his refusal to resign, keeping his Consistory Court running the Diocese in parallel with that of the Bishop until his own death], Hon. Canon of Carlisle 1857-68. Died 8/4/1887 aged 96, leaving £8,354-0-4d. [C64. Boase] Married Canterbury 5/6/1819 Eliza W. Boteler, with issue.

BURTON (Edward) Born Shrewsbury, Shropshire 13/2/1804, s. Edward Burton and Dorothy Eliza Blakeway. Christ Church, Oxford 1812, Student [Fellow] 1813, BA1815, MA1818, dn20 (Ox.), p21 (Ox.), BD1828, DD1829. Regius Professor of Divinity, Oxford University (w. Canon of 5th Prebend in Christ Church Cathedral annexed and) R. Ewelme, Oxon. 1829 (where he introduced open seats instead of pews) to death 19/1/1836 aged 42 [C11129. ODNB] Married Longnor, Shropshire 12/5/1825 Helen Corbett (dau. of an Archdeacon). Brother Robert Lingen Burton, below.

BURTON (Henry) Born Atcham, Shropshire 21/8/1803, s. Rev. Henry Burton and Mary Gittins. Christ Church, Oxford 1822, BA1826, dn26 (C&L), p27 (C&L), MA1831. R. Upton Cressett, Shropshire 1829-73, V. Condover, Shropshire 1829-73, (succ. his father as) V. Atcham 1831-73, RD of Shrewsbury 1853. Died (a widower) 6/9/1873 aged 70, leaving £10,000 [C9773. LFBI] Married St George's Hanover Square, London 28/1/1845 Hon. Charlotte Belasyse Barrington (dau. of Rev. George, 5th Viscount Barrington). Antiquarian.

BURTON (Robert Lingen) Born Shrewsbury, Shropshire, s. Edward Burton and Dorothy Eliza Blakeway. Christ Church, Oxford 1820 (aged 17), BA1824, dn25 (C&L), p26 (C&L), MA1827. V. Shrewsbury Holy Cross w. St Giles 1826 to death 11/12/1887, leaving £9,835-1s-11d. [C9774] Married (1) Eccleston, Chorley, Lancs. 18/8/1829 Everilda Rigbye (d.1833) with child (2) Shrewsbury 1835 Mary Anne Elizabeth Pine-Coffin (d.1850) with issue (3) 1859 Beatrice Julia Leigh; clerical son. Brother Edward, above.

BURTON (Thomas) Bapt. Carleton in Craven, Yorks. 13/8/1769, s. Thomas and Jane Burton. Glasgow University, MA1792, dn93 (Car. for York), p94 (York). PC. Rastrick, Yorks. 1799 to death 6/5/1837 aged 67 [C4573. YCO] Married Halifax, Yorks. 12/11/1825 Mrs Ann Wheatley.

BURY (William) Born Salford, Lancs. 24/2/1792, s. John Bury and Margaret Kenyon. Literate: dn25 (Bristol for York), p25 (York). PC. Horton in Ribblesdale, Yorks. 1825-66 (res.), R. Burnsall (both Medieties), Yorks. 1839 to death (Gristhorpe Hall, Filey, Yorks.) 8/2/1867 aged 77, leaving £2,000 [C130913. YCO. BBV] Widow Elizabeth.

BUSFIELD (Johnson Atkinson) Bapt. Bingley, Yorks. 8/8/1775, s. Johnson Atkinson (physician) and Elizabeth Busfield. Clare, Cambridge 1791, BA1796, dn98 (Llandaff for York), p99 (York), MA1800, DD1812. R. St Michael Wood Street w. St Mary Staining, City of London 1821 to death 12/1/1849 [C3678. YCO] Married (1) Manchester 18/7/1798 Mary Susanna Prestley (d.1819) (2) Clerkenwell, London 21/8/1820 Charlotte Mary Irving; w. clerical son.

BUSH (James) From Southampton, s. James Bush. Oriel, Oxford 1808 (aged 16) [admitted Lincoln's Inn 1811] BA1814, MA1816. R. (and patron) South Luffenham, Rutland 1828 to death (Bradninch, Devon) 11/12/1849 aged 58 [C110012] Clerical sons James, jun. and Paul Bush. Lord Byron's fag at Harrow School. Friend of Southey.

BUSHBY (Edward) Born Bothel Hall, Torpenhow, Cumberland 20/10/1793, s. Benjamin Bushby (farmer) and Margaret Charters. St John's, Cambridge 1811, BA1816, Fellow 1818-77, dn18 (Ely), MA1819, p20 (Ely), BD1827, tutor 1830-42. S/M Bury St Edmunds G/S 1818; V. Impington, Cambs. 1832 to death (St John's) 8/10/1877, leaving £100,000 [C6598] 'Took a keen interest in the political affairs of Europe. At an advanced age visited the Continent to view the battlefield of Sedan.' Brother below.

BUSHBY (Joseph) Born Bothel Hall, Torpenhow, Cumberland 23/6/1781, s. Benjamin Bushby (farmer) and Margaret Charters. Magdalene, Cambridge 1799, BA 1804, dn04 (York), p05 (York), MA1814. PC. Holbeck, Leeds 1815 to death 3/3/1835 aged 53 (CCEd thus) [C87153. YCO] Married Ireby, Cumberland 5/6/1800 Rachel Hind, with issue. Brother above.

BUSHELL (William) Bapt. Gloucester 5/1/1773, s. William and Hannah Bushell. Pembroke, Oxford 1788, BA1792. R. Tibberton, Glos. (a family living) 1803-[37]. Died? [C137899]

BUSHNELL (John) Bapt. Wasing, Berks. 29/12/1785, s. Rev. Thomas Hext Bushnall and Jane May [*her surname*]. Pembroke, Oxford 1803, BA1808, dn09 (Salis.), p09 (Salis.), MA1810. V. (and patron of) Beenham Valence, Berks. 1810 to death 4/8/1839 [C91489] Married (1) Thatcham, Berks. 29/8/1811 Eleanor Slade (d.1813), 1s. (2) Thatcham, Berks. 10/11/1814 Sarah Butler, with issue.

BUSSELL (John Garrett) Bapt. Plymouth 26/8/1769, s. Joseph Bussell and Mary Garrett. Oriel, Oxford 1788, BA1792, dn92 (C&L for Ex.), p96 (Salis.), MA1809. R. Beaford, Devon 1800 'for 21 years', Died IoW 24/6/1848 [C9779] Married Portsea, Hants. 11/11/1799 Sarah Carter, with issue (inc. clerical son of father's name).

BUSSELL (William John) Bapt. Kenton, Devon 17/3/1804, s. Joseph and Sarah Bussell. Pembroke, Oxford 1822, BA1826, dn27 (Ex.), p28 (Ex.), MA1830. PC. Chillington, Som. 1832 and PC. Seavington St Mary, Som. 1832-51 (with S/M Chard G/S), Chap. *R.N.* Incumbent Dingwall, Scotland 1859-89. Died Winchester 18/12/1893, leaving £2,666-5s-4d. [C41932. Bertie] Married Exeter 30/8/1832 Anne Nowell.

BUTCHER (Thomas) From Lancs., s. Rev. William Butcher. St John's, Cambridge 1775, BA1780, dn80 (C&L) [S/M Rugby School 1780-1] p89 (Chester). PC. Stalmine, Lancs. 1794-[99], PC. Hambleton, Lancs. 1803 to death 10/3/1835 (CCEd says 10/6/1835) [C9621] Married Warton, Lancs. 5/4/1790 Alice Lancaster, with issue.

BUTCHER (William) Born Cambridge c.1770, s. Joseph (attorney at law) and Ann Butcher. St John's, Cambridge 1786, BA1791, dn92 (Ely), MA1794, p94 (Ely). R. Lidgate, Suffolk 1799, R. Burrow Green, Cambs. 1799, R. Ropsley, Lincs. 1804 to death 14/11/1845 [C46450] Married Cambridge 19/2/1795 Catherine Scott.

BUTLAND (Gilbert) Bapt. Painton, Devon 3/7/1800, s. Gilbert Butland and Elizabeth Hunt. Pembroke, Oxford 1819, BA1822, dn24 (Lin. for Ex.), p25 (Ex.). R. (and patron) of Ringmore, Devon 1828-60, then unbeneficed. Died (Higher Yelverton, Devon) 17/10/1877 aged 77, leaving £7,000 [C46451] Married Edmonton, Middx. 4/3/1834 Sarah Jane Brant, with issue.

BUTLER (George) Born Pimlico, London 5/7/1774, s. Rev. Weeden Butler (V. Chelsea, London, *q.v.* ODNB) and Anne Giberne. Sidney, Cambridge 1790, BA1794 (Senior Wrangler), Fellow 1794 [incorporated Lincoln's Inn 1794] MA1797, dn00 (Lin.), p00 (Lin.), BD1804, DD1805, tutor and lecturer, incorporated at Oxford 1834. H/M Harrow School 1805-29 ('essentially a failure'); R. Calverton, Bucks.1814-21, R. Gayton, Northants. 1814-53, Chancellor of Peterborough 1836-42, then Dean of Peterborough 1836-42. Died (almost blind and with heart trouble) 30/4/1843 [C46452. ODNB. Boase] Married Bloomsbury, London 18/3/1818 Sarah Maria Gray, and together 'they perpetuated a fruitful dynasty of academics and public servants'. 'A brilliant mathematician and distinguished classical scholar; gifted with remarkable versatility of mind'. He rescued a woman from drowning in 1843, he being about seventy at the time.

BUTLER (Samuel, *later* Bishop of Lichfield and Coventry) Born Kenilworth, Warwicks. 20/1/1774, s. William Butler (draper) and Lucy Brossell. St John's, Cambridge 1791, BA1796, dn97 (London), Fellow 1797-8, p98 (London), MA 1799, DD1811, incorporated at Oxford 1830. The great H/M of Shrewsbury School 1798-1836, 'he can be said to have changed education in England'; PC. Bewick Chapel, Shrewsbury 1801-15, V. Kenilworth 1802-36, Prebend of Wolvey in Lichfield Cathedral 1807-36, Archdeacon of Derby 1821-36, Bishop of Lichfield and Coventry 1836 to death 4/12/1839 [C9782. ODNB. Samuel Butler [*grandson*], *The life and letters of Dr Samuel Butler* ... (1824. 2v.)] Married Cambridge 4/9/1798 Harriet Apthorp (a clergy dau.), with issue.

BUTLER (Thomas) Bapt. Lancaster 27/11/1767, s. Edmund Butler (attorney). Trinity, Cambridge 1785, BA1790, Fellow 1791, dn92 (Ely), MA1793, p21 (Chester). PC. Poulton (le Sands), Morecombe, Lancs. 1825 to death 8/1/1839 [C99606] Married Lancaster 16/1/1793 Rebecca Stout, with issue.

BUTLER (William) Bapt. Okeford Fitzpaine, Dorset 29/8/1762, s. Rev. Duke Butler and Mary Raufe Freke. Wadham, Oxford 1780, dn85 (Ox. for Bristol), BCL1787, p87 (Ox. for Bristol). R. Langton Long, Dorset 1787-92, V. Sturminster Newton, Devon 1791-9, V. Frampton, Dorset 1800-43, R. Bettiscombe, Dorset 1801, R. Seaborough, Som. 1806, PC. Nether Cerne, Dorset 1817-24. Died Frampton 13/8/1843 aged 81 [C23605. LBSO] Port. online. 'Billy Butler, the fox-hunting parson.'

BUTLER (William Joseph) Born Chesterfield, Derbys. 14/5/1797, s. Joseph and Sarah Butler. St John's, Cambridge 1815, BA1820, dn23 (Lin.), MA1824, p25 (York). R. Nottingham St Nicholas 1825-66, R. Thwing, Bridlington, Yorks. 1828 to death (Woodford, Essex) 5/9/1869, leaving £12,000 [C46456. YCO] Married Nottingham 18/4/1827 Lucy Atternborrow, with clerical issue.

BUTLIN (William) Bapt. Great Brington, Northants. 16/3/1855, s. John Butlin and Elizabeth Rushall. Lincoln, Oxford 1774 (aged 19), BA1778, dn78 (Peterb.), p80 (Ely for Peterb.), MA1780. PC. Roade, Northants. 1783-1840, PC. Hartwell, Northants. 1791-1840, R. Cogenhoe, Northants. 1796-1812 (res.). Died Roade 21/4/6/1840 aged 85 [C107995] Married Roade 26/2/1788 Ann Hoare, w. issue.

BUTT (Edward) Bapt. Wimborne Minister, Dorset 4/10/1764, s. Rev. Edward, sen. and Martha Butt. Merton, Oxford 1784, BA1787, dn87 (London for Bristol), p90 (Bristol). R. Hinton Parva, Dorset 1811-30, V. Toller Fratrum, Dorset 1824 to burial (Wimborne) 25/4/1842 [C52142]

BUTT (John Martin) Born Donnington, Shropshire 7/6/1774 (CCEd thus), s. Rev. George and Martha Butt. Christ Church, Oxford 1792, BA1796, dn97 (Chester), p98 (Wor.), MA1799. R. Oddingley, Worcs.1806-24 (res.), V. East Garston, Berks. 1806-[46]. Buried Worcester 23/10/1831 [C91491] Wife Mary, and clerical son Henry Francis Butt.

BUTT (John William) Born Whissenden, Rutland 6/5/1767, s. John Butt. S/M Uppingham School. St John's, Cambridge 1804, then Sidney 1808, BA1809, dn10 (Peterb.), p11 (Peterb.), MA1825. V. Lakenheath, Suffolk 1819, R. Southery, Norfolk 1825-37, V. King's Langley, Herts. 1836 to death 12/1/1855 aged 66 (in debt, having lost £7,000 in a tithe case). [C99607] Had issue.

BUTT (Thomas) Born Ryton, Shropshire 30/10/1776, s. Rev. Simon Butt and Elizabeth Congreve. Christ Church, Oxford 1795, BA 1799, dn99 (C&L), p00 (C&L), MA1802. PC. Arley, Staffs. 1800, PC. Trentham, Staffs. 1806, R. Kynnersley, Shropshire 1816 to death. Dom Chap. to Duke of Sutherland. Died Dover St., London 14/6/1841 aged 67 [C0786] Married Catherine Bormhead (a clergy dau.), w. issue.

BUTTERFIELD (Henry) Bapt. Lambeth, Surrey 25/1/1802, s. John Boddy Butterfield and Sarah Smallwood. Christ's, Cambridge 1820, BA1825, dn25, p26 (Chich.), MA1837. R. Brockdish, Norfolk 1825-42, Minor Canon of Windsor Chapel 1828-67, R. Fulmer, Bucks. 1842 to death 23/8/1875, leaving £2,000 [C111876] Married Newtimber, Sussex 30/11/1824 Charlotte Wigney, and had issue.

BUTTS (William) Bapt. London 8/5/1752, s. Rev. Robert Butts (R. Glemsford, Suffolk) and Jane Clarke. Trinity, Cambridge 1772, BA1777, dn78 (Nor.), p78 (London for Nor.), MA1779. R. Glemsford 1778-1833, R. Claydon w. Akenham, Suffolk 1782-1802 (res.). Died Le Havre, France 7/8/1833 aged 81 (CCEd says 7/9/1833) [C111880] Married Norwich 26/2/1781 Amy Drury (a clergy dau.), w. clerical s. Edward Drury Butts.

BUXTON (George Pocock) Bapt. Upton cum Chalvey, Bucks. 3/3/1794, s. George and Sarah Buxton. Trinity, Cambridge 1813, BA1817, dn17 (Lin.), p19 (Lin.), MA1820. R. Mildenhall, Wilts. 1822 to death 3/12/1854 aged 60 [C46462] Married Mildenhall 10/10/1827 Rose Shephard.

BUXTON (Thomas) Literate: dn83 (Chester), p85 (Chester). PC. Kirby Ravensworth, Yorks. 1804 to death 17/3/1838 aged 80 [C168440] Widow Hannah, with issue.

BYAM (Richard Burgh) Bapt. Southampton and Antigua, West Indies 26/1/1785, s. Capt. William Byam (68th Regt.) and Mary Ann Burgh. King's, Cambridge 1804, 1806 [admitted Lincoln's Inn 1806] BA1808, Fellow 1807, MA 1811, dn14 (Nor.), p15 (London for Nor.), tutor 1822-8, etc. R. Sampford Courtney, Devon 1827-8 (and Preacher throughout the Diocese of Exeter 1827), R. Kew and Petersham, Surrey 1828 to death. Chap. to HRH the Duke of

Sussex. Died 1/3/1867 aged 82, leaving £5,000 [C6602] Married Antigua, West Indies 18/12/1805 Frances Watkins.

BYDE (John Peacock) Born Ware Park, Herts., s. Thomas Hope Byde and Elizabeth Peacock. Pembroke, Cambridge 1821, BA1825, dn25 (Lin.), p26 (Lin.), MA1828. V. Bengeo, Herts. 1829-48, R. Edworth, Beds. 1836 to death (Bath) 14/2/1854 aged 51 [C46450] Married Havering (-atte-Bower), Essex 2/2/1827 Emma Robinson, with issue.

BYRON (Samuel) Bapt. Great Limber, Lincs. 29/6/1764, s. Joseph (or Joshua) Byron. Magdalene, Cambridge 1782, BA1786, dn86 (Lin.), p88 (Lin.), MA1789. V. Keelby, Lincs. 1792 and V. Killingholme, Lincs. 1842 to death 10/4/1844 [C46493. Kaye]

BYRTH (Thomas) Born Devonport, Plymouth 11/9/1793, s. John Byrth (of Co. Westmeath, a Quaker) and Mary Hobling (a Cornish Wesleyan); bapt. 21/10/1819. Apprentice chemist and druggist. S/M Magdalen Hall, Oxford 1818, dn23 (Bristol for Ex.), p23 (Ex.), BA and MA1826, BD and DD1839. PC. Latchford, Cheshire 1827-36-, R. Wallasey, Cheshire 1834 to death 28/10/1849 [C52145. ODNB. G.R. Moncreiff, *Remains of Thomas Byrth, Rector of Wallasey. With a memoir of his life* (1851)] Married 19/6/1827 Mrs Mary (Stewart) Kingdom, 7 ch. survived (for whom £4,000 was collected on death).

BYTHESEA (George) Bapt. Trowbridge, Wilts. 19/1/1773, s. Henry Bythesea and Fanny Whittaker. Trinity, Oxford 1810, no degree, dn16 (B&W), p18 (Glos.). R. (and patron) of Freshford, Som., 1818 to death 13/12/1853 [C33632] Brother, below.

BYTHESEA (Henry Frederick) Born Trowbridge, Wilts. 10/4/1780, s. Henry Bythesea and Fanny Whittaker. BNC, Oxford 1799, BA1802, dn12 (B&W). R. Nettleton, Wilts. 1813 to death (Bath) 2/7/1850 [C33634] Married Plymouth 18/10/1808 Eliza Meredith. Brother, above.

BYTHESEA (John Lewis) From Week House, Bagindon, Wilts., s. Thomas Bythesea and Elizabeth Lewis. Merton, Oxford 1779 (aged 18), dn83 (Ox.), p85 (Ox.), migrated to Trinity Hall, Cambridge, LLB1794. R. Leigh Delamere, Wilts. 1786, R. Bagendon, Glos. 1794 to death. Lived at Week House, Wilts. Died 24/4/1845 aged 85, *s.p.* [C24299] J.P., D.L. Wilts.

BYWATER (John) Born Madeley, Shropshire 2/2/1808, s. Thomas and Martha Bywater. St John's, Cambridge 1825, dn31 (Chester), BA 1832, p32 (Chester), MA1844. PC. Huddersfield St Paul 1833-4, R. Morleigh, Devon 1834-44, PC. St Simon and St Jude, Salford 1844-57, PC. St Botolph, Boston, Lincs. 1858-63. Died York 21/6/1865 aged 63. Will not traced [C136760]

CABBELL (John) Born Taunton, Somerset 5/11/1770, s. John Cabbell (physician) and Mary Burridge. Exeter, Oxford 1791, dn94 (B&W), SCL, p95 (B&W). PC. Cudworth, Som. 1808, V. Luppitt, Devon 1809 to death (Taunton) 3/1/1856 [C29051]

CADDY (Thomas) Bapt. Colton, Lancs. 26/12/1784, s. James Caddy (a yeoman farmer) and Agnes Harper. S/M Browedge School, Lancs. 1804. Literate: dn08 (Chester), p09 (Chester). PC. Dendron, Lancs. 1809-18 (res.), PC. Whitbeck, Cumberland 1825 to death (Ulverston, Lancs., a widower) 28/9/1847 aged 62 [C168443] Married Birmingham 25/6/1823 Elizabeth Dixon, with issue.

CAGE (Charles) Born Bearsted, Kent, s. Lewis Cage and Annette Coke. Emmanuel, Cambridge 1787, BA1791, dn92 (C&L for Cant.), p93 (Lin. for Cant.), MA1802. V. Bredgar, Kent 1794-95 and again 1802, PC. Leeds w. Bromfield, Kent 1794-5, V. Bearstead, Kent 1795, R. Leybourne, Kent 1798 to death. Dom. Chap. to Elizabeth, Duchess of Manchester 1802. Died 24/1/1849 aged 79 [C196] Married Canterbury 5/10/1792 Elizabeth Graham (a miliatry dau.). Brother, below.

CAGE (Edward) Bapt. Bearsted, Kent 31/10/1764, s. Lewis Cage (of Milgate, Kent) and Annette Coke. Emmanuel, Cambridge 1782, BA1786, dn87 (C&L for Cant.), MA1789. R. Farringdon, Hants. 1789-97, R. Eastling, Kent 1796, V. Newnham, Kent 1803-35, R. Badlesmere w. Leaveland, Kent 1818 to death. Dom. Chap. to 7th Baron Reay 1803-18. Died Eastling 17/7/1835 (CCEd says 25/8/1835) aged 70. [C9624] Married London 26/3/1790 Jane Van (Monmouthshire), w. issue. Brother above. Port. online.

CALCOTT (John) From Oxford, s. William Calcott. Lincoln, Oxford 1809 (aged 17), BA 1814, dn15 (Ox.), MA1816, p17 (Ox.), Fellow to death, BD1825, Lecturer in Greek. PC. Oxford St Michael 1823-[49]. Died 30/1/1864, leaving £12,000 [C24302]

CALCRAFT (John Neville Lucas-]Bapt. Ancaster, Lincs. 9/7/1801, s. John Charles Lucas Calcraft (Ancaster Hall) and Sophia eville Birch (a clergy dau.). Clare, Cambridge 1820, BA1824, dn25 (Lin.), p26 (Lin.), MA 1828. R. Haceby, Lincs. 1832 to death 14/7/1887, leaving £337-2s-10d. [C46496. Bennett1] Married 17/5/1842 Marianna Sophia Mansell, 8 children.

CALTHORP (John) Born Gosberton, Lincs. 16/2/1783, s. John George Calthorp and Ann Spurr. BNC, Oxford 1801, BA1805, dn06 (Lin.), p07 (Lin.), MA1808. R. Faldingworth, Lincs. 1807-10 (res.), V. Gosberton 1830 to death (Isleham, Cambs.) 14/1/1859 aged 64. Married City of London 23/7/1807 his cousin Barbara Calthorp Bonner, with issue. J.P. Lincs. and Cambs. and Chairman of the Bench.

CALVERT (Frederic) Bapt. Darlton, Notts. 15/1/1793 s. William Calvert and Elizabeth Collingham. Jesus, Cambridge 1810, BA1815, Fellow 1815-24, MA1818, tutor, dn23 (Lin. for Ely), p23 (Ely). R. Whatfield, Suffolk 1823-52, R. Chelsworth, Suffolk 1831 to death 1/8/1852 aged 59 [C6606] Married Chattisham, Suffolk 3/5/1827 Sarah Ann Hicks, with issue.

CALVERT (George) From London, s. George Calvert. University, Oxford 1804 (aged 17), BA 1809, dn12 (Win.), p13 (Salis.), MA1814. R. Boscombe, Wilts. 1815-18 (res.), R. Beeby, Leics. 1818 to death. Chap. to HRH Duke of York 1819. Died 22/10/1865, leaving £25,000 [C46641] Married Bathwick, Som. 4/4/1812 Eliza Ann Dundas, w. issue. Port. online.

CALVERT (John) Born Redmire, Bolton, Yorks. 12/9/1762, s. of William Calvert (a farmer). Sidney, Cambridge 1783, BA1788, dn88 (Lin. for York), p89 (York), MA1791. V. Foston on the Wolds, Yorks. 1803 and PC. Bolton cum Redmire 1803 to death. Chaplain to William 1V. Died (unm.) 14/2/1856 aged 93 ('of natural decay') [C46643. YCO] www.redmire.net/book/redmire-book_25.html

CALVERT (Nicolson Robert) Born Brighton, Sussex 4/8/1800, s. Nicholson Calvert and Frances Pery. St John's, Cambridge 1818 [adm. Lincoln's Inn 1820] BA1822, MA1825, dn27 (London), p28 (London). R. Childerley, Cambs. 1832-71 [income £20], R. Stocking Pelham, Herts. 1832-44, R. Hunsdon. 1832-45 (res.). Lived at Quintin Castle, Portaferry, Co. Down. Died (Forli, Romagna, North Italy) 31/3/1871, leaving £1,500 [C6607. Foster corrected] Married St George's Hanover Square, London

10/4/1826 Elizabeth Blacker (dau. of an Archdeacon of Armagh), w. issue.

CALVERT, *born* JACKSON (Thomas) Born Preston, Lancs. 27/12/1775, s. of William Jackson and Mary Newsham. St John's, Cambridge 1792, BA1797, dn98 (Lin.), Fellow 1798-1823, MA1800, p00 (London), BD1807, tutor 1814, DD1823 (as Calvert 'after being left a fortune'). Norrisian Professor of Divinity, Cambridge 1815-24. R. Wilmslow, Cheshire 1820, V. Holme on Spalding Moor, Yorks. 1822-40 and Warden of Manchester Collegiate Church 1823 [C168444] to death 4/6/1840 aged 65 [C67082 under both Calvert and Jackson. ODNB] Married West Wratting, Cambs. 24/9/1824 Juliana, dau. of Sir Charles Watson, 1st Bart. (of Wratting Park, Cambs.), 3s. Changed his surname 1817. 'His serene manner and gentle deportment made him very popular', etc. Bought Woodplumpton estate, St Michael on Wyre, 'but usually resided at Ardwick, Manchester'.

CAMBRIDGE (George Owen) Bapt. Twickenham, Middx. 19/8/1756, s. Richard Owen and Mary Trenchard. Queen's, Oxford 1774, BA1778, then Merton, MA1781, p82 (Ely). R. Chillingham, Northumberland 1782-1827, R. Hurstbourne Priors, Hants. 1783-7, R. East Lavant, Sussex 1786-1805 (res.), R. Myland St Michael, Essex 1791-5 (res.), (Sinecure) R. Elm, Cambridge 1795-1840 (res.) [value £1,641], Canon of 2nd Prebend in Ely 1795-1841, Archdeacon of Middlesex 1806-40 (res.). Died Twickenham 1/5/1841 aged 85 [C5102] Married Marylebone, London 13/1/1795 Cornelia Kuyck Van Mierop, *s.p.*

CAMERON (Charles Richard) Bapt. Worcester 7/5/1799, s. Rev. Charles Cameron and Ann Ingram. Christ Church, Oxford 1796, BA1800, dn03 (Wor.), MA1803, p04 (Wor.). PC. Wombridge, Shropshire 1808-56, R. Swaby, Lincs. 1831-65, PC. Donnington Wood, Shropshire 1832 (res.). Died 10/1/1865, leaving £2,000 [C9798. Boase] Married Worcester 12/6/1806 Lucy Lyttleton Butt, 12 ch. (some clerical).

CAMIDGE (Charles Joseph) Born York 26/2/1801, s. Matthew Camidge (organist of York Minster) and Mary Shaw. St Catherine's, Cambridge 1820, BA1824, dn24 (Lin. for York), p25 (Lin. for York), MA1827. PC. Nether Poppleton, Yorks. 1826-55 (with Chap. to York Poor Law Union 1849), V. Wakefield All Saints 1855-75, Hon. Canon of Ripon Cathedral 1861, RD of Wakefield 1869-75. Retired to Leamington, Warwicks., dying there 10/2/1878 aged 76, leaving £4,000 [C46644. YCO. Boase. BBV] Married Hull 3/7/1828 Charlotte Hustwick.

CAMPBELL (Archibald Montgomery-) From London, s. Archibald Montgomery Campbell, *H.E.I.C.*, and Ann Humphries. St John's, Cambridge 1807, BA1811 [admitted Lincoln's Inn 1812] dn13 (C&L), p14 (C&L), MA1816, Fellow. R. Little Steeping, Lincs. 1818-59 (non-res.), PC. Paddington St James, London (and Prebend of Caddington Major in St Paul's Cathedral, London) 1829 to death 23/5/1859, leaving £1,500 [C9626. Bennett2] Married Benington, Herts. 16/8/1814, Elizabeth Julia Chesshyre, with issue. Engraved port. online.

CAMPBELL (Augustus) Bapt. St Olave, City of London 4/4/1786, s. William Campbell and Anne Pitcairn. Trinity, Cambridge 1803, BA 1807 [barrister Lincoln's Inn 1809-12] dn11 (Nor.), p12 (Nor.), MA1812. R. Wallasey, Cheshire 1814-24, V. Childwall All Saints, Liverpool (and Preacher throughout the County of Lancaster) 1824 and R. Liverpool (1st Mediety 1829, then both Medieties 1855) [total income in CR65 £1,800] to death 15/5/1870 aged 84, leaving £70,000 [C111886. Boase] Married Liverpool 10/12/1816 Elizabeth Aspinall, with clerical son. 'Strongly anti-Catholic and anti-Irish'.

CAMPBELL (Charles) Bapt. Weasenham, Norfolk 9/10/1791, s. Rev. Charles Campbell, sen. Caius, Cambridge 1809 [in the army for three years] no degree, dn17 (Nor.), p18 (Nor.). (succ. his father as) V. Weasenham St Peter 1822 and R. Beachamwell All Saints w. Shingham, Norfolk [both blank in ERC] 1822 to death 20/5/1878, leaving £35,000 [C111887] Married Chesterfield, Derbys. 25/9/1820 Sarah Jane Thomas, w. clerical son.

CAMPBELL (Colin Alexander) Born Ardchattan, Argyll 23/9/1796, s. Lt.-Gen. Colin Campbell (a former Governor of Gibraltar) and Mary Louisa Johnstone. Trinity, Cambridge 1815, BA1819, dn20 (Chester), p21 (Chester), MA1825. R. Widdington, Essex 1821 and R.

Brooksby, Leics. 1835 to death 29/4/1860, leaving £2,000 [C46649] Married Felbrigg Hall, Norfolk 29/11/1820 Hon. Beatrice Byng (dau. of 5th Viscount Torrington), *s.p.* Brother James Thomas, below.

CAMPBELL (Daniel) Born Soho, London, 2 s. Robert Campbell and Frances Jones. Adm. Gray's Inn 1795. Trinity Hall, Cambridge 1799 (aged 20), SCL1804, dn04 (London) p13 (Ex.), LLB1827. V. Crowcombe, Somerset [blank in ERC] (and Preacher throughout the Diocese of B&W) 1827 to death (Fordington, Dorset) 15/5/1853 aged 75 [C41935] Married Thorpe, Surrey 30/4/1807 Elizabeth Fisher, w. issue.

CAMPBELL (James Thomas) Bapt. Marylebone, London 9/4/1800, s. of Lt.-Gen. Colin Campbell (a former Governor of Gibraltar) and Mary Louisa Johnstone. Wadham, Oxford 1819, migrated to Queens', Cambridge 1824, dn26 (C&L), BA1827, p27 (C&L), MA1832. R. Tilston, Cheshire 1829-50. Died Jersey 1866 (1st q.)? [C9628] Married (1) Edinburgh 29/3/1827 Jane Maxwell, dau. of David Dale of New Lanark (she d.1851) (2) Elizabeth de Gruchy (of Jersey: he was 71, she 32 in 1871). Brother Colin Alexander, above.

CAMPBELL (Robert) [NiVoF] R. Skirbeck, Boston, Lincs. 1818 to death 6/3/1834 (CCEd thus)[C46652]

CAMPBELL (Robert Caleb) Born Jamaica 20/12/1759. Literate: dn (Lin.), p00 (York). PC. Skelbrooke w. V. Owston, Yorks. 1800 to death 30/8/1833 aged 75 (CCEd says 22/10/1833) [C87935 and YCO as Robert. C130919 as Robert Caleb] Confusion here.

CANDLER (Philip) Bapt. Blofield, Norfolk 25/6/1740, s. Rev. Philip Candler, sen. (*'alias Gillet'*) and Mary Heath. Caius, Cambridge 1758, BA1762, dn62 (Nor.), p64 (Nor.). R. Lammas w. Little Hautbois, Norfolk 1764-1832, R. Burnham Overy, Norfolk 1773-1832, R. Brampton, Cambs. 1774-1826, R. Letheringsett, Norfolk 1826 to death 29/12/1832 aged 91 [C111890] Married Coltishall, Norfolk 9/10/1770 Charlotte Mallison.

CANE (William Augustus) Born Dublin 1755, s. Lt.-Col. Maurice Cane. [A drummer boy and fifer from the age of 8; Lt. 2nd Foot 1777].

Literate: dn90 (Win.), p91 (Car. for Bristol), then St Alban Hall, Oxford 1791 (aged 35), then Exeter, BA1794, MA1797. R. Ingram, Northumberland 1791-1801 (non-res. as completing his degree in Oxford), PC. Doddington, Northumberland 1798 and R. St Mary at Hill w. St Andrew Hubbard, City of London 1812 to death. Chap. to Duke of Northumberland; and to HRH Duke of Cumberland 1808-12. Died London 5/10/1834. [C116666] Married Alnwick, Northumberland 22/12/1777 Dorothy Ogle.

CANNING (Thomas) From Elsenham, Essex 20/5/1792, s. Rev. Thomas Canning and Hester Welch. Christ's, Cambridge 1810, BA1815, dn15 (London), p16 (Salis. for London). (succ. his father as) V. (and patron) of Elsenham 1818 to death (unm.) 11/11/1855 [C91494] 'A strong, stoutly built man, fond of shooting and boxing.'

CANNING (William) Born London 4/11/1778, s. of Stratford Canning (a merchant, and brother of 1st Viscount Stratford de Redcliffe, and cousin of the statesman) and Mehitabel ('Hitty') Patrick. Sidney, Cambridge 1797, BA1801, dn02 (London), p05 (London). V. West Heslerton, Yorks. 1817-47, Canon of Windsor Chapel 1828 to death 2/3/1860, aged 82 (the funeral being postponed 'since the appearances usually following death have not appeared'), leaving £30,000 [C116668] Married Clewer, Berks. 5/5/1818 Mary Ann Birch, *s.p.*

CANTERBURY (Archbishop of) see under **HOWLEY, William**

CANTRELL (William) Bapt. Hope, Derbys. 23/1/1772, s. Thomas Cantrell and Jane Mellor (or s. Hugh Cantrell, King's Newton, Derbys.?). Queens', Cambridge 1791, BA1795, dn96 (Lin.), p98 (Lin.). PC. Thrumpton, Notts. 1811 to death 10/4/1856 aged 83 (living at Alvaston Field, Derby) [C9803] Married Stapleford, Notts. 1808 Anne Smith (a clergy dau.)

CAPARN (John) From Lincoln, s. Daniel Caparn. Lincoln, Oxford 1772 (aged 18), BA 1776, dn76 (Lin.), then Corpus Christi, Cambridge MA1797, p78 (Lin.). R. Toft next Newton, Lincs. 1779 and R. Leverton (North and South Moieties), Lincs. 1797 to death. Dom. Chap. to 5th Duke of Ancaster and Kesteven

1797. Died 17/9/1834 aged 80 (CCEd says 13/1/1835) [C46907]

CAPE (Jonathan) Born Uldale, Cumberland, s. Rev. Joseph Cape. Trinity, Cambridge 1812, BA1816, dn16 (Salis. for Win.), p18 (Salis.), MA1821. [Assistant Professor, Naval College, Portsmouth. Professor of Mathematics at Addiscombe College 1822-61 ('an excellent teacher and disciplinarian with a keen sense of humour')]. (succ. his father as) R. (and patron) of Uldale 1830-3 [C4578. Boase. Platt] Died (an unm. lodger) Croydon, Surrey 9/9/1868 aged 75, leaving £12,000. *F.R.S.* (1852). Photo. online.

CAPEL (William Robert, Hon.) Born 28/4/1775, s. William, 4th Earl of Essex and Harriet Blaydon. Merton, Oxford 1794, BA 1798, MA1799. V. Watford, Herts. 1799 (where the bishop pursued a legal case against him for neglect of duty) and R. Rayne, Essex (both family livings) 1805 to death. Chap. in Ordinary 1814 to death (Watford) 3/12/1854 aged 79 [C116669. Boase] Married 7/6/1802 Sarah Salter (a brewer's dau.), with issue. A noted cricketer, foxhunter, and drinker. https://en.wikipedia.org/wiki/William_Capel (sportsman)

CAPPER (George) Born. Earl Soham, Suffolk 15/12/1767, s. Rev. Francis Capper and Elizabeth Peirson. Trinity, Cambridge 1783, BA1789, dn90 (Nor.), Fellow 1791, p92 (Nor.), MA1792. R. Little Blakenham, Suffolk 1794, R. Knodishall w. Buxlow, Suffolk 1799-1801, R. Gosbeck St Mary, Suffolk (non-res.) 1803, V. Wherstead, Suffolk 1815 to death (London) 4/6/1847 [C111898. LBSO] Married 1805 Anne Reid (of Jamaica), *s.p. J.P.* and Chairman of Quarter Sessions. A well-known hunting parson, and a keen yachtsman.

CAPPER (James) Born Rugeley, Staffs. 23/1/1754, s. William Capper (mercer and draper) and Rebecca Smallwood. St John's, Cambridge 1775, BA1779, dn79 (Roch.), p79 (B&W), MA1792. V. Wilmington, Sussex 1785-1835, sequestrator of Lullington, Sussex 1805, Fittleworth Prebend in Chichester 1802 and R. Ashurst, Kent 1802 to death (London) 2/3/1835 (CCEd says 13/3/1835) aged 81 [C73] Married (1) Burton-under-Needwood, Staffs. 18/1/1781 Catherine Jane Biddulph (d.1787), w. issue (2) Hackney, London 4/19/1804 Ann Nicklin.

CARD (Henry) Bapt. Egham, Berks. 14/6/1779, s. John Edward and Mary Card. Pembroke, Oxford 1796, BA1800, MA1805, dn12 (Salis.), p12 (Win.), BD and DD1823. V. Wolferlow, Heref. 1812-13, R. Upper Sapey, Worcs. 1812-16 (res.), V. Great Malvern, Worcs. 1815 and V. Dormington w. Bartestree, Heref. 1832 to death. Dom. Chap. to Susanna Maria, Viscountess Gage 1812. Died (Great Malvern) 4/8/1844 ('from the consequencies of the amputation of his leg') [C71269] Married (1) Finsbury, London 16/9/1789 Mary Anne Buckley, *s.p.* (2) Liverpool 6/6/1809 Christian Fletcher, 2s, 3 dau. *F.R.S.* (1820), *F.S.A.*

CARDALE (George) Born Rothley, Leics. 9/9/1761, s. Rev. George Cardale, sen. St John's, Cambridge 1781, BA1785, dn85 (Lin.), p87 (Lin.), MA1788. R. Millbrook, Beds. 1790 and V. Flitwick, Beds. 1820 to death (a widower) 1/1/1843 aged 83 [C46903] Married Leicester 26/5/1791 Judith Carter, with clerical son George Carter Cardale.

CARDEW (John Haydon) Born St Erme, Cornwall 16/2/1773 (CCEd says 8/3/1773), s. of Rev. Cornelius Cardew and Elizabeth Bruton. Exeter, Oxford 1790, BA1794, dn95 (Ex.), p97 (Ex.), MA1797, BD 1813. R. Curry Mallet, Som. 1797 and V. Salcombe Regis, Devon 1813 to death 8/11/1853 aged 81 [C33639] Married St Gluvias, Cornwall 4/9/1798 Mary Pollet, w. many ch. Port. online.

CARDWELL (Edward) Born Blackburn, Lancs. (bapt. Wigan 19/8/1787), s. Richard Cardwell and Jane Hodson. BNC, Oxford 1806, BA1809, Fellow 1809, MA1812, dn12 (Ox.), p13 (Ox.), BD1819, DD 1831. Camden Professor of Ancient History, Oxford 1825-61. Principal of St Alban's Hall, Oxford 1831-61. R. Stoke Bruerne, Northants. 1828-[36]. Declined the Deanery of Carlisle 1844. Died 23/5/1861 aged 73, leaving £45,000 [C24313. ODNB as church historian] Married Sussex 5/3/1829 Cecilia Feilden, with issue. An excellent administrator. *F.S.A.*

CAREW (Thomas) Born Haccombe, Devon 15/2/1788, s. Sir Thomas Carew, 6th Bart. and Jane Smallwood (a clergy dau.). Sidney, Cambridge 1805, BA1809, MA1812, dn15 (B&W), p15 (Bristol), BD1819, Fellow. R. Haccombe 1824 and R. Bickleigh, Devon 1826 to death 13/11/1848 aged 60. Lived at Colliprest House, Tiverton, Devon [C41991] Married Cullompton, Devon 12/1820 Holway Baker, with clerical son Robert Baker Carew in same parish.

CAREY (Nicholas) Born St Peter Port, Guernsey, Channel Islands 12/1/1772, s. John Carey and Marie Le Ray. Pembroke, Oxford 1787, BA1792, dn94 (C&L), MA1796. S/M Guernsey G/S 1795; R. Guernsey St Martin 1796, R. Guernsey St Peter Port 1832 (and Dean of Guernsey) to death. Royal Chap. at St James's Palace. Died 4/3/1858, leaving £25,000 [C9838. Boase] Married (1) Guernsey 7/9/1795 Sarah Anne Gosselin (d.1801), w. issue (2) Guernsey 1/12/1812 Mrs Harriet (Le Marchant) MacGregor (a military widow, d.1817), with further issue (3) Guernsey 24/2/1820 Martha La Serre.

CAREY (Richard) Bapt. Worcester 12/10/1763, s. Richard Carey. Worcester, Oxford 1780, BA 1784, MA1787, dn87 (Wor.), p88 (Wor.). R. Barrowden, Rutland 1795-1840 [C110026 as Cary], PC. Newland, Worcs. 1803, Prebend of Knaresborough in York Minster 1815 to death 9/4/1840 aged 73 [C120570] Wife Sarah, with clerical son below. Brother of William Carey, Bishop of St Asaph.

CAREY (William Sherlock) Bapt. Barrowden, Rutland 9/11/1799, s. Rev. Richard and Sarah Carey (above). Christ Church, Oxford 1816, BA1820, dn22 (Ox.), MA1823, p23 (Ox.). R. St Peter Tavy, Devon 1824, R. Ashburton, Devon 1825-35 (res.), R. Lezant, Cornwall 1830 to death. Dom. Chap. to Bishop of Exeter 1830. Died Canterbury 1847 (1st q.) [C24316] Married Brighton, Sussex 3/8/1825 Eliza Caroline Schneider.

CARLES (Richard Simcoe) Bapt. Birmingham 26/2/1768, s. Joseph and Sarah Carles. University, Oxford 1787, dn90 (C&L), BA1791, p92 (C&L). V. (and patron of) Aston Cantlow, Warwicks. 1800, V. and R. Haselor, Warwicks. 1809 to death 8/5/1846 (or burial 30/4/1846?) aged 78 [C9840]

CARLETON (Hugh Casement) Born Lisburn, Ireland 25/9/1872, s. Cornelius Carleton and Elizabeth Casement. Worcester, Oxford 1801, BA1805, dn05 (Heref. for Wor.), p06 (C&L for Wor.), MA1808. PC. Preston on Stour, Glos. 1806, R. Arrow, Warwicks. 1807-62, R. Exhall w. Wixford, Warwicks. 1815. Dom. Chap. to 1st Viscount Carleton 1815. Died (Arrow) 2/12/1862, leaving £12,000 [C9841] Married Alcester, Warwicks. 27/10/1818 Sarah Aynsworth.

CARLETON (Richard, Hon.) Born Marylebone, London 10/2/1792, s. Gen. Guy Carleton, 1st Baron Dorchester (then aged 67) and Lady Maria Howard (dau. of 2nd Earl of Effingham). Trinity Hall, Cambridge 1811 (re-adm. 1825), BA1811, MA1811, dn15 (Heref.), p15 (Heref.). R. Boughton, Northants. 1815-43, R. Nately Scures, Hants. 1819. Lived in London. Died Brighton 2/2/1869, leaving £600 [C71276. Boase] Married Marylebone, London 20/7/1820 Frances Louisa Horton (Catton Hall, Derbys.), with issue. *F.R.S.* (1826).

CARLISLE (Bishop of) see under **PERCY (Hugh, Hon.)**

CARLISLE, 8th Earl of see under **HOWARD (William George, Hon.)**

CARLISLE (William) Probably born Sedbergh, Yorks. 1/7/1762, s. William Carlisle. Literate: dn85 (Chester), p87 (C&L), then Magdalen, Oxford 1791, BA1798, MA1799. R. Ipstones, Staffs. 1789-1833, PC. Earl Sterndale, Derbys. 1789 and R. and V. Sutton [in the Dale] cum Duckmarton, Staffs. 1806 to death 29/7/1833 (CCEd thus) [C9805] Married Ipstones 31/1/1791 Frances Wolfe, with issue.

CARLOS (James) Bapt. Blofield, Norfolk 24/4/1773, s. Rev. James Carlos, sen. and Mary Fromenteel. Caius, Cambridge 1789, BA1790, MA1787, dn95 (Nor.), p97 (Nor.). R. Drinkstone, Suffolk 1804, R. Thorpe next Haddiscoe, Norfolk 1804-44, PC. Wangford, Suffolk 1831 to death 20/1/1851 [C111903] Married Norwich 29/5/1809 Lydia Louisa Bond.

CARLYLE (Irving) Literate: dn19 (Chester), p21 (Chester). PC. New Mills, Glossop, Derbys. 1831 to death 1847 aged 54 [C168449] Married New Mills 28/6/1837 Mrs Barbara Benson.

CARLYON (Philip) Born Truro, Cornwall 15/5/1769, s. Rev. John Carlyon and Mary Winstanley. Pembroke, Cambridge 1787, BA 1792, dn93 (Ex.), p93 (Ex.), MA1795. R. (and patron) of St Mawgan in Pyder, Cornwall 1806 to death 21/3/1846 aged 76 [C140542] Married Clovelly, Devon 7/10/1808 Mary Phear, with clerical son.

CARLYON (Thomas Stackhouse) Born Probus, Cornwall 15/6/1802, s. Rev. Thomas Carlyon and Mary Stackhouse. Pembroke, Cambridge 1818, BA1823, dn25 (Ex.), p26 (Ex.), MA1829. R. Truro St Mary, Cornwall 1826-39 and V. (St) Feock, Cornwall 1828-33, V. Egloshayle, Cornwall 1833-49, R. Glenfield, Leics. 1849-72. Dom. Chap. to Earl of Falmouth 1828. Died Bath 15/3/1877 aged 74, leaving £12,000 [C136725] Married Kenwyn, Cornwall 26/2/1832 Emily Carlyon [*thus*] (w), w. issue.

CARNEGIE (James) Born Chichester 1795, s. Col. John Carnegie and Catherine Tireman. Emmanuel, Cambridge 1812, BA1817, dn18, p19 (Salis.), MA1820. V. Littlehampton, Sussex 1823, V. Sutton cum Seaford, Sussex 1824 to death 6/2/1864 aged 69, leaving £7,000 [C62736] Widow Phoebe, *s.p.*

CARPENDALE (William) Born Armagh 20/6/1802, s. Rev. Thomas Carpendale (H/M Armagh College) and Jane Maxwell. TCD1818, then St John's, Cambridge 1822, BA1826, dn25 (Ely for Bristol), p26 (Bristol), MA1838. PC. Wincanton, Som. 1829-38, R. Silton, Dorset at death 13/8/1838 [C6612. Al.Dub.] Married Walton in Gordano, Som. 12/8/1828 Emma Coulson, and had issue.

CARPENTER (William) Born Queen's Co., s. Thomas Carpenter. Adm. Gray's Inn. TCD 1820 (aged 15), BA1828, dn31 (Ossory), p32 (Kildare), Hon. DD1840 (TCD). Chap. Braddon St Barnabas, Douglas, IoM 1832-48, V. Liverpool St Jude 1849-50, V. Christ Church, Moss Side, Manchester 1850-64, V. Paul, Cornwall 1864 ('for health reasons') to death 24/12/1865 aged 60, leaving £2,000 [C7445. Al.Dub. Gelling] Married (said to have eloped with) Jane (w), dau. of Sir William Forbes, of Cragievar, Aberdeenshire, 5th Bart., with issue.

CARR (Charles) Born Knaresborough, Yorks. 3/8/1793, s. Charles Carr (a physician) and Elizabeth Smith. University, Oxford 1811, BA 1815, Fellow, dn16 (York), p17 (York), MA 1818. R. Burnby, Yorks. 1818-61 and R. Headbourne Worthy, Hants. 1824 to death (Burnby) 25/4/1861, leaving £3,000 [C130927. YCO] Married Lockington, Yorks. 1840 (1st q.) Elizabeth Agnes Lundy (a clergy dau.).

CARR (Christopher) Born Horton-in-Ribblesdale, Yorks. 28/9/1788, s. John Carr. Literate: dn12 (Nor.), p13 (Nor.). PC. Newborough, Northants. 1830-51-. Died? [C111889]

CARR (Edmund) Born Chelsea, London c.1786, s. Edmund Carr. Trinity. Oxford 1806 (aged 20), BA1810, dn10 (London), p10 (Glos.), MA1812. R. Quatt, Shropshire 1817, R. Wolstanton, Shropshire 1817 to death 12/9/1864, leaving £18,000 [C9844] Married Quatt 5/3/1813 Anna Maria Whitmore.

CARR (James) Born Gilling, Yorks. 18/4/1794, s. William and Hannah Carr. Literate: dn20 (Lin. for Durham), p21 (Durham), then St John's, Cambridge 1829 (a Ten Year Man). PC. Durham St Giles 1831, PC. South Shields St Hild, Jarrow, Durham 1831-62, PC. Westoe, Durham 1853-62, Hon. Canon of Durham 1860 (and Master of Sherburn Hospital [almshouses], Durham 1862) to death. Dom. Chap. to Marquess of Londonderry. Died 29/3/1874 aged 79, leaving £4,000 [C24373. Boase]. Married Bishopwearmouth, Durham 21/10/1824 Catherine Haslewood (w) (a clergy dau.), with clerical son.

CARR (John) From Selston, Notts., s. Rev. Anthony Carr. St John's, Cambridge 1763, BA 1767, dn67 (Chester), MA1770, p70 (Peterb.), BD1778, Fellow 1768, Tutor. R. Great Oakley, Essex 1783-1833 (non-res.), Prebend of Moreton and Whaddon in Hereford Cathedral 1805-7 (res.), V. Hatfield Broad Oak, Harlow, Essex 1817 and PC. Holbrooke, Derbys. 1820 to 'natural death' 23/8/1833 (CCEd thus) [C9806] Married Ellenhall, Staffs. 28/9/1764 Anne Stubbs, Abbey House, Ranton, Staffs.

CARR (John) Probably bapt. Giggleswick, Yorks. 18/3/1785, s. William Carr and Margaret Bagot. Trinity, Cambridge 1803, BA1807, Fellow 1808, MA1810, dn13 (Durham), p14 (Durham). S/M 1811 then H/M Durham G/S 1833; V. Brantingham, Yorks. 1818-33.

Appointed Professor of Mathematics, Durham College but died 30/10/1833 (CCEd says 2/11/1833) aged 47 [C134146] Married 8/1/1817 Rosetta Anne Hopper (Witton Castle, Durham), with issue. A fine port. in D. Cross, *Joseph Bouet's Durham: drawings from the age of reform* (Durham, 2005) note 75. Another person of this name ordained Durham with possible confusion.

CARR (John Addison) Bapt. Swannington, Norfolk 14/6/1762, s. George and Elizabeth Carr. Jesus, Cambridge 1778, BA1783, dn85 (Nor.), p86 (Bangor for London), MA1786. R. Hadstock, Essex 1786 to death (London) 1/8/1838 aged 76 [C101146] Married Newmarket 20/10/1788 Susanna Brand, with issue.

CARR (John Edmund) Born Leicester 25/9/1796, s. Rev. George Carr. St John's, Cambridge 1817, BA1821, dn22 (Chester for C&L), p22, MA1824. PC. Alsop-en-le-Dale, Derbys. 1822-33 (res.), R. Parwich, Derbys. 1822-33 (res.), V. Darley (Abbey), Derby 1825-60. Died (Outwoods House, Duffield, Derbys.) 31/7/1872, leaving £45,000 [C9632. Austin] Married Derby 23/11/1822 Ellen Evans (of Darley), with clerical son Edmund Carr.

CARR (Robert James, Bishop of Worcester) Born Twickenham, Surrey 9/5/1774, s. Rev. Colston Carr and Elizabeth Bullock. Worcester, Oxford 1792, BA1796, dn96 (Salis.), p98 (Salis.), MA1806, BD and DD1820. V. Brighton, Sussex 1798 (where he attracted the attention of the Prince Regent, who became his patron, and at whose deathbed he was present), Prebend of Salisbury Cathedral 1819-24, Dean of Hereford 1820, Prebend of Chichester 1821-24, Prebend of Pretum Majus in Hereford Cathedral 1822-4. Clerk of the Closet (dismissed by Victoria). Bishop of Chichester (w. Canon of St Paul's *in commendam*, and where he was the first bishop to visit his diocese since 1755) 1824-31. Bishop of Worcester 1831 to death (Hartlebury Palace) 24/4/1841. The wish of the diocesan clergy to attend his funeral was declined by his family [C31117. ODNB] Married Twickenham 28/4/1796 Nancy Wilkinson ('a lady of good fortune'), w. issue.

CARR (Samuel) Bapt. Colchester, Essex 20/6/1792, s. Samuel Pupplett (?) Carr and Sarah Oliver. Queens', Cambridge 1809, BA 1814, dn15 (London), p15 (Nor.), Fellow 1817, MA1817. PC. Ipswich St Mary at the Quay, Suffolk 1822-30, V. Great Eversden and Little Eversden, Cambs. 1825-54, V. Colchester St Peter, Essex 1830 (church destroyed by fire 1842) to death. Chap. to HRH Duke of Sussex. Surrogate for Rochester. Died 17/6/1854 aged 63 [C6613] Married Hampstead, London 7/2/1826 Martha Diana Henning, w. issue.

CARR (Thomas) Bapt. Tosside Chapel, Gisburn, Yorks. 14/10/1753, s. Thomas Carr. Literate: dn77 (York), p79 (York). S/M 1782; then V. Thorner, Leeds 1805 to death 22/9/1837 [C87965. YCO]

CARR (William) Born Bolton Abbey, Yorks. 27/5/1763, s. Rev. Thomas Carr. University, Oxford 1781, BA1785, dn85 (Glos. for York), p87 (Ox. for York), then Magdalen MA1788, BD1795. R. Bolton Abbey 1789-1843 (and S/M Bolton Abbey G/S), R. Wydiall, Herts. 1797, R. Aston Tirrold w. Tubney, Berks. 1802-31. Died Bolton Abbey 23/7/1843 aged 80 [C24378, YCO] Author of a Craven dialect dictionary; and breeder of the famous Craven Heifer in 1807 (at 317 stone the largest such beast ever recorded).

CARRIGHAN, *born* GOSLI (Arthur Judd) Born Stamford, Lincs. 11/5/1780, s. Stamford Carrighan. St John's, Cambridge 1798, BA1803, dn03 (B&W), Fellow 1804-43, p05 (Peterb.). BA1806, BD1813. R. Barrow, Suffolk 1832 to death 13/3/1845 aged 64 [C41958 under Gosli] Married Great Saxham, Suffolk 27/8/1833 Julia Mills (Great Saxham Hall). 'A gentleman and a scholar'.

CARRINGTON (Caleb) Literate: dn80 (C&L for Salis.), p81 (Cant.), possibly a Ten Year Man at Pembroke, Cambridge? V. Berkeley, Glos. 1799 [sequestrated] to death 29/5/1837 aged 79 [C9634 suggests confusion] Had issue. His 'Carrington's Life Pills' were still advertised in 1842 as a cure for colds, rheumatism, gout and indigestion.

CARRINGTON (Robert Palk) Born Ide, Devon 31/3/1781, s. Rev. James Carrington and Frances Welland. Oriel, Oxford 1799, dn03 (Ex.), BA1805, p05 (B&W). R. Bridford, Devon 1805 to death. Dom. Chap. to 1st Duke of Buckingham & Chandos 1815. Died 7/7/1842

[C33674] Married (1) Exeter 28/10/1814 Dorothea Williams (d.1817), w. issue (2) Marylebone, London 1/6/1819 Camilla Anne Adair (Tillington, Sussex, d.1822), w. further issue.

CARROW (Richard) From Warren, Pembrokeshire, s. Richard Carrow. Corpus Christi, Cambridge 1791 (aged 17), then Pembroke, BA1797, p99 (Bristol), MA1802. R. Broxholme, Lincs. 1805, PC. North Carlton, Lincs. 1805, PC. Westbury on Trym, Glos. 1810. Probably died Redland, Bristol 26/2/1847 [C8205] Married Redland, Bristol 1806 Mary Elton (dau. of a merchant), with issue.

CARTER (Claude Jamineau) Born Sudbury, Suffolk 17/12/1763, s. William and Sarah Carter. Literate: dn87 (Peterb. for Ely), p10 (Ely). R. Great Henny, Essex 1811 to death 25/6/1833 (CCEd thus) [C99610] Married Stepney, London 28/6/1815 Sybilla Mendham.

CARTER (George) From Oxford, s. William Carter [*pleb*]. Chorister Magdalen, Oxford 1802-7; matr. Christ Church, Oxford 1810 (aged 18), BA1813, then New, Chap. 1815-18, dn16 (London), p16 (London), MA1816. Minor Canon of Norwich Cathedral 1816 (Precentor 1831) to death, V. Trowse w. Lakenham, Norfolk 1817, V. Bawburgh, Norfolk 1829. Died 20/2/1860, leaving £800 [C11595] Married St Mary in the Marsh, Norfolk 26/12/1820 Anne Murray Brown (w), with isssue.

CARTER (James) Born Dublin 1781, s. Oliver Carter. St Alban Hall, Oxford 1806, SCL1807, dn07 (B&W). [Bristol City Librarian? 1809-15] PC. Churchdown, Som. 1814-26, V. Bathford w. Bathampton >< Bath, Som. 1824 to death 1854 (2nd q.) [C33676]

CARTER (John) Bapt. Halifax, Yorks. 21/6/1801, s. Jeremiah Carter. St John's, Cambridge 1819, BA1824, dn25 (York), p26 (York), MA1827, DD1841. PC. Saxton, Yorks. 1832 (and H/M Queen Elizabeth's School, Wakefield 1841-51) to death (a widower) 9/11/1878 aged 77, leaving £2,000 [C136762. YCO] Wife Anne, with issue.

CARTER (Joseph) Bapt. Norwich 16/1/1788, s. Joseph Chamberlain Carter and Emily Smith. St John's, Oxford 1806, BA1810, dn10 (Nor.), p11 (Nor.), MA 1817, BD1821, Fellow 1834. V. Oxford St Giles 1828-33 (res.) [blank in ERC], V. Bainton, Driffield, Yorks. 1833-[43] Died? [C24493]

CARTER (Matthew Inman) Bapt. Kendal, Westmorland 12/11/1775, s. Roger Carter and Elizabeth Inman. Christ Church, Cambridge 1796, BA1800, dn02 (Chester), p03 (Chester), MA1805. PC. Rusland, Lancs. 1803-9, PC. Torver, Ulverston, Lancs. 1807 to death (unm., Kendal) 15/2/1864 aged 87, leaving £1,500 [C168452]

CARTER (William) Bapt. Bolton upon Swale, Yorks. 24/6/1768, s. Robert Carter. Literate: dn91 (Glos. for York), p92 (York). V. Weston, Otley, Yorks. 1829 ['for 26 years'?]. Died? [C135375. YCO] Note: a John Carter was at Weston in 1816.

CARTER (William) Eton. [MA but NiVoF]. V. Hullavington, Wilts. 1827 to death (a widower) 21/2/1864, leaving £10,000 [C91501] Had issue.

CARTER (William) [NiVoF] PC. Wolstanton, New Chapel, Staffs. 1832-41. Died? [C9848]

CARTER (William Drayton) Born Portsmouth, Hants., s. William Grover Carter and Ann Opie. Magdalen, Oxford 1818 (aged 22), no degree, dn19 (C&L for Win.), p21 (Salis.). PC. Wye, Kent 1832-[58]. Died Kirkby Moorside, Yorks. 1/12/1864, leaving under £200 [C9849] Married 1822 Emma Bingham Gauntlet (w), w. issue.

CARTMEL (George) From Farlton, Westmorland, s. Thomas Cartmel. Pembroke, Cambridge 1823, BA1827, dn28 (London for Cant.), p29 (London for Cant.), MA1830. R. Milton (next Canterbury), Kent 1829-34, R. Pwllcrochan, Pembroke 1834 to death 24/6/1857 [C116679]

CARTWRIGHT (Edmund) Born Marnham, Notts. 2/12/1773, s. Rev. Edmund Cartwright (inventor of the power loom) and Alice Whitaker. Balliol, Oxford 1788, BA1792, MA 1795. [An officer in the West Yorkshire Militia]. R. North Scarle, Lincs. 1802-5, R. Kilvington. Notts. 1803-5, R. Earnley and Almodington,

Sussex 1803-33, R. Storrington, Sussex 1805, R. Parham, Sussex 1819-25 (res.), Ferring Prebend in Chichester Cathedral 1826-33, V. Lyminster, Sussex 1833 to death. Chap. to HRH Duke of Gloucester 1819. Died 18/3/1833 (CCEd says 27/3/1833) [C47154] Married (1) St George's Hanover Square, London 13/4/1795 Sophia Wombwell (d.1796) (2) Pulborough, Sussex 16/5/1808 Ann Tredcroft (a clergy dau.), with issue.

CARTWRIGHT (Stephen Ralph) Born Aynhoe, Northants. 20/4/1807, s. Lt.-Col. William Ralph Cartwright (militia), M.P., and Hon. Emma Mary Maude (dau. Viscount Hawarden). Christ Church, Oxford 1824, BA 1828, dn29 (Peterb.), p30 (Peterb.), MA1831. R. Aynhoe 1830 to death 9/8/1862, leaving £5,000 [C110025] Married Lyndhurst, Hants. 2/8/1838 Fanny Hay, 1 dau.

CARTWRIGHT (Theodore John) Born Preston Bagot, Warwicks., s. Rev. John Cartwright. University, Oxford 1824 (aged 17), BA1828, dn29 (Chester), p30, MA1831. (succ. his father as) R. (and patron) of Preston Bagot 1831-67, R. Boylestone, Derbys. 1834. Died Lucerne, Switzerland 5/10/1867, leaving £4,000 [C9854] Married Newent, Glos. 13/7/1836 Anna Cecilia Onslow, w. clerical s. of father's name.

CARTWRIGHT (William Henry) Born Cawnpore, India, s. Capt. William Parry and Frances Cartwright. Trinity, Oxford 1817 (aged 18), BA1821, dn22 (Chester for C&L), p23 (Chester for C&L), MA1826. PC. Kingswinsford, Staffs. 1832, V. Dudley, Worcs. 1835, PC. Butcombe, Som. 1848-77. Died (Wrington, Som.) 29/10/1880, leaving £20,000 [C9855] Married Clun, Shropshire 1854 (2nd q.) Harriet Rogers, w. clerical sons Henry Antrobus, and Arthur Rogers Cartwright.

CARUS-WILSON (Roger Carus-) see under **WILSON**

CARUS-WILSON (William Carus-) see under **WILSON**

CARVER (Charles) Bapt. Long Stretton, Norfolk 14/3/1769, s. Rev. Charles Carver, sen. Caius, Cambridge 1786, BA1791, dn92 (Nor.), p93 (Nor.). PC. Aslacton, Norfolk 1793, V. Horning, Norfolk 1809-1855, R. Winfarthing, Norfolk 1814-16 (res.), R. Snetterton, Norfolk 1814-16 (res.). Died 11/7/1855 [C112036] Clerical son, also Charles.

CARWARDINE (Charles William) Bapt. Preston Wynne, Heref. 24/3/1775, s. Rev. Thomas Carwardine (Earls Colne Priory, Essex) and Ann Holgate. St John's, Cambridge 1792, BA1797, dn97 (Nor.), p99 (London), MA 1803. (succ. his father as) V. Cavenham, Suffolk 1805-41, R. Tolleshunt Knights, Essex 1805 to death 20/5/1857 [C112042. LBSO] Married Tolleshunt Knights 25/2/1812 Sarah Frances [*surname*] (Heybridge Hall, Essex), w. clerical sons Thomas William, and Henry Alexander. Brother, below.

CARWARDINE (John Bryan) Born Earls Colne Priory, Essex 15/2/1795, s. Rev. Thomas Carwardine and Ann Holgate. Emmanuel, Cambridge 1813, BA1818, dn18 (Nor.), p20 (Nor.), MA1822. V. Earls Colne 1824-29, R. Newland St Lawrence >< Essex 1829 to death 15/11/1871, leaving £30,000 [C116681] Married Earls Colne 18/1/1826 Anne Rogers, with issue. Brother, above.

CARWITHEN (William) Born Manaton, Devon 13/5/1783, s. Rev. William Carwithen and Mary Somers. St Mary Hall, Oxford 1800, BA1804, dn06 (B&W), p07 (Ex.), MA 1811, BD and DD1830. R. Exeter St Mary Steps, 1811, R. (and patron) of Manaton 1824, R. Exeter Allhallows on the Walls 1835, R. Bovey Tracey, Devon 1835, R. Stoke Climsland, Cornwall 1841. Chap. to County Debtors' Prison, 1816, and to County of Devon Gaol and House of Correction 1831. Died Exeter 19/4/1850 [C33680] Married Exeter 7/1/1812 Mary Melhuish Ford, with issue.

CARY (Charles Thomas) Bapt. Kingsbury, Warwicks. 9/5/1806, s. Rev. Henry Francis Cary (below) and Jane Ormsby. Magdalen, Oxford 1825, BA1829, dn30 (C&L), MA1832. V. Kingsbury 1832-75. Died 15/6/1881 aged 75, leaving £336-18s-9d. [C9892] Married Kingsbury 15/3/1863 Sarah Wilmot Cave-Browne-Cave (w).

CARY (Henry Francis) Born Gibraltar 6/12/1772, s. Capt. William Cary (1st Regiment of Foot) and Henrietta Brocas (dau. of a Dean of Killala, Ireland). Christ Church, Oxford 1790, BA1794, MA1796, dn96 (C&L). V. Abbots Bromley, Staffs. 1797-1844, V. Kingsbury, Warwicks. 1800-32 (res.) [Assistant Keeper, British Museum 1826]. Dom. Chap. to 1st Marquess of Anglesey 1812. Died 14/8/ 1844 (buried Westminster Abbey) [C9894. ODNB. H. Cary, *Memoir of the Rev. Henry Francis Cary, MA* (1847)] Married Dublin 20/8/1796 Jane Ormsby, with son above. His translation of Dante's *Divine Comedy* was standard for a long time.

CARY (John Henry Spelman) Bapt. South Lynn, Norfolk 9/7/1771. Christ's, Cambridge 1787, BA1792, dn94 (Nor.), p95 (Nor.), MA 1795. PC. Fernhurst, Sussex 1796 to death aged 81. Probate granted 12/5/1852 aged 81 [C112044] Married Thorpe-by-Ashbourne Derbys. 21/5/1810 Harriett Lloyd, with issue.

CASE (Isham) Born Bury St Edmunds c.1792, Suffolk, s. Philip James Case (solicitor). Jesus, Cambridge 1809, BA1814, dn15 (Ely for Nor.), p16 (Nor.), MA1817. R. Quarrington, Lincs. 1821-5, V. Metheringham, Lincs. 1825 and R. Springthorpe, Lincs. 1826 to death. Dom. Chap. to 9th Duke of St Albans 1826. Died 21/2/1863 aged 71, leaving £4,000 [C6618] Married Wyberton, Lincs. 22/2/1827 Catherine Sheath, with issue.

CASSAN (Stephen Hyde) Born Calcutta 8/10/1828, s. Stephen Cassan (barrister) and Sarah Mears. Magdalen Hall, Oxford 1811 [adm. Middle Temple 1811] BA1815, dn15 (Chester), p16 (Ely), MA1818. PC. Bruton, Som. 1831 and PC. Wyke Champflower, Som. 1831 to death. Chap. to HRH Duke of Cambridge; and to Earl of Caledon. Died 19/7/1841 aged 51 (apoplexy) [C41995] Contracted a 'stolen marriage' 27/12/1820 to Frances Ireland (a clergy dau.), with many ch. *F.S.A.* 'His mind gave way under the pressure of disease and pecuniary embarrassment, and he was obliged to be removed from the service of his benefice'. The *Gentleman's Magazine* has one of its most uncomplimentary obituaries.

CASSELS (Andrew) Born Lancaster 12/3/1806, s. Timothy Cassels (a physician) and Mary Hodgson. St John's, Cambridge 1822, BA 1829, dn29 (Chester), p30 (Chester), MA1832. V. Morley, Leeds 1831-9, V. Batley, Yorks. 1839 (living at Staincliffe Hall nearby, but latterly in Edinburgh 'for health reasons') to death 12/8/1874, leaving £10,000 [C136764] Married Edinburgh Hannah Cassels Anderson ('a Scottish lady half his age') 21/1/1857, with clerical son. Surrogate. Freemason. He was the 'vulgar and intrusive visitor' to the Bronte parsonage in Feb. 1850.

CASSON (Ferdinando) Bapt. Ulpha, Cumberland 19/8/1781, s. of Ferdinand Casson (a farmer) and Ann Atkinson. Literate: dn04 (Chester), p05 (Chester). TCD1821 (aged 38), BA1824, incorporated at Cambridge 1825. PC. Donative of Hargrave, Tarvin, Cheshire 1807 (and Minor Canon Chester Cathedral 1825) to death 22/3/1838 aged 56 [C168464. Al.Dub. Venn is possible] Married Bury, Lancs. 14/7/1808 Mary Ortt, with clerical son. Kept a boys' boarding school in Chester in 1834.

CASTELL (William) Born Brook, Norfolk, s. John Castell. Caius, Cambridge 1790, BA1795, dn95 (Nor.), Fellow 1796-8, p97 (Nor.), MA 1798. V. Brooke 1797 and V. (and patron) of Thuxton, Norfolk 1797 to death 24/10/1846 [C112097] Freeman of the City of Norwich 1794.

CASTLEY (Thomas) Bapt. Malew, IoM 3/7/1765, s. Rev. Thomas Castley, sen. (schoolmaster) and Janet Hamilton Nicholas. Jesus, Cambridge 1783, BA1787, Fellow 1789-1810, MA1790, p95 (Ely). PC. Cambridge St Clement 1795-1835, V. Cambridge All Saints 1798-1808, R. Cavendish, Suffolk 1808 to death 19/5/1860 aged 94, leaving £9,000 [C99612 has his father's date of death] Married Pentloe, Essex 7/5/1810 his housekeeper Susannah Griggs, 6 ch. Known as 'Ghastly Castley': www.castley.info/thomas1765.htm

CASTLEY (Timothy) Bapt. Skelton in Cleveland, Yorks. 8/6/1782, s. Timothy Castley and Mary Bryan. Literate: dn05 (York), p08 (Durham). R. Sneaton, Whitby, Yorks. 1827 to death 1848 (3rd q.) aged 66 [C87983. YCO] Married Sneaton 26/7/1830 Mary Havelock.

CASWALL (Robert Clarke) Born Swalecliffe, Oxon. 17/10/1768, s. Rev. John Caswall and Elizabeth Clarke Pryor. Balliol, Oxford 1785, then St John's, BCL1792, dn93 (Ox.), p94 (Ox.). PC. Llandogo w. PC. Penterry, Monmouth

1805-10 (res.), V. Yateley, Hants. 1814 (res.), V. West Lavington, Sussex 1828 to death 4/9/1846 [C3689] Married (1) Reading, Berks. 6/3/1794 Harriet Deane, with issue (died 'after barely a year of marriage') (2) Savoy Chapel, London 8/8/1809 Mary Burgess, with clerical son of father's name.

CATHCART (Archibald Hamilton, Hon.) Born 25/7/1764, s. of Charles, 9th Baron Cathcart and Jane Hamilton. Balliol, Oxford 1782, BA1786, dn86 (Lin.), p88 (Lin.), MA 1788. R. Ravenstone, Bucks. 1789-1823, V. Foscott, Bucks. 1791-7, R. Clifton Reynes, Bucks. 1791-1805, R. Taplow, Bucks. 1796-1805, Prebend of Barmby on the Moor 1800-2, then of Langtoft 1802-41 in York Minster, R. Methley, Yorks. 1805 and V. Kippax, Yorks. 1811 to death 10/10/1841 aged 77 [C47165] Married Marylebone, London 3/6/1790 Frances Henrietta Fremantle, with issue.

CATOR (Charles) Born Beckenham, Kent 25/8/1786, s. Joseph Heinz Carter and Diana Bertie ('reputed dau. of Lord Albemarle Bertie'). BNC, Oxford 1805, BA1810, dn10 (York), p11 (York), MA1814. R. Beckenham 1829-35 (res.), V. Carshalton, Surrey 1829-35 ('imprisoned for debt and forced to resign'), R. Stokesley, Yorks. 1835 [income in CR65 £1,400] to death 17/12/1872 aged 86, leaving £450 [C6725. YCO] Married (1) Marylebone, London 2/5/1809 Philadelphia Osbaldestone (d.1840), w. issue (2) Paddington, London 1/3/1849 Amelia Langford, w. further issue. Brother below.

CATOR (Thomas) Born Beckenham, Kent 19/2/1790, s. Joseph Cator and Diana Bertie ('reputed dau. of Lord Albemarle Bertie'). BNC, Oxford 1810, migrated to Trinity, Cambridge 1813, BA1815, dn15 (Roch.), p16 (Roch.), MA 1818. V. Womersley, Yorks. 1817-35, V. Woodbastwick w. Panxworth, Norfolk 1821-36, R. Emley (or Elmley), Yorks. 1827-30, R. Kirk Smeaton, Yorks. 1829 to death 24/8/1864 aged 74, leaving £200. Lived at Skelbrooke Park, Doncaster [C1742] Married Womersley 12/10/1825 Lady Louisa Frances Lumley Savile (dau. of Rev. the [7th] Earl of Scarborough), with clerical son. J.P. West Riding. Brother above.

CATTELL (Thomas) Possibly bapt. Warwick 23/10/1765, s. John Cattell. St John's, Oxford 1782, BA1786, dn88 (Ox.), MA1789, p89 (Chester for Ox.), BCL1792. R. Berkswell, Warwicks. 1791 to death 1836 aged 69 [C9896]

CATTLEY (Stephen Reed) Born Camberwell, Surrey c.1808, s. Stephen Cattley and Jane Isabella Reed. Queens', Cambridge 1825, BA 1830, dn30 (Lin.), p31 (Lin.), MA1834. R. Bagthorpe, Norfolk, 1832-57, PC. Clapham St George 1857-68, R. Fittleworth, Sussex 1868 to death. Chap. to Rev. the [7th] Earl of Scarborough; Chap. to Female Orphan Asylum Lambeth, Surrey. Died 21/5/1876, leaving £10,000 [C47166] Married 1830 Mary Ann Thomlinson, w. issue.

CATTLOW (John Stevenson) Bapt. Eccleshall, Staffs. 24/2/1768, s. Rev. Joseph Cattlow. St John's, Cambridge 1786, BA1790, dn92 (C&L), p92 (C&L), MA1793. PC. Chapel Chorlton, Staffs. 1796-1806, PC. then R. Whitmore, Staffs. 1796-1808, PC. 1796 then V. Madeley, Staffs. 1819-33, R. Coppenhall, Cheshire 1805 to death (Hereford) 10/1/1833 (CCEd says 10/9/1833) [C9812] Married Newcastle under Lyme, Staffs. 25/1/1797 Jane Ford, with issue.

CAULFIELD (Edward Warren) Born London 5/7/1796, s. Capt. Wade Toby Caulfield and Anne Cope. Queen's, Oxford 1815, BA1819, dn20 (Heref.), MA1822. R. Beechingstoke, Wilts. 1830 to death (Weston super Mare, Som.) 30/6/1871, leaving £30,000 [C91506] Married (1) Swainswick, Somerset 7/11/1825 Anne Pybus (d.1841), w. issue (2) Clifton, Bristol 20/10/1843 Millicent Hellicar (w), w. further issue.

CAUNTER (John Hobart) Born Dittisham, Devon 21/6/1792, s. George Caunter (Governor of Penang, Malaya) and Harriet Georgina Hutchings. [Cadet with 34th Regiment of Foot in India 1809]. Peterhouse, Cambridge 1817 (a Ten Year Man, BD1828), dn24 (York), p27 (London). Curate St Paul's, Foley Place, Marylebone, London 1825-44, PC. Portland Chapel [later St Paul's], Great Portland Street, London 1836-43, R. Hailsham, Sussex 1843-6, Min. of a Proprietary Chapel in Kensington, London 1846-8. Dom. Chap. to Earl of Thanet. Died London 14/11/1851 aged 57 [C116658. ODNB as minor poet and miscellaneous writer. Boase. YCO] Married (1) Marylebone, London

13/5/1815 Matilda Killick (of Penang, d.1838) (2) St Pancras, London 25/7/1845 Caroline Bartlett, with issue left 'unprovided for'. 'Well-known in London as the fashionable preacher of his day'.

CAUSTON (Thomas) Born Highgate, London 25/1/1869, s. Charles Causton and Susanna Thomas. St John's, Cambridge 1787, BA1791, dn91 (C&L for Salis.), p93 (Bristol for Salis.), MA1794, DD1820. Canon of Westminster Abbey 1799-1842, R. Turweston, Bucks. 1804 to death. Chap. to House of Commons. Died Bournemouth 5/11/1842 [C47170] Married St George's Hanover Square, London 1/6/1799 Mary Ann Balchen, with clerical son, below (and Rev. Charles Purefroy Causton).

CAUSTON (Thomas Henry) Born Westminster, London 9/3/1800, s. Rev. Thomas Causton (above) and Mary Ann Balchen. Christ Church, Oxford 1819, BA1823, dn23 (Lin.), p24 (Ox.), MA1825. PC. St Botolph without Aldersgate, City of London 1824-38, Minister of St Michael's, Highgate, London 1838 to death 15/5/1854 aged 54 [C24500] Married (1) Hampstead, London 5/4/1831 Hon. Frances Esther Powys (dau. 2nd Baron Lilford, she d.1840), w. clerical s. Thomas Lilford Neil Causton (2) Highgate 7/4/1842 Frances Louisa Tatham, *s.p.* Port. online: www.saxonlodge.net/getperson.php?personID= I1623&tree=Tatham. (port.)

CAUTHERLEY (Samuel) Bapt. Richmond, Surrey 30/8/1772, s. Samuel Cautherley and Susannah Blanchard. Literate: dn07 (Nor.), p07 (Nor.). V. Royston, Herts. 1808 to death 18/2/1841 aged 69 [C112103] Married Kenwyn, Cornwall 17/4/1801 Thomasine Tippet, w. issue.

CAUTLEY (Richard) Bapt. York 5/1/1763, s. Thomas Cautley and Hannah Watson. Trinity, Cambridge 1780, BA1784, dn85 (Ely for London), MA1787, p87 (Peterb.). R. Whatcote, Warwicks. 1787, R. Yardley Hastings, Northants. 1799-1805 (res.), R. Moulsoe, Bucks. 1828 to death. Dom. Chap. to 4th Viscount Galway 1785; to 1st Marquess of Northampton 1799, and to 2nd Marquess 1828. Died 26/2/1842 aged 70 [C46661] Married (1) York 10/6/1789 Elizabeth Bluitt (d./1800), 1 ch. survived (2) Bramham, Yorks. 1/8/1805 Octavia Oldfield, 5s., 1 dau.: www.saxonlodge.net/getperson.php?personID= I5277&tree=Tatham

CAUTLEY (Thomas) From Dunnington, Yorks., s. Edward Cautley. Jesus, Cambridge 1781, dn85 (Ely), BA1786, p88 (Ely), MA1791, BD1803, Fellow. V. Cambridge St Clement 1806-35, V. Griston, Norfolk 1812 to death 30/11/1835 aged 73 [C82171 says died 1817, so must have 2 men here] Married Anne Priscilla Henson (a clergy dau.), w. issue (inc. Sir Proby Thomas Cautley, civil engineer in India). Known as 'Og, King of Bashan' as very tall and large.

CAUTLEY (William Grainger) Bapt. Chapel, Essex 29/4/1782, s. Rev. John Cautley (V. Messing, Essex). Pembroke, Cambridge 1801, BA1805, dn05 (Nor.), p06 (Nor.), then Clare, Fellow 1808-31, MA1809. Chap. to the Forces 1809-18 [present at Battle of Waterloo]; Chap. at Madeira. R. Earsham, Norfolk 1831 to death (unm.) 26/3/1855 aged 72 [C111896. Boase]

CAVE, *later* **CAVE BROWNE CAVE (William Astley)** Born Stretton-en-le-Field, Derbys. 3/8/1799, s. Rev. Sir William Cave, 9th Bart. and Louisa Wilmot. BNC, Oxford 1818, BA1821, dn22 (Chester for C&L), p23 (Chester), MA1824. PC. Flixton, Lancs. 1823-42, R. (and patron of) Stretton-en-le-Field 1843 to death (Penmaenmawr, Carnarvon) 13/6/1862 aged 62, leaving £4,000 [C9899] Married (1) Stroud, Glos. 21/5/1828 Elizabeth Martha Wathen (d.1828) (2) Stoke on Trent, Staffs. 25/3/1830 Julia Minton, with clerical son William Cecil Cave Brown Cave.

CAVENDISH-BENTINCK see under **BENTINCK**

CAWOOD (John) From Matlock, Derbys., the 'poor son' of Thomas Cawood (a small farmer - *pleb*). St Edmund Hall, Oxford 1797 (aged 22), dn00 (Bristol), BA1801, p01 (Glos.), MA 1807. PC. Bewdley, Worcs. 1814 to death 1852 (4th q.) [C52227]

CAYLEY (Arthur) Born Archangel, Russia 1/11/1775 (but from Brompton, Yorks.), s. Arthur Cayley and Anne Eleanor Schulz. Trinity, Cambridge 1792, BA1796, dn13 (York), p13 (York). R. Normanby, Yorks. 1814 to death (York) 22/4/1848 aged 72 [C130935. ODNB as a biographer is slight. YCO] Married 30/5/1803 his cousin Lucy Cayley (a clergy dau.).

CECIL (William) Born Holborn, London 16/9/1792, s. Rev. Richard and Jenny Cecil. Trinity, Cambridge 1809, then Magdalene 1810, BA1814, Fellow 1814, MA1817, dn19 (Salis. for Ely), p20 (Nor.). R. Long Stanton St Michael, Cambs. 1823 to death 10/2/1882 aged 89, leaving £3,493-6s-4d. [C6620. Boase] Now regarded as the inventor of the (theory of the) internal combustion engine in 1820, but only Venn notes this.

CHALLEN (John Gratwick) Bapt. Chichester 6/3/1765, s. John Challen (Shermanbury Park, Chichester, Sussex) and Cassandra Lintott Farncombe. University, Oxford 1780, BA 1784, dn87 (C&L for Chich.), MA1787, BD & DD 1823. R. Shermanbury 1789 and R. Bressingham, Norfolk 1800 (and Selsey 1817, then Waltham Prebend of Chichester Cathedral 1817) to death 6/12/1835 [C9901] Married Chichester 23/6/1801 Sophia Diggens, *s.p.*

CHALLIS (James) Born Bocking End, Essex. 12/12/1803, s. John Challis (stonemason). Trinity, Cambridge 1821, BA1825 (Senior Wrangler), Fellow 1826-31 (re-elected 1870), MA1828, dn30 (C&L for Ely), p30 (Peterb. for Ely), incorporated at Oxford 1847. Plumian Professor Astronomy, Cambridge 1836-82 (who just failed to discover the planet Neptune). R. Papworth Everard, Cambs. 1829 to death 3/12/1882, leaving £781-14s-8d. Director of the Cambridge Observatory 1836-61 [C6621. ODNB. Boase] Married 12/7/1831 Mrs Sarah (Chandler) Copsey, of Braintree, with clerical son. *F.R.A.S.* (1836) *F.R.S.* (1848).

CHALONER (Henry) Bapt. Guisborough Priory, Guisborough, Yorks. 26/11/1791, s. William Chaloner and Emma Harvey. Trinity, Cambridge 1808, BA1813, dn16 (York), p20 (Chester). V. Alne w. Aldwark, Yorks. 1820 to death. Chap. to HRH Duke of Sussex. Died 26/11/1850 aged 59 [C130985. YCO] Wife Jane, with issue.

CHAMBERLAIN, CHAMBERLAINE (George Thomas) From London, s. Thomas Chamberlain. Corpus Christi, Oxford 1797 (aged 18), then Worcester, BA1801, dn02 (Salis.), p03 (Salis.), MA1803. V. Kenton, Devon 1810 (with Preacher throughout the Diocese of Exeter 1812)-36, R. Ansford, Som. 1836 to death (Seend, Wilts.) 21/10/1858 aged 80, leaving £6,000 [C91508] Married 21/9/1818 Harriet Woodforde (w), and issue. Confusion.

CHAMBERLAIN (Thomas Hughes, *born* Thomas Chamberlain HUGHES) Bapt. Radway, Warwicks. 9/9/1772, s. Rev. Edward Hughes and Rebecca Chamberlain. Oriel, Oxford 1790, BA1793, dn96 (Glos.), MA1796, p97 (Ox.). R. Broughton, Oxon. 1813-14 (res.), R. Churchover (o/w Over), Warwicks. 1819-51 (as T.C.H.). Died? [C10336. Foster under Hughes] Married [as T.C.H.] 7/7/1802 Tidmington, Warwicks. Ann Snow. Confusion: were T.H.C. and T.C.H. two people marrying different women?

CHAMBERLAYNE (George) From Tiverton, Devon, s. George Chamberlayne. Christ Church, Oxford 1782 (aged 19), BA1786, dn87 (Chester for London), p87 (Chester for London). R. Ramsden Crays, Essex 1787-1801, V. Wherwell, Hants. 1801-19, R. Wyke Regis w. Weymouth, Dorset 1809. Died 9/10/1837 aged 74 (as Chamberlaine) [C71712] Married St George's Hanover Square, London 1/11/1787 Susannah Long.

CHAMBERLAYNE (John) Born Hatfield Broad Oak, Essex 25/8/1791, s. Stanes Chamberlayne (of Ryes, Essex). Jesus, Cambridge 1808, BA1814, dn15 (London), p16 (Ely for London), MA1817. PC. Norton Mandeville, Essex 1816, Master of St John's Port's Hospital [almshouses], Derby 1821-31, R. Estwick, Harlow, Herts. 1825 to death 26/11/1867 aged 77. Will not traced [C6622]

CHAMBERS (John) Bapt. Spernall, Warwicks. 29/4/1753, s. Thomas and Mary Chambers. Worcester, Oxford 1771, dn75 (Ox.), p77 (Ox.), BA1778, MA1778, Fellow 1822. V. Coughton w. Sambourne, Warwicks. 1785-1814, R. Spernall 1799, R. Neen Sollars w. Milson, Shropshire 1814-36. Dom. Chap. to 2nd Marquess of Hertford 1813. Buried Spurnell 24/3/1836 [C24530]

CHAMBERS (John Peter) Bapt. Norwich 19/3/1774. Corpus Christi, Cambridge 1801, BA1806, dn07 (Nor.), p08 (Nor.). R. (and patron of) Hedenham, Norfolk 1812 to death

11/12/1858 aged 74 [C112105] Married London 13/5/1819 Anna Maria Maxwell.

CHAMBERS (Thomas) Bapt. Radway, Warwicks. 15/2/1783, s. Rev. Thomas, sen. and Mary Chambers. Worcester, Oxford 1801, BA 1805, MA1808, Fellow 1836. H/M Royal Naval School Peckham; V. Studley, Warwicks. 1825. Found *drowned* 'after serious depression of spirits accompanied with marked proofs of eccentricities' 28/3/1836 (unm.) aged 53 [C120599]

CHAMBERS (William) From Stratford on Avon, Warwicks., s. William Chambers. Oriel, Oxford 1804 (aged 17), then Magdalen, BA 1807, dn09 (Ox.), MA1810, p10 (Ox.), Fellow 1815-23, BD1818. V. Ashbury, Berks. 1823 to death 29/5/1860 aged 74, leaving £9,000 [C10004]

CHAMPION (John) Bapt. Edale, Derbys. 6/7/1802, s. John Champion and Frances Beresford. Clare, Cambridge 1821, BA1826, dn26 (C&L), p27 (C&L), MA1829. PC. Edale, Derbys. 1827-45 (and V. there again 1867-72), V. Keyworth, Notts. 1833-4 (res.) [C130921 as Campion], V. Taxal, Cheshire 1842-53. Died Ventnor, IoW 17/3/1872, leaving £1,500 [C9815] Married Arngask, Fife 12/9/1844 Margaret Elizabeth Murray (w), with issue.

CHAMPION DE CRESPIGNY see under **DE CRESPIGNY**

CHAMPNES(S) (Charles) Born Westminster, London 17/5/1783, s. Samuel Champnes and Ann Cornwall. Exeter, Oxford 1807 (aged 20), then St Alban Hall, BA1811, p12 (Lin.), MA1825. V. Ogbourne St George Wilts. 1820-6, R. St George Botolph Lane w. St Botolph Billingsgate, City of London >< 1825, R. Wywardisbury w. Langley, Bucks. 1829. Minor Canon of Windsor (after 1835). Probate granted 11/8/1855, living at Herne Bay, Kent [C47668] Brother below.

CHAMPNES(S) (Thomas Weldon) Born Westminster, London 5/5/1773, s. of Samuel Thomas Champnes and Ann Cornwall. Trinity, Cambridge 1792, BA1796, dn96 (Salis.), p97 (Lin.), MA1799. Minor Canon of Westminster Abbey 1800, Minor Canon of Windsor Chapel 1803-41, V. Upton cum Chalvey, Bucks. 1806-11, V. Sutton Courtenay w. Appelford, Beds. 1806-11, V. Ogbourne St George, Wilts. 1811-20, R. Cottisford, Oxon. 1820, V. Wywardisbury (o/w Wraysbury), Bucks. 1821-4, R. Fulmer, Bucks. 1823 to death 21/12/1841 aged 68 [C24539] Married (1) Bermondsey, London 27/12/1795 Mary Macnamara (d.1813), with issue (2) Eton, Berks. 11/1/1825 Elizabeth Langford (a clergy dau.). Brother above.

CHAMPNEYS, *born* **BURT (Henry William)** Born Rochester, Kent 26/5/1760, s. John Burt and Harriet Champneys. Christ's, Cambridge 1788, BA1793, dn96 (Glos. for Cant.), p96 (Glos. for Cant.), MA1796. V. Leigh, Lancs. 1798-1800 (res.), R. Canterbury St Margaret 1803-6, V. Rainham, Kent 1804-7, V. Welton cum Melton, Yorks. 1807-45, V. Canterbury St Mary Bredin 1807-21 (res.), R. Badsworth, Yorks. 1821 to death. Dom. Chap. to 9th Earl of Dalhousie 1821. Died 18/2/1845 aged 74 [C138156] Married St George's, Hanover Square, London 3/5/1796 Lucy Hornby (a clergy dau.), at least 10 ch. Changed surname on inheriting the Westernhanger estate in 1781. He was 'wild' when at university.

CHANDLER (George) Born Lucknow, India, s. Henry John Chandler. Oriel, Oxford 1795 (aged 17), BA1799, MA1802, dn02 (Win.), then New, Fellow, p08 (Bristol), LLD 1835. R. Treeton, Yorks. 1809 to death 20/2/1846 [C71717] Married Marylebone, London 15/6/1809 Jane Osbaldeston (w).

CHANDLER (George) From Witley, Surrey, s. John Chandler. New, Oxford 1796 (aged 16) [Student Middle Temple 1803] BCL1804, dn07 (Ex.), Fellow 1816, p08 (Bristol), DCL1824. PC. Marylebone Christ Church, London 1825-47, R. Marylebone All Souls Langham Place, London 1825-47 [net income £1,186], Dean of Chichester 1830 (w. R. Felpham, Sussex 1832 annexed: he heavily restored the Cathedral). Dom. Chap. to 4th Duke of Buccleuch 1808. Died (unm.) 3/2/1859 aged 80, leaving £20,000 [C8213. Boase] *F.R.S.* (1833).

CHANDLER (John Flutter) From Stoke, Guildford, Surrey, s. John Chandler (attorney) and Dorothy Roker. BNC, Oxford 1779 (aged 17), BA 1783, dn84 (Ox. for Win.), then University, p86 (Lin. for Win.), MA1786. V. Woking, Surrey 1786 and V. (and patron of)

Witley, Surrey 1815 to death 26/1/1837 aged 75. Dom. Chap. to 2nd Earl of Onslow 1814 [C24542] Married Godalming, Surrey 25/2/1805 Mary Currie, w. issue.

CHANTER (William) Born North Tawton, Devon 9/6/1766 (CCEd thus), s. Moses Chanter and Grace Hawkins. Oriel, Oxford 1785, BA 1789, p90 (Ex.). PC. Hartland, Devon 1797-1859 (71 years) and PC. Welcombe, Devon 1821 to death 3/5/1859 aged 93, leaving under £200 [C140556] Married Bedminster, Bristol 14/5/1794 Mary Wolferstan (d.1824), with issue.

CHAPLIN (Edward) Bapt. Tathwell, Lincs. 1/2/1770, s. Charles Chaplin and Elizabeth Thoroton. Emmanuel, Cambridge 1787, migrated to Merton, Oxford 1788, BA1796, dn96 (York), MA1797, p97 (York). V. Norwell, Notts. 1797-1833 (both Moieties), V. Dagenham, Essex 1798-1801, R. Blankney, Lincs. 1801 to death. Dom. Chap. to 1st Earl Amherst. Died (unm.) 5/9/1853 aged 86 [C47677. YCO. Kaye] Brothers, below.

CHAPLIN (Robert) Bapt. Tathwell, Lincs. 15/10/1758, s. CharlesChaplin and Elizabeth Thoroton. Emmanuel, Cambridge 1776, dn81 (Peterb.), p82 (Peterb.), LLB 1783. V. Tathwell 1783-1837, R. Raithby w. Hallington, Lincs. 1783-92, V. Haugham, Lincs. 1784-91, R. Averham w. Kelham, Notts. (and Preacher throughout the Diocese of York) 1792, and Prebend of Norwell Pallishall in Southwell Collegiate Church 1823) to death 30/5/1837 aged 78 [C47680] Married Southwell 29/1/1796 Anne Georgina (dau. of Sir Richard Sutton, 1st Bart., Norwood Park, Notts.) with clerical son. Described as 'wealthy, influential, and well-connected'; brothers above and below.

CHAPLIN (William) Born Tathwell, Lincs., s. Charles Chaplin and Elizabeth Thoroton. Christ Church, Oxford 1783 (aged 18), then Magdalen, BA1787, dn87 (Lin.), p89 (Lin.), MA1794. V. Wispington, Lincs. 1789-94, R. Raithby w. Hallington, Lincs. 1792, V. Haugham, Lincs. 1792, R. North Coates, Lincs. 1794-1818, R. West Halton w. Gunhouse, Lincs. 1814 to death. Dom. Chap. to Archbishop Charles Manners-Sutton 1794-1814. Died 11/12/1835 (CCEd says 22/12/1835) [C47681] 2 brothers, above.

CHAPLIN (William) Bapt. Norwich St John's Maddermarket 23/4/1796, s. William Chaplin and Mary Harvey. Queens', Cambridge 1825, BA1829, dn29 (Nor.) and p29 (Nor.) the same day. PC. Low Ford (later South Hylton), Durham 1833 to death 7/6/1834 [this parish noted twice in ERC: see also here under James Mellor Brown 1831-3] [C47682]

CHAPMAN (Benedict) Born Norwich, s. Charles Chapman. Caius, Cambridge 1787 (aged 17), BA1792, Fellow 1792-1820, dn94 (Ely), MA1795, p96 (Ely), DD1840, etc. Master of Caius College 1839-52 (which he endowed). R. Ashdon, Essex 1818 to death (unm.) 23/10/1852 aged 82 [C99614. Boase]

CHAPMAN (Benjamin) Born Daglingworth, Glos. 10/7/1798, s. Robert Chapman. Christ's, Cambridge 1824 [adm. Lincoln's Inn 1825] BA1828, dn28 (Ely), p28 (Ely), MA1832. R. Westley Waterless (or Waterleys), Cambs. 1829-36, V. Leatherhead, Surrey 1837 to death 29/4/1871, leaving £1,500 [C6625] Married Tooting, London 25/9/1832 Laura Maria Wilson.

CHAPMAN (John) Born Daglingworth, Glos., s. Rev. Joseph Chapman. Chorister Magdalen, Oxford 1764-8; matr. Corpus Christ, Oxford 1768 (aged 15), then Trinity, BA1772. R. Daglingworth 1797 to 'natural death' 9/12/1833 (CCEd thus) [C138189]

CHAPMAN (Richard) Bapt. Orton, Westmorland 26/3/1754, s. James and Barbara Chapman. Literate: dn77 (York), p78 (York). V. Tannington w. Brundish, Suffolk 1817. Died? [C88032. YCO]

CHAPMAN (Richard Henry) Born London 8/10/1781, s. Richard and Sarah Chapman. Queens', Cambridge 1799 (re-adm. 1803), BA 1807, dn07 (Ex. for York), p07 (Bristol for London), MA1810. V. Tinsley, Yorks. 1809-12, R. Cuxton, Kent 1811-31, Curate Marylebone Parochial Chapel, London 1823 and R. Kirby Wiske, Yorks. 1830 to death (Marylebone) 26/1/1845 aged 64 [C1748. YCO] Married Marylebone 24/4/1819 Emily Anne Allen, w. issue.

CHAPMAN (Roger) Bapt. Ingleton, Yorks. 10/2/1801, s. Rev. Robert Chapman. St Bees

College adm. 1825, dn26 (York), p27 (York). PC. Burton in Lonsdale, Yorks. 1831-66. Died there 25/8/1868 aged 67, leaving £3,000 [C130987. YCO] Married Settle, Yorks. 1842 Mary Tatham, w. issue.

CHAPMAN (Thomas) Born Stoneleigh, Warwicks., s. Thomas Chapman (agent to Lord Leigh). St John's, Cambridge 1817, BA1821, dn22, p23 (Chester), MA1824. PC. Milverton, Warwicks. 1831-43, V. Radford Semele, Warwicks. 1843 to death 6/11/1861 aged 63, leaving £3,000 [C9817] Widow Sarah Catherine.

CHAPMAN (William Emerson) Born Boston, Lincs. 21/10/1796, s. William Chapman and Susannah Emerson. St John's, Cambridge 1816, BA1820, dn20 (Lin.), p21 (Lin.), MA 1825. Chap. of the Donative of Edenham, Lincs. (where he lived) 1821, V. Swinstead, Lincs. 1821-32, V. Skendleby, Lincs. 1828-33, V. Somerby w. Great Humby, Lincs. 1832 to death. Dom. Chap. to Lord Gwydir 1820. Died 6/12/1860 aged 64 ('while proposing a toast at the wedding of his daughter'), leaving £2,000 [C47730. Bennett2] Married Godmanchester, Hunts. 13/11/1822 Eliza Martin, with clerical son Edward Martin Chapman.

CHARD (George William John) Born Winchester 30/11/1796, s. George and Amelia Chard. Trinity, Oxford 1815, BA1819, MA 1823. V. Blandford Forum, Dorset 1821 to death 12/6/1836 aged 39 [C52230] Married Blandford 26/5/1823 Elizabeth Frances Diggle, w. issue.

CHARGE (John) Bapt. Middleton Tyas, Yorks. 1/2/1789, s. Christoper Charge and Ann Bonner. Literate: dn12 (Chester), p13 (Chester). R. Copgrove, Yorks. 1813 (and RD) to death 8/5/1870 aged 81, leaving £2,000 [C168475] Married (1) Anne Crossland, with issue (2) Stockton on Tees, Co. Durham 21/1/1823 Margaret Alexander Crowe (w).

CHARLESWORTH (Beedam) Born Leeds 15/8/1804, s. John Beedam Charlesworth and Ann Gomersall. Trinity, Cambridge 1821, BA 1827, dn30 (Roch. for York), p30 (London for York), MA1830. V. Darfield (2nd Moiety), Yorks. 1830-62, PC. St James (Hensman Memorial) Church, Clifton, Bristol 1862 to death 8/1/1876 aged 71, leaving £16,000 [C116737. YCO] Married Birstall, Yorks. 12/1/1831 his cousin Sarah Gomersall Walker.

CHARLESWORTH (John) Bapt. Ossington, Notts. 16/7/1783, s. Rev. John Charlesworth, sen. 'Practiced with a surgeon', Clapham, Surrey 1804. Literate: dn14 (Nor.), p14 (Nor.), then Queens', Cambridge 1820-3 (a Ten Year Man, BD1826). R. Flowton, Suffolk 1815-44, R. Blakenham Parva, Suffolk 1819, R. St Mildred Bread Street, City of London 1844 to death 22/4/1864, leaving £300 [C112113. Boase. DEB. J.P. Fitzgerald, *The quiet worker for good: a familiar sketch of the late John Charlesworth ...* (1865)] Married Clapham 10/8/1809 Mary Beddome, with issue.

CHARLETON (John Kynaston) Bapt. Olveston, Glos. 3/11/1803, s. Rev. Robert John Charleton (below) and Mary Webb. Queen's, Oxford 1822, BA1826, dn26 (Bristol), p28 (Bristol). V. Elberton, Glos. 1828 to death 1/7/1872, leaving £14,000 [C8214] Married Olveston 10/8/1837 Georgiana Henrietta Gordon (w), with clerical son.

CHARLETON (Robert John) Born Walcot, Bath 8/12/1768, s. Rev. Rice Charleton and Mary Wright. Queen's, Oxford 1784, BA1788, MA1791, dn92 (Salis.), p92 (Salis.), BD and DD1810. V. Olveston and Elberston, Glos. 1799. Died Thornbury, Glos. 1844 (4th q.) [C33777] Married (1) Walcot, 3/7/1797 Mary Webb (d.1825), w. clerical son, above. (2) Walcot 29/12/1834 Caroline Sibley.

CHARNOCK (Joseph) Bapt. Todmorden, Lancs. 25/5/1766, s. of Thomas Charnock (handloom weaver, of Illingworth, Halifax, Yorks.). Literate: dn93 (York), p94 (York). PC. Heptonstall, Yorks. 1803 (and S/M Heptonstall G/S 1825) to burial 30/12/1847 [C88047. YCO] Married (1) Halifax 29/12/1793 Hannah Bates (d.1827), 10 ch. (including clerical son of father's name) (2) Ripon, Yorks. 1837 (3rd q.) Mary Horner Reynard.

CHATFIELD (Robert) Born London 2/10/1775, s. Robert Chatfield (Croydon, Surrey). Emmanuel, Cambridge 1795 [adm. Middle Temple 1796] dn01 (Ely for Glos.), p03 (Ely), LLB1805, LLD1811. V. Chatteris, Cambs. [net income £1,370] 1802-45. Died (Brighton) 10/8/1853 aged 77 [C99615] Married Much

Marcle, Heref. 17/7/1800 Susannah Money, with clerical son (below). *J.P.* Isle of Ely and Cambs.

CHATFIELD (Robert Money) Born Brighton, Sussex 3/11/1804, s. Rev. Robert Chatfield (above) and Susannah Money. Trinity, Cambridge 1823, BA1827, dn28 (S&M), p29 (S&M), MA1831. V. Wilsford and Woodford cum Lake, Wilts. 1830 to death 21/9/1882 aged 78, leaving £1,919-14s-4d. [C7234] Married Kirkmichael, IoM 18/6/1829 Anna Maria Jesson (Hill Park, Kent), with issue.

CHAUNCY (Charles) Born Ayot Mount Fitchet, Herts. 4/6/1778, s. Rev. Charles Chauncy (R. Ayot St Peter, Herts.) and Susannah Cayton. Peterhouse, Cambridge 1797, BA1801, dn02 (Lin.), MA1804, p13 (Lin.). V. Walden St Paul, Herts. 1814 to death 20/3/1835 (CCEd says 19/6/1835) aged 57 [C48073] Married Welwyn, Herts. 11/8/1806 Rebecca Ann Crawley, w. issue.

CHAUVEL (Arthur Robinson) Born Westminster, London 27/2/1758, s. James and Mary Chauvel. Pembroke, Cambridge 1776, dn80 (Ely for Nor.) LLB1785, p88 (Lin. for London). R. Great Stanmore, Middx. 1788-1847, Pancratius Prebend of St Paul's Cathedral, London 1817-47, V. (and patron) of Chigwell, Essex 1833 to death. Dom. Chap. to 1st Baron Southampton 1781; to 1st Baron Lyndhurst 1833. Died 21/1/1847 aged 88 [C48074] Port. online.

CHAVE (Edward) Bapt. Exeter 2/2/1769, s. Edward Chave. St John's, Cambridge 1787, then Peterhouse 1788, BA1791, dn91 (Ex.), p93 (Ex.), MA1794. Priest-Vicar Exeter Cathedral 1799-1823, R. Exeter St Mary Arches 1815 to death. Chap. to Bodmin County Gaol and House of Correction 1815-23. Died 21/7/1840 aged 71 [C140558] Married Bristol 17/11/1798 Hannah Penny Summers, and had issue.

CHAVE (William) Born Exeter 18/9/1803, s. George Chave (merchant). Caius, Cambridge 1821, then Sidney 1822, BA1826, dn26 (Ex.), p27 (Ex.). PC. Bath St Mark 1832 (w. Chap. to Bath Female Home, Penitentiary and Lock [venereal diesese] Hospital 1831-4). British Chap. at Paris, Zurich, and Munich; Secretary to the Colonial Church Society. Died Munich 9/1/1866, leaving £74,000 [C41998 and 140560] Married London 25/1/1839 Albinia Jackson Bowden (w), with issue.

CHEALES (John) Bapt. Sleaford, Lincs. 3/7/1800, s. Benjamin Cheales and Mary Ann Jane Spurr. BNC, Oxford 1819, BA1822, MA 1825, dn25 (Ex. for Bristol), p25 (Bristol). V. Firsby w. Great Steeping, Lincs. 1828, V. Witham on the Hill, Lincs. 1829-35, V. Skendleby, Lincs, 1840 to death 19/4/1865, leaving £3,000 [C8215. Bennett2] Married 9/5/1826 Mary Ann Bellingham (dau. of a baronet), with issue. Poor photo. online.

CHEAP (Andrew) Born Holborn, London 4/1/1775, s. Thomas Cheap and Grace Stuart. Magdalen Hall, Oxford 1800, migrated to Trinity Hall, Cambridge 1805, dn00 (York), p01 (C&L for York), LLB18089. R. Elvington, Yorks. 1801-41, V. Knaresborough, Yorks. 1804 to death. Dom. Chap. to 2nd Earl of Rosslyn 1809. Died 28/8/1851 aged 76 [C9820. YCO says literate. DEB. *A short memoir of the Rev. Andrew Cheap, LLB, Vicar of Knaresborough, Yorkshire* (1856 - untraced pamphlet)] Married Kirk Hamerton, Yorks. 9/10/1809 Eliza Fisher.

CHEESE (Benjamin) From Tenbury, Worcs., s. John Cheese. Balliol, Oxford 1801 (aged 28), BA1806, dn08 (Heref.), p08 (Heref.), MA 1809, BD1822, Fellow 1823. R. Tendring, Essex 1822 to death. Dom. Chap. to Anne, Countess of Galloway 1811; to 5th Duke of Marlborough 1815. Died 30/8/1838 [C24554] Married Harwich, Essex 15/9/1828 Helen Pattison (of Congleton, Cheshire), with clerical son.

CHEESEBROUGH, CHESEBOROUGH (Isaac) Bapt. Penrith, Cumberland 13/6/1793, s. Jacob Cheesebrough and Grace Kendal. Literate: dn16 (York), p17 (York). Min. at the French Protestant Church, Lausanne, Switzerland 1821, V. Northorpe, Lincs. 1827 to death (Wigton, Cumberland.) 1853 (1st q.)? [C130991. YCO] Married Bolton, Westmorland 13/6/1793 Mary Slack, w. issue.

CHENERY (Walter) Bapt. Eye, Suffolk 2/4/1801, s. Thomas Chenery and Sarah Sharman. Jesus, Cambridge 1820, BA1825, dn26 (Nor.), p27 (Nor.), MA1828. R. Stuston, Suffolk 1832 to death 3/12/1859 aged 58, leaving £3,000 [C112116] Married Norwich 10/4/1834 Emily Christiana Chapman (w).

CHEPMELL (William John) Born Guernsey, Channel Islands 16/10/1783, s. William ('The Brave') Chepmell and Elizabeth Effard Courtart. Pembroke, Oxford 1800, BA1804, MA1807, p08 (Win.). V. Vale, Guernsey 1816 and R. St Sampson, Guernsey 1816 to death 26/3/1859, leaving £3,000 [C71729 has wrong date of death] Married Newton Longville, Bucks. 2/3/1809 Harriet Le Mesurier (w), w. issue.

CHERRY (Henry Curtis) Born Surat, India 16/12/1798, s. John Hector Cherry and Catherine Stratton. Trinity, Cambridge 1817 (did not reside), then Clare 1817, BA1821, dn21 (Win.), p23 (Nor.), MA1824, incorporated at Oxford 1850. R. Burghfield, Berks. 1827-64, V. Beenham, Berks. 1840. Dom. Chap. to Lord de Saumarez 1847. Died 6/11/1864 aged 66, leaving £26,000 [C71730] Married Chelsea, London 28/10/1822 Anne Alicia, dau. of Maj-Gen. Sir John Cameron, with military issue.

CHESSHYRE (John Peter Henry) Bapt. Benington, Herts. 16/3/1791, s. John Caesar Cholmondeley and Julia Chesshyre. St John's, Cambridge 1808, BA1812, dn15 (B&W), p15 (B&W), MA1819. R. Little Easton, Essex 1815, Curate Tilty, Essex -- to death (Bath) 2/8/1855 aged 64 [C42000] Married Benington, Herts. 17/1/1816 Charlotte Frances Commeline, w. issue. Sold the inherited manor of Benington in 1826.

CHESTER (Bishop of) see under **SUMNER (John Bird)**

CHESTER (Charles) Born 31/12/1768, s. Robert Chester (of the Middle Temple). Christ Church, Oxford 1787, migrated to Emmanuel, Cambridge 1791, dn92 (Nor. for Ely), p93 (Nor.), LLB1795. R. Rousham, Oxon. 1797-1804, R. Barley, Herts. 1803-14 (res.), R. Ayot St Peter, Herts. 1804-37 and R. Rettendon, Essex (and Preacher throughout the Diocese of London) 1814 to death 19/5/1837 aged 68 [C6631] Married 1791 Catherine Roberts, w. clerical son Robert (below).

CHESTER (Matthew) Bapt. Bolton, Westmorland 3/8/1793, s. Thomas Chester (a blacksmith) and Elizabeth Longmire. Literate: dn17 (Chester for Durham), p18 (Durham). PC. (Bishop) Auckland St Helen, Durham 1822 to death 18/7/1871 aged 77, leaving £3,000 [C130354] Married Wolsingham, Durham 8/11/1824 Joyce Deighton Ion (a clergy dau.), with issue.

CHESTER (Robert) Bapt. Sutton, Cambs. 31/3/1794, s. Rev. Charles Chester (above) and Catherine Roberts. Emmanuel, Cambridge 1812, BA1817, dn18 (London), MA1820, p20 (London). R. Elsted, Sussex 1822 to death. Dom. Chap. to 3rd Baron Selsey 1819. Died 7/5/1833 aged 39 (CCEd says 22/12/1833) [C62850] Married 19/12/1815 Mary Lee, w. issue.

CHESTER (William) Born Chicheley, Bucks. 27/5/1775, s. Charles Chester and Catherine Legge (dau. Rev. Sir Henry Wilson, 10th Baron Berners after 1838). Christ Church, Oxford 1793, BA1797, then Merton, MA1800, dn00 (St Asaph), p01 (Ox.). R. Woolstanton, Staffs. 1803-7, R. Woodrising, Norfolk 1805-31 (res.), R. Denton, Norfolk 1807-38, R. Langford, Norfolk 1817-24 (res.), R. Walpole St Peter, Norfolk 1824 to death (Torquay) 22/11/1838 [C10026] Married Kirby Cane, Norfolk 8/1/1810 Elizabeth (dau. 4th Baron Berners), w. clerical s.

CHETWODE (George) Born Oakley, Staffs. 1/11/1791, s. Sir John Chetwode, 4th Bart. and Lady Henrietta Grey (dau. 5th of Earl of Stamford and Warrington). BNC, Oxford 1809, BA 1814, dn14 (Ox.), MA1815, p16 (C&L for London). PC. Stratton Audley, Bucks. 1816-31, R. Ashton under Lyne St Michael, Lancs. 1816-29 [net income £1,407], PC. Chilton, Bucks. 1829 to death (Chilton House) 4/8/1870 aged 79, leaving £16,000 [C10027] Married (1) Cannock, Staffs. 26/8/1818 Charlotte Anne Walhouse (d.1837), with issue (2) Marylebone, London 1/9/1840 Mrs Anna Maria (Shipley) Jones, dau. of a Dean of St Asaph (d.1843?) (3) Chilton, Bucks. 27/2/1849 Mrs Elizabeth Anne (Deane) Trotman (d.1861) (4) Chilton, Bucks. 30/4/1868 Mrs Elizabeth Sophia (Aubrey) Ricketts. *J.P.* Brother, below.

CHETWODE (Henry) Born Oakley, Staffs. 26/11/1798, s. Sir John Chetwode, 4th Bart. and Lady Henrietta Grey (dau. of 5th Earl of Stamford and Warrington). Trinity, Oxford 1817, dn24 (Bristol for Chester), p25 (C&L for Chester). PC. Nether (or Lower) Whitley, Great Budworth, Cheshire 1825 and V. (Princes) Harwell, Berks. 1829 to death 5/4/1843 [C8159]

Married Liverpool 30/10/1827 Mary Anne Highfield, *s.p.* Brother, above.

CHEVALLIER (John) Bapt. Aspall Hall, Aspall, Suffolk 30/8/1774, s. Rev. Temple Fiske Chevallier and Mary Syer Fiske. MD. dn17 (Nor.), p17 (Nor.). PC. (and patron) of Aspall 1817 and V. Cransford, Suffolk 1831 to death 14/8/1846 aged 71 [C112125. ODNB] Married (1) 1808 Caroline Heoburn (of Wisbech, she fell from a carriage and d.1815), with issue (2) Black Notley, Essex 22/10/1816 Emily Blomfield Syer (d.1819), with further issue (3) Black Notley 3/1/1821 Elizabeth Cole (with clerical son, and also the mother of 1st Earl Kitchener). An important early psychiatrist, having patients living in (part of) his extensive Aspall Hall. Also developed Chevallier barley for brewing - still going today. Step-brother, below. *J.P.*

CHEVALLIER (Temple) Born Badingham, Suffolk 19/10/1794, s. Rev. Temple Fiske Chevallier, sen. and Sarah Edgcumbe. Pembroke, Cambridge 1812, BA1817, dn19 (Ely), Fellow, MA1820, p20 (Ely), St Catharine's, Fellow and Tutor 1820, BD1828, incorporated at Oxford 1847. R. of the Donative of Cambridge St Andrew the Great 1825-35 (res.), PC. Esh, Durham 1835-69 (and RD 1858). Professor of Mathematics and Registrar of Durham College (then University) 1835-71 (with Professor of Astronomy 1841-71). Hon. Canon of Durham Cathedral 1840, then Canon Residentiary 1865 to death (Harrow Weald, Middx.) 4/11/1873, leaving £12,000 [C6632. ODNB. Boase] Married Cambridge 4/10/1825 Catherine Wheelwright, with issue. *F.R.A.S.* (1839). Step-brother, above. Photo. online.

CHICHESTER (Bishop of) see under **MALTBY (Edward)**

CHICHESTER (Charles) Born Shirwell, Devon, s. Rev. Robert Chichester (below) and Sarah Cawsey. Exeter, Oxford 1803 (aged 18), Fellow 1807, dn09 (Ox.), BA1810, p10 (Ox.), MA1812, BD1820. Prebend of Exeter Cathedral 1817 and R. West Worlington, Devon 1822 (probably to death) unm. 13/4/1842 [C24601]

CHICHESTER (James Hamilton John) Born Arlington Court, Arlington, Devon 3/9/1798, s. Col. John Palmer Chichester and Agnes Hamilton. Magdalene, Cambridge, BA1822, dn23 (Ex.), p24 (Ex.), MA1825. R. Arlington 1823 and R. Loxhore, Devon 1825 to death. Dom. Chap. to 9th Earl of Dalhousie 1825. Died Arlington Court 11/3/1884 aged 85, leaving £6,519-6s-3d. [C140561] Married (1) 20/3/1829 Mary Elizabeth Bateman (d.1830), w. issue (2) Dawlish, Devon 1/5/1832 Louisa Blencow (d.1833), 1 dau. (3) Flintham, Notts. 5/7/1836 Mary Ann Gertrude Whyte (d.1858), w. issue (4) St George's Hanover Square, London 1861 (4th q.) Mary Anne Hildyard.

CHICHESTER (Robert) Bapt. Bishop's Tawton, Devon 1/4/1752, s. Charles Chichester. Exeter, Oxford 1771, BA1774, dn75 (Ex.), p79 (Ex.). V. Chittlehampton, Devon 1803 (and Preacher throughout the Diocese of Exeter 1812) to death 1841 (4th q.) [C140563] Married Atherington, Devon 11/7/1781 Sarah Cawsey, with clerical son Charles, above.

CHILCOTT, CHILCOTE (Joseph) Born Tiverton, Devon 22/2/1770, s. William and Ann Chilcote. Balliol, Oxford 1789, BA1793, dn93 (Ex.), p94 (Ex.).V. Dean Prior, Devon 1802-[33] and R. Thurleston, Devon 1806. Dom. Chap. to Cassandra, Dowager Baroness Hawke. Died Brixham, Devon 1834 [C140563] Married (1) Tiverton, Devon 7/10/1795 Miriam Perkins (2) Brixham 29/1/1805 Elizabeth Gillard; with issue.

CHILCOTT, CHILCOTE (Samuel) Bapt. Tiverton, Devon 7/1/1779. Sidney, Cambridge 1792, BA1797, dn99 (Ex.), MA1800, Fellow, p00 (Lin), BD1807. R. Otterham, Cornwall 1810. Buried 27/2/1850 aged 76 [C48088] *J.P.* Cornwall.

CHILD (Charles) Probably bapt. Calverley, Yorks. 4/7/1773, s. Charles Child. Literate: dn00 (Ex. for York), then St John's, Cambridge 1800 (a Ten Year Man), p01 (Peterb.), BD1811. R. Orton Longueville w. St Botolphbridge, Hunts. 1826 to death 4/5/1835 aged 63 [C71835 says 11/7/1835] Married St George's Hanover Square, London 29/7/1802 Lydia Maria Thompson.

CHILDERS (Charles Walbanke-) Born Cantley Hall, Doncaster, Yorks. 17/5/1806, s. Col. John Childers and Selina Gideon Eardley. Christ Church, Oxford 1825, BA1829, dn30

(Lin.), p31 (Lin.), MA1833. R. Mursley, Bucks. 1831-3, V. Cantley, Yorks. 1833-43, R. Armthorpe, Yorks. 1884-6. British Chap. at Nice 1843-84 ('a post to which he clung, limpet-like'), Canon of Gibraltar 1866. Died (Florence) 15/2/1896 aged 90, leaving £12,501-15s-4d. [C49091] Married (1) Hatfield, Herts. 4/1/1834 Dulcibella Chester (a military dau., d.1865), with issue (2) 10/6/1869 Mrs Augusta (Le Poer) Trench (dau. of the Earl of Clanricard, and a clergy widow). Grandfather of the Fenian novelist Erskine Childers.

CHILDERS, *later* WALBANKE-CHILDERS (William Walbanke-) Bapt. 16/5/1775, s. of Childers Walbanke (-Childers) (Moat Hall, Little Ouseburn, Yorks.) and Mary Thompson. Trinity, Cambridge 1792, BA 1796, dn01 (York), MA1802, p02 (York). V. Cantley, Yorks. 1803 and R. Beeford w. Lissett and Dunnington, Yorks. 1812 (with Canon of 6th Prebend in Ely Cathedral 1824) to death (unm.) 8/2/1833 (CCEd says 12/3/1833) [C5167. YCO]

CHINN (Henry Barrow) From Lichfield, s. Henry and Ann Chinn. BNC, Oxford 1821 (aged 19), dn24 (C&L), BA1825, p26 (C&L). H/M Tideswell G/S 1832; R. Carsington, Derbys. 1832, Inc. of Peak Forest, Tideswell, Derbys. -- to death 14/1/1859 aged 57. Will not traced [C10030] Widow Ann.

CHISHOLM (Charles) Bapt. Blandford Forum, Dorset 17/11/1783, s. Rev. George Chisholm (a Scot) and Jane Fowle. Worcester, Oxford 1802, Fellow, BA1806, dn06 (Ox.), p07 (Ox.), MA1809. R. Eastwell, Kent 1812, V. Preston next Faversham, Kent 1820, R. Southchurch, Essex -- (and RD). Chap. to HRH Duke of York and Albany 1820. Probate granted 13/4/1849 [C24602] Married Ibornden, Kent 20/3/1823 Mary Jane Tylden Pattenson,(a clergy dau.), with issue. Brother below. *J.P.*

CHISHOLM (George) Bapt. Blandford Forum, Dorset 9/1/1797, s. Rev. George Chisholm, sen. (a Scot) and Jane Fowle. Worcester, Oxford 1809, BA1814, dn18 (Salis. for Bristol), MA1818, p20 (Salis. for Bristol), BD and DD1827. R. Ashmore, Dorset 1826 and PC. Fulham St Peter, Hammersmith, London 1831 to death 9/3/1854 aged 58 [C52235] Brother above.

CHISLETT (John) Bapt. Horncastle, Lincs. 31/5/1769, s. John (a surgeon) and Sarah Chislett. Trinity Hall, Cambridge 1788, SCL, dn91 (Lin.), p93 (Lin.). V. Thornton, Lincs. 1795 to death (Rushton, Northants.) 20/11/1850 aged 82 [C48093]

CHOLMELEY (Humphrey) Bapt. South Stoke, Easton, Lincs. 1/10/1784, s. Sir Montague Cholmeley, *M.P.* (of Easton Hall) and Sarah Sibthorpe. University, Oxford 1804, migrated to King's, Cambridge 1804, Fellow 1807-25, BA1809, dn10 (Ely), p10 (Ely), MA 1812. V. Marnham, Notts. 1824, R. Hempstead w. Lessingham, Norfolk 1824-8 (res.), R. Saltfleetby, Lincs. 1824 and R. Troston St Mary, Suffolk 1828 to death (unm.) 31/1/1841 aged 56 ('from a gun accident') [C48095]. Brother, below.

CHOLMELEY (Robert) Bapt. South Stoke, Easton, Lincs. 7/9/1780, s. Sir Cholmeley, *M.P.* (of Easton Hall) and Sarah Sibthorpe. Corpus Christi, Oxford 1796, BA1800, MA1803, dn03 (Ox.), p04 (Ox.), Fellow 1809-42, BD1812. R. Wainfleet All Saints, Lincs. 1817 and PC. Wainfleet St Mary, Lincs. 1829. Died 30/7/1842 [C1752] Married Woolwich, Kent 26/3/1813 Maria Ann Miller, w. issue. Brother, above.

CHOLWICH (William) Bapt. Westminster, London 12/3/1767, s. William Cholwich. Oriel, Oxford 1784, BA1789, dn91 (Ex.), p91 (Ex.). (Sinecure R. 1791 then) V. Ermington w. Kingston, Devon 1796 to death. Probate granted 19/2/1834 [C140566. Foster as Cholwick. ERC says Cholwich] Married Elizabeth Lambton.

CHOPPIN (Frederick) From London, s. Frederick Choppin. St John's, Oxford 1804 (aged 19), BA1808, dn08 (Ox.), p09 (Ox.), MA1810. R. Bicknor, Kent 1827. Probate granted 5/4/1849 (Brompton, London) [C24690]

CHRISTOPHERSON (John Russell) Bapt. Kings Lynn, Norfolk 13/7/1769, s. Thomas Christopherson and Mary Russell. Corpus Christi, Cambridge 1787, SCL, dn92 (Lin.), LLB1794, p94 (Lin.). PC. Guyhirne w. Ringsend, Cambs. 1795-1801, V. Eagle, Lincs. 1800 and V. Grainsby, Lincs. 1800 to death (Wisbech, Cambs.) 20/10/1844 [C6635] Married Stamford

Baron, Northants. 11/6/1826 Mrs Mary Caroline (Jackson) Marshall.

CHURCH (William) From Hatfield, Herts. Emmanuel, Cambridge 1813, dn16 (Lin.), p17 (Lin.), LLB1819. R. Kerneys Inferior, Monmouth 1823 and R. Woolsthorpe (o/w Woolstrop) w. Stainworth), Lincs. 1830 to death ('in Sackville Street, London') 20/4/1830 (CCEd says 29/4/1830) aged 56 [C3695] An Oxford man of the same name.

CHURCHILL (Benjamin) Bapt. Deddington, Oxon. 17/8/1778, s. Samuel Churchill and Priscilla Froome. Queen's, Oxford 1794, BA 1798. MA 1801, p02 (Win.), Fellow 1812. V. North Leigh, Oxon. 1810-38, PC. Appledram (o/w Apuldram), Sussex 1820 and R. Wilcote, Oxon. 1822 [but 'out of the Kingdom' in ERC] to death. Dom. Chap. to 6th Earl Waldegrave 1816. Died Honfleur, Calvados, France 12/6/1838 [C24695] Married Salisbury Cathedral 24/10/1809 Eliza Harriet Froome.

CHURCHILL (Fleetwood) Bapt. Erpingham, Norfolk 15/5/1792, s. Rev. Joseph Dixie Churchill (below) and Sarah Primrose. Pembroke, Cambridge 1813, no degree, dn16 (Nor.), p17 (Nor.). V. Roughton, Norfolk 1817 and V. Selston, Notts. 1836 to death (apoplexy) 11/2/1855 aged 63 [C6636]

CHURCHILL (Joseph Dixie) Bapt. Lichfield, Staffs. 21/5/1761, s. Joseph Churchill (a Peterborough chemist) and Mary Dixie. Pembroke, Cambridge 1779, BA1783, dn83 (Lin. for London), p85 (Nor.), MA1787. R. Willingham St Mary, Suffolk 1799-1810, R. Colby, Norfolk 1799-1802, R. Blickling, Norfolk 1802-36, R. Cadeby, Leics. 1810, V. Selston, Notts. 1810-36 and R. Henstead, Suffolk 1810-36 and R. Erpingham, Norfolk 1819 to death 8/3/1836 [C48101] Married (1) Wrentham, Surrey 7/8/1787 Sarah Primrose (d.1807), with clerical son Fleetwood (above) (2) Erpingham 24/11/1811 Sarah Chapman, with further issue.

CHURCHILL (William) Born Winterbourne Stickland, Dorset 28/5/1803, s. Rev. William Rush Hallet Churchill (Colliton House, Dorchester, Dorset, below) and Martha Tanner. Worcester, Oxford 1821, BA1825, dn27 (Llandaff for Bristol), p27 (Ely). R. Winterbourne Stickland 1828-84. Died (Drayton House, Radipole, Dorset) 1/7/1886, leaving £75,661-3s-6d. [C3696] Married Bath 26/11/1839 Julia Charlotte Mackenzie Gordon (d.1857), two clerical sons.

CHURCHILL (William Rush Hallet) Born Colliton House, Dorchester, Dorset 16/7/1774, s. William Sampson Churchill and Mary Marsh. Worcester, Oxford 1792, then All Souls, BA 1795, dn97 (Ox.), p99 (Bristol), MA1806. R. Bettiscombe, Dorset 1799-1801, R. Witherstone, Dorset 1799, R. Shaftesbury, Dorset 1800-6, V. Winterbourne St Martin (o/w Martinstown), Dorset 1806-13, R. Winterbourne Anderson, Dorset 1813. Died 11/1/1847 [C24698 as WRC and C8216 as WRHC. Foster incomplete] Married 28/5/1798 Martha Tanner, with son William, above. Port. online.

CHURTON (John) Born Whitchurch, Shropshire, s. John Churton and Elizabeth Parson. Magdalene, Cambridge 1786 (aged 16), BA 1791, dn92 (C&L), p93 (C&L). PC. Aldermaston, Berks. 1798, R. Burwarton, Shrop-shire 1800, R. Wheathill, Shropshire 1800, V. Tenbury, Worcs. 1839 to death 4/5/1860, leaving £1,500 [C9825] Married Moreton Say, Shropshire 6/12/1796 Catherine Elizabeth Holland, with clerical son Bernard.

CHURTON (John Frederick) Bapt. Marylebone, London 1/10/1798, s. of William Churton and Elizabeth Bray. Downing, Cambridge 1827, dn30 (C&L for Ely), SCL1830, p30 (Lin. for Ely), LLB1833. PC. Threapwood, Flint (Chester Diocese) 1832-40. In Auckland, New Zealand from 1840 to death 27/1/1853 [C6637] Married (1) Shrewsbury, Shropshire 21/11/1821 Letitia Hughes (d.1826), with issue (2) St Pancras, London 2/9/1826 Mary Charlotte Falwasser, many ch. The online *Blain Biographical Directory of the Anglican Clergy of the South Pacific* notes constant and serious disagreements with Bishop Selwyn of New Zealand; yet there is memorial obelisk in Auckland to his 'worth'. Port. online

CLACK (Thomas) Bapt. Okehampton, Devon 24/5/1774, s. Rev. Thomas Clack, sen. and Bridget Diana Stone. Exeter, Oxford 1792, SCL, dn97 (Ex.), p99 (Ex.), BCL1804. R. Milton Damerel, Devon 1799 to death (Holsworthy, Devon) 1852 (3rd q.) [C140571] Married St

Martin-in-the-Fields, London 29/12/1795 Elizabeth Sadler, with issue. Brother, below.

CLACK (William [Charles]) Bapt. Okehampton, Devon 31/8/1782, s. Rev. Thomas Clack and Bridget Diana Stone. University, Oxford 1801, no degree, dn06 (Ex.), p08. R. Moretonhampstead, Devon 1807 (w. Chap. of the Donative of Wolborough, including Newton Abbot) 1821) to death 30/9/1865, leaving £7,000 [C140572] Married West Alvington, Devon 31/7/1810 Anne Naylor, with clerical son William Courtenay Clack. Brother, above. Online port.

CLAPHAM (Charles) Born Leeds, Yorks. 20/10/1791, s. Thomas Clapham and Hannah Vincent. Trinity, Cambridge 1809, BA1815, dn15 (Chester for York), p16 (York), MA1818. PC. Armley, Leeds 1822 to death 13/7/1848 aged 57 [C6638.YCO] Freemason.

CLAPHAM (John) Bapt. Giggleswick, Yorks. 2/7/1758, s. of Thomas Clapham. Christ's, Cambridge 1774, BA1779, dn81 (Peterb. for York), MA1782, p82 (York). V. Giggleswick 1782 to death 21/5/1839 aged 80 [C88061. YCO] Married Old Hutton, Kendal, Westmorland 28/11/1785 Mary Bateman, with issue.

CLAPHAM (John Henry) Born Maryland, USA. Clare, Cambridge 1779, BA1783, Fellow 1783-91, MA1786, p87 (Peterb.). V. Sibertswold, Kent 1790-2, R. Isfield, Sussex 1792-1835; 'for many years Rector of Port of Spain, Trinidad', dying there 3/1/1835 aged 76 (CCEd says 13/3/1835) [C62841]

CLAPP (John Charles) Born Long Benton, Northumberland 31/5/1795, s. John Squarey Clapp and Susan Stukes Hoblyn. St John's, Cambridge 1814, BA1818, dn18 (Ex.), p19 (Ex.). R. East Coulston, Wilts. 1824 to death 18/5/1858 aged 62, leaving £6,000 [C91649] Married Falmouth, Cornwall 23/8/1825 Emma Lawrence, with issue. Oil painting online.

CLARE (George Boodle) Bapt. Bushbury, Suffolk 13/2/1799, s. Rev. John Clare (below) and Mary Boodle. Worcester, Oxford 1819, BA 1823, dn23 (Chester), p24 (C&L). PC. Bushbury 1824, PC. Shareshill, Staffs. 1825-59, (first) PC. Wolverhampton St George 1835. Died 16/11/1859, leaving £4,000 [C10032] Married Milverton, Warwicks. 18/9/1838 Mary Jane Brearley (w).

CLARE (John) Bapt. Ribbesford, Worcs. 16/8/1764, s. Timothy Clare and Mary Jasper. Worcester, Oxford 1780, BA1784, dn87 (Ox.), MA1787, p98 (C&L). V. Bushbury, Staffs. 1800, PC. Wednesfield, Staffs. 1811. Died 11/7/1839 [C10033] Married Mary Boodle 26/8/1793, w. clerical son (above). *J.P.* Staffs.

CLARK (Francis Foreman) Born Holborn, London 24/5/1800, s. Francis Clark and Lucy Ann Pollard. Queens', Cambridge 1822, BA 1827, dn27 (C&L), p28 (C&L). S/M Newcastle under Lyme Free G/S 1834; (first) PC. Coseley, Staffs. 1830-3, PC. Hartshill, Staffs. 1842-56 (w. RD Stoke on Trent 1841), PC. Malpas, Monmouth [*not* Cheshire, *q.v.* CCEd] 1858 to death there 26/8/1862 aged 62, leaving £1,500 [C10036] Married (1) St George's Hanover Square, London 7/4/1822 Martha Sitch, with issue (2) Sedgley, Staffs. 24/8/1833 Sarah Russell (w).

CLARK (Henry) Born Leicester 2/11/1785, s. Henry Clark and Martha Johnson. Queens', Cambridge 1803, BA1808, dn08 (Lin.), p10 (Lin.), MA1811. V. Rowston, Lincs. 1821 and V. Harmston, Lincs. 1821 to death (Torquay, Devon) 2/7/1862. Will not traced [C48110. Kaye] Married Wirksworth, Derbys. 30/5/1828 Mary Blackwall, with issue, including Robert, missionary in India (*q.v. Robert Clark of the Panjab* (1907, with splendid photographs). A magnificent family group photo. onlne.

CLARK (John) Born Brent Eleigh, Suffolk. Clare, Cambridge 1791, BA1796, Fellow 1796, dn97 (Nor.), MA1799, p99 (Nor.). V. Duxford St John's, Cambs. 1811 to death (Lowestoft, Suffolk) 13/2/1852 aged 76 [C6639]

CLARK, CLARKE (John) Probably bapt. Malpas, Cheshire 3/10/1790, s. Charles Clark and Hester ?Stephens. Literate: dn15 (Chester for York), p15 (Chester). R. Barrow, Cheshire 1816 to death 17/1/1862 aged about 71, leaving £1,000 [C168485. YCO] Wife Elizabeth (w), with issue.

CLARK (Thomas) Born 1783. Literate: dn09 (Chester), p18 (Chester). PC. (and patron) of Gedney Hill, Lincs. 1812 to death 28/2/1870, leaving £800 [C48119] Wife Mary Ann, and clerical son of same name. Bee keeper.

CLARK (William, *nicknamed* 'Bone') Born Newcastle upon Tyne 5/4/1788, s. of John Clark, M.D. (*q.v.* ODNB) and Susannah Heath. Trinity, Cambridge 1803, BA1808, Fellow 1809, MA1811, dn18 (B&W), p18 (Salis.), MD1827. Professor of Anatomy, Cambridge 1817-66. V. Arrington, Cambs. 1824-5, V. Wymeswold, Leics. 1825-6, V. Guiseley, Leeds 1825-59 (non-res. for nine months of the year, 'but took pains to select a good curate'). Died Cambridge 15/9/1869 aged 81, leaving £35,000 [C6640. ODNB as an anatomist. Boase] Married Marylebone, London 20/7/1827 Mary Willis (a medical dau.), 1s. survived. F.R.C.P. (1830), F.R.S. (1836). A 'friend' of Byron.

CLARKE (Anthony James) Bapt. Alfreton, Derbys. 6/4/1790, s. Nathaniel Gooding Clarke and Constance Elizabeth Stephenson. Christ's, Cambridge 1810, BA1814, dn14 (C&L), p15 (C&L), MA1817. Min. Birmingham St Peter --, R. Porlock, Som. 1831 to death 22/5/1838 aged 48 [C10042] Married Hackthorn, Lincs. 16/9/1828 Elizabeth Langton (a clergy dau.), with clerical son James Langton Clarke.

CLARKE (Edward John) Bapt. Saltash, Cornwall 19/1/1779. St Mary Hall, Oxford, SCL1803, dn03 (Ex.), p05 (Ex.). R. St Dominic, Cornwall 1803. Buried 7/3/1835 aged 56 [C140577. Not in Foster]

CLARKE (George Ford) Born Bedale, Yorks. 1/5/1791, s. Rev. Richard Clarke. Christ Church, Oxford 1809, migrated to Pembroke, Cambridge 1812, SCL, p15 (Nor. for Chester), LLB 1816. R. Thornton Watlass, Yorks. 1815 and PC. Hutton Bonville, Yorks. 1823 to death (London) 17/4/1842 aged 52 [C112179] Married Richmond, Surrey 12/10/1812 Elizabeth Mary Peirse, with issue. A sporting parson.

CLARKE (George Somers) Born London 1754, s. Somers Clarke. Trinity, Oxford 1774, BA 1778, dn81 (Ox.), MA1781, p82 (Ox.), DD1803. R. Great Waltham, Herts. 1797 to death 5/2/1837 in Chelmsford Gaol aged 82 (having been sent there in 1824 for contempt of the Ecclesiastical Court, and for 'brawling in Church') [C25146] Married 27/8/1797 Dorothea Sophia Goodeve, w. clerical s. Christopher Somers Clarke.

CLARKE (James Stanier) Born Minorca 17/12/1766, s. Rev. Edward Clarke (R. Buxted, Sussex) and Anne Greenfield. St John's, Cambridge 1784, dn89 (Chich.), p90 (Chich.), then Jesus 1804, LLB1805, LLD1816. Chap. R.N. 1795-9; V. Preston w. Hove, Sussex 1790-1834, R. Coombes, Sussex 1804-8, Canon of Windsor 1808 and R. Tillington, Sussex 1816 to death. Chap. in Ordinary 1799, Deputy Clerk of the Closet 1816 (and Librarian 1805, and Historiographer to the King 1816). Co-edited the *Naval Chronicle* for 20 years. Died Brighton (unm.?) 4/10/1834 aged 67 [C62973. ODNB. C. Viveash, *James Stanier Clarke, librarian to the Prince Regent, naval author, friend of Jane Austen* (Winchester, 2006)] F.R.S.

CLARKE (John) Born Trimlett, Somerset 24/8/1786, s. Rev. Thomas Edward Clarke (R. Clayhindon, Devon). Sidney, Cambridge 1804, BA1808, dn09 (Ex.), p10 (Ex.), MA1811. R. (and patron) of Clayhindon 1814-47, R. Dunkeswell, Devon 1814 and R. Chaffcombe, Som. 1822 all to death 24/12/1847 aged 61 [C140579]

CLARKE (John Thomas) Bapt. Jurby, IoM 10/11/1798, s. William Clarke and Mary Munn. Literate: dn22 (S&M), p22 (S&M). Chap. Malew St Mark, IoM 1828-64, Chap. Mariners' Church, Swansea 1872, V. Caerleon, Dolgellau, Merioneth 1876 to death 2/2/1888 aged 89, leaving £54-14s-3d. [C7248. Gelling] Married (1) Santan, IoM 26/9/1822 Elizabeth Clucas (d.1862), with issue (2) Santan, IoM 2/9/1864 Catherine Clucas (w). Manx speaker.

CLARKE (Joseph) Bapt. Lorton, Cumberland 12/7/1757. Literate: dn80 (Chester), p81 (Chester). V. Ilkley, Yorks. 1830 to death 4/3/1842 aged 84 [C135849]

CLARKE (Lancelot Christopher) Bapt. Stanhope, Durham 2/7/1793, s. Canon John Clarke. Emmanuel, Cambridge 1811, BA1816, dn16 (Durham), p18 (Durham). PC. Bellingham, Durham 1816-31, PC. Wolviston, Co. Durham 1823 to death 30/12/1864 aged 71. Will not traced [C130362] Married Birmingham 10/8/1819 Isabella White, with issue.

CLARKE (Liscombe) From London, s. Christopher Clarke. New, Oxford 1804 (aged 19), BA1808, dn08 (Win.), p08 (Win.), MA 1812, Fellow to 1815; Fellow of Winchester College. H/M Twyford School, Winchester 1809-15; V. Biddestone w. Slaughterford 1819-32 (res.), Prebend of Bartonsham in Hereford Cathedral 1821-31 (res.), V. Downton, Wilts. 1824, Archdeacon of Sarum 1827 1836 (res.), Prebend of Minor Pars Altaris in Salisbury Cathedral 1827-8, then of Netheravon 1828-34 (res.), Canon Residentiary 1832 (with Treasurer and Prebend of Calne annexed 1834) to death 17/4/1841, aged 55 [C71741] Married Clifton, Bristol 22/4/1819 Mary Stonhouse.

CLARKE (Robert) Bapt. Sebergham, Cumberland 10/3/1776, s. of John (a yeoman farmer) and Mary Clarke. Literate: dn02 (York), p03 (York). PC. High Worsall, Yorks. 1802, PC. Ebchester w. Medomsley, Durham 1820 to death 24/12/1837 aged 60 [C88110. YCO] Married Newcastle upon Tyne 20/6/1815 Mary Grey (of Morpeth, Northumberland, d.1818).

CLARKE (Thomas) From Chiswick, London, s. Thomas Clarke [*pleb*]. Christ Church, Oxford 1775 (aged 16), BA1780, MA1784. R. Tusmore, Oxon. 1799-1841, R. Bedwardine, Worcs. 1799-1839, R. Overbury, Worcs. 1821-39. Died London 5/1/1841 aged 73 [C25150]

CLARKE (Thomas) Born Cork, s. William Clarke and Sarah Farren. TCD1811 (aged 23), BA1814, dn14, p15. V. Micheldever, Hants. 1816 (and RD1830) to death (Southampton) 9/1/1870. Will not traced [C71743. Al.Dub.] Married (1) London 21/3/1814 Anna Maria Grey (d.1827), with clerical son (2) Hartley Witney, Hants. 28/10/1830 Anne Agnes Husband (d.1858), w. further clerical son and many other ch. (3) Islington, London 5/1/1820 Frances Marie Winkup (d.1864).

CLARKE (Thomas Brooke) Born Dublin 1757 (bapt. 4/10/1763), s. Nathaniel Clarke. TCD1773, BA 1779, MA1787, DD. 'Held livings in Ireland in which he was non-resident'; R. Dinton, Bucks. 1833 (then V. 1833) to death. Chap. in Ordinary (and Secretary to the Prince of Wales' Library). Died 13/7/1833 (CCEd says 18/10/1833). Tutor to George FitzErnest (natural s. of Duke of Cumberland). [C48141. Al.Dub.] Married (1) Ireland 1787 Helen Johnson, w. issue (2) 1830 Helen Witney, w. further issue. Auditor of the Naval Asylum at Greenwich (for naval orphans) 1805-21: collections.rmg.co.uk/collections/objects/497855.html

CLARKE (Unwin) Bapt. Sudbury, Suffolk 11/7/1764, s. Stockdell Clarke and Mary Unwin. Wadham, Oxford 1782, dn89 (Nor.), p89 (Car. for B&W), BA1792, MA1792. R. Monksilver, Som. 1789-1803, Archdeacon of Chester 1801-47 (w. Canon and Vice-Dean of Chester Cathedral), V. Eastham, Cheshire 1827-36-, V. Neston, Cheshire 1827. Chap. to HRH Duke of Clarence 1827. Died Great Broughton, Yorks. 3/2/1847 [C5767] Was married.

CLARKE (William) Bapt. Hull 31/1/1765, s. Marmaduke Clarke (merchant). Clare, Cambridge 1782, BA1787, dn87 (York), p89 (York), MA1790. V. Burstwick cum Skeckling >< Hull 1811 to death 1852 [C135850. YCO] His educational charity survives.

CLARKE (William) Literate: dn15 (Chester), p16 (Chester), then Queens', Cambridge 1824, a Ten Year Man (BD1834). PC. Chester St John's the Less (or Little St John's Hospital [almshouses] Chapel), 1828 to death (Rhyl, Flintshire) 5/10/1864 aged 72, leaving £4,000 [C168507. Not in Venn?] Widow Christiana, and clerical s.

CLARKE (William Edward) [BA but NiVoF] R. Great Yeldham, Essex 1831-[43]. Died? [C116767] Had issue.

CLARKE (William Henry) Bapt. Portsmouth 12/10/1791, s. William Clarke and Elizabeth Woodyer. Exeter, Oxford 1810, BA1814, dn15 (Peterb.), p16 (Peterb.), MA1817. V. Seaford, Sussex 1816, R. Cold Higham, Northants. 1816 to death 16/6/1875, leaving £1,000 [C62972] Married Pattishall, Northants. 6/7/1844 Elizabeth Welch (w), w. issue. J.P. Northants. 50 years.

CLARKE (William Henry) Bapt. Cranbrook, Kent 16/3/1799, s. William and Mary Clarke. St Catharine's, Cambridge 1825, BA1829, dn30 (Nor.), p31 (Nor.), MA1832. PC. Great Yarmouth St Peter, Norfolk 1833-46, PC. Herringfleet, Sussex 1846, PC. Skipton Christ Church, Yorks. 1862 to burial 24/11/ 1885 aged 85, leaving £6,100-7s-0d. [C112196] Married

Bloomsbury, Londfon 22/10/1827 Sarah Ann Heeson, w. issue.

CLARKSON (Christopher) Born Tynemouth, Northumberland 1796, s. Christopher Clarkson. Trinity, Cambridge 1814, BA1819, dn19 (Chester for Wor.), p21 (Chester for C&L), MA1823. PC. Mellor, Blackburn, Lancs. 1831-44, R. Elworthy, Som. 1835-44, R. Ringsfield, Suffolk 1845-48, R. (and patron) of Holsworthy, Devon 1860 [income £1,000] to death (Plymouth) 19/10/1869 aged 73, leaving under £200 [C10053] Widow Susan.

CLARKSON (Isaac) Bapt. 6/4/1795, s. Richard (a farmer) and Elizabeth Clarkson. Literate: dn18 (York), p19 (York). V. Wednesbury, Staffs. 1829-51-, V. Sandal Magna, Yorks. 1855 to death (York) 28/5/1860 aged 65, leaving £5,000 [C130996/C31920. YCO] Clerical son John Cowper Addison Clarkson.

CLARKSON (John) From Brackenthwaite, Lancs., s. Thomas Clarkson. Trinity, Cambridge 1800, BA1805, Fellow 1806, MA1808, dn10 (Bristol), p11 (Bristol). V. Great Barford w. Roxton, Beds. 1817 to death 16/3/1847 aged 68 [C8162] Had issue.

CLARKSON (Thomas Bayley) Born Wakefield, Yorks. 24/1/1794 (nonconformist baptism), s. Thomas Clarkson and Sarah Bayley. Literate: dn25 (York), p26 (York). PC. Chapelthorpe, Yorks. 1827-43, Chap. to West Yorkshire Asylum, Wakefield 1843 to death (Boston Spa, Yorks.) 1873. Death not in BMD and Will not traced [C130998. YCO] Married (1) Thornhill, Wakefield 17/10/1821 Mary Penelope Bedford (d.1862), with issue (2) Doncaster 4/2/1871 Sophia Laughton.

CLARKSON (Townley) Bapt. Heysham, Lancs. 2/10/1771, s. Rev. Townley Clarkson, sen. Jesus, Cambridge 1789, BA1794, dn94 (Ely), MA1798, Fellow 1798-1807, p03 (Ely). V. Hinxton, Cambs. 1805-25, V. Swavesey, Cambs. 1806-33, PC. Cambridge St Andrew the Great 1814, Chap. of the Donative of Cambridge St Andrew the Less 1825, R. Acton Scott, Shropshire 1825-30, V. Hauxton, Cambs. 1830 (only), R. Beyton, Suffolk 1830 to death 27/1/1833 (CCEd says 30/5/1833) [C6644] Married Covent Garden, London Sarah Dabbs, with issue. *J.P.* Cambs.

CLARRYVINCE (John) Bapt. (Great) Yedham, Suffolk 4/9/1785, s. John (a farmer, Fordham, Essex) and Sarah Clarryvince. Caius, Cambridge 1805, BA1810, dn10 (Ely), MA1813, p19 (Nor.). S/M Colchester School; H/M Woodbridge School, Suffolk 1815-22 (res. after being blamed for neglect of his pupils); PC. Pontesbright, Great Tey, Essex 1824 to death 1866 (3rd q.) aged 86. Will not traced [C66842] Married Woodbridge 21/1816 Sarah Tyrer (Camden Town, London).

CLAVELL, *born* RICHARDS (John) Bapt. Winfrith, Dorset 4/6/1760 (a twin), s. William Richards and Margaret Clavell. St John's, Cambridge 1777, dn81 (Nor. for Bristol), BA1781, p82 (Bristol), MA1788. V. Church Knowle, Dorset 1782-1833, V. East Lulworth, Dorset 1787-1832. Dom. Chap. to 5th Duke of St Albans 1787. Died (unm.) 14/6/1833 (CCEd says 12/11/1833) [C52246 as Richards] *J.P.* Dorset; changed name 1817 on inheriting Smedmore House, Isle of Purbeck, where he built the Clavell Tower observatory and folly at Kimmeridge Bay, Dorset: en.wikipedia.org/wiki/Clavell_Tower

CLAVERING (John) Bapt. Northampton 5/1/1779, s. Robert Clavering. BNC, Oxford 1797, BA1801, dn03 (Wor.), p04 (Wor.), MA 1806. PC. Moreton Morrell, Warwicks. 1805 and V. Stow Bardolph, Norfolk 1834 to death. Will proved 3/1/1852 [C120608]

CLAY (Benjamin) Bapt. Southwell, Notts. 29/7/1763, s. of William (an attorney) and Jemima Clay. St John's, Cambridge 1780, BA 1784, Fellow 1784-92, dn86 (Lin.), MA1787, p87 (York). R. Hockerton, Notts. 1787 (non-res.) and R. East Worlington, Devon 1796 to death (Torquay, Devon) 7/12/1851 aged 88 [C48247. YCO] Married Huntingdon 20/10/1791 Jennetta, dau. of Rev. Castel Sherard (*q.v.*), w. clerical son, below.

CLAY (Pelham Fellowes) Born Eggesford, Devon 15/10/1796, s. Rev. Benjamin Clay (above, R. East Worlington, Devon) and Jennetta Sherard. Sidney, Cambridge 1815, BA 1819, dn20 (Ex.), p21 (Ex.), MA1823. R. Eggesford 1821 and R. Chawleigh, Devon 1821 to death (Newton Abbot, Devon) 10/3/1879 aged 82, leaving £800 ('county banker the sole executor', so probably unm.?) [C140585]

CLAYTON (Augustus Philip) Born Marlow, Bucks. 11/10/1799, s. Sir William Clayton, 4th Bart. and Mary East. Caius, Cambridge 1819, BA1824, dn25 (Bristol for Salis.), p26 (Salis.), MA1827. R. Garveston, Norfolk 1828-45; then lived at Sevenoaks, Kent. Died (Fyfield House, Bray, Berks.) 2/2/1871, leaving £7,000 [C8163] Married St George's Hanover Square, London 4/9/1828 Georgina Elizabeth Talbot (dau. of a Dean of Salisbury), with issue.

CLAYTON (John) From Chipping Campden, Glos., s. John Clayton. Pembroke, Oxford 1805 (aged 16), BA1820, MA1823. Curate Redditch Chapel, Tardebigge, Worcs. 1820-[41]. Died? [C120609] Married Dymock, Glos. 13/5/1830 Anne Cam Thackwell (who remarried).

CLAYTON (Thomas) Bapt. Deane, Bolton, Lancs. 29/3/1776, s. Christopher Clayton. BNC, Oxford 1797, BA1801, MA1803, dn04 (Ox.), p04 (Ox.), BD1811, Fellow 1816. R. Cottingam, Northants. 1815 (and RD 1840) to death 15/1/1866, leaving £2,000 [C25155] Liverpool Married 1815 Mary Hodgson (a clergy dau.).

CLAYTON (William Ray) Bapt. Finningham, Suffolk 18/12/1777, s. Samuel Clayton and Anne Way. Emmanuel, Cambridge 1797, BA 1800, dn00 (Ex. for Nor.), p02 (Lin.). R. Great Ryburgh w. Little Ryburgh, Norfolk 1820-58, V. Norwich St Mary Coslany 1832-51. Died Norwich 12/8/1858 aged 81, leaving £35,000 [C48252] Married Whitechapel, London 23/10/1802 Ann Smyth.

CLEATHING (John) Bapt. Leghorn, Tuscany 20/11/1765, s. John Cleathing. Trinity, Cambridge 1784, BA1788, dn88 (York), MA1791, p91 (Lin.). V. Thorpe Arnold, Leics. [blank in ERC] 1791 to death 17/8/1841 aged 75 [C48253. YCO] Married Scarborough, Yorks. 20/6/1792 Sarah Travis. 'A generous benefactor to the S.P.C.K.'

CLEAVER, later PEACH (James Jarvis) Born Leeds 31/1/1776, s. Rev. John Cleaver. BNC, Oxford 1793, BA1797, MA1799, p00 (Chester for York). V. Appleton le Street w. Amotherby, Yorks. 1800-31, PC. Huttons Ambo, Yorks. 1804-32, V. Crambe, Notts. 1804-23, R. Holme Pierrepoint w. Adbolton, Notts. 1814-64, Prebend of Oxton Prima in Southwell Collegiate Church 1820-51-, PC. Sutton on Derwent, Yorks. 1823, R. Hawerby cum Beesby, Lincs. 1831. Dom. Chap. to 2nd Earl Manvers 1816. Died Olveston, Glos. 17/2/1864, leaving £8,000 [C48503. Foster under Peach. YCO] Married Olveston 24/6/1820 Ellen Sybilla Peach (with name change 1845), and had issue.

CLEAVER (John) Bapt. Rothwell, Yorks. 3/1/1777, s. Rev. John Clever [*sic*]. BNC, Oxford 1795, BA1799, dn01 (York), MA1802, p02 (York), BCL and DCL1811. V. Edwinstowe w. Carburton, Notts. 1802-34, R. South Leverton, Notts. 1807-34, R. Weston, Notts. 1811 to death 27/8/1834 (CCEd says 2/10/1834) aged 57 [C88131. YCO] Online confusion with another cleric of this name.

CLEAVER (John Francis) Born Oxford, s. of Rt. Rev. William Cleaver (Bishop of Bangor) and Anne Asheton. Christ Church, Oxford 1805 (aged 17), BA1809, MA1811, dn12 (B&W), p12 (Lin. for St Asaph). R. (and Sinecure R.) Corwen, Merioneth 1812, R. Newtown, Montgomery 1814-15 (res.), Cursal Canon of John Griffith in St Asaph Cathedral 1815, V. Great Coxwell, Berks. 1815 to death 12/3/1861, leaving £8,000 (3 spinster daus. the executrixes) [C33871]

CLEEVE (John Kingdon) Bapt. Silverton, Devon 23/10/1765, s. William Cleeve and Mary Elizabeth Kingdon. Balliol, Oxford 1783, BA 1787, dn88 (Ex.), p89 (Ex.), MA1818, BD and DD1818. R. Exeter St Edmund 1817, R. Exeter St George 1818 to death 18/11/1841 [C140655] Married Broadhembury, Devon 23/9/1800 Elizabeth Sanders, with issue.

CLEMENTSON (Enoch) Born Giggleswick, Yorks. 27/4/1783, s. William Clementson and Elisabeth Silverwood. Literate: dn06 (York), p07 (Car. for York). Chap. of the Donative of Church Minshull, Cheshire 1819 to death. Dom. Chap. to 1st Earl of Roden 1816 . Buried 24/12/1836 [C109600. YCO] Married Mellor, Lancs. 27/8/1808 Mary Critchley, with issue.

CLEMENTSON (John) [Perhaps] Bapt. Bridekirk, Cumberland 8/5/1781, s. Wilfrid and Margaret Clementson. Literate: dn09 (Chester), p10 (Chester). V. Wolvey, Warwicks. 1830 to death (Leamington, Warwicks.) 24/1/1859, leaving £1,100 (unadministered until 1881) [C10069] Widow Charlotte.

CLEMETSON (Dacre) Bapt. Moresby, Whitehaven, Cumberland 27/6/1794, s. Wilfrid and Margaret Clemetson. St Alban Hall, Oxford 1813, BA1817, dn17 (B&W), p18 (Salis.), MA 1819. R. [sequestrator] Chilcombe, Dorset 1833 [blank in ERC] to death. Chap. Dorchester Prison 1825; Chap. Dorset County Lunatic Asylum 1833. Died 26/4/1866, leaving £3,000 [C8218]

CLEMINSON (William) Born Ulverston, Lancs., s. George and Mary Cleminson. Queen's, Oxford 1817 (aged 19), BA1821, dn21 (London), p22 (Ox.). PC. Tranmere, Bebington, Cheshire 1831, R. Wasing, Berks. 1847 to death (Walmer, Kent) 30/1/1857 aged 59 [C25163] Married Ulverston 2/2/1841 Eleanor Boardman.

CLEOBURY (John) From Abingdon, Berks. s. Rev. John Cleobury, sen. BNC, Oxford 1809 (aged 17), BA1813, dn14 (Heref. for London), p15 (Lin.), MA1816. PC. Piddington, Oxon. 1822 to death 1853 (2nd q.) [C25190]

CLERKE (Charles Carr) Born Bury, Lancs. 23/12/1798, s. Rev. Sir William Henry Clerke, 8th Bart. and Byzantia Cartwright. Christ Church, Oxford 1814, Student [Fellow] 1814-37, BA1818, dn23 (Ox.), MA1821, p24 (Ox.), BD1830, DD1847. V. Oxford St Mary Magdalen 1827-34, Archdeacon of Oxford 1830 (with Canonry of Christ Church Cathedral, Oxford annexed 1846-77), R. Milton, Berks. 1836-75 [total income in CR65 £1,063]. Chap. to Samuel Wilberforce as Bishop of Oxford, then of Winchester. Died 23/12/1877 aged 79, leaving £25,000 [C24379. Boase] Married New Forest, Hants. 15/4/1847 Caroline Ashhurst, *s.p.* Brother, below.

CLERKE (Francis) Bapt. Bury, Lancs. 10/9/1797, s. Rev. Sir William Henry Clerke, 8th Bart. and Byzantia Cartwright. BNC, Oxford 1814, BA1818, then All Souls, Fellow 1818-27, dn21 (Ox.), MA1822, p22 (Ox.). R. Eydon, Northants. 1826 to death (Nice) 29/1/1853 [C25191] Married City of London 18/6/1842 Jane Elizabeth Lynch. Brother, above.

CLEVELAND (Henry) Bapt. Upper Shadwell, Middx. 1/4/1803, s. Reuben Cleveland and Elizabeth Forster. St John's, Cambridge 1821, BA1825, dn26 (York), p27 (Ely), MA1828. R. Barkstone (o/w Barkerston), Lincs. 1829-50, R. Romaldkirk, Yorks. 1850 to death 27/7/1889 aged 86, leaving £5,441-13s.-6d. [C6648. YCO] Married Grantham, Lincs. 10/11/1830 Margaret Potchett, w. clerical son. Surrogate. *J.P.* North Riding.

CLIFTON, *born* BEESON (John Clifton) Born Grantham, Lincs. 15/6/1805, s. John Beeson and Frances Clifton. St John's, Cambridge 1822, BA1827, dn28 (York), p29 (York), MA1831. V. Willoughby on the Wolds, Notts. 1831-6, R. Tilton on the Hill, Leics. 1831-41. Retired to South Clinton, Notts. Died 6/3/1843 aged 39 [C130830. Boase. YCO as Beeson. Venn wrongly says alive 1882] Married Scrayingham, Yorks. 5/7/1827 Mary King (of Silbey, Leics.)

CLIFTON (Robert) Born Worcester 3/8/1783, s. John Clifton and Mrs Elizabeth (Stevens) Browning. Worcester, Oxford 1800, BA 1804, dn06 (Glos.), p07 (Heref.), MA1810. V. Brookthorpe, Glos. 1809-17, R. Matson, Glos. 1817-31, R. Worcester St Nicholas 1819, R. Somerton, Oxon. 1831-40. Chap. at Bruges *c.*1843-64-. Dom. Chap. to Elizabeth, Baroness Monson 1819. Died Flanders 2/5/1863 aged 79 No will traced [C120689] Clerical son Robert Cox Clifton (*q.v.* ODNB).

CLINTON, *or* FYNES-CLINTON (Charles John Fynes-) Born Welwyn, Herts. 16/4/1799, s. Rev. Charles Fynes (Prebend of Westminster Abbey) and Emma Brough. Oriel, Oxford 1818, BA1822, dn23 (Chester for York), p24 (Chester for York), MA1825. V. Strensall w. Osbaldwick, Yorks. 1824-27, V. Orston w. Thoroton, Notts. 1827-55, R. Cromwell, Notts. 1828 to death. Dom. Chap. to 4th Duke of Newcastle 1827. Died London 10/1/1872 aged 72 (pleurisy), leaving £20,000 [C130999. ODNB. Boase. YCO] Married (1) Burton on Trent, Staffs. 16/3/1826 Caroline Clay (d.1827) (2) Orston 20/5/1829 Rosabella Mathews (of North Shields), 7s.

CLISSOLD (Henry) Bapt. Stonehouse, Glos. 29/1/1796, s. Stephen Clissold (Hill House, Glos.) and Diana Mortimer. Exeter, Oxford

1814, BA1818, dn19 (Ex.), p21 (Ely for London), MA1821. PC. Stockwell, Lambeth, Ssurrey 1824, R. Chelmondiston, Suffolk 1830-58. Died Paddington, London 1/1/1867, leaving £14,000 [C6649. Boase] Married St Giles, London 22/6/1826 Marianne Bayley, with clerical son Henry Bayley Clissold. Brother below.

CLISSOLD (Stephen) Bapt. Reading, Berks. 25/9/1789, s. of Stephen Clissold (Hill House, Glos.) and Diana Mortimer. Clare, Cambridge 1814, BA1819 [adm. Lincoln's Inn 1819] MA 1822, dn26 (London [for Nor.?]), p28 (Nor.). R. Wrentham, Suffolk 1830 (RD and Hon. Canon Norwich Cathedral 1848) to death 12/5/1863, leaving £60,000 [C112205. ODNB. Boase] Married Bramfield, Suffolk 17/6/1824 Charlotte Matilda Gooch, w. clerical son Edward Mortimer Clissold. Brother above.

CLIVE (Archer) Born Marylebone, London 16/3/1800, s. of Edward Bolton Clive and Hon. Harriet Archer. BNC, Oxford 1817, BA1820, MA1823, dn25 (Heref.), p26 (Heref.). Chap. of the Donative of Wormbridge, Heref. 1829, R. Solihull, Warwicks. 1829-47, Prebend of Pyon Parva in Hereford Cathedral 1850. Died Whitfield, Heref. 17/9/1878 aged 78, leaving £25,000 [C10073. Boase] Married 10/11/1840 Caroline Meysey-Wigley, with issue. *J.P., D.L.*

CLIVE (George Arthur) Bapt. Moreton Say, Shropshire 23/12/1803, s. William Clive, *M.P.* (Leigh Hall, Shropshire) and Elizabeth Clive Rotton. St John's, Cambridge 1821, BA1827, dn28 (St Asaph), p28 (Heref.), MA1835. PC. Clunton w. Clunbury >< Shropshire 1828, V. Bishop's Castle, Shropshire 1835, R. Montford, Shropshire 1835 and R. Shrawardine, Shropshire 1840 to death (unm.) 8/11/1881, leaving £58,343-7s-6d. [C10074] Brother, below.

CLIVE (William) Born Styche, Shropshire 14/3/1795, s. of William Clive, *M.P.* (Leigh Hall, Shropshire) and Elizabeth Clive Rotton. St John's, Cambridge 1813, BA1818, dn18 (Wor. for C&L), p19, MA1821. V. Welshpool, Montgomery 1819-65, R. Montford, Shropshire 1831-5, R. Shrawardine, Shropshire 1835-40, Archdeacon of Montgomery 1844-61, Prebend of St Asaph's Cathedral 1849 (then Residentiary Canon 1854-61), R. Blymhill 1865 (and RD) to death. Dom. Chap. to Duke of Northumberland 1824. Died 24/5/1883, leaving £94,679-7s-10d. [C10076. Boase] Married Betley, Staffs. 28/10/1829 Marianne Tollet (Betley Hall), with issue. Brother, above.

CLOSE (Francis) Born Frome, Somerset 11/7/1797, s. Rev. Henry Jackson Close and Mary Waring. St John's, Cambridge 1816, BA 1820, dn20 (Chester), p21 (Chester), MA 1824, DD1856 (Lambeth). PC. Cheltenham, Glos. 1826-56, R. Hatford, Berks. 1832-35, Dean of Carlisle 1856-81 [income in CR65 £1,400] (and PC. Carlisle St Mary 1865-8). Died (Penzance, Cornwall) 18/12/1882, leaving £1,764-3s-1d. [C10077. ODNB. Boase. DEB. A. Munden, *A Cheltenham Gameliel: Dean Close of Cheltenham* (Cheltenham, 1987)] Married (1) 24/2/1820 Anne Diana Arden (Longcroft Hall, Staffs., a clergy dau., she d.1877), 5s, 4 dau. (2) Christchurch, Hants. 2/12/1880 Mrs Mary (Antrim) Hodgson. A popular Evangelical preacher, who 'bitterly opposed horse racing and the theatre' (but who erected a monument to his dead dog). Romilly2 describes him as 'a pudding faced unintellectual looking man with coarse features: he … has a fine head of brown hair [which] is (I am told) curled daily.'

CLOSE (Richard) Born Shap, Westmorland 13/4/1766. Literate (but CCEd says MA, so a Ten Year Man?): dn92 (Durham), p93 (Durham). PC. Hunstanworth, Durham 1811 to death before 28/8/1834 [C134147] Married Slaley, Northumberland 6/9/1793 Mary Teasdale, with issue.

CLOSE (William) Bapt. Winston, Durham 27/6/1784, s. William Close. Literate: dn14 (Durham for York), p16 (Durham for York). PC. Skelton cum Brotton (o/w Skelton in Cleveland), Yorks. 1816 to death 1857 (3rd q.), leaving £1,764-3s-11d. [C130365. YCO]

CLOWES (John) Born Manchester 1/5/1777, s. Samuel Clowes. Trinity, Cambridge 1794, BA 1799, MA1805, dn06 (C&L), p07 (C&L). Fellow of Manchester Collegiate Church 1809-33 (res.), R. Grindon, Staffs. 1816-36. Succ. to the family estate of Broughton Old Hall, Salford, where he died (unm.) 28/9/1846 [C10078] An important horticulturalist and art collector.

CLOWES (Robert) Bapt. Bermondsey, Surrey 26/1/1788, s. Charles Clowes (of Delaford

Park, Bucks. and Langley Hall, Cheshire) and Ann Dawson. Magdalene, Cambridge 1809, BA 1811, dn13, p14 (Lin.), MA1814. V. (Nether) Knutsford, Cheshire 1824 (where he inaugurated the first May Fair in 1864) to death 13/10/1864 aged 76, leaving £25,000 [C48527] Married Knutsford 6/9/1824 Catherine Jee/Gee (w) (a clergy dau., Thaxted, Essex), with issue.

CLOWES (Thomas) Bapt. Caistor, Norfolk 14/12/1800, s. Thomas Clowes (solicitor, Great Yarmouth, Norfolk). Queens', Cambridge 1818, BA1823, dn24 (Chester), p25 (Nor.), Fellow 1825, MA1826. Chap. Great Yarmouth St Mary, Southtown 1830 (and H/M of a prep. school 1833-41), R. St Lawrence, Norfolk 1844-50, V. Ashbocking, Suffolk 1849 to death 27/2/1862 aged 61, leaving £5,000 [C3699] Married London 26/3/1828 Caroline Pratt, w. issue.

CLUTTERBUCK (James Charles) Born Watford, Herts. 11/7/1801, s. Robert Clutterbuck and Marianne Capper. Exeter, Oxford 1820, Fellow 1822-31, dn26 (Ox.), p26 (Ox.), BA1826, MA1827. V. Long Wittenham (o/w Wittenham Earls ><), Berks. 1830 (and RD of Abingdon 1868) to death 31/5/1885, leaving £14,878-16s-9d. [C25202. Boase] Married Watford, Herts. 21/3/1831 Louisa Capel, w. clerical s. Francis Capper Clutterbuck. 'A great authority on all questions relating to water.'

CLUTTON (John) Bapt. Birmingham 1/8/1760, s. Henry and Margaret Clutton. St John's, Oxford 1778, p82 (Heref.), p84 (Heref.), BA1782, MA1789, BD1809, DD1810. R. Kinnersley, Heref. 1784-1838, Prebend of Warham in Hereford Cathedral 1794-1838 (and Canon Residentiary 1813-1838), R. Winforton, Heref. 1794-1818 (res.), V. Lydney, Glos. 1818-31 (res.), V. (and patron) of Lugwardine, Heref. 1831 (and Master St Ethelbert's Hospital [almshouses], Hereford 1831) to death. Dom. Chap. to Bishop of Peterborough 1794. Died 7/5/1838 aged 77 (CCEd says 7/5/1838) [C10081] Clerical son, also John. 'A very active and useful magistrate'.

COATES, COTES (Henry) Bapt. Sherborne, Dorset 14/8/1759, s. Rev. Edward and Ann Coates. University, Oxford 1777, BA1781, dn82 (Ox. for Bristol), p83 (C&L). V. Bedlington, Durham 1788 to death 7/2/1835 [C10144. Foster as Cotes] Edited the text of Thomas Bewick's *Water Birds*. A sporting parson who buried his dog in a grave with a tombstone and an elegy.

COATES (James) Born Stalling Busk, Yorks. 14/5/1788, s. James and Ann Coates. Literate: dn11 (York), p12 (York). PC. Sheldon, Derbys. 1814 and PC. Chelmorton, Derbys. 1815 to death 28/1/1870, leaving under £450 [C21517. YCO] Clerical son.

COATES (John) Bapt. Huddersfield, Yorks. 12/5/1790, s. Rev. John Coates, sen. and Mary Dutton. Literate: p20 (York), p21 (York). PC. Langwood, Huddersfield 1822 (and H/M King James G/S, Almondbury, Huddersfield) to death 8 *or* 15/4/1847 aged 57 [C131001. YCO] Married Kendal, Westmorland 8/1/1815 Hannah Fayrer (d.1817), 2 ch. Freemason.

COATES (Robert Trotman) Bapt. Chipping Sodbury, Glos. 1/2/1764, s. Rev. Robert Coates and Sarah Gold. Corpus Christi, Oxford 1781, BA1785, MA1789, dn89 (Glos.), p89 (Ox.), BD 1798. PC. Stow in Lindsey, Lincs. 1790-1814 (res.), V. Box, Wilts. 1797-99, V. Yarnton, Oxon. 1800-3, R. Steeple Langford, Wilts. 1802 and R. Sopworth, Wilts. 1809 to death 1853 (2nd q.) [C25203] Married St Marylebone, London 21/12/1806 Rebecca Barten. Online photo.

COATES see also under **COTES**

COBB (Robert) Bapt. New Romney, Kent 5/10/1796, s. Benjamin Cobb and Jane Smith. Caius, Cambridge, BA1819, dn19 (Chester for Cant.), p20 (London for Cant.), MA1822. R. Burmarsh, Kent 1825 and V. Detling, Kent 1831 to death. Dom. Chap. to Anne, Baroness Harris 1831. Died 22/9/1870 aged 73, leaving £6,000 [C83 and Venn confuse him with another man of Christ's] Married Dartford, Kent 20/3/1828 Harriet Cooke.

COBB (Samuel Wyatt) Bapt. Sittingbourne, Kent 22/10/1803, s. Rev. Thomas Cobb. Oriel, Oxford 1821, BA1825, dn26 (London), p27 (London). R. Ightham, Kent 1827 to death 23/12/1856 [C116782] Married Tonbridge, Kent 28/10/1828 Frances Augusta Atkins-Bowyer (w), with issue.

COBBOLD (Edward) Bapt. Ipswich, Suffolk 23/11/1798, s. John Cobbold (a wealthy brewer and banker) and Elizabeth Knipe. Trinity, Oxford 1816, then St Alban Hall, BA1820, dn22 (Nor.), MA1823, p24 (Nor.). R. Watlington, Norfolk 1824 [blank in ERC] and R. Long Melford, Suffolk 1829 (parish sequestrated for debt) to *suicide* (Hatchett's Hotel, Piccadilly, London) 27/9/1860 aged 62, leaving £450 [C112210] Married Marylebone, London 15/6/1824 Louisa Plestow (w), with issue. Brother Richard, below. Port. online.

COBBOLD (Francis) Bapt. Eye, Suffolk 9/11/1803, s. John Wilkinson Cobbold and Harriet Temple Chevallier. Caius, Cambridge, BA1827, dn27 (Nor.), p28 (Nor.), MA1830. R. Hemley, Suffolk 1831, PC. Ipswich St Mary-le-Tower, Suffolk 1831 and R. Hemley, Suffolk 1831 to death 6/4/1844 [C112211] Married Old Catton, Suffolk 19/1/1832 Mary Anne Cobbold, 1 dau.

COBBOLD (John Spencer) Bapt. Occold, Suffolk 25/7/1768, s. Rev. Thomas Cobbold (R. Woolpit, Suffolk) and Ann Savage Rust. Caius, Cambridge 1785, BA 1790, dn90 (Nor.), Fellow 1790-8, MA1793, p93 (Ely), Hebrew Lecturer 1797-8. S/M The Perse School, Cambridge 1793-4; S/M Nuneaton School 1794; (succ. his father as) V. Shelland, Suffolk 1793 and R. (and patron) of Woolpit 1831 to death 3/4/1837 aged 69 [C99736] Married Anstey, Warwicks. 26/12/1798 Dorothy Homer (a clergy dau.), with issue. Brother William Rust, below.

COBBOLD (Richard) Bapt. Ipswich 7/9/1797, 20th ch. of John Cobbold (a wealthy brewer and banker) and Elizabeth Knipe. Caius, Cambridge 1814, BA1820, dn20 (Nor.), p21 (Nor.), MA1823. V. (and patron) of Wortham Everard, Suffolk (a wedding present from his father) 1824 to death. RD Hartismere 1844-69. Author of *The history of Margaret Cathchpole* (1845). Died 5/1/1877, leaving £12,000 [C112212. ODNB. Boase. D. Dymond (ed.), *Parson and people in a Suffolk village: Richard Cobbold's Wortham, 1824-77* (Wortham, 2007) is probably the most important single document on any rural parish for this period] Married Hollesley, Suffolk 27/11/1822 Mary Anne Waller, 3s (2 clerical), 2 dau. Brother Edward, above.

COBBOLD (William Rust) Bapt. Wilby, Suffolk 2/4/1773, s. Rev. Thomas Cobbold and Anne Savage Rust. Trinity, Oxford 1792, then Magdalen, BA1794, dn95 (Nor.), p97 (Ox.), MA1797, BD1805. V. Horspath, Oxon. 1810, R. Selborne, Hants. 1813 to death (Ludgate Hill, London) 19/8/1841 [C25207] Married Biddlesden, Bucks. 3/2/1814 Maria Mabbott (Biddlesdon Park), *s.p.* Brother John Spencer, above.

COBLEY (Charles James) Born Cheddar, Som. 20/12/1789, s. Rev. John (below) and Elizabeth Cobley. Sidney, Cambridge 1810, BA 1814, dn15 (B&W), p16 (B&W), MA1817. V. Winscombe, Som. 1828-63. Died 26/4/1859, leaving £8,000 [C32049]

COBLEY (John) Born Durnsford, Exeter 22/11/1755, s. Rev. Benjamin Cobley (R. Dodbrooke, Devon). Sidney, Cambridge 1779, dn81 (Lin.), p83 (B&W), LLB 1786. Priest-Vicar Wells Cathedral 1796-1829, V. Cheddar, Som. 1804 to death 11/5/1836 aged 82 [C27197] Wife Elizabeth, and s., above.

COCKBURN (George Alexander) Born 'at sea' 5/11/1806, *either* s. Alexander Cockburn ('envoy and minister to Columbia'), *or* the adopted (illegitimate?) s. of Vice-Admiral Sir George Cockburn, 10th Bart. St John's, Cambridge 1824, then Sidney 1826, BA1828, dn29 (York), p30 (York), MA1832. V. Ellerburn w. Wilton, Yorks. 1831-8, V. Pocklington, Yorks. 1834-40 (w. Kilnwick Percy 1836), R. Rhôscrowther, Pembroke 1842-50, V. Pickering w. Newton upon Rawcliffe, Yorks. 1858-64. Died Stow, Suffolk 21/9/1881 aged 74. Will not traced [C131004. YCO. E. Royle, *A church scandal in Victorian Pickering* (York, 2010)] Married Knaresborough, Yorks. 6/9/1836 Mary Anna Terry (d.1884), dau. of a Ripon banker, with issue. Nephew of the man below. Finally suspended from July 1864 following a long and adulterous relationship with one Jane Wardell (with whom he was living as his wife in 1881).

COCKBURN (William, Sir, 11th Bart. of Langton) Born 2/6/1773, s. Sir James Cockburn, 8th Bart., *M.P.*, and Augusta Anne Ayscough. St John's, Cambridge 1791, BA1795, Fellow 1796-1806, MA1798, dn00 (Lin.), p01 (Lin.). BD and DD1823. Minister St George, Tavistock Square, London 1811, PC. Fazeley, Tamworth, Staffs. 1812-18, R. Thelbridge,

Devon 1821-9, Dean of York 1823-58, V. Ellerburn, Yorks. 1830-1, V. Thornton, Yorks. 1831-6, V. Kelston, Bath ('where he generally spent half the year') 1832 to death 30/4/1858 aged 84, leaving £20,000 [C10082. Boase]. Married (1) 30/12/1805 Elizabeth (d.1828), dau. of Sir Robert Peel, 1st Bart., with issue (2) Hatley St George, Cambs. 14/8/1830 Margaret Emma Pearse (w) (dau. of an army officer), *s.p.* 'A rapacious nepotist', the Archbishop tried to deprive and depose him as Dean for simony, but an appeal in 1841 to the Judicial Committee of the Privy Council prohibited this from being carried out. Succeeded to title 1853.

COCKERELL (Henry) Bapt. Westminster London 24/7/1801, s. Samuel Pepys Cockerell and Anna Whetham. Trinity, Oxford 1819, BA1824, dn24 (London), p25 (Chich. for London), MA1827. R. Edgcott, Bucks. 1826-8 (res.), V. North Weald, Essex 1827 to death 8/2/1880, leaving £5,000 [C49546] Married Great Waltham, Essex 16/5/1827 Elizabeth Fanny Tudnell (w), with clerical son.

COCKERTON (Robert Blackburn) Born Dalton in Furness, Lancs. 13/12/1801, s. George Cockerton and Amelia Blackburn. Emmanuel, Cambridge 1823, p27 (Chester). PC. Cartmel Fell, Lancs. 1829 to death 17/7/1861 aged 58, leaving £800 [C168527] Married 1833 Eleanor Birket, with issue.

COCKIN (William) Bapt. Bristol 1/4/1765, s. John and Mary Cockin. BNC, Oxford 1784, BA1787, dn88 (Glos.), p89 (Glos.), MA1790. R. Cherington, Glos. 1804 [net income £1,193], R. Minchinhampton, Glos. 1806 to death. Dom. Chap. to 11th Duke of Norfolk 1806. Died 1841 (1st q.) [C142282]

COCKS (Henry Somers) Born London 16/12/1803, s. Hon. Reginald Cocks and Ann Pole. Christ Church, Oxford 1821, BA1824, MA1827. R. Leigh w. Bransford, Warwicks. 1828 to death 25/11/1856 aged 52 [C120692] Married 1/1/1829 Frances Mercy Bromley, with clerical son Henry Bromley Cocks.

COCKS (James Somers, Hon.) Born 9/1/1790, s. 1st Earl Somers and Margaret Nash (a clergy dau.). BNC, Oxford 1806, BA1809 [adm. Lincoln's Inn 1809] MA1814 [In army. *M.P.* for Reigate 1818, 1821-3] dn23 (Heref.). Prebend of Pratum Majus in Hereford Cathedral 1824-56, V. Neen Savage, Shropshire 1826, 3rd Prebend in Worcester Cathedral 1830 to death (unm.) 5/7/1856, living at Mathon, Heref. [C103959]

CODD (Charles) Bapt. East Dereham, Norfolk 23/10/1796, s. Edward Codd and Aurora Fayerman. Clare, Cambridge 1816, BA1820, dn21 (Nor.), p25 (Nor.). R. Cley-next-the-Sea, Norfolk 1830-52, R. Letheringsett, Norfolk 1832-52. Died Ottawa 15/10/1870 (having moved there 1855 'in consequence of pecuniary embarrassment' [C112216] Married Norwich 13/12/1821 Susan Ann Howes, w. clerical son.

CODDINGTON (Henry) Born Oldbridge, Co. Meath 20/2/1799, s. Rev. Latham Coddington (Timolin, Co. Kildare) and Ann Bellingham. Trinity, Cambridge 1816, BA1820 (Senior Wrangler), Fellow 1820, Tutor 1822-33, MA 1823, dn23 (Lin. for Ely), p26 (Bristol). V. Ware w. Thundridge, Herts. 1832 [sequestrated in ERC] to death (at Rome, caused by 'the stress of dealing with dissension within his parish [which] evidently led to a burst blood vessel') 1/3/1845 aged 45 [C6653. ODNB] Married Great Amwell, Herts. 17/12/1833 Priscilla Batten, with clerical son. *F.R.S.* (1829) for his work on optics; a good linguist, an excellent musician and botanist.

CODRINGTON (Thomas Stretton) Bapt. Wroughton, Wilts. 23/9/1798, s. Rev. William Codrington and Mary Palmer Lewsley. BNC, Oxford 1816, BA1820, dn22 (Ely for Salis.), p23 (Ely for Salis.), MA1824. V. Wroughton 1827 [blank in ERC] to death (Clifton, Bristol, 'suddenly, of apoplexy') 12/12/1839 aged 41 [C6654] Married Clifton 31/7/1828 Elizabeth Jemima White (w), with clerical son John Edward Codrington.

COFFIN (Charles Pine-) see under **PINE-COFFIN**

COFFIN (James) Bapt. Exeter 22/8/1756, s. Thomas Coffin (goldsmith) and Ann Hewish. Trinity, Cambridge 1774, then Sidney 1775, BA1779, dn79 (Ex.), p80 (Ex.), Fellow, MA 1782. V. Linkinhorne, Cornwall 1780 to death 12/4/1833 aged 76 [C140661] Married

Callington, Cornwall 29/3/1781 Jean Hamilton Walker, w. clerical s. John Newton Coffin.

COGAN (Thomas White) Bapt. Islington, London 6/3/1768, s. Thomas Cogan and Philadelphia Stephens. Trinity, Oxford 1790, BA1794, dn94 (C&L for Nor.), p94 (Nor.), MA 1798. V. East Dean, Sussex 1795-1856, R. [sequestrator] Chichester All Saints, Sussex 1805-35. Died 1856 (2nd q.) [C10087] Married Wanstead, Essex 28/8/1806 Sarah Parker, with issue.

COGSWELL (Norris) Born Littleborough, Lancs., s. John (or Job) Cogswell (merchant) and Elizabeth Parry. St John's, Cambridge 1822, BA1827, dn27 (Lin.), p29 (Lin.), MA1831. V. Holton le Cley, Lincs. 1833 and V. Immingham, Lincs. 1837 to death 24/4/1883, leaving £334-15s-4d. [C49553. Kaye] Married Birmingham 11/5/1831 Margaret Johnson, and had issue.

COKBURNE (Hugh) see under **KER**

COKE (George) Born Eardisley, Heref. 8/1/1797, s. Rev. Francis Coke (R. Aylton, Heref.) and Anne Whitcombe. St John's, Cambridge 1814, BA1820, dn20 (Heref.), p21 (Heref.), MA1823. (succ. his father as) R. Aylton 1821-44, PC. Marstow, Heref. 1825-31, R. Piddlehinton, Dorset 1844 to death (Erdlsley, Heref.) 20/4/1863 aged 66, leaving £2,000 [C103961] Married Eardisley 25/12/1825 Anne Elizabeth Hodgson (a clergy dau.), w. clerical son. J.P. Heref. Brother, below.

COKE (William) Born Eardisley, Heref. 2/11/1803, s. Rev. Francis Coke (R. Aylton, Heref.) and Anne Whitcombe. Trinity, Cambs. 1823, BA1827, dn27 (Heref.), p28 (Heref.). PC. Marstow w. Pencoyd, Heref. 1831 to death (Llangarron, Heref.) 2/12/1892 aged 90, leaving £6,773-8s-8d. [C103963] Brother, above.

COKER (John) Born Bath, Somerset, s. Cadwallader Robert Coker ('annuitant') and Margaret Clutterbuck. New, Oxford 1811 (aged 17), BCL1816, dn21 (Ox.), p21 (Ox.), Fellow until 1825. R. Radclive, Bucks. 1824 to death 24/11/1863, leaving £7,000 [C25340] Married Edinburgh 22/8/1825 Charlotte Sophia Dewar (a military dau.).

COKER (Walter King) Born Taunton, Som. 11/2/1794, s. Rev. William Coker and Elizabeth King. Oriel, Oxford 1811, BA1815, dn18 (Ex.), p18 (Ex.), MA1818, BD1825. V. North Curry >< Som. 1820 to death 22/9/1845 [C33884]

COLBY (Samuel) Bapt. Great Yarmouth, Norfolk 18/10/1780, s. of Dover Colby (a mercer) and Charlotte Fisher. University, Oxford 1798, BA1802, dn03 (Ely), p05 (Nor.). R. (and patron) of Great Elingham w. Little Elingham, Norfolk 1814-60, R. (and patron) of Thelnetham, Suffolk 1816 to death 2/4/1860, leaving £25,000 [C99739] Brother below.

COLBY (William) Bapt. Great Yarmouth, Norfolk 14/3/1791, s. of Dover Colby (a mercer) and Charlotte Fisher. Caius, Cambridge 1808, BA1813, dn14 (Nor.), p15 (Nor.). R. Clippesby, Norfolk 1820 to death (Southtown, Great Yarmouth) 2/4/1860 aged 69, leaving £25,000 [C112291] Brother above.

COLDHAM (George) Bapt. Anmer, Norfolk 2/4/1804, s. Capt. James Coldham and Elizabeth Waller Wright. Caius, Cambridge 1821, BA 1825, dn27 (Nor.), p28 (Nor.), MA 1828. R. Pensthorpe, Norfolk 1829-32, R. Gayton Thorpe w. East Walton, Norfolk 1831-80, R. Glemsford, Suffolk 1833 to death 26/6/1887 [total income in CR65 £1,500], leaving £1,744-12s-11d. [C112292] Married (1) Brighton 2/1/1832 Mary Anna Mansfield Clarke (dau. of a surgeon baronet, she d.1841) (2) Sudbury, Suffolk April 1844 Henrietta Faulkner (a clergy dau., of Long Melford), w. clerical son Henry Roe Coldham. Brother below.

COLDHAM (John) Bapt. Dersingham, Norfolk 24/3/1790, s. of Capt. James Coldham and Elizabeth Waller Wright. Trinity Hall, Cambridge 1808, BA1812, dn13 (Nor.), p14 (Nor.). R. Anmer, Norfolk 1815-79, R. Snettisham, Norfolk 1815 and R. Stockton, Norfolk 1815 (and RD of Hitcham 1846) to death 2/1/1878 aged 87, leaving £5,000 [C112293] Had issue. Brother above.

COLDWELL (Thomas) Born Middlethorpe Hall, York 18/8/1781, s. Thomas Coldwell and Sarah Hanson. Literate: dn27, p29 (C&L). V. Abthorpe, Northants. 1832-51-. R. Green's Norton, Northants. 1853 to death. Dom. Chap. to Duke of Grafton. Died Newport, IoW

17/11/1887, leaving £485-19s-6d. [C10091] Married Stafford 28/8/1829 Harriet Tunnicliffe, with issue. Brother below.

COLDWELL (William Edward) Bapt. Wakefield, Yorks. 8/4/1795, s. Thomas Coldwell and Sarah Hanson. St Catharine's, Cambridge 1814, BA1818, dn18 (Nor.), p19 (Nor.), MA1821, incorporated at Oxford 1854. PC. Drypool, Yorks. 1820-7 (res.), R. Stafford St Mary 1822-67, V. High Offley, Staffs. 1826-8 (res.), V. Sandon, Staffs. 1827-67, RD. Prebend of Pipa Parva in Lichfield Cathedral 1843 to death. Dom. Chap. to Earl of Roden, and to Duke of Marlborough. Commissary for Lichfield Diocese. Died Marlborough, Wilts. 13/4/1867 aged 72, leaving £4,000 [C10092] Married Mistley, Essex 29/7/1819 Mary Norman, 4 clerical sons (one taking the surname Thicknesse). Brother above.

COLE (Benjamin Thomas Halcott) Born Norwich 9/10/1782, s. Benjamin and Ann Cole. Trinity, Cambridge 1798, then Magdalene 1801, BA1803, Fellow 1803 [adm. Lincoln's Inn 1803] MA1807, dn12 (Peterb.), p13 (Bristol), incorporated at Oxford 1843. H/M Maidstone G/S, Kent 1819-21; R. Warbleton, Sussex 1815 to death (Bangor, Wales) 1/8/1850 [C8166] Married (1) Maidstone 30/12/1820 Ann Jane Allen (2) Hastings, Kent 9/8/1838 Maria Grantham Foyster.

COLE (Samuel) Bapt. St Hilary, Cornwall 28/11/1766, s. Humphrey Cole and Phyllis Maugham. Exeter, Oxford 1785, BA1789, dn89 (Ex.), p91 (Ex.), MA1811, BD and DD1819. V. Sithney, Cornwall 1819, Chaplain R.N. and First Chaplain to Royal Hospital, Greenwich. Chap. to HRH Duke of Clarence. Buried St Hilary, Cornwall 26/11/1838 aged 71 [C140671] Married Jane Griffith?

COLE (Samuel) Born Portsea, Hants., s. William Cole. Magdalen Hall, Oxford 1787 (aged 19). Chaplain on HMS *London* at the time of the Spithead Mutiny (1797), about which he wrote an account. R. Brettenham, Suffolk 1798 to burial 19/8/1858 aged 91. Will not traced [C112296] Wife Charlotte.

COLE (Thomas) Literate: dn94 (Peterb.), p95 (Peterb.). Curate Watford, Northants. 1795-1831 (res. over financial difficulties). V. Long Buckby, Northants. 1802 to death 20/5/1834 (CCEd thus) [C110078]

COLE (William Hodgson) Bapt. Guildford, Surrey 4/1/1771, s. Rev. Samuel Cole and Mary Hodgson. Magdalen, Oxford 1788, BA1792, dn93 (St David's), p94 (C&L for Win.), MA 1797. S/M Guildford Free G/S to 1819; V. Wonersh, Surrey 1806 and R. West Clandon, Surrey 1822 (and RD) to death. Chap. to HRH Duke of Gloucester 1802. Buried (a widower) 28/7/1852 [C10094] Married Guildford 29/4/1798 Frances Ann Sibthorpe, with son, below.

COLE (William Sibthorpe) Born Windlesham, Surrey 13/3/1799, s. Rev. William Hodgson Cole (above) and Frances Ann Sibthorpe. Worcester, Oxford 1816, BA1820, MA1822, dn22 (Ox.), p23 (Ox.). Chap. of the Donative of St Martha-on-the-Hill, Guildford, Surrey 1824, V. Westcliffe, Dover, Kent 1830-46, Min. Trinity Church, Dover, Kent 1835-46, R. Ryther, Yorks. 1846 (and RD of Selby 1869-82, 1884) to death. Chap. to the Warden of the Cinque Ports 1837. Died Tadcaster, Yorks. 16/1/1892 aged 92, leaving £1,163-0s-0d. [C25344. Boase] Married St James's, Piccadilly, London 7/6/1831 Mary Maule (w), with clerical son.

COLEBY (George) Bapt. Knapton, Norfolk 19/10/1766, s. Charles Coleby and Rebecca Pye. Caius, Cambridge 1791, no degree, dn93 (Nor.), p96 (Nor.). V. Thorpe Market, Norwich 1798 and R. Colby, Norfolk 1802 to death 22/8/1842 aged 75 [C112297] Married Wymondham, Norfolk 10/10/1793 Martha Tillot, w. clerical son, also George.

COLEMAN (Charles John) Born Basingstoke, Hants. 12/5/1774, s. Rev. Charles Coleman and Sarah Woodyer. St Edmund Hall, Oxford 1807 (aged 33), no degree, dn10 (Salis.), p12 (Salis.). (succ. his father as) R. (and patron) of Winterbourne Gunner, Wilts. 1815-51-. Posssibly died 1856 (but not in BMD). Will not traced [C91797] Married Newchurch, Hants. 27/12/1802 Alice Jerome, with clerical son George Coleman.

COLEMAN (James Sherard) Bapt. Leicester 26/5/1779, s. Henry Coleman and Christian Sharpe. St John's, Cambridge 1799, BA1803, dn04 (Peterb.), p05 (Peterb.), MA1809. R. Houghton-on-the-Hill, Leics. 1808 to death 29/10/1855 [C52489] Married Draughton, Northants. 18/9/1807 Elizabeth Bosworth, with issue.

COLERIDGE (Edward) Born Ottery St Mary, Devon 11/5/1800, s. Col. James Coleridge and Frances Duke Taylor. Corpus Christi, Oxford 1818, BA1822, then Exeter, Fellow 1823-6, dn24 (Ox.), p26 (Ox.), MA1827. Assistant Master Eton College 1825-50, Head of Lower School 1850-7, Fellow of Eton College 1857. R. Monksilver, Som. 1825-43, V. Mapledurham, Berks. 1862 to death (Bradfield, Berks.) 18/5/1883, leaving £10,739-16s-6d. [C25345. Boase] Married (1) Eton Mary Keate 3/8/1826 (dau. of H/M of Eton, she d.1859), w. clerical son Alfred James (2) Crickhowel, Breconshire 4/9/1862 Mary Caroline Bevan. Brother James Duke, below. Raised £30,000 for the building of St Augustine's Missionary College, Canterbury.

COLERIDGE (Edwin Ellis) Born Ottery St Mary, Devon 24/5/1803, s. Rev. Edward Coleridge and Ann Bowden. Trinity, Oxford 1821, BA1825, dn26 (Ex.), p27 (Ex.). V. Buckerell, Devon 1829 to death 1/2/1870 aged 66, leaving £10,000 [C140676] Married (1) Broad Clyst, Devon 20/7/1831 Elizabeth Tucker (d.1840) (2) Bloomsbury, London 8/12/1841 Ellen Sophia Patteson.

COLERIDGE (George May) Bapt. Ottery St Mary, Devon 27/11/1798, s. Rev. George Coleridge and Jane Hart. Christ Church, Oxford 1816, BA1820, dn22 (Chester), p22 (Ex.), MA 1824. Prebend of Whitchurch in Wells Cathedral 1823 and V. St Marychurch, Devon 1827 to death 5/6/1847 [C33890]

COLERIDGE (James Duke) Born Tiverton, Devon 13/6/1789, s. Col. James Coleridge and Frances Duke Taylor. Balliol, Oxford 1808, dn12 (B&W), p13 (B&W), BCL1821, DCL 1835. V. Kenwyn w. St Kea, Cornwall 1823-8, Prebend of Exeter Cathedral 1825-57, R. Lawhitton, Cornwall 1826-39, V. Lewannick, Cornwall 1831-41, V. Thorverton, Devon 1839 to death 26/12/1857, leaving £14,000 [C33892. ODNB. Boase] Married Heavitree, Exeter 9/6/1814 Sophia Susanna Baldock (w), with issue (inc. Lord Coleridge, Lord Chief Justice of England). Brother Edward, above.

COLES (George) From Surrey, s. William Coles. Peterhouse, Cambridge 1817 (aged 18), BA1821, dn22 (London), p23 (London for Cant.), MA1824. V. Croydon St James, Surrey 1829 (w. Master and Chap. of Whitgift's Hospital [almshouses] 1843) to death (Dorking, Surrey) 22/1/1865, aged 65, leaving £600 [C116787] Had issue.

COLES (John) From Ditcham Park, Buriton, Hants., s. Charles Coles. University, Oxford 1805 (aged 18), BA1809, dn10 (Salis.), MA1812, p12 (Salis.). R. Silchester, Hants. 1812 to death (London, a widower) 16/4/1865, leaving £3,000 [C71831]

COLES (Thomas Henry) Born Westminster, London, s. John Coles (Washingley Hall, Stilton, Hunts.) and Susannah Apreece. Clare, Cambridge 1800, BA1803, dn03 (Peterb.), p05 (Win.), MA1806, DD1818. V. Honington, Grantham, Lincs. 1805 to death 24/10/1867, leaving £25,000 (all of which he bequeathed to his College, subject to a life annuity of £300 to his son) [C51591. Boase. Kaye] Married Knaresborough, Yorks. 14/9/1805 Harriet Brooke Oliver (of Low Leighton, Essex), with son.

COLLETT (Anthony) Bapt. Walton, Suffolk 6/4/1770, s. of Anthony Collett. University, Oxford 1787, BA1790, dn92 (Nor.), MA1793, p94 (Lin.). V. Cratfield, Suffolk 1794-1803 (res.), PC. Aldringham w. Thorpe, Suffolk 1800-38, PC. Linstead Magna, Suffolk 1800-38 (w. PC. Linstead Parva, Suffolk 1800-32), R. Heveningham, Suffolk 1803-38. Died Leamington, Warwicks. 27/2/1838 aged aged 67 [C52493] J.P. Suffolk.

COLLETT (William) Bapt. Swanton Morley, Norfolk 17/8/1796, s. Rev. William Collett and Anna Carthew. Trinity, Cambridge 1814, then Sidney 1816, BA1819, dn19 (Nor.), p20 (Nor.), MA1825. V. (and patron) of Surlingham St Mary w. Surlingham St Saviour, Norfolk 1821-36, PC. Thetford St Mary, Norfolk 1828-62. R. Bressingham, Norfolk 1836-41. Chap. Morden College, Blackheath, Kent. Died (Whitby, Yorks.) 11/9/1865 aged 69, leaving £3,000. [C112300] Married (1) Great Yarmouth, Norfolk 24/10/1820 Phillis Preston Reynolds (d.1831), w. issue (2) 1835 Ellen Clarke Bidwell; clerical son; and also Sir Henry Henry Collett (q.v. ODNB).

COLLIER (Charles) Bapt. Romford, Essex 3/12/1789, s. John Collier. A baker in Bury St Edmunds. Literate: dn15 (Nor.), p16 (Nor.), then St Catharine's, Cambridge 1822 (a Ten Year Man). V. Hambleton, Rutland 1822 and V. Riby, Lincs. 1822 to death (Hambledon) 14/6/1845 aged 56 [C52497]

COLLIN (John) Born Saffron Walden, Essex 21/9/1775, s. John Collin and Ann Martin. Christ's, Cambridge 1794, BA1798, dn98 (London), p01 (London), MA1801. R. Quendon, Essex 1802 to death there 18/11/1861 aged 86, leaving £4,000 [C106681] Married Linton, Cambs. 10/4/1804 Anne Fisher, with clerical son, also John.

COLLINS (Caleb) From Middlesex. St John's, Cambridge 1818, BA1823, dn23 (Win.), p25 (Win.), MA1826. R. Stedham cum Heyshott, Sussex 1826 to death 5/9/1879, leaving £1,500 [C63031] Married Westminster, London 20/12/1831 Isabella Bushnan, with issue.

COLLINS (Charles) Bapt. Holborn, London 18/5/1800, s. Charles Collins. St John's, Cambridge 1818, BA1822, dn23 (Nor.), p24 (Peterb.), MA1825. R. (and patron) of Frinsted, Kent 1831-42, R. (and patron) of Milstead, Kent 1831-42, R. Milton next Canterbury, Kent 1842-7, V. Faversham, Kent 1847 (and Chap. to Borough Gaol) to death. Dom. Chap. to 1st Viscount Lorton 1831. Died 18/5/1866 aged 66, leaving £3,000 [C110081] Married at Golden, Co. Tipperary 18/6/1823 Anne Matilda Creaghe, with clerical son Charles Creaghe Collins.

COLLINS (Charles Edward) Bapt. Tamworth, Staffs. 13/8/1781, s. Rev. Simon Collins and Catharine Asbury. Worcester, Oxford 1798, BA1802, dn04 (C&L), p05 (C&L), MA1809, Fellow to 1823. V. Lullington, Derbys. 1810 to death 1841 (3rd q.) [C10102] Married Lullington 9/11/1822 Elizabeth Whetton, with issue.

COLLINS, *later* COLLINS-TRELAWNY (Charles Trelawny) Bapt. Pennycross, Devon 23/4/1792, s. Capt. George Collins, *Royal Marines*. Christ Church, Oxford 1810, then Balliol 1812, BA1815, Fellow 1816-26, MA 1818, dn21 (Ox.), p23 (Ox.), etc. R. Timsbury, Som. 1825-41, PC. North Newton (o/w Newton Placey), Som. 1828 to death 19/4/1878, leaving £4,000 (as Charles Trelawny Collins-Trelawny) [C42059. Boase and F. as Trelawny] Widow Elizabeth Ayliffe. Name changed 1839.

COLLINS (James) [LLD but NiVoF] R. Thorpe Abbots, Norfolk 1812-[38]. Dead by 1840 [C112301] Had issue.

COLLINS (Oliver Levey) Bapt. Northam, Devon 26/6/1795, s. Thomas Collins and Mary Levey. Literate: dn24 (York), p25 (York). PC. Dewsbury, Yorks. 1827, PC. Ossett cum Gawthorpe, Yorks. 1827 to death 15/6/1858, leaving £4,000 [C131008. YCO] Married (1) Rosetta Warren (d.1834), with issue (2) Edgbaston, Warwicks. 1/12/1836 Eliza Guest (w), with further issue.

COLLINS (Thomas) Born Knaresborough, Yorks. 9/12/1780, s. James Collins. University, Oxford 1798, BA1801, dn03 (Ox.), p04 (Ox.), then Magdalen, Fellow 1804, MA1804, BD 1811. R. Horsington, Lincs. 1815-16, R. Barningham, Yorks. 1816-29 (res.), PC. (and patron) of Farnham, Yorks. 1818 (and RD of Boroughbridge) to death 7/5/1870 aged 89. Will not traced [C25468] Married Skipton, Yorks. 25/8/1818 Anne Bramley, with issue. J.P. West and North Ridings.

COLLINSON (Henry King) Bapt. East Sheen, Surrey 16/9/1806, s. Rev. John Collinson (below) and Amelia King. Queen's, Oxford 1823, BA1827, dn27 (Durham), p28 (Durham), MA1833. PC. Castle Eden, Durham 1828-38, V. Trinity Church, Stockton on Tees, Durham 1838-[45], V. Stannington, Northumberland 1845 to death (a widower) 20/2/1867 aged 62, leaving £8,000 [C130366] Married 1827 Sophia Baker, with many ch. 'He was much addicted to the bottle, a disgrace to his high calling'.

COLLINSON (John) Born Bristol, s. Rev. Richard Collinson. Queen's, Oxford 1798 (aged 17), BA1803, dn03 (Bristol), p05 (Win. for Cant.), MA1806. R. Great Ponton, Lincs. 1808 [C16678], R. Gateshead, Durham 1810-40 (with Master of Gateshead Hospital [almshouses]), PC. Lamesley, Durham 1820, R. Tynemouth, Northumberland 1820-4 (res.), R. Boldon, Durham 1840 (and Hon. Canon of Durham Cathedral 1844) to death 17/2/1857 aged 76

[C8221 and 130367. Boase] Married Alveston, Glos. 20/4/1802 Amelia King (a clergy dau.), with clerical son (above).

COLLINSON (Robert) Bapt. Bowness, Westmorland 15/2/1793, s. Robert Collinson. Queen's, Oxford 1812, BA1816, dn17 (Win.), p19 (Win.), MA1819, Fellow 1827-47. PC. Holm Cultram, Cumberland 1822-42 (res.). Died Oxford 1847 (3rd q.) [C5776. Platt]

COLLINSON (Thomas) Born Windermere, Westmorland. H/M Crosthwaite G/S, Cumberland 1796-9. Literate: dn98 (Car.), p99 (Car.). PC. Threlkeld, Crosthwaite 1799 to death 11/10/1857 aged 83, leaving under £100 [C5777. Platt] Married 18/12/1800 Jane Bell, with issue.

COLLIS (William Blow) Bapt. Old Swinford, Worcs. 26/11/1778, s. George Collis and Ann Robins. Worcester, Oxford 1795, BA1799, dn01 (Wor.), MA1802, p03 (C&L), DCL. PC. Norton Canes, Staffs. 1814 to death. Buried 4/8/1855 [C10106] Married Walsall, Staffs. 27/6/1805 Phoebe Maria Sheldom, with issue.

COLLYER (John Bedingfeld) Born Wroxford Hall, Drayton, Norfolk 26/1/1777, s. Rev. Daniel Collyer. Clare, Cambridge 1794, BA 1798, dn99 (Nor.), p01 (Nor.), MA1808. V. Wroxham w. Salehouse, Norfolk 1801 and Archdeacon of Norwich 1844 to death (Hackford Hall, Norfolk) 29/3/1857 [C112308. Boase] Married Bury St Edmunds, Suffolk 18/3/1800 Catherine Alexander (of London), with clerical son, below.

COLLYER (Robert) Born Norwich 8/5/1804, s. Rev. John Bedingfeld Collyer (above) and Catherine Alexander. Clare, Cambridge 1823, then Trinity 1824, BA1827, dn27 (Nor.), p28 (Nor.), MA1830. V. Dersingham, Norfolk 1828-40. R. Gisleham, Suffolk 1840-4, R. Waterden, Norfolk 1844-6, R. Warham, Norfolk 1844 (and Hon. Canon of Norwich Cathedral 1856) to death (unmarried) 16/3/1874, leaving £7,000 [C112309]

COLLYER (Thomas) Bapt. Westminster, London 25/7/1771, s. Nathaniel Collyer and Mary Harrap. Christ Church, Oxford 1790, BA1794, dn94 (Nor.), p95 (Lin.), MA1798. R. (and patron) of Gislingham, Suffolk 1797 to death 1/11/1850 [C52586] Married Shoredith, London 10/5/1798 Sophia Harrison, w. clerical son of father's name in same place.

COLLYNS (Charles Henry) Bapt. Exeter 5/5/1790, s. Charles Collyns and Mary Dunsford. Balliol, Oxford 1807, BA1811, p14 (Ex.), MA1814, BD and DD1824. S/M throughhout the Diocese of Exeter 1815; R. Stokeinteignhead, Devon (and Preacher throughout the Diocese of Exeter) 1829, R. Farringdon, Devon 1838 to death. Chap. to Exeter Gaol 1815-24. Died Farington, Devon 3/6/1862, leaving £3,000 [C140685] Married (1) Kenton, Devon 5/5/1814 Dorothy Collyns (d.1832), with issue (2) Poole, Dorset 17/1/1840 Sarah Slade, with further issue. Brother, below.

COLLYNS (John Martyn) Born Exeter 23/10/1792, s. Charles Collyns and Mary Dunsford. Exeter, Oxford 1810, BA1814, dn15 (Ex.), p16 (Ex.), MA1817. R. Exeter St John 1822, V. Sancreed, Cornwall 1851 to death 31/12/1878 aged 86, leaving £800 [C140686] Married Clyst St George, Devon 20/6/1826 Sophia Saltren, with clerical son. Brother, above.

COLMAN (John) Bapt. Wymondham, Norfolk 15/6/1752, s. John Colman and Catherine Gallard. Corpus Christi, Cambridge 1769, BA 1774, dn75 (Nor.), p81 (Nor.). R. Langham St Mary, Suffolk 1776-1824, R. Knapton, Norfolk 1788-1837, V. Oulton, Norfolk 1794-8 (res.), R. Hempstead, Norfolk 1803, R. Swafield, Norfolk 1806 to death (Wicklewood, Norfolk) 12/8/1837 [C112310] Married (1) Wymondham 6/1/1778 Hannah Tawell (d.1793), with issue (2) Diss, Norfolk 2/10/1794 Martha Catchpole, w. further issue.

COLMAN, born SUMMERS (Samuel Summers) Born Holborn, London 28/12/1766, s. Thomas Summers. Caius, Cambridge 1785, dn89 (Nor.), BA1790, p91 (London for Nor.), MA 1811. Chap. Fort William, Bengal 1810-13; R. Rushmere, Suffolk 1791 to death (Boulogne), 22/5/1842 aged 75 [C112311] Married Cambridge 4/3/1788 Margaret Davey. Name changed 1786.

COLMER (John) Bapt. Chard, Somerset 31/1/1766, s. Robert Colmer (surgeon) and Catherine Syndercombe (a clergy dau.). Merton,

Oxford 1784, then Wadham, BA1787, p89 (B&W), MA1802. R. Askerswell, Dorset 1789-1842, PC. Cudworth, Som. 1798-1808, R. Cricket Malherbie, Som. 1801, Preacher throughout the Diocese of Bristol 1805, R. Symondsbury, Dorset 1805-6 (res.), R. Littleton Drew, Wilts. 1807. Died Askerwell 10/1/1842 aged 77. Dom. Chap. to 1st Viscount Bridport 1802-5 [C8222]

COLPOYS, *born* GRIFFITH (James Adair Griffith-) Born Devonport, Devon 1800, s. Vice-Admiral Sir Edward Griffith (later Colpoys) and Mrs Mary Anne (Adair) Wilson. Exeter, Oxford 1818 18), BA1824, dn25 (Heref. for Win.), MA1826, p26 (Salis.). R. North Waltham, Hants. 1831, R. Droxford, Hants. 1831 [income £1,050] to death (Southampton) 8/3/1868, leaving £14,000 (while living at St Leonards, Sussex) [C71836] Married Mapledurham, Oxon. 14/10/1828 Anne Sumner (sister of the Bishop of Chester, later Archbishbp of Canterbury, she d.1833), with issue.

COLSON (John Morton) Bapt. Studland, Dorset 8/9/1762, s. Rev. Thomas Colson and Jane Morton. Balliol, Oxford 1781, SCL, dn85 (Ox. for Bristol), p86 (Bristol), MA1804. S/M Milton Abbas G/S, Dorset 1804; R. Studland 1786, R. Little Gransden, Cambs. 1808-09 (res.), R. Piddlehinton, Dorset 1809 to death 17/12/1838 aged 75 [C52305. F. is mixed-up w. the man below] Married Sherborne, Dorset 29/8/1786 Elizabeth Hobson, and had issue. dorset-ancestors.com/?p=1889

COLSON (John Morton) Bapt. Dorchester, Dorset 28/4/1791, s. Rev. Thomas Morton Colson (R. Pilsdon, Dorset and R. Linkenholt, Hants) and Mary Dampier. Balliol, Oxford 1809, then Jesus, Cambridge 1814, dn14 (Chester for Bristol), SCL, p16 (Salis.), LLB 1817. R. Little Peatling (Peatling Parva), Leics, 1822, R. Dorchester St Peter 1822 and R. Linkenholt 1830 to death. Dom. Chap. to Lord Wynford. Died 14/9/1863 aged 72, leaving £4,000 [C52304. F. is mixed-up with the man above] Married 27/4/1826 Julia Story, Stockton-on-Tees, Co.Durham, 2 ch.

COLSTON (Thomas Edwards) Born Henley, Oxon. 24/10/1771, s. Rev. Alexander Colston and Louisa Minshull Elers. Trinity, Oxford 1790, BA1794, dn94 (Ox.), p95 (Ox.), MA1797. V. Bradwell, Oxon. 1796, R. West Lydford, Som. 1797. Probate granted 18/4/1845 [C25488] Married (1) St George's Hanover Square, London 10/5/1809 Ann King Morris (d.1812) (2) Salisbury 26/8/1813 Henrietta Judith Head Tinny. Brother below.

COLSTON (William Hungerford) Born Henley, Oxon. 2/10/1773, s. Rev. Alexander Colston and Louisa Mynshull Elers. St Mary Hall, Oxford 1792, BA1796, dn96 (Salis.), p97 (Salis.), MA1799, BD & DD1811. R. West Lydford, Som. 1797, R. Clapton in Gordano, Som. 1811, R. Keinton Mandeville, Som. 1830 to death. Buried (West Lydford) 16/10/1855 aged 82 [C34015] Married (1) Margaret Molyneux 18/9/1798 (d.1812) (2) Ludford 22/7/1813 Mary Morris (d.1829) w. clerical s. William Hungerford Morris Colston (3) Aisholt, Som. 5/12/1831 Mary Ann Heath Brice. Brother above. In April 1840 Colston was tried for alleged indecent assault on Anne Cook, but the case was seen to be an attempt at extortion.

COLTMAN (Joseph) Born Hull 8/9/1776, s. John (a merchant) and Isabella Coltman. Trinity, Cambridge 1793, BA1798, dn00 (Lin.), p01 (Lin.), MA1802. R. Sharnford, Leics. 1799, R. Hameringham w. Scrayfield, Lincs. 1801-37, V. Beverley Minster Church of St John's w. St Martin, Yorks. 1813-37, V. Kirkbymoorside, Yorks. 1810-11. Died (Beverley) 10/6/1837 aged 60 [C52593] Married Nov. 1802 a Mrs Barrat. J.P. East Riding. 'A few years before his death he weighed 32 stone 8 pounds' (520 pounds); 'the velocipede was his favourite mode of transport'.

COLTON (William Collins) Bapt. Shrivenham, Berks. 29/11/1787, s. Barfoot Colton and Elizabeth Collins. Literate: dn12 (Salis.), p15 (Glos.). PC. Lyneham, Wilts. 1826. V. Baston, Lincs. 1836 to death (Cheltenham, Glos.) 15/3/1860, leaving £5,000 [C91804] Married Marguette Louisa Colton, w. clerical son.

COLVILE (Augustus Asgill) Born Marylebone, London 24/4/1794, s. Robert Colvile (Newton, Cambs.) and Amelia Angelina Asgill. Christ Church, Oxford 1813, Student [Fellow] 1813-28, BA1817, MA1820, dn21 (Ox.), p22 (Ox.). PC. Market Harborough, Leics. 1825, V. Midsomer Norton, Som. 1827-33, R. (and patron) of Great Livermere w. Little Livermere,

Suffolk 1832 to death 27/6/1865, leaving £12,000 [C25491] Married (1) Bathwick, Som. 9/11/1830 Maria Broderip (d.1835), with issue (2) British Embassy, Paris 10/8/1839 Mary Ann Hemings, with further issue.

COLVILE (Nathaniel) Born Hemingstone, Suffolk 26/4/1771, s. Richard Colvile. St Mary Hall, Oxford 1788, BA1793, dn95 (Bangor), MA 1795, p95 (Nor.), BD &DD1818. R. Baylham, Suffolk 1795-1828, R. Lawshall, Suffolk 1801-47, R. Brome, Suffolk 1810-28. Died Geneva 17/12/1860, leaving £1,500. Married (1) Bath 30/9/1794 Amy Letitia Purvis (d.1816), w. clerical s. below (2) Westminster, London 9/5/1840 Alicia Mary Massey (w).

COLVILE (William) Bapt. Lawshall, Suffolk 9/8/1804 (or 15/9/1804?), s. Rev. Nathaniel Colvile (above) and Amy Letitia Purvis. St John's, Cambridge 1822, BA1827, dn27 (Nor.), p28 (Nor.), MA1830. R. Baylham, Suffolk 1828-59 and (succ. his father as) R. Brome, Suffolk 1828 to death (Baylham) 28/4/1859, leaving £18,000 [C112312] Married Lawshall 15/5/1834 Louisa Marianne Susan Frances Kelso (w) (dau. of a general), with issue. *J.P.*

COMBE (Edward) Bapt. Marylebone, London 9/6/1794, s. Richard and Ann Combe. Christ Church, Oxford 1792 [adm. Lincoln's Inn 1795] BA1796, MA1803, dn04 (B&W), p04 (B&W). R. Barrington, Som. 1810, PC. Drayton, Somerset 1816, R. Earnshill, Som. 1821, R. Donyatt, Som. 1821. Probably died 1848 (2nd q.) [C34020]

COMBER (Thomas) Born East Newton, Yorks. 3/3/1765, s. Rev. Thomas Comber, sen. and Mary Brooke. Jesus, Cambridge 1782, BA 1787, dn88 (Roch. for B&W), p93 (B&W). V. Creech St Michael, Som. 1806-13 (res.), R. Osbaldwick, Yorks. 1813 to death 7/8/1835 [C1761] Married St George's Hanover Square, London 30/5/1792 Elizabeth Coote, with clerical son. *J.P.* Deputy Grand Chaplain of the Orange Order 1823.

COMINS (William) Bapt. Witheridge, Devon 26/12/1783, s. William Comins. Balliol, Oxford 1802, BA1806, dn06 (Ex.), p07 (Ex.), MA1808. PC. Leighland, Som. 1816-19, V. Hockworthy, Devon 1832 and R. Rackenford, Devon 1832 both to death 'on or about' 5/2/1861, leaving £5,000 [C34028]

COMMELINE (James, sen.) Bapt. Haresford, Glos. 1/12/1762, s. Rev. James Commeline. Pembroke, Oxford 1781, BA1784, dn87 (Glos.), p88 (Glos.), then Jesus, Cambridge, MA1793. V. Cowley, Glos. 1796 and R. Redmarley D'Abitot, Worcs. 1800 to death. Dom. Chap. to Charlotte, Dowager Countess of Suffolk 1800. Died 8/5/1837 aged 75 [C142514] Married Hempstead, Glos. 24/4/1788 Ann Farmer Newton (w), with son below.

COMMELINE (James, jun.) Born Redmarley d'Abitot, Worcs., s. Rev. James Commeline (above) and Ann Farme Newton. St John's, Cambridge 1807, BA1811, dn12 (B&W), p13 (Heref.), MA 1814, BD1821, Fellow. V. Norton St Philip, Som. 1819, (succ. his father as) R. Redmarley D'Abitot 1837 and R. Colesbourne, Glos. 1837 to death 26/1/1853 aged 53 (*burnt to death*, having fallen asleep while reading in bed) aged 63 [C34030]

COMMELINE (Thomas) Bapt. Gloucester 24/2/1791, s. Thomas Commeline and Sarah Cother. St Alban Hall, Oxford 1819, dn19 (Ely for Nor.), p20 (Glos.), BA1823, MA1825. PC. Pauntley, Glos. 1820-34, PC. St Bartholomew's Hospital [almshouses] Gloucester 1827, PC. Upleadon, Glos. 1830-4, V. Claverdon w. Norton Lindsey, Warwicks. 1833 to death (Pauntley) 31/7/1842 [C6658] Married (1) Ripon, Yorks. 16/9/1824 Anne Frances Newton (d.1831), 1 dau. (2) Newent, Glos. 12/12/11833 Anne Frances Onslow (dau. of an Archdeacon of Worcester), w. futher issue.

COMMINS (Joseph Edyvean) Born Bodmin, Cornwall 24/10/1804, s. Thomas Commins and Lydia Edyvean. St Catharine's, Cambridge 1823, BA1827, dn27 (Ex.), p28 (Ely), MA1838. V. North Shoebury, Essex 1830 and V. Little Wakering, Essex 1838 to death. Chap. to Earl of St Germans. Died Matlock, Derbys. 29/3/1866 aged 61, leaving £1,000. [C6659] Married 1831 Deborah Lilburn (w), with issue.

COMPSON (James Edward) Bapt. Cleobury Mortimer, Shropshire 15/3/1793, s. James and Martha Compson. Oriel, Oxford 1811, then Trinity, BA1815, p17 (C&L), MA1826. PC. Sibdon Carwood, Shropshire 1824-33, V. Shrewsbury St Chad, Shropshire 1826 to death 16/2/1835 (CCEd thus) [C10112] Married

Ludlow, Shropshire 15/5/1818 Elizabeth Baxter.

COMPTON (John Combe) From Bisterne, Hants., s. John Compton. Merton, Oxford 1809 (aged 17), BA1813, Fellow 1814-29, dn16 (London for Win.), p16 (Ox.), MA1817. R. Minstead, Hants. 1816-35 and R. Maperton, Dorset 1820-35, (Sinecure R. Farleigh, Surrey 1828 and Sinecure R. Gamlingay, Cambs. (Moeity) 1828). Dom. Chap. to 18th Earl of Erroll 1819. Died 25/4/1835 (CCEd says 18/6/1835) [C6660]

COMPTON (William) Born Carham, Northumberland, s. Rev. William Compton, sen. Trinity, Oxford 1821 (aged 18), BA1825, dn26 (Durham), p27 (Durham), MA1828. PC. Carham, Northumberland 1826-43, R. Exeter St Olave 1835-[40] [C140717. ERC links]. Died Holy Island, Northumberland 12/6/1843 [C130369] Married Carham 9/11/1801 Mary Stow Lundie, with clerical son William Compton-Lundie.

COMYN (Henry) Born London 5/6/1775, s. Stephen Comyn (a merchant) and Mary Wilson. Christ Church, Oxford 1795, BA 1799, dn08 (Ex.), MA1808. V. Manaccan, Cornwall 1821, V. Sancreed, Cornwall 1837 to death 30/7/1851 [C140718] Married Boldre, Hants. 24/6/1814 Philadelphia Heylyn, with issue. Made important records of life in Boldre parish in 1817 when curate. Brother, below.

COMYN (Stephen George) Bapt. 25/1/1764, s. Stephen Comyn (a merchant) and Mary Wilson. Trinity, Cambridge 1782, BA1788. Chaplain R.N. 1798 [and present at the Battles of the Nile and Copenhagen]. R. Bridgham, Norfolk 1802-39, and V. Roudham, Norfolk [blank in ERC] 1826-35. Died 3/3/1839 [C72075] Married 25/10/1793 Charlotte Carter (of Rochester, Kent); Lord Nelson ('who was much attached to him') stood sponsor for his son Horatio Nelson William Comyn. Brother, above:
https://en.wikipedia.org/wiki/Stephen_George_Comyn

COMYNS (John) Bapt. Bishopsteignton, Devon 15/5/1765, s. Thomas Comyns. Oriel, Oxford 1795, dn99 (Ex.), BA1800, p01 (Nor. for Ex.), MA1801. V. Bishopsteignton 1801 and R. (and patron) of Zeal Monachorum, Devon 1801 to death. Dom. Chap. to 4th Earl of Mayo 1801. Died 3/7/1856 aged 82 [C140721] Married Axmouth, Devon 1802 Maria Hallett, with issue.

CONEY (Thomas) Bapt. City of London 21/11/1759, s. Bicknell Coney (a Director of the Bank of England) and Rebecca Roberts. Pembroke, Cambridge 1784, dn87 (Lin.), p88 (Lin.), LLB 1789. R. Batcombe w. Upton Noble, Som. 1790, R. (and patron) of Chedzoy, Som. 1811 to death (Batcombe) 29/12/1840, aged 81 [C34040] Married Binsford, Som. 5/6/1795 Elizabeth Jeane, w. issue. *J.P. & D.L* Somerset.

CONINGTON (Richard) Bapt. Horncastle, Lincs. 3/7/1796, s. James Conington and Jane Codd. Lincoln, Oxford 1815, BA1819, dn19 (Lin.), p20 (Lin.), MA1822, BCL1826. PC. Boston St Aidan, Lincs. 1822, R. Fishtoft, Lincs. 1826-34 (res.). Died 25/9/1861, leaving £10,000 [C52602] Married Jane Thirkell (before 1825) (w). His son John was a noted philologist.

CONSTABLE (John) Born Burwash, Sussex 1779, s. William Constable. University, Oxford 1798, BA1801, dn02 (Chich.), p03 (Chich.), MA1807. R. Ringmer, Lewes, Sussex 1812 to death 22/3/1863, leaving £20,000 [C63124] Widow Frances. West Sussex Record Office holds typed transcripts of his diaries for 1825-52. Doubtless related to the man below?

CONSTABLE (Richard) Bapt. Burwash, Sussex 11/9/1756. Peterhouse, Cambridge 1773, BA1778, dn79 (Nor. for Chich.), p80, MA1781, Fellow 1782-3. V. Selmeston, Sussex 1795-1801, V. Heathfield, Sussex 1795-1801, Prebend of Wisborough in Chichester Cathedral 1796-1839, V. Cowfold, Sussex 1801 and V. Hailsham, Sussex 1804 to death. Dom. Chap. to 2nd Earl Harcourt 1780. Died 5/10/1839 aged 83 [C63125] Married Winchelsea, Sussex 8/5/1786 Mary Luxford. Doubtless related to the man above?

COOK (James Tobias) Born Mildenhall, Suffolk 5/5/1783, s. of James (a farmer) and Ann Cook. St John's, Cambridge 1803, BA1807, Fellow 1809-12, dn09 (Lin.), p09 (Ely), MA 1810. V. Whittlesey St Andrew, Cambs. 1815 to death 22/9/1845 aged 62 [C6663] Married (1) Hackington, Kent 20/8/1811 Fanny Desbrosses (dau. of a Paris wine merchant and emigré), w. issue (2) Whittlesey 1838 (2nd q.) Mary Ainger. Archaeologist; geologist. Engaged in a 14-year law suit over tithes with the Lord of the Manor. J.P. Cambs., 'an excellent magistrate, having a sound knowledge of the law'.

COOK (John) From Grantham, Lincs., s. James Cook. St John's, Cambridge 1800, then Clare 1801, BA1804, dn06 (Ex. for Cant.), MA 1807, p07 (Cant.), BD1815, R. Ockley, Surrey 1817 to death (London) 13/12/1864 aged 83, leaving £600 [C140723. Not in Venn] Widow Lucy.

COOK (Joseph) Bapt. Shilbottle, Northumberland 21/11/1759, s. Samuel Cook (Newton Hall). Queens', Cambridge 1778, BA1782, Fellow 1783, dn84 (Nor.) [CCEd adds *MD* 1784] MA1785, p85 (Durham). V. Chatton, Northumberland 1799-1831-, V. Shilbottle 1803 to death 24/5/1844 aged 85 [C112318] Married Morpeth, Northumberland 6/8/1786 Sarah Brown, with clerical son.

COOK (Joseph George) Born Holborn, London 13/3/1784, s. Gen. William Cook, *H.E.I.C.* Trinity, Cambridge 1802, BA1807, dn07 (Win.), p08 (Win.), MA1810. V. Theddingworth, Leics. 1810-41. Died Calcot Park, Tilehurst, Berks. 17/2/1856 [C52991] Married South Stoneham, Hants. 13/2/1809 Maria Hoadley Ash, *s.p.*

COOK, COOKE (Stephen) Bapt. Knapton, Norfolk 23/9/1774, s. Stephen Cook (farmer) and Lorina Deys. Caius, Cambridge 1791, BA 1797, dn97 (Nor.), p98 (Nor.). V. (and patron) of Oulton, Norfolk 1798-1854, V. Paston, Norfolk 1854 to death 28/9/1861 aged 87, leaving £3,000 [C112319] Married Walcott, Norfolk 28/12/1801 Maria Atkinson (w), and issue.

COOKE, COOK (Alexander) Bapt. Warmsworth, Doncaster,Yorks. 17/5/1767, s. Rev. George Cooke(-Yarborough) (R. Darfield, Yorks.) and Mary Newsome.Christ Church, Oxford 1784, BA1788, LLB 1791, dn91 (London for York). R. Warmsworth 1791 (and Preacher throughout the Diocese of York 1791-6), R. Darfield (1st Mediety 1791-6 [blank in ERC], V. Arksey, Yorks. 1831 (only). Died 14/6/1849, living at Loversall Hall, Doncaster, Yorks. [C109454. YCO] Married Warmsworth 19/9/1811 Catherine Esther Buck, with issue. Brother Henry, below.

COOKE, COOK (Bell) Bapt. Hackford w. Whitwell, Norfolk 23/1/1796, s. Thomas Cooke and Mary Harpley. Literate: dn20 (Nor.), p21 (Nor.). PC. Norwich St Paul w. St James 1826 to death (Heigham, Norfolk) 20/2/1869 aged 74, leaving £5,000 [C1041] Married Norwich 8/5/1826 Mary Anne Harris, w. clerical sons.

COOKE (Charles) Born Semer, Suffolk 25/2/1762, s. Rev. Thomas Cooke. Caius, Cambridge 1780, dn84 (Nor.), p86 (Nor.), BA 1787, MA 1787. R. Bromeswell, Suffolk 1790, (succ. his father as) R. and patron of Semer 1793 to death 23/3/1838 [C112320] Married Clare, Suffolk 22/8/1797 Elizabeth Young, with issue. J.P. Suffolk. Brother Thomas, below.

COOKE (Edward) Born Demerara, British Guiana 22/12/1800, s. John and Catherine Cooke. St Bees adm. 1822, dn24 (Bristol for Durham), p25 (Chester for Durham). V. Bywell St Peter, Northumberland 1828 to death (Clifton, Bristol) 7/3/1845 ('of deep consumption') aged 45 [C8170. LBSO] Married South Shields 1841 (2nd q.) Fanny Wallis (w). Claimed compensation for slave ownership.

COOKE (George) Bapt. Barnborough, Yorks. 4/2/1760, s. John Cooke and Catherine Cooke. Christ Church, Oxford 1778, BA1782, then All Souls, Fellow, SCL1783, dn85 (York), BCL 1786, p86 (York) [CCEd adds LLB by 1788]. R. Warmsworth, Yorks. 1788-91, R. Sprotbrough, Yorks. (and Preacher throughout the Archdiocese of York) 1790 to death (Great Malvern, Worcs.) 6/5/1837 [C109453. YCO] Married 1795 Anne Burward, with issue.

COOKE (George) From Gloucester, s. John Cooke. Oriel, Oxford 1777 (aged 16), BA1780, dn86 (Ox.), MA1786, p87 (Ox.), BD1790, DD 1796. V. Oxford St Mary the Virgin 1796-7, V. Moreton Pinckney, Northants. 1797-1800, R. Tortworth, Glos. 1799 and R. Didmarton w. Odbury-on-the-Hill, Glos. 1803 to death 17/9/1840 aged 80 [C25562] *J.P., D.L.* Glos. and Wilts.

COOKE (George Leigh) Born Bookham, Surrey 1/7/1779, s. Rev. Samuel Cooke and

Cassandra Leigh. Balliol, Oxford 1797, then Corpus Christi, BA1800, Fellow 1800-15, MA 1804, dn04 (Win.), p05 (Ox.), BD1812. Sedleian Professor of Natural Philosophy, Oxford 1810-53. Keeper of the University Archives 1818-26. V. Rissington Wyck >< Glos. 1811-53, R. Broadwell w. Adelstrop 1818-20, V. Cubbington, Warwicks. 1820-53, PC. Hunningham, Warwicks. 1820 to death (Cubbington) 29/3/1853 aged 73 [C10114. ODNB. Boase] Married Bloomsbury, London 26/19/1815 Ann Hay. Brother Theophilus Leigh, below.

COOKE (Harry) Bapt. Kirk Sandal, Yorks. 14/10/1777, s. George Cooke. Trinity, Cambridge 1793. BA1798, dn00 (York), p01 (York), MA1801. R. Sandy, Beds. (and Preacher throughout the Diocese of Lincoln) 1814 to death 13/8/1858, leaving £8,000 [C53517. YCO]

COOKE, COOK (Henry) Bapt. Everton, Notts. 22/6/1771, s. Rev. George Cooke (R. Darfield, Yorks.) and Mary Cooke. Queens', Cambridge 1790, then Clare 1790, BA1795, dn95 (York), p95 (York). R. (and patron) of Darfield (1st Moiety) 1796-1835 [blank in ERC], R. Black Notley, Essex 1834-5 (res.). Died 1842 aged 72 [C109455. YCO] Married (1) Mary Bowen, Woodbridge Hall, Suffolk (d.1833), with clerical son below (2) Elizabeth Cope. Brother Alexander, above.

COOKE (Henry Bowen) Born Darfield, Yorks. 29/3/1797, s. Rev. Henry Cooke (above) and Mary Bowen. Trinity Hall, Cambridge 1816, BCL, dn20 (York), p21 (Chester for York), LLB 1821. PC. Worsborough, Darfield 1821-35, (succ. his father as) R. (and patron) of Darfield (1st Moiety) 1835-79 [income £1,600] Also Incumbent of Annan, Dumfriesshire in the Scottish Episcopal Church 1845-63. Died (Darfield) 27/2/1879 aged 81, leaving £4,000 [C131011. YCO. Bertie] Married (1) Burneston, Yorks. 27/6/1822 Juliana Mary Serjeantson (d.1862), w. clerical s. Henry Pennant Cooke (2) Kelton, Kirkcudbright 29/9/1864 Georgina Helen Elizabeth Whigham (w), *s.p. J.P.* West Riding.

COOKE (John Constantine) Born Greenwich Hospital, Kent. 5/2/1776, s. Rev. John Cooke. Trinity, Cambridge 1792, then Christ's 1794, BA1797, dn98 (Nor.), p00 (Nor.), MA1800. V. Swilland, Suffolk 1806 and R. Kings Ripton, Hunts. 1818 to death. Dom. Chap. to 1st Viscount Templeton 1807; to 7th Earl of Sandwich 1820. Died Ipswich 22/10/1842. [C53515]

COOKE (Theophilus Leigh) Born Bookham, Surrey 13/4/1778, s. Rev. Samuel Cooke and Cassandra Leigh. Balliol, Oxford 1794, then Magdalen, Fellow, BA1798, MA1801, p02 (Win.), BD1812. PC. Beckley, Oxon. 1802-46, PC. Little Ilford, Essex 1803 and R. Brandeston, Norfolk 1815 to death 11/10/1846 [C25566] 'Liberal and kind'. Brother George Leigh Cooke, above.

COOKE (Thomas) Born Semer, Suffolk, s. Rev. Thomas Cooke, sen. Caius, Cambridge 1771, BA1776, MA1779, Scholar 1771-6, dn76 (Nor.). V. Westbury, Wilts. 1813-45. Died 20/1/1848 'aged 90' [Not in CCEd or Venn] Married Elsworth, Cambs. 13/5/1777 Elizabeth Holworthy, w. issue. Inherted the estate of Modrydd, Llansbyddyr, Brecon. Brother Charles, above.

COOKE (Thomas) Bapt. Gloucester 4/5/1791, s. Charles Cooke. Oriel, Oxford 1809, BA1813, MA1816, dn16 (Glos.), p17 (Glos.). PC. Brighton St Peter's Chapel of Ease, Sussex 1828-73 [C63130], V. Brigstock w. Stanion, Northants. 1824-74, V. Grafton Underwood, Northants. 1829-[54]. Dom. Chap. to 2nd Earl of Malmesbury 1829. Died Brighton. Sussex 18/12/1874, leaving £7,000 [C111568] Married (1) St George's Hanover Square, London 17/12/1827 Jane Finch (d 1858), with issue (2) Marylebone, London 12/1/1860 Esther Goldsmid (d.1865) (3) Brighton 3/7/1866 Eliza Juliana Musgrave.

COOKE (William) Born Hereford 2/8/1785, s. John Cooke [*pleb*] and Mary Hughes. New, Oxford 1802, BA1806, dn08 (Heref.), p09 (Heref.), MA1810. S/M Hereford Cathedral G/S 1807 and in 1824; H/M Bromyard G/S, Heref. 1835; Vicar-Choral Hereford Cathedral 1808 (and other Cathedral posts there through life); PC. Brockhampton, Heref. 1810-13 (res.), V. Pipe and Lyde, Heref. 1813-34 (res.), (Sinecure R. Bromyard (3 Portions) 1825), V. Ullingswick w. Little Cowarne, Heref. 1829 and V. Bromyard 1834 (and RD 1839) to death. Dom. Chap. to 7th Viscount Molesworth 1834.

Died 18/10/1854 [C103986] Married Bridgnorth, Shropshire 13/12/1810 Mary Anne Murray, with issue. Photo. online.

COOKSON (Christopher) Born Leeds, Yorks. 19/5/1758, s. Thomas Cookson (merchant and alderman). St John's, Cambridge 1777, BA1781, dn82 (Lin.), p83 (Lin.). R. & V. Stamford St Michael w. St Andrew w. St Stephen, Lincs. 1787-1808, V. Cherry Willingham, Lincs. 1806-32 (res.), R. Wittering, Northants. 1808-36. Died 12/9/1844 [C53538] Married (2?) Dowsby, Lincs. 23/3/1818 Martha Foster (a clergy dau.), with issue.

COOKSON (Edward) Born Leeds 21/10/1802, s. John Cookson (merchant). St Catharine's, Cambridge 1820, then Trinity 1820, BA1825 [adm. Lincolns Inn 1825] MA1828, p31 (Lin.), p31 (Lin.). PC. Leeds St Mary, Quarry Hill, 1833-48, PC. Sharrow, Ripon, Yorks. 1839-52, V. Holy Trinity, Leeds 1855 to death (Ticehurst, Surrey) 28/1/1862 aged 59, leaving £9,000 [C53541. BBV] Married Leeds 10/7/1832 Elizabeth Chorley (w) (dau. of a surgeon), with clerical son of father's name.

COOKSON (Francis [Thomas]) Born Leeds 5/3/1786, s. William Cookson. Trinity, Cambridge 1805, BA1809, dn09 (Durham), p10 (Durham), MA1813. PC. Leeds St John's the Evangelist 1810 to death. Dom. Chap. to 4th Viscount Midleton 1810. Died 20/12/1859, leaving £4,000 [C134148. BBV] Married Leeds 23/3/1820 Mary Ellen Fawcett (w) (a clergy dau.), with issue.

COOKSON (George) Bapt. Fornsett, Norfolk 29/7/1793, s. Rev. William Cookson (Canon of Windsor Chapel) and Dorothy Cooper. St John's, Cambridge 1812, BA1816, dn16 (Salis.), p17 (Salis.), MA1819. R. Deptford St Paul, Kent 1818-19 (res.), R. Writhlington, Som. 1819, V. Powerstock, Dorset 1832 to death. Chap. to HRH Duke of Sussex 1819. Died 15/2/1848 aged 54 [C1765] Brother William, below.

COOKSON (James) Bapt. Martindale, Westmorland 14/4/1751, s. John Cookson. Literate: dn74 (Car. for Win.), p75 (Win.), then Queen's, Oxford 1777, BA1781, MA1786. R. Colmer w. Prior's Dean, Hants. 1775-1835, (Sinecure R. [blank in ERC] 1795 then) V. Harting, Sussex 1805 to death 22/1/1835. Dom. Chap. to 1st Baron Garvagh 1819 (CCEd thus) [C5778. ODNB] *F.S.A.* (1814).

COOKSON (William) Bapt. Fornsett, Norfolk 27/9/1793, s. Rev. William Cookson (Canon of Windsor) and Dorothy Cooper. BNC, Oxford 1811, BA1815, dn16 (Salis.), p17 (Salis.), MA 1818. V. Hungerford, Berks. 1818 and V. Broad Hinton, Berks. 1834 [total income in CR65 £1,000] to death. Dom. Chap to Charlotte, Dowager Countess of Antrim 1834. Died 21/5/1866 (St Helier, Jersey, where he seems to have been a frequent visitor), leaving under £100 [C91840] Married Exeter 10/6/1819 Caroline Mary Neave (b. India), with issue. Brother George, above:

COOPER (Allen) Born Bloomsbury, London, 17/8/1793, s. Allen Cooper and Susanna Maria Moule. Oriel, Oxford 1809, BA1813, MA1815, dn17 (London for Cant.), p17 (London for Cant.). Min. St Mark, North Audley Street [Proprietary Chapel], London 1808 to death. Dom. Chap. to 2nd Marquess of Exeter 1817. Died Brighton, Sussex 5/1/1851 aged 57 [C116804] Married (1) Clifton, Bristol 26/4/1820 Harriot Ann Turner (a clergy dau., d.1833) (2) Rochester 30/3/1842 Harriet Grace (dau. of Sir John Gregory Shaw, 5th Bart.).

COOPER (Augustus) Bapt. Woodbridge, Suffolk 18/12/1789, s. Robert Cooper. Pembroke, Cambridge 1808, dn12 (Nor.), BA1813, p13 (Nor.). R. Billingford w. Thornham Parva >< Norfolk 1823-64, PC. Syleham, Suffolk 1833 (living at Syleham Hall). Died (Upper Norwood, Surrey) 22/8/1877 aged 89, leaving £20,000 [C112327] Married Stoke Ash, Suffolk 7/11/1816 Jane Maria Wood, with clerical son.

COOPER (Blakley) Bapt. Yetminster, Dorset 3/7/1783, s. Rev. Edward Cooper and Mary Fort. Wadham, Oxford 1802, dn06 (Bristol), BA1806, p07 (Bristol), MA1809. V. Yetminster 1807 and R. East Chelborough, Dorset 1809 to death. Dom. Chap. to 2nd Earl of Radnor 1809. Died 1849 (1st q.) [C8224] Married (1) Marylebone, London 28/7/1805 Charlotte Mary Bacon, w. issue (2) Yetminster 5/8/1847 Jane Connock.

COOPER (Charles Beauchamp) Born Chipping Ongar, Essex 31/1/1802, s. Beauchamp Newton Cooper and Frances Adams.

University, Oxford 1820, BA1824, dn26 (Lin.), p27 (Lin.), MA1828. R. (and patron) of Morley St Botolph w. Morley St Peter, Norfolk 1832 (and RD of Hingham 1844-8) to death 21/1/1878, leaving £18,000 [C53553] Married Great Stanmore, Middx. 31/7/1828 Harriet Harvey, with issue.

COOPER (Edward Dolman) Bapt. Droitwich, Worcs. 23/10/1765, s. Rev. Edward and Hannah Cooper. Worcester, Oxford 1783, BA1787, dn88 (Ox.), Fellow, p91 (Wor.), MA 1792. R. Hamstall Ridware, Staffs. 1799-[1849], R. Rous Lench, Worcs. 1804, R. Yoxall, Staffs. 1809 to death. Dom. Chap. to 2nd Baron Northwick 1804.. Died 1848 (1st q. as Dorman) [C10119 - where death date is obviously wrong] Married Saintbury, Glos. 29/10/1801 Mary Cooper, with clerical son. Jane Austen connections.

COOPER (Edward Philip) Born Harpsden, Oxon. 27/10/1794, s. Rev. Henry (*or* Edward) Cooper and Caroline Isabella Powys. St John's, Oxford 1811, BA1815, MA1819, dn21 (Ox.), p22 (Ox.), BD1825. V. Long Itchington, Warwicks. 1826, V. Little Dalby, Leics. 1852 to death (Leamington, Warwicks.) 29/11/1864, leaving £12,000 [C10120] Married Whitchurch on Thames, Oxon. 19/7/1825 Caroline Louisa Powys, with issue.

COOPER (James) [NiVoF] R. West Thorney, Sussex 1785 to death 12/4/1833 (CCEd thus) [C63135]

COOPER (James) Bapt. Aldingham, Lancs. 1802. St Bees adm. 1824, p29 (Chester). PC. Houghton, Leyland, Lancs. 1824 to (burial) 4/7/1833 [C168545]

COOPER (John) [NiVoF] R. Newton Bromswold, Northants. 1788 to death (Leicester) 21/4/1841 aged 80 [C110101]

COOPER (John Mawbey) Born Burbage, Leics. c.1787, s. Rev. William Cooper and Martha [Mawbey?]. Queen's, Oxford 1807, migrated to Trinity Hall, Cambridge 1808 dn11, BA1812, p12 (Salis.), MA1815. R. Peckleton, Leics. 1814 to death. Dom. Chap. to 3rd Baron Montfort of Horseheath 1815. Died (at his home at Deeping St James, Lincs.) 18/1/1864 aged 76, leaving £1,500 [C53564] Married Frolesworth, Leics. 5/8/1817 Christian Staresmore Marvin (of Frolesworth House), w. clerical s. William Henry. *J.P.* Leics. & Lincs.

COOPER (Robert Jermyn) Born Dursley, Glos. 2/11/1795, s. Robert Bransby Cooper and Anne Purnell. Christ Church, Oxford 1812, BA1816, dn18 (Glos.), p20 (Glos.), MA1820. V. Leigh, Glos. 1826-51-, R. West Chiltington, Sussex 1835 to death. Chap. Gloucester County Gaol 1823. Died 19/5/1873 aged 77. No will traced [C142818] Married Dursley 8/9/1817 Arabella Harriet Wallington, with clerical son of father's name, and 2 dau.

COOPER (Samuel) Born Wistow, Hunts., s. Rev. Samuel Cooper, sen. and Ann Pyke (a clergy dau.). St John's, Cambridge 1795, BA 1799, dn99 (Lin.), MA1802, p05 (Lin.), PC. Upwood w. Great Raveley, Hunts. 1821-50, R. Wood Walton >< Hunts. 1827 to death (Wistow) 2/1/1856 [C53568] Brother William, below.

COOPER (Thomas Lovick) Bapt. Shotesham, Norfolk 6/9/1801, s. Rev. Samuel Lovick Cooper (Letheringham Abbey) and Sarah Leman Rede. Magdalene, Cambridge 1819, dn24 (Nor.), p25 (Nor.), BA1826, MA1829. R. (and patron) of Ingoldisthorpe, Norfolk 1825-31, Min. South Lambeth Proprietary Chapel, Surrey 1826-31, R. Hawkshead, Lancs. 1830-4, R. (and patron) of Mablethorpe w. Stane, Lincs. 1831-92, V. Empingham, Rutland 1831 [total income in CR65 £1,150] to death 29/5/1892 aged 90, leaving £6,061-2s-6d. [C53572] Married (1) Norwich 18/6/1821 Emily Mary Sophia Swinfen (dau. of Sir Thomas Durrant, 2nd Bart., she d.1838), with issue (2) St George's Hanover Square, London 15/7/1841 Harriette Ricardo, with further issue.

COOPER (William) Born Wistow, Hunts., s. Rev. Samuel Cooper and Ann Pyke (a clergy dau.). St John's, Cambridge 1788, BA1792, dn92 (Lin.), Fellow 1794-1810, MA1795, p95 (Ely), BD1802. R. Waddingham St Peter, Lincs. 1808-56 (non-res.), (succ. his father as) R. West Rasen, Lincs, 1802 (and RD) to death. Dom. Chap. to Earl of Macclesfield; Chap. in Ordinary 1830. Died 24/8/1856 [C53575. Kaye] Married Swinhope 2/12/1822 Anne Alington, with issue. Brother Samuel, above.

COPLESTON (John Gaius) Born Offwell, Devon 5/4/1778, s. Rev. John Bradford Copleston and Margaret Gay. Pembroke, Oxford 1795, then Corpus Christi, BA1799, dn00 (Ex.), MA 1802, p03 (Ex.). R. (and patron) of Offwell 1804-41 and V. Upottery, Devon 1814-41, V. Kingsey, Bucks. 1827-33, R. Lamyatt, Som. 1833. Dom. Chap. to Elizabeth, Baroness Graves of Gravesend 1814. Died 20/7/1841 [C140727] Married Offwell 27/4/1801 Harriet Townsend, with son, below.

COPLESTON (William James) Bapt. Offwell, Devon 28/12/1804, s. Rev. John Gaius Copleston (above) and Harriet Townsend. Corpus Christi, Oxford 1822, BA1825, then Oriel 1822, Fellow 1826-40, MA1828, dn28 (Ox.), p29 (Ox.). V. Exeter St Thomas the Apostle, Devon 1831, R. Cromhall, Glos. 1839 to death 3/2/1874 aged 69, leaving £12,000 [C25815] Widow Elizabeth Ann.

COPNER (Cornelius) A Welshman. Literate: dn82 (St David's), p84 (St David's). R. Naunton Beauchamp, Worcs. 1815 to death 7/9/1839 aged 70 [C120829] Married Carmarthen 26/12/1781 Sarah Bloom, w. issue.

COPPARD (William Isaac) Bapt. Wartling, Sussex 2/11/1786, s. Rev. William Coppard (R. Graveley, Cambs., who was 'indicted by the College for neglect of his livings'). Emmanuel, Cambridge 1805, BA1809, dn09 (Roch.), p11 (Roch.), MA1818. PC. Plympton St Mary, Devon 1817 to death. Dom. Chap. to Earl of Morley 1840-53-. Died 25/2/1865, leaving £800. [C1768] Married Plympton 9/6/1836 Charlotte Sarah (w), dau. Rear-Admiral Samuel Peter Forster. Antiquarian

CORBETT (Andrew) Born Hillington, Middx. 16/3/1805, s. William Corbett (Darnhill, Cheshire) and Jane Eleanor Ainslie. Trinity, Cambridge 1824, BA1828, dn28 (Lin.), p29 (Lin.), MA1831. V. Sixhills, Lincs. 1829-64, V. Great Ludford (Ludford Magna) and Elsham, Lincs. 1829-31, R. Benniworth, Lincs. 1831 and R. South Willingham, Lincs. 1838 to death 9/5/1864, leaving £12,000 [C53631] Married 5/1/1839 Marion (dau. Sir Matthew White-Ridley), w. issue. *J.P.* Lindsey.

CORBETT, *born* PLYMLEY (Joseph) Born Longnor Bank House, Shropshire 7/2/1794, s. Ven. Joseph Plymley (*later* Corbett), Archdeacon of Salop (and abolitionist) and Martha Collins. Pembroke, Oxford 1810, BA1814, MA1816. R. Tugford, Shropshire 1822 and PC. Clee St Margaret, Shropshire 1823 to death (a bachelor) 1/12/1860, leaving £450 [C19266 is his father, with whom there is much confusion] Brother Waties, below.

CORBETT (Stuart) Born London, s. Capt. Andrew Corbett (Horse Guards) and Lady Augusta Stuart (d. 1778, a granddaughter of 3rd Earl of Bute, the Prime Minister). Merton, Oxford 1792 (aged 18), BA1796, dn97 (Lin.), p98 (Lin.), MA1800, BD and DD1816. V. Luton, Beds. 1798-1804 (and Preacher throughout the Diocese of Lincoln 1798), PC. Wortley, Leeds, Yorks. 1802 (living at Conduit House there), R. Kirk Bramwith, Yorks. 1804-45, R. Ordsall, Notts. before 1812, R. Scrayingham, Yorks. 1816, Archdeacon of York 1837-45 (w. Prebend of Strensall 1841-4). Dom. Chap. to 2nd Marquess of Bute 1816. Died (Wortley) 25/8/1845 aged 71 [C53633] Married Loughborough, Leics. 25/10/1798 Ann King, w. clerical s. James Wortley Corbett. *J.P.*

CORBETT, *born* PLYMLEY (Waties) Born Longnor Bank House, Longnor, Shropshire 25/12/1796, s. Ven. Joseph Plymley (later Corbett, Archdeacon of Salop, the abolitionist) and Martha Collins. Trinity, Cambridge 1814, dn20 (Heref.), BA1821, MA1824. PC. Leebotwood w. Longnor, Shropshire 1822-55, R. Coreley, Shropshire 1821-35, R. Acton Scott, Shropshire 1833 (and Prebend of Moreton Parva in Hereford Cathedral 1836 and Chancellor of Hereford Diocese 1837) to death (Longnor) 30/12/1855 aged 59 [C10131. Boase] Brother Joseph, above.

CORFIELD (Richard) Born Shrewsbury, Shropshire 24/1/1781, s. Richard and Sarah Corfield. Clare, Cambridge 1797, BA1802, dn03 (Heref.), p05 (C&L), MA1806. PC. Norton Canes, Staffs. 1811-15, R. Pitchford, Shropshire 1812 and R. Waters Upton, Shropshire 1822 to death (Llangattock, Monmouth) 26/12/1865, aged 84. Will not traced [C10132] Married Shrewsbury, Shropshire 15/12/1802 Diana Margaretta Peele, with issue.

CORNISH (George James) Born Ottery St Mary, Devon 7/6/1794, s. George Cornish and

Sarah Kestell. Corpus Christi, Oxford 1810, BA1814, MA1817, dn18 (Ox.), p21 (Ex.). R. Kenwyn w. Kea, Cornwall 1828 (and Prebend of Exeter Cathedral) to death 10/9/1849 [C25949] Married Chaddesden, Derbys. 3/7/1818 Harriott Wilmot, with issue.

CORNISH (Sidney William) Born Exeter before 9/6/1801, s. Robert Cornish and Frances Ann Squire. Exeter, Oxford 1818, BA1822, Fellow 1822-8, dn24 (Ox.), MA1825, p25 (Ox.), BD and DD1836. H/M King's School, Ottery St Mary, Devon 1824-63 and V. Ottery 1841-74, R. South Newington, Oxon. 1827. Died (Seaton, Devon) 1/8/1874, leaving £4,000 [C25951. Boase] Married Exeter 17/6/1829 Jane Kingdon (w), with issue. Surrogate 1841.

CORNISH (Thomas) Born Kingston, Som., s. Thomas Cornish. Magdalen Hall, Oxford 1781 (aged 17), BA1785, dn86 (B&W), p87 (Ex. for B&W). R. (and patron) of Heathfield, Som. 1787 to death 28/11/1841 aged 77 [C34084]. Wife Elizabeth, and clerical son Thomas Merton Cornish. Well-known for his cider making!

CORNISH (William Floyer) Bapt. Totnes, Devon 6/12/1769, s. James Cornish and Sarah Searle. Wadham, Oxford 1788, then Exeter, BA1799, dn99 (Ex.), p01 (Ex.). R. Thornton Watless, Yorks. 1804-7 (res.), R. Hooke, Dorset 1827. Died (Berry Pomeroy, Devon) 30/8/1858, leaving £20,000 [C53633] Married Totnes 1/5/1804 Elizabeth Marshall (w), w. issue.

CORNTHWAITE (Thomas) Bapt. Wyresdale Chapel, Lancs. 10/4/1763, s. William and Elizabeth Cornthwaite, Literate: dn89 (York), p90 (York) [C88289]. V. Crich, Derbys. (non-res.) 1801-38 (res.). Died Derby 6/5/1838 aged 75 [C10138. YCO. Austin] An 'eccentric': www.crichparish.co.uk/webpages/vicar.html

CORNU, *or* LE CORNU (John) Bapt. Jersey, Channel Islands 14/6/1760, s. Phillippe and Anne Le Cornu. Literate: dn92 (York). V. Hathersage, Derbys. 1796 and PC. Derwent, Derbys. 1807 to death 19/6/1844 [C10139. YCO]

CORNWALL (Alan Gardner) Born Hendon, Middx. 16/7/1798, s. John Cornwall and Susannah Hall Gardner. Trinity, Cambridge 1816, BA1821, dn21 (Win.), p23 (Win.), MA 1824. V. Stanstead Mountfitchet, Essex 1827-8, R. Newington Bagpath, Glos. 1827-72, R. Newent, Glos. 1827, R. Beverston w. Kingscote, Glos. 1839 [total income in CR65 £1,070] to death. Chap. in Ordinary to the Queen. Died 5/8/1872, leaving £5,000 [C142821] Married 29/4/1828 Caroline Marianne Kingscote, w. clerical s. Alan Kingscote Cornwall.

CORRANCE (Francis Thomas) From Wolverhampton, Staffs, s.William Corrance. Trinity Hall, Cambridge 1801 (re-adm. 1807), LLB 1809, dn09 (Win.), p10 (Salis. for Win.). V. Glen Magna cum Great Stretton, Lincs. 1814 to death 25/10/1850 aged 69 [C53642] Wife Katharine, and issue.

CORRIN (William) Born Arbory, IoM 1795. Literate: dn17 (S&M), p19 (S&M). V. Rushen, IoM 1824 to death 5/2/1859 aged 64. Will not traced [C7254. Gelling] Wife Isabella, 5s., 8 dau. Caught cholera in 1832. 'A strong evangelical'; and 'an excellent classical scholar'.

CORRY (Robert) Born Ellesmere, Shropshire 27/3/1770, s. Robert Corry. BNC, Oxford 1788, BA1791, p92 (Wor.), MA1794, p94 (Wor.); 'Fellow of Dulwich College'. R. Tarrant Hinton, Dorset 1821 to death 2/2/1838 aged 57 [C52313] Widow Louisa.

CORSELLIS (Joseph Goodall) Bapt. Wivenhoe, Essex 4/8/1764, s. Rev. Nicholas Corsellis. Jesus, Cambridge 1783, BA1787, dn87 (C&L for London), MA1792, p92 (Nor.). Chap. to the Forces 1809; R. Wivenhoe 1826 to death (unm.) 6/4/1835 aged 70 (CCEd says 1/5/1835) [C9635]

CORSER (Thomas) Born Whitchurch, Shropshire 9/7/1793, s. George Corser (a banker) and Martha Pythian. Balliol, Oxford 1811, BA 1815, dn16 (C&L), p17 (C&L), MA1818. V. Stand, Prestwich, Lancs. 1826-76, RD of Prestwich 1852, V. Norton (by Daventry), Northants. 1828 to death (Stand) 24/8/1876 aged 84, leaving £25,000 [C10141. ODNB. Boase] Married Prestwich 24/11/1828 Ellen Lyon (a clergy dau.), with issue. Literary scholar with a major library of early English poetry which sold after his death for £20,000.

CORT (Robert) Born Brigham, Cumberland, s. Robert Cort and Rebecca Stainton. Literate:

dn92 (Chester), p93 (Chester). PC. Formby, Lancs. 1793, PC. Arkholme, Lancs. 1793, PC. Kirkby St Chad, Lancs. 1793 to death 23/1/1850 aged 87 [C168553] Married Formby, Lancs. 12/8/1794 Elizabeth Rose, with issue. In ERC twice (once blank, and again as Kirby)

CORY, CORRY (Charles) Born Kettlestone, Norfolk 1775/6, s. Rev. James Cory and Charlotte Whaites. Caius, Cambridge 1793, BA 1798, dn98 (Nor.), p00 (Ely for Nor.), MA1801. R. Tunstall, Yorks. 1832-36, V. Skipsea, Yorks. 1834 (and Chap. of the Donative of Stainborough, Wentworth Castle, Yorks. c.1844) to death (a widower) 17/2/1862 aged 86, leaving £300 [C99747. BBV] Married Manchester 20/11/1817 Sarah Girt (Stainborough Hall, Barnsley), 8 ch. in 1832. Brother below.

CORY (James) Born Kettlestone, Norfolk 29/4/1772, s. Rev. James Cory and Charlotte Whaites. Corpus Christi, Cambridge 1789, BA 1794, dn94 (Nor.), p96 (Nor.). R. Shereford (o/w Sheringford), Norfolk 1796 and R. Kettlestone, Norfolk 1796 to death 5/5/1864 aged 92, leaving £1,500 [C112347] Married Fakenham, Norfolk 25/11/17895 Jane Erratt, w. issue. Brother above.

CORY (John James) Bapt. Limehouse, London 11/4/1790, s. John Cory (a wine merchant). Trinity, Cambridge 1808, BA1813, p14 (Ely), MA1816, then Sidney, Fellow 1817, BD1823. V. Orton on the Hill, Leics. 1831 and V. Aylsham, Norfolk 1834 to death (Rickmansworth, Herts.) 22/8/1834 (CCEd says 8/7/1834) aged 43 [C6670] Married Rickmansworth 25/1/1832 Catherine Dawbiney.

CORY (Richard) Bapt. Fowey, Cornwall 9/10/1760, s. Rev. Nicholas Cory. Christ Church, Oxford 1780, BA1783, dn83 (Ex.), p85 (Ex.). V. Egloshayle, Cornwall 1804 and R. St Keyne, Cornwall 1804 to death 13/7/1833 aged 72 [C140733] Married Landrake, Cornwall 4/11/1784 Jane Boger, with issue.

COSENS (William Burrough) From Ipplepen, Devon, s. Rev. William Cosens. Magdalen Hall, Oxford 1818 (aged 26), dn20 (Ely for Salis.), p20 (Salis.), BA1824, MA1825. R. Monkton Farleigh, Wilts. 1824, V. Berry Pomeroy, Devon 1834 (where he was involved in a pamphlet war with his patron) to death 27/10/1861 aged 70, leaving £1,000 [C6672] Married Warminster, Wilts. 9/7/1821 Marianne Rowlandson (w).

COSSERAT (George Peloquin) Bapt. Exeter 6/8/1780, s. Nathaniel Elias Cosserat and Elizabeth Lewis. Exeter, Oxford 1798, BA 1802, dn03 (B&W), p05 (Ex.), Chap. 1806-9 (res.), MA1808. R. Exeter St Martin 1827 and Exeter St Pancras 1830, R. Shelley, Suffolk 1844-[52]. Died Stow, Suffolk 18/12/1858. Will not traced [C34114] Married before 1816 Jane Graham Howarth, with clerical son George Peloquin Graham Cosserat.

COSWAY (Samuel) Probably born Tiverton, Devon, s. Thomas Cosway. Queens', Cambridge 1826, BA1830, dn30 (London for Cant.), p31 (London for Cant.). PC. Bilsington, Kent 1832-44, V. Chute, Wilts. 1838 to death 31/10/1880, leaving £6,000 [C116814] Widow Harriot.

COTES (Charles Grey) Born Woodcote, Shropshire 22/1/1801, s. John Cotes and Lady Maria Booth Grey (dau. of 5th Earl of Stamford and Warrington). Christ Church, Oxford 1820, BA 1823, dn24 (Ox.), p25 (Ox.), MA1826. R. Stanton St Quintin, Wilts. 1826 to death 28/12/1866, leaving £45,000 [C91891] Married Shifnal, Shropshire 4/4/1839 Fanny Henrietta Pigot (dau. of military baronet), with issue.

COTES (Peter) From Tickton, Yorks., s. Peter Cotes. Wadham, Oxford 1820 (aged 17), BA 1824, dn26 (London), MA1827, p27 (London). R. Litchfield, Hants. 1832 to death 24/8/1865 aged 62, leaving £5,000 [C72510]

COTES see also under **COATES**

COTTERILL (Henry) [NiVoF]. (first) PC. Oakamoor Chapel, Cheadle, Staffs. 1833-[36]. Died? [Not in CCEd] Could possibly be the Bishop of Grahamstown, then of Edinburgh, but if so, this charge not noted.

COTTERILL (Joseph) Born Stafford c.1780, s. Rev. Thomas Cotterill and Susan Dunlop. St John's, Cambridge 1804, BA1808, dn08 (B&W), p08 (Win. for B&W), Fellow 1809-11, MA1812. R. Ampton, Suffolk 1811-26, R. Cockthorpe w. Blakeney cum Glanford w. Little Langham, Norfolk 1824 (w. RD of Holt 1844 and Hon.

Canon of Norwich 1846) to death 15/2/1858 aged 78, leaving £7,000 [C34116] Married (1) Somerset 14/3/1811 Anne Boak (d.1826), w. issue (2) Chelsea, London 26/4/1826 Anne Robina Hare (a clergy dau., Dicking Hall, Norfolk), w. clerical s. Joseph Morthland Cotterill. Port. online.

COTTINGHAM (James) Bapt. Little Neston, Cheshire 2/10/1803, s. Thomas Cottingham and Elizabeth Cooper. Clare, Cambridge 1823, BA 1827, dn27 (Chester), p28 (Chester). PC. Shotwick, Cheshire 1831 to death (Chester) 11/10/1890 aged 87 (for 59 years). Will not traced [C168573] Married (2?) Wirral, Cheshire 1873 (4th q.) Annie Roberts, with issue.

COTTLE (Henry Wyatt) Born Wallingford, Berks. 11/6/1801, s. Rev. Wyatt Cottle and Lucretia Games. Worcester, Oxford 1820, migrated to Sidney, Cambridge 1822, BA1826, dn26 (Salis.), p27 (Salis.). R. Watford, Northants. 1831-54, R. Harford, Devon 1854-71 (on permanent leave of absence). In New Zealand (his travel diary survives): a priest near Auckland until his death 10/3/1871 aged 70, leaving £2,000 [C91894. Blain] Married Long Buckby, Northants. 9/2/1843 Alice Worster, many children.

COTTON (Ambrose Alexander) Born Madingley, Cambs. 28/7/1764, s. Sir John Hynde Cotton, 4th Bart., *M.P.*, and Ann Parsons. Pembroke, Cambs. 1782, BA1786, dn87 (Peterb. for Ely), p88 (Ely), MA1789. R. Meesdon, Herts. 1790-1812, V. King's Langley, Herts. 1791-1807, R. Girton, Cambs. 1807-46, R. Great Hallingbury, Essex 1812-38. Dom. Chap. to Anne, Countess of Radnor 1791; to Elizabeth, Duchess of Beaufort 1807-12. Died 9/3/1846 aged 82 [C53654] Married 16/6/1807 Maria Houblon (Hallingbury Place, Essex), with issue.

COTTON, *born* GREEN (Charles Evelyn) Born Etwall Hall, Derbys. 14/9/1782, s. Joseph Green and Elizabeth Cotton. Emmanuel, Cambridge 1799, LLB1806, dn06 (C&L), p07 (C&L). R. Dalbury, Derbys. 1807 and R. Trusley, Derbys. 1818 to death (Dalbury) 18/3/1857. Lived at Etwall Hall [C11273. Austin] Married 3/3/1828 Frances Maria Bradshaw (w) (Bradshaw Hall, Derbys., she d. leaving £450), and had issue: mappingbirmingham.blogspot.com/2012/06/portugal-house.

COTTON (Henry Calveley) Bapt. Marylebone, London 7/5/1789, s. Henry Calveley Cotton and Matilda Lockwood. Merton, Oxford 1806, BA 1810, dn12 (Lin.), MA1813, p13 (Lin.). R. Penn, Bucks. 1813-23, R. (and patron) of Hinstock, Shropshire 1820 and V. Great Ness, Shropshire 1823 (and RD) to death 9/12/1850 (or 4/10/1850?) [C10154] Married Marylebone, London 24/5/1815 Eloisa Mostyn-Owen, with issue. Brother Richard Lynch, below.

COTTON (Horace Salusbury) From Reigate, Surrey, s. Robert Salusbury Cotton. Wadham, Oxford 1791 (aged 17), BA1795, dn96 (Salis.), p97 (Salis.). S/M Cuckfield G/S, Sussex 1805; V. Desborough, Northants. 1800, Chap. Newgate Prison 1814-37 (where he detailed all 413 executions that took place there, *q.v.* online article). Died Reigate, Surrey 1846 (2nd q.) [C63147. Foster calls him Horatio] Married 1803 Marylebone, London Caroline Amelia Merriam. with son of father's name: www.bbc.co.uk/news/uk-england-london-19193935 presents him very unfavourably.

COTTON (Joseph Aldrich) Bapt. Lichfield 13/1/1762, s. William Cotton (surgeon and apothecary) and Sarah Aldrich. Christ Church, Oxford 1780, BA1784, dn85 (C&L), p87 (C&L), MA1788. V. Ellesmere, Shropshire 1790 to death 9/2/1845 [C10156] Married Ellesmere 3/3/1795 Sarah Harries, with issue.

COTTON (Nathaniel) Born Northampton 23/8/1789, s. Rev. Nathaniel Cotton, sen. and Mary Wright. Jesus, Cambridge 1808, BA1812, dn13 (Lin. for Peterb.), p14 (London [for Peterb.?]), MA1820. (succ. his father as patron and) R. Thornby, Northants. 1814 and R. Misterton, Leics. 1830 to death. Dom. Chap. to 1st Viscount Exmouth 1830. Died 29/12/1840, aged 51 [C53658] Married Leyton, Essex 24/7/1817 his cousin Charlotte Cotton, with issue.

COTTON (Richard Lynch) Born Woodcote, Oxon. 14/8/1794, s. Henry Calveley Cotton and Matilda Lockwood. Worcester, Oxford 1811, BA1815, Fellow 1816-38, dn17 (Ox.), MA1818, p18 (Ox.), tutor 1822. Provost of Worcester College, Oxford 1839-80, BD and DD1839.

Vice-Chancellor of Oxford 1852-6. V. Denchworth, Berks. 1823-39. Dom. Chap. to Earl of St Germans 1824. Died 8/12/1880 aged 86, leaving £12,000 [C26098. ODNB. Boase. DEB is long] Married St George's Hanover Square, London 18/6/1839 Charlotte Bouverie Pusey (w) (sister of Edward Bouverie Pusey, the Tractarian leader), with issue. Brother Henry Calveley, above.

COTTON (William) Born Combermere Abbey, Cheshire, s. Sir Robert Salusbury Cotton, 5th Bart., *M.P.*, and Frances Stapleton. Trinity Hall, Cambridge 1795, LLB1801, dn02 (Chester), p02 (Chester). V. Audlem, Cheshire 1802-36 [blank in ERC], PC. Burley Dam, Acton, Cheshire 1802-53 [blank in ERC], R. Hinstock, Shropshire 1810-20, R. Adderley, Shropshire 1820 to death (unm., Burley Dam) 16/6/1853 [C10158] Foster is confused.

COULCHER (William Bedell) Bapt. New Brentford, Middx. 21/5/1794, s. Rev. Martin Coulcher and Elizabeth Bedell. Emmanuel, Cambridge 1818, no degree, dn18 (Nor.), p20 (Nor.). V. Bawdsey, Suffolk 1822-51-, R. Ryburgh 1832-3, R. Bircham, Newton and Bircham Tofts 1833-5, R. Longham 1835-43, R. Whaddon, Cambs. 1843-53, PC. Bradninch, Exeter 1853-63. Died (Diss, Norfolk) 14/1/1873 aged 78, leaving £450 [C112351] Married 1/7/1823 Harriet Ann Twiss, w. issue.

COULSON (Henry Tonkin) Bapt. Penzance, Cornwall 16/12/1796, s. Henry Coulson and Margaret Tonkin. Queens', Cambridge 1814, BA1817, dn20 (Ex.), p21 (Ex.), MA1821. R. Landewednack, Cornwall 1828 and R. Ruan Major, Cornwall 1828 to death. Dom. Chap. to 2nd Earl of Minto 1828. *Drowned* 8/7/1840 aged 43 [C136731] 'An able and useful magistrate'.

COULTHURST (Edward) Born Gargrave, Craven, Yorks. 22/7/1795, s. John Coulthurst and Margaret Reed. Peterhouse, Cambridge 1814, BA 1818, dn18 (Durham), p19 (Durham). R. Linton in Craven (2nd Mediety), Yorks. 1821 to death (Machynlleth, Montgomery) 16/9/1849 [C129747]

COULTON (James) Born c.1760, s. John Coulton and Mary Hogg. [NiVoF] V. North Wootton, Norfolk 1804 to death (King's Lynn, Norfolk) 14/2/1834 aged 74 [C112354] Wife Ellen, and issue.

COURTENAY (Francis John) Bapt. Kensington, London 20/11/1800, natural s. Lady Valentia Courtenay and John Bellenden Ker Gawler (and for whose emotionally tangled lives see: edpopehistory.co.uk/entries/gawler-john-bellenden/1793-03-24-000000). Peterhouse, Cambridge 1825, dn29 (London), BA 1830, p31 (B&W for Ex). R. North Bovey, Devon 1831-59, R. Exeter St Sidwell in 1850. Died Long Marton, Westmorland 11/5/1859 aged 59, leaving £600 [C42066] Married Weyhill, Surrey 9/6/1831 Emma Camilla Kilner (w), with issue.

COURTHOPE (William) From Whiligh, Sussex, s. George Courthope (of the Middle Temple). St John's, Cambridge 1787 (aged 19), BA1791, dn91 (Win.), p92 (Chich.), MA1794. V. Plumpton, Sussex 1796, V. Brenchley, Kent 1802-47, R. Lewes St John's the Baptist, Southover, Sussex 1805-21, R. Westmeston, Sussex 1821 to death. Dom. Chap. to 2nd Earl of Chichester 1805-21. Died 29/10/1847 aged 69 [C116]

COURTNEY (John) Bapt. Beverley, Yorks. 27/6/1769, s. John Courtney, *J.P.*, and Mary Smelt. Trinity, Cambridge 1788, BA1792, dn94 (Ely for York), p95 (York), MA1795. R. Goxhill, Yorks. 1801-8, again 1818-45, V. Warlingham w. Chelsham, Surrey 1805-18, R. Sanderstead, Surrey 1818, 1821 to death. Dom. Chap to Anne Isabella, Dowager Countess Hawarden 1810. Buried 26/3/1845 aged 76 [C72519. YCO] Married (1) Winestead, Holderness, Yorks. 24/1/1810 Caroline Mary Ferrers (d.1811), with issue (2) Wanstead, Essex 29/6/1814 Sophia Elizabeth Catherine Poggenpohl ('of St Petersburg'), with further issue. Brother Septimus, below.

COURTNEY (John Classon) An Irishman. TCD, BA1820. (first) PC. Lindley, Huddersfield, Yorks. 1833-5. Then in Canada. Left the CoE and joined the [Plymouth] Brethren. In New Zealand from 1851. Died there 26/61882 aged 85 [C131019. Al.Dub.] Married Dublin 1839 Sarah --, 2s. and 7 dau. alluded to.

COURTNEY (Septimus) Born Beverley, Yorks. 25/5/1779, s. John's Courtney, *J.P.*, and

Mary Smelt. St John's, Cambridge 1796, BA 1801, MA1804, dn04 (Peterb. for York), p04 (York), Fellow 1804. R. Chesterton w. Haddon, Hunts. 1814-19, Min. Plymouth Charles 1829 to death. Dom. Chap. to 9th Marquess of Huntly 1814. Died 6/3/1843 [C53721. YCO] Married (1) 11/8/1807 Gedling, Notts. Dorothy Smelt (a clergy dau., d.1821) w. issue (2) 15/3/1831 Elizabeth Wiltshire, w. further issue. Brother John, above.

COVE (Edward, sen.) From Dunsford, Devon, s. Rev. Edward Cove. Balliol, Oxford 1794 (aged 18), BA1797, dn98 (B&W), p00 (Salis.), MA1800. R. Woolhampton, Berks. 1800-27, V. Brimpton, Berks. [blank in ERC] 1800 to death 20/2/1840 aged 64 [C34129] Clerical son, below.

COVE (Edward, jun.) Born Woolhampton, Berks. 1803, s. Rev. Edward Cove, sen. (above). Worcester, Oxford 1821, BA1825, dn30 (Lin.), p31 (Lin.). R. Thoresway, Lincs. 1831 to death 17/3/1875, leaving £2,000 [C53722]

COVENTRY (Thomas Henry, Hon.) Born Streatham, Surrey 18/9/1792, s. George William, 7th Earl of Coventry and Margaret Pitches. Christ Church, Oxford 1811, BA 1815, dn16 (Salis.), MA1827. R. Croome D'Abitot w. Pirton, Worcs. 1816-69, R. Croome Hill >< Worcs. 1827 and R. Severn Stoke, Worcs. 1833 to death. Dom. Chap. to 7th Earl of Coventry 1816-23. Died 20/8/1869 [total income, £1,060], leaving £4,000 [C91896]

COVENTRY AND LICHFIELD (Bishop of) see under **RYDER (Henry, Hon.)**

COWARD (William) Born Lowick, Lancs. St Bees adm. 1818. Literate: dn19 (Chester), p20 (Chester) [C142933]. PC. Westoe, Northumberland 1830 and PC. Harton, South Shields, Durham 1843 to death (unm.) 29/4/1853 [C129749]

COWDELL (Henry) From Ludlow, Shropshire, s. Richard Cowdell. Worcester, Oxford 1811 (aged 18), BA1816, dn16 (Heref.). R. Cold Weston, Shropshire 1816-64- [pop .36]. Died (Oreleton, Heref.) 6/6/1875 aged 82, leaving £1,500 [C103999]

COWE (James) Perhaps from Fordyce, Banff? King's College, Aberdeen 1776-80, dn85 (Lin. for London). V. Sunbury on Thames, Middx. (and RD) 1790-1839. Died 6/3/1842 [C53724] Married 1786 Elizabeth Palmer Wollaston (a clergy dau.). Kept a meteorological diary, published 1889.

COWELL (Joseph) Born Leeds 26/2/1790, s. Richard Cowell. Literate: dn20 (York), p21 (York). PC. Todmorden, Rochdale, Lancs. 1821 to death (Preston, Lancs.) 4/2/1846 [C131021. YCO] Married Tong, Yorks. 28/1/1815 Agnes Hammerton, with issue.

COWLARD (William) Bapt. Oxford 5/10/1788, s. William (of Wellington, Somerset) and Ann Cowlard. Pembroke, Cambridge 1814, dn20 (Nor.), p23 (Ex.), BA1824. PC. Laneast, Cornwall 1826, PC. Werrington, Devon 1842 to sudden death (Dolsdon, Cornwall) 17/6/1844 aged 55 [C112358] Married (1) Launceston, Cornwall 6/3/1810 Sarah Lethbridge (d.1825), with issue (2) Chelsea, London 21/6/1827 Frances Elizabeth Falkland (d.1829), with further issue (3) 4/7/1835 Sarah Phillis Clode Bradden. Foster has a different person of this name (Balliol 1798, d.1858), also PC Laneast (n.d.).

COWLING (William) Bapt. Fenstanton, Hunts. 21/11/1765, s. Peter and Mary Cowling. St John's, Cambridge 1784, BA1788, dn89 (Lin.), p90 (Lin.). MA1791. R. Wicken Bonhunt, Essex 1807-14, V. Albury, Herts. 1811 and R. Newton Blossomville, Bucks. 1814 to death. Dom. Chap. to 3rd Earl of Hardwicke 1811. Died 1846 [C53726] Married 14/12/1809 Letitia Bridget Ambrose (a clergy dau.).

COWPLAND (William) Literate. Christ's College, Cambridge 1823 (aged 24) as a Ten Year Man ('but did not follow through'). R. Acton Beauchamp, Worcs. 1828 to death. Probate granted 29/12/1854 [C120833. Possibly in YCO as born Kendal, Westmorland 14/2/1798?]

COX (Charles Henry) Born Oxford 16/11/1797, s. Richard Cox (banker and Mayor of Oxford) and Sarah Adams. Christ Church, Oxford 1816, Student [Fellow] 1816-34, BA 1820, dn20 (Ox.), p21 (Ox.), MA1822. [At Bodleian Library 1826-8] V. Oxford St Mary

Magdalen 1823-7 (res.), PC. Benson (or Bensington), Oxon. 1828-34, PC. South Littleton, Worcs. 1834-45, R. Oulton, Suffolk 1845 to death 1/10/1850 [C26129]

COX (Frederick) From Oxford, s. Charles Cox [*pleb*]. Lincoln, Oxford 1813 (aged 17), BA 1818, MA 1819, dn19 (Ely for Cant.), p20 (Chester for Cant.). H/M Aylesbury G/S 1840; R. Upper Winchendon, Bucks. 1821 to death. Chap. Aylesbury County Gaol 1834. Died Kilburn Park, Middx. 24/4/1879, leaving £16,000 [C6677] Clerical son.

COX (James) Born Allington, Dorset, s. Joseph Cox [*pleb*] and Jane Tuck. Wadham, Oxford 1789 (aged 20), BA1793, MA1796, p04 (Lin.), BD and DD1809. S/M King's Norton Free G/S, Worcs. 1806; R. Litton Cheney, Dorset 1824-33, RD of Bridport, Dorset 1832, V. Hoxne w. Denham St John's, Suffolk 1832. Died Palgrove, Suffolk 16/12/1848 [C52318] Married (1) Bristol 24/12/1794 Elizabeth Hodges (d.1812), with clerical son, below (2) Chelsea, London 3/1/1833 Ann Fisher Green.

COX (James Septimus) Born 1805, s. Rev. James Cox (above) and Elizabeth Hodges. Corpus Christi, Cambridge 1825, BA1829, dn29 (Lin.), p30 (Lin.), MA1833. PC. Harpswell, Lincs. 1830-3, (succ. his father as) R. Litton Cheney, Dorset (and Preacher throughout the Diocese of Bristol) 1833 to death there 28/11/1874, leaving £3,000 [C8174] Married 30/8/1836 Mary Ann Palmer Sweeting (w), with issue.

COX (John) From Crewkerne, Som., s. John Cox. St John's, Oxford 1805 (aged 19), migrated to Jesus, Cambridge 1806, dn09 (Ex.), p10 (B&W), LLB 1811. R. Stockland, Dorset 1812 and R. Cheddington, Dorset 1816 to death (Bath) 24/2/1846 [C34198]

COX (John) Bapt. Kingston on Thames, Surrey 1/11/1791, s. Charles William Cox and Mary Munnings. Christ's, Cambridge 1808, BA1813, dn15 (Ex. for Ely), MA1816, p17 (Ely). R. Otton Belchamp >< Essex 1820-33, V. Poslingford, Suffolk 1833-7, R. Fairstead w. Witham, 1837 to death 12/1/1863 aged 73, leaving £7,000 [C6678] Married Clare, Suffolk 13/1/1829 Mary Hughes Elwes (w), w. clerical son Charles William Cox.

COX (Richard Symes) Born Beaminster, Dorset 20/6/1794, s. Samuel Cox and Ann Symes. Exeter, Oxford 1813, BA1817, dn17 (B&W), p18 (Salis.). R. Wayford, Som. 1819, V. North Poorton, Dorset 1819 to death (Chard, Som.) 1/7/1845 [C34196] Married Seaborough, Dorset 20/7/1818 Maria Elizabeth Perkins, with issue.

COX (Robert) Born Wisbech, Cambs. St John's, Cambridge 1803, then Queens' 1804, dn06 (Win.), BA1806, p07 (Bristol for London), MA1811. R. Broughton Astley, Leics. 1807-12 (res.), PC. Bridgnorth St Leonard 1819-24 (res.), PC. East Stonehouse, Devon 1828 to death. Dom. Chap. to Marquess of Sligo. Died 1/10/1833 [C8175]

COX (Robert Albion) Bapt. Hackney, Middx. 23/11/1801, s. Robert Albion Cox and Mary Snowden. Merton, Oxford 1821, BA1826, dn26 (B&W). PC. Charminster w. Stratton, Dorset 1830, V. Montacute, Som. 1833, PC. Seavington w. Dinnington, Som. 1838, R. Hinton St George, Som. 1838. Probate granted 2/11/1846 [C42068] Married Marston Magna, Somerset 15/4/1834 Frances Williams.

COX (Thomas) Bapt. Leek Wootton, Worcs. 18/6/1788, s. Rev. Thomas Cox and Elizabeth Amy Clarke. Trinity, Oxford 1806, BA1810, dn11 (C&L), p12 (C&L), MA1813, BD &DD 1824. R. (and patron) of Atherstone on Stour, Warwicks. 1814-68, R. Oxhill, Warwicks. 1824-62. Died (Atherstone) 10/1/1868, leaving £3,000 [C10377] Widow Sarah.

COX (Thomas) [NiVoF] V. Coldridge [Coleridge in ERC], Devon 1816 to death. Probate granted 24/8/1838 [Not yet in CCEd. Foster has options]

COXE (Charles Batson) From Wroughton, Bucks., s. Rev. Richard Coxe. Merton, Oxford 1798 (aged 18), BA1802, dn02 (Salis.), p04 (Chester for Salis.), MA1810. R. East Shefford, Berks. 1804, R. Avington, Berks. 1810 to death. Dom. Chap. to 1st Viscount Anson 1806. Died Feb. 1846 aged 66 [C91898] Married 4/8/1808 Eliza Anne butler, with issue.

COXE (George) From London, s. William Coxe (physician) and Martha d'Aranda. Pembroke, Cambridge 1775, BA1780, dn83 (Ely for B&W), p96 (Lin. for Win.), MA1792. 'Travelled in Europe as a tutor. Held a living in Ireland'. PC. Lincoln St Peter in Eastgate w. St Margaret in the Close 1800-10 (res.), R. Withcall, Lincs. 1807 and R. Winchester St Michael, Wilts. 1810 to death (Twyford, Hants.) 30/7/1844 aged 88 [C53964] Married Chatham, Kent Mrs Mary (Hamilton) Lyon (a military widow), *s.p.* Jane Austen links.

COXE (Richard Charles) Bapt. Bucklebury, Berks. 25/3/1800, s. Rev. Richard and Susanna Coxe, Worcester, Oxford 1817, BA1821, Fellow 1823-5, dn23 (Ox.), MA1824, p24 (Lin. for Cant.). Chap. Archbishop Tenison's Proprietary Chapel, London (o/w St Thomas, Regent Street) [blank in ERC] 1824/9-41, V. Newcastle upon Tyne 1841-53, Archdeacon of Lindisfarne (w. V. Eglingham annexed) 1842-65, Hon. Canon of Durham Cathedral 1843-58, then Canon Residentiary 1858 [income in CR65 £1,000] to death 25/8/1865, leaving £3,000 [C26144. ODNB. Boase] Married Dover, Kent 23/6/1825 Louisa Arabella Maule (a clergy dau.), with issue: https://en.wikipedia.org/wiki/Richard_Coxe_(priest)

COXWELL (Charles) Born Ablington Manor, Birbury, Glos., s. Rev. Charles Coxwell and Mary Small. Exeter, Oxford 1788 (aged 16), BA1791, MA1794, dn94 (Glos.), p95 (Glos.). R. Dowdeswell, Glos. 1826 to death 30/8/1854 [C143037] Married Gloucester 17/6/1796 Anne Rogers, with issue. Brother, below.

COXWELL (Thomas Tracey) Born Ablington Manor, Birbury, Glos. 14/8/1778, s. Rev. Charles Coxwell and Mary Small. Worcester, Oxford 1796, then Pembroke, BA1799, dn01 (Glos.), MA1803, p03 (Glos.). V. Great Marlow, Bucks. 1811, PC. Eastleach Turville, Glos. 1807-51-, R. Horton, Bucks. 1850. Died 8/12/1854 [C26146] Brother, above. Surrogate.

COYLE (Miles) Bapt. Ludlow, Shropshire 14/3/1779, s. Miles and Ann Coyle. Worcester, Oxford 1797, BA1800, dn01 (Glos.), MA1803, p03 (Heref.). PC. Brimfield, Heref. 1807-32, R. Monnington on Wye, Heref. 1825-32, V. Gladestry, Radnor 1831 and V. Blockley, Worcs. 1831 to death 23/10/1832 (CCEd thus) [C104004] Clerical son, also Miles.

COYTE (James) Bapt. Ipswich, Suffolk 12/4/1796, s. Rev. James Coyte, sen. and Ann Parker. Caius, Cambridge 1814, BA1818, dn19 (Nor.), p20 (Nor.), MA1822. PC. Farnham, Suffolk 1827-40, R. Boyton, Suffolk 1837-40, R. Polstead, Suffolk 1840 to death there 28/5/1886 aged 90, leaving £32,073-9s-1d. [C112361] Married Great Yarmouth, Norfolk 11/12/1823 Mary Anne Reynolds, with issue.

CRABTREE (James) Bapt. Newchurch in Rossendale, Lancs. 23/3/1755, s. James Crabtree and Sarah Cunliffe. Schoolmaster. Literate: dn84 (C&L), p86 (C&L). V. Laughton-en-le-Morthen, Yorks. 1818-35, PC. Anston cum Membris, Worksop, Notts. 1818 and PC. Thorpe St John's, Notts. 1818 to death 13/1/1835 aged 80 [C10382] Married (1) Newchurch 24/8/1776 Ellen Ashworth ('below age', she d.1787), with issue (2) Gawsworth, Cheshire 31/5/1797 Edna Rathbone (d.1816), with further issue.

CRABTREE (William) From Halifax, Yorks., s. John Crabtree [*pleb*]. University, Oxford 1803 (aged 18), BA1807, MA1810, tutor 1816, Fellow to 1821. R. Checkendon, Oxon. 1820 to death (Greenwich, Kent) 22/10/1864, leaving £4,000 [C26147]

CRACROFT (John) Born Dawlish, Devon 4/10/1784, s. John Cracroft (Hackthorne, Lincs.) and Penelope Anne Weston. BNC, Oxford 1803, BA1807, dn07 (Salis.), p09 (Ex. for London), MA1812. Chaplain to the Forces 1812-42 [invalided home from the Peninsula; on half-pay from 1819]. R. West Keal, Lincs. 1821-2 (non-res.), V. Hackthorne 1821-7 (his father owning the Hackthorne estate from 1797), R. Ripley, Yorks. 1822-42. Died and buried Neuwied-on-the-Rhine 21/9/1842 [C53969. Bennett2] Married (1) London 22/12/1807 Eliza Lewis (d.1811), 1 dau. (2) Lincoln 10/11/1814 Jane Brown, 6 ch.

CRAGG (Richard) Bapt. Dent, Yorks. 17/9/1768, s. Joseph (a grazier) and Jane Cragg. St John's, Cambridge 1790, BA1794, dn94 (York), p96 (Lin.). R. Wymondham, Leics. 1823 (and S/M Wymondham G/S) to death 27/2/1849 aged 80 [C53971. YCO]

CRAIG (John Kershaw) Born St Pancras, London 22/10/1801, s. Walter (or William)

Marshall Craig and Elizabeth Worrall. Magdalen Hall, Oxford 1824, BA1828, dn28 (Win. for York), p29 (York). PC. Oulton, Leeds 1830-5 [blank in ERC], PC. then V. Burley, Hants. 1839-86 (where he was charged by a parishioner with performing his duties in an irregular manner 1848). Died there 17/9/1889, leaving £181-3s-2d. [C72611. Boase. YCO] Married Brixton, Surrey 6/9/1831 Mary Tudor Phillips, with 4 clerical sons.

CRAINE (Edward) Born IoM 1785, s. Robert Craine and Elinor Gick. Literate. V. Onchan, IoM 1810 to death 26/4/1847 aged 61 ('after an illness of 6 months') [C7258. Gelling] Married Onchan 1/11/1812 Isabella Moore. Manx speaker.

CRAKELT (Isaac) Probably bapt. Kendal, Westmorland 2/10/1768, s. Isaac Crakelt and Elizabeth Dockray. Literate: dn94 (Car.), p95 (Car.). H/M Ambleside G/S, Westmorland 1795-1810; General Preacher throughout the Diocese of Carlisle 1794, PC. Newlands Chapel, Crosthwaite, Cumberland 1795 (only), PC. Skelton, Yorks. 1810-33 and PC. Marton le Moor, Yorks. 1811-33 (res.). Died Marton le Moor 9/1/1846 aged 78 [C5788] Wife Elizabeth, with clerical son.

CRAMER (John Anthony) Born Mittoden, Switzerland c.1793, s. John Anthony Cramer. Christ Church, Oxford 1811, Student [Fellow] 1811-24, BA1814, MA1817, dn18 (Ox.), p19 (Ox.), BD1830, DD1831. Principal New Inn Hall, Oxford (which he rebuilt) 1831-47. Regius Professor of Modern History, Oxford 1842-8. PC. Binsey, Oxon 1822. Dean of Carlisle 1844 to death (Scarborough, Yorks.) 24/8/1848 [C26150] Married Childwall, Liverpool 27/5/1823 Harriet Ashton, w. issue.

CRANE (Robert Prentice) Bapt. Colchester, Essex 7/5/1856, s. Robert Crane and Mary Rachell Pollett. Clare, Cambridge 1802, BA 1808, dn09 (Salis. for London), p10 (London), MA1811. V. Great Tolleshunt (o/w Tolleshunt Major), Essex 1810-56, V. Heybridge St Andrew, Essex 1833 to death. British Chap. at Rio de Janeiro for 15 years; Dom. Chap. to 1st Baron Stuart de Rothesay 1833. Died 21/10/1856 aged 72 [C72612] Married Colchester 14/4/1812 Jane Gurr, w. issue. Port. online.

CRANE (Samuel) Bapt. Worcester 7/4/1792, s. John Crane and Elizabeth Harris. Magdalen, Oxford 1810, dn18 (Nor.), BA1820, p21 (Chester for C&L). Min. Bordesley Holy Trinity, Aston, Warwicks. 1823-[41]. Died c.1841 [C10390]

CRAWFORD (William Henry) Born Haughley Park, Stowmarket, Suffolk, s. William and Elizabeth Dorothea Crawford. Peterhouse, Cambridge 1809, BA1813, dn14 (Peterb.), MA 1816, p16 (Ely for Cant.). Fellow 1816-64-. V. Sandwich St Clement, Kent 1826-30, V. Linsted, Kent 1830-9. Died Haughley Park 18/4/1868 aged 77, leaving £80,000 [C6680] Married Bath 1853 (3rd q.) Laura Taylor (a clergy dau., of Biddlesham, Som., 35 years his junior), s.p.

CRAWLEY (Charles) Born Flaxley,m Glos. 25/4/1756, s. Thomas Crawley and Susanna Lloyd. Balliol, Oxford 1776, dn82 (Heref.), p82 (Heref.), BCL1786. V. Broadway, Worcs. 1784 and R. Stow Nine Churches, Northants. 1789 to death 4/1/1849 aged 93 [C104040] Married Exeter, Devon 12/4/1784 Mary Gibbs, with issue. Doubtless related to the man below.

CRAWLEY (Charles) Born Flaxley Abbey, Glos. 28/11/1780, s. Sir Thomas Boevey Crawley, 2nd Bart. and Ann Savage (a clergy dau.). Pembroke, Oxford 1799, BA1804, dn05 (Win.), p06 (Win.). PC. Flaxley 1808, V. Hartpury, Glos. 1838 (and Hon. Canon of Gloucester Cathedral and RD) to death 17/1/1856 aged 75 [C72615] Married Cornwood, Devon 30/8/1811 Catherina Yonge (a clergy dau.), with clerical son. Brother John Lloyd (below). J.P., D.L. Brother Jophn Lloyd, below. Doubtless related to the man above.

CRAWLEY (Edmund Jones) From Llanbeblig, Carnarvon, s. Edmund Jones. Jesus, Oxford 1809 (aged 17), BA1813, dn14 (Ex.), p15 (Ex.), MA1818. PC. Walcot Holy Trinity, Bath 1822, Prebend of Taunton in Wells Cathedral 1840 to death Bath 31/1/1871 aged 79, leaving £18,000 [C42069. Foster corrected]

CRAWLEY (John Lloyd) Born Flaxley Abbey, Glos. 21/2/1775, s. Sir Thomas Boevey Crawley, 2nd Bart. and Ann Savage (a clergy dau.). St Mary's Hall, Oxford 1794, BA1798, then King's, Cambridge, MA1801, R. (and patron) of Heyford, Northants. 1800 and R.

Holdenby, Northants. 1809 to death (Swalcliffe Park, Oxon.) 18/10/1850 aged 75 [C110108] Married Glos. 21/4/1806 his cousin Anne Crawley (a clergy dau.), 3 clerical sons. Brother Charles, above.

CRAWLEY (Richard, sen.) Born Smyrna, Turkey 19/12/1756, s. Samuel Crawley (British Consul there) and Maria Dunant (who remarried Baron de Hochepied). University, Oxford 1775, BA1779, dn80 (Ox. for Win.), MA1782, p82 (Roch.). R. Rotherfield, Sussex 1785-1837, V. Frant, Sussex 1784-1805-Sussex [net income £1,454], R. St Mildred Poultry w. St Mary Colechurch, City of London 1807 to death. Dom. Chap. to Wilhelmina Catherina, Baroness King 1784; to 1st Earl Whitworth 1807. Died Rotherfield 2/11/1837 aged 80 [C1774] Married 12/7/1796 Mary Clutton, 3s. (one clerical s. of same name below) and 7 dau.

CRAWLEY (Richard, jun.) Born 31/5/1810, s. Rev. Richard Crawley, sen. (above) and Mary Clutton. Trinity, Cambridge 1810, then Magdalene, BA1814, Fellow and tutor 1814-29, dn15 (Ely), p16 (Ely), MA1817. V. Steeple Ashton, Wilts. 1828 (and Prebend of Salisbury Cathedral 1843) to death (unm.) 9/12/1869, leaving £16,000 [C6681]

CREED (Henry Knowles) Bapt. Hackney, London 7/5/1785, s. Henry Creed. Literate: dn16 (Chester for Nor.), p16 (Chester for Nor.), then Trinity, Cambridge 1816 (a Ten Year Man, BD1826). V. Corse, Glos. 1828 to death (Sudbrook Park, Petersham, Surrey) 26/10/1855 aged 70 [C72616] Married Chelsea, London 2/10/1813 Catherine Herries (a military dau., d.1818), w. issue (and another possible marriage 1836). J.P.

CREGOE (John) Bapt. Gerrans, Cornwall 10/10/1755, s. Edward Cregoe. Exeter, Oxford 1775, no degree, dn80 (Heref.), p81 (Heref.). R. St Ewe, Cornwall 1777. Buried 10/3/1836 aged 80 [C104043]

CREIGHTON (Archibald) Bapt. Yarborough, Lincs. 20/1/1789, s. Rev. John and Ann Creighton. Lincoln, Oxford 1807, BA1811, dn12 (Win. for C&L), p14 (C&L), Fellow 1816-23, MA1817. V. Stallingborough, Lincs. 1830 to death 4/3/1871 aged 82, leaving £450 [C10395. Kaye] Married (2) Grimsby, Yorks. 27/9/1866 Mary Ann Kirkland, w. issue.

CREMER (Cremer) Bapt. Cringleford, Norfolk 5/7/1795, s. Cremer Cremer (formerly Woodrow), Beeston Hall, Norfolk and Ann Buckle. St John's, Cambridge 1812, BA1818, dn18 (Nor.), p27 (B&W). R. Runton w. Aylmerton >< Norfolk 1827-38, R. Felbrigg w. Metton, Norfolk 1827-38, R. Beeston Regis, Norfolk 1837 to death 6/5/1867 aged 71, leaving £3,000 [C42071] Married Felbrigg 22/7/1829 Marianne Charlotte Wyndham (Cromer Hall, Norfolk), with issue.

CRESPIN (Abraham John) Bapt. Dunstable, Beds. 9/9/1771, s. Daniel Crespin and Barbara Filkes. Trinity, Cambridge 1788, BA1793, dn93 (Ely), p97 (Lin.). V. Renhold, Beds. 1798 and V. Ravensden, Beds. 1817 to death (a widower) 25/12/1850 aged 79 [C53979] Married (1) Renhold 31/3/1807 Mrs Mary (Newman) Cuming, of Great Barford (d.1832) (2) Bedford 28/11/1834 Mary Nash.

CRESSWELL (Daniel John) From Wakefield, Yorks., s. Rev. Daniel Cresswell. Trinity, Cambridge 1792, BA1797, Fellow 1799, MA 1800, p00 (Peterb.), DD1823, etc. PC. Cambridge St Mary the Great 1817-25, PC. Enfield St Andrew, Middx. [net income £1,174] 1823 to death 21/3/1844 [C6682. ODNB] Married Enfield 1827 Anne Thompson. J.P. Middx. 1823. F.R.S. (1823) for mathematical work.

CRESSWELL (Edward) Bapt. Nottingham 18/10/1757, s. of Samuel Cresswell (owner of the *Nottingham Journal*, pleb) and Rebecca Wilkinson. Christ Church, Oxford 1774, BA 1778, dn80 (C&L), p82 (Lin. for York), then St Catharine's, Cambridge 1806, MA1806. V. Lenton, Notts. 1803 and R. Radford, Notts. 1803 to death (Basford, Notts.) 29/4/1840 aged 88 [C10398] Married Newark, Notts. 2/2/1797 Sara Gunthorpe, with issue.

CRESSWELL (Francis) Born Babworth, Notts. 26/4/1763 (CCEd thus). Clare, Cambridge 1780, BA1785, Fellow 1785, dn86 (C&L), MA1788, p92 (Nor.), BD1796, Tutor. V. Duxford, Cambs. 1789-1806, V. Great Waldingfield, Suffolk 1807 to death 17/11/1841 aged 79 [C10397]

CRESSWELL (Henry) Born Bibury House, Bibury, Glos. 14/3/1787, s. Estcourt Cresswell, *M.P.*, and Mary Gregory. Wadham, Oxford 1804 (aged 17), BA1809, dn10 (Salis.). V. Creech St Michael, Som. 1813 to death 2/8/1849 [C34221] Married Taunton, Som. 14/3/1815 Sophia Smith, w. issue. Brother Sackville, below.

CRESSWELL (Oswald Joseph) Born Charlton, Kent, s. Francis Easterby (*q.v.* ODNB) and Frances Dorothea Cresswell. Corpus Christi, Oxford 1820, BA1824, dn26 (Durham), p27 (Ely for Durham), MA1827. V. Seaham, Durham 1827-43, R. Hanworth, Middx. 1846 to death 7/6/1871 aged 68, leaving £5,000 [C129519] Married Brompton, London 10/1/1837 Anna Maria Strong (a clergy dau.), with issue. In USA 1831.

CRESSWELL (Sackville) Bapt. Bibury House, Bibury, Glos. 14/5/1785, s. Estcourt Cresswell, *M.P.*, and Mary Gregory. Pembroke, Oxford 1802, SCL, dn08 (Glos.), p09 (Glos.). V. ('Commissary') Bibury w. Winson 1809 to death 7/4/1843 [C143048] Married Bibury 29/4/1812 Emily Jane Tombs. Brother Henry, above.

CREWE (Charles) Bapt. Barthomley, Cheshire 25/6/1779, s. Rev. Randulph Crewe and Frances Glynne. BNC, Oxford 1797, BA1801, MA1804, dn07 (Chester), p08 (Chester). V. Longdon, Worcs. 1815 to death 26/5/1864, leaving £14,000 [C120837] Related to Offley, below.

CREWE (Henry Robert) Born Calke Abbey, Derbys. 4/9/1801, s. Sir Henry Crewe (formerly Harpur), 7th Bart. and his former mistress Ann (Nanny) Hawkins (a lady's maid, 'an unfortunate connection'). Trinity, Cambridge 1820, BA1826, dn27 (Lin.), p28 (C&L), MA 1830. R. Swarkestone, Derbys. 1828-30 (res.), R. Stanton by Bridge, Derbys. 1828-30 (res.), R. Breadsall, Derbys. 1830 to death 29/8/1865, leaving £1,500 [C10400. Boase] Married Bladingwood, Staffs. 25/9/1827 Frances Caroline Jenney, with clerical son.

CREWE (Offley) Bapt. Warmingham, Cheshire 26/2/1752, s. Rev. Randulph Crewe and Ann Read. BNC, Oxford 1768, BA1772, dn75 (Chester), MA1776, p77 (Chester). R. Barthomley, Cheshire 1777-82 (res.), R. Warmingham 1777-82, R. Muckleston (o/w Muxton), Shropshire 1782-1830, R. Astbury, Cheshire [net income £1,485] 1782 to death (Muckleston) 19/2/1836 aged 71 [C10414] Married Warmingham 15/8/1779 Harriet Assheton Smith, with issue. Related to Charles, above.

CREWE (Willoughby) Bapt. Richmond, Surrey 4/4/1792, s. Maj.-Gen. Richard Crewe and Milborough Alpress ('a West Indian dawdling beauty', *divorced* 1802). Christ Church, Oxford 1810, then St Alban's Hall, p15 (Chester), p16 (Chester), BCL1819. R. Warmingham, Cheshire 1816 [income £1,000], R. Barthomley, Cheshire 1819-50, R. Muckleston, Shropshire 1836, R. Astbury, Cheshire 1836 to death. Dom. Chap. to 5th Earl Ferrers 1777; to the Bishop of Peterborough 1782. Died 9/4/1850 aged 58 [C154986. LBSO] Married Southampton 30/7/1816 Catherine Harvey, with issue.

CREYKE (Stephen) Born East Stonehouse, Devon 24/9/1796, s. Richard (Governor of the Royal Naval Hospital Plymouth) and Ann Creyke. Corpus Christi, Oxford 1812, BA1816, MA1820 and Fellow 1821-3, dn20 (York), p21 (York). V. Warter, Yorks. 1826, V. Snaith, Yorks. 1828, V. South Cave, Yorks. 1828, V. Ergham, Yorks. 1829, PC. Marton cum Moxby (o/w Marton in Galtres), Yorks. 1830, V. Wiggington, Yorks. 1834-44, V. Sutton on the Forest, Yorks. 1837-44, Prebend of South Newbold in York Minster 1841-83, Canon Residentiary 1857-73, R. Beeford, Notts. 1844-65, Archdeacon of York 1845-66 (res.), R. Bolton Percy, Yorks. 1865 [total income in CR65 £1,040] to death 11/12/1883 aged 87, leaving £127,436-14s-10d. [C131032. Boase. YCO] Married York 5/9/1823 Sarah Hotham, with issue. Portrait online.

CRICK (Thomas) Bapt. Little Thurlow, Suffolk 1/6/1801, s. Rev. Thomas sen. and Mary Crick. St John's, Cambridge 1818, BA 1823, dn24 (Nor.), p25 (Nor.), Fellow 1825-48, MA1826, Tutor 1831-46, BD1833, incorporated at Oxford 1834. President St John's College, Oxford 1839-46. (succ. his father as) R. Little Thurlow 1825-48, R. Staplehurst, Kent 1848 [income £1,202] to death there 1/6/1876, leaving £20,000 [C112372. Boase] Married Eastbourne, Sussex 1848 (3rd q.) Frances Catherine Cooper (w) (a clergy dau.), with issue.

CRIGAN (Alexander) Bapt. Liverpool 22/12/1780, s. Rt. Rev. Claudius Crigan (Bishop of Sodor and Man, an Irishman) and Mary Crump (dau. of a West Indian slave owner). MD (?) 1803. Literate. R. Long Marston, Ainsty of York 1821-6 (res.), R. Escrick, Yorks. 1826-[48], V. Skipwith w. Riccall, Yorks. 1848 to death (Sidmouth, Devon) 25/1/1863, leaving £1,000. Married Kensington, London 2/2/1821 Mary Smelt (dau. Lt.-Governor, IoM) (w), w. issue.

CRIPPS ([Richard] Henry) Bapt. Cirencester, Glos. 5/12/1788, s. Joseph Cripps and Elizabeth Harrison. Merton, Oxford 1805, BA 1809, dn11 (Salis.), MA1812. V. Preston All Saints, Glos. 1817 and V. Stonehouse, Glos. 1826 to death 7/11/1861, leaving £9,000 [C91961] Married 7/7/1812 Judith Lawrence, w. issue.

CRIPPS (Thomas) Born Witney, Oxon. 26/8/1763, s. Thomas Cripps and Ann Morris. Lincoln, Oxford 1782, BA1786, dn86 (Lin.), p88 (Salis), MA1790. H/M Witney Free G/S, Oxon. 1802; 'Perpetual V'. Asthall, Oxon. 1806 to death 10/3/1834 (CCEd thus) [C26185] Married (1) Warminster, Wilts. 24/1/1791 Elizabeth Phillipa Hill (d.1792 in childbed) (2) Sarsden, Oxon. 12/7/1813 Ann Cauley Saunder, w. further issue.

CROBY (George) [MA but NiVoF] R. Bond-leigh (o/w Bundeligh), Devon 1832-42-. Died? [Not yet in CCEd] Surname not in FreeBMD. Problem man.

CROCKETT (Robert) From Church Eaton, Staffs., s. Henry Crockett. BNC, Oxford 1791 (aged 18), BA1795, MA1797, dn98 (C&L), p99 (C&L). R. Marton in Craven, Yorks. 1804-10 (res.), then 1816-22 (res.), R. Nailstone, Leics. 1821-[52]. Died? [C10415]

CROFT (James) Born Rowley, Yorks. 4/7/1784, s. Rev. Robert Croft and Elizabeth Bowes. Peterhouse, Cambridge 1802, BA1807, dn09 (York), p10 (York), MA1812. R. Ingold-mells, Lincs. 1810-12 (res.), R. Saltwood w. Hythe, Kent (and Preacher throughout the Diocese of Canterbury) 1812, R. Great Chart, Kent 1814-18, 3rd Prebend of Ely Cathedral 1815-32 (res.), R. Cliffe at Hoo, Kent [net income £1,297] 1818-69, 4th Prebend of Canterbury Cathedral 1822 and Archdeacon of Canterbury 1825 to death. 'Entrusted with the care of' the Hospitals [almshouses] of St Nicholas Horbledown, Kent (1787-1803) and St John's Northgate, Canterbury (1827). Dom. Chap. to 4th Earl Fitzwilliam 1812. Died 9/5/1869 [his total income in CR65 £3,205] [C5408. Boase. YCO] Married 5/10/1812 Charlotte Manners-Sutton (dau. of an Abp of Canterbury), with issue. J.P. East Kent. Brothers Stephen, and Thomas Hutton, below.

CROFT (John) Bapt. Richmond, Yorks. 29/8/1791, s. George Croft. Trinity, Cambridge 1809, BA1814, then Christ's, Fellow 1816-39, MA1817, dn19 (Salis.), p19 (Nor.), etc. R. Fen Drayton, Cambs. 1828-35, R. Eaton Bishop, Heref. 1838, V. Catterick, Yorks. 1840 to death. Chap. to Archbishop of York. Died 13/1/1869, leaving £4,000 [C91962] 'A good man of business', and a university reformer.

CROFT (Stephen) Born Rowley, Yorks. 14/8/1794, s. Rev. Robert Croft and Elizabeth Bowes. Trinity, Cambridge 1812, BA1817, dn20 (Nor.), p20 (Ely for Nor.), MA1821. R. Ipswich St Mary Stoke, Suffolk 1820 (and RD) to death 23/6/1868, leaving £25,000 [C6683] Married 1/1/1836 Georgina, dau. Sir Cornelius Cuyler, 1st Bart., with issue. Brothers James, and Thomas Hutton, here.

CROFT (Thomas Hutton) Born Aldborough Hall, Boroughbridge. Yorks. 19/8/1797, s. Rev. Robert Nicholas Croft (Prebend of York) and Elizabeth Bowes. Trinity, Cambridge 1816, dn22 (York), p22 (Durham for York), BA 1823, MA 1827. V. Stillington, Yorks. 1822, V. Hutton Buscell (o/w Bushell), Yorks. 1827 (and Prebend of Stillington in York Minster 1831, and part RD of Ridall) to death (London) 23/6/1873 aged 75, leaving £45,000 [C26192. YCO] Married Sept. 1828 Eliza Mary Thompson (of Kirby Hall, Yorks.), with issue. J.P. Brothers James, and Stephen, above.

CROFTS (Daniel) Born Lewes, Sussex c.1781, s. Peter Guerin Crofts and Sarah Strudwick. Christ's, Cambridge 1804 (aged 24), dn08 (Win. for Peterb.), BA1809, p10 (Peterb.), MA1813. R. Shelton, Beds. 1813 to death 11/4/1866, leaving £45,000 [C54047] Married Leighton Bromswold, Hunts. 13/10/1808 Mary Russel. Brother Peter Guerin Crofts, below.

CROFTS (Henry) Born North Grimston, Yorks. 18/4/1809, s. Rev. William Crofts and Dorothea Carr. University, Oxford 1826, BA 1830, dn33 (Ely for York), p33 (Glos. for York). R. Linton (1st Mediety), Skipton, Yorks. 1833-55 [blank in ERC] Died Munich 23/4/1857 aged 47. Probate granted 2/6/1885 [*sic*], leaving £631-5s-0d. [C131036. YCO] Married Burnley, Lancs. 16/10/1855 Elizabeth Somervell (w).

CROFTS (John) From Bristol, s. John Crofts. Christ Church, Oxford 1785 (aged 18), BA1789, dn90 (Cant.), p91 (Glos. for Cant.), MA1792. Curate Marylebone St Paul's Chapel, London 1803, R. Great Berkhampstead, Herts. 1810 to death 1851 (1st q.) [C54050]

CROFTS (Peter Guerin) Bapt. Hertford 2/3/1775, s. Rev. Peter Guerin Crofts, sen. (V. Lewes, Sussex) and Sarah Strudwick. Queens', Cambridge 1794, BA1798, MA1813. V. Lewes St John's w. Lewes sub Castro 1800 to death (South Malling, Sussex) 16/7/1859 aged 84, leaving £30,000 [C72617. Venn is confused] Married (1) Lewes 20/1/1812 Harriet Campion (of Oporto, Portugal, she d.1813), 1 ch. (2) Little Horsted, Sussex 30/4/1816 Elizabeth Frederica Law (w), with issue. Brother Daniel, above.

CROKER (Frederick) From Liskeard, Cornwall, s. Richard Croker. Exeter, Oxford 1790 (aged 18), dn94 (Ox.), BA1794, p95 (London). V. Lowdham w. Petistree, Suffolk 1807 (w. S/M Lavenham, Suffolk 1816) and V. Goxhill, Lincs. 1808 to death 14/8/1834 (CCEd thus) [C26190]

CROMPTON (Thomas) Bapt. Walpole, Norfolk 27/6/1758, s. John (Halesworth, Suffolk) and Rebecca Crompton. Merton, Oxford 1781, dn84 (Ox.), BA1786, p86 (Nor.), MA1788. R. South Bergh (or Southburgh), Norfolk 1802-28, R. Craneworth w. Letton, Norfolk 1802-32 (res.), R. Hackford, Norfolk 1832-[38]. Died St Pancras, London 8/8/1838 [C26191] Married Elizabeth Foster (a clergy dau.).

CROOK (Charles) From Bath, s. Charles (doctor and alderman) and Ann Crook. Oriel, Oxford 1806 (aged 18), BA1809, p11 (B&W), MA1812. V. Bath St Peter and St Paul (Abbey Church), etc. 1815 and Prebend of Combe X111 in Wells Cathedral 1832 to death. Chap. in Ordinary 1818. Died 2/12/1837, aged 49 (36 clergy at his funeral) [C34251] Married St James's, Westminster, London 23/11/1821 Charlotte Mary Worthington (dau. of a barrister).

CROOK (Henry Simon Charles) Born Bath, s. Henry and Sarah Crook. Lincoln, Oxford 1825 (aged 19), BA1828, dn28 (B&W), p29 (B&W), MA1833, incorporated at Cambridge 1859. PC. Walcot St Saviour, Bath 1832, V. Upavon, Wilts. 1840-70. Inspector of Schools 1860-70. Died 4/8/1884, leaving £6,760-16s-7d. [C42083] Married (1) Walcot 6/10/1836 Margaret Catherine Douce (d.1840) (2) Notting Hill, London 3/12/1862 Janet Macdowall. *J.P.* Wilts.

CROOME (John) Bapt. Cirencester, Glos. 12/11/1778, s. Robert Croome and Margaret Bennett. St Mary Hall, Oxford 1801, BA1805, dn05 (Peterb.), p06 (Peterb.), MA1808. R. Bourton on the Water, Glos. 1816 to death 9/4/1834 (CCEd says 26/9/1834) [C110114] Married Stratton, Glos. 1808 Anne Matilda Daubeney, with issue.

CROPLEY (Edward Hatch) Born Witchford, Cambs. 1801, s. Edward Cropley (farmer) and Kezia Hatch. Sidney Sussex, Cambridge 1820, then Trinity, BA1825, dn25 (London), p26 (London). MA1828. PC. Wicken, Cambs. 1826 (a family living) to death 31/12/1837 aged 68 [C54062]

CROSBY (Robert) Bapt. Kirkby Thore, Appleby, Westmorland 30/12/1770, s. Robert and Hannah Crosby. Queen's, Oxford 1789, BA1793, dn96 (Salis.), MA1797. PC. Haggerston St Mary, Shoreditch, London 1827 to death 31/12/1837 aged 68 [C91964]

CROSLAND (John) Born Holbeck, Leeds, s. Thomas Crossland (merchant). Magdalene, Cambridge 1820 (aged 20), BA1824, dn24 (St David's for Ely), p25 (Ely), Fellow, MA1827. PC. Grainsthorpe, Lincs. 1830-74. Died Leeds 10/7/1883. No will traced [C6685]

CROSS (Joseph) From Bristol, s. Thomas Cross. Magdalen Hall, Oxford 1812 (aged 18), BA1816, dn17 (B&W), p18 (Glos.), MA1819. V. Merriott, Som. 1832 to death 1855 (3rd q.) [C42084] Married (1) Clapham, Surrey Anne

Hadley (d.1842) (2) Langport, Som. 1846 (4th q.) Caroline Mary Richardson, with issue.

CROSS (Samuel) Bapt. Wisbech, Cambs. 26/10/1763, s. Edward Cross and Sarah Massey. Peterhouse, Cambridge 1782, BA1787, dn87 (Peterb.), p93 (Nor. for Peterb.), Fellow 1798, MA1790. V. Hunstanton, Norfolk 1791-1845. Died 15/5/1847 aged 84 [C99771]

CROSSE (Edward) Born Cullompton, Devon 27/7/1750, s. John (a lawyer) and Mary Crosse (and brother of Richard Crosse, the miniature painter). Sidney, Cambridge 1774, BA1776, dn76 (B&W), p78 (B&W). S/M Colchester G/S 1806; R. Tolland, Som. 1780-1835, V. Pawlett, Som. 1789-1827, R. Mount Bures, Essex 1812-18 (res.), PC. Leyer de la Hey, Essex 1826, PC. Berechurch, Essex 1826 and R. Kingsdon, Som. 1827 to death 5/6/1835 (CCEd says 10/10/1835) [C34253]

CROSSE (John Dudley Oland) Born Bridgwater, Somerset, s. John Webber Crosse and Eliza Lawrence Reeder. Exeter, Oxford 1822 (aged 18), BA1826, dn27 (B&W), p27 (B&W), MA1830. V. Pawlett, Som. 1827 to death 12/7/1875, leaving £1,500. Inspector of Schools 1871 [C42087] Married Tiverton, Devon 23/9/1834 Margaret Jane Brown (a clergy dau.), with issue.

CROSSE (John Thomas Godsalve) Bapt. Newcastle upon Tyne 6/8/1797, s. John Crosse Godsalve (later Crosse) and Mary Sutherwood. Wadham, Oxford 1818, migrated to Jesus, Cambridge 1820, BA1824, dn26 (London), p26 (London). V. Rainham, Essex 1826 to death 2/10/1846 aged 48 [C116843 - not Godalve] Married by 1833 Eliza Morris, with issue.

CROSSMAN (George Brickdale) Born West Monkton, Somerset 18/7/1791, s. Rev. George Crossman and Elizabeth Brickdale. Magdalen, Oxford 1812, BA1814, MA1814, dn14 (B&W), p15 (B&W). R. Blagdon, Som. 1815-19, PC. Leighland, Som. 1819. Lived in Florence many years, dying there 27/2/1854, leaving £2,000 (as a layman) [C34262] Married Ann Oakes, 2 dau.
genforum.genealogy.com › Surnames › Crossman Family Genealogy Forum

CROUCH (Isaac) Bapt. Bradford-on-Avon, Wilts. 25/4/1756, s. of Isaac William Crouch and Elizabeth Anne Newton. St Edmund Hall, Oxford 1774, BA1777, dn78 (Ox. for Wor.), p80 (Ox. for Salis.), MA1780, Chap. Merton 1796-1817. R. Narborough, Leics. 1814 to death 30/10/1835 (CCEd says 6/12/1835) [C26194. DEB is long] Married (1) 1787 Jane -- (2) *c.*1830 Mrs Mary Anne Hancock; *s.p.*

CROUGHTON (Robert Fleetwood) Born Battersea, Surrey 29/11/1797, s. Samuel Croughton and Jane Fleetwood. Jesus, Cambridge 1818, BA1822, dn22 (Lin.), p23 (Lin.), MA1854. Chap. of the Donative of Little Wymonsbury, Herts. 1822, V. Melton Mowbray, Leics. 1839 to death. Chap. of the Newmarket Poor Law Union 1859. Died (Newmarket, Cambs.) 11/6/1866 aged 68, leaving £7,000 [C54230] Married Aston, Herts. 3/6/1822 Sarah Crooke Godfrey (w).

CROWE (Henry) Bapt. Stoke Ferry, Norfolk 24/3/1769, s. Rev. Henry Crowe (R. Burnham Deepdale, Norfolk). Caius, Cambridge 1785, BA 1790, dn91 (Lin. for Nor.), p93 (Nor.), then Clare, Fellow 1793-1800, MA1794. V. St Nicholas at Wade, Kent 1808-9, V. Buckingham 1808 (non-res. for 32 years 'due to ill-health') to death (London) 18/12/1851 aged 83 [C54232]

CROWTHER (James) Probably from Kingston on Thames, Surrey. Jesus, Cambridge 1816, BA1820, MA1824. V. Kingsbury Episcopi, Som. 1820 to death 7/9/1849 [C34266]. But see also a James Crowther, of Trinity, Cambridge as only one J.C. occurs in the *Clergy List* for 1846 and 1849.

CROWTHER (Thomas) Born Thornton in Craven, Yorks. 10/7/1794, s. of James Crowther (a weaver) and Elizabeth Browne. Literate: dn21 (York), p22 (York). PC. Halifax St John's in the Wilderness (o/w Briers Chapel) 1822 to death 18/11/1860, leaving £600 [C131043. YCO. BBV] Married Thornton in Craven 6/1/1815 Phoebe Wilkinson (w), with issue.

CRUMBY see under CUMBY

CRUMP (Charles Collins) Bapt. Worcester 20/7/1792, s. Richard Crump and Elizabeth

Roberts. Exeter, Oxford 1811, BA1814, dn15, p16. R. Halford, Warwicks. 1826-[59]. Died Ilfracombe, Devon 29/5/1876, leaving £14,000 [C120841] Married Ludlow, Shropshire 5/3/1823 SarahWade Browne, with issue.

CRUTTENDEN (William Cruttenden) Born Esher, Surrey 3/7/1776, s. William Courtenay Cruttenden (an army officer) and Ann Thurston. Sidney, Cambridge 1795, BA1799, MA1802, dn03 (Peterb.), p04 (Ely), Fellow to 1806, Tutor. PC. Macclesfield Christ Church, Cheshire 1811-28 (res.), R. Normanton, Lincs. 1821-9, PC. Macclesfield St Michael 1828-47. R. Alderley, Cheshire 1847 to death 24/10/1863 aged 87, leaving £25,000 [C54236] Married Bury St Edmunds 13/6/1806 Theophila Mills (a clergy dau.), with issue. J.P. and local worthy.

CRUTTWELL (Richard) Bapt. Sherborne, Dorset 17/12/1776, s. William Cruttwell and Martha Wickham. Lincoln, Oxford 1796, then Exeter, dn01 (Ex. for York), p01 (York), BCL 1803. Chap. *R.N.;* PC. Holmfirth, Yorks. 1801-32 (res.), R. Spexhall, Suffolk 1821 to death (London) 12/11/1846 [C88430. ODNB as a financial writer. YCO]

CUBITT (Benjamin) Bapt. Stalham, Norfolk 26/6/1769, s. Benjamin Mullenger Cubitt (farmer) and Hannah Mack. Caius, Cambridge 1788, BA1793, dn93 (Nor.), MA1796, p98 (Nor.). V. (and patron) of Stalham 1801-43, R. Sloley, Norfolk 1841-3. Died (Sloley) 25/4/1852 [C112413] Married (1) Smallburgh, Norfolk 6/8/1798 Mary Ann Mack (d.1823), with issue (2) Lakenham, Norfolk 23/8/1827 Frances Maria White (sister of Henry Kirk White, poet), with further issue. Port. online.

CUBITT (Francis William) Bapt. Honing Hall, Norfolk 6/5/1799, s. Capt. Thomas Cubitt and Catherine Spencer. St John's, Cambridge 1817, BA1821, dn22 (Nor.), p23 (Nor.). R. (and patron) of Fritton, Suffolk 1831 (and living at Fritton House). Died 22/6/1882, leaving £3,122-5s-9d. [C112415] Married 1/10/1833 Jane Mary Astley (w) (a clergy dau., East Barsham, Norfolk), with issue. J.P. Norfolk & Suffolk.

CUBITT (John) Bapt. Hickling, Suffolk 22/9/1767, s. John Cubitt and Anna High.

Caius, Cambridge, dn92 (Nor.), Fellow, p93 (Nor.). R. Hinderclay, Suffolk 1819-33, R. Waxham w. Palling, Norfolk 1808-41, R. Overstrand, Norfolk 1822-41, R. Palling, Norfolk 1822 (only), R. Oxwick, Norfolk 1833. Died 25/6/1841 aged 74 [C112416] Married South Walsham, Norfolk 19/11/1799 Bridget Jary, with issue.

CULLUM (Thomas Gery, Sir, 8th Bart.) Born Hardwick House, Bury St Edmunds, Suffolk 23/10/1777, s. Sir Thomas Gery Cullum, 7th Bart. (surgeon, botanist, antiquarian) and Mary Hanson. Pembroke, Cambridge 1795, BA1799, dn00 (Nor.), p01 (Nor.), MA1802. R. Knodishall w. Buxlow, Suffolk 1801-35. Chap. to HRH Duke of Sussex 1805. Died 26/1/1855 [C112418] Married (1) Woodford, Essex 27/8/1804 Mary Ann Eggers (d.1830) (2) 30/4/1832 Ann Lloyd Hanford-Flood (Flood Hall, Kilkenny). Succ. to title 1831. Baronetcy extinct on his death. Doubtless related to the man above.

CUMBY, CRUMBY (Anthony) Bapt. Richmond, Yorks. 2/11/1803, s. William Bryce Cumby (*R.N.*) and Ann Metcalfe. Corpus Christi, Cambridge 1822, BA1827, dn29 (York), MA1830, p30 (Chester). PC. Hudswell, Catterick, Yorks. 1831-3. V. Bolton on Swale, Yorks. 1836-80 (and H/M Scorton G/S 1836-76) to death (Richmond) 31/5/1881 aged 77, leaving £6,524-8s-2d. [C136069 as Crumby/C168622 as Cumby. Boase. YCO] Married Bolton on Swale 14/1/1836 Anne Jane Bowe (a clergy dau.), with issue.

CUMING (Joseph) Bapt. Totnes, Devon 14/6/1757, s. Samuel Cuming. St Alban Hall, Oxford 1785, BA1789, dn89 (Wor.), p90 (Wor.). V. Totnes 1795 to death 30/12/1836 aged 80 [C120843] Married Old Swinford, Worcs. 1792 Eleanor Haden.

CUMMING (James) Born Westminster, London 24/10/1777, s. James Cumming and Alice Atherton. Trinity, Cambridge 1796, BA 1801, Fellow 1803, MA1804, dn04 (Lin.), p07 (Lin.), incorporated at Oxford 1832. Professor of Chemistry, Cambridge Univ. 1815. R. North Runcton w. Hardwick w. Setchey, Norfolk 1819 to death 10/1/1861, leaving £7,000 [C54243. ODNB. Boase] Married Cambridge 17/2/1820 Sarah Humfry, clerical s. and 2 dau. *F.R.S.* and

F.R.G.S. (1816). 'A photograph of Cumming in old age shows that he was well built and clean shaven and had thick white hair, but was partially bald. He was a kind, honest man with a genial nature. Clear thinking and well read, he had the ability to grasp the essentials of any problem, and an aptitude for quotation. He liked to discuss all manner of topics, and he and his wife sometimes invited friends to a soirée, when a singer would provide entertainment.' (ODNB)

CUMYNS (Robert Heysham) Bapt. Holborn, London 3/9/1768, s. of George Cumyns and Elizabeth Thornton. All Souls, Oxford 1786, BA1790, dn91 (Cant. for Glos.), MA1792, p92 (Glos.), p20. S/M Portsmouth G/S; Min. Portsea St Mary, St George's Chapel 1820-1 (res.), (first) Min. Portsea St Mary All Saints Chapel 1829 to death 1838 (2nd q.) [C72623] Married Maria Greenstreet 26/7/1807 (annulled on grounds of non-consummation: https://books.google.co.uk/books?id=Ao80AA AAIAAJ

CUNDILL (James) Bapt. Alne, Yorks. 8/8/1780, s. James Cundall and Susannah Waters. Literate: dn04 (Chester), dn07 (Chester). V. Stockton upon Tees, Durham 1820-32, V. Coniscliffe, Durham 1832-49, PC. Durham St Margaret 1842. Died Darlington, Co. Durham 25/11/1849 aged 70 [C130051] Married Staindrop, Durham 28/12/1809 Maria Watson, with clerical son.

CUNLIFFE (George) Born Acton Park, Wrexham, Denbigh/Flint 3/6/1795, s. Sir Foster Cunliffe, 3rd Bart. and Harriet Kinloch (dau. of a Scottish bart.). Balliol, Oxford 1814, BA1817, dn18 (St Asaph), p20 (St Asaph), MA 1822. R. Petton, Shropshire 1821-64, V. Wrexham 1826-75, Cursal Canon of St Asaph 1835. Died Denbigh 31/1/1884, leaving £18,345-4s-6d. [C10420] Married 8/2/1821 Dorothea Townshend, s.*p*. A social and sanitary reformer, 'he gained notoriety as the man who stopped the racing at Wrexham Racecourse'.

CUNNINGHAM (Francis) Born Paddington, London 1785 27/7/1785, s. John Cunningham and Ann Hardy. Queens', Cambridge 1809, dn13 (Bristol), p13 (Bristol), BA1815, MA 1818. R. Pakefield, Suffolk (2 Medieties) 1814-30, V. Lowestoft, Suffolk 1830 (and Hon. Canon of Norwich) to death (Lowestoft, Suffolk) 8/8/1863 aged 78, leaving £18,000 [C8181. DEB] Married Earlham Hall, Norfolk 31/1/1816 Richenda Gurney (a sister of Elizabeth Fry). 'During a fever epidemic in 1824 he risked his own life by personal attendance on the sufferers.' Photo. online.

CUNNINGHAM (John William) Born London 3/1/1780, s. Francis Cunningham (a hatter and hosier) and Agnes Bicket. St John's, Cambridge 1798, BA1802, dn03 (Win.), p03 (Win.), MA1805. V. Harrow (on the Hill), Middx. 1811 to death. Dom. Chap. to Lord Northwick. Died 30/9/1861 aged 81, leaving £12,000 [C72624 - not Oxford. ODNB. Boase. DEB is excellent] Married (1) Farnham, Surrey 30/7/1805 Sophia Williams (Moor Park, d.1821), with clerical s. Francis Macaulay Cunningham (2) Rickmansworth, Herts. 24/7/1827 Mary (dau. of Gen. Sir Harry Calvert, 1st Bart.), with further issue (15 in all). 'A strong supporter of the Evangelical party; said to have taken great pride in the fact that he had influenced the election of headmasters of Harrow belonging to the Evangelical school. Nicknamed 'Velvet Cunningham 'after the publication of his novel *The Velvet Cushion*.

CURGENVEN (William) Born St Michael Penkevil, Cornwall 26/11/1769, s. Rev. William Curgenven and Abigail Pearce . St John's, Cambridge 1789, BA1793, dn93 (Ex.), p94 (Ex.). R. Lamorran, Cornwall 1803 to death 3/1/1848 aged 76 [C140810] Married (1) Truro, Cornwall 12/6/1800 Laura Martyn (d.1806), with issue (2) Truro 1807 Grace Buckland, 1s, 4 dau.

CURRIE (James) St Bees adm. 1822, dn23 (Car.), p24 (Car.), then Queens', Cambridge 1825 (aged over 24), a Ten Year Man. PC. Newlands, Crosthwaite, Cumberland 1826-40, V. Dearham, Cumberland 1839 to death (unm.) 18/12/1876 aged 77, leaving all his £200 to his housekeeper [C5791. Platt]

CURRIE (Thomas) Bapt. Bungay, Suffolk 13/9/1803, s. James Currie (surgeon). Emmanuel, Cambridge 1821, BA1826, dn26 (Nor), p27 (Nor.). V. Little Melton, Norfolk 1832-9, R. Bridgham. Norfolk 1839 and V. Roudham, Norfolk 1841 to death 22/12/1875, leaving £1,500 [C112423] Married Great Yarmouth, Norfolk 18/6/1829 Maria Elizabeth Wall, and had issue.

CURSHAM (Thomas Leeson) Born Ashover, Derbys. 9/5/1785, s. Rev. Thomas Cursham and Ann Leeson. Lincoln, Oxford 1801, BA 1807, dn08 (York), p09 (York), MA1813, DCL 1825, LLD 1826. V. Mansfield, Notts. 1813-68, PC. Annesley, Notts. 1819-47, V. Blackwell, Derbys. 1826 to death (Mansfield) 31/7/1868 aged 83, leaving £6,000 [C10454. YCO] Married (1) Lenton, Notts. 27/10/1810 Sabina Stretton (d.1854), with issue (2) London St Pancras 25 or 26/1/1860 Marianne Sarah Sidney Ashby.

CURTEIS (Thomas) Born Sevenoaks, Kent, s. John and Martha Curteis. Jesus, Cambridge 1805 (aged 18), BA1810, then Clare, Fellow 1810-16, dn11 (Cant.), p12 (Cant.), MA1815. PC. Smallhythe, Kent 1812-61, R. (and Sinecure R. and patron) of Sevenoaks 1831 to death. Dom. Chap. to 1st Earl Amherst 1817. Died Bradfield, Berks. 2/8/1861 aged 73, leaving £6,000 [C123489] Married Wilbury, Kent 138/12/1815 Sarah Ann Lipscombe (a clergy dau.), with issue. J.P. Kent.

CURTEIS (Whitfield) Born London 5/12/1777, s. William Curteis and Elizabeth Whitfield. Trinity, Cambridge 1797, BA1801, dn01 (London for Cant.), p02 (Nor.), MA1804. R. Burwash, Sussex 1806-21, R. Smarden, Kent 1821 to death (Bath) 31/7/1834 (CCEd says 14/10/1834) [C63189] Married Ashford, Kent 16/4/1807 Mary Thorne.

CURTIS (George William) Born Colney Hatch, Middx. 4/11/1788, s. Capt. George Curtis, *H.E.I.C.*, and Anne Delicia Windsor. St John's, Cambridge 1807, BA1811, dn10, p11, MA1814. V. Leominster, Heref. 1819-24, R. Padworth, Berks. 1823-65, R. Wennington, Essex 1826-65, R. Farndish, Beds. 1850-60. Died 1/7/1865, leaving £6,000 [C104068] Married Dawlish, Devon 1822 Caroline Georgina Perkins (a clergy dau.), w. clerical sons Francis Henry, and Philip Windsor Curtis.

CURTIS (John) From Ashby-de-la-Zouche, Leics. Literate: dn16 (Lin.), p17 (Lin.), then Trinity, Cambridge 1817 (a Ten Year Man). H/M Ashby-de-la-Zouche G/S 1814; PC. Smisby, Derbys. 1831-56. Lived latterly in Jersey and died there 28/1/1870 aged 83. Will not traced [C10455]

CURTOIS (Peregrine) Born Branston, Lincs. 4/4/1776, s. Rev. Peregrine Harrison Curtois and Barbara Bagge. Trinity Hall, Cambridge 1793, dn98 (Lin.), LLB1800, p01 (Lin.). R. Potter Hanworth, Lincs. 1801-47, R. (and patron) of Branston, Middx. 1815 to death 16/1/1847 [C54254. Kaye] Married Edmonton, Middx. 22/12/1802 Anne (dau. Sir James Winter Lake, 3rd Bart.), w. clerical son, also Peregrine. Port. online.

CURTOIS (Rowland Grove) Bapt. Sixhill, Lincs. 3/7/1786, s. Rev. Rowland Curtois (Longhills Hall, Branston, Lincs.) and Mary Dales. Corpus Christi, Oxford 1803, BA1807, MA1811, dn11 (Ox.), p12 (Salis.), Fellow 1814-21, BD1820, DD1841. Chap. to the Forces 1812 -West Indies - Canada - Gibraltar - Chatham 1832-46; V. Oving, Sussex 1826-7 (res.), PC. Hannah w. Hagnaby, Lincs. 1828. Dom. Chap. to Marquess of Queensbury. Died Rochester 23/1/1849 [C26208] Married (1) Chichester 31/1/1821 Louisa Georgina (dau. Lt-Gen. Sir David Tining-Widdrington, she d.1826), 2 military sons (2) Rochester 7/5/1839 Mrs Mary (Scholes) Farquhar (a clergy widow). www.chradams.co.uk/Curtois/rowlandgrove.html

CURWEN (John Christian) Born Unerigg Hall, Maryport, Cumberland 15/4/1799, s. John Christian Curwen, *M.P.*, and Isabella Gale. Literate: dn22 (Chester), p23 (Chester). R. Harrington, Cumberland 1823-40, PC. Workington, Cumberland 1823, R. Plumbland, Cumberland 1834 to death 25/2/1840 aged 40 [C5792. Platt] Married (1) 1818 Ann Cookson (2) Plemstall, Cheshire 19/5/1824 Marianne Baldwin, with issue. Port. online.

CURZON (Alfred, Hon.) Born 17/4/1801, s. Nathaniel, 2nd Baron Scarsdale and Felicité Anne Josephe de Wattines ('a Flemish lady'). BNC, Oxford 1819, BA1822, MA1824, dn24 (C&L), p25 (C&L). R. Norton juxta Twycross, Leics. 1829, R. Kedleston, Derbys. 1832 to death 12/1/1850 aged 48 [C10456] Married Nuthall, Notts. 14/7/1825 Sophia Holden, with issue. Brother below.

CURZON (Frederic Emmanuel Hippolyte) Born 5/2/1795, s. Nathaniel, 2nd Baron Scarsdale and Felicité Anne Josephe de Wattines ('a Flemish lady'). Oriel, Oxford 1813, then

Magdalene, Cambridge 1819, MA1820, dn20 (Chester), p20 (Chester). V. Mickleover, Derbys. 1820-71, R. Kedleston, Derbys. 1850-5. Died 18/12/1871 aged 76, leaving £450 [C10411. LNCP] Married Heanor, Derbys. Dec. 1836 Augusta Marian Mundy (Shipley Hall, Notts., d.1827). Brother above. Photo. online.

CUST (Henry Cockayne, Hon.) Born Belton, Lincs. 28/9/1780, s. Sir Brownlow Cust, 1st Baron Brownlow and Frances Bankes. Trinity, Cambridge 1799, MA1803, dn04 (Peterb.), p05 (Peterb.). R. Scott Willoughby >< Lincs. 1805, R. Cockayne Hatley >< Beds. 1806-61, R. Sywell, Northants. 1806-61, V. Middle Rasen Drax, Lincs. 1806-32 (res.), Canon of Windsor 1813 to death 19/5/1861 aged 80, leaving £12,000 [C54360] Married 20/6/1816 Lady Anna-Maria Needham (dau. of 1st Earl of Kilmorey), with issue. Brother below.

CUST (Richard, Hon.) Born 26/8/1785, s. Brownlow Cust, 1st Baron Brownlow and Frances Bankes. Oriel, Oxford 1804, BA1807, dn09 (Lin.), p10 (Lin.), MA1810. R. Belton, Gainsborough, Lincs. 1810-64, R. Faldingworth, Lincs. 1811-14, R. Snelland, Lincs. 1814, V. Hough on the Hill, Lincs. 1814-22 (res.), RD. Prebend of Lincoln Cathedral 1846 to death. Dom. Chap. to 1st Earl Brownlow 1810. Died 17/7/1864, leaving £40,000 [C54361. LNCP] Brother above. Interesting port. at: www.bbc.co.uk/.../the-honourable-and-reverend-richard-cust-17851864.

CUSTANCE (Frederic(k)) Born Kidderminster, Warwicks. 7/12/1802, s. George Custance and Bridget Betts. Trinity, Cambridge 1819, BA1825, dn25 (Bristol), p26 (Chester for Bristol), MA1839. R. Steeple, Essex 1828-40, PC. Ripponden, Halifax, Yorks. 1830-40, R. Colwall, Heref. 1840 (and Prebend of Putson Minor in Hereford Cathedral 1861, and part RD of Frome, Heref.) to death (a widower) 29/3/1867 aged 64, leaving £18,000 [C8182] Married Wellingborough, Northants. 28/8/1828 Penelope Corrie, with clerical son.

CUTCLIFFE (Robert) Born Westleigh, Devon 24/10/1760, s. Charles Cutcliffe and Elizabeth Dene. Exeter, Oxford 1779, BA1783, dn83 (Ex.), p85 (Ex.). V. Seaton and Beer, Devon 1791 to death 12/1/1838 aged 77.

Married Exeter 1793 Elizabeth Grainger, with issue [C140812] ERC says Richard Cutliffe.

CUTLER (John) Bapt. Eton, Bucks. 19/5/1756, s. Roger Cutler and Mary Bold. Exeter, Oxford 1775, BA1779, dn79 (Ox. for Win.), p86 (C&L), then King's, Cambridge 1790, BA1790, MA1790. S/M Rugby School 1784-7; S/M Dorchester 1787; S/M King's School, Sherborne, Dorset 1792, H/M 1815; R. Patney, Wilts. 1815 to death. Naval Chap. on HMS *Hero* with Sir Edward Hughes at the East Indies Station. Died ('in Sackville St., London') 28/2/1833 (CCEd says 20/3/1833). [C10458] Married 17/17/1786 Sarah Elizabeth Guise, with clerical son.

DADE (Thomas) Born Ryburgh, Norfolk 6/6/1776, s. Thomas Dade (farmer) and Sarah Turner. Caius, Cambridge 1783, dn98 (Nor.), BA1798, p00 (Nor.), Fellow 1801-20, MA1801. R. Bincome w. Broadway, Dorset 1820 to death 9 /11/1860, leaving £10,000 [C52343] Married Great Yarmouth, Norfolk 27/3/1820 Jane Lloyd (Bawdeswell Hall, Norfolk). *J.P.* Dorset.

DAINTRY (John) Born Macclesfield, Cheshire 17/11/1795, s. John Smith Daintry and Elizabeth Ryle. Trinity, Cambridge 1812, BA1817 [adm. Inner Temple 1817] MA1820, dn28 (Win.), p29 (Win.). Curate Shedfield, Droxford, Hants. 1833, PC. (and patron) of North Rode, Congleton, Cheshire 1849-63. Died (North Rode) 7/9/1869, leaving £6,000 [C72765] Married Lanlivery, Cornwall 5/9/1821 Elizabeth Hext.

DAKINS (John) From Romsey, Hants., s. William Dakins and Sarah Davenport. Literate: dn95 (Nor.), p97 (Cant. for Glos. and Ex. - *sic*). R. Colchester St James, Essex 1799 to death 14/2/1839 (where 2,000 people attended his funeral) [C112442] Brother, below.

DAKINS (William Whitfield) Born Romsey, Hants. 4/2/1767, s. William Dakins and Sarah Davenport. St AlbanHall, Oxford 1789, SCL 1792, dn92 (Lin.), BA 1794, p94 (Roch.), DD 1812 (Lambeth). R. St Michael Crooked Lane, City of London 1816, V. Asheldham, Essex 1817, Minor Canon and Precentor of Westminster Abbey. Chap. to Brigade of Guards; Chaplain General to the Forces 1830-44; and founder of Royal Military Chapel, Wellington Barracks, London. Died 10/1/1850 (buried Westminster Abbey) [C116857. Foster as William only] Married Witney, Oxon. 24/11/1792 Susanna Shorter, w. clerical issue. *F.S.A.* Brother, above.

DALBY (John, 'Jack') Possibly bapt. Sutton Bonnington, Notts. 12/11/1772, s. John Dalby (a solicitor) and Ann Kirkland. Queen's, Cambridge 1790, BA1794, Fellow, dn94 (Lin.), p97 (Lin.), MA1797. V. Belton, Leics. 1803-8, V. Castle Donington, Leics. 1807 and R. Long Whatton, Leics. 1822 to death. Dom. Chap. to Flora, Marchioness of Hastings 1810-22. Died 1/9/1852 aged 82 [C52105] Married Tissington, Derbys. 16/2/1803 Mary Ann Bakewell (d.1815), w. issue.

DALBY (William) Bapt. Stoke Damerel, Devon 20/5/1792, s. Capt. Thomas Dalby, *R.N.*, and Anna Maria Carteret. Exeter, Oxford 1808, Fellow 1811-26, BA1814, MA1815 [adm. Lincoln's Inn 1815] dn18 (Ox.), p18 (Ox.). V. Warminster, Wilts. 1825 (with Prebend of Warminster in Salisbury Cathedral 1832-61), R. Compton Bassett, Wilts. 1841 to death (Bournemouth) 3/12/1861, leaving £3,000 [C26211] Married Frome Selwood, Som. 1/6/1826 Harriet Byard Sheppard, w. clerical s.

DALE (Peter Steel) Born Liverpool 8/4/1782, s. of John Dale (merchant) and Elizabeth Norris. Queen's, Oxford 1803, no degree, dn05 (Chester), p06 (Chester). PC. Burtonwood, Lancs. 1829 (only), PC. Hollinfare, Warrington, Lancs. 1829 to death 30/6/1871 aged 89, leaving £6,000 [C168632] Married Eccles, Lancs. 2/4/1823 Mary Ann Garven, w. issue.

DALES (Edward) Bapt. Cheapside, London 16/11/1764, s. Samuel (linen merchant) and Elizabeth Dales. Sidney, Cambridge 1782, BA 1786, dn88 (C&L), p89 (C&L), MA1789. PC. Smethwick Chapel, Harborne, Staffs. [blank in ERC] 1815 to death 17/2/1850 aged 85 [C10424]

DALLAS (Alexander Robert Charles) Born Malden, Essex 29/3/1791, s. Robert Charles Dallas and Sarah Harding. Treasury Clerk 1810-20. [Present at Battle of Waterloo]. Worcester, Oxford 1820, no degree, dn21 (London), p21 (Salis.), MA Lambeth. V. Ardeley (o/w Yardley), Herts. 1827-8, R. Wonston, Hants. (and Preacher throughout the Diocese of Winchester) 1828-69, Prebend in Llandaff Cathedral? [total income in CR65 £1,028] Chap. to Bishop Sumner of Winchester. Died Blackheath, Kent 12/12/1869 aged 80 (CCEd says 18/12/1828), leaving £4,000. [C26212. ODNB. Boase. [A. B. Dallas], *Incidents in the life and ministry of the Rev. Alex. R.C. Dallas ...* (1871)] Married (1) Morden, Surrey 4/5/1818 (the wealthy) Mrs Mary Ann (Ferguson) Edge (d. 1847), with issue (2) Holton, Oxon. 18/12/1849 Anne Briscoe Tyndale (w) (a clergy dau.), with further issue. Founder and Hon. Sec. of the Society for Irish Church Missions to Roman Catholics 1848. Port. online.

DALLAWAY (James) Born Bristol 20/2/1763, s. James Dallaway (a banker) and Martha Hopton. Trinity, Cambridge 1778, BA1782, MA1784, dn85 (Ox.), p93 (Glos.), MB

1793. R. South Stoke, Sussex 1799-1804, R. Slinfold, Sussex 1803-34, R. Llanmaes, Glamorgan --, V. Leatherhead, Surrey 1804-34, Prebend of Huve Ecclesia in Chichester Cathedral 1811-17, then Ferring Prebend 1817-26. Chap. and physician to the British Embassy in Constantinople, and the author of two travelogues. Dom. Chap. to 2nd Earl of Ludlow 1804. Died 6/6/1834, leaving £10,000 [C1455. ODNB as antiquary] Married 26/6/1800 Harriet Anne Jefferis, 1 child. Heraldic writer, and Secretary to the Earl Marshal from 1797 to death, and thus *F.S.A.* (1789): ttps://en.wikipedia.org/wiki/James_Dallaway

DALLIN (James) Born Hendon, Middx. 10/1/1776, s. Robert Dallin and Elizabeth Cartwright. Magdalene, Cambridge 1795, BA 1800, dn00 (Ex. for York), p01 (York), MA 1805. V. York Holy Trinity Goodramgate w. St Maurice and St John Del Pike 1803-38 (with Vicar-Choral in York Minster 'for 35 years', and Librarian to the Dean and Chapter), V. Rudston, Yorks. 1823-33 (res.). Dom. Chap. to 1st Baron Howden 1823. Died York 28/11/1838 aged 62 [C91365. YCO] Married 8/11/1826 Elizabeth Jenkinson.

DALTON (Charles) Born Bury St Edmunds, Suffolk 8/5/1775, s. William Dalton (a mercer) and Bridget Squire. Caius, Cambridge 1791, BA 1796, MA1799, dn99 (Nor.), Fellow 1799-1802, p00 (Nor.). V. West (or Bishop's) Lavington, Wilts. 1803-4, V. Kelvedon, Essex 1804 to death 20/12/1858, leaving £8,000 [C83689] Married Rochester 17/8/1802 Jane Brown (a clergy dau.), with issue.

DALTON (Henry) Born Dublin, s. George Forster Dalton and Dorothy Catherine Worrall. TCD1822 (aged 17), dn26, p27, BA 1827, MA 1845, incorporated at Trinity, Oxford 1852. PC. Bridgnorth St Leonard, Shropshire 1833-35 (depr.). Became an Apostle in the Catholic Apostolic Church ('in charge of France'). Dom. Chap. to Duke of Leinster 1846 to death (Albany, Surrey, the headquarters of the Church) 6/11/1869, leaving £450 [C10462. Boase. Al.Dub.] Married Kneeton, Notts. 17/10/1836 Alice Spick, with issue. Brother two below.

DALTON (John) Born Fulham, Middx., s. Edward Dalton and Dinah Whittle. St Mary Hall, Oxford 1822 aged 25, dn28, p28; TCD 1828 (?). PC. Warlingham cum Chelsham, Surrey 1829 to death 19/1/1862 aged 67, leaving £800 [C72769] Wife Ann (w), and dau. Elfrida (a spinster missionary). Online references.

DALTON (William) Born Co. Down 1801, s. George Forster Dalton and Dorothy Catherine Worrall. TCD1818, BA 1823, MA1832, then Pembroke, Oxford 1840, BD1846. (first) Min. Liverpool St Jude, Edge Hill 1831-35 (res.), V. Wolverhampton St Paul 1835-59, Prebend of Sandiacre in Lichfield Cathedral 1856-80, (first) PC. (and patron) of Wolverhampton St Philip 1859-80 (and RD of Wolverhampton 1857) to death (London). A professional Protestant and anti-Catholic. Died 13/5/1880 aged 79, leaving £25,000 [C10463. Al.Dub. DEB] Married (1) St James, Piccadilly, London June 1831 Mrs Sarah (Fereday) Marsh ('a young Wolverhampton heiress', she d.1862) [W. Dalton, *A brief memoir of a beloved wife* (1862)] (2) St John's, Paddington, London 16/6/1864 Mary Isabelle Chalfont, (Asprey Lodge, Beds.) 'half his own age' [actually 70/41 years in 1871 Census], with clerical s. Brother above. Web article w. port.

DALZELL, DALZIEL (Anthony) Born Cumberland 1771, s. Anthony Dalziell and Elizabeth Wildridge. Literate: dn95 (Chester), p96 (Chester). PC. Clifton, Workington, Cumberland 1804-50, V. Dearham, Cumberland 1813-14 (res.). Died Workington 20/1/1850 aged 78 [C5798] Married Workington 6/5/1811 Mary Russell, with issue.

DAMPIER (John) Bapt. Wareham, Dorset 20/1/1763, s. John Dampier and Mary King. Wadham, Oxford 1780, BA1784, dn85 (Ox.), p87 (Chester), MA1787. R. Codford St Peter, Wilts. 1790 and R. Langton Maltravers, Dorset 1808 to death. Dom. Chap. to 3rd Earl of Massereene 1808. Died 14/10/1839 [C26625] Married City of London 5/3/1791 Jane Browne, with issue.

DAMPIER (John) Bapt. Hinton St Mary, Dorset 3/5/1778, s. John Dampier and Elizabeth Simpson. Balliol, Oxford 1795, SCL1801, dn01 (Salis.), BCL1802, p02 (Win. for Salis.), LLB 1813. PC. North and South Brewham, Som. 1813 and PC. Pitcombe, Som. 1819 to death 16/1/1841 [C5480] Married Kilmington, Som. 22/9/1810 Mary Charlotte Digby (w), and had issue.

DANDRIDGE (John Strange) Bapt. Worcester 12/4/1765, s. John Dandridge and Letitia Strange. Christ Church, Oxford 1782

[Student of Middle Temple 1788] migrated to Emmanuel, Cambridge 1793, dn96 (Glos.), Fellow, p96 (Glos.), LLB 1799. R. Syresham, Northants. 1797 and R. Rousham, Oxon. 1804 to death (Woodstock, Oxon.) 11/1/1841 aged 76 [C26628] Married 11/10/1792 Catherine Chester (dau. of a lawyer), with clerical son, also John Strange. 'Constitutionally indolent - his sister a good churchwoman among the poor.'

DANIEL (Henry) Bapt. Llangeitho, Cardigan 17/5/1791, s. John and Anne Daniel. Jesus, Oxford 1812, no degree, dn21 (York), p30 (Nor.). V. Swinstead, Lincs. 1832 to death 30/7/1840 aged 48 [C54555. YCO. Bennett2]

DANIEL (John Edge) Born Walton, Suffolk 1805, s. Rear-Admiral G. H. (Hierarchus) Daniel and Amn Edge. Christ's, Cambridge 1823, BA 1827, dn28 (Nor.), p29 (Nor.), MA 1830. V. (and patron) of Weybread, Suffolk 1829-45, PC. Wingfield, Suffolk 1845-7. Chap. to the County Prison at Ipswich in 1864. Died Ipswich 17/10/1888 aged 84, leaving £4,194-0s-4d. [C112446] Married Woolpit, Suffolk 1/1/1830 Ann Aldrich, w. issue.

DANSEY (William) Bapt. Blandford, Dorset 9/1/1792, s. John Dansey and Jane Jones. Exeter, Oxford 1810, BA1814, MA1817, MB 1818, dn19 (Ely for Salis.), p19 (Salis.). R. (and patron) of Donhead St Andrew, Wilts. 1820-41, RD and Bishopstone Prebend in Salisbury Cathedral 1841 to death (Weymouth, Dorset) 7/6/1856 [C6692. ODNB. Boase] Married Hackney, London 28/5/1818 Sarah Warburton, w. issue.

D'ARBLAY (Alexander Charles Louis) Bapt. Great Bookham, Surrey 11/4/1794, s. *Comte* Alexandre Piochard D'Arblay (an exiled French general) and Fanny Burney (the 'esteemed' diarist and novelist). Caius, Cambridge 1813, then Christ's 1816, Fellow 1818, BA1818, dn18 (Salis.), p19 (Chester for Salis.), MA1821. PC. Camden Town All Saints, London 1824-37 [now the Greek Orthodox Cathedral], Min. of Ely Chapel, High Holborn, London 1836 to death (tuberculosis) unm. but engaged 19/1/1837 [C91971] A fine mathematician and a chess fanatic: www.vukutu.com/blog/2011/03/the-matherati-alexander-darblay/

DARBY (John Wareyn) Born. Diss, Norfolk 7/1//1792, s. John Darby (a surgeon) and Elizabeth Kett. Christ's, Cambridge 1809, then Caius 1810, BA1814, MA1817, dn19 (Nor.), p19 (Nor.). V. Wicklewood, Norfolk 1823-32, R. Shottisham, Suffolk 1832 to death [C112452] 'An ecclesiastical antiquary'. Brother below.

DARBY (Martin Baylie) Born Diss, Norfolk 10/1/1803, s. John Darby (a surgeon) and Elizabeth Kett. St John's, Cambridge 1820, BA1826 (Nor.), p28 (Nor.). V. Wicklewood, Norfolk 1832, R. Hackford, Norfolk 1838 to death (Hingham, Norfolk) 15/3/1880, leaving £25,000 [C112453] Widow Charlotte Isabella. Brother above.

DARBY (Thomas) Born Aston, Herts., s. Edmund Darby. Trinity, Cambridge 1822, then Downing, dn27 (Lin.), BA1828, p28 (Lin.). R. Swaton w. Spancy, Lincs. 1828 to death 9/10/1840 [C54562]

DARCEY (John) Bapt. Marton, Congleton, Cheshire 23/10/1768, s. Thomas Darcey and Ann Thornicroft. BNC, Oxford 1788, BA1792, Fellow 1792-1813, dn93 (Ox.), p93 (Chester), MA1794, BD1808, Fellow. PC. Marton 1806 and R. Tedston Delamere, Hereford 1812 to death (Macclesfield, Cheshire) 10/6/1844 aged 75 [C26631] Married (1) Prestbury, Cheshire May 1812 Ellen Brindley, with issue (2) Newcastle under Lyme, Staffs. 8/2/1821 Mary Nickisson (dau. of a Macclesfield banker); with clerical s., also John.

DARCH (William) Born Huish Champflower, Som., s. Richard Darch and Wilmot Lock. Queen's, Oxford 1781 (aged 23), p86 (B&W), BA1788, migrated to Sidney, Cambridge, MA1807. V. Milverton, Som. 1790-1819 (res.), R. Raddington, Som. 1807 and R. Huish Champflower 1823 to death. Dom. Chap. to 15th Lord Somerville 1807; to Bishop of Gloucester, then Bath & Wells 1823. Died 4/1/1833 (CCEd thus) [C34443] Clerical s. Richard Darch.

DARNELL (William Nicholas) Born Newcastle upon Tyne 14/3/1776, s. William Darnell (wine merchant) and Frances Cook. Corpus Christi, Oxford 1792, BA1796, MA 1800, dn01 (Ox.), p02 (Ox.), BD1806 and Fellow. V. Durham St Mary-le-Bow 1809-15, V. Stockton upon Tees, Durham 1815-20, V. Lastingham, Yorks. 1815-27 (non-res.), 9th Prebend of Durham 1816-20, then 6th Prebend 1820-31, PC. St Margaret w. Eastgate, Durham 1820-8, V. Norham, Northumberland 1827-31, R. Stanhope w. Roothorpe, Durham 1831 [gross income £6,000, net income £4,843, the second richest living in England] to death 19/6/1865 aged 89, leaving £60,000 [C26632. ODNB. Boase] Married Scorton, Lancs. 15/6/1815 Elizabeth Bowe (a clergy dau.), with issue.

D'ARVILLE (Frederick Luke) From Bristol, s. Rev. George D'Arville (below) abd Ann Shortland. Christ's, Cambridge 1821, BA1826, dn26 (B&W), p27 (Bristol). R. Littleton on Severn, Glos. 1830 to death (w. ubsuccessful s/m Thornbury G/S 1827). Died 23/8/1842 aged 40 [C42093] Online entry.

D'ARVILLE (George) Bapt. City of London 12/12/1767, s. Edward and Ann D'Arville. St Alban Hall, Oxford 1787, BCL1812, dn14 (Ely for Bristol), p15 (B&W for Bristol). H/M Thornbury, G/S, Bristol 1822 (w. s/m Thornbury G/S 1822-7). PC. Rangeworthy, Glos. 1825-34 (res.). Died 9/7/1853 aged 85 [C6688. Foster as Darvill] Married 25/1/1791 Ann Shortland, w. son above. Online entry.

DASHWOOD (Augustus) Bapt. New Windsor, Berks. 13/4/1795, s. Sir Henry Dashwood, 3rd Bart. and Mary Helen Graham. Pembroke, Cambridge 1823, no degree, dn25 (Nor.), p25 (Ely for Nor.). PC. Quy, Cambs. 1825, R. Bintree w. Themelthorpe, Norfolk 1826, R. Thornage w. Brinton, Norfolk 1826 to death 12/7/1863 aged 68, leaving £8,000 [C6693] Married 16/6/1825 Esther Astley (dau. of a baronet), with issue.

DASHWOOD (Henry) Born Halton, Bucks., s. Sir John Dashwood [-King], 4th Bart. and Mary Anne Broadhead. Trinity, Oxford 1817 (aged 17), BA1823, dn25 (Lin.), p25 (Lin.), MA1826. R. Halton, Bucks. 1826 and V. West Wycombe (Wickham), Bucks. 1832 to death. Dom. Chap. to 9th Duke of St Albans 1832. Died 4/1/1833 (CCEd thus) [C54566] Married 19/9/1825 Anne Leader, w. issue.

DASHWOOD (Samuel Vere) Born Stanford-on-Soar, Notts. 3/11/1804, s. Rev. Samuel Francis Dashwood and Lydia Boughton Lister. BNC, Oxford 1823, BA1826, dn29 (Roch. for York), p29 (London for York). R. (and patron) of Stanford on Soar 1829 (living at Stanford Hall) to death 10/11/1876 aged 72, leaving £7,000 [C116864. YCO] Married (1) Eccleshall, Norfolk 18/10/1828 Caroline Hammond (d.1840) (2) Clifton, Bristol 25/1/1844 Elizabeth Edith Hawkshaw; 17 ch. in all (some clerical).

DAUBENY (Edward Andrew) Bapt. Stratton, Glos. 21/7/1785, s. Rev. James Daubeny and his cousin Helena Daubeny. [A midshipman wounded at the Battle of Copenhagen 1801] St Mary Hall, Oxford 1802, then Corpus Christi 1806, BA1806, dn07 (Glos.), p08 (Glos.), MA 1809. R. Hampnett w. Stowell, Glos. 1818 [blank in ERC]. PC. Ampney St Peter, Glos. (w. V. Ampney Crucis 1829-64) 1820-69 [total income in CR65 £1,116]. Died 26/3/1877 aged 92, leaving £40,000 [C136732] Married Cirencester, Glos. 22/8/1811 Jane Croome, w. clerical son Edward Daubeny. *J.P.* Hunts.

DAUBENY (James) Bapt. Clifton, Bristol 21/7/1801, s. Rev. Andrew Daubeny and Elizabeth Innys. BNC, Oxford 1820, BA1824, dn25 (B&W), p25 (B&W), MA1827. R. Publow, Som. 1834 [blank in ERC]. Died Charlton Kings, Glos. 16/4/1882, leaving £16,749-15s-8d. [C42100] Married St George's Hanover Square, London 2/6/1825 Eleanor Browne Clayton (w), with issue.

DAUBUZ, DAUBREZ (John Claude) Bapt. Truro, Cornwall 17/4/1803, s. Lewis Charles Daubuz and Wilmot Arundell. Exeter, Oxford 1821, BA1825, dn27 (B&W), p28 (B&W). R. (St) Creed, Cornwall 1829-57. Dom. Chap. to Earl of Rosslyn 1803. Died Killow, Cornwall 24/9/1883 aged 80, leaving £140,900-12s-3d. [C42399. Daubuz in CR65] Married 1836 Mary Uzella Foster (a banker's dau.), w. issue: hompi.sogang.ac.kr/anthony/Family/DaubuzFamily.html

DAVENPORT (Charles) Bapt. Stratford-on-Avon, Warwicks, 23/6/1796, s. Rev. James Davenport (below) and Margaret Webb. Worcester, Oxford 1814, BA1818, p20 (Glos.), MA1842. R. Welford, Glos. 1820 to death 12/10/1864, leaving £1,500 [C120876] Married Stratford on Avon, Warwicks. 19/3/1822 Caroline Johnson, with issue.

DAVENPORT (Edmund Sharington) Born Worcester 6/5/1778, s. Rev. Edward Davenport and Catherine Taylor. Oriel, Oxford 1796, then St Alban Hall, BA1801, MA1805. V. Worfield, Shropshire 1803 and R. Lydham, Monmouth 1830 to death. Died 4/1/1833 (CCEd thus). Died 4/1/1833 (CCEd thus) [C10476] Married Worfield 7/8/1806 Elizabeth Tongue, w. issue.

DAVENPORT (James) Born Reading, Berks. 14/8/1750, s. William Davenport and Elisabeth Marshall. St John's, Oxford 1769, BA1773, dn73 (Ely for Wor.), p74 (Wor.), MA1776, BD1783, DD1791. V. Weston on Avon, Glos. 1774, V. Stratford-on-Avon, Warwicks. 1787 to death 16/8/1841 aged 91 [C10478] Married Stratford 5/7/1791 Margaret Webb, with clerical son Charles (above). J.P. Warwicks.

DAVERS (Robert) Born Rushbrook, Suffolk, the natural s. of Sir Charles Davers, 6th Bart. and a Frances Treice (with whom he had 5s. and 3 dau.). Caius, Cambridge 1790, BA1794, dn94 (Nor.), p95 (Nor.). R. Little Whelnetham, Suffolk 1796-1802, R. Nowton, Suffolk 1798-1802 (res.), R. Rougham, Suffolk 1800-53, R. Bradfield St George w. Rushbrooke 1802-53, R. Bradfield St Clare, Suffolk 1815-24 (res.). Died 26/1/1853 [C112462] Married Stepney, London 10/5/1801 Mary Ellis.

DAVEY (Bartholomew) Bapt. Nymet Tracey, Devon 10/7/1760, s. Rev. Bartholomew Davey, sen. and Honour Hutchings. Balliol, Oxford 1779, BA1783, dn83 (Ex.), p84 (Ex. for B&W). V. Bampton, Devon 1785 and R. Calverley, Devon 1803 to death 11/7/1841 aged 81. Married Tiverton, Devon 21/11/1810 Jane Govett, and had issue [C140847]

DAVIDSON (John) Born Torpenhow, Cumberland, s. Rev. John Davidson, sen. Literate: dn05 (Car.), p06 (Car.). PC. Barnard Castle, Durham 1815 (with Master of the Hospital [almshouses] of St John the Baptist 1822-7) to death 14/7/1847 aged 68 [C5800] Married 1807 Elizabeth Wilson (Kelso, Roxburghshire), with clerical s., also John (in the same place?).

DAVIDSON (John Noah) Bapt. Marylebone London 12/4/1796 (and apparently re-baptised Holborn, London 26/4/1820), s. James and Ann Davidson. Queens', Cambridge 1817, BA 1821, dn21 (Glos.), p21 (Glos.), MA1824. V. East Harptree, Som. 1831-53 (ret.). Died St John's Wood, London 7/8/1871, leaving £14,000 [C42101] Married (1) Roxwell, Essex 3/12/1828 Charlotte Bramston (d.1841), w. issue (2) Kensington, London 17/8/1857 Anne Catherine Tate (w).

DAVIE (Charles) Bapt. Buckland Brewer, Devon 15/8/1765, s. John Davie and Eleanora Basset. Trinity, Oxford 1784, BA1788, dn88 (Ox.), p89 (Ex.), MA1790. V. Buckland Brewer 1789 and R. Heanton Punchardon, Devon 1791 (and Prebend of Exeter Cathedral 1803) to death. Dom. Chap. to 9th Earl of Devon 1791. Died 7/2/1836 aged 70 [C26638] Married St George's Hanover Square, London 2/6/1801 Bridget Boyfield.

DAVIES (Charles Greenall) Born Tewkesbury, Glos. 14/11/1804, Rev. Daniel William Davies (V. Cranbrook, Kent) and Louisa Greenall. St Mary Hall, Oxford 1823, BA1827, dn30, p31, MA1834. Curate Bradstow Chapel, Broadstairs, Kent 1830, V. Tewkesbury 1846-77 (and RD of Gloucester and Chap. to Tewkesbury Poor Law Union), PC. Walton Cardiff, Tewkesbury 1847, Hon. Canon of Gloucester Cathedral 1854 to death 13/4/1877 aged 72, leaving £3,000 [C63222] Married (1) Broadstairs, Kent 26/4/1831 Mary Ellen Torre (d.1832) (2) Tewkesbury 18/11/1856 Christiana Jane Douglas (w), with clerical s. Charles Douglas Percival Davies. Port. online.

DAVIES (David) From Carmarthen. Corpus Christi, Cambridge 1779 (aged 24), no degree, dn86 (St David's), p87 (St David's). V. Tannington w. Brundish, Suffolk 1811-13, R. Cliddesden cum Farleigh Wallop, Hants. 1813-29, R. Willersey, Glos. 1813-14 (res.), Chap. of the Donative of Marston Chapel, Yardley, Worcs. 1830. Dom. Chap. to 3rd Earl of Portsmouth 1816. Died 22/12/1840 [C143281] Wife Lettice. Had a major library.

DAVIES (Edward Lutwyche) From Hay on Wye, Brecon, s. James Davies. Jesus, Oxford 1822 (aged 19), BA1826, dn26 (Heref.), p27 (Heref.), MA1828. PC. Kenderchurch, Heref. 1828, PC. Kilpeck, Heref. 1835, R. Thurrock Parva (Little Thurrock), Essex 1860-7. Died (Clifton, Bristol) 15/12/1895 aged 91, leaving £93-7s-10d. [C104154] Married Mary Ann Davis, w. issue.

DAVIES (George) From Cranfield, Beds., s. Rev. George Davies. University, Oxford 1803 (aged 17), BA1808, dn09 (Ely for Roch.), p10 (Roch.), MA1811. V. (and patron) of (Isle of) Grain St James, Kent 1813-60, Curate Flamstead, Herts. 1816-[58]. Died Rochester 8/12/1860, leaving £14,000 [C1782. YCO]

DAVIES (George John) Born Stony Stratford, Bucks. 1/2/1779, s. Rev. Thomas Davies (R. Little Woolstone, Bucks.). Sidney, Cambridge 1796, BA1802, dn02 (Lin.), p03 (Lin.), MA 1805.

S/M Hull G/S 1812-22; PC. Upper Gravenhurst, Beds. 1808, PC. Sutton (in Holderness), Yorks. 1819-39, PC. Marfleet, Yorks. 1824-7. Died Hull 19/5/1839 aged 60 [C54591] Was married, with issue.

DAVIES (Howel) From Gwenddwr, Breconshire, s. David Davies. Wadham, Oxford 1789 (aged 26), no degree, p82 (C&L). PC. Fitzhead, Som. 1808-34, PC. Kinver, Staffs. 1814-34, R. Tarrington, Heref. 1814-32, R. Stoke Edith, Heref. 1819 to death there 28/2/1834 aged 75 (CCEd thus) [C10434]

DAVIES (James) From Newland, Glos., s. James Davies, Oriel, Oxford 1804 (aged 18), BA 1808, dn09 (Glos.), p10 (Glos.), MA1811. R. Little Barrington, Glos. 1820, V. Sherborne w. Windrush, Glos. 1829, R. Abbenhall, Glos. 1837 (and RD of Forest, Second Part) to death (English Bicknor, Glos.) 27/8/1881, leaving £347-2s-1d. [C143205]

DAVIES (Jemson) Bapt. Leicester 23/5/1795, s. Richard Davies and Mary Jemson. Trinity, Cambridge 1814, then Clare 1816, BA1818, dn18 (Lin.), p19 (Lin.), MA1822. V. Evington, Lincs. 1819, V. Leicester St Nicholas 1841 (and Confrater of Wyggeston's Hospital [almshouses], Leicester 1820) to death 15/2/1873, leaving under £100 [C54599] Married by 1830 Mary Elizabeth Oliver, with issue.

DAVIES (John) From Cwmddytha, Radnor, s. of Rice Davies [*pleb*]. Jesus, Oxford 1785 (aged 18), BA1789, dn95 (Heref.). V. St Nicholas at Wade, Thanet, Kent 1814 to death 9/6/1833 aged 65 (CCEd says 27/6/1833) [C104174]

DAVIES (John) From Holborn, London, s. James (*or* John) Davies. St John's, Cambridge 1784 (aged 16) [Venn says Trinity], BA1789, dn89 (St David's), MA1792. V. Glooston, Leics. 1802, R. Stanton Wyville, Leics. 1820 to death. Dom. Chap. to 5th Duke of Buccleuch and Queensberry 1820. Died 29/12/1847 [C128964]

DAVIES (John) From Rendcombe, Glos., s. William Davies. Pembroke, Oxford 1810 (aged 19), BA1814, MA1817. PC. Upleadon w. Pauntley, Glos. 1824-30, PC. Gloucester St Nicholas (w. St Bartholomew's Hospital [almshouses]) 1830 to death 11/6/1843 aged 51 [C143426] Died? [C10568]

DAVIES (John) Born Rock, Stourport, Worcs., s. Rev. David Davies. Worcester, Oxford 1808 (aged 19), BA1812, MA 1815. R. Worcester St Clement (w. the Worcester Episcopal Floating Chapel) 1816-32 [C120881], PC. Nether Worton w. Over Worton, Oxon. 1825. Died (Bredwardine, Heref.) 12/7/1858, leaving £1,500 [C26655. G. Lea, *Memoir of the Rev. John Davies, MA, Rector of St Clement's, Worcester* (1859)]. Widow Selina. Worked with canal men and watermen:
www.users.totalise.co.uk/~fortroyal/WorcestershirePast/people/watermenskn.html

DAVIES (John) Born Llanddewi-Brefi, Cardigan 1795 ('of well-to-do parents'). Queens', Cambridge 1820 (a Ten Year Man, BD1831), DD1844. R. Chichester St Pancras. Sussex 1830-40 (and kept a boarding school). R. Gateshead, Co. Durham 1840 (and Hon. Canon of Durham Cathedral 1853) to death (Ilkley) 21/10/1861, leaving £12,000. Master of King James's Hospital [almshouses], Durham 1840 [C63282/63281. Boase] Married 9/7/1823 Mary Hopkinson (w), with issue (including Emily Davies, feminist and founder of Girton College).

DAVIES (Richard) From Llanwrog, Montgomery, s. Andrew Davies [*pleb*]. Jesus, Oxford 1787 (aged 19), dn91 (Nor. for C&L), p91 (C&L), BA1793, MA and BD1801. V. Welton, Northants. 1800, V. Leicester St Nicholas 1813. Died? [C10568]

DAVIES (Richard) From English Bicknor, Glos., s. James Davies. Oriel, Oxford 1814 (aged 18), MA1821, dn21 (Heref.). R. Dixton, Monmouth 1822-33 (res.), R. Staunton, Glos. 1823-57 (and Hon. Canon Gloucester Cathedral 1853) to death 1857 aged 61. Dom. Chap. to 2nd Baron Sherbourne 1823 [C138805]

DAVIES (Robert) Bapt. Denbigh 23/5/1787. Clare, Cambridge 1806, dn10 (Nor.), BA1811, p11 (Nor.), MA1828. R. Llanddulas, Denbigh 1819-23, PC. Newmarket, Flintshire 1823-8, R. Gwaenysgor, Flintshire (Chester Diocese) 1823, (first) PC. Liverpool St David 1828 (a Welsh-speaking congregation) [C168665], PC. St Paul, Liverpool 1842 to death. Dom. Chap. to 6th Earl of Cardigan 1827. Died 1/8/1850 aged 63 [C111981] Had issue.

DAVIES (Samuel) From Llandovery, Carmarthen, s. Arthur Davies. Wadham, Oxford 1787 (aged 18), BA1791, dn91 (Nor. for Win.), p92 (Salis. for Win.), MA1809. PC. Egremont, Carmarthen 1794-1812, R. Llanmadog, Glamorgan 1795-1810 (res.), V. Llandeilo Talybont, Glamorgan 1797, R. Llanedi, Carmarthen 1809, PC. of the Donative of Northaw, Herts. 1810 to death. Dom. Chap. to 1st Viscount Hood 1809. Died 11/2/1845 [C72804. ERC links].

DAVIES (Thomas) Born Pentrefoelas, Denbigh, s. John Davies. Jesus, Oxford 1799 (aged 18), BA1802, MA1805, Fellow 1806-44, BD1813, etc. Chap. *R.N.*; R. Besselsleigh, Berks. 1817 to death 9/2/1844 [C91978]

DAVIES (Thomas) [MA but NiVoF]. V. Mamble w. Bayton, Worcs. 1816-[45]. Died? [C138836]

DAVIES (William) From Eastington, Glos., s. Rev. William Davies, sen. Worcester, Oxford 1782 (aged 16), then Magdalen, BA 1789, dn91 (Glos.), MA1792, p93 (Glos.), BD & DD1817. PC. Stone, Glos. 1797 and R. Rockhampton, Glos. 1819 to death 26/1/1849 aged 79 [C143520] *J.P., D.L.* Wilts.

DAVIS (Charles) [NiVoF] Chap. of the Donative of Whitcombe, Dorset 1832. Died? [Not yet traced in CCEd] Problem man.

DAVIS (Evan) Bapt. Havershan, Bucks. 23/7/1790, s. Evan and Hannah Davies. Wadham, Oxford 1807, BA1812, MA1812, dn13 (B&W), p14 (B&W). S/M Dorchester Free G/S 1813-24. R. Dorchester All Saints, Dorset 1818. Dom. Chap. to 6th Earl of Shaftesbury 1816. Died Kelvedon, Essex 1866 (2nd q.) aged 76 [C52354] Married (1) Burnham-on-Sea, Som. 13/7/1815 Sophia Dods, with issue (2) Melcombe Regis, Dorset 22/9/1831 (d.1835) Harriet Oakley.

DAVIS (Henry, 'Harry') From Bloxham, Oxon., s. Rev. John Davis. Trinity, Oxford 1780 (aged 18), dn84 (Ox.), then Merton, BA1785, p86 (Ox.). PC. Barford St Michael (or Great Barford), Oxon. 1826. Died? [C28164]

DAVIS (Henry) [BA but NiVoF] V. ('Treasurer') Somerton, Som. 1795-1833, R. Keinton Mandeville, Som. 1809-10. Died 27/5/1833 (CCEd says 13/6/1833) [C34684]

DAVIS (John) From New Church, Carmarthen, s. John Davis. Exeter [Foster says Jesus], Oxford 1789 (aged 18), BA1793, MA 1795, dn98 (Nor. for Salis.), p99 (Bristol). V. Cerne Abbas, Dorset 1812 [C52362] w. R. Melcome Horsey, Dorset 1814 to death 4/12/1840 [C52351 as John David]

DAVIS (John) Born Danyrallt, Carmarthen, s. Evan Davis (farmer). Pembroke, Cambridge 1792 (aged 18), BA1793, MA1796, p98 (Chich.). R. Bellingham, Northumberland 1815-32 (res.). Died? [C130376]

DAVIS (John) From Llangadwaladr, Denbigh, s. John Davis. Jesus, Oxford 1800 (aged 19), BA1804. R. Kilkhampton, Cornwall 1804 and V. Poughill, Cornwall 1810 to death 8/1/1857 aged 77 [Not yet in CCEd]

DAVIS (John) Born Poole, Dorset, s. John Davis. Exeter, Oxford 1812 (aged 19), then Trinity Hall, Cambridge 1815, SCL, dn16 (B&W), p17 (B&W), LLB1820. PC. Ashwick, Bath 1826-70. Died Ashwick (a widower) 17/4/1874 aged 81. No will traced [C42115] Had issue.

DAVIS (Richard Francis) From Worcester, s. Thomas Davis. Worcester. University, Oxford 1784 (aged 17), BA1788, dn90 (Wor.), MA1791, p91 (Wor.), BD and DD1810. R. Worcester All Saints 1795 and R. Pendock, Worcester 1810 to death 25/12/1844 [C120990]

DAVIS (Robert) Bapt. Minehead, Somerset 24/7/1794. Queens', Cambridge 1813, BA1817, dn18 (Nor.), p19 (Nor.), MA1820. V. Cannington, Som. 1825 to death 21/6/1865, leaving £12,000 [C42116] Clerical son.

DAVISON (Edward, sen.) Born Durham 30/6/1760, s. Edward Davison and Elizabeth Bird. Lincoln, Oxford 1777, BA1781, dn82 (Durham), p84 (Durham). PC. Trimdon, Durham 1785 to death (Auckland, Durham) July 1839 aged 79 [C129516] Married 1784 Hannah Bell, with clerical son (below). An active *J.P.* Co. Durham. Mayor of Durham 1815. 'Extremely rich.'

DAVISON (Edward, jun.) Born Brancepath, Co. Durham 13/4/1788, s. Rev. Edward Davison (above) and Hannah Bell. Corpus Christi, Oxford 1803, BA1807, University, Fellow 1807-16, MA1810, dn11 (Ox.), p12 (Ox.). R. Harlington, Middx. 1816-55, PC. Durham St Nicholas 1821-56 (his father was

Lecturer here, so some confusion) to death 22/5/1863, leaving £30,000 [C28173. Boase] Married (1) Durham 23/7/1815 Isabella Ann White, with issue (2) Durham 11/5/1824 Mrs Margaret (Pearson) Wolfe Butler, w. clerical s. Charles Henry Davison. Alderman of Durham.

DAVISON (John) Born Morpeth, Northumberland 25/5/1777, s. John (schoolmaster - *pleb*) and Mary Davison. Christ Church, Oxford 1794, BA1798, then Oriel, Fellow 1798-1818, MA1801, p03 (Salis.), BD1818. R. Seagry, Wilts. 1803-5 (res.), R. Sutterton, Lincs. 1817-19, R. Washington, Co. Durham 1819, Sneating Prebend in St Paul's, London 1824-31 (res.), Canon of 5th Prebend in Worcester Cathedral 1825-34, R. Upton upon Severn, Worcs. 1826-34, V. Old Sodbury, Glos. 1829-31 (res.), V. Wichenford, Worcs. 1831 to death (Cheltenham) 6/5/1834 [C55238. ODNB as theologian of the Noetic group] Married 20/7/1819 Mary Thorpe, w. clerical son John Robert Davison

DAVISON (Thomas) Born Stokesley, Yorks. 5/101753, s. Rev. William Davison and Catherine Vane. University, Oxford 1772, BA 1776, dn77 (Durham), p78 (Durham), MA 1780. V. Crowmarsh Gifford, Oxon. 1778-89, V. Combe, Hants. 1789-1833, V. Brantingham, Yorks. 1793-4 (res.), V. Hartburn, Northumberland 1794 to death 4/7/1833 aged 79 (CCEd says 10/12/1833) [C130378] Married (1) Castle Eden, Co. Durham 24/2/1785 Elizabeth Webster, with issue (2) 1808 Sarah Hall.

DAVISON (Thomas Francis) Born 1792. [NiVoF] V. Donnington, Sussex 1795 and R. Chichester St Peter the Less [sequestrator] 1805, Treasurer and Wigthring Prebend in Chichester Cathedral 1792 to burial 21/4/1834 (CCEd says 16/5/1834) [C63223] Married Chichester 14/12/1791 Emily Caroline Hutchinson, with issue.

DAVISON (W.) [NiVoF] Curate of Worthing, Surrey 1812. Died? [Not in CCEd]

DAVY (Charles) Bapt. Eye, Suffolk 4/10/1757, s. Rev. Charles Davy (R. Benacre, Suffolk) and Jane Nunn. Caius, Cambridge 1776, MB1781, Fellow 1782-92, dn84 (Nor.), p91 (Lin.). S/M The Perse School, Cambridge 1786-91; R. Creeting St Peter, Suffolk 1792-1818 (res.), V. Wickham Market, Suffolk 1803-27, R. Combs w. Barking and Darmsden, Suffolk 1818 and PC. Badley, Suffolk 1818 to death 7/3/1836 [C55241] Married Ipswich, Suffolk 12/12/1792 Anne Freeman, w. issue. 'A very ingenious naturalist'.

DAVY (Charles) From Winkleigh, Devon, s. Rev. William Davy. [NiVoF?] 'Perpetual V'. Preshult, Wilts. 1829-34, V. Inglesham, Wilts. 1834 to death 1836 [C91987 - but consider 141284]

DAVY (Martin) Bapt. Ingoldisthorpe, Norfolk 28/1/1763, s. William Davy and Jane Oldman. Caius, Cambridge 1787, Fellow 1791, MB1792 and MD1797 (both Edinburgh) and practised medicine in Cambridge. dn10 (Bristol for Ely), p10 (Bristol for Ely), DD 1811, the 'despotic' Master of Caius College, Cambridge 1803-39, Vice Chancellor of Cambridge 1803, 1827. R. Cottenham, Surrey 1827 and Heathfield Prebend of Chichester Cathedral 1832 to death 18/5/1839 [C17373 - same as below. Total confusion here. ODNB] Married 16/5/1811 the heiress Ann Stevenson (Eccleshall, Staffs., she d. the same year), 'By his own request his papers were destroyed, which was done by boiling them in the large copper vessel of the college kitchen' (ODNB). *F.R.S.* (1801). But see also below.

DAVY (Martin) Bapt. Ingoldisthorpe, Norfolk 3/6/1791, s. Rev. William and Elizabeth Davy. Trinity, Oxford 1810, then Magdalen, Fellow 1815-33, BA1814, MA1817, BD1824, etc. V. Waterperry, Oxon. 1817 to death (Ingoldisthorpe) 20/8/1833 (CCEd says 21/12/1833) [Noted only in C17373 - which differentiated him from his namesake (above), but the two men are still hopelessly confused in CCEd]

DAVYS (George, *later* Bishop of Peterborough) Bapt. Loughborough, Leics. 2/11/1780, s. John Davys (R. Rempstone, Notts.) and Sophia Wigley (a clergy dau.). Clare, Cambridge 1798, BA1803, dn06 (Nor.), MA 1806, then Christ's, Fellow 1806-14, p07 (Nor.), DD 1831. Tutor to Princess Victoria 1827-37. V. Willoughby on the Wolds, Lincs., Notts. 1811-31, V. All Hallows on the Wall, City of London 1829-30, Dean of Chester 1831-9, Bishop of Peterborough 1839 to death (bronchitis) 18/4/1864, leaving - as George Peterborough - £80,000 [C23491. ODNB. Boase] Married Bury St Edmunds 18/1/1814 Marianne Mapletoft (a clergy dau.), w. clerical sons Edward, and Owen William Davys. Photo. online.

DAVYS, *born* RICHARDS (Morgan Richards) Bapt. Carmarthen 2/10/1800, s. Morgan David Richards and Sarah Thomas. Literate: dn26 (Bristol for York), p26 (York). V. Theddlethorpe All Saints w. Mablethorpe, Lincs. 1829-30, PC. Alvingham w. North Cockerington, Lincs. 1831. Died? [C52367. YCO] Married Builth, Brecon 1845 (3rd q.) Margaret Powell.

DAWES (Charles Thomas) Born Camberwell, Surrey 21/7/1793, s. Charles Thomas Dawes (physician) and Mary Halford. Magdalene, Cambridge 1811, BA1816, dn17 (Nor.), p20 (Nor.). PC. Adbaston, Staffs. 1826, V. Dilhorne, Staffs. 1836 to death (Leamington, Warwicks.) 8/8/1863 aged 70, leaving £200. Lived on the Mount Ephraim estate, Faversham, Kent [C11130] Married (1) Cannock, Staffs. 7/5/1818 Jane Butler Barber (a clergy dau., d.1822) (2) Bredwardine, Worcs. 30/12/1826 Mary Henrietta Sherwood (w) (a military dau.), with issue.

DAWES (John) Bapt. Ambleside, Westmorland 30/3/1766. Literate: dn92 (Chester), p93 (Chester). PC. Ambleside 1811 to death 17/8/1845 aged 79 [C168675] The young Hartley Coleridge attended his school; 'a kindly and liberal-minded pedagogue'.

DAWES (Richard) Bapt. Hawes, Yorks. 13/4/1793, s. James Dawes (farmer) and Isabella Cockbone. Trinity, Cambridge 1813, BA1817, MA1820, dn20 (Chester for Ely), p20 (Ely), then (the new) Downing College 1818-36. V. Tadlow, Cambs. 1820-40, V. East Hately, Cambs. 1826-40, R. King's Somborne, Hants. 1836 (where he had a school), Dean of Hereford 1850 (income £1,000, and where he restored the Cathedral) to death. Master of St Catherine's Hospital [almshouses], Ledbury, Heref. 1861. Died 10/3/1867, leaving £3,000 [C17405. ODNB. Boase. W.C. Henry, *A biographical notice of the late Very Rev. Richard Dawes, Dean of Hereford* (1867)]. Married 1836 Mary Helen Gordon (w) (Logie, Aberdeenshire). Brother, below. A major educationalist, his model school run on radical lines attracted much attention.

DAWES (Septimus) Born Hawes, Yorks., s. James Dawes and Isabella Cockbone. Emmanuel, Cambridge 1822 (aged 19), then Caius, BA1827, dn27 (Lin.), p29 (Lin.), MA 1830. PC. Long Sutton St James, Beds. 1830 [income £65] to death 14/11/1874 aged 71, leaving £1,000 [C55244. Kaye] Married Long Sutton 9/4/1839 Emma Ricardo Wilkinson, with issue. Brother, above.

DAWKINS (Edward Henry) Bapt. Chipping Norton, Oxon. 25/6/1794, s. Henry Dawkins, *M.P.*, and Augusta Clinton. BNC, Oxford 1812, then All Souls, Fellow 1815-35, BCL1819, dn19 (Ox.), p20 (Ox.), DCL1824. V. West Markham (or Markham Clinton), Notts. 1828 to death (Moggerhanger House, Beds.) 18/5/1859, leaving £40,000 [C28180] Married Marylebone, London 14/5/1835 Mrs Elizabeth (Cooper) Dawkins (dau. of his cousin Rev. Sir William Henry Cooper, 4th Bart.), with issue.

DAWNAY (Thomas, Hon.) Born Leatherhead, Surrey? 30/6/1779, s. John, 4th Viscount Downe and Laura Burton. Christ Church, Oxford 1797, BA1803, dn03 (Peterb.), p03 (Peterb.). R. Ashwell, Rutland 1803 to death (unm.) 8/1/1850 [C110141] Brother, below.

DAWNAY (William Henry, 6th Viscount Downe). Bapt. Leatherhead, Surrey 15/9/1772, s. John, 4th Viscount Downe and Laura Burton. Christ Church, Oxford 1790, BA1795, MA 1796, dn98 (Cant. for York), p98 (York). R. Sessay and Thormanby, Yorks. 1798-1836. Died York 23/5/1846 aged 73, leaving £70,000 [C91377. YCO] Married St George's Hanover Square, London 6/6/1811 Lydia Heathcote (of Conington Castle, Yorks.), with issue (incl. Payan Dorney). Inherited Beningbrough Hall, Yorks. in 1827. Brother, above. Succ. to title 1832.

DAWSON (Ambrose) Born Liverpool 11/6/1787, s. Pudsey Dawson (Langcliffe Hall, Settle, Yorks.) and Elizabeth Ann Scott. BNC, Oxford, 1805, BA1809, MA1811, Fellow 1811-48, dn13 (Ox.), p14 (Bangor), BD1819. (joint) PC. Liverpool St Philip 1816-26, (joint) Min. Liverpool St Michael 1826-35 (res.), RD. Chap. to HRH Frederick, Duke of York and Albany 1814. Died unm. at Langcliffe Hall 12 or 19/10/1848 aged 61. [C28181]

DAWSON (Birkett) Bapt. Troutbeck, Westmorland 7/5/1775, s. of Thomas Dawson (a landowner) and Dinah Adamson. S/M Crosby on Eden, Cumberland 1798. Literate: dn99 (Chester), p00 (Chester), then Emmanuel, Cambridge 1801, a Ten Year Man (BD1812). PC. Bradshaw, Lancs. 1822-44. Died (unm.) Chipping Barnet, Herts. 7/5/1853 [C168679] Brother Isaac, below. Freemason.

DAWSON (Edmund) Bapt. Garsdale, Yorks. 4/8/1776, s. William Dawson and Elisabeth Hodgson. Literate: dn00 (C&L), p02 (Durham). V. Alford w. Rigsby w. Ailby, Lincs. 1808 and V. Sutton le Marsh, Lincs. 1808 to death (Alford) 12/3/1852 aged 76 [C10439] Wife Mary Ann, and issue.

DAWSON (Edward Henry) Born Bedford 24/7/1804, s. John Thomas Dawson and Mary Higson Leach. Emmanuel, Cambridge 1823, BA1828, dn29 (Lin.), p29 (Lin.), MA1835. R. Studeley Manor, Glos. 1832-4 (res.), V. Winchcombe, Glos.1832-4 (res.), R. Otten Beauchamp, Essex 1840 to death 8/12/1861 aged 55, leaving £6,000 [C55247] Widow Mary, and issue.

DAWSON (Francis) Bapt. Newmarket, Suffolk 27/4/1788, s. Francis Dawson (a breeder of racehorses) and Catherine Frances Thoroton. Trinity, Cambridge 1807, BA1812, dn12 (Cant.), p13 (Cant.), MA1816, BD1825. PC. Folkestone, Kent 1813-15, R. Hawkinge, Kent 1813-15, R. Chislehurst, Kent 1815-46, (Sinecure R. Orpington, Kent 1827), R. Hayes, Kent 1827-31 (res.), Canon of 3rd Prebend in Canterbury Cathedral 1833-52, (Sinecure R. and) R. All Hallows Lombard Street, City of London 1834, V. East Peckham, London 1846 to death (Canterbury) 24/10/1852 aged 64 [C1785] Married Nov. 1833 Alice Weldon, with issue. Brother George Francis Dawson, below.

DAWSON (George Augustus) Bapt. Lambeth, Surrey 19/2/1791, s. Thomas Dawson (Edwardstone Hall, Boxford, Suffolk) and Anne Manning. St John's, Cambridge 1809, then Clare 1810, BA1814, dn15 (C&L), MA 1819. V. Edwardston, Suffolk 1817 to death. Dom. Chap. to Earl of Belmore 1841. Died 18/1/1848 aged 56 [C10440] Married Westminster, London 11/8/1830 Louisa, dau. Sir Thomas Pilkington, 7th Bart., with issue.

DAWSON (George Francis) Bapt. Newmarket, Suffolk 6/10/1794, s. Francis Dawson (a breeder of racehorses) and Catherine Frances Thoroton. [In army]. TCD1826, BA 1829, p29 (Win.). (joint) Curate Guernsey St James, Channel Isles 1829, V. Hurstbourne Priors, Hants. 1834-[43]. V. Orpington, Kent at death 11/10/1850 ('disease of the heart') [C72818. Al.Dub.] Married Southampton, Hants. 21/7/1829 Anna Maria Hennen, with issue. Brother Francis, above.

DAWSON (Henry) Born 24/8/1791 (bapt. Marylebone, London 3/6/1795), s. William Dawson and Sophia Aufrere. Oriel, Oxford 1811, BA1815, MA1818. R. Bunwell, Norfolk 1821-84, R. Hopton, Suffolk 1827. Died Torquay, Devon 21/12/1889 aged 98, leaving £66,526-0s-4d. [C112575] Married (1) Marylebone, London 13/7/1818 Juliana Buxton (d.1825), with issue (2) Clapham, Surrey 12/3/1835 Susanna Rebecca Jackson (w), with further issue; clerical son William.

DAWSON (Isaac) Bapt. Troutbeck, Westmorland 9/9/1770, s. Thomas Dawson (landowner) and Dinah Adamson. Literate: dn99 (York), p00 (York). V. (St Stephens by) Saltash, Cornwall 1815-33 (and S/M there). Died Modbury, Devon 18/9/1855 [C143063. YCO] Married (1) Elizabeth Appleby (2) Elizabeth Hawkins, 1 dau. Brother Birkett, above.

DAWSON (John) Bapt. Greystoke, Westmorland 29/12/1754, s. Anthony Dawson. Usher at Witherslack Free G/S, Beetham, Westmorland in 1777. Literate: dn77 (Chester), p79 (Chester). PC. Witherslack 1799 to death 18/6/1843 aged 88 [C168682] Was married w. issue.

DAWSON (John Frederick) Bapt. Bedford 31/7/1802, s. John Thomas Dawson and Mary Higson Leech. Trinity, Cambridge 1821, dn26 (Lin.), p26 (Lin.), LLB1827. R. Toynton St Peter w. Toynton All Saints, Lincs. (non-res.) 1827 to death (Clapham, Surrey) 16/10/1870, leaving £6,000 [C55250. Bennett2] Married (1) Eaton Socon, Beds. 1/5/1827 Hester Wade-Gery (a clergy dau., d.1860) (2) Brighton 22/6/1861 Alice Proctor, his housekeeper (w); with issue.

DAWSON (Joseph) Bapt. Allendale, Northumberland 26/12/1773, s. Hugh Dawson. And Elizabeth Waugh. Literate: dn00 (York), p01 (York). R. Edmundbyers and Muggleswick >< Co. Durham 1810-37. Probate granted 27/6/1837 [C91513. YCO]

DAY (Charles) Bapt. Norwich 10/12/1780, s. Rev. John Day and Cecilia Maria Weston. New, Oxford 1799, BA1803, dn03 (Ox.), p07 (Nor.). PC. Playford, Suffolk 1827-51-, R. Norwich St Swithin 1843 to death 18/1/1856 [C28184] Married Gretna Green, Dumfries-shire 15/5/1806 (then again at Norwich 10/6/1806) Marianne Harvey, with issue.

DAY (Charles) From Sussex. St John's, Cambridge 1817, dn22 (Lin.), p23 (Lin.), LLB1824. V. Rushmere St Andrew, Suffolk 1826-35 (res.), PC. Wedmore Chapel, Theale, Som. 1835 (only), Min. Trinity Chapel, St George's in the East, London --, V. Mucking, Essex 1842 to death there 18/3/1868 aged 74, leaving £3,000. Chap. to City of London Poor Law Union [C42123]

DAY (Edmund) Bapt. Scarborough, Yorks. 29/3/1790, s. of Edmund (merchant) and Charlotte Day. Sidney, Cambridge 1821, a Ten Year Man (BD1832), dn13 (York), p14 (York). V. Rillington cum Scampton, Yorks. 1831, PC. (and patron) of Norton, Yorks. 1834-74, V. Willerby, Scarborough 1836 to death (New Malton, Yorks.) 6/2/1874 aged 84, leaving £12,000 [C131063.YCO] Married (1) Rillington 13/11/1817 Elizabeth Catherine Gilbert (d.1828), w. issue (2) Foxholes, Yorks. 28/2/1833 Hannah Todd, w. further issue; clerical son.

DAY (Edward) Bapt. Horsford, Norfolk 9/11/1791, s. Rev. John Day. Trinity, Oxford 1808, BA1812, dn14 (Nor.), p15 (Nor.). R. Kirby Bedon. Norfolk 1821 to death 24/3/1875, leaving £3,000 [C112677] Had issue.

DAY (George) Born Norwich 7/12/1792, s. Starling Day and Margaret Framlingham. Corpus Christi, Cambridge 1811, BA1815, dn15 (Nor.), p16 (Nor.), MA1819. R. Barton Bendish St Mary and All Saints, Norfolk 1817-64, Minor Canon Norwich Cathedral 1817-64, V. Eaton, Norwich 1817-64, PC. Hemblington, Norfolk 1826-64, PC. Norwich St Peter Parmentergate 1829-58. Died 28/12/1864, leaving £33,000 [C1043] Married Heveningham, Suffolk 13/10/1819 Carolina Elfrida Geering (w), with issue.

DAY (Jeremiah Ives) Bapt. Norwich 11/8/1768, s. Benjamin Day and Mary Ives. Trinity, Oxford 1786, then Magdalen 1788-92, BA1790, dn80 (Nor.), p92 (Nor.), Fellow 1792-5, MA 1793. PC. Seething. Norfolk 1797, R. Mundham, Norfolk 1797, R. Yelverton w. Alphington, Norfolk 1800 to death (Loddon, Norfolk) 16/9/1837 [C112679] Married Bury St Edmunds, Suffolk 26/3/1795 Hannah White, with clerical son.

DAY (Jeremy) Bapt. Ilketshall St John, Suffolk 3/8/1773, s. Richard Day (farmer) and Sarah Dresser. Caius, Cambridge 1790, BA1795, dn96 (Nor.), Fellow 1797-1821, p98 (Nor.), MA1799, etc. R. (and patron) of North Tuddenham, Norfolk 1813, R. Hethersett w. Canteloff, Norfolk (w. Chap. of Cantley) 1820 to death 1/11/1855 [C112680] Inherited the Blythfor Manor estate 1822. Nephew below.

DAY (John Tomlinson) Born St Neots, Hunts., s. William Day and Elizabeth Wallman. Corpus Christi, Cambridge 1826, BA1830, dn30 (Lin.), p31 (Lin.), MA1834. V. Riseley, Beds. 1831-2, R. Bletsoe, Beds. 1832 to death (St John's Wood, London) 4/5/1881, leaving £1,209-12s-3d. [C56167] Married Clapham, Beds. 6/7/1841 Ellen Mary Dawson, with issue. Appears to have been in Bedford Gaol in 1872.

DAY (Samuel Emery) From Bengworth, Worcs./, s. Rev. William Day and Grace Esterbrook. St Edmund Hall, Oxford 1817 (aged 19), BA1820, dn20 (Glos.), p21 (Bristol), MA1823, V. Bristol St Philip and St Jacob 1833 (w. Trinity Chapel 1832) to death 24/1/1864, leaving £16,000 [C52369. Kaye] Married Bristol 4/7/1826 Olivia Louisa Hoare (w) (a clergy dau.), with clerical son Arthur Benjamin Day.

DAYMAN (Charles) Bapt. Poughill, Cornwall 18/9/1786, s. John and Mary Dayman. Balliol, Oxford 1805, BA1809, then Exeter, Fellow 1809-17, dn10 (Ox.), p11 (Ox.), MA1814. Chap. to the Forces in Portugal 1811. V. Poundstock, Cornwall 1809 and V. Tintagel, Cornwall 1810, V. Great Tew w. Little Tew, Oxon. 1830 to death 19/8/1847 [C28187] His wife became a Catholic.

DAYMAN (John) Born St Columb Major, Cornwall 23/6/1803, s. John Dayman and Jane Arthur. Trinity, Cambridge 1819, then Corpus Christi, Oxford 1819, BA1823, Fellow 1825-31, MA1826, dn28 (Ox.), p29 (Ox.). R. Skelton, Cumberland 1831 (with RD of Greystoke). Died 'in a cab between Holloway and Tavistock Hotel, Covent Garden', London 8/7/1871 aged 69, leaving £7,000 [C5804. Boase. Platt] Married Holborn, London 15/10/1831 Levina Elizabeth Angelo, with issue. Scholar and Italian linguist. Surrogate.

DAYRELL (Thomas) Born Hutton Buscel, Yorks. 28/5/1802, s. Marmaduke Dayrell (of Shudy Camps Park, Cambs.) and Mildred Rebecca Lawley. Magdalene, Cambridge 1821, BA1825, dn25 (York), p26 (York), MA1830. R. Long Marston, Ainsty of York 1826 to death (Shudy Camps Park) 18/5/1866 aged 64, leaving

£10,000 [C131064. YCO] Married 9/6/1828 Maria Hawksworth (a clergy dau.), with issue. *J.P.* and *D.L.* for Cambs. and West Riding.

DE CHAIR (Richard Blackett) Born Sibertswold, Kent 13/6/1760, s. Rev. John de Chair (Westminster, London) and Julia Wentworth. Oxford: St Mary Hall 1783, dn86 (Glos.), p86 (Glos.), BCL1790, LLB. R. East Horsley, Surrey 1788-92, V. Postling, Kent 1792, V. Sibertswold w. Coldred 1792, V. Hibaldstow, Lincs. 1814. Died Sibertswold 26/3/1851 aged 90 [C56293. Foster under Chair] Married St James, Piccadilly, London 10/7/1786 Isabella Beauvoir, with clerical son.

DE CRESPIGNY (Heaton Champion-) Born Drayton Cerne, Wilts. 23/5/1796, s. Sir William Champion de Crespigny, 2nd Bart. and Lady Sarah Windsor (dau. of 4th Earl of Plymouth). Trinity Hall, Cambridge 1815, dn19 (Nor.), p22 (Chester), LLB1825. [Saw active service in Royal Navy] V. Neatishead, Norfolk 1822, R. Stoke Doyle, Northants. 1822-33. In gaol in Leicester 1822 'in danger of transportation'. Fought a duel 1828 at Calais with Long Wellesley, 4th Earl of Mornington. Imprisoned 6 months for debt of £7,500 in 1833. Lived at Plas Bodegroes [House], Caernarvon. Died Ballarat, Victoria, Australia 15/11/1858 aged 62, leaving £1,000 - 'and also gold miner'! [C110142] Married 19/7/1820 Caroline Bathurst (dau. of a Bishop of Norwich), with issue.

DE GREY (Thomas, 4th Baron Walsingham) see under **WALSINGHAM**

DE HAGUE (George) Born Norwich 31/5/1761, s. Elisha de Hague (Town Clerk of Norwich, of Huguenot descent) and Mary Ganning. Corpus Christi, Cambridge 1778, BA1783, dn83 (Nor.), Fellow 1786-1806, MA 1786, p86 (Nor.), BD1794. R. Little Wilbraham, Cambs. 1806 to death 14/9/1847 aged 86 [C99823]

DE PASSOW (John Claus) Bapt. Bromley, Kent 10/10/1772, s. Christian Albrecht de Passow and Jane/Jenny Children [*sic*]. Trinity, Oxford 1792, BA1796, dn99 (Salis.), p99 (Salis.), MA1799. R. Hever, Kent 1799 to death 23/2/1850 [C91992 as de Passon. Foster under Passow]

DE SAUMAREZ (James, 2nd Baron de Saumarez) see under **SAUMAREZ**

DE WITT see under **WITT**

DEACLE (Thomas) From Halcot, Northants., s. Rev. John Deacle and Elizabeth Levett. Lincoln, Oxford 1789 (aged 18), BA1793, dn83 (Lin. for Peterb.), MA1796. R. Uphill, Som. 1795 to death 10/7/1843 [C34520] Married Clifton, Bristol 30/5/1796 Harriott Watson, with issue. And a possible second marriage?

DEACON (James) Bapt. Norwich 13/8/1780, s. Rev. John Deacon and Jane Sparrow. Caius, Cambridge 1798, BA1803, dn04 (Nor.), MA 1805, p11 (Nor.). (succ. his father as) R. Norwich St Peter Northgate 1819-65, PC. Norwich St Etheldreda 1822 and V. South Walsham St Mary, Norfolk 1832 to death 20/1/1865, leaving £600 [C112686] Married Norwich 14/10/1806 Anne Starling, with clerical son.

DEACON (Thomas) Born Clerkenwell, London 21/6/1796, s. John Deacon. St Alban Hall, Oxford 1813 (aged 27), no degree, dn17 (London for Roch.), p19 (Nor. for Roch.). R. Strood, Kent 1832 to death 4/12/1846 [C151]

DEALTRY (William) From Yorkshire, s. John Dealtry. Jesus, Cambridge 1764, BA1768, Fellow 1769-76, dn69 (London), MA1771, p72 (Peterb.). R. Skirpenbeck, Yorks. 1774-1834, R. Barnby(upon Don), Yorks. 1785, Prebend of Norwell Tertia in Southwell Collegiate Church 1785-1834, V. Bishop Wilton >< Yorks. 1786, R. Hatcliffe, Lincs. 1786-1834, R. Wigginton, Yorks. 1786 to death. Dom. Chap. to 12th Lord Gray 1784 and to Lady Gray 1786. Died 18/1/1834 (CCEd says 15/12/1834). [C136776] Married (1) 6/2/1776 Elizabeth Frances Barber, with issue (2) Darrington, Yorks. 19/7/1803 Henrietta Sotheron (of Darrington Hall).

DEALTRY (William) Born Whitgift, Yorks. 20/7/1775, s. William Dealtry (Swinefleet. Yorks.) and Margaret Nicholson. St. Catharine's, Cambridge 1792, then Trinity 1793, BA1796, Fellow 1798, MA1799, dn99 (Peterb.), p00 (Peterb.), tutor 1801-6, BD1812, DD1829. Professor of Mathematics at East India College, Haileybury 1805-13. R. Clapham Holy Trinity, South London 1813-43, R. of Hatfield Broadoak, Essex 1814-17, R. of Watton at Stone, Herts. 1816-30, R. of Clothall, Herts. 1816-30, Canon of 7th Prebend in Winchester Cathedral 1830-47 (and Chancellor of Diocese of Winchester 1830-45), Archdeacon of Surrey

1845 to death (Brighton) 15/10/1847 [C72834. ODNB. DEB] Married St James, Westminster, London 17/8/1814 Harriet Stainforth, w. issue. *F.R.S.* (1810).

DEAN (James) Bapt. Manchester 1/5/1785, s. Thomas [*pleb*] and Catherine Dean. BNC, Oxford 1804, BA1808, MA1810, dn12 (Win. for C&L), p12 (C&L). PC. Worthington, Lincs. 1819 to death 21/4/1832 [C10581. Foster corrected - or two men here?]

DEAN (John) Probably bapt. Manchester 15/5/1769, s. James [*pleb*] and Ellen Dean. BNC, Oxford 1791, BA1794, Fellow 1795-1815, MA 1797, dn01 (Ox.), p02 (Bangor), BD1808, DD 1816. Principal of St Mary Hall, Oxford 1815 to death. Canon of Vaynol (and Precentor) in St Asaph Cathedral (w. Sinecure R. Corwen, Merioneth 1808-9 (res.)), R. Old (o/w Wolde), Northants. 1815-33. Died 12/4/1833 (CCEd says 19/7/1833) [C28196]

DEAN (Thomas) Literate: dn19 (Salis.), p19 (Chester). S/M Colwall G/S, Heref.; PC. Berrow, Worcs. 1819, PC. Little Malvern, Worcs. 1830, V. Warton, Lancs, 1844 (and RD of Tunstall 1844) to death 25/11/1870 aged 75, leaving under £300 [C91996] Widow Mary.

DEANE (George) Born Ropley, Hants. 25/1/1797, s. Thomas Deane (Hyde Abbey, Winchester) and Susannah Noyes. St Mary Hall, Oxford 1819, BA1822, dn23 (Heref.), p23 (Heref.), MA1825. R. Bighton, Hants. 1827 to death 11/3/1872, leaving £7,000 [C72836] Married by 1829 Mary Grant, with issue.

DEANE (George Henry) Bapt. Walcot, Bath 24/3/1775, s. Anthony Deane and Ann Sophia Whitmore. Merton, Oxford 1793, BA1798, MA 1800, dn00 (Ox.), dn01 (Ox.). V. Bentley, Suffolk 1815, R. Great Wenham 1819-30 (res.), V. Eckington, Worcs. 1830-1 (res.). Died Leamington, Warwicks. 14/2/1855 [C28798] Married Belvidere Harriet Tolley, with issue.

DEANE (Henry) Bapt. Sholden, Kent 13/9/1799, s. Henry Boyle Deane and Elizabeth Wyborn. New, Oxford 1819, Fellow 1819-33, BCL1826, dn26 (Heref.), p26 (Heref.), tutor 1826, etc. V. Gillingham, Dorset 1832 [net income £1,313], RD. Prebend of Alton Australis in Salisbury Cathedral 1842 to death 6/4/1882, leaving £11,717-10s-1d. [C52375] Married (1) West Lavington, Wilts. 18/6/1833 Jane Caswall (d.1850), with issue (2) Battersea, Surrey 29/7/1851 Katherine Mary Smyth; w. clerical sons.

DEANE (William Henry) Bapt. Erwarton, Suffolk 20/5/1798, s. William Deane and Elizabeth Sewell. University, Oxford 1816, BA 1820, dn21 (Peterb. for Nor.). R. Hintlesham, Suffolk 1822 to death 30/11/1854 [C110146] Married Warwick 2/11/1837 Elizabeth Christian Anstruther (dau. of a general), with issue. Port. online.

DEANS (Joseph) Born Tynemouth, Northumberland 5/12/1803, s. Joseph Deans and Sarah Davidson. Christ's, Cambridge 1823, BA 1827, dn27 (Lin.), p29 (Lin.), MA1830. PC. Chellaston, Derby 1830-72, V. Melbourne, Derby. 1831 (and RD of Stanton by Bridge 1870-9) to death (a widower) 20/4/1888 aged 84, leaving £835-14s-0d. [C10586] Had issue. 'A scholarly gentleman, but of indolent and retiring character'.

DEANS (William) Marischal College, Aberdeen, MA, dn85 (Chester), p85 (Chester). V. Aughton w. East Cottingwith, Selby, Yorks. 1786 to death 22/6/1838 [C136223]

DEAR (William Smith) Born Laverstoke, Hants. 11/12/1803, s. Richard Dear and Sarah Goodman. Wadham, Oxford 1821, BA1825, dn27 (Ely), p28 (Ely). MA1828. R. Abdon, Shropshire 1829, R. Albourne, Sussex 1850 to death (unm.) 25/6/1878 aged 75, leaving all £3,000 to his spinster sister [C17411]

DEASON (Thomas) Bapt. Durham 13/11/1771, s. Canon James Deason. Lincoln, Oxford 1788, BA1792, dn94 (York), p95 (Bristol for York). PC. Whitworth, Durham 1797 to death (Camden, London) 12/12/1833 aged 62 [C52376. YCO] Married Islington, London 2/4/1809 Margaret Dobson (dau. of a wine merchant).

DEBARY (Peter) Born Hurstbourne Tarrant, Hants. 24/9/1764, s. Rev. Peter Debary, sen. and Ann Hayward. Trinity, Cambridge 1783, BA 1787, dn87 (Salis.), Fellow 1789, MA1790, p90 (Roch.), BD 1830. Usher at Westminster School 1788-96; R. Eversley, Hants. 1823 (res.), (Sinecure R. Orwell, Cambs. 1830-41). Died London 9/10/1841 aged 77 [C1786, where death date is that of the father].

DEBRETT, DE BRETT (Henry Symonds) Born Westminster, London 5/1/1802, s. John Debrett and Sophia Granger. Downing, Cambridge 1822, dn24 (Lin. for Cant.), SCL, p26 (London for Cant.), LLB 1827, BCL1830. R. Broughton, Lincs. 1830 to death 26/1/1842 aged 40 (living in London) [C56175]

DEEDES (John) Bapt. Hackington, Kent 8/1/1767, s. William Deedes and Mary Bramston. Christ Church, Oxford 1785, BA 1790, then Oriel, MA1792, dn99 (Glos.). R. East Mercea, Essex 1802-6 (res.), R. Langenhoe, Essex 1809-46, R. St Mary Hoo, Kent 1806-9 (res.), R. Willingale Dow w. Shellow Bowels, Essex 1806 to death. Dom. Chap. to 4th Earl of Buckinghamshire 1806-13. Died 2//7/1846 aged 76 [C1787] Married Hastings, Sussex 18/9/1798 Sophia Forbes, with issue.

DEEDES (Julius) Bapt. Hythe, Kent 25/5/1798, s. William Deedes and Sophia Bridges. Trinity, Oxford 1814, BA1819, MA 1821, dn23 (Ely for Cant.), p25 (Lin. for Cant.). R. Orlingbury, Northants. 1825-7 (res.), R. Wittersham, Kent 1828, V. Marden, Kent (and RD) 1846 to death 24/10/1879, leaving £14,000 [C17412] Married West Peckham, Kent 14/5/1829 Henrietta Charlotte Dering (w), with issue.

DEEKER (Robert) Bapt. Little Walsingham, Norfolk 9/2/1795, s. Robert Deeker and Mary Buchanan. Trinity, Cambridge 1821, dn23 (Nor.), BA1825, p25 (Nor.). R. Wakerley, Northants. 1828-53, R. Lyndon, Rutland 1853 to death 21/2/1862, leaving £4,000 [C56295]

DELL (John) Born Aylesford, Bucks. 9/12/1755, s. John and Elizabeth Dell. New, Oxford. 1775, Fellow 1775, dn79 (Ox.), p81 (Ox.), BCL1783, LLB 1803, DCL. R. Totternhoe, Beds. 1782-1803, R. Weston Longueville, Norfolk 1803 to death 7/10/1838 aged 81 [C28207] Married Chenies, Bucks. 15/12/1778 Elizabeth Grant, w. issue.

DEMAINBRAY (Stephen George Francis Tribouday) Bapt. Ealing, Middx. 18/8/1759, s. Rev. Stephen Charles Tribouday Demainbray (*q.v.* ODNB) and Sarah Horne. Hertford Oxford 1775, then Exeter, Fellow 1778-99, BA1781, MA1782, dn82 (Ox.), p85 (Ox.), BD 1793. Succ. his father as Superintendent of Kew Observatory, Richmond, Surrey 1782-1840. V. Long Wittenham, 1794, R. Great Somerford (Somerford Magna), Wilts. 1799 to death. Dom. Chap. to 3rd Baron Ducie 1786; and to the King. Died Malmesbury Wilts. 6/7/1854 aged 94 [C28210. Boase] Married St Pancras, London 7/2/1803 Mary Tomkins.

DENE (John) Bapt. Horwood, Devon 23/4/1779, s. John Dene. Balliol, Oxford 1798, BA1801, dn01 (Ex.), p03 (B&W). R. Horwood 1803-57, R. Newton Tracey, Devon 1832, R. Bittadon, Devon 1828 to death. Dom. Chap. to 20th Baron Dacre 1803. Died 1857 (4th q.) aged 78 [C34541] Married Barnstaple, Devon 30/3/1807 Maria Barston Wavell.

DENISON (Edward, *later* Bishop of Salisbury) Born Marylebone, London 13/3/1801, s. John Denison (born Wilkinson), of Ossington, Notts., *M.P.*, and Charlotte Estwick (dau. of a West Indies planter). Oriel, Oxford 1818, BA 1822 [Student Middle Temple], then Merton, Fellow of 1826-37, MA 1826, dn27 (Ox.), p28 (Ox.), DD1836. PC. Wolvercott, Oxon. 1829, V. Radcliffe on Trent, Notts. 1830-3 [C136776], Prebend of Norwell Tertia in Southwell Collegiate Church 1834, PC. Oxford St Peter in the East 1834, Bishop of Salisbury 1837 (aged 36) to death 6/3/1854 aged 52 (of black jaundice or leptospirosis) [C28211. ODNB. Boase] Married (1) St George's Hanover Square, London 27/6/1839 Louisa Mary Ker Seymer (d.1841), with issue (2) Lambeth, Surrey 10/7/1845 Clementina, dau. Ven. Charles Baillie-Hamilton, Archdeacon of Cleveland.

DENISON (William) Born Oxford 6/1/1763, s. Rev. William Denision, sen. Magdalen Hall, Oxford 1780, BA1783, then Lincoln, dn86 (Ox.), MA1786, p87 (Ox.), BD1796, Fellow 1806. R. Cublington, Bucks. 1805 to death 5/9/1834 (CCEd says 3/3/1835), living at Fenton House, Beds. [C28214] Married Aspley Guise, Beds. 10/8/1808 Caroline Mary Tipping Aveling, with issue.

DENNIS (John) From Newcastle-under-Lyme, Staffs., s. Stephen Dennis. St Edmund Hall, Oxford 1779 (aged 21), no degree, dn79 (C&L). V. White Notley, Essex 1804 to death 13/9/1843 [C10591]

DENT (William) Born Thirsk, Yorks. 15/3/1784, s. William Dent (apothecary) and Mary Coats. Trinity, Cambridge 1801, BA1806, dn07 (Heref. for York), p08 (York), MA1809. PC. Sowerby, Notts. 1827-43, R. Carlton

Miniott, Thirsk 1834 to death (Crosby Hall, Northallerton, Yorks.) 13/6/1843 [C104392. YCO] Married Herts. 14/7/1806 his second cousin Sophia Louisa Dent, with issue. *J.P.* North Riding and Chairman of Quarter Sessions. Below?

DENT (William) Born Thirsk, Yorks, s. Robert Dent (surgeon). Clare, Cambridge 1813, BA1818, dn18 (Chester), p20 (Chester). R. Lassington, Glos. 1830 [to death] (unmarried) 1845 [C143968] Above?

DENTON (Isaac) Bapt. Crosthwaite, Cumberland 4/7/1786, s. Rev. Isaac Denton, sen. and Sally Robson. Queen's, Oxford 1806, BA1810. PC. Wythburn, Crosthwaite 1812 and V. Wingrave, Bucks. 1816 to death 17/5/1850 aged 64 [C5809. Platt] Married Newbold Percy, Warwicks. 5/4/1817 Mary Kay (of Wigton, Cumberland).

DENYS (Thomas) Born London, s. Peter Denys. Magdalen Hall, Oxford 1788 (aged 25), BA1793, dn93 (Peterb.), p95 (Nor. for Peterb.), MA1796. V. Easton Neston, Northants. 1795-1807, V. Bourne, Lincs. 1807 to death (St John's Wood, London) 22/1/1842 [C56304. Bennett1] Married (2?) Southwark, Surrey 3/9/1821 Elizabeth Musson.

DERING (Cholmeley Edward John) Born Brighton, Sussex 18/3/1790, s. Cholmeley Dering and Charlotte Elizabeth Yates. Christ Church, Oxford 1808, BA1812, dn13 (Salis. for Cant.), p14 (Salis. for Cant.), MA1815. PC. Goodnestone, Kent 1814-15 (res.), R. West Deeping, Lincs. 1814-18, R. Pluckley, Kent 1816, R. Fairstead, Essex 1817-27, Tottenhall Prebend in St Paul's Cathedral, London 1827 to death. Chaplain in Ordinary; Dom. Chap. to 2nd Earl of Onslow 1814. Died 12/8/1848 [C56506] Married Marylebone, London 27/5/1817 Maria Price, with issue.

DES VOEUX, DESVOEUX (Henry) Born Dublin 1786, s. Sir Charles Philip Vinchon Des Voeux, 1st Bart., *M.P.* (of Queen's County and Yorks.) and Mary Anne Champagné. TCD1803, BA1807, p10 (C&L), incorporated at Cambridge 1820. V. Stapenhill, Staffs. 1813-[37]. Lived at Leamington, Warwicks. Dom. Chap. to 1st Marquess of Anglesey 1812. Died Interlaken, Switzerland ('as the result of an accident') 30/9/1857 [C10442. Al.Dub.] Married (1) Burton on Trent, Staffs. 1/12/1812 Frances Dalrymple (d.1827), with issue (2) Norwell, Notts. 3/5/1828 Frances Elizabeth Hutton (d.c.1838), with further issue (3) Marylebone, London 1839 (2nd q.) Julia Grace Denison (with yet more children?).

DETHICK (Thomas) Born Bombay 20/8/1764, s. Thomas and Elizabeth Dethick. St John's, Oxford 1782, BA1786, dn87 (Ox.), MA1788, p01 (Bristol for 'The Commissary of the Peculiar Jurisdiction of Bridgnorth'). PC. Bridgnorth St Mary Magdalen, Shropshire 1804 and R. Oldbury, Shropshire 1822 to death. Surrogate to the Commissary 1830. Died 21/12/1833 [C25574]

DEVERELL (John Robert) Born Leicester 15/3/1779, s. James and Susanna Deverell. Queens', Cambridge 1797, SCL1802, dn02 (Lin.), p05 (Lin.), MA1826. R. Careby, Lincs. 1826 to death. Dom. Chap. to Duke of Ancaster. Died Bourne, Lincs. 14/9/1844 ('after a long illness') aged 65 [C56508. Bennett2] Married Lincoln 31/3/1797 Susannah Ann Ruding, 3 ch.

DEW (John Worgan [*not* Morgan]) Bapt. 8/3/1797, s. George Worgan (of Poolway House, Coleford, Glos.) and Anne Dew. Literate: dn24 (York), p25 (York), then Trinity, Cambridge 1822 (a Ten Year Man). (first) V. Halifax St James, Yorks. 1831 to death. Dom. Chap. to Viscount Strathallan. Died ('lamented') 5/9/1834 aged 36 [C131069. YCO] Married Knaresborough, Yorks. June 1826 Anne Wormald, with clerical son.

DEWDNEY (Edmund) Bapt. Dorking, Surrey 2/5/1798, s. James and Mary Dewdney. St John's, Cambridge 1822, BA1827, dn27 (Ox.), p28 (Ox.), MA1830. PC. Portsea St John, Hants. 1833 to death (Florence) 18/6/1847 [C28222] Married Bath 21/1/1829 Emily Letitia Lindsey, w. issue.

DEWDNEY (George) Bapt. Dorking, Surrey 27/10/1797, s. George Dewdney and Sophia Jameson. Queen's, Oxford 1816, BA1822, dn22 (Salis.), MA1824. R. Fovant, Wilts. 1828, R. Gussage St Michael, Dorset 1830 to death 28/6/1869 aged 71, leaving £5,000 [C52380] Left issue.

DEWE (James Byam) Born Breadsall, Derbys. 19/3/1792, s. Rev. John James (V. Alstonfield, Staffs.) and Sarah Dewe. St John's, Cambridge

1811, BA1817, dn17 (C&L), p17 (York). PC. Ravenfield, Yorks. 1817 to death 11/3/1840 [C10443. YCO]

DEWE (Samuel) Born Appleby, Leics. 10/11/1795, s. of Rev. Samuel Dewe, sen. (V. Buntingford, Herts) and Lucy Mills. St John's, Cambridge 1814, BA1818, dn18 (Lin.), p20 (Lin.), MA 1821. S/M Devonport Classical and Mathematical School, Devon 1824; Minor Canon of Rochester Cathedral 1832-64, V. Chart Sutton, Kent [blank in ERC] 1833-6, V. Allhallows, Kent 1835, V. Rochester All Saints 1836 (only), R. Kingsdown w. Mappiscombe 1836 to death 10/9/1885 aged 89, leaving £7,290-13s-6d. [C202] Married Layston, Herts. 8/3/1824 Frances Mary Cork (of Buntingford, Herts.), with clerical son Francis Avarne Dewe.

D'EYE (Nathaniel) Bapt. Eye, Suffolk 29/5/1771, s. Nathaniel D'Eye (attorney) and Ann Rust. Caius, Cambridge 1789, BA1793, dn94 (Nor.), MA1796, p96 (Nor.). R. Occold, Suffolk 1796-1805 (res.), R. Thrandeston, Suffolk 1800-44, R. Burlingham St Andrew, Norfolk 1808-19 (res.). Died (influenza) 10/2/1844 aged 73 [C112434] Married Cambridge 23/2/1796 Ann Halfhide Green, with issue. *J.P. Suffolk.*

DIBDIN (Thomas Frognall) Born Calcutta 1776, s. Capt. Thomas Dibdin, R.N., and Elizabeth Compton. St John's, Oxford 1793 [adm. Lincoln's Inn 1794] BA1801, MA1802, dn05 (Win.), p05 (Win.), BD & DD1825. V. Exning, Cambs. 1823, R. St Marylebone St Mary Bryanston Square, London 1824 to death. Chaplain in Ordinary. Died ('after a long illness, of paralysis on the brain') 18/11/1847 [C73002. ODNB. E.J. O'Dwyer, *Thomas Frognall Dibdin: bibliographer and bibliomaniac extraordinary, 1776-1847* (Private Libraries Association, 1967)] Married Camden, London 8/7/1797 Sophia Humphreys (a clergy dau.), with issue. The famous bibliographer, and a founder of the Roxburghe Club. *F.R.S.* (1821), *F.S.A.*

DICKEN (Aldersey) Born Witheridge, Devon 28/2/1794, s. Rev. Perry Dicken and Mary Vere. Sidney, Cambridge 1811, BA1815, then Peterhouse, Fellow 1816-33, dn17 (Ely), p18 (Ely), MA1818, BD1826, DD1831. H/M Blundell's School, Tiverton, Devon 1823; V. Milton, Cambs. 1821-31 (res.), R. Norton, Suffolk 1831 to death (Bournemouth, Dorset) 2/2/1879, leaving £14,000 [C17725] Married 25/2/1838 Caroline Mary Huddleston, with naval issue.

DICKES (Thomas) From Middlesex. Jesus, Cambridge 1788, BA1793, dn94 (Cant.), p96 (Cant.), MA1797, Fellow 1797-8 (res.). V. Comberton, Cambs. 1810-30, V. Whittlesford, Cambs. 1830 to death 23/1/1845 aged 75. Joint 'Registrar of the Archepiscopal Consistory Court of Commissioners at Canterbury' 1802-45 [C17726]

DICKINS (Watson William) Bapt. Marylebone, London 30/3/1789, s. Francis Dickins and Diana Manners-Sutton. Merton, Oxford 1808, BA1812, dn13 (Glos.), p13 (Glos.), MA1819. R. Hawkinge, Kent 1815-18, PC. Folkestone, Kent 1815-18, R. Adisham w. Staple, Kent 1818 and Prebend of Wellington in Lichfield Cathedral 1822 to death 27/8/1862, leaving £5,000 [C10617. Foster as William Watson] Married Lambeth, Surrey 20/6/1818 (some say 8/1/1818) Mary Knatchbull, with issue.

DICKINSON, DICKENSON (John) Born Kaber, Westmorland. [NiVoF] V. Compton Dundon, Somerset 1829-51-[63]. Died? [C42169] Married 31/8/1829 Frances Elizabeth Salmon (of Wells), w. issue. At least two men of this name.

DICKINSON (Robert) [NiVoF] V. Ilfracombe, Devon 1804 (probably non-res. as he was also Sunday Afternoon Lecturer, Newington Butts, Surrey 1797), both to death 13/2/1836 aged 80 [C155053] Had issue. Or two men?

DICKINSON (Robert) Bapt. Crosthwaite, Cumberland 14/8/1769, s. Robert Dickinson [*pleb*] and Elizabeth Turner. Queen's, Oxford 1786, BA 1791, dn94 (Ox.), Fellow, MA1795, p98 (Roch.). Probably PC. Milton, Hants. 1822 [C73004], R. Headley, Hants. 1818 to death 1/11/1847 [C1794] Wife Henrietta Maria.

DICKINSON (Thomas Gustavus) Bapt. St Pancras, London 7/12/1788, s. Thomas Dickinson. Magdalen Hall, Oxford 1814, no degree, dn14 (Nor.), p15 (Nor.). R. Alpheton, Suffolk 1816-48. Died 26/11/1865. No will traced [C112763] Married City of London 28/1/1817 Elizabeth King.

DICKSON (George Stevens) From Sunderland, Co. Durham, s. George Stevens Dickson. University, Oxford 1823 (aged 18), BA1827, dn28 (Lin.), p29 (Peterb.). PC. Lincoln St Swithin 1830 to death 7/10/1863, leaving £3,000 [C56528]

DICKSON (Michael) From Taunton, Som., s. Michael Dickson. Oriel, Oxford 1781 (aged 24), no degree, p82 (Nor. for B&W). PC. Bishop Hull, Som. 1785, PC. Trull, Som. 1788 and V. Pitminster, Som. 1790 to death 22/2/1837 [C34560]

DICKSON (Thomas Briggs) Born Poulton-le-Fylde, Lancs. 19/12/1804, s. Richard Dickson and Margaret Briggs. Emmanuel, Cambridge 1823, BA1828, dn31 (Chester), MA1831, Fellow 1831-42, p33 (Chester), BD1838. PC. Whittle le Woods, Leyland, Lancs. 1831-9, PC. Marple, Cheshire 1842-58, R. Eastchurch, Kent 1858 [income £1,750] to death 6/5/1870 aged 65, leaving £6,000 [C168705] Married Liverpool 13/12/1842 Jane Swainson, with clerical son.

DIGBY (Charles) Born Westminster, London 31/5/1775, s. Col. Hon. Stephen Digby (Meriden Hall, Warwicks.) and Lady Lucy Fox-Strangways. Christ Church, Oxford 1793, then St Mary Hall BA1798, dn99 (B&W), p00 (Salis.), MA1801. R. Penselwood, Som. 1806-32 (res.), R. Chiselborough, Som. 1807-41, R. Middle Chinnock, Som. 1807-41, Canon of Windsor (2nd Stall) 1808-41, R. Bishop's Caundle, Dorset 1810-41, RD of Shaftesbury, Dorset 1824. Dom. Chap. to 3rd Earl Digby 1810. Died Windsor 23/6/1841 aged 66. [C27003] Married St George's Hanover Square, London 8/6/1801 Mary Somerville (a military dau.), with issue.

DIGBY (William) Born Durham 25/2/1774, s. Very Rev. Hon. William Digby (Dean of Worcester, then of Durham) and Charlotte Lepell Cox. Christ Church, Oxford 1791, BA 1795, dn98 (Ox.), MA1798, p99 (Chester for Ox.). PC. Offenham, Worcs. 1800, PC. South Littleton w. North and Little Littleton, Worcs. 1807, Canon of 1st Prebend in Worcester Cathedral 1813-48, V. Wolveley, Worcs. 1813-14 (res.), R. Harvington, Worcs. 1814-18 (res.), R. Cropthorne, Worcs. 1818-26 (res.), V. Wichenford, Worcs. 1826-31, V. Coleshill, Warwicks. 1831, R. Sheldon, Warwicks. 1831. Master of St Oswald's Hospital [almshouses], Worcester 1833. Died (Kingston, Surrey) 21/1/1848, s.p. [C10621] Married (1) Bisham, Berks. 20/8/1800 Almeria Augusta Cary (d.1811) (2) 3/1/1813 Charlotte Elizabeth Digby (d.1820 'of rapid consumption': a fine seated marble monument of her by Chantrey in Worcester Cathedral and online).

DIGHTON, DEIGHTON (William) Bapt. Wolsingham, Co. Durham 11/5/1764, s. Seymour Dighton [*pleb*] and Joyce Thompson. Lincoln, Oxford 1785, dn88 (Durham), BA 1789, p89 (Durham). R. Whinburgh w. Westfield, Norfolk 1805, V. Carbrooke, Norfolk 1816. Died 29/8/1843 [C112712]

DIKES see under **DYKES**

DILLON (Henry Luke) Born London (or Poole, Dorset?) 10/1/1786, s. Luke Dillon (army officer) and Lady Margaret Augusta de Burgh (dau. 11th Earl of Clanricarde). Worcester, Oxford 1804, BA1808, dn09 (Salis. for Bristol), p10 (Salis. for Bristol), migrated to Trinity Hall, Cambridge 1825, MA1825. R. Lytchett Maltravers, Dorset 1810-31 (res.), PC. Corhampton, Wilts. 1823-31 (res.). Died March 1845 [C52383] Married Bloomsbury, London 29/6/1815 Phoebe Hawkins, with issue.

DILLON (Robert) Bapt. St Gluvias/Gulval, Cornwall 28/6/1754, s. Robert Dillon and Hannah Cock. Exeter, Oxford 1773, dn76 (Ex.), BA1777, p78 (Ex.). R. Redruth, Cornwall 1804, V. Bodmin, Cornwall 1813, V. Gulval 1819 to death (a widower) 6/1/1839 aged 84 ('at 8 o' clock in the morning'). Probate granted 11/3/1874 for under £20 [C143071] Married Gulval 20/4/1791 Alida Van Horne, with issue.

DILLON (William Edward) Bapt. Falmouth, Cornwall 14/4/1762, s. William Dillon and Anne Ragland. Trinity, Oxford 1780, BA 1784, dn84 (Ex.), p86 (Ex.). R. St Endellion, Cornwall 1795 and PC. Cornelly, Cornwall 1805 to death 21/4/1833. Married Creed, Cornwall 11/5/1790 Anna Moore, with issue [C143072]

DIMOCK (Charles) Bapt. Chipping Norton, Oxon. 17/11/1770, s. Rev. Henry Dimock and Susanna Barker. Oriel, Oxford 1788, BA1792, dn93 (London), MA1794, p94 (London). V. Headcorn, Kent 1801-3, R. Great Mongeham, Kent 1802 to death 3/2/1849 [C116935] Brother below.

DIMOCK (Henry) Born Chipping Norton, Oxon., s. Rev. Henry Dimock and Susanna

Barker. Pembroke, Oxford 1781 (aged 16), then Corpus Christi, Fellow, BA1785, MA and Chap. 1789, dn89 (Glos.), p89 (Ox.). R. Halstead, Suffolk 1797-1801, R. Monks Eleigh, Suffolk 1800-12, PC. Ash, Kent 1810-12, R. Monks Risborough, Bucks. 1811 to death 3/10/1839 aged 75. Principal Register and Chief Actuary of the Province of Canterbury 1798-1803 (res.) [C1795] Brother, above.

DIMOCK (John Giles) Born Stonehouse, Glos. 21/3/1773, s. John Dimock and Betty Cole. Pembroke, Oxford 1790, then University, BA 1794, dn97 (Glos.), MA1800, p00 (Glos.). V. Clanfield, Oxon. 1800-23, V. Uppingham, Rutland 1817 to death 15/12/1858, leaving £20,000 [C28233] Married St James, Piccadilly, London 18/4/1797 Sarah Humphries, with clerical son.

DINELEY (George, sen.) Bapt. Peopleton, Worcs. 7/5/1751, s. Josiah Dineley and Mary Perkins. Worcester, Oxford 1769, BA1773, dn73 (Heref.), p75 (Heref. for Wor.), MA1776, BD 1786. R. Spetchley, Worcs. 1777-1811, R. Churchill (in Halfshire), Worcs. 1781 and R. (and patron) of Peopleton 1786 to death 11/5/1844 aged 93, living at Crowle, outside Worcester [C104390] Married Peopleton 2/12/1779 Elizabeth Green, with clerical son (below).

DINELEY (George, jun.) Bapt. Crowle, Worcs. 20/12/1786, s. Rev. George Dineley, sen. (above) and Elizabeth Green. Worcester, Oxford 1805, BA1809, MA1811, BD1828. (succ. his father as) R. Spetchley, Worcs. 1811-44, (succ. his father as) R. Churchill (in Halfshire), Worcester 1844-63. Died South Hayes, Worcs. 4/7/1863, leaving £3,000 [C56532 has confusion with the father] Married Winchester 15/11/1814 Maria Coates.

DISBROWE (Henry John) Bapt. Launceston, Cornwall 29/4/1792, s. Edward Disbrowe and Charlotte Hobart. Christ Church, Oxford 1813, BA1816, All Souls, Fellow 1816-21, BCL1819, dn19 (Ox.), p20 (Ox.). R. Welbourn, Lincs. 1820 to death 24/3/1867, leaving £5,000 [C28236] Married Manchester 5/9/1823 Elizabeth Slater (d.1829), w. clerical son Henry Sharp Disbrowe.

DISTURNELL (Henry Josiah) Born Bermondsey, London 10/3/1743/4, s. John Disturnell. Pembroke, Cambridge 1763, BA 1767, dn67 (Ex. for Nor.), p68 (Nor.), MA 1770. R. Wormshill, Kent 1792 to death 9/12/1834 (CCEd says 17/3/1835) [C112766]

DITCHER (Joseph) Literate: dn18 (London), p18 (London), then Queens', Cambridge 1829 (a Ten Year Man), MA1837 Lambeth. British Chap. at Belize, Honduras 1819-22; PC. Bitton Holy Trinity (o/w Kingswood), Glos. 1821-33 (res.), V. South Brent, Somerset 1841 to death 28/11/1875 aged 82, leaving £3,000. Principal Acting Surrogate and Judge of the Episcopal Court, Bath and Wells Diocese 1836-41 (and it was he who prosecuted Archdeacon Denison over his Eucharistic doctrine) [C42172. Boase. DEB. Selina Ditcher, *Brief memorial of the Rev. Joseph Ditcher, addressed to his late parishioners, South Brent, Somerset* ([1876])]. Married (2) Widcombe, Som. 7/1/1864 Selina Thompson (w).

DIXON (Anthony) Born Cumberland. Literate: p92 (Car.), p93 (Car.). PC. Maryport, Cumberland 1800-45 (res.), PC. St Bridget, Calder Bridge, Beckermet w. St John, Beckermet, Cumberland 1816-43. Died there (unmarried) 23/4/1847 aged 78 [C5813. Platt]

DIXON (George) Born Kirkby Moorside, Yorks. 10/12/1793, s. Rev. George, sen. and Margaret Dixon. St Catharine's, Cambridge 1812, BA1816, dn16 (York), p17 (York for Durham), MA1819. V. Wawne (o/w Waghen), Yorks. 1827-69, PC. Kirkdale w. Nawton, Yorks. 1830, V. Helmsley w. Sproxton, Rievaulx and Carlton, Yorks. 1830-69 [C135857], PC. Cold Kirby, Yorks. 1830, Prebend of Bugthorpe in York Minster 1846 (and part RD of Ridall) to death 30/7/1869 aged 75, leaving £3,000 [C131071 has some dates of the father. YCO] Married (1) 1824 Sarah Lambert (dau. of an attorney), with issue (2) by 1851 Ann Maria (w); had clerical son. Surrogate.

DIXON (Henry) Born Walton on Thames, Surrey 14/10/1776. Literate: dn99 (Chester), p01 (Chester), then Sidney, Cambridge 1804 (a Ten Year Man, BD1814). V. Harrold w. R. Souldrop, Beds. 1817-22, V. Millom, Cumberland 1822 to death 13/6/1836 aged 58 [C56541] Married St Bees, Cumberland 15/1/1809 Catherine Fox, w. issue.

DIXON (Henry) From Sullington, Sussex, s. Rev. Joseph Dixon. BNC, Oxford 1817 (aged 19), BA1820, dn21, p22, MA1823, incorporated at Cambridge 1857. V. Ferring, Sussex 1832 to death (a widower) 6/11/1870, leaving £1,000 [C63318]

DIXON (John) Bapt. Wakefield, Yorks. 9/6/1768, s. John Dixon (a book keeper). Queens', Cambridge 1788, BA1792, dn92 (Car. for York), p92 (York), MA1795. PC. Ingleby Greenhow, Yorks. 1797-1846, PC. Bilsdale, Helmsley, Yorks. 1810. Died Ingleby Greenhow 5/3/1846 [C5816. YCO] Married 1830 Eliza Barnet (of Barry, Glamorgan), w. issue.

DIXON (John) Bapt. Ulverston, Lancs. 6/4/1787, s. James Dixon (a hatter) and Peggy Jackson. Literate: dn11 (Chester), p12 (Llandaff). PC. Crosthwaite and Lyth, Westmorland 1830 (and S/M Crosthwaite G/S 1827) to death 6/11/1861 aged 74, leaving £450 [C168710 and 3830] Married (1) Windermere, Westmorland 16/1/1816 Mrs Jane (Jackson) Gaskarth (d.1834), with issue (2) Crosthwaite 30/12/1839 Margaret/Mary Airey (w).

DIXON (Jonathan) Bapt. Lamplugh, Cumberland 6/1/1753, s. John Dixon. Literate: dn75 (Chester), p77 (York), MA by 1816 (a Ten Year Man>). R. Kirby Grindalythe, Yorks. 1781-9, V. Burton Pidsea, Yorks. 1788-1831, V. Humbleton w. Elsternwick, Yorks. 1792 and V. Garton in Holderness w. Grimston, Yorks. 1792 to death. Dom. Chap. to 9th Duke of St Albans 1816. Died 21/12/1831 aged 79 (CCEd says 2/6/1832) [C109804. YCO]

DIXON (Matthew) Bapt. Tickhill, Yorks. 8/4/1784, s. Rev. Matthew, sen. and Elizabeth Dixon. St Catharine's, Cambridge 1805, dn10 (Salis. for Chester), p10 (Salis. for Chester - but CCEd and YCO say p32 (Lin. for York)). PC. Wellow, Notts. 1832-40. Died 1848 (1st q.) [C56550 appears to conflate father and a son of same name? YCO]

DIXON (Richard) Bapt. Whitehaven, Cumberland 5/5/1780, s. Robert Joshua and Ann Dixon. Queen's, Oxford 1796, BA1799, dn02 (Peterb.), p03 (Chester), MA1803, Fellow to 1829, etc. PC. Clifton, Cumberland 1803-4 (res.), R. Godshill w. Niton >< IoW 1828 to death 13/5/1858, leaving £40,000 [C73009. Boase] *F.R.S.* (1811).

DIXON (Richard Samuel) Bapt. City of London 24/4/1795, s. Richard and Elizabeth Dixon. Trinity Hall, Cambridge 1817, SCL, dn21 (Ely for London), p21 (London), LLB1821, LLD1833. R. (and patron) of Flempton w. Hengrave, Suffolk 1826 and (Sinecure R. Great Tey, Essex 1828-45). Died 2/8/1845 [C17732]

DIXON (Thomas) Born Cliburn, Westmorland 9/1/1798, s. Joseph Dixon. St John's, Cambridge 1815 (re-adm. 1816), dn21 (Nor.), BA 1822, p22 (Nor.), MA1825. V. Tibenham, Norfolk 1825 to death 16/4/1863, leaving under £200 [C17727] Widow Charlotte.

DIXON (Thomas) Born St Bees, Cumberland 18/10/1795, s. Thomas and Phoebe Dixon. [NiVoF], dn18, p19. V. Stokesay, Shropshire 1829-44, R. Stckleigh Englsh, Devon 1844. Died ('late of Lydbury North', Shropshire) 18/2/1872, leaving £450 [C10639] Married Mary Ann Marston (w), and had issue.

DIXON (William) Literate: dn98 (Car.), p99 (Car.). V. Appledore, Kent 1829 to death 8/9/1844 aged 71 [C5815] Wife Mary, and issue.

DIXON (William) [NiVoF] PC. East Ardsley >< Leeds, Yorks. 1808 to death 24/2/1844 aged 67 [Not yet in CCEd. Possibly in YCO] Married Leeds 21/6/1808 Rachel Thompson (w). Not the same man as either of the two other men of this name here.

DIXON (William) Bapt. Dalton in Furness, Lancs. 7/3/1790, s. Robert and Agnes Dixon. Literate: dn13 (Chester for York), p14 (Chester). PC. Kirkby on the Moor, Yorks. 1814, PC. Broughton, Preston, Lancs. 1817 to death 23/3/1872 aged 82, leaving £5,000 [C168716. YCO] Wife Jane, with issue.

DIXON (William) Born Walton on the Hill, Liverpool 16/7/1803, s. Henry Dixon and Catherine Townley Plumbe. BNC, Oxford 1823. BA1827, dn29 (Chester), p30 (Chester). V. Ellel, Cockerham, Lancs. 1832-5, R. Tong, Bradford, Yorks. 1835 to death 27/2/1854 [C168718] Confusion in the various sources.

DIXON (William Henry) Born Wadworth, Doncaster, Yorks. 2/11/1783, s. Rev. Henry Dixon and Anne Mason (a clergy dau.). Pembroke, Cambridge 1800, BA1805, dn07 (Ex. for York), p08 (York), MA1809. Canon (5th Stall) in Ripon Collegiate Church 1815-24 (then in the new Cathedral 1836-52), V. Mapleton, Yorks. 1818-21, PC. Bradfield, Yorks. 1819, V. Wistow and Cawood, Yorks. 1821-9, V. Bishopthorpe, York 1824-34, Prebend of Weighton in York

Minster 1825 (Residentiary Canon 1831-54), V. Topcliffe w. Dalton, Yorks. 1828-34, V. Sutton in the Forest, Yorks. 1834-37, R. Etton, Yorks. 1837 (and RD of York 1842) to death. Dom. Chap. to Archbishop of York 1828-54. Died (York) 17/2/1854 [C121207. ODNB (where several dates of incumbencies differ). Boase. YCO. C.B. Norcliffe, *Memoir of the late Rev. W.H. Dixon, MA, FSA* (York, 1860)] Married (1) Loversall, Doncaster 9/1/1809 Mary Anne Fenton (d.1830) (2) York 2/2/1832 Mary Anne, dau. of Rear-Admiral Hugh Robinson. Instrumental in blocking the revival of the Convocation of York. *F.S.A.* 'Wealthy'.

DOBRÉE (Daniel) Born St Peter Port, Guernsey, Channel Islands 13/10/1806, s. Henry Dobrée and Applegarth Budd [*sic*]. Pembroke, Oxford 1825, BA1828, dn30 (Chich.), MA1831, p31 (Glos.). S/M Elizabeth College, Guernsey; Curate Guernsey Holy Trinity 1833, R. Guernsey (The) Forest and Torteval 1836 to death 12/4/1867, leaving under £100 [C63319] Married Mrs Mary Perchard (Mansell) Power.

DOBRÉE (John Gale) Born Hackney, London 28/2/1786, s. Samuel Dobrée (merchant) and Elizabeth Hankey. Pembroke, Cambridge 1814, BA1818, dn19 (Ely for London), p20 (Nor.), MA1821. R. Fleet Marston, Bucks. 1829-32, R. Newbourn, Suffolk 1832-55, R, Holton St Mary, Norfolk 1855 to death 26/4/1879 aged 83, leaving £15,000 [C17728] Married Capel St Mary, Suffolk 3/5/1821 Emily Elizabeth Tweed (a clergy dau.), with clerical son James Bonamy.

DOBRÉE (Nicholas Peter) Born St Peter Port, Guernsey, Channel Islands 17/3/1755, s. Nicholas Dobrée and Elizabeth Le Pelley. Jesus, Oxford 1776, dn78 (Ox.), p79 (Ox.), BA 1780, MA1783. R. Guernsey St Saviour 1784 (only), R. Guernsey Castel 1784, R. Wigginton, Oxon 1789-1835 (res.), R. Furtho, Northants. 1789 to death there 5/2/1843 [C28243] Married July 1789 Charlotte de Saumarez, with issue.

DOBSON (John) Bapt. Lowther, Westmorland 20/6/1765, s. Richard and Margaret Dobson. S/M Kirkby Lonsdale G/S, Westmorland 1786 for 47 years. Literate: dn91 (York). PC. Hutton Roof, Westmorland 1799-1838. Died Kirkby Lonsdale 26/4/1842 aged 78 [C124882 and C168722. YCO] Married Kirkby Lonsdale 6/1/1790 Mary Harrison, with issue.

DOBSON (John) Born Colchester, Essex. St John's, Cambridge 1794, BA1798, Fellow 1799, dn99 (Lin.), MA1801, BD1808, p13 (Lin.), Fellow 1823-31. R. Brandesburton, Yorks. 1829 to death 1/2/1847 [C56556]

DOBSON (Robert) Bapt. Corney, Cumberland 5/2/1786, s. Robert Dobson and Mary Dixon. Literate: dn15 (Chester), p16 (Chester). PC. Great Harwood, Blackburn, Lancs. 1819 to death (Samlesbury, Lancs.) 4/4/1861 ('after a long illness'), leaving £4,000 [C168723. Not the person noted in Venn] Married Bolton, Lancs. 19/4/1825 Hannah Haworth, with issue.

DOCKER (William) Born Kirby Morland, Westmorland 1/12/1790, s. William Docker and Jane Betham. Literate: dn14 (Car.), p15 (Car.), then St Catharine's, Cambridge 1830, a Ten Year Man. PC. Martindale, Westmorland 1817-18 (res.), (first) PC. Southport, Lancs. 1821 to death 10/7/1849 aged 58 [C5819. Venn has a reference. Platt] Married Asby, Westmorland 16/1/1816 Charlotte Jane Henderson, Newcastle upon Tyne. Kept a boarding school near Southport. Fine portrait online.

DODD (Henry Allison) Born Aspatria, Cumberland 13/12/1798, s. Rev. John and Mary Dodd. Queen's, Oxford 1815, BA1819, MA 1822, dn26 (Ox.), p26 (Ox.), Chaplain, Fellow, etc. 1829-42. PC. Newcastle upon Tyne St John 1826-34, V. Sparsholt w. Kingston Lisle, Berks. 1841 to death 28/6/1869 aged 70, leaving £16,000 [C28246] Surrogate.

DODD, DOD (Henry Hayman) Born Taunton, Somerset 27/5/1803, s. Henry Dod and Susanna Dell Hayman. Worcester, Oxford 1821, BA 1825, dn28 (B&W), MA1828, p30 (Chich.). V. Arlington, Sussex 1830 to death 10/8/1833 (CCEd says 12/2/1833) [C42173] Married Chichester 20/4/1829 Frances Elizabeth Holland, with issue.

DODD (John) Literate: dn93 (Car.), p94 (Car.). V. Wigton, Cumberland 1804-26, V. Newcastle upon Tyne St Nicholas 1826 to death. Dom. Chap. to Earl of Galloway. Died 31/12/1840 aged 71 [C5821. Platt] Married Stanwix, Cumberland 18/2/1798 Mary Carrick, with clerical son.

DODD (Moses) From Northend, Bucks., s. John Dodd [*pleb*] and Elizabeth Green. Corpus Christi [*not* Christ Church], Oxford 1785 (aged

18), then Hertford, BA1789, dn90 (Bristol for Salis.), p91 (Ox.), MA1791. Highley Prebend in Chichester Cathedral 1802-24, V. Chidham, Sussex 1804-5, R. Fordham, Essex 1804 to death 3/12/1839 [C28247] Married Ealing, Middx. 11/8/1795 Penelope Sturges, with issue.

DODD (Philip Stanhope) Born Camberwell, London 3/4/1775, s. Rev. Richard Dodd (R. Cowley, Middx.) and Elizabeth Sanderson. Magdalene, Cambridge 1792, BA1796, dn97 (London), Fellow, MA1799. Min. Lambeth Chapel, South London 1803-7, R. St Mary at Hill w. St Andrew Hubbard, City of London 1807-12, (Sinecure R. Aldrington, Sussex 1812-52 - 'church destroyed'), R. Penshurst, Kent (and Preacher throughout the Diocese of Canterbury) 1819 (and RD of Malling 1846) to death. Chap. to Lord Mayor of London 1806; Dom. Chap. to 6th Duke of Leeds 1819. Died 22/3/1852 aged 77 [C63322. ODNB. Boase] Married Swine, Yorks. 4/8/1814 Martha Wilson (a military dau.), and had issue.

DODDS, DODS (George) Born Rokeby, Yorks. 20/3/1798, s. George Dodds and Elizabeth Ellis. Literate: dn22 (York), p23 (York), then Pembroke, Cambridge 1823 (a Ten Year Man), BD 1834, DD1839. V. Corringham, Lincs. 1831 and PC. Harpswell, Lincs. 1844 to death. Died 22/3/1852 aged 77. Dom. Chap. to Duke of Cleveland c.1865-79. Died 22/3/1852 aged 77 [C56563. YCO] Married Liverpool 23/8/1821 Ann Jacques, with issue. Antiquarian; geologist.

DODGSON (Charles) Born Hamilton, Lanark 2/11/1800, s. Charles Dodgson (officer in 4th Dragoon Guards) and Lucy Hume. Christ Church, Oxford 1818, Student [Fellow] 1818-28, BA1822, dn23 (Ox.), MA1824, p26 (Ox.). PC. Daresbury, Cheshire 1827-43, R. Croft, Darlington, Yorks. 1843 (w. Canon Residentiary of Ripon Cathedral 1852 and Archdeacon of Richmond 1854 to death. Chap. to Bishop of Ripon 1836-56; and to Archbishop of Canterbury 1862-8. Died 21/6/1868 aged 67, leaving £8,000 [C28250. Boase. BBV] Married his cousin Frances Jane Lutwidge 5/4/1827, and had clerical s. Charles Lutwidge Dodgson, *aka* 'Lewis Carroll'.

DODGSON (William Jacob Thomas) Born Ulverston, Lancs. (others say of Demerara, British Guiana, his mother's home), s. William Dodgson and Martina Esther Thomas. Queen's College, Oxford 1823 (aged 29), BA1828, p29 (London). Chap. to the Imperial Brazilian Mining Association 1829; (first) PC. Ulverston Holy Trinity 1832-9, V. Arksey, Yorks. 1839-[44], R. St Peter, Essequibo, British Guiana at death there ('insolvent') on or around 3/12/1845 [C116946. LBSO] Married (1) Liverpool 25/7/1825 Christiana Kenny (a minor, she d.1844) (2) Leguan Island, British Guiana 21/4/1845 Rebecca Glorvina Trotz. Freemason.

DODS (Richard) From Burton, Lincs., s. Joseph Dods and Sarah Arnall. BNC, Oxford 1795 (aged 18), BA1799, dn99 (Lin.), p01 (Lin.). R. Faldingworth, Lincs. 1806-7, R. Fleet, Lincs. [net income £1,057] 1807 to death 1/8/1853 [C56565] Married Fleet 17/7/1810 Mary Stanger, with issue.

DODSLEY (Christopher) Born Willington, Derbys. 29/9/1783 (bapt. 25/5/1795), s. Rev. Richard Dodsley and Dorothy Greaves. BNC, Oxford 1801, no degree, dn08 (York), p09 (York). R. (and patron) of Swinnerton, Staffs. [blank in ERC] 1822 to death 31/7/1851 [C10640. YCO] Married Barrow w. Twyford, Derbys. 20/1/1811 Joyce Elizabeth Beaumont, w. child.

DODSON (Christopher) Bapt. Burton on Trent, Staffs. 18/5/1792, s. Rev. John Dodson and Frances Dawson. University, Oxford 1810, BA1813, MA1817, dn17 (Ex. for Chich.), p18 (Glos.). R. Grateley, Hants. 1819, R. Penton Mewsey, Surrey 1832 to death there. Dom. Chap. to Maria, Countess of Guilford 1817; to Louisa, Countess of Craven 1832. Died 14/4/1876 aged 83, leaving £2,000 [C10642] Widow Eleanor.

DODSON (John) Born Lancaster 8/7/1807, s. John Dodgson and Harriet Potter. Trinity, Cambridge 1826, BA1831, dn31 (Cant.), p32 (Lin. for Cant.), MA1835. PC. Overton, Lancs. 1832, V. Cockerham, Lancs. 1835-48. 'Retired to his estate in Littledale Hall, Lancs. where he opened a Baptist Church and ministered for thirty years'. Died Eastbourne, Sussex 23/4/1890 aged 84 leaving £35,050-19s-9d. [C56568. DEB] Married 1831 Elizabeth Ann Salisbury, with issue.

DODSON (Nathaniel) Bapt. Hurstpierpoint, Berks. 19/11/1787, s. Rev. John Dodson and Frances Dawson. St John's, Cambridge 1805, BA1809, dn19 (York for C&L), p11 (York for

C&L), MA1812. R. Buttermere, Wilts. 1818 and R. Abingdon St Helen w. St Nicholas, Berks., 1824 (and Prebend of South Scarle in Lincoln Cathedral 1824) to death. Dom. Chap. to 1st Earl of Sheffield 1814-24. Died 13/8/1867 aged 79 [total income in CR65 £1,287], leaving £12,000 [C10644. YCO] Married East Hendred, Oxon. 17/6/1829 Mary Anne Wapshere, w. issue.

DODSON (William) From Yoxhall, Staffs., s. Rev. John Dodson. St John's, Oxford 1800 (aged 18), BA1804, dn04 (Ox.), p06 (Ox.), MA1808, Fellow to 1812, BD1817. R. Well w. Dexthorpe and Claxby, Lincs. 1812 and V. Edlington, Lincs. 1817 to death 17/10/1852 [C28473]

DODSWORTH (John) From Carlton, Yorks., s. John Dodsworth. Queens', Cambridge 1818, dn22 (Lin. for Ely), BA1823, MA1827, p27 (London for York). PC. Roundhay, Leeds, Yorks. 1827 to death 28/9/1839 (aged 46?) ('from mortification' following a compound fracture after 'leaping from' his gig) [C17730. YCO]

DOLBEN, *born* SKINNER (Thomas) From Ipsley, Warwicks., s. Thomas Skinner and Margaret Harris. St John's, Oxford 1803 (aged 18), SCL, dn17 (Ex.), p17 (Ex.). V. King's Coughton, Warwicks. --, R. (and patron) of Ipsley 1829 to death 1/11/1839 aged 53 (as Thomas Dolben-Dolben) [C143076] Married Coventry, Warwickshire 26/11/1816 Anne Chambers (w), and had issue.

DOLIGNON (John) Bapt. 6/9/1774, s. John Dolignon (a London wine merchant) and Elizabeth Delamare. Trinity, Cambridge 1792, BA1797, dn98 (Lin.), MA1800, p06 (Nor.). R. Gooderstone, Norfolk 1816-54, (Sinecure R. Wimbish, Essex 1816-38), R. Hilborough, Norfolk 1838 to death 12/12/1856 aged 82 [C56576] Married Swaffham, Norfolk 24/1/1811 Eliza Jane Yonge (a clergy dau.), with issue.

DOLPHIN (John) Born Bourton-on-the-Water, Glos. 26/8/1804, s. Rev. John Dolphin and Martha Rollinson. Trinity, Cambridge 1824, BA1828, dn28 (London), p29 (London). (succ. his father as) R. Pebmarsh, Essex 1831-42, R. Antingham St Mary, Norfolk 1830 (and RD of Repps 1869-87) to death 21/6/1889 aged 84, leaving £18,068-17s-8d [C155063. Boase]

Married Walcot, Bath 13/8/1833 Mary, dau. Admiral Thomas Western (Tattingstone Park, Ipswich), with clerical s. John Maximilian. Cricket Blue and member of Norfolk County Eleven 1828-42: ttps://en.wikipedia.org/wiki/John_Dolphin_(cricketer)

DOMETT (Joseph) Bapt. Bovey Tracey, Devon 22/9/1756, s. of Rev. Philobeth Domett. Pembroke, Oxford 1775, dn79 (Ex.), BA1779, p80 (Ex.), then King's, Cambridge, MA [but not in Venn?]. V. Bovey Tracey 1780, V. Lyme Regis, Dorset 1787-98, (succ. his father as) R. Shepton Beauchamp, Som. 1798 to death. Dom. Chap. to 11th Earl of Caithness 1787; to 4th Earl of Macclesfield 1798. Died 29/10/1835 aged 80 [C34569] Married (1) West Teignmouth, Devon 17/5/1805 Susanna Bickford (2) Ideford 17/5/1810 Laura Bradford.

DOMVILE, DOMVILLE (Henry Barry) Born Tallow, Co. Dublin, s. Charles (or John) Pocklington Domville and Mary Sheppard. Oriel, Oxford 1798 (aged 19), dn04 (Glos. for Win.), BA1804, p05 (Glos. for Win.), MA1811. R. Leigh w. Bransford, Worcs. 1811-28 (res.), R. Pencombe, Heref. 1830-56, PC. Marston Stannett, Heref. 1832-33. Died 20/1/1856 [C10648] Brother below.

DOMVILE (William) Born Tallow, Co. Dublin 26/12/1783, s. Charles (*or* John) Pocklington Domvile and Mary Sheppard. St Mary Hall, Oxford 1804, BA1808, MA1814. R. Munsley, Heref. 1814, R. Winforton, Heref. 1818 to death. Dom. Chap. to 11th Earl of Caithness 1787; to 4th Earl of Macclesfield 1798. Died (a widower) 5/11/1858, leaving £6,000 [C104479] Had issue. Brother above.

DONALD (John) Literate: dn05 (Car.), p06 (Car.). PC. Crosscanonby, Cumberland 1806 to death 28/3/1853 aged 70 [C5826. Platt]

DONALD (Matthewman Hodgson) Born Warwick Hall, Longcroft, Cumberland 22/10/17192, s. William Donald and Mary Hodgson. Queen's, Oxford 1811, BA1815, dn18 (Salis.), MA1818, p19 (Salis.) R. Iford w. Kingston >< Sussex 1822 to death (a widower) 19/8/1864, leaving - nothing [C63328] Married Iford 4/4/1823 Mary Lucy Hurley.

DONCASTER (John) Bapt. Nottingham 8/7/1772, s. John Doncaster and Elizabeth

Caunt. Trinity, Cambridge 1789, BA1794, Greek Lecturer 1794, dn94 (Cant.), p96 (Cant.), Fellow, etc. 1796-1815, MA1797, Hebrew Lecturer 1800-2, DD1816. S/M then H/M Oakham School 1808-46; R. Navenby, Lincs. 1814 to death. Chap. Oakham House of Correction, Rutland 1816. Died (Brighton) 5/10/1858 aged 86, leaving £25,000 [C56649] Married (1) Widmerpool, Notts. 29/5/1816 Elizabeth Wright (d.1842) (2) Ancaster, Lincs. 26/1/1843 Helen Nettleship.

DONCASTER (William) Bapt. Ollerton, Notts. 12/9/1774, s. Charles and Ann Doncaster. University, Oxford 1794, then Magdalen, Fellow 1797-1819, BA1797, dn97 (York), MA 1799, p99 (Chester for Ox.), BD 1807. V. Normanton upon Trent, Notts. 1804-47, R. Horsington, Lincs. 1814-15 (res.), R. Winterbourne Bassett, Wilts. 1818 to death (Warwick) 29/12/1847 [C28477. YCO]

DONNE (James) From Oswestry, Shropshire, s. Rev. James Donne (H/M Oswestry School). St John's, Cambridge 1813, BA1817, dn19 (St Asaph), p19 (Salis.), MA1820, BD1836. PC. South Carlton, Lincs. 1819, V. Bedford St Paul 1824-61, V. Clapham, Surrey 1843 to death. Dom. Chap. to 5th Baron Monson 1819. Died 17/1/1861, leaving £8,000 [C56654] Widow Mary.

DONNE (John) Born St Donat's, Glamorgan 22/2/1789, s. Matthew Donne and Ann Bowen. V. Houghton Regis, Beds. 1819 to death 28/7/1846 [C56656] Married Houghton Regis 24/9/1817 Dinah Haslehurst.

DORNFORD (Joseph) Born Deptford, Kent 9/1/1794, s. Sir Josiah Dornford and Esther Fawcett. Trinity, Cambridge 1809 ['left suddenly' to fight in the Peninsular War 1811], migrated to Wadham, Oxford 1813, BA 1816, then Queen's, Fellow 1817-19, then Oriel, Fellow 1819-36, MA1820, dn21 (Ox.), p22 (Ox.). PC. Moreton Pinkney, Northants. 1827-32, R. Plymtree, Devon 1832 (and Prebend of Exeter Cathedral 1847) to death 18/1/1868 aged 74, leaving £7,000 [C28479. ODNB. Boase] Married Gravesend, Kent 31/5/1855 Emma Louisa Dornford (*thus*) (w), 1s. 'In his bearing he was more of a soldier than a priest, and his talk ran much on war. He was a man of strong will, generous impulses and pugnacious temper'; and a ladies' man. Mountaineer.

DOUGLAS (Henry) Born Whitbourne, Hereford 17/4/1793, s. Rev. Robert Douglas (R. Salwarpe, Worcs.) and Frances Jeffreys. St John's, Cambridge 1811, BA1815, MA1818. V. Newland, Glos. 1822-32, RD, Precentor and Prebend of Master Henry Hicman in Llandaff Cathedral 1825-34, R. Whickham, Durham 1832-44, 7th Prebend of Durham Cathedral 1834-59, R. Salwarpe 1849 to death (Durham City) 15/7/1859 aged 66, leaving £30,000 [C3833] Married Newland 30/9/1823 Eleanor Birt (w) (a clergy dau.), 17 ch. (inc. clerical). George Richmond painted his portrait; his undergraduate diary survives.

DOUGLAS (James, 4th Baron Douglas) Born 9/7/1787, s. Archibald Douglas, 1st Baron Douglas (of Castle Douglas) and Lady Frances Scott (dau. of Earl of Dalkeith). Christ Church, Oxford 1807, BA1810, dn11 (Salis. for Heref.), p12 (Salis. for Heref.), MA1816. R. Marsh Gibbon, Bucks. 1819-48 and R. Broughton St Andrew, Northants. 1825 to death. Dom. Chap. to 5th Baron Monson 1819. Died (Bothwell Castle, Lanark) 6/4/1857 aged 69 [C56664] Married 18/5/1813 Wilhelmina Murray (a military dau.), *s.p.* Succ. to title 1848 which became extinct on his death.

DOUGLAS (John) Born St Bees, Cumberland 29/5/1791, s. James Douglas (farmer) and Ann Dixon. Literate: dn16 (Chester), p17 (Chester). PC. Nether Wasdale, Cumberland 1827 to death 28/6/1856 [C168731] Married 1834 Ellen Sarah Plymton.

DOUGLAS (Philip William) Born Cambridge, s. Rev. Philip Douglas (Master of Corpus Christi College) and Mary Mainwaring. Christ Church, Oxford 1817 (aged 17), Student [Fellow] 1817-29, BA1821, MA1824, dn25 (Bristol), p27 (Ox.). V. Bonby, Lincs. 1828-35 (res.), V. Horkstow (Hawkstow) Lincs. 1828-34, PC. Escot, Devon 1840. Lived at Ryde, IoW. Died Weymouth, Dorset 11/2/1872, leaving £6,000 [C28482] Married (1) Shoreditch, London 7/1/1813 Susannah Aplin (d.1826) (2) Brighton, Sussex 19/1/1830 Charlotte Barber; with issue.

DOVELL (John) Bapt. Parracombe, Devon 19/12/1755, s. John Dovell and Mary Knight. Exeter, Oxford 1776, BA1780, dn80 (Ex.), p81 (Ex.). R. Martinhoe, Devon 1789. Died 1839 (3rd q.) [C143079] Married North Molton, Devon 31/10/1786 Elizabeth Burgess, w. issue.

DOVETON (Frederick) Bapt. Blackheath, Kent 23/12/1787, s. Frederick Doveton and Mary Slade. Corpus Christi, Oxford 1805, BA 1809, dn11 (Win.), p11 (Win.), MA1813. V. Woodham Walter, Essex 1812-18, V. Steeple, Essex 1813-19, R. South Normanton, Derbys. 1819 to death. Dom. Chap. to 6th Earl of Shaftesbury 1813. Died 15/4/1871 (but living - and dying - in Calvados, France), leaving £8,000 [C100674] Wife Mary Honel.

DOVETON (John Frederick) Born Chudleigh, Devon 9/8/1774, s. Richard Doveton and Elizabeth Farthing. Oriel, Oxford 1792, then Exeter, dn99 (B&W), p00 (Salis.), BCL1804, MA1811. R. West Monkton, Som. 1804-12, R. Blagdon, Som. 1804-15, V. (East) Betchworth, Surrey 1815, R. Burnett, Som. 1815, R. Mells, Som. 1824-45 (and Preacher throughout the Diocese of B&W) 1824. Chap. to HRH Duke of Kent 1811. Died (Topsham, Devon) 9/1/1857 aged 82 [C34598] Married West Mockton, Som. 28/7/1803 Elizabeth Crossman, with clerical son. *J.P. & D.L* Somerset.

DOWBIGGIN (John) Born Stoke Goldington, Bucks. 20/7/1766, s. Rev. Robert Dowbiggin and Elizabeth Green. St John's, Cambridge 1784, BA1790, dn90 (Lin.), p92 (Lin.). V. Skellingthorpe, Lincs. 1795 to death 1838 (1st q.)? [C56683] Married Lincoln 8/3/1799 Mary Bennett, with issue.

DOWDESWELL (Charles) Bapt. Bromsgrove, Worcs. 28/3/1771, s. John and Abigail Dowdeswell. Worcester, Oxford 1788, BA1792, dn93 (Wor.), p95 (Wor.). V. Beoley, Worcs. 1828 to death 28/6/1839 [C120910]

DOWDESWELL (Edward Christopher) From Pull Court, Worcs., s. Hon. John Robert William Dowdeswell, *M.P.*, and Bridget Codrington (dau. of a baronet). Christ Church, Oxford 1780 (aged 15), BA1783, then All Souls, Fellow, dn87 (Ox.), MA1787, p88 (Chester for Ox.), BD1795, DD1799. PC. Bushley, Glos. 1791-1809, V. Alne w. Aldwark, Yorks. 1793, R. Stanford Rivers, Essex [net income £1,007] 1802-49, R. Langham, Essex 1807-29 (res.), Canon of 4th Prebend in Christ Church Cathedral, Oxford 1808 to death (London) 1/8/1849 [C28484] Married St Pancras, London 23/12/1800 Ann Gellas.

DOWELL (Stephen Wilkinson) Bapt. Highgate, London 22/1/1802, s. of Stephen Dowell and Elizabeth Longman. Exeter, Oxford 1820, then Worcester, BA1824, dn25 (Lin.), p26 (Lin.). V. Shorwell, Hants. 1830-40, R. Mottistone, Hants. 1830-40, V. Gosfield, Essex 1848 to death (Bournemouth, Dorset) 21/12/1870 aged 68, leaving £7,000 [C56687] Married Bathwick, Som. 21/1/1832 Julia Beasley, w. clerical son Arthur Giro Dowell.

DOWKER (Edmund) Born Salton, Yorks. 9/2/1795, s. John Dowker (a farmer) and Mary Woodcock. Trinity, Cambridge 1813, BA1813, dn18 (York), p19 (York), MA1821. V. Salton 1819-36, PC. Sinnington, Yorks. 1819 and V. Willerby, Yorks. 1830 to death (Scarborough) 12/4/1836 aged 41 [C131082. Venn has him living until at least 1849. YCO] Married Melton Mowbray, Leics. 16/5/1833 Mary Anne Clark.

DOWLAND (John James Golden) Bapt. Winterbourne Whitchurch, Dorset 20/11/1795, s. Rev. James Dowland and Dorothy Bestland. Wadham, Oxford 1814, dn18 (London for Bristol), SCL1818, LLB1818, BA1819, p19 (Chester for Bristol), V. Winterbourne Whitchurch 1820, V. Turnworth, Dorset 1820-29, V. Broadwindsor, Dorset 1828 to death 14/3/1838 [C52396] Married Shaftesbury, Dorset 27/7/1824 Harriet Buckland.

DOWNE (Thomas) Bapt. Eltham, Kent 5/11/1770, s. George Downe and Mary Mantell. Corpus Christi, Cambridge 1787, BA1794, dn94 (Cant.), p96 (Bristol for Cant.). V. Lydden, Kent 1814 to death 8/6/1838 [C52397] Married 1800 Mary Lord, with issue.

DOWNE (6th Viscount) see under **DAWNAY (William Henry)**

DOWNES (Richard) Bapt. Ardley, Oxon. 2/5/1777, s. Rev. Robert and Hannah Downes. New, Oxford 1794, BA1797, dn00 (Ox.), p01 (Ox.) MA1801, Fellow, etc. to 1827. PC. Wheatley, Oxon. 1823 (only), R. Berwick St John, Wilts, 1826 to death 1/3/1855 [C24278] Brother below.

DOWNES (Robert) Bapt. Ardley, Oxon. 17/8/1795, s. Rev. Robert, sen. and Hannah Downes. Worcester, Oxford 1815, BA1819, dn19 (Heref.), MA1821. V. Leamington, Warwicks. 1824-39, R. Fletcham, Surrey 1839. Died Leamington 19/10/1859 aged 65, leaving

£6,000 [C10677] Married Leamington 7/11/1826 Philadelphia Hopper (w). Brother above.

DOWNES (Samuel) Bapt. Birmingham 15/10/1779, s. Charles Downes (schoolmaster-*pleb*) and Catherine Rhodes. Wadham, Oxford 1796, BA1800, dn02 (Lin.), p04 (Lin.). S/M Durham School 1804, S/M Tamworth G/S, Staffs.; V. Kilham, Yorks. 1823 to death (Islington, London) 25/7/1845 [C56692] Married Newport, Hants. 3/9/1812 Frances Mary Phillips, with issue. Freemason.

DOWNES (William) Bapt. Sheffield, Yorks. 23/8/1751, s. Rev. Henry Downes. Literate: dn75 (York), p76 (York). R. Harworth, Bawtry, Notts. 1780 to death. 'Day Chaplain' to Juliana, Dowager Duchess of Leeds. Died 19/2/1841 aged 89 [C109810. YCO] Married Sheffield 1781 Ann Hawksley, w. clerical son below - and confusion with him.

DOWNES (William Henry) Born Harworth, Notts. 14/2/1794, s. Rev. William Downes (above) and Ann Hawksley. St John's, Cambridge 1811, dn17 (Ex. for York), p18 (Chester for York). V. Melchbourne, Beds. 1818-21, PC. Thorpe Salvin, Yorks. 1818 and PC. Wales, Sheffield, Yorks. 1832-40, Master of St Mary Magdalen Hospital [almshouses], Bawtry, Yorks. 1834, R. Dinnington, Yorks. 1835 to death (Dublin) 8/9/1840 [C56693. YCO] Confusion with the father, wrongly called William Henry.

DOWSING (Horatio, *or* Horace) From Hunts. Corpus Christi, Cambridge 1773, BA 1779, dn79 (Nor.), p81 (Nor.), MA1788. V. Hindringham, Norfolk 1783-1843, R. North Barsham >< Norfolk 1788 and R. Aldeby, Norfolk 1790 to death 18/1/1843 aged 83 [C1044] Married 1810 Ann Jones.

D'OYLY (George) Born Buxted, Sussex 31/10/1778, s. Ven. Matthias D'Oyly (Arch deacon of Lewes) and Mary Pougher. Corpus Christi, Cambridge 1796, BA1800, Fellow, etc. 1801-13, dn02 (Chich.), MA1803, p03 (B&W), BD1811, DD1821. V. Herne Hill, Kent 1815-16, V. Buxted w. Uckfield, Sussex 1815-20, R. Lambeth St Mary, Surrey 1820 [net income £2,227] and R. Sundridge, Kent 1820 to death. Dom. Chap. to Archbishop of Canterbury 1813. Died 8/1/1846 [C63211. ODNB] Married 9/8/1813 Chetwynd, Shropshire Maria Frances Bruere, with issue. One of the principal promoters of King's College, London.

DRAGE (William Henry) Bapt. Buntingford, Herts. 22/6/1787, s. William Drage and Elizabeth Judkins. Emmanuel, Cambridge 1815, BA1819, dn19 (Chester for Roch.), p19 (Chester for Roch.), MA1822. V. Halling, Kent 1824-32, Minor Canon of Rochester Cathedral 1831, V. Wilmington, Kent 1832-40, V. Rochester St Margaret 1832 to death there 10/2/1869, leaving £9,000 [C158] Married 18/4/1828 Mary Jane Lindsay (w), with issue.

DRAKE (Charles Digby Mackworth) Born Wells, Somerset, s. Francis Drake and Elizabeth Anne Mackworth (dau. of a baronet). St John's, Cambridge 1819, BA1826, dn26 (C&L), MA 1828, p28 (C&L). R. Dalham, Suffolk 1830-5, R. Huntshaw, Devon 1834 to death 24/3/1874 aged 73, leaving £9,000 [C10665] Married Huntshaw 12/3/1835 Arthurina Maria Dene (w), w. dau. of same name.

DRAKE (Francis) Bapt. Womersley, Yorks. 1/4/1766, s. Rev. Francis Drake, sen. University, Oxford 1784, BA1787, then Magdalen, Fellow, MA1790, dn90 (Ox.), p90 (Nor.), BD 1797, DD1812. R. St Mary Hoo, Kent 1809-16, PC. (and patron) of North Frodingham, Yorks. 1809-32, R. Langton upon Swale, Yorks. 1812 to death 7/5/1847 aged 81 [C1800] Wife Ann Sophia, with clerical son William (below).

DRAKE (George Tyrwhitt) Born Shardeloes [House], Amersham, Bucks. 19/10/794, s. Thomas Tyrwhitt-Drake, *M.P.*, and Anne Wickham. BNC, Oxford 1812, migrated to Jesus, Cambridge 1815, MA1818, LLB 1818, dn18 (Heref. for Win.), p19 (Salis. for Win.), DCL1826. V. Deptford St Nicholas, Kent 1826-30, R. Malpas, Cheshire (Higher Mediety w. St Chad) [net income £1,000] 1830 to death (Hitchin, Herts.) 6/3/1840 [C104190] Married Ibberton, Dorset 14/8/1827 Jane (dau. of Joseph Halsey, *M.P.*, Gaddesden Park, Herts.), with issue. Brother John Tyrwhitt Drake, below.

DRAKE (James) Born 16/9/1770, Halifax, Yorks., s. James Drake and Jane Atkinson. St John's, Cambridge 1788, BA1792, dn93 (Ex. for Chester), p94 (Chester), MA1795. Prebend of Lledrod in Brecon Collegiate Church 1801-36-, V. Clyro, Brecon 1803-10, Chancellor 1803 and Prebend of Llanufydd in St Asaph Cathedral

1810, V. Warmfield, Yorks. 1810 to death (Harrogate, Yorks.) 19/8/1837 aged 67 [C111997] Married Bramham, Yorks. 27/8/1801 Caroline Assheton (a clergy dau.), w. clerical son.

DRAKE (John) Born Shardeloes [House], Amersham, Bucks. 7/6/1780, s. Rev. John Drake, sen. (R. Deptford, Kent) and Mary Wickham. BNC, Oxford 1798, BA1802, then All Souls, BCL1805, LLB1806, dn06 (Ox.), p06 (Ox.), LLD. R. Deptford St Paul 1807-8 (res.), PC. Nettleden, Bucks. 1823-34 (res.), PC. Deptford St Nicholas, Kent 1830, R. Stourton, Wilts. 1846 to death 8/2/1858, leaving £12,000 [C1802] Had issue. Brother William Wickham Drake, below.

DRAKE (John Tyrwhitt) From Chadlington, Oxon., s. Thomas Tyrwhitt Drake and Anne Wickham. BNC, Oxford 1808 (aged 17), BA 1812, MA1815, dn16 (Salis.), p17 (Ex. for Salis.). R. Aylesby, Lincs. 1821 and R. Amersham w. Coleshill, Bucks. 1826 to death 26/6/1860, leaving £25,000 [C28493] Married (1) 7/8/1826 Mary Annesley (d.1827) (2) London 2/11/1830 Emily Drake Garrard, with issue. Brother George Tyrwhitt Drake, above.

DRAKE (Thomas) Bapt. City of London 28/11/1761. Queens', Cambridge 1781, BA 1785, dn85 (Nor.), p86 (Nor.), MA1788, R. Intwood w. Keswick, Norfolk 1789-1842, R. Hackford w. Whitwell 1797-1812 (res.). Died 9/5/1842 [C112784]

DRAKE (William) From Grafton Regis, Northants., s. Rev. Christopher and Elizabeth Drake. Pembroke, Cambridge 1776 (aged 19), dn79 (Peterb.), BA1780, p81 (Lin.), MA1784. V. Binbrook St Gabriel, Lincs. 1783-95, V. Kirton-in-Lindsey, Lincs. 1788-1812, V. Oadby, Leics. 1794 to death (Stoke Goldington, Bucks.) 1840 aged 85 [C56963]

DRAKE (William) Born Walkington, Yorks. 19/4/1806, s. Rev. Francis (above) and Anne Sophia Drake. Lincoln, Oxford 1825, BA1829, dn31 (York), p31 (York), MA1832. (succ. his father as) V. (and patron) of North Frodingham, Driffield, Yorks. 1832-[56], V. Bradwell, Bucks. 1833-65-, and R. Moulsoe, Oxon. 1842-65-. Perhaps died Hull 1868 (3rd q.) aged 63. No will traced [C131086. YCO]

DRAKE (William Fitt) Bapt. Norwich 14/5/1786, s. Christian Drake (manufacturer) and Rebecca Fitt. Caius, Cambridge 1807, then Corpus Christi 1808, dn10 (Nor.), p10 (Nor.), BA1811, MA1823. Minor Canon of Norwich Cathedral 1811-35, V. Norwich St Stephen 1811-31 (res.), V. Stoke Holy Cross, Norfolk 1814-38, V. Norwich St Gregory 1831-6, R. West Halton w. Gunhouse and Conisby, Lincs. 1835 to death 5/5/1874 aged 87, leaving £4,000 [C1045] Married Norwich 4/3/1811 Harriet Tomlinson, and had issue. J.P. for Lindsey.

DRAKE (William Wickham) Born Bucks. 17/7/1778, s. Rev. John Drake (R. Deptford, Kent) and Mary Wickham. BNC, Oxford 1796, dn01 (Lin.), p02 (Lin.), BA1800, MA1807. R. (and patron) of Malpas, Cheshire (Lower Mediety 1802, 2nd Mediety 1816) and PC. Harthill, Cheshire 1816 (w. Prebend of Welton Ryval in Lincoln Cathedral 1810-13) to death. Dom. Chap. to 4th Earl of Macclesfield 1816. Died 28/11/1832 (CCEd says 26/4/1833) aged 54. [C56966] Married Malpas 13/8/1807 Eliza Susanna Tarleton (of Bolsworth Castle, Cheshire), w. clerical son. Brother John Drake, above.

DRAPER (James) Bapt. Crewkerne, Som. 19/1/1763, s. Richard Draper and Mary Gray. Wadham, Oxford 1779, BA1783, dn85 (Ox. for Bristol), p87 (B&W). R. Easthams, Crewkerne, Som. 1800 to death (Drimpton, Dorset) 25/7/1836 aged 75 [C28494] Had issue.

DREYER (Richard) Bapt. City of London 22/2/1763, s. Maurice Dreyer and Margaret Christian. Trinity, Cambridge 1779, then Trinity Hall 1781, LLB1785, dn87 (Lin.), p88 (Lin.). R. Woughton on the Green, Bucks. 1796-1823 (res.), R. Thwaite, Norfolk 1800 to death (Bungay, Suffolk) 1838 [C56972] Married Great Yarmouth, Norfolk 3/1/1797 Eliza Bonhote.

DRIFFIELD (Charles George Thomas) Born East Bergholt, Suffolk 17/11/1771, 'assumed' s. Rev. Walter Wren Driffield and Elizabeth Townshend. King's, Cambridge 1790 (aged 18), Fellow 1793, dn94 (Lin.), BA1795, p96 (Lin.), MA1798. PC. Little Maplestead, Essex 1799-1841, V. Prescot, Lancs. 1815 to death there. Dom. Chap. to 2nd Marquess Cornwallis 1815. Died 17/12/1847 aged 76 [C56973] Married Prescot 23/7/1826 Letitia, dau. of Vero Kemball (Maldon, Essex), with issue.

DRIFFIELD (Joseph Charles) Born London 19/2/1791, s. Edward Mills (Driffield, Yorks.) and Sarah Corneck. Clare, Cambridge 1809, BA1814, dn14 (London), p17 (London). R. Tolleshunt D'Arcy, Essex 1819 to death 19/1/1874 leaving £1,000 [C117338] Married Maldon, Essex 9/5/1820 Mary White, and issue.

DRUMMOND (Arthur) Born London 20/8/1797, s. Charles Henry Drummond (banker, Charing Cross, London) and Frances Dorothy Lockwood (a clergy dau.). Balliol, Oxford 1816, BA1820, dn21 (Chester for Win.), p22 (Win.), MA1826. R. Charlton next Woolwich Kent 1826 to death (Maidenhead, Kent) 26/2/1862 aged 64, leaving £600 [C6730] Married (1) Charlton next Woolwich 13/5/1830 Margaretta Maria Wilson (dau. of a baronet, she d.1854), with clerical son (2) Brighton, Sussex 14/9/1857 Mrs Caroline Eliza (Moring) Grey, a clergy widow.

DRUMMOND (James) Born Bombay *or* Calcutta 3/10/1799, s. James Drummond and Harriet Castell. Christ Church, Oxford 1818, BA1823, dn24 (Lin.), MA1825, p26 (London for Cant.). PC. Downe, Kent 1828 [where he leased Down House to Charles Darwin], Hon. Canon of Peterborough 1853, R. Gaulby, Leics. 1859-77. Died (Tunbridge Wells, but 'formerly of Stellenberg', South Africa) 18/11/1882, leaving £8,011-1s-9d. [C56979] Married 11/5/1830 Hon. Mary Powys (dau. of 2nd Baron Lilford), with distinguished issue.

DRUMMOND (Robert) Born Bath, Som. 22/6/1804, s. Vice-Adm. Sir Adam Drummond and Lady Charlotte Murray (dau. 4th Duke of Atholl). Jesus, Cambridge 1823, then Trinity 1823, BA 1827, dn27 (Lin.), p28 (Lin.), MA1831. V. Feering, Essex 1829-66. Died 14/4/1883 (living at St Catharine's Court, Bath), leaving £8,215-5s-1d. [C56980] Married 19/1/1841 Hon. Charlotte Olivia Elizabeth Strutt (w) (dau. of Baroness Rayleigh).

DRURY (Benjamin Heath) Born Harrow, Middx. 18/9/1782, s. Rev. Joseph Drury (H/M Harrow School) and Louisa Heath. King's, Cambridge 1801, Fellow 1804-7, BA1805, MA 1808, dn09 (Ely), p09 (Ely). S/M Eton College 1804-23 ('but forced to resign owing to his addiction to boxing', and to the theatre, and to London night-life); V. Tugby w. East Norton, Leics. 1810 to death (Haute-Garonne - to escape creditors?) 20/2/1835 (CCEd says 30/5/1835) [C56982. ODNB under his father] Married (1) Bloomsbury, London 30/7/1807 Anna Dorothea Hollamby (dau. of a West Indian planter, she d.1817), with issue (2) Charmouth, Devon 30/3/1820 Catherine Sarah Bateman Bean (Clapham House, Surrey), with further issue. Brothers, below.

DRURY (Charles) Bapt. Harrow, Middx. 10/6/1788, s. Rev. Joseph Drury (H/M Harrow School) and Louisa Heath. Oriel, Oxford 1806, BA1810, then Queen's, Fellow 1811-24, dn13 (Ox.), MA1813, p15 (Ox.). R. Pontesbury (1st & 2nd Portions, then 2nd Portion only), Shropshire 1824 (and Prebend of Warham in Hereford Cathedral 1842) to death 15/1/1869, leaving £12,000 [C28496] Brothers, above and below.

DRURY (Henry Joseph Thomas) Born Harrow, Middx. 27/4/1778, s. Rev. Joseph Drury (H/M Harrow School) and Louisa Heath. King's, Cambridge 1796, Fellow 1799-1808, BA1801, MA1803, dn11 (London for Ely) p19 (Lin.). S/M Harrow School 1801-33, Master of Lower School 1833-41; R. Fingest, Bucks. 1820 to death 5/3/1841 [C56984. ODNB] Married Marylebone, London 23/12/1808 Ann Caroline Taylor (of Boreham Wood, Herts.), with issue. A classical scholar and book collector, and 'noted for the charm of his conversation.' Two brothers, above. Port. online.

DRURY (Mark) Born Harrow, Middx. 27/4/1759, s. Thomas Drury and Elizabeth Hilton. Trinity, Cambridge 1776, BA1782, dn82 (Lin.), MA1792, p01 (Lin.). S/M Harrow School 1785, then Under/Second Master 1789-1826 (and candidate for H/M in 1805); R. Caldecote, Herts. 1801-6, 1816-35, R. Edworth, Beds. 1806, 1819 to death. Chap. in Ordinary 1819. Died (Brussels) 22/7/1835 aged 75 [C56985. ODNB] Married May 1790 Catherine Elizabeth Angelo, with issue.

DRYDEN (Henry Turner, Sir, 3rd Bart.) Born London 7/7/1787, s. Sir John Turner, 1st Bart. (of Canons Ashby, a Tudor manor house) and Elizabeth Dryden. Trinity, Oxford 1805, BA 1809, dn10 (Glos.), MA1812, p14 (Heref. for Glos.). V. Ambrosden, Oxon. 1821 and V. Leek Wootten, Warwicks. 1824 to death 17/11/1837 aged 50 [C10686] Married Canterbury Cathedral 13/7/1817 Elizabeth Hutchinson (a clergy dau.), with issue. Fine portrait online. A lengthy and platitudinous obituary in *Gentleman's Magazine*. Succ. to the title 1818.

DU BOULAY (James Thomas Houssemayne) Born Walthamstow, Essex 4/3/1801, s. Francis Houssemayne du Boulay and Elizabeth Paris. Exeter, Oxford 1818, BA1822, MA1824, dn24 (Ox.), p26 (Ox.). R. Heddington, Wilts. 1831 to death (Ventnor, IoW) 13/6/1836 [C28191. F. under Boulay] Married Camberwell, London 1/6/1825 Susannah Maria Ward, with issue.

DU CANE (Henry) Born Coggeshall, Essex 30/8/1786, s. Rev. Edward Du Cane and Louisa Desmadryll. Oriel, Oxford 1804, BA 1808, dn10 (Win. for London), p11 (London), MA1811. R. St Peter Paul, Wharf, City of London 1824. Died 22/11/1855 [C73036. F. under Cane] Married Offley, Herts. 3/2/1825 Mary Sowerby, with issue. *J.P.*

DU HEAUME (George) Bapt. Jersey, Channel Islands 1770, s. Peter du Heaume and Sarah Bertram. Pembroke, Oxford 1790 (aged 19), dn93 (Ex. for Win.), p94 (Ex. for Win.), BA1795, MA1818. R. Jersey St Ouen (Owen) 1795-1815, R. Jersey St Lawrence 1812. Buried 17/3/1842 ged 73 [C73037. F. under Heaume]

DU PRÉ, DUPRÉ (William Maxwell) Born Beaconsfield, Bucks. 24/9/1804, s. James du Pré and Madelina Maxwell. Christ Church, Oxford 1824, BA1828, dn29 (London), p30 (London), MA1830. V. Wooburn, Bucks. 1831 to death 16/10/1855 [C56987] Married London 6/7/1837 Louisa Emily Frances Lydia Baring, with issue.

DU SAUTOY (William Stevens) Bapt. East Meon, Hants. 21/12/1783, s. Peter du Sautoy and Mary Ann Stevens. Literate: dn06 (Ex. for Win.), p07 (Win.). PC. Portsea St John, Hants. 1822-33 (res.), R. Exton, Hants. 1831 to death 14/12/1861, leaving £2,000 [C73038] Married St George's-in-the-East, London *c.*1808/9 Mrs Eleanor (Rogers) Marshall Rowe (w), with clerical son William Stevens Oliver du Sautoy.

DUCK (Joseph) Born Danby, Yorks. 7/12/1781, s. Rev. Daniel Duck and Dorothy Smith. St John's, Cambridge 1801, then Sidney 1801, BA 1805, dn05 (York), p13 (York). V. Danby w. Castletown 1825-48, Chap. of the Royal Infirmary, Lunatic Asylum and Lock [venereal] Hospital, Liverpool 1853-7. Died Danby 6/6/1862, leaving £450 [C131216. YCO] Married Marton in Cleveland, Yorks. 22/4/1814 Eleanor Clifford, with issue. 'For a vivid picture of him and his strange way of life' see J.C. Atkinson (his successor), *Forty years in a moorland parish* (1891 and reprints).

DUDLEY (Edward) Bapt. Alton End, Warwicks. 19/6/1777, s. Thomas Dudley and Elizabeth Bree. Christ Church, Oxford 1795, BA1799, MA1802, dn02 (Wor.), p03 (Wor.). R. Broome, Worcs. 1810 to death 6/12/1858, leaving £4,000 [C120912] Married 9/12/1803 Christina Maria Amphlett, with clerical s. of father's name in same parish. Another son Joseph, below.

DUDLEY (John) Bapt. Humberstone, Leics. 7/12/1762, s. Rev. John and Hannah Dudley. Clare, Cambridge 1780, Fellow 1786-95, dn87 (Peterb.), BA1788, tutor 1789-94, p90 (Peterb.). (succ. his father and grandfather as) V. Humbertstone 1794 and V. Sileby, Leics. 1795 to death (bronchitis) 7/1/1856 [C56997. ODNB. Boase. Long obit. in *Gentleman's Magazine*] 'He spent a long and happy life as a retired student, occupying himself chiefly with mythological and philosophical studies.'

DUDLEY (Joseph) Bapt. Broome, Staffs. 21/5/1809, s. Rev. Edward Dudley (above) and Christina Maria Amphlett. Worcester, Oxford 1837, BA1831, dn32 (Wor.), p33 (Heref.). PC. Marston Stannett, Heref. 1833-43, R. Sarnesfield, Heref. 1834 to death (Aberystwyth, Cardigan) 28/9/1894, leaving £4,502-11s-4d. [C104702] Married Tedstone Delamere, Heref. 6/7/1840 Eliza Lane Wright, with issue.

DUFFIELD (Richard) Born Theakston, Yorks. *c.*1783, s. Richard Duffield and Ann Dawson. St John's, Cambridge 1804, BA1808, dn08 (Nor. for Ely), p10 (Salis. for Win.), MA 1811, BD1819, incorporated at Oxford 1851. V. Impington, Cambs. 1824-32, R. Frating w. Thorington >< Essex 1832 and RD 1833 to death 2/2/1863 aged 79. Will not traced [C17733] Married Cambridge 2/5/1832 Sophia Barbara Kerrich (a clergy dau.).

DUGARD (George) Born Radnor 1798, s. Thomas Dugard (Doverdale, Worcs.) and Mary Oseland. St John's, Cambridge 1824, BA1828, dn28 (Chester), p30 (Chester), MA1835. Minister Manchester St Andrew, Ancoats 1831-42 (where he commended himself during the cholera epidemic) [Librarian at Chetham's Library, Manchester 1834-37] PC. Birch in Rusholme, Manchester 1841-6, PC. Holt,

Denbigh 1841-6, PC. Barnard Castle 1847-65 (with Master of St John's Hospital [almshouses] from 1850), Hon. Canon of Durham Cathedral 1850 to death (Colwall, Hereford) 13/7/1865 aged 67, leaving under £600 [C168745] Married Prestwich, Lancs. 16/5/1837 Mary Lyon (a clergy dau.). *J.P.* Active in public health issues.

DUGDELL, DUGDALE (John William) Bapt. Westminster, London 11/2/1781, s. John and Elizabeth Dugdale. Clare, Cambridge 1802, BA1806, dn07 (Bristol), p09 (Ex.), MA 1810. V. Throwley, Kent 1811-29, R. Winchelsea, Sussex 1822-9, R. Kington Magna (Great Kington), Dorset 1829 to death 13/8/1862 aged 80, leaving £1,000 [C52403] Married Greenwich, Kent 1/6/1809 Charlotte Ann Tarbutt, with issue.

DUGGAN (William) Born Malew, IoM 21/6/1795, s. William Duggan and Elinor Cubbon. Literate: dn19 (S&M), p20 (S&M). Chap. St Mark, Malew 1820-7, V. Marown, IoM 1827 to sudden death 2/3/1862. Will not traced [C7270. Gelling] Wife Mary, with issue.

DUGMORE (Henry) Bapt. Swaffham, Norfolk 23/8/1797, s. John Dugmore and Elizabeth Woodrow. Caius, Cambridge 1814, BA1818, dn19 (Nor.), MA1821, p21 (Nor.). R. Beachamwell, Norfolk 1829-30 (and living at Beachamwell Hall), R. Pensthorpe, Norfolk [pop. 12, no church] 1832 to death 24/2/1869, leaving £25,000 [C112793] Married Horsham St Faith, Norfolk 13/10/1846 Cecilia Rachel Thomlinson (w), with issue.

DUKINFIELD (Henry Robert, Sir, 7th Bart.) Born Sulham, Berks. 1/6/1791, s. Sir Nathaniel Dukinfield, 5th Bart. and Katherine Ward. Christ Church, Oxford 1800, Student [Fellow] 1809-16, BA1813, dn14 (Ox.), MA 1816, p16 (London). PC. Ruscombe, Berks. 1816-17 (res.), V. Waltham St Lawrence, Berks. 1816-34, V. Reading St Giles, Berks. 1816-34, Prebend of Winterbourne Earls in Salisbury Cathedral 1833-56 (res.), V. St Martin-in-the-Fields, Westminster, London 1834 to death 24/1/1858, leaving £20,000 [C28500. Boase. DEB. Jane C. Dukinfield, *A memoir of the Rev. Sir Henry Dukinfield, Bart.* (1861)] Married Barham, Suffolk 29/8/1836 Mrs Jane (Craufurd) Chowne (dau. of a Scottish baronet, and widow of a general), *s.p.* Succ. to title 1836, title then extinct.

DUMARESQ (Clement) Born Jersey, Channel Islands, s. Rev. Clement Dumaresq [C73042] and Elizabeth Reissier. Pembroke, Oxford 1799 (aged 18), BA1803. R. Jersey St Clement 1788-1822, R. Jersey St Mary 1804 to death 1837 [C73042] Married Elizabeth Mallet, with issue.

DUNCALF (John) Bapt. Macclesfield, Cheshire 1/6/1781, s. John and Elizabeth Duncalf. Literate: dn07 (Car. for York), then St John's, Cambridge 1809, p10 (Chester), a Ten Year Man, BD1819. Chap. Peak Forest, Derbys. 1812 to death 24/9/1836 aged 53 [C136241. YCO] 'A man of the greatest mathematical ability', who also ran a private school. Wife Mary, and issue.

DUNCOMBE (Edward) Born Grimston Hall, Kirkby Wharfe, Yorks. (bapt. 23/5/1802), s. Thomas Duncombe and Emma Hinchliffe (Yorks.). BNC, Oxford 1820, BA1824, dn25 (York), p26 (York), MA1828. R. Newton Kyme, Yorks. 1831-[50], R. Barthomley, Cheshire 1850-80. Died there (a widower) 25/3/1888 aged 85, leaving £955-17s-3d. [C131224. YCO] Married Chester 22/11/1825 Susan Mainwaring (a clergy dau.), with issue. Brother, below.

DUNCOMBE (Henry John) Born Laughton-en-le-Morthen, Yorks. 9/12/1796, s. Thomas Duncombe (Grimston Hall, Yorks.) and Emma Hinchliffe. Trinity, Cambridge 1814, BA1818, dn21 (York), p22 (Salis.), MA1822. R. (and patron) of Kirby Sigston, Yorks. 1824-67, R. Kirkby Misperton, Yorks. 1833-38. Dom. Chap. to 2nd Earl of Glengall 1833. Died Kirby Sigston 17/7/1867 aged 71, leaving £3,000 [C92121. YCO. ATV] Married Darlington, Yorks. 10/11/1831 Georgiana Nesham (w), and had issue. Brother, above.

DUNCUMB (John) Bapt. Shere, Surrey 20/9/1764, s. Rev. Thomas Duncumb and Ann Holland. Trinity, Cambridge 1783, BA1787, dn91, p92 (C&L for Win.), MA1796. R. Talachddu, Brecon 1793-6 (res.), R. Frilsham, Bucks. 1793-1809, R. Tortington, Sussex 1809, R. Abbey Dore >< Heref. 1809 and V. Mansel Lacy, Heref. 1815 to death 19/9/1839 aged 74 [C10670. ODNB] Married Holmer, Heref. 29/3/1792 Mary Webb, with clerical son, below. *J.P., F.S.A.* (1809). Historian of Hereford (unfinished) and agricultural writer; Secretary of the Herefordshire Agricultural Society.

DUNCUMB (William George) From Hereford, s. Rev. John Duncumb (above) and Mary Webb. BNC, Oxford 1825 (aged 19), BA 1829, dn29 (Heref), p30 (Heref.). V. Kilpeck, Heref. 1830 and V. Kenchester, Heref. 1833 to death (unm.) 22/11/1835 [Not yet in CCEd]

DUNDAS (Thomas Lawrence, Hon.) Born Upletham, Yorks. 12/10/1775, s. Thomas Dundas, 1st Baron Dundas of Aske and Lady Charlotte Fitzwilliam (dau. of 3rd Earl Fitzwilliam). Trinity, Cambridge 1796, MA1796, dn98 (York for London), p99 (London), LLD 811. R. Tankersley, Yorks. 1799-1803, R. Harpole, Northants. 1803 and R. Keyston, Hunts. 1807 to death 17/3/1848 aged 72 [C57641. YCO] Married Dallington, Yorks. 25/7/1816 Mary Jane Bousquet (a clergy dau.), w. clerical son Robert Bruce Dundas.

DUNKIN (William) Bapt. Dublin 16/11/1767, s. William Dunkin. Trinity, Cambridge 1785, then Trinity Hall 1786, BA 1789, dn91 (Nor.), p92 (Lin.), MA1792. R. Pilham, Lincs. 1792 to death 13/3/1838 aged 72 [C57632]

DUNNE (Charles) Born Martley, Worcs. 14/5/1783, s. of Rev. Thomas Dunne. Balliol, Oxford 1801, BA1806, dn07 (Glos. for Wor.), p07 (C&L for Wor.), MA1808. R. Earl's Croome, Worcs. 1807, (succ. his father as) R. Martley 1807, V. Eldersfield, Worcs. 1813-26 (res.). Dom. Chap. to Frances, Countess of Clermont 1812. Died 5/10/1850 aged 67 [C10694] Married White Ladies Aston, Worcs. 3/12/1822 Letitia Beauchamp, *s.p. J.P.* Worcs.

DUNNINGTON, *later* **DUNNINGTON-JEFFERSON (Joseph Dunnington)** Born Thices Hall, Thorganby, Yorks. 17/7/1807, s. Joseph Dunnington and Mary Toutill. St John's, Cambridge 1825, BA1830, dn31 (York) p32 (York), MA1833. PC. (and patron) of Thorganby 1832 (and Prebend of Osbaldwick in York Minster 1852) to death (Thicket Priory) 31/7/1880 aged 73, leaving £160,000 [C131229. YCO] Married 23/5/1837 Anna Mervinia, dau. Gen. Sir Henry Maghull Mervyn Vavasour, 2nd Bart., with issue. *J.P.*

DUNSFORD (James Hartley) Born Ashburton, Devon 2/2/1786, s. James Dunsford and Catherine Sophia Elias Jacquery. Wadham, Oxford 1801, BA1805, dn09 (Salis.), p10 (Salis.), MA1810. V. Frampton on Severn, Glos. 1813, V. Fretherne, Glos. 1824-34 (res.). Moved to Canada 1838. Dom. Chap. to 16th Earl of Suffolk 1824. Died (Peterborough, Upper Canada) 25/7/1852 [C92122] Married Highworth, Wilts. 22/2/1814 Mary Crowdy, with issue: www.lostlangtons.co.uk/humogen/family/humo_/F3361/I46952/

DUNTZE (Samuel Henry) Born Sherborne, Dorset 10/10/1800, s. James Nicholas Duntze and Jane Harriott Cockburn. BNC, Oxford 1818, BA1822, dn22 (Glos.), p23 (Glos.), MA 1826. V. Thornton w. Allerton, Yorks. 1825-31, V. Weaverthorpe w. Helperthorpe, Yorks. 1831 to death (Cardigan) 15/10/1855 aged 56 [C42182] Married Exeter 11/10/1827 Frances Palmer (dau. of a Dean of Cashel), with issue. Heir-Presumptive to Sir J.T. Duntze, 3rd Bart.

DUPPA (John Wood) Bapt. Culmington, Shropshire 30/4/1762, s. William Duppa and Susanna Wood. Christ Church, Oxford 1779, BA1783, dn84 (Heref.), MA1785, p86 (Heref.). PC. Hatfield, Heref. 1812, R. (and patron) of Puddleston w. Whyle, Heref. 1823 (living at Puddleston Court). Died 10/8/1840 aged 79 [C104708] Had issue. An active *J.P.*

DUPRÉ (John) Bapt. Jersey 28/5/1752, s. Rev. John Dupré, sen. and Marie Millais. Pembroke, Oxford 1769, then Exeter, Fellow 1773-83, dn75 (Win.), BA1776, MA1776, p76 (Ox.), BD and DD1790. S/M Berkhamsted School 1789; R. Bow Brickhill, Berks. 1795-1820, R. Mentmore, Berks. 1784-1834 [blank in ERC], R. Toynton St Peter, Lincs. (non-res.) 1820-7. Died Wyke Regis, Dorset 12/12/1834 'after a long career of usefulness' [C28510] Married Tring, Herts. 23/5/1782 Eleanor Bayley, with clerical son Thomas Dupré (below).

DUPRÉ (Philip) Literate: dn13 (Chester for Win.), p16 (Salis. for Win.). R. Jersey St John/ St Jean, Channel Islands 1819 to burial there 24/10/1848 aged 57 [C73051]

DUPRÉ, DU PRÉ (Thomas) Bapt. Tring, Herts. 22/6/1784, s. Rev. John Dupré (above) and Eleanor Bayley. Exeter, Oxford 1799, no degree, dn07 (Lin. for Win.), p15 (C&L for Win.). S/M Great Berkhamsted G/S, Herts. 1816; R. Willoughby-in-the-Marsh, Lincs. [net income £1,060] (and Preacher throughout the Diocese of Lincoln) 1815 to death 16/4/1861, leaving £20,000 [C10696] Married before 1806 Sarah Dunscombe, with issue.

DUPUIS (George) Bapt. City of London. 7/7/1757, s. Abraham Dupuis and Frances Batchelor. Merton, Oxford 1776, then Christ Church Student [Fellow] 1777, BA1780, dn80 (Ox.), p81 (Glos.), MA 1784. R. Wendlebury, Oxon. 1789 to death 5/3/1839 [C28512] Married Hanwell, Middx. 12/9/1793 Caroline Ann Stevens, with clerical son, below. *J.P.* Oxon.

DUPUIS (George John) Born Wendlebury, Oxon. 12/12/1795, s. Rev. George Dupuis (above) and Caroline Ann Stevens. Exeter, Oxford 1815, then King's, Cambridge 1815, Fellow 1818-31, BA1820, MA1823, dn24 (Ely), p31 (Chich. for Ely). Ass. Master Eton College 1818-40 (Fellow from 1838, Vice-Provost 1868-84); R. Hemingby, Lincs. 1831-40, R. Creeting St Mary, Suffolk 1840-62, R. Worplesdon, Surrey 1862-78 (res.). Died 22/11/1884 aged 88, leaving £6,640-0s-7d. [C17734. Boase] Married 2/8/1831 Julia Maria Roberts (dau. of the clerical Vice-Provost of Eton), with clerical and naval issue.

DURAND (Haviland) Born Guernsey, Channel Islands 17/9/1799, s. Rev. Daniel Francis Durand and Ann de Jersey. Pembroke, Oxford 1816, BA1821, dn23 (Win.), MA1823, p24 (Win.). R. Guernsey St Mary de Castro (o/w Catel) 1832 (and Chap. to Forces there) to death 5/1/1843 aged 43 [C73054] Married Catel Maria Caroline Maingay, w. clerical son, also Haviland. Port. online.

DURELL (David) Born St Saviour, Jersey, Channel Islands 18/6/1762, s. Thomas Durell and Mary Hilgrove. Christ Church, Oxford 1781, BA1785, dn86 (Ox.), p86 (Ox.), MA1789, DD. R. Mongewell, Oxon. 1791-1852, R. Twyning, Glos. 1792-1802, R. Crowmarsh Gifford, Oxon. 1793-1843, Canon of 8th Prebend of Durham Cathedral 1809 to death. Dom. Chap. to Bishop of Llandaff/ Salisbury/ and Durham. Died 15/1/1852 [C28514] Married 1792 Ann Robin, w. clerical s. Thomas Vavasor Durell, below.

DURELL (Edward) Born Jersey, Channel Islands 26/12/1781, s. Edward Durell. Pembroke, Oxford 1799, BA1803, dn05 (Glos.), p05 (Glos.), MA1809. S/M Bodmin, Cornwall 1816; R. Jersey St Saviour 1819. Died 23/2/1848 'from causes induced by domestic affliction' [C73084]

DURELL (Thomas Vavasor) Born Mongewell, Oxon. 29/4/1799, s. Rev. David Durell, (above) and Ann Robin. Christ Church, Oxford 1818, Student [Fellow] 1820-33, BA1821, dn22 (Ox.), p23 (Ox.), MA1824. Fellow of St Peter's College, Radley. V. Pyrton (Pirton), Oxon. 1832, (succ. his father as) R. Mongewell 1852 to death 28/5/1879 aged 80, leaving £70,000 [C28515] Married 1/5/1826 Maria Le Breton, w. issue.

DURHAM (Philip) Born Ipswich, Suffolk 15/2/1782, s. Robert Stones Durham (attorney, Fordham, Essex) and Sarah Dykes. Pembroke, Cambridge 1809, p12 (Ely), BA1813, MA1816. S/M Ely Cathedral School 1816-33 (res.); Minor Canon of Ely Cathedral 1816, PC. Ely Holy Trinity 1816 and V. Witchford, Ely 1824 to death July 1842 aged 60 [C17735] Married Ely 5/9/1818 Anne Golborne, with issue.

DURHAM (Bishop of) see under **VAN MILDERT (William)**

DURNFORD (Richard) Born and bapt. City of London 12/12/1766, s. Richard Durnford and Elizabeth Durnford (Betchworth, Surrey). Pembroke, Oxford 1784, BA1788, dn89 (Win.), p90 (Win.), BCL1791. R. Wherwell, Hants. 1830-5, V. Goodworth Clatford >< Hants. 1830-5 [Foster adds R. Middleton, Lancs. 1835]. Died London 25/1/1835 (CCEd says 26/3/1835) [C73086] Married Merton, Surrey 30/9/1801 Louisa Mount, with issue.

DURY (Theodore) Born Hadley, Middx. 31/10/1778, s. Col. Alexander Dury and Lucy Maria Bowles. Jesus [Venn says Pembroke], Cambridge 1807, BA1811, dn12 (London), p13 (Glos.), MA1830. R. Keighley, Yorks. 1814-40, R. Bolton by Bowland, Yorks. 1830-1 [blank in ERC], R. Westmill, Herts. 1840 to death. Dom. Chap. to 6th Duke of Devonshire 1830. Died 2/10/1850 [C117375] Married (1) Monken Hadley, Barnet, Herts. 31/3/1814 Caroline Bourchier (d.1820), 1s., 1 dau. (2) 22/10/1822 Anne Greenwood, 5s. (inc. clerical), 2 dau.

DUTHY (William) Born Ropley, Hants. 18/8/1796, s. John and Harriett Anne Duthy, St Mary's Hall, Oxford 1816, then Queen's, BA 1820, dn20 (London), p21 (Heref.), MA1823. R. Sudborough, Northants. 1823 to death 11/9/1889, leaving £7,904-4s-0d. [C73089]

Married 12/11/1834 Emma Robinson (w), with clerical issue. *J.P.*

DYER (Nicholas) Bapt. East Looe, Cornwall 5/10/1762, s. Rev. James and Thomasine Dyer. Christ Church, Oxford 1780, dn85 (Ex.), p87 (Ex.). PC. Landkey w. Swimbridge, Devon 1787 and V. St Allen, Cornwall 1793. Died 1847 (1st q.) [C143091] Married Swimbridge 7/8/1801 Emma Nott, with issue.

DYER (Thomas) From Abbess Roding >< Essex, s. Rev. William Charles Dyer. Wadham, Oxford 1800 (aged 17), BA1804, dn05 (Roch.), p06 (Ox.), Fellow to 1814, MA1809. R. Abbess Roding 1828-52, V. Norton w. Lunchwick, Worcs. 1828. Died 23/10/1852 [C1807]

DYKE (Henry Thomas) From Westminster, London, s. John Hart Dyke. Oriel, Oxford 1822 (aged 18), BA1826, dn27 (London), p28 (London for Cant.), MA1831. V. Pelynt, Cornwall 1829 to death 10/5/1841 aged 38 [C117378] *J.P.* Cornwall

DYKE (Jerome) Bapt. Chiseldon, Wilts. 22/9/1771, s. William and Elizabeth Dyke. Queen's, Oxford 1790 (aged 18), BA1793, dn94 (Salis.), MA1796, p96 (Salis.). R. Aston Flamville w. Burbach, Leics. 1797 (and Preacher throughout the Diocese of Lincoln) to death 17/6/1837 [C57651] Married Swindon, Wilts. 28/6/1798 Mary Sheppard, w. issue. *J.P.* Leics. 1806.

DYKE, or HART-DYKE (Thomas Hart-) Born Lullingstone Castle, Kent 11/12/1801, s. Sir Perceval Dyke, 5th Bart. and Anne Jenner. Christ Church, Oxford 1820, BA1824, dn25 (Ox.), p26 (Ox.), MA1827. R. Lullingstone 1828-66 (a family living) and R. Long Newton, Durham 1832 [total income £1,014] to death 25/6/1866 aged 64, leaving £50,000 [C6736] Married Newton Kyme, Yorks. 31/1/1833 Elizabeth Fairfax (w), w. clerical son.

DYKES, DIKES (Thomas) Born Ipswich, Suffolk 21/12/1761, s. Philip Dykes (merchant) and Sarah Jarvis. Magdalene, Cambridge 1785, LLB1791, Fellow, dn88 (Lin. for York), p89 (York). (builder and first) PC Hull St John 1791 (and Master of the Charterhouse [almshouses], Hull 1833) and V. North Ferriby, Yorks. 1834 to death 23/8/1847 aged 85 [C56531. ODNB. YCO. DEB is long. J. King, *Memoir of the Rev. Thomas Dykes, LLD, incumbent of St John's Church Hull*, ed .W Knight (1849 and port). Married Leeds 15/3/1789 Mary Hey (dau. of a surgeon), w. issue. Anti-slaver; friend of Wilberforce; 'a great benefactor to the town of Hull'.

DYMOKE (John) Bapt. Scrivelsby, Lincs. 8/10/1804, s. Rev. John Dymoke, sen. (Scrivelsby Court) and Jane Alice Amelia Elphinstone. Trinity, Cambridge 1823, BA 1828, dn18 (Lin.), MA1829 Lambeth, p29 (Lin.). (succ. his father as) R. Scrivelsby w. Dalderby 1829 and R. Haltham, Lincs. 1829-67. Resigned Orders. Died (Naples) 22/11/1873, leaving £2,000 [C57655. Boase] Married 22/11/1830 Mary Anne Madeley (a clergy heiress), with issue. He succeeded his brother as The Honourable the Queen's Champion in 1865, when the Honour became extinct.

DYNEVOR (5th Baron) see under **RICE (Francis William)**

DYSON (Charles) Bapt. Acton, Middx. 11/6/1787, s. Jeremiah (Clerk in the House of Commons) and Elizabeth Dyson. Corpus Christi, Oxford 1804 , BA1808, MA1812, Fellow 1815-19, dn16 (Ox.), p17 (Ox.). Rawlinson Professor of Anglo-Saxon at Oxford Univ. 1812-16 (delivered one lecture only). R. Nunburnholme, Yorks. 1818-28 (res.), R. Nazeing, Essex 1828-33 (res.), R. Dogmersfield, Hants. 1836 to death 24/4/1860 aged 73, leaving £9,000 [C38520. OBNB. Boase] Widow Elizabeth. Brother, below.

DYSON (Francis) From Compton, Hants., s. Jeremiah (Clerk in the House of Commons) and Elizabeth Dyson. Merton, Oxford 1802 (aged 17), BA1806, dn08 (Ox.), MA1809, p09 (Ox.), Fellow to 1817. R. Minstead, Hants. 1815-16 (res.), R. South Tidworth, Hants. 1816-58, R. Dogmersfield, Hants. 1824-8 (res.), 1817, Prebend of Salisbury Cathedral, R. North Tidworth, Wilts. 1829 to death. Chap. in Ordinary to Prince of Wales 1824. Died (Cheltenham) 30/11/1858 aged 73, leaving £9,000 [C28521. Boase] Married Marylebone, London 15/4/1816 Charlotte Compton, w. clerical son, also Francis. Brother, above.

DYSON (Henry) Born 5/8/1765, s. Jeremiah Dyson, *M.P.* (and 'Cofferer to His Majesty's Household', *q.v.* ODNB) and Dorothy Dyson [*sic*]. King's, Cambridge 1784, Fellow 1787-92, BA1789, MA1792, p92 (Linc.). R. Baughurst, Hants. 1796-1842, R. Wexham, Bucks. 1814 to death 16/6/1846 [C57660]

EADE (Charles) Bapt. Badingham, Suffolk 22/9/1776, s. Rev. John Eade (R. Cotton, Suffolk) and Ann Stevens. Sidney, Cambridge 1795, BA1799, dn99 (Nor.), p00 (Nor.). Chap. Metfield, Suffolk [C112807]1808 to death 24/1/1835 [C112807] Had issue. Brother below.

EADE (Peter) Bapt. Badingham, Suffolk 8/11/1769, s. Rev. John Eade (R. Cotton, Suffolk) and Ann Stevens. Emmanuel, Cambridge 1788, BA1792, dn92 (Nor.), p95 (Nor.). V. Stow Bedon, Norfolk 1795 and (succ. his father as) R. (and patron) of Cotton 1811 to death 27/7/1847 aged 77 [C112808] Married Badingham 1/11/1792 Hannah Smith, with issue. Brother above.

EADES (John) From Worcester, s. John Eades. St Alban Hall, Oxford 1796 (aged 25). R. Abbots Morton, Worcs. 1796 to burial 5/2/1835 (CCEd says died 11/3/1835) [C120938]

EAGLES, *later* WARRE (John King) Born Clifton, Bristol 7/11/1806, s. Rev. John Eagles (V. Halberton, Devon) and Harriet King. Wadham, Oxford 1823, migrated to St John's, Cambridge 1825, then Trinity 1827, BA1831, dn31 (B&W), p32 (B&W). PC. Hillfarrance, Taunton, Som. 1832-77. Died (Pitminster, Som.) 27/12/1880, leaving £12,000 [C42187. F. and Boase as Warre] Married Bathwick 11/5/1839 Helena Georgiana Crampton, with issue. Name changed 1873.

EAMONSON (Benjamin) Born Barwick in Elmet, Yorks. 5/5/1788, s. Benjamin Eamonson and Eleanor Powell. Trinity, Cambridge 1806, then Queens' 1806, BA1810, dn12 (York), p12 (York), MA1813. PC. Cawthorne, Yorks. 1813-14, PC. Wetherby, Yorks. 1816-33 (res.), PC. Bilbrough, Yorks. 1821-54, V. Collingham, Yorks. 1839 to death 11/5/1867 aged 79, leaving £12,000 [C131236. YCO] Married (1) Newton Kyme, Yorks. 24/4/1813 Louisa Chaloner (dau. of a Lincoln surgeon, she d. same year) (2) Spofforth, Yorks. 1/7/1831 Catherine Sarah Ann Medhurst, with issue.

EARLE (Henry John) Born High Ongar, Essex, s. Rev. Edward Henry Earle and Susannah Taylor. Christ Church, Oxford 1818 (aged 19), then St John's, Cambridge 1820, dn22 (London), BA1823, p23 (London). (succ. his father as) R. (and patron) of High Ongar 1823 to death [net income £1,282]. Died 9/12/1881, leaving £10,294-9s-5d. [C177384] Married High Ongar 18/1/1823 Charlotte Sperling (a clergy dau., of Monks Hall, Essex), with clerical son Walter. *J.P.* Essex. 2 photos. online.

EARLE (James Henry) Born London 1788, s. of Sir James Earle (surgeon, *q.v.* ODNB) and Mary Pott. Jesus, Cambridge 1818, SCL, dn23 (London), p24 (London), LLD1825. (builder of and first) PC. Ide, Devon 1832. Probate granted 30/1/1856 [C117385] Married Shoreditch, London 1834 Mary Wootton.

EARLE (John) Bapt. Appleby, Westmorland 20/8/1780, s. Rev. John, sen. and Hannah Earle. Literate: dn03 (York), p04 (York). S/M Morland, Westmorland; PC. Watton, Great Driffield, Yorks. 1823-39, PC. Barlby, Selby, Yorks. 1826, V. Aughton, Yorks. 1838 to death (Watton Abbey, Hutton Creswick, Yorks.) 9/5/1839 aged 59 [C121275. YCO] Was married with issue.

EARLE (Robert) Born Unthank, Cumberland. St John's, Cambridge 1810, dn12 (Car.), p15 (Car.). V. Minster Lovell >< Oxon. 1818-?72 [blank in ERC], V. Wateringbury, Kent to death (Malling, Kent) 10/10/1877, leaving £6,000 [C5830] Married Wateringbury 11/1/1830 Susanna Selby, with clerical son, also Robert Earle.

EAST (John) Bapt. Westminster, London 28/7/1793, s. William and Ann East. St Edmund Hall, Oxford 1811, dn17 (Glos.), p17 (Glos.), BA1816, MA1819. R. Croscombe, Som. 1828, R. Bath St Michael 1843 to death (Malling, Kent) 26/2/1856 [C42188] Married (1) Bristol 16/9/1823 Ann Day (d.1836), w. issue (2) Wells, Som. 26/2/1838 Mary Ann Brookes, w. further issue. Hymn writer.

EASTON (William) From Salisbury, Wilts., s. James Easton. Wadham, Oxford 1785 (aged 18), BA1789, dn89 (Salis.), p91 (C&L for Salis.). R. Eldon, Hants. 1793-1834 ['church dilapidated and unfit for services'], PC. Swallowcliffe, Wilts. (w. Swallowcliffe Prebend in Heytesbury Collegiate Church, Wilts.) 1804-34, PC. West Somerton, Norfolk 1802-34, V. Hurstbourne Priors (w. St Mary Bourne), Hants. 1817 to death 20/11/1834 (CCEd says 10/12/1834) [C10706]

EATON (Joseph) Bapt. Chester 7/2/1770, s. Rev. Joseph Eaton, sen. St Catharine's, Cambridge 1789, BA1793, dn93 (Nor. for Chester), p94 (Chester), MA1796. PC. Chester St Michael 1796-1831, Minor Canon and Precentor of Chester Cathedral 1803-50, V. Chester St Oswald 1819-27, R. Handley, Cheshire 1827-50, PC. Farndon, Cheshire 1833-[44]. Died Chester 5/4/1850 aged 80 [C112811] Married Aug. 1800 Anne Boydell, Trevallyn Hall, Denbigh. 'An excellent mathemetician'.

EATON, *later* BROWNE (Richard) Born Elsing, East Dereham, Norfolk 23/6/1787, s. Rev. Richard Eaton, sen. and Frances Barney. St John's, Cambridge 1805, BA1809, dn10 (Nor.), p11 (Nor.). (succ. his father as) R. Elsing 1820 (living at Elsing Hall) to death 10/10/1851 aged 66 [C112814] Married Swaffham, Norfolk 30/10/1827 Caroline Susan Marcon, w. issue. Name changed 1845?

EBDON (Thomas) Born Marylebone, London 22/1/1787, s. Christopher Ebdon. Trinity, Cambridge 1805, BA1810, dn10 (Durham), p11 (Durham). Minor Canon (and Sacrist) of Durham Cathedral 1811-15, 1823-34, V. Pittington, Durham 1815-22, V. Merrington, Durham 1822-31, V. Billingham, Durham 1831 to death (unm.) 18/11/1853 aged 65 [C130396]

ECHALAZ (John Manuel) Born Clapton, Middx. 12/7/1800, s. Joseph Echalaz (from the Basque region of Spain) and Mary Alsager. Trinity, Oxford 1818, BA1822, dn23 (London), MA1824, Fellow 1829-31, p30 (Lin.), tutor 1830, etc. R. Appleby, Leics. 1830 (and RD of Sparkenhoe 1838, and Hon. Canon of Peterborough 1844) to death 16/5/1877, leaving £16,000 [C57671] Married Streatham, Surrey 13/12/1832 Charlotte Lloyd (w), probably w. clerical s. Theophilus Sidney. J.P. Leics.

ECKLEY (Edmund) Bapt. Credenhill, Heref. 21/4/1759, s. Rev. Richard and Susanna Eckley. St John's, Oxford 1776, no degree, dn81 (Heref.), p83 (Heref.). (succ. his father as) R. Credenhill 1785 to death 24/9/1835 (CCEd thus) [C104711] Doubtless related to the man below.

ECKLEY (John) Bapt. Credenhill, Heref. 7/5/1784, s. John Eckley and Sarah Powcock. Trinity, Oxford 1802, BA1806, dn13 (Heref.), p13 (Heref.), V. Burghill, Heref. 1821-35, R. Credenhill 1835 to death there 2/3/1867, leaving £7,000 [C104712] Married Glasbury, Brecon 30/7/1807 Elizabeth Williams, with issue. J.P. Heref. Doubtless related to the man above.

EDDOWES (John) Born Barrow-on-Soar, Leics. 20/12/1762, s. Rev. Richard Eddowes and Rose Beaumont. St John's, Cambridge 1779, BA1783, dn85 (York), p87 (Lin.). V. Belton, Leics. 1810 to death 3/4/1840 [C57672. YCO] Married (1) Great Glen, Leics. 6/5/1789 Elizabeth King (d.1819) w. issue (2) Alice Whitehead (a clergy dau.).

EDDY (John) Bapt. Lydney, Glos. 9/11/1757, s. Thomas [*pleb*] and Hannah Eddy. Wadham, Oxford 1778, then All Souls, BA1781, p82 (Heref.), MA1787. R. Whaddon, Wilts. 1784-88, V. Didbrook w. Pinnock, Glos. 1788, V. Toddington w. Stanley Portlarge, Glos. 1788, R. Fugglestone w. Bemerton Wilts. 1830-[6]. Died 9/11/1842 [C92259] Married Bathwick, Som. Sept. 1795 Anne Allen, w. clerical s., also John Eddy.

EDEN (John) From Warrington, Lancs., s. James Eden. St Alban Hall, Oxford 1789 (aged 23), BA1792, dn92 (Lin. for Bristol), p92 (Bristol), MA1798, BD1803. V. Bristol St Nicholas w. St Leonard 1799 to death 25/12/1840 [C52407]

EDEN (Robert John, 3rd Baron Auckland, *later* Bishop of Sodor and Man, *then* of Bath and Wells) Born Beckenham, Kent 10/7/1799, s. William, 1st Baron Auckland and Eleanor Elliot. Magdalene, Cambridge 1817, MA1819, Fellow, dn22 (Nor.), p23 (Wor.), BD and DD 1847. R. Eyam, Derbys. 1823-26, R. Hertingfordbury, Herts. 1825-35, V. Battersea, South London 1835-47, Bishop of Sodor and Man 1847-54, then Bishop of Bath and Wells 1854-69 (res.). Chap. in Ordinary 1831-49. Died 25/4/1870 aged 70, leaving £100,000 [C10721. ODNB. Boase] Married Eyam 15/9/1825 Mary Hurt (Alderwasley, Derbys.), 5s, 5 dau. Succ. to title 1849. Wonderful coloured drawing of him online; and a photo.

EDEN (William, Hon.) Born Berlin 7/11/1792, s. Morton Frederick Eden, 1st Baron Henley and Lady Elizabeth Henley (dau. 1st Earl of Northington). Christ Church, Oxford 1810, BA 1815, dn16 (London for Win.), dn16 (Salis. for Win.), MA1817. R. Harbledown, Kent 1820 and V. Bekesbourne, Kent 1820, R.

Bishopsbourne, Kent 1845 to death there 5/1859 aged 65, leaving £12,000 [C73093] Married Coventry, Warwickshire 18/1/1820 Anna Maria Kelham, Baroness Grey de Ruthin (w), with clerical son.

EDGAR (John) Born The Red House, near Ipswich, Suffolk (bapt. 8/12/1761), s. Mileson and Elizabeth Edgar. Sidney, Cambridge 1785, then Jesus 1786, dn90 (Nor.), BA1791, p91 (Nor.), MA 1794. V. Falkenham, Suffolk 1796-1842, R. Spexhill, Suffolk 1806, R. Kirton, Suffolk 1820 to death (Felixstowe, Suffolk) 2/8/1842 aged 79 [C112816] Brother, below.

EDGAR (Mileson Gery) Bapt. Grundisburgh, Suffolk 3/8/1784, s. Mileson Edgar and Elizabeth Edgar. Caius, Cambridge 1801, BA 1807, dn07 (Nor.), p08 (Nor.), MA 1810. PC. Ipswich St Nicholas 1812 and R. Trimley St Mary, Suffolk 1815 to death. Dom. Chap. to 2nd Marquess Cornwallis 1809. Died 3/8/1853, *s.p.* [C112819] Married (1) City of London 19/2/1818 Mary Ann Bickwood (Dulwich, Kent) (2) Ipswich, Suffolk 2/6/1840 Elizabeth Arkell. Brother, above. *J.P.* Suffolk.

EDGCOMBE (John) Bapt. Barnstaple, Devon 13/6/1778, s. Rev. William Edgcombe. Pembroke, Oxford 1797, BA1801, dn01 (Ex.), p03 (Ex.). R. Thornbury, Devon 1803 to death 16/3/1838 [C143331] Married Northam, Devon 26/2/1805 Elizabeth Anna Maria Heywood (a clergy dau.), with issue.

EDGE (John Webb) Bapt. Strelley, Notts. 24/11/1790, s. Thomas Edge (Strelley Hall) and Elizabeth Webb. Exeter, Oxford 1810, migrated to St John's, Cambridge 1812, BA 1814, dn14 (York), p15 (York), MA1817. PC. Sherbourne, Warwicks. 1819, R. Bilborough w. Strelley 1819 to death. Dom. Chap. to Henrietta, Dowager Countess of Brooke and Warwick 1816. Died (Cheltenham) 30/4/1842 aged 51 [C120941. YCO] Married Mapperley, Notts. 11/2/1824 Anne Neville, dau. of Ichabod Wright, *s.p.*

EDGE (William) Bapt. Ipswich, Suffolk 10/12/1786, s. Rev. Peter Edge and Elizabeth Singleton. Emmanuel, Cambridge 1804, BA 1809, dn09 (Nor.), p10 (Nor.). R. (and patron) of Naughton, Suffolk 1810-71, V. Weybread, Suffolk 1814 (only), R. (and patron) of Nedging, Suffolk 1822 to death (Nedging Hall) 10/1/1871 leaving £35,000 [C112821] Married (1) 1812 Lydia Growse (d.1828), w. clerical s. William John (2) Ipswich, Suffolk 1831 Jane Burman.

EDGECOMBE, EDGCOMBE (John) Born Barnstaple, Devon 13/6/1778. Rev. William Edgcombe, sen. Pembroke, Oxford 1797, BA 1801, dn01 (Ex.), p03 (Ex.). R. Thornbury. Devon 1803 to death 16/3/1838. [C14331 as Edgcombe]

EDGELL (Edward) Bapt. Frome, Somerset 10/5/1782, s. Chaffin Edgell and Eleanor Lucretia Rishton. Wadham, Oxford 1800, BA 1804, dn04 (B&W: 'declared void as under canonical age'), p05 (B&W). Prebend of Combe X1 in Wells Cathedral 1806-60, V. West Alvington (o/w Allington), Devon 1807, PC. Rodden, Som. 1835 to death 2/4/1860, leaving £30,000 [C38228] Married (1) Frome 19/6/1804 Frances Wickham (d.1811), 2 clerical s. (2) Bathwick, Som. 28/4/1814 Elizabeth Wilson (w).

EDIE (Arthur) Born St Andrews 18/4/1775, s. Arthur Edie and Margaret Gib. St Andrew's University 1789, MA, dn10 (Nor.), p11 (Nor.). V. Rodbourne Cheney, Wilts. 1821 and V. Seagry, Wilts. 1827 to death 12/10/1847 aged 72 [C112823. Smart]

EDISON (George Thomas) Bapt. City of London 7/5/1762, s. John and Mary Barbara Edison. Queens', Cambridge 1779, p87 (Lin.). R. Stock Harvard w. Ramsden Belhouse, Essex 1787 to death. Dom. Chap. to 18th Baron Dacre 1786. Died 3/3/1839 [C57656] Married Marylebone, London 29/9/1789 Catherine Mary Master (of Greenwich), w. clerical son Edward John Edison in same parish.

EDMEADES (William Henry) Born Cobham, Kent 27/8/1803, s. William Edmeades and Elizabeth Allen. Merton, Oxford 1822, BA 1826, dn26 (Roch.), p27 (Roch.), MA1830. R. Ifield, Kent 1828, R. (and patron) of Nursted, Kent 1828 to death (Strood, Kent) 13/6/1886, leaving £50,059-5s-6d. [C6731] Married Thanet, Kent 14/11/1832 Sarah Mary Jane Isacke, with issue. 'This stone marks the spot upon which the Revd W.H. Edmeades suddenly expired on his way to perform divine service, Whitsunday, June 13th 1886'.

EDMEADS (John) Born Trottiscliffe, Kent 23/5/1779, s. John Edmeads and Elizabeth Higgins. Literate: dn17 (Chester), p18 (Chester).

R. Cricklade St Mary, Wilts. 1827-34, 'Perpetual V.' Preshute, Wilts. 1834 to death (Marlborough) April 1849 aged 69 [C92310] Married London 13/9/1809 Louisa Frances Grimaldi.

EDMONDES (Thomas) From Cowbridge, Glamorgan, s. John Edmondes and Margaret Deere. Jesus, Oxford 1792 (aged 17). R. Ashley w. Silverley, Cambs. 1831-[35]. Probably died Cowbridge 12/9/1845 [C112824] Married 1802 Mary David, s. clerical s of same name.

EDMONDS (George) From Dublin, s. Edward Edmonds. TCD1819 (aged 18), BA 1823, then incorporated at Christ Church, Oxford 1859, MA1859. V. Madeley, Shropshire 1831-41, R. Little Wenlock, Shropshire 1841 to death 20/4/1889, leaving £20,552-7s-2d. [C104715. Al.Dub.]

EDMONDS (Robert) Born July 1797, perhaps s. Robert Edmonds, Boughton House, Kettering, Northants. St John's, Cambridge 1816, BA 1820, dn20 (Peterb.), p22 (Peterb.), MA1826. R. Church Lawford w. Kings Newnham, Warwicks. 1825 to death 14/2/1863 aged 65, leaving £25,000 [C110163]

EDMONSTONE (George) Born Marylebone, London 12/12/1768, s. Sir Archibald Edmonstone, 1st Bart., *M.P.* (Duntreath Castle, Stirling) and Susanna Mary Harenc (of French extraction, but from Kent). Trinity, Cambridge 1781, BA 1785, MA1788. V. Addington, Surrey 1789, V. Potterne, Wilts. 1807-37 (and RD Potterne 1819). Dom. Chap. to 3rd Viscount Sydney 1813. Probate granted 10/11/1855 [C73096]

EDMUNDS (Payne) Bapt. Peterborough 2/7/1777, s. George Edmunds and Henrietta Bertie. Magdalene, Cambridge 1796, then Clare, SCL, dn00 (Lin.), p01 (Lin.), LLB1805. R. Theddlethorpe St Helen w. Mablethorpe St Peter, Lincs. 1810 to death. Dom. Chap. to 9th Earl of Lindsey 1810. Died 21/7/1861, leaving £25,000 [C57683] Married (1) Cartmel, Lancs. 1811 Louisa Richardson (niece of the Earl of Lindsey), with issue (2) Cartmel 8/7/1840 Charlotte Burgh, with further issue.

EDSALL (John) Bapt. Canterbury 1/4/1782, s. Simon and Mary Edsall. Exeter, Oxford 1800, BA1804, dn05 (Ex.). PC. Woodbury, Devon 1807 to death 15/8/1846 [Not yet in CCEd] Married Topsham, Devon 15/1/1810 Caroline Sydney Dodd, and had issue.

EDWARDS (Bartholomew) Bapt. Hethersett, Norfolk 20/3/1789, s. Rev. Bartholomew Edwards, sen. and Catherine Smith. St John's, Cambridge 1807, BA1811, dn12 (Nor.), p13 (Nor.), MA1814. R. (and patron) of Ashill, Suffolk [net income £1,017] 1813 (and RD of Breckles and Thetford, 1820-87) to death 21/2/1889 aged 99, leaving £27,000-6s-5d. [C112829. Boase] Married Weston Longville, Norfolk 12/2/1811 Emily Custance, *s.p. D.L.* Norfolk.

EDWARDS (Edward) From Ruthin, Denbigh., s. Edward Edwards [*pleb*]. Christ Church, Oxford 1778 (aged 21), dn80 (Nor.), p82 (Lin.), BA1784. S/M Huntingdon G/S 1786; R. Syderstone, Norfolk 1785 [ERC makes the link here], V. Orby, Lincs. 1795-1803, R. Offord Cluny, Hunts. 1803-34, R. Huntingdon All Saints w. St John 1803-34. Prebend of Welton Beckhall 1808-23, then of Leighton Ecclesia 1823 in Lincoln Cathedral to death. Dom. Chap. to 7th Lord Elibank 1803. Died 27/6/1834 (CCEd says 29/7/1834) [C57685] Possible clerical sons James, and John, below.

EDWARDS (Edward) Born Clenchwarton, Norfolk 2/2/1766, s. John Edwards and Catherine Sommersby. Trinity, Cambridge 1782, then Corpus Christi 1784, BA1787, Fellow 1788-96, dn88 (Nor.), p90 (Ely), MA 1790. R. North Lynn, Norfolk 1799 (and Hon. Canon Norwich Cathedral 1841) to death 15/3/1849 [C112830. DEB] Married Sculcoates, Hull 3/2/1796 Anne Pead, with issue. Port. online.

EDWARDS (Edward) Bapt. Llansantffraid, Montgomery 16/8/1788, s. David and Gwen Edwards. Literate: dn21 (York), p22 (York). PC. Marsden, Almondbury, Yorks. 1823-[39], R. Penegoes, Montgomery 1849 to death 1/9/1869, leaving £600 [C131239. YCO] Married Lancaster 8/4/1829 Sophia Dawson (Aldcliffe Hall, Lancaster), with issue.

EDWARDS (Edwin) From Suffolk. Jesus, Cambridge 1817, BA1821, dn21 (Nor.), p23 (Nor.). PC. Ashfield w. Thorpe, Suffolk 1823 to death (Watford, Herts.?) 5/12/1852 [C112833]

EDWARDS (Evan) From Llanymawddey, Merioneth, s. Thomas Evans [*pleb*]. Jesus, Oxford 1774 (aged 22), dn75 (Ox. for St Asaph), p79 (Ely for Chich.), BA1805. V. Warnham, Sussex 1805 to death 20/1/1839 aged 86 [C26772]

EDWARDS (Henry) Bapt. Chard, Som. 12/10/1792, s. Charles and Martha Edwards. Wadham, Oxford 1809, then Trinity Hall, Cambridge 1813, dn15 (B&W), LLD1816, p16 (Bristol), incorporated at Oxford 1829. V. Wappenbury, Warwicks. 1818, R. Wambrook, Dorset 1818-50 to death (Chard) 27/3/1859 leaving under £100 [C10766] His son of same name was also Rector there.

EDWARDS (James) From Fairford, Glos., s. Rev. Edward Edwards. Magdalen, Oxford 1818 (aged 17), BA1822, MA1825. R. Britwell Prior, Newington, Oxon. 1830 to death 27/5/1845 [C136750]

EDWARDS (John) Bapt. Berry Pomeroy, Devon 12/9/1751. Caius, Cambridge 1776, dn78 (Ex.), p79 (Ex.), LLB1783. V. Berry Pomeroy 1781 to death (Blagdon, Som.) 28/4/1834 aged 82 [C143339]

EDWARDS (John) Bapt. Hethersett, Norfolk 11/6/1790, perhaps s. Rev. Edward Edwards (above, S/M Huntingdon G/S). St John's, Cambridge 1805, then Jesus 1809, BA1810, dn11 (Lin.), p12 (Lin.), MA1813. S/M Richmond School 1814-21; S/M Harrow School 1826-8; H/M Bury St Edmunds School 1828-41. Professor of Greek and Classical Literature, Durham University 1841-62 (and often acting Sub-Warden). R. South Ferriby, Lincs. 1814 (wholly non-res.) and Prebend of Durham Cathedral 1841 to death. Dom. Chap. to 2nd Baron Bridport 1816. Died 1/4/1862, leaving £12,000 [C57690] Had clerical son George. Known as 'Poppo'.

EDWARDS, *later* BAGOT DE LA BERE (John) From Bristol, s. Edward Edwards. Worcester, Oxford 1819 (aged 18), BA1823, dn23 (Glos.), p24 (Glos.), MA1825. V. (and patron) of Prestbury, Glos. 1825-60. Died Cheltenham, Glos. 5/2/1886, leaving £21,791-7s-6d. [C144662. Foster as de Bere] Name changed 1879. Clerical son of father's name.

EDWARDS (John Robert) Born Oswestry, Shropshire 5/8/1789, s. Rev. Turner and Sarah Edwards. Pembroke, Oxford 1808, BA1813, dn13 (Ox.), MA1815, p17 (St Asaph), Fellow 1822-41-, PC. Holt, Wrexham, Denbigh (Chester Diocese) 1825 to death 17/4/1877 aged 87, leaving £6,000 [C26781]

EDWARDS (Thomas) Born Chester, s. Thomas Edwards. BNC, Oxford 1791 (aged 17), BA1795, MA1797, dn98 (Chester), p98 (Chester). R. Aldford, Cheshire 1832 to death 4/7/1842 aged 68 [C168768] Wife Mary Ann, w. clerical s. George Robertson Edwards..

EDWARDS (Vincent) From Wolverhampton. Staffs., s. Vincent Edwards and Elizabeth Tucker. Trinity, Oxford 1787 (aged 18), BA 1791, dn91 (C&L), p93 (C&L), MA1794. R. Darlaston, Staffs. 1793-6 (res.), V. Broomfield, Essex 1796-1843, R. Colchester St Giles, Essex 1810-12 (res.), R. Nevendon, Essex 1814. Died Broomfield 17/1/1843 [C10773] Married Holborn, London 9/12/1812 Jane Tindal.

EEDLE (Edward) Born Great Missenden, Bucks. 31/6/1795, s. William Eeedle [*pleb*] and Kitty Blackwell. Christ Church, Oxford 1813, BA 1817, dn20 (Salis.), p20 (Salis.), MA1821. V. South Bersted, Sussex 1824-75, RD1852, Sutton Prebend of Chichester Cathedral 1855 to death 3/3/1875, leaving £5,000 [C63362] Married Marylebone, London 22/7/1822 Amelia Stert.

EGERTON (Charles) Bapt. Chelmsford, Essex 1/7/1765, s. John Egerton and Ann Abigail Chandler. Queen's, Oxford 1782, BA1786, p88 (Lin.), p90 (Ex.). V. Thorncombe, Devon 1790-1844. Died Theydon Garnon, Essex 26/4/1845 aged 80 [C57700] Married Thorncombe 5/3//1795 Mary Coker, and has issue.

EGERTON-BRYDGES (Anthony) see under **BRYDGES**

EGERTON-WARBURTON (James Francis) see under **WARBURTON**

EGREMONT (Edward) Bapt. Wakefield, Yorks. 19/5/1801, s. John Egremont and Hannah Crowther. Trinity, Cambridge 1819, BA1823, dn24 (Kilmore), p26 (C&L), MA1826. V. Wroxeter, Shropshire 1828 to death 31/8/1884, leaving £3,478-14s-8d. [C10723] Married Durham 1834 Sarah Maude, w. issue.

EGREMONT (Godfrey) Bapt. Whitgift, Yorks. 25/3/1772, s. John Egremont and Margaret Godfrey. St Catharine's, Cambridge 1790, dn96 (York), p97 (York), LLB1797. V. (and patron) of Crowle, Lincs. 1798 and R. Welton le Wold, Lincs. 1813 to death 6/6/1842 aged 70 [C57705. YCO] Married York 1/6/1794 Maria Frances Cataneo, with son, below.

EGREMONT (Godfrey George) Born Howden, Yorks. s. Rev. Godfrey Egremont (above) and Maria Frances Cataneo. St Catharine's, Cambridge 1815, BA1810, dn19 (Lin.), p20 (Lin.), MA1822. V. Barrow upon Humber, Lincs. 1828 to death (Brigg, Lincs.) 10/3/1848 aged 53 [C57706] Married Kirk Ella, Yorks. 18/6/1829 Emily Barkworth.

EKINS (Frederick) Born Quainton, Bucks. 25/9/1767, s. Very Rev. Jeffery Ekins (Dean of Carlisle, *q.v.* ODNB) and Anne Baker. New, Oxford 1786, Fellow, BA1790, dn90 (Ox.), p91 (Salis.), MA 1794. V. Brampton, Cumberland 1791-2, R. Morpeth, Northumberland 1791 [net income £1,611] to death 29/3/1842 [C5836] Married Whalton, Northumberland 23/8/1802 Jane Ogle Tyler, with clerical son Jeffrey.

EKINS (Robert) Bapt. Newton Toney, Wilts. 20/12/1785, s. Very Rev. John Ekins (Dean of Salisbury) and Harriet Baker. King's, Cambridge 1804, Fellow 1807-10, BA1809, dn10 (Chich. for Salis.), p09 (Salis.), MA1812. V. Godalming, Surrey 1810-33, R. Folke, Dorset 1833-43, PC. North Wootton, Norfolk 1843-54. Died Prestbury, Glos. 17/11/1874, leaving £6,000 [C73102] Married Newton Toney 30/7/1812 Eliza Malet, with issue.

ELERS (Carew Thomas) Bapt. Camden, London 28/1/1791, s. Carew Elers and Susanna Farrow. Sidney, Cambridge 1816 (a Ten Year Man), dn17 (Nor.), p18 (C&L), BD1827. R. (and patron) of Rishangles, Suffolk 1821, V. Bickenhall, Warwicks. 1823 to death 19/2/1863 aged 72, leaving £1,500 [C10724] Married Coleshill, Warwicks. 25/2/1821 Sarah Palmer (w), with son of father's name.

ELFORD (William) Born Tavistock, Devon, 18/2/1753, s. Ralph Elford. Balliol, Oxford 1772, BA1776, dn76 (Ex.), p78 (Ex.), migrated to Sidney, Cambridge MA1795. R. Lew Trenchard, Devon [blank in ERC] 1786-1833, V. North Petherwin, Cornwall 1796 [sequestrated in ERC] Dom. Chap. to 5th Duke of Bedford 1796. Died 1833 [C143350] Married Minster, Cornwall 9/2/1781 Margaret Hoskyns, w. issue.

ELIOT (Lawrence William) Born Hambledon, Surrey 16/3/1777, s. Rev. Edward Eliot and Mary Chandler. Peterhouse, Cambridge 1797, MA1817. R. Alford, Surrey 1801-17, R. Peper Harow, Surrey 1801 and R. Shipton Oliffe w. Shipton Sollars, Glos. 1817 to death 19/3/1862 aged 85, leaving £6,000 [C73105] Married St George's Hanover Square, London 2/4/1811 Matilda Elizabeth Halsey (Henly Park, Surrey), with issue.

ELLA (John Gaskarth) Born Wath, Yorks. 6/11/1765, s. Rev. Richard Ella and Sarah Gaskarth. St John's, Cambridge 1783, BA1788, dn88 (Chester), then Peterhouse, p90 (Chester), Fellow 1791-1809, MA1791. R. Higham Gobion, Beds. 1807-13, R. Wootton St Martin, Kent 1813 to death. Dom. Chap. to Margaret, Countess Poulett 1819. Died 21/11/1834 (CCEd is wrong here) [C26791]

ELLAM (William) Literate: dn85 (Chester), p86 (Chester). S/M Prescot G/S, Lancs. 1786; PC. Rainford, St Helens, Lancs. 1807 to death 12/2/1846 aged 86 [C168770]

ELLERTON (Edward) Born Downholme, Yorks. 30/1/1771, s. Richard Ellerton [*pleb*] and Catherine Whitelock. University, Oxford 1787, BA1792, dn93 (Glos.), MA1795, p95 (Lin.), then Magdalen, Fellow 1803-51, BD and DD1815, Tutor 1822, etc. S/M Magdalen College School 1799; PC. Horspath, Oxon. 1814, R. Tilehurst w. Theale, Berks. 1831 and PC. Sevenhampton, Glos. 1825 to death 26/12/1851 [C26793. ODNB. Boase] Founded several scholarships.

ELLERTON (Joseph) Born Bootle, Cumberland, s. Edward Ellerton and Martha Munday. Literate: dn90 (Chester), p92 (C&L). Usher Stafford G/S 1805-26 (H/M 1826 only); PC. Marston w. Whitegreaves, Staffs. 1805, V. Berkswich w. Walton on the Hill (o/w Baswick), Staffs. 1817 to burial 6/5/1836 (CCEd says died 16/6/1836) [C10727] Married Bootle 1783 Hannah Thompson, with issue.

ELLICE (James) Born Auchterless, Aberdeenshire 7/8/1787, s. Alexander Ellice [Foster adds: St James', Westminster: he d. Bath 1805 leaving £175,000] and Ann Russell. University, Oxford 1804, BA1808, MA1811, dn14 (Roch.), p14 (London). R. Watton at Stone, Herts. 1814-16 (res.), R. Aston, Herts. 1815-16, R. Clothall, Herts. 1816 to death. Dom. Chap. to 1st Earl Duncan of Camperdown 1814. Died 5/6/1856 [C1814. LBSO] Had issue. Received slave compenstion.

ELLICOMBE (Richard) Bapt. Exeter 23/3/1780, s. Rev. William Ellicombe and Hannah Rous. Exeter, Oxford 1798, BA1802, p04 (Ex.), MA1811. Prebend of Exeter 1812 and R. (and patron of) Alphington, Devon 1831 to death 4/8/1851 [C143354] Married Kenton, Devon 6/4/1820 Eliza Swete (a clergy dau., Oxton House), with issue. Brother, below

ELLICOMBE (William Rous) Bapt. Thorverton, Devon 21/2/1774, s. Rev. William Ellicombe and Hannah Rous. Exeter, Oxford 1790, BA1795, dn97 (Ex.), MA1800, p00 (Ex.). R. (and patron) of Clyst St George, Devon 1810 to death 21/8/1849 [C143356] Married Chudleigh, Devon 1793 Elizabeth Trott, with issue. Brother, above.

ELLICOTT (Charles Spencer) Born Little Hallingbury, Essex 6/2/1793, s. Rev. John Ellicott (V. Exton, Rutland) and Frances Jones. Trinity Hall, Cambridge 1814, SCL, dn17 (Lin.), p18 (Lin.), LLB 1821. R. Whitwell, Rutland 1818-77 and V. Threckingham, Lincs. 1829-77 (non-res.), RD of Oakham 1848-64. Lived latterly at Cheltenham, then Clifton, Bristol, dying there 5/6/1880 aged 87, leaving £12,000 [C57721] Married Marylebone, London 22/7/1818 Ellen/ Eleanor Jones (w), with clerical son Charles John Ellicott, Bishop of Gloucester (*q.v.* ODNB).

ELLIOT (Gilbert) Born Dresden, Saxony 17/3/1800, s. Hugh Elliot (former Governor of Madras) and Margaret Jones. St John's, Cambridge 1818, BA1823, dn23 (Bristol), p24 (Heref.), then Trinity Hall, MA1828, DD1850 (Lambeth). R. Newington Butts. Kent 1824-33, R. Barming, Kent 1832-4, R. Kirkby Thore, Westmorland 1833 (w. Brougham 1834) -45 (res.), Martock, Somerset. R. Wivenhoe, Essex 1845-6, R. Holy Trinity Marylebone, London 1846-50, Dean of Bristol 1850 to death. Chap. to HRH Duke of Cambridge 1834; to Archbishop of Canterbury 1850. Proluctor of the Lower House of Convocation 1857-64. Died 11/8/1891, leaving £27,553-8s-0d. [C5837. Boase. Platt. Not in DEB in spite of his 'passionate Evangelicalism'. J. Bettey, 'Contrasting clerics in nineteenth-century Bristol: Dean Gilbert Elliot and Canon John Pilkington Norris' *in* J. Bettey (ed.) *Historic churches & church life in Bristol: essays in memory of Elizabeth Ralph, 1911-2000* (Bristol, 2001)] Married (1) 20/8/1825 Williamina Brydore (d.1853), with issue (2) Dec. 1863 the (much younger) writer Mrs Frances Vickriss (Dickenson) Geils - this marriage failed and she left him to live in Italy, *q.v.*: https://en.wikipedia.org/wiki/Frances_Minto_Elliot . A fine effigy in Bristol Cathedral.

ELLIOT (William) Born Greenwich, Kent 11/11/1773, 'son of a Danzic merchant'. Literate: dn96, p97 (Win.). Chaplain *R.N.*; R. Thorneyburn, Northumberland 1819-29, R. Simonburn, Northumberland 1829 [as BA] to death 26/1/1841 [C130401] Married 1819 Grace Johnstone, with issue.

ELLIOTT (Edward Bishop) Bapt. Paddington, London 27/8/1793, s. Charles Elliott (a prominent member of the Clapham Sect) and Eling ('Nelly') Venn. Trinity, Cambridge 1811, BA1816, Fellow 1817-24, MA1819, dn21 (Ely), p22 (Nor.) [in Italy 1817-20]. V. Tuxford, Notts. 1824-40, Prebend of Hill Deverill in Heytesbury Collegiate Church 1826-64-, PC. Brighton St Mark's [Proprietary Chapel] (and Prebend of Salisbury Cathedral) 1853 to death 30/7/1875 aged 82, leaving £40,000 [C17741. ODNB. Boase. DEB is long] Married (1) Torwood, Sussex 26/4/1826 Mary King, with clerical s. (2) Cheltenham, Glos. 3/10/1835 Harriette Emily (w), dau. of Sir Richard Steele, [3rd?] Bart., Co. Dublin, 1s., 2 dau. A decided evangelical, and apocalyptic writer. Brother, below.

ELLIOTT (Henry Venn) Bapt. 29/2/1792, s. Charles Elliott and Eling ('Nelly') Venn. Trinity, Cambridge 1809, BA1814, Fellow 1816, MA 1817 [touring in Europe and Middle East 1817-20] dn23 (Ely), p24 (Nor.), Warden of St John the Baptist Hospital [almshouses], Wilton, Wilts. 1826-31, (first) Minster of Brighton St Mary [Proprietary Chapel] 1827 to death there 24/1/1865, leaving £40,000 [C17742. ODNB. Boase. DEB is very long. J. Bateman, *The life of the Rev. Henry Venn Elliott, MA, Perpetual Curate of St Mary's, Brighton* (1868)] Married Ullswater, Lancs. 31/10/1833 Julia Marshall (d.1841), with issue. A rigid Sabbatharian. Brother, above. Photo. online.

ELLIOTT (John) Born Stonehouse, Glos. 19/12/1791, s. John Elliott (schoolmaster) and Mary Holder. St Edmund Hall, Oxford 1814, dn17 (Glos.), BA1818, p18 (Glos.), MA1820. (first resident minister of) R. Randwick, Stroud, Glos. 1819 (V. 1866) to death 4/1/1891 (aged 100), leaving £10,715-14s-1d. [C144830. Boase] Married Martha Wells before 1828, with 5 ch.:

www.sandford.plus.com/Randwick2/Fennemore/Chapter_5.html

ELLIS (Francis) Bapt. Nottingham 9/11/1758. Queens', Cambridge 1781, BA1785, dn85 (Nor.), p86 (Nor.), Fellow 1787, MA1788, BD 1796. R. Rockland St Mary, Norfolk 1808-28, V. Langham Episcopi (o/w Bishop's Langham), Norfolk 1822. Died London 8/6/1838 aged 79 [C26797]

ELLIS, *later* JERVOISE (Francis) Born London as Francis Ellis. Corpus Christi, Cambridge 1796, then Queens' 1798, BA1800, dn02 (Lin.), p03 (Lin.), MA1807. V. Long Compton, Warwicks. 1803, R. Shalstone, Bucks. 1809-22, R. Lasham, Hants. 1822 to death 28/2/1848 [C57783] Married (1) Britford, Wilts. 18/5/1807 Mary Purefoy Jervoise (a clergy dau., d.1849), w. issue (2) Basingstoke, Herts. 14/5/1850 Sophia Roe, *s.p.*. Changed name in 1848.

ELLIS (James) Born Southwark, Surrey 23/7/1771, s. Thomas and Elizabeth Ellis. St John's, Oxford 1790, BA1794, dn95 (York), p96 (York), MA1797. R. Ashurst, Surrey 1806 to death aged 64. Probate granted 8/6/1836 [C63404. YCO]

ELLIS (John) Bapt. Ledenham, Lincs. 19/1/1767, s. Rev. Jeremiah Ellis. Merton, Oxford 1785, then King's, Cambridge 1786, Fellow 1789-1809, BA1792 [travelled in Europe and may have been interned by the French] MA1796, dn00 (Lin.), p01 (Ely). V. Wootton Wawen, Warwicks. 1809 to death 25/2/1854 aged 88 [C57788] Married Beaconsfield, Bucks. 13/11/1809 Ann Pearch, with issue. J.P.

ELLIS (John) Bapt. Pickering, Yorks. 14/10/1770, s. John Ellis. Literate: dn96 (York), p98 (York). V. Yedingham, Yorks. 1832 to death 27/9/1847 aged 77 [C136779. YCO] Married before 1803, with issue.

ELLIS (John Joseph) Born Shoreditch, London 25/8/1769, s. John Ellis and Sarah Belknap. St John's, Oxford 1788, BA1792, dn92 (London), p95 (London), MA1795. Second Master, Merchant Taylors' School; London; R. St Martin Outwich, City of London 1821 to death ?20/4/1855 aged 86 [C117402] Married by 1798 Elizabeth Hockaday, w. clerical son of father's name.

ELLIS (Robert) Born York 23/1/1790, s. William Ellis. Trinity and Ann Elizabeth Butler. Cambridge 1808, BA1813, dn13 (York), p14 (York), MA1816. V. Burton Leonard, Yorks. 1814-34, R. Escrick, Yorks. 1825-26, V. Acaster Malbis, Ainsty of York 1829-68 ('Mr Ellis has not officiated for years') [C136947], PC. Birdsall, Yorks. 1831-80, V. Wharram-le-Street, Yorks. 1832-77. Died North Grimston, Yorks. 19/12/1880 aged 90, leaving £100,000 [C131251. YCO. ATV] J.P. North and East Ridings.

ELLIS (Thomas) From Ruthin, Denbigh, s. Edward Ellis [*pleb*]. Jesus, Oxford 1783 (aged 20), then Christ Church, BA1786, dn86 (C&L), p86 (C&L), MA1791. PC. Little Compton, Glos. 1797-1842, V. Great Milton, Oxon. 1800-48. Probate granted 9/10/1848 [C10782] Married (1) Reading, Berks. 1/7/1789 Catherine Willats (d.1790), with clerical s. Charles Willats Ellis (2) Burghfield, Berks. 1/3/1798 Mary May, with clerical son William May Ellis.

ELLIS (Valentine) Born Hundon, Suffolk, s. Rev. William Ellis (R. Molesworth, Hunts.). Sidney, Cambridge, BA1797, dn97 (Lin.), p98 (Lin.), MA1811. R. (and patron) of Barnardiston, Suffolk 1803 and V. (and patron) of Walton, Bucks. 1821 to death 16/3/1851 [C57793] Married Cambridge 6/10/1803 Charlotte Bullen, with issue.

ELLIS (William) From London, s. James Ellis. Trinity, Cambridge 1779, dn83 (Lin.), p86 (Lin.), LLB1787. PC. Thames Ditton, Surrey 1791-34, R. Charlwood, Surrey 1794 (only), PC. East Molesey, Surrey 1797 to death 1/11/1834 (CCEd says 20/11/1834) [C57794]

ELLISON (Noel Thomas) Born Newcastle upon Tyne 16/2/1791, s. Rev. Nathaniel Ellison and Jane Furye. Corpus Christi, Oxford 1808, BA1811, MA1815, dn15 (Ox.), Balliol, Fellow 1815-24, etc., p15 (C&L). R. Whalton, Northumberland 1816-24, R. Huntspill, Som. (and Preacher throughout the Diocese of B&W) 1823-58, Canon and Prebend of Warminster in Wells Cathedral 1841 and R. Nettlecombe, Som. 1831 to death. Dom. Chap. to 8th and 9th Lords Napier 1831. Died 12/8/1858, leaving £25,000 [C10785] Married St James's, Westminster, London 7/6/1828 Maria Jane Trevelyan (dau. of a baronet) (w).

ELLISON (Robert) Bapt. Thorp, Surrey 3/7/1768, s. Stanhope Ellison and Sarah Wilby. King's, Cambridge 1787, Fellow 1790-3, BA1791, dn91 (Lin.), p93 (C&L), MA1794. Tutor to sons of Bishop of Lichfield. V. Penn, Staffs. 1793-1800, Prebend of Willenhall in Wolverhampton Collegiate Church 1793, R. Slaugham, Surrey 1805-1839, R. Ardingley, Sussex 1804, R. Southease, Sussex 1805 to death 26/7/1839 [C10730] Married Chertsey, Surrey 30/7/1793 Sarah Potter.

ELLISON (Thomas) Bapt. London 28/8/1754, s. Thomas Ellison. King's, Cambridge 1773, BA1778, Fellow 1776-90, MA1783, dn86 (Ely), p87 (Peterb.). R. Haddiscoe w. Monks Tofts >< Norfolk 1790 and R. Denton, Sussex 1825 to death May 1837 [C57799] Note a contemporary Oxford namesake.

ELLMAN (Henry John) Bapt. Glynde, Sussex 19/3/1800, s. John Ellman and Constantia Davies. Wadham, Oxford 1819, BCL1828. R. Carlton w. Chellington, Beds. 1829 to death (London) 3/2/1862 aged 62, leaving £3,000 [C57801] Married Paddington, London 21/8/1840 Elizabeth Simmons (w).

ELMS (Edward) Bapt. Reading, Berks. 19/9/1785, s. Edward [*pleb*] and Rachel Elms. Christ Church, Oxford 1804, BA1808, dn08 (Salis.), p09 (Heref.), MA1820. Min. Fulham St Mary North End Parochial Chapel, London 1814, R. Itchingfield, Sussex 1821 to death 3/5/1845 [C63411] Married Fulham, London 6/9/1815 Jane Fielding, with issue.

ELSDALE (Robinson) Born Surfleet, Lincs. 26/3/1783, s. Robinson Elsdale and Anne Gibbons. Corpus Christi, Oxford 1801 ('where he used to study 16 hours a day'), BA1805, MA 1807, dn09 (Ox.), p09 (Ox.), Fellow, BD & DD1838. S/M Manchester G/S 1808-36; PC. Stretford St Matthew, Manchester 1819-[50], High Master Manchester G/S 1836-40. Dom. Chap. to Ann, Countess Manvers 1818. Died Wrington, Som. 8/8/1850 aged 67 [C26857] Married Wrington 24/7/1810 Marianne Leeves (a clergy dau.), 13 ch. (7 lived).

ELSLEY (Heneage) Born Patrick Brompton, Yorks. 13/12/1745, s. Charles Elsley and Elizabeth Dering. Peterhouse, Cambridge 1763, BA1768, dn71 (Chester), p74 (Salis.), MA1780. R. St Benet Gracechurch w. St Leonard Eastcheap, City of London 1778-89 (res.), R. Burneston, Yorks. (and Public Preacher within the Diocese of Chester) 1789 to death 20/12/1833 aged 87 [C92319] Married Great Shefford, Berks. 20/10/1774 Miriam Lockey (a clergy dau.), with issue.

ELSTON (Henry) Bapt. West Down, Devon 16/12/1780, s. Rev. Philip Elston and Stuart [*sic*] Seddon. St John's, Cambridge 1800, BA 1804, dn06 (Win.), p06 (Ex. for Win.). PC. Tidcombe and Fosbury, Wilts. 1821-36. Died? [C73120] Married Owslebury, Hants. 10/12/1807 Sarah Young.

ELTON (William Tierney) Born Bath, s. Isaac Elton and Catherine Bayard. Worcester, Oxford 1821 (aged 18), BA1825, dn26 (B&W), p27 (B&W), MA1840. R. White Staunton, Som. (living at the Manor house) 1827 to death 30/8/1874, leaving £6,000 [C42194] Married The Hague, Netherlands 2/1/1828 Lucy Caroline, dau. Sir Abraham Elton, 6th Bart., with 14 ch. (including s. Frederick Cockayne Elton who won the Victoria Cross in 1855).

ELWES (Frederic) Born Clare, Suffolk 29/12/1806, s. Lt.-Gen. John Timms Hervey-Elwes and Frances Payne. Pembroke, Cambridge 1825, BA1830, dn30 (Lin. for Ely), p31 (Lin. for Ely). R. Wixoe, Essex 1831-80, (Sinecure R. 1846 and) V. Guestingthorpe, Essex 1848 to death 27/7/1887, leaving £21,996-6s-6d. [C17743] Married 27/2/1830 Mary Wilfred Armstrong, with issue.

ELWIN (Caleb) Born Baconsfield, Sussex 13/1/1774, s. Thomas Elwin (farmer). Caius, Cambridge 1791, then Pembroke 1792, BA 1796, dn97 (London), p99 (London), MA1809. R. Bayfield, Norfolk 1799-1849, (Sinecure R. and) V. Ringstead St Andrew (Little Ringstead), Lincs. [blank in ERC] 1801-49, R. Bootton, Norfolk 1804 and R. Melton Constable w. Little Burgh, Norwich 1811 to death. Dom. Chap. to (and resident with) his relation Sir Jacob Astley (Lord Hastings). Died 30/5/1849 aged 75 [C112865]

ELWIN (Fountain) Born Marylebone, London, s. Hastings Elwin and Elizabeth Diana Woodhead. St Edmund Hall, Oxford 1809 (aged 25), no degree, dn10 (Salis. for Bristol), p11 (Salis. for Bristol). Min. Octagon (St Michael) Proprietary Chapel, Bath --, V. Bristol Temple (o/w Holy Cross) 1816. Died Bath (a widower)

22/5/1869, leaving £1,500 [C38258] His dau. began the Bath Home for Deaf and Dumb Women. Doubtless related to the men below.

ELWIN (Robert Fountain) Bapt. Reepham, Norfolk 7/9/1783, s. Robert Elwin and Virtue Baldwin. Caius, Cambridge 1801, BA1805, dn07 (Nor.), p07 (Nor.). R. Wilby and Hargham, Norfolk 1810-53, R. Norwich St Margaret (de Westwick) 1825-48. Died Leeds 21/2/1853 [C112866] Married Scottow, Norfolk 8/10/1810 Theodora Martha Blake. Doubtless related to the men above and below.

ELWIN (Thomas Henry) Born Edmonton, Middx. 8/6/1788, s. Fountain Elwin (financier) and Mrs Anne Maria (Gibson) Mathews. Worcester, Oxford 1807, BA1811, dn11 (Lin.), p14 (Lin.), MA1822. R. Wormingford, Essex 1822-25 (res.), R. Bradfield St Clare, Suffolk 1824, R. East Barnet, Herts. 1827 [net income £1,042] and RD to death 17/7/1866, leaving £2,000 [C57807] Married Enfield, Middx. 15/1/1812 Eliza Leonora Monk, with issue. Doubtless related to the men above.

ELWYN (William) Bapt. Canterbury 26/7/1790, s. Richard Elwyn and Mary Noble. Corpus Christi, Cambridge 1808, BA1812, dn13 (Chester for Cant.), Fellow 1814, p14 (Cant.), MA1815. PC. Loose, Kent 1816 to death 1/5/1854 aged 65 [C92321] Married Sandwich, Kent 15/8/ 1816 Fanny Curling, with issue.

ELY (Bishop of) see under **SPARKE (Bowyer Edward)**

EMPSON (Richard) Bapt. Wraby, Lincs. 10/4/1792, s. of Amaziah Empson and Ann Kelk. St John's, Cambridge 1811, BA1817, dn17 (Lin.), p19 (Lin.). PC. West Butterwick, Lincs. 1824 to death (Scotton, Lincs.) 3/1/1835 [C57812]

EMRA (John) From St Kitts, West Indies, s. John Emra and Lucy Manners. St Alban Hall, Oxford 1794 (aged 25), dn94 (St David's for B&W), p95 (B&W), BA1798. V. Bristol St George 1809 to death 19/9/1842 [C38260] Married Minehead, Devon 11/12/1795 Elizabeth Bastone Blake (a naval dau.), with clerical son , also John. 'A poet and gifted painter'.

ENGLAND (William, sen.) Born Blandford, Dorset 26/8/1767, s. John England. St John, Cambridge 1774, BA1778, dn80 (London for Bristol), p81 (Ex. for Bristol), MA1782, DD 1814. R. Great Yeldham, Essex 1782-1804, R. Winterbourne Came, Dorset 1804-20, Archdeacon of Dorset 1815-35, R. Owermoigne 1808 and R. West Stafford, Dorset 1820 to death 13/11/1835 [C52416] Married Shudy Camps, Cambs. 1/1/1787 Margaret Bridge, w. clerical son (below).

ENGLAND (William, jun.) Born Sept. 1793, s. Rev. William England, sen. (above) and Margaret Bridge. St John, Cambridge 1813, LLB1817, dn17 (B&W), BA1818, p19 (Salis. for Bristol). (succ. his father as) R. Winterbourne Came, Dorset 1820 to death 25/12/1846 aged 54 [C42195]

ENGLAND (William Henry) Born Kensington, London 13/6/1800, s. Joseph England and Mary Frances Hunt. Pembroke, Oxford 1819, BA1824, dn26 (B&W), MA1828, p29 (Peterb.). R. Ellesborough, Bucks. 1832 to death (Milan) 6/10/1858, leaving £50,000 [C42196] Married Holborn, London 20/8/1827 Mary Prevost, with clerical son.

ERRINGTON (Ralph) Bapt. Walwick Grange Warden, Northumberland 11/12/1776, s. John Errington and Mary Stoddart. Christ's, Cambridge 1794 [Captain 20th and 98th Regiments] dn22 (Nor.), p22 (Nor.). PC. Widdrington, Northumberland 1828-40 [followed by another unrelated minister of the same name], PC. Swallowcliffe, Wilts. 1801 [Not in ERC], V. Mitford, Northumberland 1844 to death (Morpeth, Northumberland) 30/5/1853 aged 75 [C112873] Married Newcastle-upon-Tyne 27/10/1802 Margaret Diana Watson, 5s. (including clerical), 8 dau.

ERSKINE (Henry David, Hon.) Born 1786, s. Thomas Erskine, 1st Baron Erskine (a Scottish M.P.) and Frances Moore. Edinburgh, then Trinity, Cambridge 1806, MA 1810, p12 (Salis. for Chich.), DD1852 (Columbia College, New York). R. Loddington, Northants. 1816, R. Swithland, Leics. 1817-41, V. Leicester St Martin 1830, R. Kirby Underdale, Yorks. 1840-7, Prebend of Warthill in York 1845-7 (res.), Dean of Ripon 1847 to death 27/7/1859 aged 72, leaving £4,000 [C10791. Boase. YCO] Married Chiswick 4/5/1813 Lady Mary Harriet Dawson (dau. of 1st Earl of Portarlington), with issue. 'A great promoter of Mechanics' Institutes'.

ERSKINE (Thomas, Hon.) Birth 'registered' Alloa, Clackmannan 6/8/1784], s. John Francis Erskine, 7th Earl of Mar and Frances Floyer. Trinity, Cambridge 1804, dn08 (York), p10 (York), MA1811. V. Beighton, Derbys. 1821 to death (Rotherham, Yorks.) 1/1/1859 aged 74, leaving £2,000 [C10792. YCO. Austin] Married 4/6/1817 Charlotte Watson (w) (a military dau.), with issue.

ESCOTT, *or* SWEET-ESCOTT, *born* SWEET (Thomas Sweet-, sen.) Born Hartrow Court, Tiverton, Devon, s. Rev. George Sweet and Catherine Richards. Balliol, Oxford 1782 (aged 18), BA1786, MA1789. R. Riseholme w. Grange de Lings, Lincs. 1797, R. Mark Teys 1802, Prebend of Wedmore III in Wells Cathedral 1819-42, R. (and patron) of Brompton Ralph, Som. 1802-42, R. Kittisford, Som. 1802-42, R. Combe Florey, Som. 1824-9. Dom. Chap. to 1st Viscount Hood 1802; to 2nd Viscount Clifden 1824-31. Died 17/4/1842 [C38271] Married Wells Cathedral 1799 Mary Escott, with clerical sons Thomas Sweet-Escott, jun., and William Sweet Escott (both below), and Charles Sweet.

ESCOTT, *or* SWEET-ESCOTT, *born* SWEET (Thomas Sweet-, jun.) Born Brompton Ralph, Som. 11/5/1801, s. of Rev. Thomas Sweet, sen. (above) and Mary Escott. Balliol, Oxford 1818, BA1822, then Lincoln, Fellow 1824-30, dn24 (B&W), MA1825, p25 (B&W). R. Foston, Yorks. 1829-35 [exchanged with Sydney Smith for Combe Florey, Som.], V. Gedney, Lincs. 1835 to death 6/8/1856 [C42199] Married (1) Elizabeth Chapman (2) Ann Young; with issue. Suspended 1840 for refusing to bury a baby girl baptised in a Wesleyan chapel. Brother below.

ESCOTT, *or* SWEET-ESCOTT, *born* SWEET (William Sweet-) Born Brompton Ralph, Somerset 17/7/1806, s. Rev. Thomas Sweet, sen. (above) and Mary Escott. New, Oxford 1825, Fellow 1825-32, SCL, dn29 (Heref.), p30 (Ox.). Oxford St Peter in the East 1831, R. Oddington, Glos. 1832, R. Carlton w. Chellington, Beds. 1863. Died Brompton Ralph 2/3/1884 aged 77, leaving £3,428-13s-6d. [C26864] Married Fairford, Glos. 7/6/1832 Lucy Horatia Rice, with clerical son. Brother above. His Will adds: 'Formerly of Foyle College, Londonderry'.

ESTCOURT (Edmund Hiley Bucknall) Born Marylebone, London 23/11/1803, s. Thomas Grimston Bucknall Estcourt, *M.P.* (Estcourt, Glos.) and Eleanor Sutton. Balliol, Oxford 1821, BA1825, then Merton, Fellow 1826-31, dn27 (Ox.), MA1828, p28 (Ox.). V. (Great) Wolford, Warwicks. 1830, R. Eckington, Derbys. 1843. Of Estcourt Park, Glos. Died 25/1/1894 aged 90, leaving £50,787-0s-10d. [C120950/C26865] Married St George's Hanover Square, London 15/4/1830 Anne Elizabeth Johnstone (dau. of a Scottish baronet), with issue.

ESTCOURT (Edmund William) Born Bath 28/4/1782, s. Thomas Estcourt and Jane Grimston. Oriel, Oxford 1800, BA1804, dn05 (Glos.), p06 (Glos.), MA1807. R. Shipton (le) Moyne, Glos. 1806 and R. Long Newnton, Wilts. 1808 to death. Dom. Chap. to 1st Earl of Verulam 1808. Died (Tetbury, Glos.) 28/5/1856 [C92324. Some say Edmond] Married Wargrave, Berks. 13/2/1811 Bertha Emmeline Wyatt, with issue.

ETHELSTON (Charles Wicksted) Born Manchester 26/12/1798, s. Rev. Charles Wicksted Ethelston, sen. (Wicksted Hall, Cheshire) and Ann Threlfall. Trinity, Cambridge 1818, BA1822, dn24 (Ex.), p25 (Ex.), MA1826. (succ. his father as) PC. Manchester St Mark, Cheetham Hill 1830-34 (res.), R. (and patron) of Uplyme, Devon 1842 to death 1/12/1872 aged 72, leaving £20,000 [C143412] Married Tormohun, Devon 2/5/1822 Ann Peel (dau. of Robert Peel, Wallington Hall, Norfolk), with clerical son. The second clerical magistrate present at Peterloo; 'pompous and loud-voiced'.

ETOUGH (Richard [Saunderson]) Born Lowick, Northants. 27/3/1785, s. Rev. Henry Etough and Martha Saunderson ('an heiress'). Sidney, Cambridge 1802, dn08 (Ely), p09 (Nor.), DD by 1819. V. Stonesby, Leics. 1820, R. Great Addington, Northants. 1831-2, R. Croxton Kerrial, Leics. 1832, R. Claydon w. Akenham, Suffolk 1832-41. Died 1853 [C57817] Married Oct. 1808 Anna Awdry Olivier (a clergy dau.), 2s, 7 dau.

EVANS (Arthur Benoni) Born Compton Beauchamp, Berks. 25/3/1781, s. Rev. Lewis Evans and Ann Norman. St John's, Cambridge 1799, BA1804, dn04 (Glos.), p05 (Glos.), MA 1820, BD and DD1828. [Professor of Classics and History at Royal Military College, Sandhurst 1805-22]. H/M Market Bosworth G/S 1829-54; R. Coln Rogers, Glos. 1807, V. Barnwood, Glos. 1809-41. Died 8/11/1854 [C92329. ODNB as misc. writer. Boase] Married Plumstead, Kent 17/6/1819 Anne Dickinson, with issue. Port. online.

EVANS (Benjamin) Bapt. Exeter 4/8/1765, s. John and Elizabeth Evans. Pembroke, Cambridge 1785, BA1789, dn89 (Lin.), Fellow, MA 1792. S/M Harrow School 1792-1826, Under Master 1826-33; R. South Elmham St Margaret and St Peter, Suffolk 1807 to death 20/6/1833 aged 68 (CCEd says 19/11/1833) [C57818] Had issue. 'One of the most charming old men that any boy could chance to live under', etc. House master to Lord Byron.

EVANS (Edward) Born Kirby Bedon, Norfolk 24/5/1791, s. Thomas Browne Evans (North Tuddenham, Norfolk), J.P., and Mary Hase. Trinity, Cambridge 1809, BA1814, dn14 (Nor.). R. Hempsted, Norfolk 1815-24, R. Eriswell, Suffolk 1815-53, R. Eccles by the Sea (Eccles on Sea), Norfolk 1815-53. Dom. Chap. to 6th Marquess of Queensbury. Died? 1815 [C112878] Brother Henry, below.

EVANS (George) Bapt. Ruyton (of the Eleven Towns), Oswestry, Shropshire 18/10/1793, s. Rev. David and Mary Evans. Christ Church, Oxford 1813, BA1817, dn17 (C&L), p18 (C&L), MA1820. R. Ruyton (of the Eleven Towns) 1823 to death 6/10/1859, leaving £1,000 [C10821] Widow Elizabeth. 'A sound scholar, a man of vigorous intellect, and a disciplinarian'.

EVANS (George Sherwood) Bapt. Micheldean, Glos. 21/2/1787, s. Thomas and Bridget Evans. Pembroke, Oxford 1804, BA1808, dn10 (Salis. for Win.), MA1811, p11 (Ox.), Fellow to 1822. PC. Temple Grafton, Warwicks. 1825, R. Hinton Waldrist, Berks. at death 22/4/1853 [C26872] Married Hinton Waldrist 22/5/1817 Penelope Symonds.

EVANS (George William David) From Middlesex. St John's, Cambridge 1812, BA1818, dn20 (Salis. for Cant.), p20 (Chester for Cant.), MA1821. V. Reculver, Kent 1832 to death 3/11/1873, leaving £1,000 [C92331] Married Broseley, Shropshire 20/7/1827 Bridget Griffiths, and had issue.

EVANS (Gowen) Bapt. Chester-le-Street, Co. Durham 6/3/1768, s. David [*pleb*] and Ruth Evans. Jesus, Oxford 1791 (aged 20), BA1795, dn95 (Heref.). V. Potterspury w. Yardley Gobion, Northants. 1827 to death 7/12/1841 aged 72 [C104786] Married Potterspury 8/7/1822 Sarah Sabin, and had issue.

EVANS (Hugh) From Denbighshire. Literate: dn13 (Chester), p15 (Chester). PC. Haigh, Wigan, Lancs. 1833 to death before June 1835 [C168791] Widow Mary, and issue.

EVANS (John) Born Langeter, Carmarthen 23/1/1808, s. Methusalem [*sic*] Evans. Literate: dn29 (York), p30 (York), Lampeter BD1853. Chap. of the Donative of Netherthong, Almondbury, Yorks. 1830, V. Crickhowell, Breconshire 1837 (and R. 1851, and Chap. to the Poor Law Union) to 1874. Died? Will not traced [C131258. YCO] Married (1) 26/8/1836 Elizabeth Philipps (Jeffreystone House, Pembroke), w. issue (2) Portland, Dorset 25/8/1867 Mrs Mary Nicholas, 2s., 1 dau.

EVANS (John) From Tottenham, London, s. of John Evans, Lincoln, Oxford 1808 (aged 21), BA1812, dn12 (C&L), p13 (C&L), MA 1816. PC. Edingale (or Edengale), Staffs. 1824-64-. Died? [C10823]

EVANS (John) Bapt. Lambeth, Surrey 25/9/1803, s. John (a mercer) and Mary Evans. Pembroke, Cambridge 1821, BA1825, dn27 (Win.), MA1828, p28 (Win.). PC. Bermondsey St James, London 1829-40, Deputy Commissary for Surrey and Judge of Commissary Court; Assistant Secretary S.P.C.K. 1840-2, then Secretary 1842-79; Acting Chaplain at the Tower of London, Preb. of St Paul's Cathedral 1869-79. Lived at Maidenhead, Berks. Died London 21/5/1879, leaving £12,000 [C73548. Boase]

EVANS (John) Born Shrewsbury, s. John Evans, physician. Clare, Cambridge 1805, BA 1809, Fellow 1809, dn11 (London for Ely), p11 (Ely), MA1812, BD1827. V. Hardingham, Norfolk 1832 to death (Tarvin, Cheshire - his brother's home) 14/12/1838 [C99952]

EVANS (John William) Literate: dn19 (Ely for Llandaff), p19 (Chester for Llandff). V. Bassingthorpe w. Westby, Lincs. 1819-68, R. Alltmawr, Brecon 1848 (living at Builth) to death 24/11/1868. No will traced [C51889 - two men here? Bennett2]

EVANS (Joseph Saville Roberts) Bapt. Lydgate, Saddleworth, Yorks. 29/3/1801, s. Thomas (of Ashton-under-Lyne, Lancs.) and Sarah Evans. Queen's, Oxford 1822, BA1826, dn26 (Durham), p27 (Chester), MA1829. PC. Rochdale, Lancs., 1828, PC. Lydgate 1829-35 (res.). Died Hastings, Kent 28/10/1861, aged 60, leaving £25,000 [C130410] Married Prescot, Lancs. 22/9/1830 Elizabeth Lees, w. issue. *J.P.*

EVANS (Robert) Bapt. Londesborough, Yorks. 9/6/1770, s. Rev. Robert, sen. and Mary Evans. Trinity, Cambridge 1788, BA1793, dn93 (York), Fellow 1795, MA1796, p00 (Win.). V. Everton, Notts. 1803-47, V. Normanton, Yorks. 1803-33, V. Misson, Notts. 1829-47 (where he also took pupils), RD of East Retford, Notts., R. Coveney, Cambs. 1847 to death (Cambridge) 12/1/1852 [C131259. YCO] Married Shrewsbury, Shropshire 13/3/1810 Charlotte Margaretta Money. *J.P.* for Notts.

EVANS (Samuel Newland) [NiVoF] R. Beguildy, Pembroke 1776-1836. King's, Cambridge 1784 (a Ten Year Man, BD1784). R. Holton St Peter, Suffolk 1807 to death 2/7/1836 aged 94. Dom. Chap. to 5th Earl of Scarborough 1782 [C112904] Married Westminster, London 10/9/1789 Martha Thackeray.

EVANS (Thomas) [NiVoF] Chap. of the Donative of Longdon-on-Terne, Shrewsbury, Shropshire 1829 to death. Probate granted 28/8/1845 [Not in CCEd] Widow Elizabeth.

EVANS (William) From Eyton Hall, Kingsland, Heref., s. Rev. Richard Evans (Prebend of Bangor Cathedral) and Jane Lloyd. Christ's, Cambridge 1787, BA1792, dn92 (Heref.), MA 1796. V. Vowchurch, Heref. 1815-31, V. Wigmore, Heref. 1821 (only), R. (and patron) of Kingsland, Heref. 1821 (succ. his brother, and was then succ. by his son) to death 1841? [C105014] Married Wirksworth, Derbys. Margaret Leaford Goodwyn, w. issue.

EVANS (William) From Llangadock, Carmarthen, s. Thomas Evans. Jesus, Oxford 1812 (aged 17), BA1815, Fellow 1817-28, MA 1818, BD1826. R. Shipston upon Stour, Worcs. 1827 to death 2/4/1873, leaving £10,000 [C120955]

EVANS (William) From Andover, Hants., s. Rev. Robert Evans. Trinity, Oxford 1820 (aged 18), BA1824, dn25 (Win.), p26 (Ely), MA1827, BD1838. R. Pusey, Berks. 1827 to death 14/2/1860, leaving £3,000 [C17745] Widow Mary Elizabeth.

EVANS (William Edward) Born Shrewsbury, Shropshire 8/6/1801, s. John Evans (physician) and Jane Wilson. Clare, Cambridge 1818, BA 1823, dn24 (Peterb.), p25 (St Asaph), MA1826. PC. Criggion, Montgomery [Heref. Diocese] 1829-37, V. Madeley, Heref. 1850-69, RD, Prebend of Nonnington in Hereford Cathedral 1841-61, Praelector 1846-61 (res.) and Canon Residentiary 1861 to death (a widower) 21/11/1869, leaving £7,000 [C105013. ODNB. Boase] Married his cousin Elizabeth Evans (who inherited Burton Court, Leominster, where they lived latterly), with issue.

EVANSON (Thomas) From Warrington, Lancs., s. William Evanson. BNC, Oxford 1765 (aged 16), BA1769, Fellow, MA1771, dn72 (Ox.), p83 (Glos.). R. Great Catworth, Hunts. 1788 to death 6/2/1835 (CCEd says 27/5/1835) [C27142]

EVANSON (William Alleyn) Born Cork, s. Charles Evanson and Harriet Alleyn. TCD 1799 (aged 14), BA1804, MA1828, incorporated at Oxford 1840. V. Blewbury, Berks. 1832, V. Inglesham, Wilts. 1836 to death 2/3/1857 aged 71 [C105773. Al.Dub.] Married Cork 24/1/1811 Lyndon McConnell, w. clerical s., also William Alleyn.

EVE (Henry) Bapt. Letchworth, Herts. 8/6/1794, s. Col. Henry Eve and Mary Long. Wadham, Oxford 1812, then Magdalene, Cambridge 1814, BA1816, dn16 (Lin. for London), p18 (London), MA1821. R. South Ockenden, Essex 1819 to death 26/5/1873, leaving £12,000 [C57839] Widow Elizabeth, and issue.

EVELEIGH (John) From Aylesford, Kent, s. Rev. William Eveleigh. Oriel, Oxford 1816 (aged 17), BA1821, dn22 (Lin. for Roch.), p23 (Win. for Roch.), MA1823. V. Darenth, Kent 1823 to death 4/2/1863 aged 64, leaving £4,000 [C1463] Married St George's Hanover Square, London 13/7/1836 Mahala Georgiana Brockwell (w). But note another unbeneficed but identically-named cleric in Kent dying in Lausanne at almost exactly the same time.

EVERARD (Daniel) Bapt. King's Lynn, Norfolk 20/11/1765, s. Daniel Everard. Oriel, Oxford 1787, BA1791, dn91 (Nor.), p92 (Nor.), MA1796. R. Stanhoe, Norfolk 1793 and R. Burnham Thorpe, Norfolk 1802 to death 23/1/1853, aged 81 [C112908]

EVERARD (Edward) Born City of London, c.1778. St John's, Cambridge 1806, then Peterhouse 1808, BA1810, dn11 (Roch.), p13 (B&W), MA1814, DD1831. R. Sutton Waldron, Dorset 1822-6, R. Holy Trinity, Shaftesbury (o/w Sharston), Dorset 1823, R. Southwick, Sussex 1825, PC. Bishops Hull, Som. 1844 to death. Dom. Chap. to Henrietta, Countess of Brooke and Warwick 1823; Chap. to the King at Brighton 1832. Died 26/9/1855, leaving £1,047-13s-3d. [C1816] Married Hitchin, Herts. 3/6/1812 Sarah Patteson, w. issue.

EVEREST (Thomas Roupell) Born Greenwich, Kent 7/12/1800, s. William Tristram Everest (Hampton Court, Middx.) and Lucetta Mary Smith. Pembroke, Cambridge 1818, BA 1822, dn25 (Lin. for Salis.), p26 (Bristol). R. Wickwar, Glos. 1830 to death 15/6/1855 aged 54 [C52424] Married 27/9/1830 Mary Ryall, with issue. An early writer on homeopathy: ueyounghistories.com/.../06/.../thomas-roupell-everest-and-homeopathy...

EVERY (Nicholas) Bapt. Bodmin, Cornwall 17/8/1794, s. John Every and Joan Cradock. Clare, Cambridge 1813, BA1817, dn18 (Salis.), p18 (Ex.), MA1820. V. St Veep, Cornwall 1823 to death there 14/4/1836 [C92342] Married Elizabeth Hickes, with clerical s. Nicholas Thomas Every.

EWART (Peter) Born Liverpool, s. of William Ewart, 'an influential Liverpool businessman'. Christ Church, Oxford 1820 (aged 19), BA1823, dn23 (Chester), p25 (Chester), MA1826. R. Kirklington, Yorks. [net income £1,034] 1828 to death 25/8/1852 [C168794] Married Childwall, Liverpool 2/5/1831 Maria Margaret Lester Salisbury, with issue.

EWBANK (Thomas) Bapt. Kirk Levington, Yorks. 28/2/1762, s. George Ewbank. St John's, Cambridge 1780, then St Catharine's 1780, BA 1784, dn84 (Durham), p86 (Durham), MA 1787. PC. Eryholme, Yorks. 1790, R. Elton, Durham 1804 to death 16/4/1840 aged 78 [C130412] Married York 7/12/1814 Frances Shillito, 1 dau. (dec.).

EWBANK (William Withers) Born Bolton Percy, Yorks. 10/2/1807, s. Rev. William Ewbank and Theodosia Cooper. Christ's, Cambridge 1826, BA1830, dn32 (York), p32 (Roch. for Durham), MA1843. V. Grindon, Durham 1832-41, PC. St George, Everton, Liverpool 1841 to death 26/3/1855 (of dysentery 'on his way from Cairo to Mount Sinai'), leaving £1,000 (left unadministered) [C130413. YCO] Married 26/12/1834 Justina Eleanor (dau. of Sir George Cooper, a judge in Madras).

EXETER (Bishop of) see under **PHILLPOTTS (Henry)**

EXTON (Richard Brudenell) Literate: dn14 (Lin.), p15 (Lin.). R. Athelington, Suffolk 1822, V. Cretingham, Suffolk 1827 to death. Dom. Chap. to Earl of Clarendon. Died 1863 (3rd q.). No will traced [C57845 as Richard only] Clerical son, also Richard.

EXTON (Thomas) Bapt. Rivington, Lancs. 26/8/1761, s. Richard Exton. S/M Blackburn Free G/S 1783. Literate: dn85 (Chester), p88 (Chester), then St John's, Cambridge 1797 (a Ten Year Man). S/M Blackburn G/S 1783; PC. Over Darwen, Lancs. 1791-1816, PC. Balderstone, Lancs. 1816 to death (*accidentally drowned* in the River Darwen) 11/2/1839 aged 78 [C168795]

EYRE (Anthony William) Born Barnbrough, Yorks. 20/11/1783, s. Rev. Anthony Fountayne Eyre and Honor Wolley. Emmanuel, Cambridge 1802, BA1806, p06 (Ex. for York), p08 (York). PC. Chadkirk, Cheshire 1808-14 (res.), PC. Marple, Cheshire 1808-14 (res.), V. Tottenhoe, Beds. 1814-19, V. Stillingfleet, Yorks. 1818-26, R. Long Riston w. Hornsea >< Yorks. 1831 to death (Bath) 17/9/1848 aged 64. Dom. Chap. to Jean Mary, Dowager Baroness Bolton (of Bolton Castle) 1809; to 6th Earl of Scarborough 1830 [C57847. YCO] Married Yarmouth 15/12/1810 Sarah Mapleton, with issue. Stepbrother Charles Wolff, below.

EYRE (Charles Wasteneys) Born Babworth, Notts. 7/3/1802, s. Ven. Charles Eyre (Archdeacon of Nottingham) and Charlotte Armytage. BNC, Oxford 1820, BA1823, dn25 (Bristol for York), p26 (C&L for York), MA 1826. R. Carlton in Lindrick, Notts. 1826-40, Prebend of Strensall in York Minster 1828-36 (res.), R. Babworth 1830, V. Sturton le Steeple, Notts. 1835-6. Died Rampton Manor, Notts.

30/10/1862, leaving £4,000 [C10831. YCO] Married York 26/4/1829 Lucy Dorothea Foulis, with issue. *J.P.*

EYRE (Charles Wolff) Born Barnbrough, Yorks. 5/1/1772, s. Rev. Anthony Fountayne Eyre and Susanna Prescot (a clergy dau.). St Catherine's, Cambridge 1790, dn94 (York for Chester), BA1794, p96 (Win. for Chester), MA 1799. V. Kildwick Percy, Yorks. 1796, (succ. his father as) V. Pocklington, Yorks. 1796, R. Hooton Roberts, Yorks. 1796-1860 and V. Sturton, Notts. 1835 to death (Hooton Roberts, unmarried) 8/8/1860 aged 88, leaving £3,000 [C101798. YCO] Step-brother Anthony William (above).

EYRE (Daniel James) Born Salisbury, Wilts.. c.1803, s. Daniel Eyre and Prudence Barbara Kinnear. Oriel, Oxford 1820 (aged 17), BA 1824, dn26 (Salis.), MA1827, p27 (Salis.). PC. Winterbourne Dauntsey, Wilts. 1827-[44], Sub-Dean of Salisbury Cathedral 1846 to death 25/2/1882 aged 79, leaving £5,921-1s-8d. [C92343]

EYRE (George Hardolph) Born Hatfield, Yorks. 20/9/1801, s. Vice-Admiral Sir George Eyre and Georgiana Cooke. Pembroke, Cambridge 1822, BA1826, dn26 (Ely for York), p26 (York), MA1836. V. Headon cum Upton, Yorks. 1826-36, R. Molesworth, Hunts. 1826-36, PC. Dalton, Rotherham, Yorks. 1849-59, V. Beighton, Derbys. 1859 to death 16/2/1865, leaving £1,000 [C57848. YCO] Married Cleobury Mortimer, Shropshire 1844 (4th q.) Cecilia Maria Hill, with issue.

EYRE (James) Born Wylye, Wilts. 4/2/1772, s. Rev. John Eyre and Susanna Layton. Exeter, Oxford 1793, then St Mary Hall, BCL1801 [CCEd adds BA1827, LLB 1829]. PC. North Dalton, Yorks. 1827-55, PC. Butterwick, Foxholes, Yorks. 1829, R. Kirk Ella, Hull 1837-46. 'Senior Assistant PC Beverley Minister'. Died 7/3/1855 aged 83 [C131260] Married Westbury, Wilts. 5/4/1806 Penelope Phipps (Leighton House, Wilts.), with clerical son.

EYRE (William) Born Ardleigh, Essex 8/9/1779, s. Rev. John Eyre (R. Sherfield on Loddon, Hants.). Sidney, Cambridge 1798, BA 1802, dn02 (Win.), p03 (Win.), MA1806. R. Sherfield on Loddon 1815 to death (a bachelor) 4/11/1859, leaving £20,000 [C73562]

EYRE (William Thomas) Born Padbury, Bucks. 9/5/1795, s. Rev. William Eyre and Mary Sayer. BNC, Oxford 1812, BA1816, dn18 (London), p19 (London), MA1819. PC. Hillesdon, Bucks. 1830 and V. Padbury 1830 to death (Sidmouth, Devon) 8/7/1868, leaving £6,000 [C57858. Foster corrected] Married Guisborough, Yorks. 26/5/1838 Frances Williamson (w), with issue.

EYTON (Charles Watkin Wynne) Born Leeswood Hall, Mold, Flintshire, s. Rev. Hope Eyton and Margaret Wynne. Jesus, Oxford 1818 (aged 19), BA1822, dn22 (Ox.), p23 (Ox.), Fellow 1823-48, MA1824, BD1834. PC. Shocklach, Cheshire 1832-[64], R. Aston Clinton, Bucks. 1848 to death 21/1/1870 aged 70, leaving £12,000 [C27156] Married Chester 2/3/1848 Mrs Philadelphia Frances Esther (Wrangham) Barnard (w).

FAITHFULL (Ferdinand) Bapt. Warfield, Berks. 24/4/1789, s. Rev. John Faithfull and Patty Boyter. St John's, Cambridge 1819, dn21 (Nor.), BA1826. p26 (London). R. Headley, Surrey 1830 to death (a widower) 5/8/1871, leaving £1,500 [C73642] Married East Barnet, Herts. 13/5/1815 Elizabeth Mary Harrison. 3 clerical brothers below.

FAITHFULL (Francis Joseph) Bapt. Winchester 10/7/1786, s. Rev. John Faithfull (of Warfield, Berks.) and Patty Boyter. St John's, Oxford 1802, dn10 (Salis.), BCL1811, p11 (Ox.), Fellow to 1813. R. Bishop's Hatfield >< Herts. [net income £2,097] (and Preacher throughout the Diocese of Lincoln) 1819-54, R. Bygrave, Herts. 1830-2 (res.). Dom. Chap to 1st Marquess of Salisbury 1811. Died Hatfield 11/11/1854. [C27168] Married Scawby, Lincs. 1/12/1813 Mary Carter Grantham, with issue. Brothers above and below. Port. online.

FAITHFULL (George David) Bapt. Winchester 30/7/1785, s. Rev. John Faithfull and Patty Boyter. Corpus Christi, Oxford 1803, BA1807, dn10 (Salis. for Win.), MA1810, p10 (Ox. or Durham?), Fellow 1812-30, BD1818, etc. R. Eastwell, Leics. 1812-30, R. Lower Hayford, Oxon. 1830 and R. Gunby St Peter, Lincs. 1830 to death 25/3/1866, leaving £8,000 [C27171 as Faithful] Married Grantham, Lincs. 18/12/1830 Anne Norris, with issue. Brothers above and below. 'A hunter - clever - careful - a farmers' man' (Wilberforce).

FAITHFULL (Robert) Bapt. Warfield, Berks. 13/7/1794, s. Rev. John Faithfull and Patty Boyter. Wadham, Oxford 1810, BA1814, dn16 (Salis.), p17 (Salis.), MA1817. V. Warfield 1824-33, V. Dengie, Essex 1818-25. Died 7/12/1833 (CCEd says 25/3/1834) [C92349] Married Warfield 10/8/1818 Sarah Maxwell Windle. Brothers above.

FALLE (Edward) Bapt. Jersey, Channel Islands 11/2/1803, s. Edward Falle and Douce Balliau. Pembroke, Oxford 1820, BA1823, dn26 (Lin. for Win.), p27 (Win.), MA1827. R. Jersey St Brélade 1829-82. Buried 21/12/1899. No will in England [C58086] Married Jersey 1842 Carterette Le Couteur Balléine, with issue.

FALLOFIELD (William) Born London 20/4/1788, s. James Peter Fallofield (chemist) and Maria Moore. Pembroke, Cambridge 1804, BA1810, dn11 (Win.), p12 (London), MA1814. PC. St Pancras Old Church, London 1822-45. Dom. Chap. to 5th Earl of Jersey 1812. Died 20/4/1858, leaving £30,000 [C73644] Married Paddington, London 14/10/1834 Sarah Helen Boaden.

FALLOWFIELD (John) Born Morland, Westmorland 21/01/178, s. Thomas Fallowfield and Sarah Bland. Literate: dn03 (Chester). PC. Oldham St Mary, Lancs. 1818-42. Died there 17/3/1846 aged 66 [C168806] Married Oldham 23/9/1822 Mary Ann Gordon.

FANCOURT (William John Lowfield) Bapt. Woodford, Northants. 2/4/1766, s. Rev. William Fancourt and Mary Harrington. Clare, Cambridge 1785, BA1789, dn89 (Lin.), p90 (Lin.), MA1800, DD1823, incorporated at Oxford 1813. S/M 1793 then H/M Southwark St Saviour's G/S, Surrey 1801-23 (*or* 28?); Prebend of Milton Ecclesia in Lincoln Cathedral 1823-42, V. Leicester St Mary and All Saints 1828 and V. Leicester St Leonard [sequestrator] 1828 to death (London) 13/5/1840 aged 75 ('Fancourt was attending a meeting of the Protestant Association in Exeter Hall when he was seized with a sudden affection of the heart, and expired without saying a word') [C57979. DEB] Married (1) Holborn, London 1/3/1794 Juliana Ann Gilder (d.1811), with issue (2) Lambeth, Surrey 11/7/1811 Mary Holland.

FANE (Edward) Born 7/12/1783, s. Hon. Henry Fane (and grandson of 8th Earl of Westmoreland) and Anne Batson. St John's, Cambridge 1802, BA1806, dn07 (Lin.), p07 (Lin.), MA1809. R. Fulbeck, Lincs. 1807-62, R. Burton by Lincoln 1813-15, R. Stubton, Lincs. 1816-19, Prebend of Clifton in Lincoln Cathedral 1821 and Prebend of Lyme and Halstock in Salisbury Cathedral 1824 to death. Died 28/12/1862, leaving £10,000. Dom. Chap. to (the later) 1st Earl of Limerick 1813 [C58088] Married Dorchester 17/10/1816 Maria Hodges, with clerical son.

FANSHAWE, FANSHAW (Charles Robert) Born Westminster, London 4/4/1780, s. Henry Fanshawe and Susannah Frances Legrys. Trinity, Oxford 1796, BA1800, dn02 (Salis.), MA1803, p04 (London). R. Dengie, Essex 1804-18 (living at Dengie Hall), R. Morton on the Hill (o/w Helmingham), Suffolk 1805-12, R. Fawley, Bucks. 1817-32 (res.), V. Coaley, Glos. 1835 to death. Chap. to HRH Duke of Clarence 1819.

Died Dursley, Glos. 7/9/1859, leaving under £450 [C58091] Married (1) Warfield, Berks. 16/4/1805 Patty Faithfull (d.1823), with clerical son (2) Chelmsford, Essex 2/8/1825 Jane Williams.

FANSHAWE, FANSHAW (John) Born Holborn, London 7/4/1773, s. John Gascoyne Fanshawe and Mary Parkinson. Christ Church, Oxford 1790, Student [Fellow] 1790-1819, BA 1795, dn96 (Ox.), MA1797, p02 (S&M). V. Frodsham, Cheshire 1818 to death 27/10/1843 (2pm) at Parsloes Manor, his seat near Dagenham, Essex [C7455] Son below?

FANSHAWE (Thomas Lewis) Born Parsoles Manor, Dagenham 21/9/1792, s. John Gascoyne Fanshawe and Mary Parkinson. St Mary Hall, Oxford 1812, BA1816, dn16 (Salis.), p16 (Salis.), MA1823. V. Dagenham, Essex 1816 to death. Dom. Chap. to 7th Earl of Kintore 1818. Died Hendon, Middx. 5/3/1858, leaving £8,000 [C92350] Married 1/10/1821 Catherine Stephens Gaspard Le Marchant (w), with issue.

FARBRACE (George Henry Teale) Born Dover, Kent 4/5/1785, s. George Fanshawe and Elisabeth Anne Teale. Christ's, Cambridge 1803, BA1808, dn09 (Ex. for Cant.), p09 (Win. for Cant.), MA1824. R. Eythorne, Dover 1809 to death 17/3/1872, leaving £5,000 [C73646] Married Deal, Kent 3/5/1810 Elizabeth Bower Poynter (w).

FARDELL (Henry) Born Lincoln 6/3/1795, s. John Fardell and Eleanor Penelope Hayward. St John's, Cambridge 1813, BA1817, dn18 (Chester for Lin.), MA1819 Lambeth, p19 (Lin.). Canon of 1st Prebend in Ely Cathedral 1819-54, R. Tydd St Giles, Cambs. 1821-9, R. Bexwell, Norfolk 1823 (only), V. Waterbeach, Cambs. 1821-54, V. Feltwell, Norfolk 1823-31, V. Wisbech St Peter w. St Mary, Cambs. 1831 to death. Chap. to the Bishop of Ely 1834. Died Ely 26/3/1854. [C15511] Married 6/1/1820 Eliza Sparke (dau. of a Bishop of Ely), with issue. J.P. Isle of Ely, Norfolk and Lincs.; Chairman of Quarter Sessions. Brother below.

FARDELL (Thomas) Born Lincoln 1/11/1791, s. John Fardell and Eleanor Penelope Hayward. St John's, Cambridge 1825, then Queens' 1825, dn28 (Ely), p28 (Ely), LLB 1832, LLD 1848. R. Boothby Pagnell, Lincs. 1831-46, V. Sutton, Cambs. 1846 to death 30/12/1860, leaving £14,000 [C17749] Married Knaresborough, Yorks. 21/1/1819 Emma Clara Anne Meyrick, with issue. Brother above.

FARINGTON (Robert) Bapt. Leigh, Lancs. 10/10/1760, s. Rev. William Farington and Hester Gilbody. BNC, Oxford 1777, BA1781, dn83 (Ox.), MA1784, p85 (Cant.), BD and DD1803. R. St George in the East, London 1802 to death 19/9/1841 [C27509]

FARINGTON, FARINGDON (William James) Born Leigh, Lancs., s. Henry Faringdon and Marion Borron. St John's, Cambridge 1816, then Clare 1816, dn17 (Chester), p18 (Chester), BA1820, MA1823. (first) PC. Rochdale St James (o/w Wardleworth), Lancs. 1821 to death 31/1/1863 aged 72, leaving £4,000 [C136781] Married Pontefract, Yorks. 31/8/1822 Mary Anne Haxby/Maxby (w), s.p.

FARISH (Henry) Born Cambridge, s. James Farish (surgeon) and Dorothy Fawcett. Queens', Cambridge 1818, BA1822, dn22 (Lin.), p23 (Lin.), Fellow 1824, MA1825. V. Sheffield St Mary 1830-53, PC. Ecclesall Bierlow, Yorks. 1853 to death 30/10/1856 aged 57 [C17750] Married (1) Marylebone, London 4/6/1830 Jane (d.1833), dau. of Hugh Farrer, H.E.I.C., with issue (2) Rotherham, Yorks. 1845 (2nd q.) Margaret Prime Upton, with further issue.

FARISH (William) Bapt. Stanwix, Carlisle 21/4/1759, s. Rev. James Farish and Elizabeth Gilpin. Magdalene, Cambridge 1774, BA1778 [Senior Wrangler], dn80 (Peterb.), MA1781, p82 (Peterb.), Fellow and tutor, BD1820. Professor of Chemistry, Cambridge 1794-1813, then Jackson Professor of Natural Philosophy 1813-37. R. Norton sub Hamden, Som. 1790-1823 (res.), V. North Clifton, Notts. 1797-1802, V. Cambridge St Giles w. St Peter 1800 and R. Little Stonham, Suffolk 1836 to death 12/1/1837 [C23777. ODNB. DEB] 'In 1792 F. developed the concept of grading students' work quantitively'.

FARLEY (William) From Westbourn, Sussex, s. Thomas Farley. Magdalen Hall, Oxford, 1776 (aged 18), BA1783, dn80 (C&L), MA1784. V. Effingham, Surrey 1793 to death 25/1/1837 [C10846] Married Horsleydown, Surrey 15/7/1788 Dorothy Meymott, w. issue.

FARMER (Thomas) From Chirbury, Shropshire, s. Thomas Farmer [pleb]. Pembroke, Oxford 1764 (aged 17), BA1768, dn68 (Heref.), p71 (Heref.). V. Chirbury 1802 to death 2/2/1838 aged 92 [C105279]

FARMER (Thomas) From Leics. Emmanuel, Cambridge 1790, BA1794, dn94 (Lin.), p95 (Lin.), MA1797. R. Skinnand, Lincs. 1801 and R. & V. Aspley Guise w. Husborne Crawley, Beds. 1813 to death 7 or 25/7/1843 aged 71 [C58097]

FARMERIE, FARMERY (Robert) Bapt. North Collingham, Notts. 8/2/1787, s. William Farmerie and Elizabeth Jones. Pembroke, Cambridge 1805, BA1809, dn10 (Ely for Wor.), MA 1813, p13 (Chester for York), LLD by 1821. V. Car Colston, Notts. 1821-38. Died Newark on Trent, Notts. 14/9/1846 aged 59 [C121032. YCO] Married South Willingham, Lincs. 14/5/1810 Rebecca Wattam, and had issue.

FARNABY (Charles Francis, Sir, 5th Bart.) Born Wickham Court, Bromley, Kent 17/10/1787, s. Sir John Farnaby, 4th Bart. and Mary Lennard. BNC, Oxford 1807, migrated to St John's, Cambridge 1814, BA1814, dn14 (Roch.), MA1814, p14 (London for Roch.). R. (and patron) of West Wickham 1814 (and RD of Dartford 1846)-48. Died Wickham Court 29/8/1859, leaving £40,000 [C1817. Boase] Married Lamberhurst, Kent 29/12/1810 Jane Eliza Morland, *s.p.* Succ. to title 1802; baronetcy extinct on his death.

FARRER (Joseph Liddell) Born Bombay 1775, s. Capt. Joseph Farrer and Anne Greening. Pembroke, Cambridge 1793, BA 1797, dn04 (Nor.), p04 (Nor.). V. Cratfield w. Laxfield, Suffolk 1804 to death (Hackney, London) 28/2/1850 [C112935] Married Clifton, Bristol 17/8/1801 Mary Jervis-White-Jervis (dau. of an Irish baronet), with issue.

FARRER (Richard) From Market Harborough, Leics., s. Rev. Richard Farrer and Jane Dalley. BNC, Oxford 1793 (aged 17), BA1797, MA 1800, dn06 (Ox.), p06 (Ox.). R. Deptford St Paul, Kent 1808-9 (res.), R. (and patron) of Ashley, Northants. 1809 and V. Fawsley, Northants. 1819 to death (Ashley) 16/4/1852 [C1818] Married Muckleston, Staffs. 23/12/1811 Anna Maria Chetwold (dau. of a baronet), with issue.

FARROW (John) Born and bapt. Kirkby Misperton, Yorks. 30/3/1798, s. Rev. Thomas and Rose Farrow. St Bees adm. 1820, dn21 (York), p22 (York). R. Upper (o/w Over) Helmsley, Yorks. 1828-68, V. Gate Helmsley, Yorks. 1851 [to death] 28/7/1871 aged 72, leaving £600 [C131265. YCO] Married York 2/1/1823 Mary Anne Rotherford, with clerical son.

FARROW (Thomas) Bapt. Rosedale, Pickering, Yorks. 23/10/1764, s. John Farrow (born Faroe) and Barbara Longhorn. Literate: dn90 (York), p91 (York). PC. Knapton, Yorks. 1804, PC. Scampston w. Rillington, Yorks. 1818-[38]. Probably died 16/2/1842 aged 77 [C98335. YCO]

FARWELL (Arthur) Bapt. Berry Pomeroy, Devon 17/11/1802, s. Rev. Arthur Farwell, sen. and Elizabeth Trist Taylor. Exeter, Oxford 1821, BA1825, dn25 (Ex.), p26 (Ex.). R. Stoke Fleming, Devon (and Preacher throughout the Diocese of Exeter) 1832 to death 16/3/1859. Will not traced [C143474] Married Modbury, Devon 20/11/1832 Laura Molloy Bartlett, w. issue.

FARWELL (William) Born Stoke Gabriel, Devon 30/4/1805, s. Christopher Farwell. Trinity, Oxford 1824, BA1828, dn29 (Bristol for Ex.), p29 (Ex.). R. St Martin by Looe, Cornwall 1830 (and Preacher throughout the Diocese of Exeter 1832) to death 10/5/1876 aged 71, leaving £18,000 [C52427] Married Walcot, Bath 11/5/1830 Mary Browne, and had issue.

FAULKNER (Henry) Born Norton juxta Kempsey, Worcs. 24/7/1789, s. Rev. William Faulkner and Mary Moore. Magdalen Hall, Oxford 1806, BA1812, dn12, p13 (Salis.). R. North Piddle, Worcs. 1819 and PC. Norton juxta Kempsey, Worcs. 1828 to death (Pershore, Worcs.) 6/3/1864, leaving £6,000 [C92352] Married Bromham, Wilts. 21/2/1813 Harriet Bayntun, w. clerical s. Henry Bayntun-Faulkner.

FAULKNER (Richard Rowland) Bapt. Clerkenwell, London 2/12/1790, s. Rev. William Elisha Law Faulkner (below) and Britannia Perkins. Literate: dn13 (Nor.), p14 (Nor.), then St John's, Cambridge 1813 (re-adm. 1844), a Ten Year Man (BD1826). V. Cambridge St (or Holy) Sepulchre 1825 and PC. Havering atte Bower, Essex 1834 to death (Romford, Essex) 9/5/1873. Will not traced [C17751] Married Clerkenwell, London 30/8/1831 Agnes Gilmour, with issue.

FAULKNER (William Elisha Law) Born Cripplegate, City of London 6/10/1758, s. William Faulkner and Lydia Skelton. [BA but NiVoF] dn81 (Lin. for Nor.), p82 (Nor. for London.). R. Clerkenwell St John, London 1814. Died 1832? [Following C58114 here, but major confusion between father and son] Married London 28/2/1786 Britannia Perkins, with clerical sons William Elisha Law Perkins Faulkner, and Richard Rowland (above

FAUQUIER (George Lillie Wodehouse) Born Hampton Court Palace, Middx. 30/11/1798, s. Thomas Fauquier and Charlotte Townshend. Pembroke, Cambridge 1817, BA 1821, dn22 (Nor.), p23 (Nor.). V. Bacton, Norfolk 1823-54, V. Bradfield, Norfolk 1831-54, V. (and patron) of West Haddon, Northants. 1854 to death there 26/2/1887, leaving £645-7s-6d. [C112929] Married (Hampton Court?) 6/9/1824 Caroline Morris (dau. of a baronet), with issue.

FAUSSETT (Godfrey) Bapt. Nackington, Kent 28/8/1780, s. Henry Godfrey Faussett and Susan Sandys. Corpus Christi, Cambridge 1797, BA 1801, then Magdalene, Fellow 1804, dn04 (Ox.), MA1804, p05 (Ox.), BD1822, DD1827, Lady Margaret Professor of Divinity, Cambridge 1827-53. Canon of 6th Prebend in Worcester Cathedral 1827-40, V. Old Sodbury, Glos. 1831, R. Worcester St Martin 1833, 2nd Canon of Christ Church Cathedral Oxford 1840-53, V. Cropthorne, Worcs. 1840-1. Died 28/6/1853 [C27513. ODNB. Boase] Married (1) Stapleton, Glos. 2/6/1808 Marianne-Elizabeth Bridges (of Thanet, Kent, d.1819), w. issue (2) Great Marlow, Bucks. 19/4/1823 Susan Wethered, w. further issue.

FAWCETT (Christopher) Born Durham 4/4/1802, s. Rev. John Fawcett and Mary Ann Bates. University, Oxford 1820, BA1824, dn25 (Durham), p26 (Durham), MA1829. V. Winterbourne Whitchurch, Dorset 1829-30, V. Turnworth, Dorset 1829-30, R. Boscombe, Wilts. 1830. V. Somerford Keynes, Wilts. 1852 to death 14/6/1880, leaving £4,000 [C52429] Married West Cholderton, Wilts. 3/10/1836 Sarah Frances Foyle, with issue. J.P.

FAWCETT (Edward) Born Scaleby, Cumberland, s. James Fawcett (a grazier) and Agnes Stephenson. Magdalene, Cambridge 1796 (aged 18), BA1801, dn01 (Car.), p02 (Car.), MA1804. R. South Fambridge, Essex 1803 and PC. Cockermouth, Cumberland 1809 to death there 24/2/1865 aged 86, leaving £600 [C5848] Married Carlisle 3/1/1803 Elizabeth Grisdale (a clergy dau.), w. clerical s. James Grisdale Fawcett.

FAWCETT (James) Bapt. Carlisle 27/2/1798, s. Rev. John Fawcett (below) and Eleanor Fawcett [*thus*]. Clare, Cambridge 1816, BA1821, dn21 (Chester for York), p22 (York), MA1824. PC. Leeds St Mark, Woodhouse 1826-51, V. Knaresborough, Yorks. 1851 to death 18/10/1873 aged 75, leaving £3,000 [C131266. YCO] Married Cambridge 7/4/1835 Isabella Farish, w. clerical son. Surrogate.

FAWCETT (John) Born Leeds 30/11/1769, s. Rev. John Fawcett, sen. Jesus, Cambridge 1787, then Magdalene 1788, BA1792, dn93 (York), p94 (York), MA1795. S/M Hull G/S 1795-1803; H/M Carlisle Cathedral G/S 1795-1803; PC. Carlisle St Cuthbert 1801-51, PC. Scaleby, Cumberland 1802-26, PC. Mallerstang, Westmorland 1832-[44]. Died Carlisle 4/12/1851 aged 83 [C3383. YCO. DEB. Platt] Married Cambridge 8/7/1795 his cousin Eleanor Fawcett, with clerical son, above. Confusion with another man of same name. 'The most prominent evangelical in Carlisle Diocese after the death of Dean Milner'. Early temperance advocate.

FAWCETT (Joseph) Born Old Hutton, Westmorland 19/5/1791, s. John Fawcett and Catherine Parker. Literate: dn15 (Chester), p16 (Chester). S/M Heversham Free G/S, Westmorland 1812-22; PC. Natland, Kendal, Westmorland 1825 to death (Ardwick, Manchester) 5/4/1866, leaving £800 [C168811] Married (1) Walton, Liverpool 23/6/1818 Harriet Gilliard (d.1823), w. issue (2) Kendal 29/12/1825 Elizabeth Haddock, with further issue. Surrogate.

FAWCETT (Richard) Born Leeds 6/1/1760, s. Rev. Richard Fawcett, sen. St John's, Cambridge 1777, BA1781, dn82 (York), p84 (York), MA1784. PC. Armley, Leeds 1791-1815, V. Leeds St Peter [net income £1,257] (and Preacher throughout the Diocese of York) 1815 to death. Dom. Chap. to 1st Earl of Harewood 1816. Died 22/1/1837 aged 77 (influenza) [C98442. YCO] Married Harewood, Yorks. 2/2/1796 Anna Maria Bainbridge (a clergy dau.), with issue.

FAWCETT (Thomas) From Newcastle upon Tyne, s. Rev. Richard Fawcett. Christ Church, Oxford 1785 (aged 17), BA1791, dn92 (Peterb.), p96 (Peterb.), MA1808. R. Bradden, Northants. 1797-1818, R. Aynhoe, Northumberland 1818-30, R. Green's Norton >< Northants. 1817 to death. Dom. Chap. to 2nd Baron Southampton 1808; to 5th Viscount Chetwynd 1815. Died 11/9/1853 [C110184]

FAWCITT (Robert) Bapt. Danby, Yorks. 16/8/1778, s. George Fawcitt. Literate: dn02 (York), p03 (York). PC. Hilton, Yorks. 1818 and V. Marton (in Cleveland), Yorks. 1829 to death 1847 (2nd q.) [C98446. YCO] Married before 1813, with issue.

FAYLE (Richard) Born Covent Garden, London 2/4/1796, s. of Benjamin Fayle (an Irish businessman) and Charlotte Adams. BNC, Oxford 1815, then St Mary Hall, BA 1820, dn20 (Glos. for Win.), p21 (Heref.), MA1822. R. Hope Mansell, Heref. 1828, R. Wareham Holy Trinity w. Lady St Mary and St Martin, Dorset 1828-41 [blank in ERC. C52440], Min. (and patron) of Holy Trinity [Proprietary] Chapel, Torquay 1838 to death 26/2/1872, leaving £30,000 [C73654] Married (1) Catherine Vigors Richards (d.1853), with issue (2) Barnstaple, Devon 1856 (3rd q.) Mrs Eleanora Elizabeth Savile (dau. of Sir Bourchier Wrey, 7th Bart.).

FAYRER (Joseph) Born Milnthorpe, Westmorland 21/1/1786, s. Capt. Joseph Fayrer and Bridget Dickinson. Trinity, Cambridge 1804, then Clare 1806, BA1809, dn09 (Llandaff), p11 (Lin.), MA1817. S/M Bodmin Free G/S 1812; S/M Chard G/S 1828; ?Prebend of 'Heredum Marney in Endellion' in Exeter Cathedral 1817, V. St Teath, Cornwall 1830-8, PC. Scavington St Mary and Chillington, Som. 1830-32. Died 10/5/1838 [C3896] Married Haddenham, Cambs. 3/4/1809 Sarah Clay, with clerical son.

FEACHAM (George) Born Winchester 28/12/1766, s. George Feacham (merchant) and Elizabeth Dale. St Mary Hall, Oxford 1785, migrated to St John's, Cambridge, BA1790, dn90 (Bristol for C&L), p91 (C&L), MA1793. V. Dorking, Surrey 1800 to death 7/2/1837 [C10855] Married Dorking 15/5/1800 Susanna Warneford (a clergy dau.), with issue.

FEARON (Devey) Bapt. Holborn, London 16/4/1769, s. Daniel Fearon and Ann Devey. Trinity, Cambridge, BA1791, MA1794, migrated to Pembroke, Oxford 1794, MB1795, MD1798 [doctor to 1807] dn07 (Win.), p07 (Win.). R. Ore (Oare), Sussex 1815 to death (Hastings, Sussex) 28/7/1847 [C63425. DEB] Married (1) 1790 Elizabeth Dorothy Rose [surname] (a clergy dau., d.1803), w. clerical s. Daniel Rose Fearon (2) Holborn 17/4/1811 Harriot Taylor, w. clerical s. William Charles.

FEARON (Isaac) Possibly bapt. Embleton, Cumberland 14/6/1761. Literate: p84 (Durham), p85 (Durham). V. Portisham, Dorset 1814 to death 10/1/1837 'at a very advanced age' [C52442]

FEAVER (George) From St Marychurch, Devon, s. Rev. George Feaver, sen. and Edith Stickland. All Souls, Oxford 1796 (aged 17), BA1799, dn00 (Bristol), MA1802, p03 (Bristol). V. Sydling St Nicholas, Dorset 1819 to death 20/12/1837 [C52443] Married Beaminster, Dorset 29/4/1806 Anna Maria Adney, with issue.

FEILD (Edward, *later* Bishop of Newfoundland and Bermuda) Born Worcester 7/6/1801, s. James (a surgeon) and Elizabeth Feild. Wadham, Oxford 1819, then Queen's, BA1823, Fellow 1825-33, MA1826, dn26 (Ox.), p27 (Ox.), Mathematics Lecturer (1828) and in History (1830), DD1844. R. English Bicknor >< Glos. [net income £1,023] 1833-44 (and an important Inspector of National Schools 1840), second Bishop of Newfoundland and Bermuda 1844 to death (Hamilton, Bermuda) 8/6/1876, leaving £9,000 in England [C27531. ODNB. Boase. *Dictionary of Canadian Biography* (online edn.). H.W. Tucker, *Memoir of the life and episcopate of Edward Field, DD., Bishop of Newfoundland, 1844-1876* (1877) with sour-looking port.] Married Biggleswade, Beds. 30/4/1867 Mrs Sophia (Bevan) Mountain (a clergy widow): https://en.wikipedia.org/wiki/Edward_Feild

FEILD (Samuel) From Evesham, Worcs., s. Benjamin Feild. Worcester, Oxford 1799 (aged 17), BA1803, dn05 (Glos.), p06 (Glos.), MA 1806. V. Hatherleigh, Devon 1831-62, R. (and patron) of Ashwater, Devon 1862 to death 9/9/1868 aged 86, leaving £18,000 [C150098] Married Hampton, Evesham, Worcs. 11/3/1806 Sarah Preedy, with clerical sons.

FEILD see also **FIELD**

FEILDE (Edward) Bapt. London 14/4/1794, s. Rev. Matthew and Mary Feilde. Literate: dn17 (London), p18 (London), then Peterhouse, Cambridge 1826 (a Ten Year Man), BA1830, MA1840. Curate Plaistow St Mary, West Ham, London 1831, PC. Rock and Rennington, Northumberland 1834-48. Living at Harrogate, Yorks. 1849 to death 15/1/1851 [C130418] Married Embleton, Northumberland 26/1/1836 Mary Ann Bosanquet. Brother below.

FEILDE, FEILD (Matthew) Born London, s. Rev. Matthew, sen. and Mary Feilde. Trinity, Cambridge 1795 (aged 16), then Pembroke 1796, BA1800. V. Lancing, Sussex 1808-[34], V. Shinfield w. Swallowfield, Berks. 1823 to death 24/10/1846 [C58230] Married City of London 15/11/1807 Mrs Hannah (Ponder) Gorton, w. issue. Brother above.

FEILDE (Thomas) Bapt. Brewood, Staffs. 20/3/1766, s. Rev. Thomas Feilde. Christ Church, Oxford 1783, BA1787, MA1789, dn92 (Ox.), p95 (London). V. Stanstead, Herts. 1796-1835, R. Graveley w. Chivesfield [no church], Herts. 1819-20 (res.), R. Netteswell, Essex 1821-35, R. Hertingfordbury, Herts. 1835 to death. Dom. Chap. to 7th Earl of Elgin 1819-21. Died 6/3/1847 [C27532]

FEILDEN (Henry James) Bapt. Prestbury Hall, Prestbury, Cheshire 20/10/1796, s. Robert Feilden and Anne Parker Mosley. BNC, Oxford 1813, BA1817, MA1820, p20 (Chester). R. Kirk Langley, Derbys. 1820 to death 21/11/1884, leaving £962-0s-4d. [C10860] Married (1) Blackburn, Lancs. 27/3/1815 Rachel Kirkham (d.1835), w. issue (2) Kirk Langley 10/10/1839 Marion Meynell, with issue. Brothers below. Photo. online.

FEILDEN (Oswald) Born Prestbury Hall, Prestbury, Cheshire 7/11/1797, s. Robert Feilden and Anne Parker Mosley. BNC, Oxford 1814, BA1818, dn21 (Chester), p22 (Chester), MA1831. R. Weston under Lizard, Staffs. 1833-59. Died Leasingham Hall, Lincs. 27/11/1872, leaving £18,000 [C10861] Brothers above and below.

FEILDEN (Randle Henry) Born Witton, Lancs. 6/1/1802, s. Henry Feilden and Fanny Hill. St John's, Cambridge 1819, BA1825, MA 1828. R. Walton le Dale, Lancs. 1827, R. Ashley, Wilts. 1830-45, R. Staplegrove, Som. 1846, R. St Lawrence, IoW 1848-52. Died Bonchurch, Hants. 1/11/1870, leaving £45,000 [C92354] Married Teddington, Surrey 22/11/1825 Phoebe Sarah Arbuthnott (dau. of a general), with issue.

FEILDEN, FIELDEN (Robert Mosley) Born Rolleston, Notts. 4/7/1794, s. Robert Feilden and Anne Mosley. BNC, Oxford 1813 [barrister at law, Lincoln's Inn 1818] then Magdalene, Cambridge 1822, BA1825, dn25 (C&L), p26 (C&L). PC. Over, Cheshire 1826, R. (and patron) of Bebington, Cheshire 1826 to death (Chester) 14/5/1862, leaving £16,000 (living at Dulas Court, Hereford) [C10862] Married Canterbury, Kent 18/2/1822 Frances Mary Ramsay (dau. of a general), with issue. Two brothers above.

FEILDING (Everard Robert Bruce, Hon.) Born 30/10/1799, s. Maj.-Gen. William Robert Feilding, Viscount Feilding (Berwick House, Pimhill, Shropshire) and Anne Catherine Powys. Oriel, Oxford 1818, BA1822, dn23 (Chester), p23 (Chester), MA 1828. R. Stapleton, Warwicks. 1824 to death there 14/9/1854 [C10863] Married 21/6/1832 Anne Henrietta Boughey, *s.p.*

FELIX (Peter) Born Aberystwyth, Cardigan 1791. Literate: dn14 (Chester), p15 (Chester), then Trinity, Cambridge 1820 (a Ten Year Man, BD1831). PC. Lledrog, Cardigan 1816, V. Easton Neston, Northants. 1825, V. Llanilar, Cardigan 1829 to death there 1/2/1861, leaving £3,000 [C110186] Wife Elizabeth, and issue.

FELL (Hunter Francis) Bapt. Caversham, Oxon. 12/4/1791, s. David Fell and Catherine Gardener. Pembroke, Oxford 1809, dn14 (Lin.), p15 (Ox.), BA1813, MA1816. PC. Islington Holy Trinity, London 1830 and PC. Goring, Oxon. 1823. Lived at Oultham, Suffolk. Died (East Worldham, Southampton) 10/11/1861, leaving £3,000 [C27533] Married London 20/4/1817 Rachel Butler Hall, w. clerical son George Hunter Fell. 'A good man' (Wilberforce).

FELL (John) Born Retford, Notts., s. John Fell. Trinity, Cambridge 1814 (aged 23), dn17 (Chester), BA1818, p18 (Lincoln), MA1821. H/M Huntingdon G/S 1823-69; PC. Wilburton, Cambs. 1822-61, R. Huntingdon St Mary and St Benedict 1861-9 and R. Thoresby, Lincs. 1868 to death. Chap. to the Huntingdon Poor Law

Union. Died 17/10/1869, leaving £450 [C58235. Boase] Had issue.

FELL (Richmond) Bapt. Chillingham, Northumberland 6/4/1761, s. Rev. John Fell. St John's, Cambridge 1779, BA1784, dn84 (Durham), p85 (Win. for Car.), MA1787. V. Warcop, Westmorland 1785-1828, R. Aikton, Cumberland 1828 to death (Aikton Hall) 28/9/1844 aged 83 [C5855. Platt] Married (1) 24/8/1798 Margaret Carmichael (a Scot) to whom he was married in two ceremonies: firstly in a Church of Scotland service, then in a Church of England service (Warcop 24/8/1798), and had issue (2) Carlisle 28/2/1832 Elizabeth Robinson, w. clerical son, also Richmond.

FELL (Thomas Cotton) Bapt. Sheepy Magna, Leics. 20/2/1776, s. Rev. William Fell and Ann Cotton. Jesus, Cambridge 1792, BA1797, dn98 (Lin.), Fellow 1799-1808, MA1800, p01 (C&L), BD 1807. Prebend of Flixton w. Offley 1800-12, then of Wellington 1812-22, then of Whittington and Berkswich 1822-55, all in Lichfield Cathedral, (succ. his father as) R. (and patron) of Sheepy (2 Moieties) 1807-55, Prebend of Monmore in Wolverhampton Collegiate Church 1820 to death 27/10/1855 [C10864] Married Sheepy Magna 10/11/1808 Maria Greene, w. clerical s. Thomas Fell.

FELLOWES (Henry) Born Minorca, Spain 27/12/1774, s. of William Fellowes (army doctor) and Mary Butler. St John's, Cambridge 1800, BA1804, dn03 (Ex.), p04 (Ex.), MA1807. V. Sidbury, Devon 1813 to death. Chap. to the Prince Regent. Died 11/2/1864, leaving £300 [C143487. LBSO] Married Littleham, Devon 10/8/1804 Mary Judith Bourke (dau. of a plantation owner), with clerical s. Edmund Fearon Bourke Fellowes.

FELLOWES (John) Born Shotesham, Norfolk 2/7/1785, s. Robert Fellowes. Jesus, Cambridge 1803, BA1807, dn08 (Nor.), p09 (Nor.), MA 1810. V. Easton, Norfolk 1809, V. Shotesham 1810, R. Beighton, Norfolk 1824-7, R. Bramerton, Norfolk 1827 [blank in ERC] and R. Mautby, Norfolk 1827 to death 20/2/1838 [C112935] Married 29/5/1811 Susan, dau. Hon. Thomas Lyon (Hetton House, Durham), with issue.

FENDALL (Henry Benson) Bapt. Matson, Glos. 29/6/1795, s. William Fendall and Jane Benson. Trinity Hall, Cambridge 1811, then Emmanuel 1814, BA1816, dn18 (Glos.), p19 (Glos.). PC. Awre w. Blakeney, Glos. 1818, V. Nazeing, Essex 1820-8 (res.), R. Nunburnholme, Yorks. 1828-39, V. Crambe, Yorks. 1839-61, PC. Huttons Ambo, Yorks. 1839-61. Travelled abroad and eventually settled in New Zealand by 1866. Died Timaru, New Zealand 27/5/1872. No will in UK [C117749. *Blain's Biographical Directory of the Clergy of the South Pacific* (online, 2011)] Married Great Parndon, Essex 10/9/1823 Anne Catherine Johnson (a clergy dau.), w. clerical s. Henry Benson Fendall.

FENNELL (John) Bapt. Madeley, Shropshire 20/6/1762, s. Thomas Fennell and Mary Hotchkiss. A Methodist lay preacher, he ran a Methodist Academy in Penzance 1812-13. Literate: dn15 (York), p15 (York), then Peterhouse, Cambridge 1824, a Ten Year Man. PC. Cross Stone, Yorks. 1819 to death 13/10/1841 aged 79 [C131273. YCO] Married (1) Madron, Cornwall 13/121790 Jane Branwell (Mrs Maria Bronte's aunt), d.1829), w. issue (2) Halifax, Yorks. 18/7/1830 Elizabeth Lister, dau. of a Leeds merchant, with further issue. I. and C. Emberson, 'Turns in the circle of friendship: "Uncle Fennell", 1762-1841', *Bronte Studies*, 30 (2) (July 2005) 141-150.

FENTON (George) Born Rothwell, Yorks. 10/2/1797, s. James Fenton and Thomasine Ibbetson. Exeter, Oxford 1813, BA1817, dn18 (Chester for York), p22 (York). Chap. of the Donative of Denton, Yorks. 1823, V. Royston, Yorks. 1836 to death (Halifax, Yorks.) 7/4/1843 [C131274. YCO] Brother William, below.

FENTON (James) From Lancashire. Peterhouse, Cambridge 1777 (aged 20), BA1781, dn82 (York for Chester), p83 (Chester), MA 1784. PC. Stalmine, Lancs. 1783-7, R. Althorpe w. Keadby, Lincs. 1787-1837 ('the ill-feeling which exists between the R. of Althorpe and the inhabitants prevents any good thing being accomplished'), R. Doddingston w. Whisby, Lincs. 1788 to death 10/10/1837 aged 82. Chap. to HRH Duke of Cumberland and Strathearn 1788 [C58242. YCO]

FENTON (John Mason) Born Stainmore, Westmorland 12/1/1759, s. Rev. James Fenton and Elizabeth Pearson. Literate: dn81 (Car.), p83 (Car.). PC. Stainmore in Brough 1784-1836, R. Brougham, Cumberland 1786-8. Died (unm.)

10/4/1836 aged 77 [C5858. Platt] Brother William Carr, below.

FENTON (John [Thomas]) Born Newcastle under Lyme, Staffs., s. Thomas Fenton. University, Oxford 1791 (aged 18), BA1795, dn96 (C&L), p97 (C&L), MA1800. V. Torpenhow, Cumberland 1801-54 [blank in ERC], V. Penrith St Andrew, Westmorland 1823-33 [blank in ERC], R. Ousby, Cumber-land 1833 to death (Greenwich, Kent). Dom. Chap. to future 1st Duke of Sutherland 1823. Died 13/10/1854 [C5859 and Foster as John only; another says Thomas] Married 4/11/1801 Anne (sister of Sir Alexander Livingstone, of West Quarter, 9th Bart.), w. clerical s. George Livingstone Fenton.

FENTON, or CARR-FENTON (William Carr) Bapt. Rothwell, Yorks. 2/9/1783, s. James Fenton and Thomasine Ibbetson. Literate: dn20 (York), p21 (Chester for York). R. Cowthorpe, Yorks. 1824 and V. Mattersey, Retford, Notts. 1835 to death 23/4/1855 aged 72 [C131276. YCO] Married Knaresborough, Yorks. 4/10/1823 Caroline May Myddleton (a clergy dau.), w. issue. Brother George, above. Founded the Yorkshire Institution for the Deaf and Dumb in Doncaster 1829.

FENWICK (Collingwood Forster) Born Eglingham, Alnwick, Northumberland July 1790, s. Nicholas Fenwick and Dorothy Forster. BNC, Oxford 1807 [Lt. Grenadier Guards] migrated to Trinity Hall, Cambridge 1812, dn15 (B&W), p17 (Glos.), LLB1817. R. Street, Som. 1820-3, V. Blidworth w. Oxton, Notts. 1823 and R. Brooke, IoW 1836 to death (Ryde, IoW) 6/12/1858, leaving £1,500 [C38407. Austin2] Married Walcot, Bath 11/3/1813 Elizabeth Christie (dau. of an admiral), with naval issue.

FENWICK (John Thomas) Born Lambton, Co. Durham 8/4/1771, s. George Fenwick (agent to the Lambton family, later Earls Grey) and Eleanor Addison. St John's, Cambridge 1789, BA1793, dn94 (Ely for Nor.), MA1796, p98 (Cant.). R. (and patron) of Northfield [net income £1,170] Worcs. 1805 to death 26/5/1833 (CCEd says 16/10/1833) [C99959] Married Burton-on-Trent, Staffs. 22/4/1813 Anne Thornewill (Dovecliff Hall, Stretton Staffs.), w. issue. J.P. Worcs., Warwicks., and Staffs.

FENWICKE (George Owsley) Born Hallaton, Leics. 7/5/1783, s. Rev. John Fenwicke and Dorothea Owsley. St John's, Cambridge 1801, BA1806, dn06 (Lin.), p07 (Lin.), MA1809. V. Kempston, Beds. 1817-34, R. Rearsby, Lincs. 1832-4, V. Aston, Birmingham 1834-52, R. (and patron) of Blaston St Giles, Leics. 1834-50. Died (Clifton, Bristol) 11/10/1864, leaving £12,000 [C10870] Married Stockerston Hall, Uppingham, Leics. 5/10/1813 Elizabeth Anne Walker, with issue. Book collector (10,000 vols.) and antiquary. 'He was a perfect gentleman, a High Churchman without any leaven of bigotry, a thorough-going conscientious Conservative, and altogether a noble specimen of the learned minister of God's Word of other days.'

FERGUSON (Daniel) Bapt. Catterick, Yorks. 25/8/1780, s. Daniel Ferguson and Elizabeth Lumlay. Emmanuel, Cambridge 1798, BA1802, dn03 (Win. for York), p05 (York). R. Broughton Sulney, Notts. 1807-8, R. (and patron of) Walkington, Yorks. 1808 to death 29/11/1859 aged 79, leaving £600 [C73659. YCO] Married Catterick 4/10/1804 Margaret Booth, with clerical son. J.P., D.L. East Riding,

FERGUSSON, FERGUSON (William Knox) Born Dublin, s. Thomas Ferguson. TCD1818 (aged 18), BA1823. MA1831.V. Scottow w. Belaugh, Norfolk 1830 to death 14/2/1834 (CCEd thus) [C112941. Al.Dub.]

FERRABY (John) Born Hull, Yorks. 13/11/1757, s. George Ferraby and Ann Saul. Clare, Cambridge 1774, BA1779, dn80 (Lin.), p82 (Lin.), MA1794. V. Impington, Cambs. 1792-1810, V. Welford and Sibbertoft, Lincs. 1810 to death 4/11/1834 aged 76 [C58257] Married Ruckland, Northants. 18/9/1793 Mary Holland, w. issue.

FERRAND (Thomas Gerrard) Born Matterset, Notts.11/8/1785, s. Rev. Thomas Ferrand (formerly Waddington) and Mary Hill. Trinity, Cambridge 1802, BA1807, MA1810, p13 (Chester). R. (and patron) of Tunstall w. Dunningworth, Suffolk 1814 to death 13/4/1859, leaving £14,000 [C112942] Married Tunstall 23/1/1834 Mrs Giorgina [*sic*] (Darby) Horton (w), with issue.

FERRERS (John Bromfield) Born Cookham, Berks. 10/2/1758, s. Edmund Ferrers (a London barrister) and Hannah Bromfield. Christ Church, Oxford 1777, BA1781, dn81 (Ox. for Nor.), p82 (Peterb. for Nor. *or* Lin. for Salis.), incorporated at St John's, Cambridge, MA1808. V. Wroughton (o/w Elrington), Wilts. 1782-3, R. Beddington, Surrey [net income £1,212] 1783 to death. Dom. Chap. to Anne Isabella, Countess Hawarden 1810. Died 6/6/1841 [C27535] Married Beddington 24/9/1799 Mrs Charlotte (Proby) Pitcairn (a military widow). Port. online.

FERRIS (Thomas) Born Battle, Sussex 12/7/1782, s. Very Rev. Thomas Ferris (Dean and V. of Battle - a Peculiar) and Mary Dixon. St John's, Cambridge 1800, then Jesus 1803, BA 1804, dn05 (B&W), MA1807. V. Dallington, Sussex 1810 to death (Leeds) 25/5/1848 aged 65 [C38413] Married Higham, Sussex 13/12/1809 Elizabeth Dorothy Lamb, w. clerical sons Thomas Boys, and Charles Francis Ferris.

FERRYMAN (Robert) Bapt. Barrow upon Soar, Leics. 2/2/1763, s. John Ferryman and Elizabeth Beaumont. [NiVoF] Literate: p96 (Glos.). R. Iping w. Chithurst Chapel, Sussex 1805 to death 29/11/1837 aged 85 [C150134] Married Westminster, London 5/2/1782 Sibylla Mary Barke, with issue. Port. online.

FESTING (Charles George Ruddock) Born Andover, Hants. 5/12/1797, s. Commander Henry Festing, R.N., and Mary Morton Colson. St John's, Cambridge 1817, dn21 (Bristol), BA 1822, p22 (Salis. for Bristol), MA1825. V. (St) Paul, Cornwall 1827 and PC. Witham Friary, Som. 1827 to death (Warminster, Wilts.) 30/8/1857 [C42219. Venn inverts first two names] Married Warminster 18/6/1833 Louisa Seagram, with clerical son.

FESTING (John [Deverell Thomas Missing]) Bapt. Wyke Regis, Dorset 20/6/1754 (CCEd says 16/8/1754), s. Rev. Michael Festing and Katherine Greene. Christ Church, Oxford 1773, BA1777, dn77 (London for Ely), p79 (Exeter) V Newnham, Herts. 1796 [to death] (York) 1837 [C108086 as John] Married Shepton Mallet, Som. 19/10/1787 Hannah Vigar Butt.

FIELD (Frederick) Born London 20/7/1801, s. Henry Field (apothecary) and Esther Barron. Trinity, Cambridge 1819, BA1823, Fellow 1824-43, MA1826, dn27 (Lin.), p28 (Ely), Hon. LLD 1875 and Hon. Fellow 1875-85. V. Over, Cambs. 1830-4, R. Reepham w. Kerdiston, Norfolk 1842-63. Died Heigham, Norwich (unm.) 19/5/1885, leaving £19,037-9s-3d

[C17755. ODNB. Boase] 'The Jerome of the Anglican Church. Edited various patristic works for Oxford and Cambridge University Presses. Member of Old Testament Revision Company, 1879-85. His name is inseparably connected with Chrysostom and Origen'. Deaf for most of his life. A direct descendant of Oliver Cromwell.

FIELD (John) Born Malton, Yorks. 4/6/1789, s. Thomas (who owned a racing stable) and Sarah Field. St John's, Cambridge 1807, BA 1811, dn12 (Bristol), MA1814, p15 (Peterb.). Kept a school at Wootton Hall, Northants. 1818-67; R. (and patron) of Braybrooke, Northants. 1829 to death. Dom. Chap. to Lord Forester. Died 24/3/1867 aged 77, leaving £7,000 [C52472] Married Hardingstone, Northants. 21/12/1818 Louisa Bousquet, with clerical son Thomas Field. #

FIELD (Robert) Bapt. Gedgrave, Suffolk 15/9/1775, s. Robert Field and Elizabeth Dove. Sidney, Cambridge 1798, BA1797, dn97 (Nor.), p07 (Nor.). V. (and patron) of Sutton, Suffolk 1807-54, PC. Ramsholt, Suffolk 1813-54, V. (and patron) of Mendlesham, Suffolk 1817-34. Died 13/9/1854 [C112945] Married by 1810 Elizabeth Chilton

FIELD see also **FEILD**

FIELDING (Charles) Born Canterbury, Kent 12/6/1791, s. Rev. Allen Fielding and Mary Ann Whittingham. St John's, Cambridge 1811, dn14 (Cant.), p15 (Cant.), LLB1817. R. Canterbury St Margaret 1822-8, PC. Stodmarsh, Kent 1823-38, V. Headcorn, Maidstone, Kent 1836-50 (res.). Died (Bucklands, Dover) 25/11/1866 aged 75, leaving £2,000 [C123666] Married 5 *or* 27/4/1825 Elizabeth Oakley Boyce (dau. of an H.E.I.C. officer), with issue. Brothers, below.

FIELDING (George) Born Canterbury, Kent 27/3/1793, s. Rev. Allen Fielding and Mary Ann Whittingham. Worcester, Oxford 1810, then St John's 1811, BA1815, dn16 (Cant.), p17 (Cant.), MA1819. PC. (Bishop) Auckland St Andrew w. St Anne, Durham 1827-45, R. North Ockendon, Essex 1845 to death 25/5/1869 aged 77, leaving £7,000 [C3897] Married Marylebone, London 17/10/1825 Mary Rebecca Hanbury Williams, w. clerical s. Geoffrey Hanbury Fielding. J.P. Durham and Essex. Brothers above and below.

FIELDING (Henry) Born Sibbertswold, Kent 12/1/1786, s. Rev. Allen Fielding and Mary Ann Whittingham. Worcester, Oxford 1805, BA1809, dn09 (Cant.), p10 (Cant.), MA1812. R. Crundale, Kent 1810-25 (res.), PC. <u>Canterbury St Cosmas and St Damien [in the Blean]</u> 1809 (V. 1816), PC. <u>Nackington</u>, Kent 1813 to death. Chap. to Prince Regent 1816. Died 7/2/1863, leaving £4,000 [C155374] Married Westbere, Kent 6/12/1827 Augusta Fagge, with issue. 2 brothers above. Photo. online.

FILLEUL (Philip(pe)) Born Jersey, Channel Islands 10/1/1792, s. Philippe Filleul and Elizabeth Nicolle. Pembroke, Oxford 1813, dn16 (Salis. for Win.), p17 (London for Win.), BA1817, MA1820. R. Jersey St Brélade 1818-29 (res.), R. <u>Jersey St Peter</u> 1829-48, R. Jersey St Saviour 1848-50, R. Jersey St Helier 1850 to death 13/10/1875. No will traced [C73664. Boase] Married Reading, Berks. 13/10/1823 Catherine Elizabeth Blanche Valpy, with clerical s. Philip Valpy Mourant Filleul. A controversial figure, he divided-up parishes, and invested parish moneys in his sons' sheep farm in New Zealand: www.theislandwiki.org/?title=Filleul

FINCH (Charles, Hon.) Born 1799, s. Heneage Finch, 4th Earl of Aylesford and Lady Louisa Thynne (dau. of the 1st Marquess of Bath) and thus brother of 5th Earl. Merton, Oxford 1817, BA1822, dn22 (Lin.), p23 (Lin.), MA 1825. R. <u>Little Packingham and Great Packingham</u> >< Warwicks, 1824 and V. <u>Meriden</u> 1830 to death (unm.?) 19/11/1859, leaving £2,000 [C10883]

FINCH (Daniel, Hon.) Born 3/4/1757, s. Heneage Finch, 3rd Earl of Aylesford and Lady Charlotte Seymour (dau. of 6th Duke of Somerset). Christ Church, Oxford 1774, then All Souls, BA1778, Senior Fellow 1778-1840, dn80 (Ox.), p81 (Ox.), MA1782, BD1790. R. Cwm, Flintshire 1790, Prebend of Bristol (then Gloucester and Bristol) 1792-1840, R. <u>Harpsden</u> (o/w <u>Harding</u>), Oxon. 1801. Died 24/10/1840 [C10884]

FINCH (Heneage) Bapt. Shifnal, Shropshire 28/6/1788, s. Charles Finch and Jane Wynne. Christ Church, Oxford 1806), BA1810, dn12 (Ox.), p12 (Win.), MA1814. R. Great Weldon, Northants. 1812-19 (res.), V. <u>Oakham,</u> Rutland 1815 (and RD) to death. Dom. Chap. to 4th Earl of Dartmouth 1815; Chap. in Ordinary. Died ('at the Conservative Club in the County of Middlesex') 5/4/1865 aged 76, leaving £16,000. [C27569]

FINCH (Henry [Ingle]) Born Little Shelford Manor, Cambs. 14/7/1782, s. William Finch Ingle (later Finch) and Betty Weldon. Christ's, Cambridge 1799, BA1805, dn06 (Win. for Ely), p06 (Ely), MA1808. R. <u>Little Shelford</u> 1806-49 [sequestrator] and V. <u>Great Shelford</u> 1812-49, V. <u>Longstanton</u>, Cambs. 1813 to death. Dom. Chap. to 5th Earl of Jersey 1813. Died 23/6/1849 [C73665 has another man in here and has wrong death date] Married Lambeth, Surrey 17/2/1807 Ann Crowe, with issue.

FINCH (Thomas) From Cambridge, s. Joseph Finch (ironmonger). Trinity, Cambridge 1769 (aged 17), MA1773, dn73 (London), p75 (Peterb. for London), MA1776. V. <u>Barrington</u>, Cambs, 1775 (w. V. <u>Hauxton (in the Isle) w. Newton</u>, Cambs. 1788) to death 20/1/1837 aged 86 [C99961] Wife Sophie.

FINCH (William) Born 14/9/1791, s. Admiral Hon. William Clement Finch and Mary Brouncker. Jesus, Cambridge 1816, MA1817, dn17 (Glos. for C&L), p18 (Chester for C&L). V. Great Hamden w. Great Kimble, Bucks. 1819-27 (res.), R. <u>Warboys</u>, Hunts. 1828 [income £1,300] to death (Kingston, Surrey) 19/10/1880 (a bachelor), leaving £70,000 [C10887]

FIOTT, *later* LEE (Nicholas) Born Totteridge Park, Herts. 5/6/1794, s. John Fiott and Harriet Lee. St John's, Cambridge 1813, BA 1817, MA1820, dn20 (Nor. for Ely), p20 (Ely), BD1828. V. <u>Edgware</u>, Middx. 1825 to death 1858 (3rd q.), living at Hartwell House, Aylesbury, Bucks. No will traced [C109511] Married 11/6/1835 Mrs Harriet Jenner (Hart) Dyke, with issue.

FIRMIN (Robert) Born Dedham, Essex 1800. Clare, Cambridge 1818, BA1823, dn23 (London), p25 (London), MA1846. V. <u>Fingrinhoe</u>, Essex 1826-46, V. (and patron) of Yoxford, Suffolk 1846 to death (Dedham) 5/4/1872 aged 72, leaving £6,000 [C66791] Married (2?) Strand, London 18/8/1861 Cassandra Raynham (w). Surrogate 1854-72.

FIRTH (William) From Oxford, s. Richard Firth. New, Oxford 1805 (aged 17), then Corpus Christi 1807, BA1810, MA1814, Fellow 1819-30, BD1822, Tutor 1822, etc. R. <u>Letcomb Bassett</u>, Berks. 1830 to death 1856 (3rd q.) [C92362]

Married Letcomb Bassett 18/10/1830 Mary Ann West.

FISH (John) Born Hollymount, Co. Mayo 31/1/1790, s. Rev. William Fish and Jane Wren. Literate: p14 (Chester) [TCD1817, BA1820?] R. Thurstaston, Cheshire 1822-[58] 'Found dead in his bed', Wangford, Suffolk 24/7/1871 aged 79. Will not traced [C168838. Al.Dub.] Married in Ireland 21/9/1818 Frances Maria Mossom, with issue.

FISHER (Charles) Bapt. Great Yarmouth, Norfolk 3/12/1782, s. John Fisher (mercer, and a privateer carrying Letters of Marque [*q.v.* Google]) and Martha Goate. Caius, Cambridge 1803, BA1808, dn08 (Nor.), p08 (Nor.), MA 1811. R. (and patron) of Ovington and Tilbury juxta Clare, Essex 1809 to death 21/12/1839 aged 57 [C112965] Married Finchingfield, Essex 9/1/1816 Frances Brise Ruggles (Spains Hall), 4 clerical sons.

FISHER (Charles) Bapt. Great Yarmouth, Norfolk 14/5/1785, s. James Fisher and Helen Kittridge. St John's, Cambridge 1803, BA1807, dn08 (Nor.), p09 (Nor.), MA1810. R. Oulton, Suffolk 1829 to death 30/1/1836 [C165056] Married Great Yarmouth 28/3/1811 his 2nd cousin Mary Anne Colby, with issue. Ports. online.

FISHER (Edmund, sen.) From Duxford, Cambs., s. Edmund Fisher and Sarah Trott. Corpus Christi, Cambridge 1792, BA1797, dn97 (Ely), p99 (Ely), MA1800. V. Linton, Cambs. 1800-44, then unbeneficed. Died 8/12/1851 aged 77 [C99965] Married Saffron Walden, Essex 18/11/1800 and Mary Collin, with son below.

FISHER (Edmund, jun.) Bapt. Linton, Cambs. 2/10/1801, s. Rev. Edmund Fisher, sen. (above) and Mary Collin. Peterhouse, Cambridge 1818, BA1823, Fellow 1825, dn25 (Ely), MA 1826, p26 (Lin.). R. Chipping Ongar, Essex 1832-68. Died Putney, Surrey 8/5/1881 aged 79, leaving £5,000 [C17756] Married High Ongar, Essex 13/5/1834 Harriet Edridge, with clerical s. Frederic Horatio Fisher.

FISHER (George Ingram) Bapt. Salisbury 27/7/1797, s. Rev. Samuel Fisher and Elizabeth Ingram. Worcester, Oxford 1814, dn19 (Salis.), BA1819, p20 (Salis.), MA1820. R. Winfrith Newburgh, Dorset 1820, PC. Ebbesbourne Wake, Wilts. 1823 (and Sub-Chanter Salisbury Cathedral 1823), V. Abbotts Kerswell, Devon 1851 to death (Bath) 19/11/1863, leaving £4,000 [C52475. LBSO] Married Bathwick, Som. 5/6/1825 Elizabeth Pendrill (whose grandfather had Jamaican slave money).

FISHER (Henry) Born York 7/12/1772, s. Samuel Fisher. St Catharine's, Cambridge 1794 (re-adm. 1798), no degree, dn95 (York), p96 (Bristol for York). PC. Kirk Hamerton, Yorks. 1798-1812, PC. Nun Monkton, Yorks. 1808-15 (res.), R. Frome Castle >< Heref. 1812 to death 1843 [C52476. YCO]

FISHER (John) From London, s. John Fisher. Hertford, Oxford 1778, migrated to Pembroke, Cambridge 1778 (aged 19), then St Alban Hall, BCL1787, dn78 (Lin.) [Called to the Bar Lincoln's Inn 1787] p80 (Lin.), BA1801. R. Brockhall (or Brockholes), Northants. 1794-1806 (res.), V. Dodford, Northants. 1801 (presented by his father-in-law) and R. Holcott, Northants. 1809-25 (res.). Dom. Chap. to Elizabeth, Viscountess Dowager Sydney 1809. Died 29/7/1837 [C60016 but possible confusion] Married Harleston, Cheshire 29/12/1791 Charlotte Andrew.

FISHER (John, sen.) Born Higham on the Hill, Leics. 1767, s. Thomas Fisher (a nephew of a Bishop of Salisbury) and Hannah Woodroffe. University, Oxford 1784, BA1788, MA1791, dn91 (Lin.), p92 (Lin.). R. Higham on the Hill, Leics. 1792-1832 (res.), R. Caldecote, Warwicks. 1797. Died Islington, London 17/5/1841 [C10983. CCEd agrees. Foster is wrong] Married City of London 21/5/1797 Matilda Wilkes, w. clerical son, also John, two below.

FISHER (John) Bapt. Bodmin, Cornwall 7/6/1774, s. Rev. John and Catherine Fisher. Pembroke, Oxford 1793, BA1797, dn97 (Ex.), p99 (Ex.), MA1824. R. Wavendon, Bucks. 1805-46, R. Haversham, Bucks. 1824-7 (res.). Dom. Chap. to 1st Duke of Buckingham and Chandos 1824. Died 23/12/1846 [C143484] Clerical son, also John Fisher.

FISHER (John, jun.) Born Higham on the Hill, Leics. 20/5/1797, s. Rev. John Fisher, sen. (two above) and Matilda Wilkes. Sidney, Cambridge 1815, BA1819, dn20 (Chester), MA1822, p22 (Lin.). R. Stoney Stanton >< Lincs. 1831, (succ. his father as) R. (and patron) of Higham on the Hill 1832 to death 3/7/1868, leaving

£9,000 [C10984] Married Sapcote, Leics. 19/1/1832 Sophia Frances Harrington (w), with clerical s. Henry Fisher.

FISHER (John) Born Ampleforth, Yorks. 3/12/1798, s. Peter and Elizabeth Fisher. Literate: dn22 (York), p23 (York). PC. Heapy, Leyland, Lancs. 1832-71 (res.). Died there 1873 (2nd q.) aged 76. Will not traced [C131278. YCO] Wife Anne, and issue.

FISHER (John Hutton) Born Thrimby, Westmorland 25/12/1794, s. John Fisher and Judith Holme. Trinity, Cambridge 1813, BA1818, Fellow 1820-31, MA1821, dn27 (Lin.), p28 (Ely). PC. Arrington, Cambs. 1829-32 (sequestrated), V. Kirkby Lonsdale, Westmorland 1831-60, RD. Dom. Chap. to Bishop of Bristol 1835. Died (unm.) Cambridge 11/3/1862 aged 67 (afflicted by a paralytic stroke, 'and sadly addicted to drinking', for which he was removed from his parish). Will not traced. [C17759] *J.P.* 1840.

FISHER (Jonathan Parker) Bapt. Peterborough 28/9/1757, s. Rev. John Fisher and Elizabeth Laurens. University, Oxford 1774, BA1778, dn79 (Ox.), MA1780, p81 (Ox.), BD 1802, DD1807. V. Eastbourne, Sussex 1785-95, R. Farringdon, Devon 1805-38, V. Rockbeare, Devon 1805, Archdeacon of Barnstaple 1805-7, Prebend, Canon Residentiary and Sub-Dean of Exeter 1807 to death (Farringdon) 31/7/1838 aged 81 [C27583] Brother of a Bishop of Salisbury, and of Philip Fisher (below).

FISHER (Joseph) Born Cockermouth, Cumberland 12/10/1798, s. Joseph Fisher (an attorney) and Maria Dorothea Radcliffe. Christ's, Cambridge 1829, BA1824, p25 (Durham). PC. Carlton in Snaith, Yorks. 1820, R. Maltby in the Marsh, Lincs. 1823 to death (Jesmond, Newcastle) 23/12/1856 aged 57 [C60023. Confusion in Venn] Had issue.

FISHER (Philip) Bapt. Peterborough 1/12/1750, s. Rev. John Fisher and Elizabeth Laurens. University, Oxford 1766, BA1770, Fellow, MA1772, dn74 (Ox.), p75 (Ox.), BD 1780, DD1804 (Lambeth). Master of the Charterhouse [School] 1804-42; R. Headbourne Worthy, Hants. 1780-1 (res.), R. Ayleston, Leics. 1787, V. Elton, Hunts. 1787, R. West Deeping, Lincs. 1792-1801, V. Whaplode, Lincs. 1801 to death, Prebend of Exeter 1808-33 (res.), Stratton Prebend 1808-10 then Ilfracombe Prebend 1810-23 in Salisbury Cathedral (and Precentor 1819-42), Canon of 1st Prebend in Norwich Cathedral 1814 to death 19/1/1842 aged 92 [C1046] Married Ealing, Middx. 24/7/1787 Mary Roberts, w. clerical s. Philip Scott, and William (below). Brother of a Bishop of Salisbury, and of Jonathan Parker Fisher, above.

FISHER (Philip Scott) Bapt. Elton, Hunts. 8/3/1804, s. Rev. Philip Fisher (above) and Mary Roberts. University, Oxford 1811 [adm. Lincoln's Inn 1812] BA1815, dn17 (Salis.), MA1817, p18 (Salis.). R. Burbage, Wilts. 1818, V. Hurstbourne Tarrant, Hants. 1818 (w. Vernhams Dean Chapel 1829). Died 1841 (1st q.) [C73668] Brother William, below.

FISHER (Ralph Watkins) Born Liverpool 26/12/1802, s. Ralph Fisher, *D.L.*, and Anne Bromfield. Clare, Cambridge 1824, BA1828, dn28 (Chester), p29 (Chester), MA1831. S/M Goudhurst G/S, Kent 1833; PC. New Hutton, Kendal, Westmorland 1830-[40]. Died Perth, Scotland 17/6/1849 aged 46 [C167719] Married Kendal 14/4/1830 Elizabeth Sleddal Tatham, with issue. *J.P.* 1840. Port. online.

FISHER (Robert Bail(e)y) Born Bradford-on-Avon, Wilts., s. William Bailey Fisher. University, Oxford 1801 (aged 15), BA1805, dn09 (Salis.), p10 (Ox.), MA1834. V. Basildon, Berks. 1814 to death 29/9/1859, leaving £5,000 [C27585] Married (1) Cholsey, Berks. 17/1/1807 Martha Harvey Hopkins (d.1837) (2) Marylebone, London 21/7/1847 Louisa Currie (w).

FISHER (Samuel) Bapt. Dublin 18/8/1792, s. Samuel Fisher. TCD1821, BA1831, p32 (Nor.). V. Corpusty, Norfolk 1833-[44]. Died? [C112969. Al.Dub.]

FISHER (Thomas) Born Ravenstone, Leics. 22/7/1760, s. Thomas Fisher. Christ Church, Oxford 1778, then St Alban Hall, BA1798, dn99 (Car.), p99 (Car.), MA1801. R. Idlicote, Warwicks. 1800. Died (North Ferriby, Yorks.) 3/8/1842 aged 82 [C5868]

FISHER (Thomas) Possibly Trinity, Cambridge 1800, BA1806, dn06, p07, MA1809. R. Roche (o/w Rock) St Gomonda, Cornwall 1819-34 (res.). R. Luccombe (o/w Luckham), Som. 1839-56. Lived in Bath. Probate granted 2/10/1856 [Not yet in CCEd]

FISHER (William) Born Elton, Hants. 20/3/1799, s. Rev. Philip Fisher (above) and

Mary Roberts. Christ Church, Oxford 1815, Student 1815-23, BA1819, MA1821, dn22 (Ox.), p22 (Ox.). V. Poulshot, Wilts. 1823-74, Prebend of Ilfracombe in Salisbury Cathedral 1823, then Canon Residentiary 1834 to death. Dom. Chap. to Bishop of Salisbury 1824. Died 9/6/1874, leaving £30,000 [total income in CR65 £1,380] [C27586] Married (1) Salisbury Cathedral 6/1/1824 Elizabeth Cookson (a clergy dau., d.1851), w. issue (2) St George's Hanover Square, London 18/11/1862 Mrs Mary Sullivan (Dalton) Preston (w). Brother Philip Scott, above.

FISHLAKE (John Roles) Born Salisbury 3/1/1790, s. John Fishlake and Elizabeth Roles. Wadham, Oxford 1806, BA1810, dn13 (Ox.), MA1813, p14 (London), Fellow 1815-23. R. Little Cheverell, Wilts. 1823 to death. Dom. Chap. to 2nd Earl of Radnor 1820. Died 25/1/1868 aged 78, leaving £12,000 [C27587. Boase] Married Salisbury, Wilts. 17/4/1823 Jane Nicholas, w. issue.

FISKE (Robert) Bapt. Fulbourn, Cambs. 23/11/1783, s. Rev. Robert Fiske and Elizabeth Fisher. St John's, Cambridge 1800, BA1804, Fellow 1805-17, MA1807, dn07 (Ely), p08 (Ely), BD1814. R. Wendon Lofts w. Elmdon, Essex 1814 and V. Great Chishall, Essex 1821 to death (Elmdon) 21/8/1839 (CCEd thus) [C99970] Married Saffron Waldon, Essex 27/8/1816 his cousin Mary Ann Fiske (dau. of a surgeon), with issue.

FISKE (Thomas) From Shimplingthorne, Suffolk, s.. John Fiske. Jesus, Cambridge 1785, BA1789, dn91 (Nor.), p94 (Nor.). (succ. his father as) R. (and patron) of Kettlebaston, Suffolk 1791-39 and R. Shimplingthorne 1800-39 [blank in ERC]. Died? [C112975] Had issue.

FITZCLARENCE (Augustus, Lord) Born London 1/3/1805, (1 of 10) natural ch. of Duke of Clarence (later William 1V) and the actress Dorothea Jordan. BNC, Oxford 1824, migrated to Trinity, Cambridge 1826, dn28 (Heref.), p29 (Chich.), LLB1832, Hon. LLD1835. 'Compelled' into Holy Orders, but 'an exemplary and generous parish priest'. V. Mapledurham, Oxford 1829 to death. Chap. in Ordinary 1829-37, and to his step-mother Queen Adelaide. Died London ('from blood poisoning') 14/6/1854 aged 49 [C27590. Boase. M. Murphy, 'Lord Augustus Fitzclarence', *History Today*, 24 (9/9/1974) claims he had a natural vocation for the stage (like his mother) rather than the church] Married Kensington Palace, London 2/1/1845 Sarah Elizabeth Catherine (aged 16/17, dau. Major Lord Henry Gordon), 6 ch. Granted the rank of the son of a Marquess 1831, and thus 'Lord'; 'Very liberal and kind, sees no society' (Wilberforce thus).

FITZHUGH (William Anthony) Born Southampton, Hants. 16/5/1795, s. William Fitzhugh and Charlotte Hamilton. Christ Church, Oxford 1811, migrated to Trinity, Cambridge 1814, dn17 (Salis. for Win.), p17 (Heref for Win.), BA1818, MA1822. R. Street, Sussex 1821-81, R. Belchford, Lincs. 1826-81, Prebend of Warminster in Wells Cathedral 1828-34 (res.), Prebend of Middleton in Chichester Cathedral 1860 to death. Dom. Chap. to Bishop of Gloucester, then of C&L 1819. Died (Hurstpierpoint, Sussex) 17/3/1881, leaving £78,323-6s-1d. [C42224] Married Chevening, Kent 15/8/1820 Mary Anne Lane, with issue.

FLAMSTEAD, *born* DODSLEY (Alvary Dodsley) Bapt. Sponden, Derbys. 28/8/1786, s. Rev. Richard Dodsley and Dorothy Greaves. Emmanuel, Cambridge 1804, BA1808, dn11 (Win. for C&L), MA1813, p14 (Chester for C&L). R. Lambley, Notts. 1819 (w. R. Radcliffe on Soar, Notts. 1830 only) to death 13/7/1842 (living at Lambley House) [C10994] Married Woodborough, Notts. 23/11/1830 Charlotte Catherine Worth, with issue.

FLAVELL (Josiah Webb) Born London 7/1/1773, s. Josiah Flavell and Agnes Webb. Christ's, Cambridge 1791, BA1795, dn95 (C&L), p97 (C&L), MA1798. R. Stody w. Hunworth, Holt, Norfolk 1801 to death there 9/9/1848 aged 75 [C10995] Married Marylebone, London 10/4/1802 Catherine Aufrère (Hoveton Hall, Norfolk), with clerical son John Webb Flavell.

FLEET (Christopher) Bapt. Tarrant Gunville, Dorset 2/6/1757, s. Rev. Edward and Mary Fleet. King's, Cambridge 1775, Fellow 1778-94, dn79 (Ely), BA1780, MA1783, p84 (Ely). R. Durweston w. Bryanston, Dorset 1793-1841, 'Dean' of the Collegiate Church of Whitchurch Canonicorum w. Stanton St Gabriel, Dorset 1824 [not in ERC], R. Lytchett Maltravers, Dorset 1832 to death 6/3/1841 aged 84 [C52539]

FLEMING (Fletcher) Bapt. Windermere, Westmorland 27/8/1795, s. Rev. John Fleming, sen. (below) and Jane Taylor. St John's, Cambridge 1815 (expelled: no degree), dn19 (Chester), p23 (Chester). PC. Lorton, Cumberland 1823-6, (first) PC. Rydal, Grasmere, Westmorland 1825-57 (living at Rydal Lodge), R. Grasmere 1857 to death 11/11/1876 aged 81, leaving £16,000 [C168857] Married 23/6/1836 Mrs Catherine Emily (Boscawen) Rowlands. Brother John, jun., below. 'A notorious drunkard' (but for a more measured tone see Dorothy Wordsworth's *Journal*).

FLEMING, born RAINCOCK (John, sen.) Bapt. Penrith, Cumberland 14/5/1768, s. Rev. William Raincock (R. Ousby, Westmorland) and Agnes Fletcher Fleming. St John's, Cambridge 1785, BA1789, MA1792. PC. Troutbeck, Westmorland 1799-1827, Prebend of St Andrew in Llandaff Cathedral 1800-35, V. Eglwysilan St Martin, Glamorgan 1802-32, V. Pentyrch, Glamorgan 1807-13, V. Brigham, Cumberland 1813-14, R. Bootle, Cumberland 1814 to death 11/1/1835 aged 66 (CCEd says 4/4/1835) [C3899] Married Whitehaven, Cumberland 20/6/1794 his cousin Jane Taylor, with clerical sons (below and above) and also Thomas, and George. Name changed 1779 on inheriting.

FLEMING (John, jun.) Bapt. Windermere, Westmorland 26/7/1800, s. Rev. John Fleming, sen. (above) and Jane Taylor. St Bees adm. 1822, dn23 (Chester), p24. PC. Ponsonby, Cumberland 1829-42, V. Llangwm, Monmouth 1835 to death 2/5/1857 aged 57 [C168861] Married Usk, Monmouth 30/5/1842 Caroline Shepperd (dau. of a solicitor). Brother Fletcher, above.

FLEMING (Richard, Sir, 6th Bart.). Born Whitehaven, Cumberland 4/11/1791, s. Roger Fleming and Isabella Hicks. St Bees adm. 1818, dn20 (Chester), p21 (Chester), then Trinity Hall, Cambridge 1822 (a Ten Year Man), MA1823. R. Grasmere, Westmorland 1822-57 (parish sequestrated 1833) and R. Windermere, West-morland 1823 to death. Dom. Chap. to 11th Earl of Strathmore and Kinghorne 1823. Died Derby 3/4/1857 aged 65. [C150456. Boase] Married Bolton-le-Sands, Lancs. 27/10/1825 Sarah Bradshaw (Alton Hall, Lancs.), with issue. Succ. to title 1821.

FLESHER (John Thomas) Born Tiffield, Northants., s. Rev. John Thomas Flesher, sen. and Rhoda Biker. Lincoln, Oxford 1818 (aged 18), BA1823, MA1825. R. (and patron) of Tiffield 1832 to death 17/10/1852 [Probably C60351] Married Ashbourne, Derbys. 19/1/1831 Elizabeth Spencer, and had issue.

FLETCHER (Horatio Samuel) Born Walsall, Staffs., s. Samuel Fletcher and Sophia Westley. Queen's, Oxford 1826 (aged 19), dn29 (C&L), BA1830, p31 (C&L). PC. Bilston St Mary, Staffs. 1830-6, PC. Bilston St Leonard 1836 to death (London) 30/4/1871 aged 75, leaving £5 [*sic*] [C11003] Married Wolverhampton, Staffs. 21/4/1835 Sarah Lester (w), with issue.

FLETCHER (John, sen.) Bapt. Gainsborough, Lincs. 7/8/1756, s. of John Fletcher (a grocer) and Sarah Sharples. St Catharine's, Cambridge 1778, then Magdalene 1778, BA1782, dn82 (York), p82 (York). V. Royston, Yorks. 1791 to (burial) 28/1/1836 aged 79 [C98684. YCO] Married (1) Ecclesfield, Yorks. 10/1/1787 Jane Carr (d.1795), with son below (2) Royston 30/8/1808 Abigail Stocks, with further issue.

FLETCHER (John, jun.) Born Royston, Barnsley, Yorks. 12/5/1791, s. Rev. John Fletcher, sen. (above) and Jane Carr. Lincoln, Oxford 1810, BA1815, dn15 (York), p16 (Salis. for York). V. Bradfield, Ecclesfield, Yorks. 1819 to death 1853 [C92368. YCO]

FLETCHER (John Kendall) Bapt. Plymouth, Devon 8/8/1763, s. John Fletcher. St Alban Hall, Oxford 1791, dn93 (Ex.), p95 (Ex.), BA, MA and BD (all 1808), DD1817. S/M Callington G/S, Devon 1803; V. Ashford, Devon 1803-61 and V. Yarnscombe, Devon 1803, V. Quethiock, Cornwall 1811-16 (res.). Chap. to Prince of Wales 1806. Died (a widower) 26/1/1861, leaving £1,000 [C143485] Married Stoke Damerel, Devon 2/6/1786 Mary Parminter, with clerical son (below).

FLETCHER (John Rooke) Born East Stonehouse, Devon, s. Rev. John Kendall Fletcher (above) and Mary Parminter. Exeter, Oxford 1803 (aged 16), BA1808, MA1810, dn10 (Ex.), p11 (Ex.), BD1818, DD1834. V. Quethiock, Cornwall 1816-68 and R. Lidford, Devon 1828-68. Died Compton Gifford, Devon 10/11/1877 aged 90, leaving £9,000 [C136525] Married before 1816 Mary Shuldham Robertson, with clerical son.

FLETCHER (Joseph) Born Newburn, Northants., s. Charles Fletcher [*pleb*.]. St Edmund Hall, Oxford 1808 (aged 21), BA1812, dn12 (Salis.), p12 (Salis.), MA1815. R. Dowles, Shropshire 1818 to death (Cheltenham, Glos.) 21/2/1871, leaving £2,000. Dom. Chap. to Earl of Huntingdon [C92369] Married (1) Westminster, London 18/4/1815 Sarah Laurens Bicknell (d.1840) (2) St Pancras, London 29/3/1856 Mary Henrietta Bickenell (w), with issue.

FLETCHER (Walter) Bapt. Calke, Derbys. 17/11/1767, s. Rev. Walter Fletcher, sen. and Mary Fletcher. Pembroke, Cambridge 1785, BA1790, dn90 (C&L), p92 (C&L), MA1793. V. Dalston, Cumberland 1793-1846, V. Swarkeston, Derbys. 1795, V. Bromfield, Cumberland 1799-1826 (res.), Chancellor and Vicar-General of the Diocese of Carlisle 1814-46, V. Lazonby, Cumberland 1826 (and Prebend of Bugthorpe in York Minster 1825) to death. Dom. Chap. to Bishop of Carlisle, later Archbishop of York 1799. Died Carlisle 1/4/1846 aged 78 [C5870. J. Platt (ed.), *The Diocese of Carlisle, 1814-1855: Chancellor Walter Fletcher's 'Diocese Book...* (Surtees Society/CWAAS, 2015 and port.), especially ppxiv-xxii. Married Dalston 11/5/1797 Mary Anne (w), dau. Rev. Browne Grisdale (his predecessor as Chancellor), with issue.

FLETCHER (William) Bapt. Wood Enderby, Lincs. 25/12/1796. St John's, Cambridge 1821, BA, dn24 (Lin.), MA, p26 (Lin.). PC. Charsfield, Suffolk 1829, V. Stone w. Bishopstone, Bucks. 1832-9, R. Foxcote (Foxcott), Bucks. 1839-43, V. Harwell, Berks. 1843 to death (Malmesbury, Wilts.) 24/3/1852. Dom. Chap. to Duke of Buckingham 1843-52 [C60359] Married Whitton w. Thurlston, Suffolk 7/7/1818 Mary Studd, with clerical issue. *J.P.* Bucks. and Berks.

FLOCKTON (Jonathan) Bapt. Westminster, London 1/4/1768, s. Jonathan Flockton and Sarah Fenton. St Edmund Hall, Oxford 1787, BA1791, dn91 (Lin.), p93 (Nor. for Win.). V. Shernborne, Norfolk 1831 to death 21/4/1835 (CCEd says 15/5/1835) [C17781] Married St James, Piccadilly, London 19/1/1792 Hannah Cole ('a minor, with consent of her natural and lawful mother'), with issue.

FLOWER (William, sen.) Bapt. York 18/9/1753, s. Hardy Flower. Literate: dn78 (York), p79 (York). R. York All Saints, Pavement 1792 to death 21/1/1837 aged 83 [C98690. YCO] Married Wheldrake, Yorks. 6/8/1779 Philadelphia Waundby, with clerical son (below).

FLOWER (William, jun.) Bapt. Hull, Yorks. 2//5//1781, s. Rev. William Flower, sen. (above) and Philadelphia Waundby. Trinity, Cambridge 1800, BA1805, dn05 (York), p06 (York), MA1808. PC. Malton Old and New, Yorks. 1822-38, R. Kirkbride, Cumberland 1835 (non-res.), Chap. of New Gaol, York Castle 1835 and R. South Hykeham, Lincs. 1838 to death (York) 10/11/1843 [C5871. YCO. Platt]

FLY (Henry) Bapt. Cripplegate, City of London 14/6/1744, s. Edward and Deborah Fly. BNC, Oxford 1762, BA1766, dn67 (Ox. for London), Fellow, p68 (London), MA1773, BD & DD 1797. R. Holy Trinity, Minories, City of London 1770-1833, Minor Canon of St Paul's Cathedral, London 1783, PC. Knockholt, Kent 1788-1820 (res.), PC. Downe, Kent 1788-1817 (res.), V. Willesden, Middx. 1821, PC. Kingsbury, Middx. 1821 to death. Chap. in Ordinary and Priest in Ordinary 1833 ('Confessor to His Majesty's Household'). Died St James Palace 10/8/1833 aged 89 (CCEd says 27/9/1833) aged 88 [C27678] Married City of London 30/11/1769 Anne Ridley. *F.S.A.*

FOLEY (John) Born Mordiford, Heref. 15/1/1775, s. Rev. Robert Foley and Anne Walwyn. Wadham, Oxford 1792, BA1795, dn97 (Wor.), p99 (Wor.), MA and Fellow 1801. R. Holt, Worcs. 1812-47, R. Shrawley, Worcs. 1823-7 (res.). Dom. Chap. to 2nd Earl of Mountnorris 1823. Died 11/8/1847 [C121040] Married 24/9/1804 Martha Hickman Hayley, w. clerical sons John, and Edward Walwyn. *J.P.* Worcs.

FOLEY (Thomas Philip) Bapt. Barrington, Cambs. 28/2/1758, s. Rev. Philip Foley (R. Shelsley Beauchamp, Worcs.) and Anne Titchmarsh. Trinity, Cambridge 1775, then Jesus 1775, BA1779, Fellow 1780-90, dn80 (Peterb.), MA1782, p85 (Peterb.). V. Hundon, Suffolk 1789-1801, V. Fordham, Cambs. 1789-1798, R. Old Swinford, Worcs. 1797 and V. Wombourn w. Trysul, Staffs. 1801 to death. Dom. Chap. to 3rd Baron Foley 1804. Died 7/10/1835 (CCEd thus) [C11014] Married St Pancras, London 6/10/1801 Elizabeth Bache (*or* Beach), with issue. A follower of Joanna Southcott!

FONNEREAU (Charles William) Bapt. Thornhaugh, Northants. 18/6/1764, s. Rev. William Fonnereau (of Christchurch Mansion, Ipswich) and Anne Williams (dau. of a baronet). [Saw action with the Royal Navy during the American War] Trinity Hall, Cambridge 1787, dn91 (Peterb.), p92 (Peterb.), LLB1793, V. (and patron) of Tuddenham St Mary, Suffolk 1796-1840, R. Hargrave, Northants. 1797-1805, PC. Ipswich St Peter 1801, PC. (and patron) of Ipswich St Margaret 1805 to death 9/1/1840 [C110203. DEB] Married Hargrave 18/7/1793 Harriet Deborah Neale (dau. of a doctor), with issue. Brother below.

FONNEREAU (Claudius Williams) Born Clopton, Northants., s. Rev. William Fonnereau (of Christchurch Mansion, Ipswich) and Anne Williams (dau. of a baronet). Clare, Cambridge 1779, dn85 (C&L for Peterb.), p85 (Peterb.), LLB1786, LLD1804. (succ. his grandfather as) R. Clopton 1785 (and Ipswich St Margaret 1804-5) to death 6/10/1845 aged 84, *s.p.* [C11015. DEB] Married Caxton, Cambs. 11/10/1805 Ann Okins. Brother above.

FOORD, FORD (Henry [John Jackson]) Born Hartford, Cheshire 10/12/1777, s. Rev. Henry Foord and Mary Rowe. Jesus, Cambridge 1796, BA1800, dn00 (York), p01 (Nor. as Henry), MA1804. R. Foxholes, Yorks. 1815 (as Ford) and V. Seamer, Yorks. 1818 to death. Dom. Chap. to 3rd Earl of Clanwilliam 1818. Died 1/2/1847 aged 69 [C88738. YCO. The two Herefordshire parishes noted in Venn are probably those of the father] Married Settrington, Yorks. 10/12/1822 Ann Todd (a clergy dau.), with clerical s. Richard Henry.

FOORD-BOWES (Timothy Fysh) see under **BOWES**

FOOT (John Strode) Born Plymouth, Devon 29/9/1749, s. Rev. Josias Foot and Mary Dixon. Balliol, Oxford 1768, BA1772, dn73 (Ex.), p06 (Ex.). V. Liskeard, Cornwall 1821 to death (Devonport), Devon 29/12/1838 aged 90 [C143489] Married 1784 Eliza Collins.

FOOT (Lundy) Born Holly Park, Dublin 3/4/1793, s. Jeffery Foot and Elinor Williams. TCD1810, BA1815, MA1824. [Called to the Bar 1817]. R. Long Breedy, Dorset 1829 (and Prebend of Netherbury in Terra in Salisbury Cathedral) 1854 to death 5/1/1873, leaving £2,000 [C52543 as Fool. Al.Dub.] Married (1) Dublin 7/11/1817 Elizabeth Vicars (d.1825), with clerical son (2) Harrow, Middx. 28/11/1827 Harriet Cunningham (a clergy dau., d.1839), with further (and clerical) issu: histfam.familysearch.org/getperson.php?personID=I252939&tree...

FOOTTIT (James) Bapt. Cromwell, Notts. 11/11/1781, s. John Foottit [*pleb*] and Sarah Falkingham. St Edmund Hall, Oxford 1800, BA1804, dn04 (Roch. for York), p05 (London for York). Vicar Choral, Southwell Collegiate Church, Notts. (and H/M Southwell G/S) 1812, PC. West Ravendale Chapel, East Ravendale, Lincs. 1813 and R. Brigsley, Lincs. 1813-22, V. Upton, Notts. 1819, V. Barnby in the Willows, Notts. 1822-49, V. Farnsfield, Notts. 1834-9, R. Gonaldston, Notts. 1840 to death (Barnby) 18/5/1849 [C1829. YCO] Married (1) Brighton 14/12/1805 Mary Walker (d.1815), with clerical son of the father's name (2) Southwell 13/1/1817 Elizabeth Flower, with further issue. Port. online.

FORD (Charles) Born Marylebone, London 26/6/1797, s. Sir Francis Ford, 1st Bart., *M.P.* (Ember Court, Thames Ditton, Surrey, and Barbados - slave money) and Mary Anson. Balliol, Oxford 1815, BA1819, dn20 (Glos.), MA1821, p21 (Glos.). R. Billingford, Norfolk 1821-50, V. North Elmham, Norfolk 1828-33 (res.), R. Postwick, Norfolk 1843 to death (Hyde Park, London) 14/5/1863 aged 65, leaving £8,000 [C112983] Married Cheltenham, Glos. 9/5/1839 Catherine Juliana Stuart, with clerical son Charles Primrose Ford.

FORD, *later* FORDE (Frederick) Born Sandbach, Cheshire 20/6/1801, s. Col. John Ford and Elizabeth Ingram. Balliol, Oxford 1819, then Trinity, Cambridge 1822, BA1825, dn27 (Chester), p28 (Chester), MA1831. R. Church Lawton, Cheshire 1831-9 (res.) [blank in ERC], V. Malvern St Peter, Worcs. 1842-5, R. Chester St Peter 1846-55 (res. ill-heath), then again 1861-73, PC. Chester Little St John without the Northgate 1873 to death (Hammersmith, London) 23/2/1881 aged 80, leaving £4,000. British Chap. Heidelberg 1856-9, then Cannes 1860-1 [C168870] Married Church Lawton 9/7/1833 Anne Twemlow (w), with issue. Secretary to The Honourable the Irish Society 1846; port. online.

FORD (Gilbert) Bapt. Bristol 16/11/1768, s. John Ford and Mary Clare. Wadham, Oxford 1786, BA1790, dn91 (C&L for Win.), p93 (Bristol for Win.), MA1798. R. North Meols, Lancs. 1793 to death 6/5/1835 [C11018] Married Ormskirk, Lancs. 9/9/1799 Elizabeth Watson.

FORD (James) Bapt. Canterbury Cathedral 29/11/1779, s. Canon James Ford and Dorothy Spearman. Trinity, Oxford 1797, BA1801, dn02 (Win. for Cant.), MA1804, p07 (Ox.), BD1812, Fellow to 1831, etc. R. Ipswich St Lawrence 1808-31, R. Hillfarrance, Som. 1820-32 (res.), R. Navestock, Essex 1830 to death 31/1/1850 aged 70 [C27706. ODNB. *Gentleman's Magazine* has a long obit. with details of his quite extraordinary funeral, *q.v.*] Married Bloomsbury, London 9/11/1830 Letitia Jermyn (dau. of an Ipswich bookseller), *s.p.* Founded the Ford Professorship of English History at Oxford.

FORD (Richard Wilbraham) Born Wincanton, Somerset 16/3/1781, s. John Ford and Margaret Bell. King's, Cambridge 1799, Fellow 1802, dn03 (Lin.), BA1804, p05 (Cant.), MA 1807. V. South Cerney, Glos. 1807-62, V. Stourpaine, Dorset 1810-54, R. Little Rissington, Glos. 1811 (and Hon. Canon of Gloucester Cathedral 1846) to death. Dom. Chap. to Anne Dorothea, Baroness Alvanley 1811. Died 24/8/1862, leaving £11,000 [C60375] Married Bath 9/5/1811 Jemima Rooke, with clerical son Charles Henry Ford.

FORD (William) Born Stockton on Tees, Co. Durham. St John's, Cambridge 1824, BA1828, dn28 (Car.), p29 (Car.). PC. Cumwhitton, Cumberland (and Minor Canon of Carlisle Cathedral) 1831 to death 1844 (1st q.) [C3385. Platt] Married Stanwix, Cumberland 18/12/1832 Eleanor Allison. His sketches of Cumbrian churches survive. Cumwhitton also in ERC under Samuel Hudson, *q.v.*

FORESTER (Townsend) Born Ross Hall, Shropshire 5/4/1772, s. Lt.-Col. Cecil Forester and Anne Townsend. Pembroke, Oxford 1792, BA1796, dn96 (C&L), p96 (C&L), MA807, BD & DD1812. R. Sheinton, Shropshire 1796-1803, R. Knockin, Shropshire 1798-1815, R. Broseley w. Linley, Shropshire 1799-1841, Canon of 8th Prebend of Worcester 1815-41, R. Pulford, Cheshire 1809-18, R. Bredwardine St John the Baptist, Worcs. 1818-41, R. Little Wenlock. Shropshire 1818-41, PC. Benthall, Shropshire 1796 to death 30/9/1841 [C11023] Married Shrewsbury, Shropshire 5/1/1786 Anne Maria Byne (a military dau.), with clerical son George Townsend Forester.

FORGE (Christopher) Bapt. Nafferton, Cumberland 10/9/1795, s. William Forge (a yeoman farmer) and Margaret Keld (but Venn says son of Sir Bateson Harvey, 1st Bart., so perhaps illegitimate?). Jesus, Cambridge 1815, BA1819, dn19 (York), p20 (York), MA1824. PC. Mapleton, Yorks. 1821-73 and R. Goxhill, Beverley, Yorks. 1845 to death (Hornsea, Yorks.) 31/3/1873 aged 77, leaving £4,000 [C131284. YCO] Married Great Driffield, Yorks. 3/7/1827 Ann Kirkby. Brother below?

FORGE (William) Bapt. Nafferton, Yorks. 31/1/1779, s. William Forge (husbandman) and Margaret Keld. Jesus, Cambridge 1800, BA 1802, dn02 (York), p03 (York), Fellow 1806-20, MA1806. R. King's Stanley (o/w Stanley Regis), Glos. 1820-57, PC. Asgarby, Lincs. 1822. Died 12/7/1857 [C60377. YCO] Married Puddlestone, Heref. 5/5/1820 Mary Hinson, with issue. Brother above?

FORMBY (James) Born Formby Hall, Formby, Lancs., s. Rev. Richard Formby and Anne Lonsdale. BNC, Oxford 1815 (aged 18), BA1819, dn20 (Chester), p21 (Chester), MA 1822. PC. Blackpool St John 1821-6, V. Frindsbury, Kent 1826 to death 14/2/1881, leaving £4,000 [C6732] Married Kirkham, Lancs. 30/7/1821 Susan Alice King, with issue. Brothers below. Good online port.

FORMBY (Miles) Born Formby Hall, Formby, Lancs. 21/9/1793, s. Rev. Richard Formby and Ann Lonsdale. BNC, Oxford 1812, BA1816, dn18 (B&W), p18 (Glos.), MA1819. PC. Liverpool Holy Trinity 1821-[47], R. West Monkton, Som. 1823-25, PC. Cothelstone, Som. 1824-31, PC. Melling, Halsall, Lancs. 1829 to death 4/5/1849 [C38875] Married Manchester 22/4/1823 Carolina Peel (dau. of Lawrence Peel, Ardwick Green, Manchester), *s.p.* [for her sister, see below]. J.P. Lancs. 1828. Brothers above and below.

FORMBY (Roger Hesketh) Born Formby Hall, Formby, Lancs. 1/12/1795, s. Rev. Richard Formby and Ann Lonsdale. Jesus, Cambridge 1814, BA1818, dn18 (Chester), p20 (Chester or Glos.), MA1820. Joint or Second Minister Liverpool St Paul 1827 to death (Cheltenham) 6/10/1842 [C150559] Married Doncaster, Yorks. 14/8/1827 Harriet Peel (dau. of Lawrence Peel, Ardwick Green, Manchester), with issue [for her sister, see above] His brothers, above.

FORSHAW (Charles) Bapt. Burtonwood, Lancs. 16/1/1793, s. Thomas Forshaw and

Mary Gorse. Literate: dn18 (Chester), then Trinity, Cambridge 1819 (a Ten Year Man), p20 (Chester). PC. Altcar, Ormskirk, Lancs. 1826 (and H/M Ormskirk G/S 1852) to burial 24/12/1855 aged 62 [C168876] Married Mottram, Cheshire 18/2/1819 Sarah Turner, with issue.

FORSTER (John) Born Halesworth, Suffolk 9/1/1758, s. Rev. Thomas Forster. St John's, Cambridge 1776, BA1780, dn80 (Nor.), p82 (Nor.), MA1785. R. Tunstead, Suffolk 1782-1837, PC. Great Yarmouth St George 1817-33 (res.). Died 1/2/1837 [C112984] Married Great Yarmouth 28/10/1800 Maria Wall, with issue. Brother Samuel, below.

FORSTER (John) Bapt. Newcastle upon Tyne 9/1/1767, s. Francis Forster and Eleanor Greave. Trinity, Cambridge 1786, BA1790, dn92 (Durham), p92 (Durham), MA1795. R. Kirk Sandall (o/w Little Sandall), Yorks. 1803 and R. Rither (Ryther), Yorks. 1805 to death. Dom. Chap. to 2nd Earl Gray 1805. Died 4/10/1846 [C134167] Married Newcastle upon Tyne 24/5/1803 Anna Latton (a clergy dau.). *J.P.* West Riding.

FORSTER (Nathaniel) From Oxford, s. Rev. Samuel Forster and Anne Keele. Worcester, Oxford 1787 (aged 17), BA1791, dn92 (Salis.), p94 (Salis.). R. and V. East and West Mersea, Essex 1797 to death 12/5/1851 [C66806] Wife Tabitha, and issue.

FORSTER (Samuel) Born Halesworth, Suffolk 30/7/1752, s. Rev. Thomas Forster. St John's, Cambridge 1772, BA1776, dn76 (Nor.), p76 (Nor.), Fellow 1776-84, MA1779, DD1791. H/M Norwich G/S 1785-1810 ('by which time the boys had dwindled to 8'); (succ. his father as) R. Tunstead (w. South Ruston), Norfolk 1776-82, R. Wainfleet, Lincs. 1783-1810, PC. Walpole, Suffolk 1784-1817 (res.), PC. St Mary Coslany, Norwich 1797-1810, V. Great and Little Chesterford, Essex 1810-17, R. Shotley St Mary (o/w Kirkton), Suffolk 1817-43, V. Rushmere St Andrew, Suffolk 1826 only, R. Quarrington, Lincs. 1826 to death (Shotley - and blind) 24/7/1843 [C60435] Married Westminster, London 1/5/1783 Elizabeth Turenne, with issue. Brother John, above. 'Private tutor to the sons of the Marquis of Bristol, accompanying the elder ones to Eton, as was the custom at that time.'

FORSTER (Thomas) From Oxford, s. Thomas Foster [*pleb*]. Chorister Magdalen, Oxford 1802-9, then [Choral] Clerk 1812-18]. New, Oxford 1812 (aged 17), BA1815, p18 (Salis.), MA1818, p19 (Heref.), Chap. New 1815-57, Chap. Christ Church 1818-24. Vicar-Choral Hereford Cathedral 1818-20, V. Cassington, Oxon. 1824 to death (Kidlington, Oxon.) 30/9/1867, leaving £10,000 [C17627] Widow Catherine Anne. 'Very poor [*sic*], no courage, but a good man' (Wilberforce).

FORSTER (William) From Rutland, s. Thomas Forster (druggist). St John's, Cambridge 1761 (aged 18), BA1765, dn66 (Lin.), p69 (Lin.), MA1781. R. Thistleton, Rutland 1771-1834, R. Ayston, Rutland 1780-1834, R. South Pool, Devon 1793-1826. Dom. Chap. to 4th Earl of Harborough 1816. Died 15/4/1834 (CCEd says 19/5/1834) aged 90 [C60436] Married Bath 23/8/1796 Lucy Winston.

FORSTER see also under **FOSTER**

FORTESCUE (George) Bapt. Exeter 25/10/1759, s. George Fortescue. Merton, Oxford 1777, dn83 (Glos.), then Jesus, BCL 1785, p89 (London for Ex.). R. St Pinnock, Cornwall 1789 and R. St Mellion, Cornwall 1793 to death 26/4/1835 [C117857]

FORTESCUE (John, Hon.) Born South Molton, Devon 5/5/1796, s. 1st Earl Fortescue, *M.P.*, and Hester Grenville. Magdalene, Cambridge 1814, Fellow, MA1816, dn19 (Salis. for Bristol), p20 (Chester for Bristol). R. Anderby w. Cumberworth, Lincs. 1821-35, Canon Residentiary of 5th Prebend in Worcester Cathedral 1834-69, R. Poltimore w. Huxham, Devon 1835 to death. Master of St Oswald's Hospital [almshouses], Worcester 1847. Died 3/1/1869, leaving £70,000 [C52575] Married Stamford, Lincs. 13/4/1842 Sophia Nevile (a clergy dau.), with clerical son.

FORTESCUE (John Faithful Grover) Bapt. Richmond, Surrey 30/9/1785, s. Admiral John Faithful Fortescue and Elizabeth Ann Fraine. Trinity, Cambridge 1805, BA1809, dn09 (London), p10 (London), MA1812. PC. Berners Roding >< Essex 1811, R. Colchester St Giles, Essex 1812-18 (res.), PC. Brentwood, Essex 1826-9 (res.), R. Snoreham, Essex 1849 to death (Terling, Essex) 16/11/1865, leaving under £300 [C117858] Married Selworthy, Som. 29/7/1812 Frances Anne Acland. Lived in

Roxwell, Essex and Castle Creke, Ross Carbery, Co. Cork.

FORTESCUE (William) Born Kingsnympton, Devon 1788, s. Capt. Hon. Matthew Fortescue, *R.N.*, and Henrietta Archer. Trinity, Oxford 1810, migrated to St John, Cambridge 1811, dn14 (Salis.), p16 (London for Salis.), LLB 1817. R. Weare Giffard, Devon 1822 and R. Kingsnympton (o/w Nymet St George) 1824 to death 3/9/1856 [C92395] Married (1) Edinburgh 6/2/1819 Isobel Barclay Christie (from Fife, she d.1826), with issue (2) Luccombe, Som. 18/2/1832 Elizabeth Gould (a clergy dau.).

FORWARD (Charles) Born Axminster, Devon 11/7/1794 ('9am'), s. Samuel Forward and Rebecca Higgins Adam. Wadham, Oxford 1812, BA1818, dn18 (Salis.), p18 (Ex.), MA 1823. V. Wappenbury, Warwicks. 1819-46, R. North Poorton, Dorset 1846-51, R. Bettiscombe, Dorset 1851 to death 24/9/1858, leaving £2,000 [C11024] Married 23/5/1831 Mary Bond, with issue. Brother below.

FORWARD (Edward Cook) Born Axminster, Devon 7/9/1781, s. Samuel Forward and Rebecca Higgins Adam. Wadham, Oxford 1799, BA1804, dn04 (Ex. for Bristol), p05 (Win. for Bristol), Fellow, MA1807. R. Wambrook, Dorset 1805-8, R. Combe Pyne, Devon 1807-36, R. Lymington, Som. 1810 to death. Dom. Chap. to 2nd Baron Graves 1810. Died Axminster 11/11/1836 [C40117] Married 1831 Mary Parker Slee Russell, with issue. Brother above.

FOSBROOKE (Philip) Born Shardlow Hall, Derbys. 13/11/1805, s. Leonard Fosbrooke and Mary Elizabeth Story. Clare, Cambridge 1825, BA1830, dn30 (C&L), p31 (Lin.). V. Lockington w. Hemington, Leics. 1831 to death (unm.) 13/1/1864, leaving £12,000 [C11026]

FOSBROOKE, *later* FOSBROKE (Thomas Dudley) Born Clerkenwell, London 27/5/1770, s. Rev. William Fosbrooke and Heather Lashbroke. Pembroke, Oxford 1785, BA1789, MA 1792, dn93 (C&L for Win.), p94 (Glos.). V. Walford, Heref. 1830 to death 1/1/1842 ('insolvent') [C11027. ODNB] Married Horsley, Glos. 11/4/1796 Harriet Howell, 4s, 6 dau. *F.S.A.*1799. Antiquarian writer and archaeologist. Freemason.

FOSTER (Aaron) Born Wells, Som. 19/4/1764, s. Rev. Aaron Foster, sen. and Ann Slade. St Mary Hall, Oxford 1784, dn86 (B&W), p88 (Bristol), BCL1791. V. (and Sinecure R.) Kingston St Mary (o/w Kingston Pitney), Som. 1791, and V. Lyng, Som. 1806 to death 28/11/1851 aged 88 [C38423] Brother of Robert (b.1766), below.

FOSTER (Aaron) Bapt. Wells, Somerset 20/8/1799, s. Rev. Edward Foster and Ann Drake. Exeter, Oxford 1817, BA1821, dn22 (Glos.), p23 (Glos.), MA1826. V. Mudford, Som. 1828 (and Priest-Vicar Wells Cathedral 1829) to death (Weston-super-Mare) 28/4/1853 [C42228] Married Sherborne, Dorset 31/1/1832 Marianne Cruttwell. Brother below.

FOSTER (Francis Drake) Born Wells, Som. 17/12/1794, s. Rev. Edward Foster and Ann Drake. Balliol, Oxford 1811, BA1814, dn17 (Glos.), p18 (Glos.), MA1819. R. Dodington, Glos. 1827-72. Died (Wells) 23/9/1882, leaving £5,537-15s-10d. [C150586] Married Batcombe, Dorset 21/6/1836 Caroline Margaret Coney. Brother above.

FOSTER (Henry) Literate: dn84 (Chester), p85 (Chester). PC. Copp, St Michael on Wyre, Lancs. 1785-1803, Prebend of Oxton (Second Part) in Southwell Minster 1796, PC. Woodplumpton, St Michael on Wyre. 1803-36. Died there 7/8/1844 aged 84 [C168878] Married Woodplumpton 2/5/1787 Alice Croft, with issue.

FOSTER (John) Bapt. Settle, Yorks. 20/5/1762, s. John Foster. Literate: dn88 (London for York), p90 (York). PC. Houghton (o/w Tossett), Gisburne, Yorks. 1790-1837. Died 18/5/1840 aged 79 [C117865. YCO] Was married with issue.

FOSTER (John) From Erringdon Park, Halifax, Yorks., s. Thomas Foster. Trinity, Cambridge 1797, BA1801, dn02 (Lin.), p03 (Lin.), MA1804. V. West Thurrock, Essex 1805 (w. Purfleet 1806), V. Sarratt, Herts. 1815. Dom. Chap. to 1st Marquess of Camden 1815. Died? [C60445]

FOSTER (John) Bapt. Ryhall, Rutland 17/1/1780, s. Rev. Thomas Foster and Sarah Baskett. St John's, Cambridge 1797, BA1801, Fellow 1802-10, dn02 (Peterb.), p04 (Lin.), MA1804. R. (and patron) of Wickersley, Rotherham, Yorks. 1804-63, V. Marton cum Grafton, Yorks. 1809 to death. Dom. Chap. to

1st Earl of Lonsdale 1809. Died (a widower) Dalton, Rotherham 14/6/1863, leaving £1,000 [C60446. Boase] Married Bath 6/6/1810 Charlotte Rooke (Langham Hall, Essex), with clerical son. Brother Kingsman, below.

FOSTER (Jonathan) Bapt. Hubberholme, Kettlewell, Yorks. 22/2/1784. St Bees adm. 1817, dn20 (Chester), p21 (Chester). R. Kettlewell 1822 to death 26/9/1866, leaving £300 [C135868] Married Kettlewell 29/6/1824 Alice Briscoe.

FOSTER (Joseph) Born Putney, London 19/8/1806, s. William and Sarah Foster. Emmanuel, Cambridge 1823, dn28 (Ely for Bristol), BA1829, p30 (Bristol), MA1838. V. Abbotsbury, Dorset 1832 and R. Winterbourne Monkton, Dorset 1838 to death 23/5/1856 [C17784. Some say William Joseph] Married 17/6/1825 Sarah Anne Lepper, with issue.

FOSTER (Kingsman) Bapt. Ryhall, Rutland 27/6/1783, s. Rev. Thomas Foster and Sarah Baskett. St John's, Cambridge 1802, BA1806, dn06 (Lin. for Peterb.), p07 (Peterb.), MA 1809. R. (and patron) of Dowsby, Lincs. 1807 to death there 18/4/1867, leaving £800 [C60448. Bennett1] Married City of London 5/3/1812 Mary (dau. of Kingsman Basket St Barbe), 13 ch. (inc. Rev. Kingsman Basket Foster). Brother John, above.

FOSTER (Richard) Bapt. Horton in Ribblesdale, Yorks. 22/4/1771, s. Thomas Foster (a yeoman farmer). St Catharine's, Cambridge 1789, BA 1793, then Clare, Fellow, dn94 (Lin.), p97 (York), MA1806. PC. Hunslet, Leeds 1808 to death 1841 (3rd q.) aged 72 [C60548. YCO] Married Almondbury, Huddersfield, Yorks. 1797 Mrs Ann (Clapham) Wilkinson, with issue.

FOSTER (Robert) Born Bath, Somerset 24/5/1766, s. Rev. Aaron Foster and Ann Slade. St Mary Hall, Oxford 1784, BA1787, dn88 (Lin. for B&W), p90 (Bristol), MA1790. V. Lyng, Som. 1796-1806, Precentor of Bristol Cathedral 1799-1810, V. Marden, Wilts. 1805-10, R. Sutton Bonnington (2nd Mediety o/w St Michael), Notts. 1810-36, Priest-Vicar 1813 and Prebend of Wedmore the Fifth in Wells Cathedral 1820 to death 206/9/1836 aged 70 [C38425] Married (1) by 1794 Eliza Manley (d.1809), with military issue (2) before 1815 Joanna Slade Foster [*thus*],with further issue. Brother Aaron (b.1784), above.

FOSTER see also under **FORSTER**

FOULIS (Henry, Sir, 9th Bart.) Bapt. 15/9/1800, s. Sir William Foulis, 7th Bart., (Ingleby Manor, Northallerton, Yorks.) and Mary Ann Turnour. St John's, Cambridge 1819, BA1823, dn23 (Lin.), p24 (Lin.), MA1825 (Lambeth). V. Wragby w. East Torring-ton >< Lincs. 1825-38, R. Panton, Lincs. 1825-34, V. Milton Ernest, Beds. 1834-5, R. Great Brickhill, Bucks. 1834-76, Prebend of Welton Westhall w. Gorehall in Lincoln Cathedral 1844 to death. Dom. Chap. 5th Viscount Downe 1825. Died (unm.), Ampthill House, Beds. 7/10/1876, leaving £60,000 [C60558. Boase] Succ. his brother to the baronetcy 1845; baronetcy thereafter extinct. 'Chairman of the Hospital for Consumption at Brompton, London, 1849-76, where the East Gallery is named after him; gave the Chapel attached to Hospital'. Port. by George Richmond.

FOULKES (Henry) Bapt. Henllan, Denbighshire 20/3/1773, s. John Ffoulkes and Margaret Clough. Jesus, Oxford 1790, BA1794, dn96 (Ox.), MA1797, p97 (Ox.), BD1804, Fellow to 1817, DD1817, Principal of Jesus College, Oxford 1817-57 (with Sinecure R. Llandysul w. Clynog Fawr, Carnarvon 1817 both appended). R. Yelford, Oxon. 1815-57, R. Besselsleigh, Berks. 1844 to death 17/9/1857 aged 84, having been 'inactive' for some time [C27729. Boase] Port. online.

FOULKES (James) From Trelydan, Montgomeryshire, s. William Foulkes. Magdalene, Cambridge 1783, BA1788, dn88 (St Asaph), p89 (St Asaph). R. Flitcham w. Appleton, Norfolk 1801, R. Crostwick, Norfolk 1804, R. Sutton, Norfolk 1804-39, V. East Winch, Norfolk 1804-9, PC. Hitcham, Suffolk 1835 to death 30/7/1839 (*drowned* 'by falling into the river whilst walking out late in the evening') [C112093]

FOULKES (Peter Davy) Born Dawlish, Devon, s. John Davy Foulkes and Elizabeth Inglett Fortescue. Exeter, Oxford 1818 (aged 18), BA1821, dn22 (Ex.), p23 (Ex.). PC. Abbots Bickington w. Bulkworthy, Devon 1823 and V. Shebbear, Devon 1829 to death 4/11/1854 [C27731] Married Meeth, Devon 13/9/1827 Catharine Lemprière, with issue.

FOUNTAINE, *born* ADDISON (William) From Dimsdale, Co. Durham, s. Rev. William

Addison. Probably University College, Oxford 1786 aged 18, BA1790. R. Middleton St George 1798 to death (Clifton, Bristol) 31/5/1837 aged 69. Married (1) York 21/4/1800 Mary Fountaine (d.1812), with clerical son William Fountaine Addison (2) Walcot, Bath 2/4/1816 Lucy Rattray (dau. of a physician).

FOWKE (Thorpe William) Born Walton on Thames, Surrey 20/10/1777, s. Holland Fowke and Anne Isabella Elisabeth Wood. Peterhouse, Cambridge 1797, BA1802, dn02 (Ely), p02 (Ely). MA1805. V. Sudbury All Saints, Suffolk 1811 to death. Dom. Chap. to 1st Earl of Craven 1797. Died 9 or 10/11/1846 ('the last man to be buried by torchlight in the family vault') [C99983] Married Toft, Cambs. 8/3/1804 Sarah Hart, with issue. 'Unaffected piety, meekness, charity and every Christian virtue marked him for a man of God', etc.

FOWLE (Fulwar Craven) Born Kintbury, Berks. 14/5/1764, s. Rev. Thomas Fowle and Jane Craven. St John's, Oxford 1781, BA1785, dn86 (Salis.), MA1788, p88 (Glos.). R. Elkstone, Glos. 1788 and V. Kintbury 1798 to death. Dom. Chap. to 1st Earl of Craven 1797. Died (a widower) 9/3/1840 [C92400] Married Enborne, Berks. 15/9/1788 Elizabeth Lloyd, with clerical son, below.

FOWLE (Fulwar William) Born Deane by Basingstoke, Wilts. 15/4/1791, s. Rev. Fulwar Craven Fowle (above) and Elizabeth Lloyd. Merton, Oxford 1809, BA1814, dn14 (Salis.), p16 (London), MA1844. R. Allington, Wilts. 1816 and R. Amesbury, Wilts. 1817 (w. RD and Prebend of Chisenbury and Chute in Salisbury Cathedral 1841) to death. Chap. to Ame-sbury Poor Law Union 1837. Died 28/6/1876, leaving £7,000. [C92401] Married (1) Kintbury, Berks. 27/3/1819 Emily Hallett (d.1833), with clerical son (2) Box, Wilts. 9/12/1833 Ann Fawcett Moor.

FOWLE (Henry) From Amport, Hants., s. William Fowle and Harriet Everett. University, Oxford 1821 (aged 18), BA1825, dn25 (Salis.), p27 (Salis.), MA1829. PC. Durrington, Wilts. 1828-[63]. Died (Chute Lodge, Wilts.) 21/1/1865 aged 62, leaving £12,000 [C73694] Married 23/8/1831 Mary Amelia Everett (w), w. issue.

FOWLE (James) Bapt. Rainham, Kent 3/5/1796, s. John Fowle. Wadham, Oxford 1813, BA1818, dn21 (Nor.), p22 (Cant.), MA 1823. PC. Queenborough, Kent 1822-6, R. Pebworth, Glos. 1825 and R. Quinton, Glos. 1826 to death. Dom. Chap. to 2nd Marquess of Salisbury 1826. Died 26/12/1875, leaving £2,000 [C112992]

FOWLER (Barnardiston Forester) Born Horncastle, Lincs. 30/7/1778, s. James Forester Fowler and Catharine Falkner. Literate: dn01 (Chester), p05 (Lin.). PC. Scamlesby, Lincs. 1805, R. Asterby, Lincs. 1805-60, V. Calkwell, Lincs. 1807. Died 9/7/1860, leaving £2,000 [C60567] Married by 1807 Mary Allison, w. issue.

FOWLER (Charles) Born Southwell, Notts. 31/3/1758, s. Rev. Charles, sen. and Mary Fowler. Chorister, Southwell Collegiate Church 1768-9; adm. St John's, Cambridge 1775, BA 1780, dn80 (York), Fellow 1781-4, p82 (York). Vicar Choral, Southwell Collegiate Church 1780-1840, PC. Morton, Notts. 1780-1840, V. Bleasby, Notts. 1782-5, V. Eaton, Yorks. 1783-1840, V. Woodborough, Yorks. 1784 and V. Rolleston, Notts. 1785 to death. Dom. Chap. to 1st Marquess of Stafford 1802. Died (Southwell) 29/3/1840 [C88739. YCO] Married 17/3/1784 Charlotte Greaves, with clerical son (two below).

FOWLER (John) Born Peterbrough 14/12/1777, s. Rev. Robert Fowler (R. Warboys, Hunts.). St John's, Cambridge 1795 (re-adm. 1803), BA1804, dn04 (Lin.), p05 (Lin.), MA 1808. R. Rampton, Cambs. 1812 to death (West End, Southampton) 28/2/1855 [C60576] Had issue.

FOWLER (Robert Hodgson) Bapt. Southwell, Notts. 16/1/1798, s. Rev. Charles Fowler (above) and Charlotte Greaves. Exeter, Oxford 1815, BA1819, dn21 (York, ordaining bishop not specified), p22 (York), MA1825. R. Brigsley, Lincs. 1822-35, PC. Edingley, Notts. 1824, R. Kirklington, Notts 1824, V. Rolleston, Notts. 1841-58, Vicar-Choral in Southwell Collegiate Church. Died Southwell 2/1/1858, leaving £2,000 [C60583. YCO] Married Lambeth, Surrey 18/1/1825 Frances Elizabeth Bish (w), with issue.

FOX (Charles) Bapt. Mapperton, Dorset 14/2/1787, s. Thomas and Elizabeth Fox. Trinity, Cambridge 1802, BA1807, dn10 (Salis.), MA1814, p14 (B&W). R. East Stoke, Dorset 1819 and R. Mapperton 1835 to death (unm.)

8/7/1864 aged 79, leaving £18,000 [C42229] Step-brothers Henry, and Thomas, below?

FOX (Henry) From Mapperton, Dorset, s. Rev. Thomas Fox and Margaret Edwards. Balliol, Oxford 1810 (aged 19), BA1814, dn14 (Salis. for Bristol), p15 (B&W for Bristol), MA 1817. PC. (and patron) of Allington, Dorset 1819-73, PC. Bothenhampton, Dorset 1824, R. Pilsdon, Dorset 1830-70. Died (Allington) 12/1/1873, leaving £16,000 [C42231] Clerical son Edward. Possibly step-brothers Thomas (below), and Charles, above?

FOX (James) Bapt. Burton in Kendal, Westmorland 7/10/1759, s. Henry and Elizabeth Fox. 'Inferior Master' Kirkham G/S, Lancs. 1786-1808 [C168884]. Literate: dn91 (Chester), p92 (Car. for Chester). PC. Warton, Kirkham 1792-1830, V. Ribby cum Wrea, Kirkham 1801 to death (Fleetwood) aged 86. Buried 19/12/1845 [C5874] Married Kirkham 16/2/1784 Alice Swann, w. clerical s. with the father's name in the same place following.

FOX (John) Born c.1764. [BA, MA but NiVoF] V. Witcham, Cambs. 1802, V. Barton Mills, Suffolk 1815 to death. Dom. Chap. to 6th Baron Middleton 1815. Buried 20/3/1845 aged 81 [C112996] Wife Fanny.

FOX (Thomas) Bapt. Finningley, Notts. 1/11/1769, s. Thomas Fox and Sarah Walker. St Catharine's, Cambridge 1789, BA1793, dn95 (Nor. for York), p96 (York), MA1796. PC. Hatfield, Doncaster, Yorks. 1816 (and H/M Hatfield G/S 1827) to death 4/3/1848 [C112997. YCO] Wife Mary, and issue.

FOX (Thomas) From Mapperton, Devon, s. Rev. Thomas Fox, sen. and Margaret Edwards. Wadham, Oxford 1797 (aged 17), BA1801, dn03 (Glos.), p04 (Ox.), MA1805. R. Abbas Combe (o/w Templecombe), Som. 1820-59, V. Compton Chamberlayne, Som. 1822-8, V. South Newton, Wilts. 1827 to death. Dom. Chap. to 11th Earl of Pembroke and Montgomery 1822; and to (the Russian) Ekaterina, Dowager Countess 1827. Died 26/8/1859, leaving £3,000 [C27784] Clerical son. Brother Henry, above, and probable step-brother Charles.

FOX-STRANGWAYS (Charles Redlynch, Hon.) Born Redlynch, Somerset 27/4/1761, s. the (homosexual) 1st Earl of Ilchester and Elizabeth Horner (married to him at 12 or 13 years of age). Christ Church, Oxford 1778, BCL1785, LLB1787, dn87 (Lin. for Bristol), p87 (London for Bristol). R. Maiden Newton, Dorset 1787-1836, R. Brympton, Som. 1788-90 (res.), R. Whatley, Som. 1789-1812, R. Kilmington, Som. 1811 to death 4/11/1836 [C49131 as Strangways] Married 2/8/1787 Jane Haines (a clergy dau.), with clerical son.

FOXLEY (Thomas) Born Manchester 1752, s. Rev. Thomas Foxley, sen. BNC, Oxford 1768, BA1772, dn75 (Roch. for London), p76 (Chester), MA1780. PC. Atherton, Lancs. 1777-1838, R. Radcliffe St Mary, Lancs. 1784 and V. Batley, Yorks. 1798 to death. Dom. Chap. to 1st Earl of Wilton 1798. Died (unmarried) at Radcliffe 13/12/1838 aged 86 [C1833]

FOXLOW (Francis) Bapt. Staveley, Derbys. 30/11/1771, s. Samuel Foxlow and Dorothy Gisborne. St John's, Cambridge 1789, BA1794, dn97 (Win. for C&L), MA1797, p99 (C&L). R. Ordsall, Notts. 1812 and V. Elmton w. Creswell, Derbys. 1822 to death (Staveley House) 13/12/1841 [C11030] Married Chesterfield 8/3/ 1798 Jane Slater (dau. of an attorney).

FOXTON (George) Bapt. Newport, Shropshire 16/9/1761, s. William Henry Foxton and Mary Hodges. Christ Church, Oxford 1779, BA1783, dn84 (Chester for C&L), MA1786, p86 (Salis.). R. Great Coxwell, Berks. 1788-1815 (res.), V. Queniborough, Leics. 1797, V. Twyning, Glos. 1802, R. Newtown, Montgomery 1815 to death (Cheltenham) 8/7/1844 aged 82 [C11052] Married Faringdon, Berks. 5/11/1793 Sarah Lardner, with son below.

FOXTON (George Lardner) Born Coxwell Magna, Berks. 24/12/1794, s. Rev. George Foxton (above) and Sarah Lardner. Worcester, Oxford 1812, migrated to Christ's, Cambridge 1816, dn18 (Glos.), p18, BA1823, MA1826. PC. Blackpool St John (formerly Layton Chapel) 1826-9 (res.), PC. Blackburn St Peter, Lancs. 1829-52, V. Worcester St Peter the Great 1839-52, V. Kempsey, Worcs. 1852 to death 12/4/1879 aged 84, leaving £3,000 [C105303] Married Bury, Lancs. 8/6/1822 Anne Hardman, with issue (some clerical).

FOYSTER (John Goodge) Bapt. St Pancras, London 8/3/1782, s. Samuel Foyster and Ann Grimes. Queens', Cambridge 1799, BA1803, dn05 (Win.), MA1806, p06 (London for Win.). R. (and patron) of Hastings All Saints, Kent (and Preacher throughout the Diocese of Chichester) 1832-49, R. Hastings St Clement 1849 to death 17/5/1855 aged 73, leaving £14,000 [C63489]

FRAMPTON (John) Bapt. Clifton, Bristol 24/10/1798, s. Thomas Frampton and Hannah Wood. Exeter, Oxford 1815, BA1820, dn21 (Bristol), MA1822, p22 (Glos. for Bristol). V. Tetbury, Glos. 1828-80, RD. Hon. Canon of Gloucester Cathedral 1848 to death 22/9/1880, leaving £10,000 [C42232] Married Tetbury, Glos. 27/7/1829 Harriette Paul, with issue.

FRANCE (Isaac Newton) Bapt. Manchester 19/4/1794, s. Richard France ('who kept the "Sir John Falstaff" in the Market Place') and Isabel Newton. Literate: dn17 (Chester), p18 (Chester). PC. Stalybridge Old St George, Lancs. 1822 to death 17/5/1850 aged 56 [C168900] Married 2/2/1826 Eliza Davies, of Dukinfield. A divisive and sectarian figure, 'he reduced the numbers in his church to six or seven'. A full Web entry on all of this: cockerhill.com/tag/isac-newon-france/

FRANCIS (John Pechey) From Wheatley, Cambs., s. John Francis and Mary Pechey. Corpus Christi, Cambridge 1796, BA1801, dn02 (Roch. for Cant.), MA1804, p04 (B&W for Cant.). V. Canterbury Holy Cross Westgate and St Peter 1804, and V. Newenden, Kent 1812 to death. Chap. to HRH Duke of York and Albany 1812. Died ('*shot himself* in his study whilst temporarily insane') 28/3/1853 aged 75 [C1836] Married Soham, Cambs. 25/9/1806 Mary Pechey [*sic*], and had issue.

FRANCIS (Robert John) Born Norwich 3/12/1774, s. Robert Francis and Mary Hangar. Corpus Christi, Cambridge 1792, BA1797, dn97 (Nor.), p99 (Nor.), MA1800. R. Churchwarton, Norfolk 1804-12, R. Kirkley All Saints, Suffolk 1812-60, R. Carleton St Peter, Norfolk 1822-60, R. Rollesby, Norfolk 1860 to death. Chap. of Beccles Gaol. Died Norwich 2/11/1869 aged 94, leaving £3,000 [C113004] Married by 1807 Catherine Bernard, w. issue.

FRANCKLIN (Fairfax) Bapt. Attleborough, Norfolk 12/5/1771, s. Rev. John Francklin and Eleanor Fairfax. Corpus Christi, Cambridge 1789, then Clare 1789, BA1793, dn93 (Nor.), Fellow 1794-1802, p95 (Nor.), MA1796. R. Barford, Norfolk 1795-1804. R. Attleborough 1803-38, V. Watton, Norfolk 1803 to death (Attleborough) 17/9/1838 aged 67 [C113005] Married 1802 Sarah Bidwell, with clerical son John Fairfax Francklin (below). Brother below.

FRANCKLIN (Henry) Bapt. Attleborough, Norfolk 2/7/1779, s. Rev. John Francklin and Eleanor Fairfax. Clare, Cambridge 1796, BA 1801, p06 (Nor.). R. Barford, Norfolk 1806 to death 16/5/1859, leaving £2,000 [C113006] Brother above.

FRANCKLIN (John Fairfax) Bapt. Attleborough, Norfolk 29/11/1803, s. Rev. Fairfax Francklin (above) and Sarah Bidwell. Clare, Cambridge 1821, BA1827, dn27 (Nor.), p28 (Nor.), Fellow 1831-5, MA1832. R. Earsham, Suffolk 1813, PC. New Buckenham, Norfolk 1829, V. West Newton, Norfolk 1842, V. Whaplode, Lincs. 1859 to death. Chap. to 16th Lincolnshire Rifle Volunteers. Died 25/11/1882, leaving £2,331-12s-11d. [C113010] Married Norwich 18/5/1835 Julia Burroughes (w) (a clergy dau., Manor House, Long Stratton, Norfolk), w. issue. Step-brothers above.

FRANK (Edward) Born and bapt. Campsall, Yorks. 6/3/1780, s. Bacon [*sic*] Frank and Catharine Hoare. Trinity, Cambridge 1798, dn05 (York), p06 (York), LLB. R. Alderton, Suffolk 1810 (sequestrator?) and R. (and patron) of Shelton w. Hardwick, Norfolk 1811 to death 14/10/1834 aged 54 (CCEd says 19/2/1835) [C113011. YCO] Married 8/3/1801 Mary Frances Sowerby (a military dau., from whom he separated because of her adultery with the 'rupture doctor' John Dickenson). In 1825 he was successfully accused of being insane in a long, sensational and explicit trial.

FRANK (Thomas) From Oswestry, Shropshire, s. Edward Frank. BNC, Oxford 1773 (aged 18), BA1777, dn77 (C&L), p79 (C&L). PC. Preston Gobalds, Shropshire 1793 to death (Shrewsbury, Shropshire) 22/1/1849 [C11054]

FRANKLIN (Frederick William) Born Westminster, London 17/2/1774, s. Frederick Franklin. Pembroke, Cambridge 1793, BA 1797, MA1800, dn01 (London), p02 (London). S/M Christ's Hospital [school], Hertford 1801-27; V. Ugley, Essex 1816 and V. Berden, Essex 1816-8, V. Horley, Surrey 1817-27, V. Albrighton, Shropshire 1827 to death. Dom. Chap. to Earl Talbot. Died 23/2/1836 [C11034]

FRANKS (James Clarke) Born Halifax, Yorks. 4/1/1793, s. Rev. James Franks and Sarah Clarke. Trinity, Cambridge 1810, BA 1815, dn17 (Ely), p17 (London for Ely), MA 1818, Chap. 1819, BD1855. PC. Boxworth, Cambs. 1817, V. Huddersfield St Peter, Yorks. 1823-40, PC. Whittlesea, Cambs. 1844-54, R. Canterbury St Margaret 1859-63. Died Huddersfield 17/4/1867 aged 74, leaving £2,000 [C17786] Married Bradford, Yorks. 24/9/1824 Elizabeth Firth (w), with clerical son. Ann and Charlotte Bronte spent a week with him.

FRASER (Hugh) Born Aberdeen 25/9/1764, s. William Fraser (of Fraserfield, Aberdeenshire) and Rachel Kennedy. Marischal College, Aberdeen 1777-79, then Glasgow University 1779-82, then Snell Exhibitioner at Balliol, Oxford 1782, BA1786, dn88 (London for Cant.), p88 (Lin. for Cant.), MA1789. R. St Martin Ludgate, City of London 1796-1805, R. Woolwich, Kent 1805 to death 1/4/1837 aged 73 [C1837 with long memorial inscription. Snell] Married Mary Lloyd (of Lambeth) 25/6/1803 (w), their children all predeceasing them.

FRASER (Peter [Lovett]) Bapt. Richmond, Yorks. 20/4/1772, s. Peter Fraser. Christ's, Cambridge 1790, BA1795, dn95 (Nor.), p97 (London), MA1798, Fellow 1802, 1813. V. Bromley by Bow, Middx. 1824-49, R. Kegworth, Leics. 1831 (and Prebend of Stow St Mary in Lincoln Cathedral 1831) to death. Chap. to HRH Duke of Cambridge. Died 16/10/1852 [C60682] Anonymous editor of *Fraser's Magazine*, he 'left his large collection of chronicles, histories and memoirs in English, French and Italian, and a bust of himself to the College Library'.

FRASER (William) Probably born Bangal, s. James Fraser. Trinity, Cambridge 1796, Chap. in Bengal Presidency 1819-[22]; PC. Pirbright, Surrey 1828-32 (res.), R. North Waltham, Hants. 1831. Probate granted 15/9/1842 [C73701] Widow Mary.

FREDERICK (Christopher) Born Burwood House, Walton, Surrey 10/12/1785, s. Sir John Frederick, 5th Bart. and Mary Garth. Trinity, Oxford 1805, migrated to Trinity Hall, Cambridge 1808, dn08 (Win.), p09 (Win.), BA1810. R. Scotton, Lincs. 1810 to death. Chap. to Prince of Wales 1809. Died (unm.) 23/9/1863, leaving £6,000 [C60683]

FREELAND (Henry) Born Aldeburgh, Suffolk 19/5/1795 (bapt. Hasketon, Suffolk 1/4/1797), s. of John Freeland (of Dedham, Essex) and Sarah Coyte. Emmanuel, Cam-bridge 1812, BA1817, dn18 (Nor.), p19 (Nor.). R. (and patron) of Hasketon 1819-40, 1843-4, R. Ovington w. Tilbury, Essex 1840 to death Jan. 1844, having been 'seized with [a] spasmodic affection and was a corpse within an hour' [C113013] Married (1) St George's Hanover Square, London 8/2/1825 Sophia Lydia Ruggles (d.1827) (2) 14/5/1829 Georgiana Frances Round (w); 'leaving 10 ch. under 14 years of age'.

FREEMAN (Edward) Bapt. Ledbury, Heref. 24/4/1776, s. Thomas Freeman and Hannah Dew. Merton, Oxford 1794, BA1798, dn04 (Heref.), p04 (Heref.). R. Donnington, Heref. 1817-31 (res.), V. Felton, Heref. 1825-50, PC. Wisteston, Heref. 1833 (only). Died Felton 2/10/1850 [C105308]

FREEMAN (John Neville) From Uxbridge, Middx., s. Robert Freeman (physician) and Santa Maria Howard. Exeter, Oxford 1782 (aged 18), BA1786, dn86 (Lin.), Fellow 1787-92, p89 (Car.), MA1791. V. Hayes, Middx. 1792 to death 13/12/1843 [C5876] Brother William George, below.

FREEMAN (Matthew) Born Foston, Leics. 15/1/1786, s. Joseph and Susannah Freeman. Literate: dn13 (Chester for York), p14 (York). PC. Mellor, Derbys. 1824 to death there 14/3/1859, leaving £300 [C11059. YCO] Married Mellor 25/9/1828 Elizabeth Ollerenshaw (w) (dau. of the previous incumbent), with clerical son.

FREEMAN (Thomas) Bapt. City of London 1/11/1756, s. Charles and Elizabeth Freeman. Sidney, Cambridge, LLB, dn92 (London for Nor.), p93 (Nor.). R. Bruntingthorpe, Leics, 1795 to death 18/4/1834 (CCEd thus) [C60694. Not in Venn]

FREEMAN (William George) Bapt. Uxbridge, Middx. 20/5/1768, s. Robert Freeman (physician) and Santa Maria Howard. King's, Cambridge 1786, BA1790, dn91 (Lin. for Car.), Fellow 1789-1812, MA1793, p96 (Salis.). S/M Eton College 1793-4; R. Christon, Som. 1806, R. Milton, Cambs. 1812-41, R. Caldecote, Warwicks. --. Dom. Chap. to 3rd Baron Lisle 1811. Died ('from the effects of being thrown from his gig') 6/7/1841 [C5877] Married Langley Marsh, Bucks. 30/1/1812 Catherine Swaybey, with issue. Brother of John Neville, above.

FREER (George) Bapt. Old Swinford, Worcs. 14/6/1794, s. William Leacroft Freer and Anna Maria Hickman. Emmanuel, Cambridge 1816, dn18 (Nor.), p19 (Nor.), BA1820, MA1824. V. Yaxley, Hunts. 1828-36. Died Sparkbrook, Birmingham 28/9/1870, leaving £800 [C60695] Married (1) Horstead, Norfolk 24/7/1821 Charlotte Postle (d.1865), w. child (2) Aston, Birmingham 23/1/1867 Mrs Hannah (Bennett) Whitehouse. Note an Oxford contemporary.

FREER (Thomas Lane) From Birmingham, s. John Freer and Jane Lane, Pembroke, Oxford 1792 (aged 15), BA1797, MA1799, dn99 (Salis.), p01 (Salis.). R. Handsworth, Birmingham 1803-35 [blank in ERC], V. Wasperton, Warwicks. 1821-6 (res.). Dom. Chap. to 5th Earl of Aylesford 1821. Died 25 *or* 28/4/1835 [C11062] Married Oxford 28/4/1800 Sarah Wetherell (a clergy dau.), w. clerical son Richard Lane Freer.

FREKE (Thomas) Bapt. Modbury, Devon 29/10/1774, s. Rev. Freeman Freke. Balliol, Oxford 1793, BA1797, dn98 (Ex.), p98 (Ex.), incorporated at Cambridge 1812. V. Spreyton, Devon 1802, V. South Tawton, Devon 1803-24, R. Down St Mary, Devon 1812 and V. (and patron) of Loddiswell, Devon 1824 to death. Dom. Chap. to 2nd Earl of Carnarvon 1812-24-. Died 1837 aged 64 [C139351]

FREMANTLE (William Robert) Born Swanbourne, Bucks, 30/8/1807, s. Vice-Admiral Sir Thomas Francis Fremantle and Elizabeth Wynne. Christ Church, Oxford 1825, BA1829, then Magdalen, dn31 (Ox.), Fellow 1831-42, MA1832, p32 (Ox.), BD & DD1876. R. Pitchcott, Bucks. 1832, V. Steeple Clayton, Bucks. 1841-68, R. Middle Claydon w. East Claydon, Bucks. 1841-76, RD 1841-76, Hon. Canon of Christ Church Cathedral 1869-76, Dean of Ripon 1876 to death (Wimbledon, Surrey) 8/3/1895, leaving £32,238-4s-11d.; his nephew William Fremantle succ. him to the Deanery [C27795. Boase. DEB] Married (1) 4/11/1835 Emily Caroline Calvert (d.1877) (2) Branston, Lincs. 9/10/1879 Caroline Leslie-Melville, w. issue. Founder of the Navvy Mission; President of the Prophetical Society. Port. online.

FRENCH (Peter Dillwy) From Reading, Berks., s. Peter William French and Mary Dillwy. Queen's, Oxford 1818 (aged 18), BA 1822, dn22 (Salis.), p23 (Salis.), MA1825. V. Burton on Trent Holy Trinity, Staffs. 1824-71. Chap. to the Burton Poor Law Union. Died Reading 14/2/1878, leaving £35,000 [C11063] Married Reading 13/10/1823 Penelope Arabella Valpy, w. issue (incl. Thomas Valpy French, Bishop of Lahore, *q.v.* ODNB*)*.

FRENCH (Pinkstan Arundel) Born London 16/1/1764, s. Rev. Hugh French and Sarah Arundel. Christ Church, Oxford 1782, BA1786, MA1789 [barrister Inner Temple 1789] dn94 (London), p95 (Ox.). Min. Sydenham, Kent 1796, PC. Hawkhurst, Kent 1797-1803, R. Odcombe, Som. 1803 and R. Thornfalcon, Som. 1821 to death 12/4/1836 [C1839] Married Westminster, London 12/8/1806 Susanna Smith.

FRENCH (Robert Nicholas) Bapt. Derby 6/7/1775, s. Richard French and Millicent Mundy. Literate: dn99 (Car.), p99 (Car.), then Trinity Hall, Cambridge 1802 ('A Twenty Four Year Man' [*sic*]). PC. Foremark, Derbys. 1800, R. Seckington, Warwicks. 1800-62, R. Osmaston by Derby 1811 and R. Weston on Trent, Derbys. 1811 to death (Regent's Park, London) 22/12/1862 aged 87, leaving £9,000 [C5878. Austin] 'Insane - a lunatic'.

FRENCH (William) Born Eye, Suffolk 1786, s. of Thomas French, 'a wealthy farmer'. Caius, Cambridge 1807, then Pembroke 1811, BA 1811, Fellow and Tutor 1811-14, dn13 (Ely), MA1814, p14 (Ely), DD1821. Master of Jesus College, Cambridge 1820-49 (where he restored the College Chapel) (w. Canon of 3rd Prebend in Ely Cathedral appended 1831), V. Cretingham, Suffolk 1824-7, R. Moor Monkton >< Ainsty of York. 1827 (non-res.) to death (Cambridge) 12/11/1849 aged 62 [C15916. ODNB which speaks of his 'forbidding formality of manner'] Married Eye, Cambs. 1/2/1821 Elizabeth Maria Wythe, w. issue.

FRERE (Edward) Bapt. Llanelly, Brecon 26/9/1805, s. Edward Frere (Clydach, Brecon). Downing, Cambridge 1824, then Trinity 1824, BA1828, dn28 (Nor.), p29 (Nor.), MA1835. R. Finningham, Suffolk 1829 to death (unm.) 23/7/1841 [C113022]

FRERE (Edward Barker) Born Hemsby, Norfolk 25/7/1782, s. Major Edward Frere and Mary Barker. Corpus Christi, Cambridge 1800, BA1805, dn05 (Nor.), p06 (Nor.), MA1825. V. Biggleswade, Beds. 1810-41, PC. Ilketshall St Lawrence, Suffolk 1830-8. Lived and died Great Yarmouth, Norfolk 11/11/1864, leaving £1,500 [C60697] Married Great Yarmouth 14/7/1825 Elizabeth Hanbury, w. clerical son Edward Hanbury Frere.

FRERE (Temple) Born London 16/5/1781, s. John Frere, *F.R.S.* (Roydon, Norfolk) and Jane Hookham. Trinity, Cambridge 1797, BA1802 ['studied divinity at Aberdeen 1802-4 under Bishop Skinner'] dn04 (Nor.), MA1805, p05 (Nor.). R. Finningham, Suffolk 1805-25 (res.), R. Roydon 1820-59 (living at Roydon Hall 1821-46), Prebend of Westminster Abbey 1838-59 (Canon 1840) to death. Chap. to House of Commons 1833. Died 7/7/1859, leaving £40,000 [C60699] Married Bloomsbury, London 16/4/1816 Jane, dau. of Sir Richard Richards (Baron of the Exchequer, Merioneth), with clerical s. Henry Temple Frere. *J.P.* Norfolk 1823, for Suffolk 1829; *D.L.* Norfolk 1826.

FRESTON (Thomas [Gordon Westfaling]) Born Bagborough, Somerset 25/9/1796. s. Rev. Anthony Brettingham Freston and Ann Hyde. Merton, Oxford 1814, migrated to Peterhouse, Cambridge 1818, BA1820, dn20 (Glos.), p20 (Nor.). PC. Needham, Norfolk 1820-34, R. Great Witcombe, Glos. 1826, R. Daglingworth, Glos. 1833 to death 25/6/1837 [C113024 has error] Married June 1824 Emily Ellen Mills, w. issue.

FRITH (William Cokayne) Bapt. North Cray, Kent 30/10/1785, s. Rev. Edward and Mary Frith. St John, Oxford 1802, Fellow 1802-18, BCL1808, dn08 (Ox.), p09 (Ox.), DCL 1814. Military chap. at some date. R. Chilfrome, Dorset 1824-32, R. Wallingford St Peter, Berks. 1828 to death 28/6/1855 [C27804] Married Oxford 6/8/1818 1818 Mary Cox (a banker's dau.), w. issue.

FROME (George Clutterbuck) From Blandford, Dorset, s. Rev. Robert Frome (below) and Jane Butler. Merton, Oxford 1796 (aged 17), BA 1800, dn03 (Bristol), p03 (Bristol), MA1808 (as George). R. Lytton Cheney, Dorset 1804-24, R. (and patron of) Puncknowle, Dorset 1804 and R. Winterbourne Clenstone, Dorset 1825 to death 22/12/1844 [C52603] Married Clifton, Bristol 15/11/1823 Mary Sophia Pleydell (d.1827), 2 dau.

FROME (Robert) Born Tollard, Wilts. 25/2/1744, s. Rev. George Frome and Arundell Clutterbuck. Wadham, Oxford 1761, dn67 (Salis.), p70 (Ox. for Bristol), BCL1770. R. Chettle, Dorset 1776-82, R. Folke, Dorset 1777 and R. Minterne Magna, Dorset 1782 and R. Goathill, Som. 1797 to death 9/4/1833 [C27806] Married Okeford Fitzpaine, Dorset 8/6/1778 Jane Butler, with clerical son (above).

FROUDE (John) Bapt. Knowstone, Devon 6/7/1777, s. Rev. John Froude, sen. and Prestwood Love Legassacke [*sic*]. Exeter, Oxford 1797, BA1801, dn01 (Ex.), p03 (Ex.). R. Knowstone 1804 to death 9/12/1852 [C143508] Married South Malton, Devon 1838 (4th q.) Mary Halse.

FROUDE (Robert Hurrell) Bapt. Aveton Gifford, Devon 12/10/1770, s. Robert Froude (Walkhampton, Devon) and Phillis Hurrell (fine painting online by Reynolds). Oriel, Oxford 1788, BA1792, dn95 (Ex.), MA1795, p96 (Ex.). R. Denbury, Devon 1798 and also R. Dartington, Devon (with Preacher throughout the Diocese of Exeter) 1799 to death, Archdeacon of Totnes 1820 to death. Dom. Chap. to Anna Maria, Duchess of Somerset 1799. Died 23/2/1859 aged 89, leaving £35,000 [C143509. Boase] Married Bassenthwaite, Cumberland 19/6/1802 Margaret Spedding, 4s. (including Richard Hurrell Froude, intimate of Newman; and James Anthony Froude historian and biographer of Thomas Carlyle), 3 dau.

FROWD (Edward) From Stratford-sub-Castle, Wilts., s. Richard Frowd. Exeter, Oxford 1817 (aged 17), BA1821, dn23 (Bristol), MA1824, p24 (Chester for Bristol). R. Upper Clatford, Hants. 1830 to death 14/8/1863, leaving £50,000 [C52605]

FROWD (Isaac) From Brinton Deverell, Wilts., s. Edward Frowd. Merton, Oxford 1772 (aged 18), BA1776, dn76 (Ox.), p77 (Salis.), MA 1779, V. Bishop's Castle, Shropshire 1777-1834, R. Shrawardine, Shropshire 1782-1834, R. Clunton w. Clunbury, Shropshire 1819. Dom. Chap. to 1st Earl of Powis 1782-1819. Died 3/12/1835 (CCEd says 6/12/1834) [C27809. Boase].

FRY (John) From Tunbridge Wells, Kent, s. John Fry. University, Oxford 1794 (aged 19), BA1798 (as Frey), dn98 (Salis.). R. Desford, Leics. 1801 to death 21/6/1849 [C60709]

FRY (Thomas) From Compton Bishop, Som., s. Peter Fry and Elizabeth Homfray. Oriel, Oxford 1792 (aged 17), BA1796, then Lincoln, dn97 (Lin.), MA1798, p98 (Ox.). R. (and patron) of Emberton, Bucks. 1804 to death. Dom. Chap. to 1st Baron Erskine 1814. Died Bath 26/3/1860, leaving £10,000 [C27814] Married (1) with issue (2) St Pancras, London 2/4/1846 Mrs Mary Ann (Bagshawe) Foster, w. further issue.

FRY (William) Bapt. Chipping Wycombe, Bucks. 27/3/1782, s. Francis Fry and Eleanor Nash. 'Self-educated.' Literate: dn15 (Chester for York), p22 (York). R. Egdean, Sussex 1832 to death (Petworth, Sussex) 5/8/1853 aged 69 [C63505. YCO] Married Stowchurch, Oxon. 7/6/1802 Elizabeth Ferguson.

FRYE (Percival) Born Bloomsbury, London 27/5/1785, s. John Ravell Frye and Sarah Pott. Oriel, Oxford 1803, BA1806, dn08 (Durham), p09 (Durham), MA1811. Minor Canon of Durham Cathedral 1808, V. Merrington, Durham 1809-12 (res.), R. (Low) Dinsdale, Durham 1812-35 (res.), PC. Brompton Holy Trinity, Kensington, London 1829, V. St Winnow, Cornwall 1834 to death 28/11/1863, leaving £3,000 [C117938] Married 1818 Laura Augusta Hastings Scott-Waring (w) (dau. of an M.P.), with issue.

FRYER (William) From Newnham, Glos., s. Thomas Fryer. Hertford, Oxford 1785 (aged 29), no degree, dn86 (Glos.), p87 (Glos.). V. Cam, Glos. 1800-34, V. Stinchcombe, Glos. 1800 and PC. Whitminster (o/w Wheatenhurst), Glos. 1813 to death 6/8/1834 (CCEd thus) [C150791]

FULFORD (Francis, *later first* Bishop of Montreal) Born Sidmouth, Devon 3/6/1803, s. Col. Baldwin Fulford and Anna Maria Adams. Exeter, Oxford 1821, Fellow 1824-30, dn26 (Nor.), BA1827, p28 (Ex.), MA1838, Hon. DD 1850. R. Trowbridge, Wilts. 1832-41, V. Croyden, Cambs. 1841-5, Minister of Curzon [Proprietary] Chapel, Mayfair, London 1845-50. Consecrated first Bishop of Montreal 25/7/1850 (and Metropolitan of Canada 1860) to death (Montreal). Chap. to HRH Duchess of Gloucester. Died 9/9/1868, leaving £8,000 [C73710. ODNB. Boase. *Canadian Dictionary of Biography* (Online Edition) with photo.] Married 18/10/1830 Mary Drummond (w) (Cadlands, Hants.), with issue. A moderate and highly respected figure.

FULLER (Robert Fitzherbert) Born Kidbrook House, East Grinstead, Kent 11/8/1794, s. John Trayton Fuller and Anne Eliott. BNC, Oxford 1813, BA1817, dn19 (Salis.), MA1819, p19 (Salis.). PC. Crowhurst w. Lingfield, Surrey 1819, PC. Chalvington, Sussex 1833. Died 23/8/1849 [C63508] Married Lingfield 7/10/1827 Maria Ursula Sheffield, with issue. Doubtless related to the man below.

FULLER (Thomas) Born Heathfield, Sussex 13/1/1755, s. John Fuller and Mary Duke. Trinity, Cambridge 1773, BA1777, p79 (Nor. for Chich.), MA1780. R. Hastings All Saints and St Clement, Sussex 1785-95, R. Chalvington, Sussex 1785-1832, V. Hooe, Sussex 1805 to death 10/12/1832 [C63509] Doubtless related to the man above.

FULLER (Thomas) Born Marylebone, London 16/3/1790, s. Rose [*sic* Ross?] and Elizabeth Fuller. St John's, Cambridge 1808, BA1812, Fellow 1812, dn13 (Ely), p14 (Ely), MA1815. Min. Curzon St. [Proprietary] Chapel, Mayfair, London 1821-7, Min. Pimlico St Peter, London 1827 to death 30/3/1871 aged 81, leaving £50,000 [C17789] Married (2) Marylebone 3/8/1827 (*or* 3/9/1827) Mrs Josephine Therese Sanders, w. clerical son John (cricketer and academic).

FURBANK (Thomas) Bapt. Leeds 6/10/1793 (in a dissenting chapel), s. Thomas Furbank and Sarah Hopkinson. Lincoln, Oxford 1813, BA1817, dn17 (York), p17 (York), MA1820. PC. Bramley, Leeds 1830 to death 13/11/1850 aged 57 [C131305. YCO] Married Shipley, Yorks. 4/2/1845 Mary Horsfall, with issue.

FUREY, FURY (Joah) Bapt. Witton, Cheshire 24/8/1774, s. John Furey and Grace Bates. King's, Cambridge 1794, dn97 (Lin.), Fellow 1797-1815, BA1798, MA1801, p01 (Nor.), etc. V. Fordingbridge, Hants. (and Preacher throughout the Diocese of Winchester) 1815 to death 9/9/1839 [C60714]

FURNEAUX (Tobias) Born Stoke Damerel, Devon 19/4/1794, s. Rev. James Furneaux and

Harriet Foot. Magdalen Hall, Oxford 1820, dn23 (Glos.), p24 (Lin. for Ex.), BA1824, MA 1832. R. St Germans, Cornwall 1828-74 and V. St Gennys, Cornwall 1829. Died 20/7/1874 aged 80, leaving £25,000 [C60716] Married Anne Richards, with clerical sons Henry, and Alan Furneaux. Surrogate 1828.

FURNESS (Thomas) Born Caistor, Lincs. Nov. 1776, s. Rev. Anthony (schoolmaster) and Elizabeth Furness. Corpus Christi, Cambridge 1795, BA1799, dn99 (Lin.), p01 (Lin.). R. Oxcombe, Lincs. 1821 to death (Hull) 13/4/1842 [C60718. Kaye]

FUSSELL (Jacob) Bapt. Mells, Somerset 20/2/1788, s. James Fussell and Ann Stone. Queen's, Oxford 1806, BA1813, dn14 (London), MA1814 (as Henry Jacob), p15 (Peterb.). V. Doulting, Som. 1823 to death 24/6/1867, leaving £25,000 [C41511] Married Banbury, Oxon. 12/7/1815 Sarah Heydon, and had issue.

FYLER (Samuel Arnot) Bapt. Twickenham, Middx. 4/10/1803, s. of Samuel Fyler (barrister) and Margaret Arnot. Trinity, Oxford 1821, BA 1825, dn27 (Durham for York), p28 (York), MA1839. PC. Durham St Giles 1831-5, R. Cornhill on Tweed, Northumberland 1834 to death (unm.) 2/11/1880 aged 77, leaving £2,000 [C130434. YCO]

FYNES-CLINTON (Charles John) see under **CLINTON**

www.ingramcontent.com/pod-product-compliance
Lightning Source LLC
Chambersburg PA
CBHW050717090526
44588CB00014B/2315